CONSUMER BEHAVIOUR

Visit the *Consumer Behaviour: A European Outlook*, Second Edition, Companion Website at **www.pearsoned.co.uk/schiffman** to find valuable **student** learning material including:

- Self-assessment multiple choice questions for each chapter
- Searchable online glossary
- Flashcards to test your knowledge of key terms and definitions

CONSUMER BEHAVIOUR

A EUROPEAN OUTLOOK

second edition

LEON G. SCHIFFMAN
St. John's University, New York, USA

LESLIE LAZAR KANUK and HÅVARD HANSEN
City University,
New York Graduate School, USA

University of Stavanger,
Norway

**Financial Times
Prentice Hall
is an imprint of**

PEARSON

Harlow, England • London • New York • Boston • San Francisco • Toronto • Sydney • Singapore • Hong Kong
Tokyo • Seoul • Taipei • New Delhi • Cape Town • Madrid • Mexico City • Amsterdam • Munich • Paris • Milan

Pearson Education Limited
Edinburgh Gate
Harlow
Essex CM20 2JE
England

and Associated Companies throughout the world

Visit us on the World Wide Web at:
www.pearson.com/uk

Published 2007, 2004, 2000, 1997, 1991 by Pearson Education Inc., Upper Saddle River, New Jersey, 07458

First published in the UK 2008
Second edition 2012

© Pearson Education Limited 2008, 2012

ISBN: 978-0-273-73695-0

British Library Cataloguing-in-Publication Data
A catalogue record for this book is available from the British Library

Library of Congress Cataloging-in-Publication Data

Schiffman, Leon G.
   Consumer behaviour : a European outlook / Leon G. Schiffman, Håvard Hansen and Leslie Kanuk. — 2nd ed.
      p. cm.
   Includes bibliographical references and index.
   ISBN 978-0-273-73695-0 (pbk.)
   1. Consumer behavior—Europe.   2. Motivation research (Marketing)—Europe.   I. Hansen, Håvard.   II. Kanuk, Leslie Lazar.   III. Title.
   HF5415.33.E85H36   2011
   658.8'342—dc22

                                                          2011013123

10 9 8 7 6 5 4 3 2
15 14 13

Typeset in 9/12 pt ITC Giovanni by 73
Printed and bound by Rotolito Lombarda, Italy

BRIEF CONTENTS

CONTENTS

SUPPORTING RESOURCES

Visit **www.pearsoned.co.uk/schiffman** to find valuable online resources
- Complete, downloadable Instructor's Manual
- PowerPoint slides that can be downloaded and used for presentations

Also: The Companion Website provides the following features:
- Search tool to help locate specific items of content
- E-mail results and profile tools to send results of quizzes to instructors
- Online help and support to assist with website usage and troubleshooting

For more information please contact your local Pearson Education sales representative or visit **www.pearsoned.co.uk/schiffman**

PREFACE TO THE SECOND EDITION

Ever since I was a second year business school student and took my first course in consumer behaviour, Schiffman and Kanuk's text has stood out as one of the best textbooks I have ever read. Later, when I found myself responsible for the same introductory consumer behaviour course as I once took myself, the choice of which textbook to use turned out to be quite simple. And certainly, when I was invited to contribute to a European adaptation of the text, I found myself facing yet another simple choice.

That being said, the term 'adaptation' needs an explanation. Given the fact that the original text is a really good introduction to the study of consumer behaviour, the contents of this European adaptation do not differ substantially from the original text. The goal has been to adapt the book to fit the needs of the European student of consumer behaviour, which means that what you are now holding is a book *for* European consumers (i.e. students) – and not a book *about* European consumers. Specifically, in line with the original text, I have kept the focus on the examination and application of consumer behaviour principles to the development and implementation of marketing strategies. From a managerial point of view, the overarching objective for a marketer is to have consumers choose its products or services instead of equivalents offered by competing firms. While simple to state, such a goal often proves hard to accomplish. In recognition of this fact, the European adaptation has increased the emphasis on consumer decision-making by placing this topic as the first chapter in the section on the consumer as an individual. By so doing, an understanding of the complexity of consumer decision-making is established early on, and the succeeding chapters on consumers both as individuals and in their social settings extend the comprehension of how decisions are influenced in a variety of ways.

OVERVIEW OF CHANGES IN THIS SECOND EDITION

The first edition text was thoroughly adapted to European conditions and somewhat revised to focus attention on critical consumer behaviour concepts, highlighting the links between inter-related principles and processes. Some of the major changes between the first and the second edition include:

- A strengthened emphasis on decision-making as an important starting point for studying consumer behaviour.
- A further update of examples from Europe, with a focus on offering examples that are both understandable and familiar to students regardless of which European country they come from.
- An inclusion of more examples related to online consumer behaviour.
- Inclusion of more theoretical models of consumer behaviour, for example the Theory of Planned Behaviour as an extension of TRA in the chapter on attitudes.

ORGANISATION OF THE TEXT

This European adaptation of *Consumer Behaviour* consists of 16 chapters, divided into four parts:

Part 1 provides the background and tools for a strong and comprehensive understanding of the consumer behaviour principles examined throughout the rest of the book

Chapter 1, An introduction to the study of consumer behaviour, sets the tone for the book. It introduces the reader to the study of consumer behaviour, its diversity, its development and the latest evolution of the marketing concept, and discusses marketing ethics and consumer responsibility. It examines how companies use past consumption behaviour as the foundation for creating and keeping satisfied and profitable lifetime customers. The chapter also introduces a simple model of consumer decision-making that provides a structural framework for understanding the interrelationships among the consumer behaviour principles examined throughout the book. Chapter 2 provides readers with an overview of the critical consumer research process and the techniques associated with consumer behaviour research. Chapter 3 presents a comprehensive examination of the newest insights into effective market segmentation.

Part 2 discusses the consumer as an individual

Chapter 4 describes how consumers make product decisions, and expands on the increasingly important practice of relationship marketing. This chapter concludes with a deeper and more comprehensive examination of a model of consumer decision-making (building on the overview model briefly introduced in Chapter 1). It includes an in-depth examination of consumer gifting behaviour, a discussion of the expanding research focus on individual consumption behaviour and the symbolic meanings of consumer possessions. Chapter 5 presents an in-depth discussion of consumer needs and motivations, exploring both the rational and emotional bases of consumer actions. Chapter 6 discusses the impact of the full range of personality theories on consumer behaviour and explores consumer materialism, fixated consumption and compulsive consumption behaviour. The chapter considers the related concepts of self and self-image and includes an expanded discussion of virtual personality or self. Chapter 7 provides a comprehensive examination of the impact of consumer perception on marketing strategy and the importance of product positioning and repositioning. Chapter 8 examines how consumers learn, and discusses behavioural and cognitive learning theories, limited and extensive information processing, and the applications of consumer involvement theory to marketing practice. Chapter 9 offers an in-depth examination of consumer attitudes. Chapter 10 demonstrates that communication is the bridge between individuals and the world and people around them, and includes a timely discussion of advertising, traditional and new media, and the effective use of persuasion.

Part 3 is concerned with the social and cultural dimensions of consumer behaviour

Chapter 11 begins with a discussion of consumer reference groups (including virtual groups and virtual communities), family role orientations and changing family lifestyles. Chapter 12 presents consumers in terms of their socio-economic and social-class standing and discusses the emergence of the 'techno class'. Chapter 13 investigates consumers in their social and cultural milieus. Societal and subcultural values, beliefs and customs in relation to consumer behaviour are also discussed in this chapter. Chapter 14 concludes this part with a discussion of cross-cultural marketing within an increasingly global marketplace.

Part 4 explores further aspects of consumer decision-making

Chapter 15 offers a comprehensive discussion of personal influence, opinion leadership and the diffusion of innovations. Chapter 16 summarises the text and ties the threads back to the decision-making model introduced in Chapter 1 and described in detail in Chapter 4.

Finally, I would like to record my great appreciation for being given the opportunity to work with such an impressive text, and it is my hope that you enjoy reading this European adaptation as much as I have enjoyed working on it.

HÅVARD HANSEN
Egersund, Norway
February 2011

GUIDED TOUR

PART 1
INTRODUCTION

PART 1 PROVIDES THE BACKGROUND AND THE TOOLS FOR A STRONG AND COMPREHENSIVE UNDERSTANDING OF CONSUMER BEHAVIOUR

Chapter 1 introduces the reader to the study of consumer behaviour, its diversity, its development and the role of consumer research. It concludes with a detailed discussion of ethical considerations in marketing and consumer practices and introduces a simple model of consumer decision-making. Chapter 2 provides an overview of the critical research process and the techniques associated with consumer behaviour research, including a discussion of positivist and interpretivist research methods. Chapter 3 presents a comprehensive examination of market segmentation and demonstrates how consumer behaviour variables provide both the conceptual framework and the strategic direction for the practical segmentation of markets.

Colourful **part openers** introduce the chapters, outlining what you can expect to learn from each section of the book.

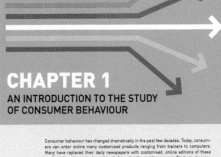

CHAPTER 1
AN INTRODUCTION TO THE STUDY OF CONSUMER BEHAVIOUR

Consumer behaviour has changed dramatically in the past few decades. Today, consumers can order online many customised products ranging from trainers to computers. Many have replaced their daily newspapers with customised, online editions of these media and are increasingly receiving information from online sources. Students choosing a university no longer rely on receiving prospectuses through the post; instead, they have online access to all the pertinent information about a university's courses and teaching staff and, in some cases, can visit, virtually, actual classes. People wanting to sell their old computers or grandmother's antique table no longer need to advertise in the local newspaper or rely on a pricey auctioneer; instead, they can sell these items via online auctions or their own personalised online advertisement. Consumers who want out-of-print books no longer have to visit out-of-the-way shops with hundreds of poorly organised dusty shelves, and those who wish to purchase a book published in another country no longer have to call foreign publishers or deal with the bureaucratic nightmare of overseas delivery; instead, they can visit online stores where they can easily locate and place orders for the books they seek. Television viewers can now avoid the advertisement breaks by using the 'skip' feature of their recorders and order on demand previously shown television programmes as well as films. All of these new ways of selling products and services became available to consumers during the past 15 years and are the result of digital technologies. And they also have another thing in common: they exist today because they reflect an understanding of consumer needs and consumer behaviour.

The term **consumer behaviour** is defined as the behaviour that consumers display in searching for, purchasing, using, evaluating and disposing of products and services that they expect will satisfy their needs. Consumer behaviour focuses on how individuals make decisions to spend their available resources (time, money, effort) on consumption-related items. That includes what they buy, why they buy it, when they buy it, where they buy it, how often they buy it, how often they use it, how they evaluate it after the purchase, the impact of such evaluations on future purchases and how they dispose of it.

Chapter introductions concisely describe the themes and issues explored in the chapter.

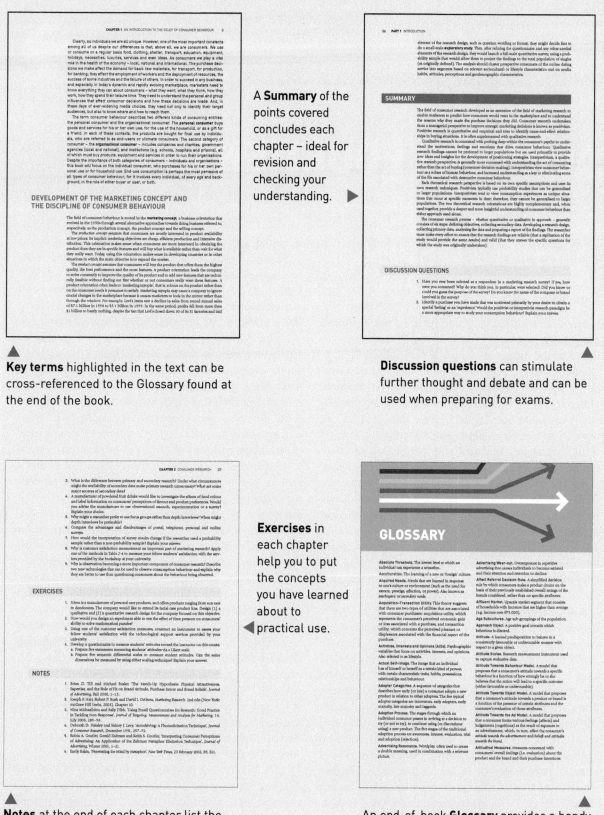

A **Summary** of the points covered concludes each chapter – ideal for revision and checking your understanding.

Key terms highlighted in the text can be cross-referenced to the Glossary found at the end of the book.

Discussion questions can stimulate further thought and debate and can be used when preparing for exams.

Exercises in each chapter help you to put the concepts you have learned about to practical use.

Notes at the end of each chapter list the sources you can use if you want to take your reading further.

An end-of-book **Glossary** provides a handy guide to important terms and concepts.

ACKNOWLEDGEMENTS

We are grateful to the following for permission to reproduce copyright material:

Figures

Figure 2.2 reprinted with permission from Customer profitability in a supply chain, *Journal of Marketing*, published by the American Marketing Association, Niraj, R., Gupta, M. and Narasimhan, C., July, 2001; Figure 3.1 from Volvo XC90 advertisement, Copyright: Volvo Personbiler Norge AS/TWBA; Figure 3.2 from Jagged Globe, reprinted with permission from Jagged Globe, Climb Trek Ski Ltd., www.jagged-globe.co.uk; Figure 3.3 adapted from SBI VALS™ segments, Reprinted with permission of Strategic Business Insights (SBI); www.strategicbusinessinsights.com/VALS; Figure 4.1 reprinted with permission from Goal setting and goal striving in consumer behaviour, *Journal of Marketing*, published by the American Marketing Association, Bagozzi, R. P. and Dholakia, U., 63, 1999, p. 21; Figure 4.3 from Search regret: Antecedents and consequences, *Journal of Retailing*, 82, 4, p. 342 (Reynolds, K. E., Garretson Folse, J. A. and Jones, M. A. 2006), Copyright 2006, with permission from Elsevier; Figure 4.5 reprinted with permission from Decision making and coping of functionally illiterate consumers and some implications for marketing management, *Journal of Marketing*, published by the American Marketing Association, Viswanathan, M., Rosa, J. A., Harris, J. E., 69, January 2005, p. 19; Figure 5.1 adapted from Observations: Translating values into product wants, *Journal of Advertising Research*, 36, 6, November (Dugree, J. F. *et al.* 1996), with permission from Warc; Figures 5.3a, 5.3b, 5.3c from Sonador Wines advertisements, www.sonadorwines.com, Branded Wines AS; Figure 6.3 from IKEA advertisement - TILLSAMMANS - together with IKEA, illustrator Lotta Kühlhorn, with agency Agent Bauer. Used with the permission of Inter IKEA Systems B.V; Figure 6.4 from Devold advertisement, Devold of Norway AS; Figure 6.5 reprinted with permission from Dimensions of brand personality, *Journal of Marketing Research*, published by the American Marketing Association, Aaker, J. L., 35, August 1997, p. 352; Figure 6.7 from LG Born to Shine advertisement, LG Electronics Nordic AB; Figure 6.8 adapted from Using self-concept to assess advertising effectiveness, *Journal of Advertising Research*, February, p. 87 (Mehta, A. 1999), with permission from Warc; Figure 7.1 from WWF advertisement. Mediterranean bluefin tuna are killed to make sushi, photographer Piet Johnson, with kind permission from WWF and Ogilvy & Mather; Figure 7.4 from AAAA advertisement, courtesy of American Association of Advertising Agencies; Figure 7.5 from PETA advertisement, image courtesy of PETA (www.peta.org); Figure 7.11 reprinted by permission from Macmillan Publishers Ltd: *Journal of Brand Management*, 11, 6, July, Measuring perceptions of brand luxury, p. 484 (Vigneron, F. and Johnson, L. W. 2004), copyright 2004 published by Palgrave Macmillan; Figure 7.12 reprinted with permission from The behavioural consequences of service quality, *Journal of Marketing*, published by the American Marketing Association, Zeithaml, V. A., Berry, L. L. and Parasuraman, A., 60, April 1996, p. 33; Figure 7.13 reprinted with permission from Effects of price, brand and store information on buyers' product evaluations, *Journal of Marketing Research*, published by the American Marketing Association, Dodds, W., Monroe, K. and Grewal, D., 28, August 1991, p. 308; Figure 8.1 from KLM BlueBiz advertisement © KLM Royal Dutch Airlines; Figures 8.3a, 8.3b, 8.4a, 8.4b from © V&S Vin & Sprit AB. Used under permission from V&S Vin & Sprit AB. ABSOLUT® VODKA. ABSOLUT COUNTRY OF SWEDEN VODKA & LOGO, ABSOLUT, ABSOLUT BOTTLE DESIGN AND ABSOLUT CALLIGRAPHY ARE TRADEMARKS OWNED BY V&S VIN & SPRIT AB; Figure 8.10 from BBC World News advertisement, BBC World News/James Day; Figure 8.11 with kind permission from Springer Science+Business Media:, *Journal of the Academy of Marketing Science*, Customer loyalty: Toward an integrated conceptual framework, 22, 2, 1994, p. 101 (Dick, A. S. and Basu, K.), Copyright © 1994, Springer; Figure 9.3 adapted from The relationship between consumer characteristics and attitude toward online shopping, *Marketing Intelligence and Planning*, 21, 1, p. 40 (Shwu-Ing Wu 2003), © Emerald Group Publishing Limited all rights reserved; Figure 9.4 adapted from Ajzen, Icek; Fishbein, Martin, *Understanding Attitudes and Predicting Social Behavior*, 1st ©1980, Printed and Electronically reproduced by permission of Pearson Education, Inc., Upper Saddle River, New Jersey; Figure 9.5 adapted from The power of feelings in understanding advertising effects, *Journal of Consumer Research*, 14, December, p. 431 (Edell, J. A. and Burke, M. C. 1987), Copyright © 1987, JCR, Inc; Figure 9.9 from Nikon advertisement, www.europe-nikon.com, Nikon BV; Figure 9.10 from Dove soap advertisement, reproduced with kind permission of Unilever [from an original in Unilever Archives]; Figure 10.5 adapted from A new model for measuring advertising effectiveness, *Journal of Advertising Research*, March/April, pp. 23-31 (Hall, B. F. 2002), with permission from Warc; Figure 10.6 from SAAB advertisement, with permission from Saab USA and Saab AB; Figure 11.3 adapted from Selecting celebrity endorsers: The practitioner's perspective, *Journal of Advertising Research*, May/June, p. 46 (Zafer Erdogan, B., Baker, M. J. and Tagg, S. 2001), with permission from Warc; Figure 11.6 adapted from Strategies for influencing parental decisions on food purchasing, *Journal of Consumer Marketing*, 21, 2, p. 135 (Marquis, M. 2004), © Emerald Group Publishing Limited all rights reserved; Figure 11.7 adapted from A modern-sized family life cycle, *Journal of Consumer Research*, 6 June, p. 17 (Murphy, P. E. and Staples, W. A. 1979), Copyright © 1979, JCR, Inc; Figure 13.1 adapted from Culture and consumption: A theoretical account of the structure and movement of the cultural meaning of consumer goods, *Journal of Consumer Research*, 13, June, p. 72 (McCracken, G. 1986), Copyright © 1986, JCR, Inc; Figure 13.4 from Unilever Bestfoods advertisement, reproduced with kind permission of Unilever [from an original in Unilever Archives]; Figure 14.2a from British Airways advertisement - Don't sit up all night before important meetings. © British Airways, reprinted with permission from British Airways Plc; Figure 15.6 reprinted with permission from Riding the saddle: How cross-market communications can create a major slump in sales, *Journal of Marketing*, published by the American Marketing Association, Goldenberg, J., Libai, B. and Muller, E., 66, April 2002, p. 5; Figure 15.9 from adidas 'Be first' advertisement. adidas, the adidas 3-Bars logo and FOREVER SPORT are registered trademarks of the adidas group, used with permission.

Tables

Table 1.3 adapted from *Beyond the Marketing Concept: From 'Make only what you can sell' to 'Let customers customize what you make'*, Working Paper, May (Wisenblit, J. 2002), The Stillman School of Business, Seton Hall University, South Orange, NJ, with permission from Joe Wisenblit; Table 2.1 reprinted with permission from Customer research, not marketing research, *Marketing Research*, published by the American Marketing Association, Pruden, D. R. and Vavra, T. G., Summer 2000, pp. 14-19; Table 3.1 adapted from VALS™ segments consumers by psychological characteristics and a few demographics. GeoVALS™ brings geography to VALS, Reprinted with permission of Strategic Business Insights (SBI); www.strategicbusinessinsights.com/VALS; Table 3.3 adapted from Segmenting global markets by generational cohorts: determining motivations by age, *Journal of Consumer Behaviour*, 1 September, p. 56 (Schewe, C. D. and Meredith, G. 2004), copyright © 2004 Henry Stewart Publications Ltd., reprinted with permission from John Wiley and Sons; Table 3.6 reprinted with permission from How to court various target markets, *Marketing News*, published by the American Marketing Association, Barlow, R. G., 9 October 2002, p. 22; Table 4.8 reprinted with permission from Decision making and coping of functionally illiterate consumers and some implications for marketing management, *Journal of Marketing*, published by the American Marketing Association, Viswanathan, M., Rosa, J. A., Harris, J. E., 69, January 2005, p. 25; Table 4.10 adapted from Gift giving in Hong Kong and the continuum of social ties, *Journal of Consumer Research*, 28, 2, September, p. 244 (Joy, A. 2001), Copyright © 2001, JCR, Inc; Table 4.11 adapted from The role of mothers as gift givers: A comparison across three cultures, *Advances in Consumer Research*, 23, edited by Kim P. Corfman and John G. Lynch, Jr., p. 26 (Hill, C. and Romm, C. T. 1996), reproduced with permission of Association for Consumer Research; permission conveyed through Copyright Clearance Center, Inc; Table 4.12 adapted from To me from me: A descriptive phenomenology for self-gifts, *Advances in Consumer Research*, 23, edited by Marvin E. Goldberg, Gerald Gorn and Richard W. Pollay, pp. 677-82 (Mick, D. G. and DeMoss, M. 1990), reproduced with permission of Association for Consumer Research; permission conveyed through Copyright Clearance Center, Inc; Table 6.1 adapted from *What Flavour is Your Personality? Discover Who You Are by Looking at What You Eat*, Sourcebooks (Hirsch, A. 2001), with permission from Dr. Alan Hirsch; Table 6.2 adapted from Consumer innovativeness: Concepts and measurements, *Journal of Business Research*, 57, 6, June, p. 674 (Roehrich, G. 2004), Copyright 2004, with permission from Elsevier; Table 6.3 adapted from Consumers' need for uniqueness: Scale development and validation, *Journal of Consumer Research*, 28, June, pp. 50-66 (Tepper Tian, K., Bearden, W. O., Hunter, G. L. 2001), Copyright © 2001, JCR, Inc; Table 6.4 adapted from A consumer values orientation for materialism and its measurement: Scale development and validation, *Journal of Consumer Research*, 19, 3, December, p. 310 (Richins, M. L. and Dawson, S. 1992), Copyright © 1992, JCR, Inc; Table 6.6 reprinted with permission from Consumer ethnocentrism: Construction and validation of the CETSCALE, *Journal of Marketing Research*, published by the American Marketing Association, Shimp, T. A. and Sharma, S., 24, August 1987, p. 282; Table 6.7 adapted from Does 'Made in ...' matter to consumers? A Malaysian study of country of origin effect, *Multinational Business Review*, Fall, p. 73 (Mohamad, O., Ahmed, Z. U., Honeycutt, Jr., E. D. and Tyebkhan, T. H. 2000), with permission from Emerald Group Publishing Ltd; Table 6.8 adapted from Colour schemes, *New York Magazine*, 2 April, pp. 22-3 (Kanner, B. 1989), Bernice Kanner/New York Magazine, New York Media; Table 6.10 reprinted with permission from Managing images in different cultures: A crossnational study of colour meanings and preferences, *Journal of International Marketing*, published by the American Marketing Association, Madden, T. J., Hewett, K. and Roth, M. S., 8, 4, 2000, p. 95; Table 6.11 adapted from Peak experiences and mountain biking: Incorporating the bike in the extended self, *Advances in Consumer Research*, 1996 (Dodson, K. J. 1996), reproduced with permission of Association for Consumer Research; permission conveyed through Copyright Clearance Center, Inc; Table 6.12 adapted from Trait aspects of vanity: Measurement and relevance to consumer behaviour, *Journal of Consumer Research*, 21, March, p. 624 (Netemeyer, R. G., Burton, S. and Lichtenstein, D. R. 1995), Copyright © 1995, JCR, Inc; Table 7.1 adapted from Capture and communicate value in the pricing of services, *MIT Sloan Management Review*, Summer, pp. 41-51 (Berry, L. L., Manjit, Y. S. 1996), © 1996 from MIT Sloan Management Review/Massachusetts Institute of Technology. All rights reserved. Distributed by Tribune Media Services; Table 7.2 adapted from Beyond reference price: Understanding consumers' encounters with unexpected prices, *Journal of Product and Brand Management*, 12, 3, p. 141 (Lindsey-Mulliken, J. 2003), © Emerald Group Publishing Limited all rights reserved; Table 8.3 adapted from A revised product involvement inventory: Improved usability and validity, *Diversity in Consumer Behaviour: Advances in Consumer Research*, Vol. 19, pp. 108-115 (McQuarrie, E. F. and Munson, J. M. 1992), reproduced with permission of Association for Consumer Research; permission conveyed through Copyright Clearance Center, Inc; Table 8.4 reprinted with permission from Whence brand loyalty?, *Journal of Marketing*, published by the American Marketing Association, Oliver, R. L., 63, 1999, pp. 33-44; Table 8.5 reprinted by permission from Macmillan Publishers Ltd:, *Journal of Brand Management*, January, A comparison of attitudinal loyalty measurement approaches, pp. 193-209 (Bennett, R. and Rundle-Thiele, S. 2002), copyright 2002, published by Palgrave Macmillan; Table 9.6 reprinted by permission from Macmillan Publishers Ltd:, *Corporate Reputation Review*, 7, 1 October, From actions to impressions: Cognitive attribution theory and the formation of corporate reputation, p. 277 (Sjovall, A. M. and Talk, A. C. 2004), copyright 2004, published by Palgrave Macmillan; Table 11.4 adapted from A cross-national study on children's purchasing behaviour and parental response, *Journal of Consumer Marketing*, 21, 4, p. 276 (Wimalasiri, J. S. 2004), © Emerald Group Publishing Limited all rights reserved; Table 11.5 adapted from The influence of children on purchases: the development of measures for gender role orientation and shopping savvy, *International Journal of Market Research*, 47, 1, p. 22 (Tinson, J. and Nancarrow, C. 2005), with permission from Warc; Table 11.6 adapted from Children's influence on family decision making: A restaurant study, *Journal of Business Research*, 54, 2, November, p. 175 (Labrecque, J. and Ricard, L. 2001), Copyright 2001, with permission from Elsevier; Table 13.5 reprinted with permission from Getting to know Y: The consumption behaviours of a new cohort, *2000 AMA Winter Educators' Conference, Marketing Theory, Conference Proceedings*, published by the American Marketing Association, Noble, S. M. and Noble, C. H.,11, p. 294; Table 13.6 adapted from The value orientation of new-age elderly: The coming of an ageless market, *Journal of Business Research*, 22, 2, March, pp. 187-94 (Schiffman, L. G. and Sherman, E. 1991), Copyright 2001, with permission from Elsevier; Table 13.7 reprinted with permission from Men and women online: What makes them click, *Marketing Research*, published by the American Marketing Association, Smith, S. M. and Whitlark, D. B., 13, 2, Summer 2001, p. 23; Table 14.5 adapted from How to turn national European brands into Pan-European Brands, Working Paper, Hagan School of Business, Iona College, New Rochelle, NY, with permission from George V. Priovolos, PhD; Table 15.2 adapted from Surrogate buyers and the new product adoption process: A conceptualization and managerial framework, *Journal of Consumer Marketing*, 14, 5, p. 394 (Aggarwal, P. and Cha, T. 1997), © Emerald Group Publishing Limited all rights reserved; Table 15.3 from Price perceptions and consumer shopping behaviour: A field study, *Journal of Marketing Research*, 30 (May), pp. 234-245 (Lichtenstein, D.

R., Ridgway, N. M., Netemeyer, R. G. 1993), used with the permission of American Marketing Association; permission conveyed through Copyright Clearance Center, Inc.

Photos

The publisher would like to thank the following for their kind permission to reproduce their photographs:

(Key: b-bottom; c-centre; l-left; r-right; t-top)

Corbis: © Swim Ink 2, LLC / CORBIS 172; **Image courtesy of The Advertising Archives:** 112, 113, 114, 117, 143, 172, 215l, 215r, 248, 249, 251, 270, 305, 346.

Every effort has been made to trace the copyright holders and we apologise in advance for any unintentional omissions. We would be pleased to insert the appropriate acknowledgement in any subsequent edition of this publication.

PART 1

INTRODUCTION

PART 1 PROVIDES THE BACKGROUND AND THE TOOLS FOR A STRONG AND COMPREHENSIVE UNDERSTANDING OF CONSUMER BEHAVIOUR

Chapter 1 introduces the reader to the study of consumer behaviour, its diversity, its development and the role of consumer research. It concludes with a detailed discussion of ethical considerations in marketing and consumer practices and introduces a simple model of consumer decision-making. Chapter 2 provides an overview of the critical research process and the techniques associated with consumer behaviour research, including a discussion of positivist and interpretivist research methods. Chapter 3 presents a comprehensive examination of market segmentation and demonstrates how consumer behaviour variables provide both the conceptual framework and the strategic direction for the practical segmentation of markets.

CHAPTER 1

AN INTRODUCTION TO THE STUDY OF CONSUMER BEHAVIOUR

Consumer behaviour has changed dramatically in the past few decades. Today, consumers can order online many customised products ranging from trainers to computers. Many have replaced their daily newspapers with customised, online editions of these media and are increasingly receiving information from online sources. Students choosing a university no longer rely on receiving prospectuses through the post; instead, they have online access to all the pertinent information about a university's courses and teaching staff and, in some cases, can visit, virtually, actual classes. People wanting to sell their old computers or grandmother's antique table no longer need to advertise in the local newspaper or rely on a pricey auctioneer; instead, they can sell these items via online auctions or their own personalised online advertisement. Consumers who want out-of-print books no longer have to visit out-of-the-way shops with hundreds of poorly organised dusty shelves, and those who wish to purchase a book published in another country no longer have to call foreign publishers or deal with the bureaucratic nightmare of overseas delivery; instead, they can visit online stores where they can easily locate and place orders for the books they seek. Television viewers can now avoid the advertisement breaks by using the 'skip' feature of their recorders and order on demand previously shown television programmes as well as films. All of these new ways of selling products and services became available to consumers during the past 15 years and are the result of digital technologies. And they also have another thing in common: they exist today because they reflect an understanding of consumer needs and consumer behaviour.

The term **consumer behaviour** is defined as the behaviour that consumers display in searching for, purchasing, using, evaluating and disposing of products and services that they expect will satisfy their needs. Consumer behaviour focuses on how individuals make decisions to spend their available resources (time, money, effort) on consumption-related items. That includes what they buy, why they buy it, when they buy it, where they buy it, how often they buy it, how often they use it, how they evaluate it after the purchase, the impact of such evaluations on future purchases and how they dispose of it.

Clearly, as individuals we are all unique. However, one of the most important constants among all of us despite our differences is that, above all, we are consumers. We use or consume on a regular basis food, clothing, shelter, transport, education, equipment, holidays, necessities, luxuries, services and even ideas. As consumers we play a vital role in the health of the economy – local, national and international. The purchase decisions we make affect the demand for basic raw materials, for transport, for production, for banking; they affect the employment of workers and the deployment of resources, the success of some industries and the failure of others. In order to succeed in any business, and especially in today's dynamic and rapidly evolving marketplace, marketers need to know everything they can about consumers – what they want, what they think, how they work, how they spend their leisure time. They need to understand the personal and group influences that affect consumer decisions and how these decisions are made. And, in these days of ever-widening media choices, they need not only to identify their target audiences, but also to know where and how to reach them.

The term consumer behaviour describes two different kinds of consuming entities: the personal consumer and the organisational consumer. The **personal consumer** buys goods and services for his or her own use, for the use of the household, or as a gift for a friend. In each of these contexts, the products are bought for final use by individuals, who are referred to as end-users or ultimate consumers. The second category of consumer – the **organisational consumer** – includes companies and charities, government agencies (local and national), and institutions (e.g. schools, hospitals and prisons), all of which must buy products, equipment and services in order to run their organisations. Despite the importance of both categories of consumers – individuals and organisations – this book will focus on the individual consumer, who purchases for his or her own personal use or for household use. End-use consumption is perhaps the most pervasive of all types of consumer behaviour, for it involves every individual, of every age and background, in the role of either buyer or user, or both.

DEVELOPMENT OF THE MARKETING CONCEPT AND THE DISCIPLINE OF CONSUMER BEHAVIOUR

The field of consumer behaviour is rooted in the **marketing concept**, a business orientation that evolved in the 1950s through several alternative approaches towards doing business referred to, respectively, as the production concept, the product concept and the selling concept.

The *production concept* assumes that consumers are mostly interested in product availability at low prices; its implicit marketing objectives are cheap, efficient production and intensive distribution. This orientation makes sense when consumers are more interested in obtaining the product than they are in specific features and will buy what is available rather than wait for what they really want. Today, using this orientation makes sense in developing countries or in other situations in which the main objective is to expand the market.

The *product concept* assumes that consumers will buy the product that offers them the highest quality, the best performance and the most features. A product orientation leads the company to strive constantly to improve the quality of its product and to add new features that are technically feasible without finding out first whether or not consumers really want these features. A product orientation often leads to 'marketing myopia', that is, a focus on the product rather than on the consumer needs it presumes to satisfy. Marketing myopia may cause a company to ignore crucial changes in the marketplace because it causes marketers to look in the mirror rather than through the window. For example, Levi's Jeans saw a decline in sales from record annual sales of $7.1 billion in 1996 to $5.1 billion in 1999. In the same period, profits fell from more than $1 billion to barely nothing, despite the fact that Levi's closed down 30 of its 51 factories and laid off 15,000 of its workers. The reason? Levi's no longer connected with younger customers, and did not offer products able to satisfy the changing needs of the market.[1]

A natural evolution from both the production concept and the product concept is the *selling concept*, in which a marketer's primary focus is selling the product(s) that it has unilaterally decided to produce. The assumption of the selling concept is that consumers are unlikely to buy the product unless they are aggressively persuaded to do so – mostly through the 'hard sell' approach. The problem with this approach is that it fails to consider customer satisfaction. When consumers are induced to buy products they do not want or need, they will not buy them again. Also, they are likely to communicate any dissatisfaction with the product through negative word-of-mouth that serves to dissuade potential consumers from making similar purchases. Today, the selling concept is typically utilised by marketers of unsought goods (such as life insurance), by political parties 'selling' their candidates aggressively to apathetic voters and by firms that have excess inventory.

The marketing concept

The field of consumer behaviour is rooted in a marketing strategy that evolved in the late 1950s, when some marketers began to realise that they could sell more goods, more easily, if they produced only those goods they had already determined that consumers would buy. Instead of trying to persuade customers to buy what the firm had already produced, marketing-oriented firms found that it was a lot easier to produce only products they had first confirmed, through research, that consumers wanted. Consumer needs and wants became the firm's primary focus. This consumer-oriented marketing philosophy came to be known as the *marketing concept*.

The key assumption underlying the marketing concept is that to be successful a company must determine the needs and wants of specific target markets and deliver the desired satisfactions better than the competition. The marketing concept is based on the premise that a marketer should make what it can sell, instead of trying to sell what it has made. Whereas the selling concept focuses on the needs of the *sellers* and on existing products, the marketing concept focuses on the needs of the *buyer*. The selling concept focuses on profits through sales volume; the marketing concept focuses on profits through customer satisfaction.

It is interesting to note that even before the evolution of the marketing concept, an intuitive understanding of consumer behaviour was the key to the growth of companies that have remained highly successful even today. Apparently, companies centred on understanding customers are the ones that continue to grow and remain leaders in their industries in spite of increased competition and changing business environments. Two anecdotes depicting two business leaders who led such companies are presented in Table 1-1.

Implementing the marketing concept

The widespread adoption of the marketing concept provided the impetus for the study of consumer behaviour. To identify unsatisfied consumer needs, companies had to engage in extensive marketing research. In so doing, they discovered that consumers were highly complex individuals, subject to a variety of psychological and social needs quite apart from their survival needs. They discovered that the needs and priorities of different consumer segments differed dramatically, and in order to design new products and marketing strategies that would fulfil consumer needs, they had to study consumers and their consumption behaviour in depth. Thus, the marketing concept underscored the importance of consumer research and laid the groundwork for the application of consumer behaviour principles to marketing strategy. The strategic tools that are used to implement the marketing concept include segmentation, targeting, positioning and the marketing mix.

TABLE 1-1 Two business leaders who understood consumer behaviour long before the development of the marketing concept

1. In the 1930s, Colonel Sanders, America's Chicken King, opened a roadside restaurant where he developed the recipes and cooking methods that are the key to Kentucky Fried Chicken's successes even today. As the restaurant grew in popularity, Sanders enlarged it and also opened a roadside motel. At that time, motels had a bad reputation and 'nice' people driving long distances generally stayed in central hotels. Sanders decided to try and overcome this image by putting a sample room of his clean and comfortable motel in the middle of his successful restaurant, and even put the entrance to the restaurant's ladies' toilet in that room. Sanders understood the importance of image and of turning an offering into a success by repositioning, long before this idea was articulated as a business objective. Later on, Sanders came up with the idea of franchising his cooking methods and chicken recipe, while keeping the ingredients of the recipe a secret, and founded KFC and a business model that has since been adopted by many other fast-food chains.[a]

2. In the 1950s, Ray Kroc met the brothers McDonald, who pioneered the idea of fast food as we know it today in a single outlet in California, and became their partner. Ray Kroc envisaged thousands of McDonald's outlets across the country. Trying to pinpoint the best locations for the new restaurants, Kroc used to fly over towns looking for church steeples. He believed that where there were churches there were good American families – the kind of people he wanted as customers. Intuitively, Kroc understood and practised market targeting. In 1961, Kroc opened Hamburger University as a training centre for the company's franchisees and their employees, and pioneered the idea of centralised training as a key to delivering standardised products across a large number of outlets with a wide geographical spread.[b]

Sources: [a]Colonel Sanders, America's Chicken King, VHS Tape, A&E Television Networks, 1998.
[b]Ray Kroc, Fast-Food McMillionaire, VHS Tape, A&E Television Networks, 1998.

The role of consumer research

Consumer research describes the process and tools used to study consumer behaviour. Broadly speaking, there are two theoretical perspectives that guide the development of consumer research methodology: the positivist approach and the interpretivist approach.

Positivists tend to be objective and empirical, to seek causes for behaviour, and to conduct research studies that can be generalised to larger populations. Consumer research designed to provide data to be used for strategic managerial decisions falls into this category.

The research done by *interpretivists*, on the other hand, tends to be qualitative and based on small samples. Although they tend to view each consumption situation as unique and unpredictable, interpretivists seek to find common patterns of operative values, meanings and behaviour across consumption situations. Chapter 2 explores the basic assumptions and methodology of each research approach in some detail.

Segmentation, targeting and positioning

The focus of the marketing concept is consumer needs. At the same time, recognising the high degree of diversity among us, consumer researchers seek to identify the many similarities – or constants – that exist among the peoples of the world. For example, we all have the same kinds of biological needs, no matter where we are born – the needs for food, for nourishment, for water, for air and for shelter from the elements. We also acquire needs after we are born. These needs are shaped by the environment and the culture in which we live, by our education and by our experiences. The interesting thing about acquired needs is that there are usually many people who develop the same needs. This commonality of need or interest constitutes a market segment, which enables the marketer to target consumers with specifically designed products and/or promotional appeals that satisfy the needs of that segment. The marketer must also adapt the image of its product (i.e. 'position' it), so that each market segment perceives the product as better fulfilling its specific needs than competitive products. The three elements of this strategic framework are market segmentation, targeting and positioning.

Market segmentation is the process of dividing a market into subsets of consumers with common needs or characteristics. The variables and methods used to form such subsets are detailed in Chapter 3. Because most companies have limited resources, few companies can pursue all of the market segments identified. Market **targeting** is selecting one or more of the segments identified for the company to pursue. The criteria for selecting target markets are detailed in Chapter 3.

Positioning is developing a distinct image for the product or service in the mind of the consumer, an image that will differentiate the offering from competing ones and squarely communicate to consumers that the particular product or service will fulfil their needs better than competing brands. Successful positioning centres around two key principles: first, communicating the benefits that the product will provide rather than the product's features. As one marketing sage pointed out: 'consumers do not buy drill bits – they buy ways to make holes'. Secondly, because there are many similar products in almost any marketplace, an effective positioning strategy must develop and communicate a 'unique selling proposition' – a distinct benefit or

TABLE 1-2 Rollerblade: Effective implementation of the marketing concept

About two decades ago, in-line skates were an off-season training tool for hockey players. In the mid-1980s, Rollerblade developed marketing strategies that positioned in-line skating as a new sport. The company sold in-line skates to bicycle and conventional skate hire stores in two trend-setting places: Miami Beach, Florida, and Venice Beach, California, and a new form of recreational sport that appeals to many age groups and social classes was born. Backed by aggressive marketing and public relations, the popularity of the new sport soared and was quickly integrated into the mainstream. As competition appeared, Rollerblade continued to lead the market with such innovations as breathable shoe liners, buckle closure systems and female-specific skates; today the company holds several hundred patented innovations.

The company's product line illustrates the utilisation of segmentation, targeting and positioning strategies. The company targets five segments and offers models that provide different benefits to the members of each segment: (1) Men can choose among models designed for expert, intermediate or demanding skaters, and among such benefits as style, technological innovation and performance. (2) Women are targeted with similar choices as men. (3) There are several models for children. (4) Street and park skaters can choose among models focused on durability, performance or attention to detail. (5) Race skaters are targeted with a model offering high-tech features and top performance. The models offered to men, women and children include brakes, whereas the models offered to street, park and race skaters do not.

Rollerblade's entire marketing mix stems from its core product. In addition to the in-line skates, the company sells helmets, skate bags, and wrist, elbow and knee protectors. The skates are priced along a range varying from very expensive models offered to aggressive and racing skaters who look for maximum performance, to value-oriented skaters, to recreational skaters. The products are distributed in a variety of outlets – both domestic and overseas – in a way that reflects the market segments targeted and the skate models' prices. The company advertises its products in the mass media, issues frequent press releases as part of its public relations, and promotes its products through athletic and event sponsorships (currently in the USA there are Rollerblade skate weekends that are called Camp Rollerblade), as well as its 'Skate School'.

The company's website also includes features that encourage skaters to revisit, such as a list of places to skate (arranged by state), a dealer locator, skating tips, tips for people who wish to take up the sport, and suggestions on skating safety. These features show that Rollerblade has a thorough understanding of customer retention as well as social responsibility, concepts that are discussed later in this chapter.

Source: Developed from material available at **www.rollerblade.com**.

point of difference – for the product or service. In fact, most of the new products introduced by marketers (including new forms of existing products such as new flavours, sizes, etc.) fail to capture a significant market share and are discontinued because they are perceived by consumers as 'me too' products lacking a unique image or benefit. In Chapter 7, the concepts and tools of positioning are explored further.

The marketing mix

The **marketing mix** consists of a company's service and/or product offerings to consumers and the methods and tools it selects to accomplish the exchange. The marketing mix consists of four elements:

1. the product or service (the features, designs, brands and packaging offered, along with post-purchase benefits such as warranties and return policies);
2. the price (the list price, including discounts, allowances and payment methods);
3. the place (the distribution of the product or service through specific retail and non-retail outlets);
4. promotion (the advertising, sales promotion, public relations and sales efforts designed to build awareness of and demand for the product or service).

Table 1-2 depicts the implementation of the elements of the marketing concept by the Rollerblade company.

CUSTOMER VALUE, SATISFACTION AND RETENTION

Since its emergence in the 1950s, many companies have very successfully adopted the marketing concept. The result has been more products, in more sizes, models, versions and packages, offered to more precisely targeted (and often smaller) target markets. This has resulted in an increasingly competitive marketplace. And in the 1990s the digital revolution enabled many marketers to offer even more products and services and distribute them more widely, while reducing the costs and barriers of entering many industries. It has accelerated the rate at which new competitors enter markets and also has speeded up the rate at which successful segmentation, targeting and positioning approaches must be updated or changed, as they are imitated or made obsolete by the offerings of new business rivals.

Shrewd marketers today realise that in order to outperform competitors they must achieve the full profit potential from each and every customer. They must make the customer the core of the company's organisational culture, across all departments and functions, and ensure that each and every employee views any exchange with a customer as part of a customer relationship, not as a transaction. The three drivers of successful relationships between marketers and customers are customer value, high levels of customer satisfaction and building a structure for customer retention.

Providing customer value

Customer value is defined as the ratio between the customer's perceived benefits (economic, functional and psychological) and the resources (monetary, time, effort, psychological) used to obtain those benefits. Perceived value is relative and subjective. For example, diners at an exclusive, Michelin-star-awarded restaurant in Copenhagen, Denmark, where a meal with drinks may cost €250 per person, may expect unique and delicious food, immaculate service and beautiful decor. Some diners may receive even more than they had expected and will leave the restaurant feeling that the experience was worth the money and other resources expended (such as a month-long wait for a reservation). Other diners may go with expectations so high that they leave the restaurant disappointed. On the other hand, millions of customers each year visit thousands of McDonald's restaurants in scores of countries around the globe, where they purchase standard, inexpensive meals from franchise owners and employees systematically trained by the McDonald's Corporation to deliver the company's four core standards: quality, service, cleanliness and value. Customers flock to McDonald's outlets repeatedly because the restaurants are uniform, customers know what to expect and they feel that they are getting value for the resources they expend.

Developing a value proposition (a term rapidly replacing the popular business phrase 'unique selling proposition') is the core of successful positioning. For example, Unilever want to bring vitality to life, and promise to meet everyday needs for nutrition, hygiene and personal care with brands that help people feel good, look good and get more out of life. Measures of customers' expectations and evaluations of products and services are discussed in Chapter 2, and the strategic applications of customers' perceptions of prices, quality and value are explored in Chapter 7.

Customer satisfaction

Customer satisfaction is the individual's perception of the performance of the product or service in relation to his or her expectations. As noted earlier, customers will have drastically different expectations of an expensive restaurant and a McDonald's, although both are part of the restaurant industry. The concept of customer satisfaction is a function of customer expectations. A customer whose experience falls below expectations (e.g. used dishes not cleared quickly enough at an expensive restaurant or cold fries served at a McDonald's) will be dissatisfied. Diners whose experiences match expectations will be satisfied. And customers whose expectations are exceeded (e.g. by small samples of delicious food 'from the Chef' served between courses at the expensive restaurant, or a well-designed play area for children at a McDonald's outlet) will be very satisfied or delighted.

A widely quoted study that linked levels of customer satisfaction with customer behaviour identified several types of customers: completely satisfied customers who are either 'loyalists' who keep purchasing, or 'apostles' whose experiences exceed their expectations and who provide very positive word-of-mouth about the company to others; 'defectors' who feel neutral or merely satisfied and are likely to stop doing business with the company; consumer 'terrorists' who have had negative experiences with the company and who spread negative word-of-mouth; 'hostages' who are unhappy customers who stay with the company because of a monopolistic environment or low prices and who are difficult and costly to deal with because of their frequent complaints; and 'mercenaries' who are very satisfied customers but who have no real loyalty to the company and may defect because of a lower price elsewhere or on impulse, defying the satisfaction–loyalty rationale. The researchers propose that companies should strive to create apostles, raise the satisfaction of defectors and turn them into loyalists, avoid having terrorists or hostages, and reduce the number of mercenaries.[2] Customer satisfaction measurement tools and techniques are discussed in Chapter 2.

Customer retention

The overall objective of providing value to customers continuously and more effectively than the competition is to have highly satisfied (even delighted) customers; this strategy of **customer retention** makes it in the best interest of customers to stay with the company rather than switch to another firm. In almost all business situations, it is more expensive to win new customers than to keep existing ones. Studies have shown that small reductions in customer defections produce significant increases in profits because:

1. loyal customers buy more products;
2. loyal customers are less price sensitive and pay less attention to competitors' advertising;
3. servicing existing customers, who are familiar with the firm's offerings and processes, is cheaper; and
4. loyal customers spread positive word-of-mouth and refer other customers.

Furthermore, marketing efforts aimed at attracting new customers are expensive; indeed, in saturated markets, it may be impossible to find new customers.[3] Today the Internet and digital marketer–consumer interactions are ideal tools for tailoring products and services to the specific needs of consumers (often termed one-to-one marketing), offering them more value through increased customer intimacy and keeping the customers returning to the company.

Marketers who designate increasing customer retention rates as a strategic corporate goal must also recognise that all customers are not equal. Sophisticated marketers build selective relationships with customers, based on where customers rank in terms of profitability, rather than strive merely 'to retain customers'. Such a marketer will closely monitor its customers' consumption volume and patterns, establish tiers of customers according to their profitability levels and develop distinct strategies toward each group of customers. For example, some stockbrokers programme their telephones to recognise the phone numbers of high-volume traders to ensure that their calls receive priority.

Customers who have purchased and registered several of a company's products should receive extensive and expedited customer support. On the other hand, for instance, a bank's less profitable customers who make little use of their credit cards should not have penalties waived for bounced cheques or late payments. Some companies also identify customer groups that are unlikely to purchase more if pursued more aggressively; such customers are often discouraged from staying with the company or even 'fired' as customers.

Classifying customers according to profitability levels goes beyond traditional segmentation methods that subdivide consumers on the basis of demographic, sociocultural or behavioural characteristics. Customer profitability-focused marketing tracks costs and revenues of individual customers and then categorises them into tiers based on consumption behaviours that are specific to the company's offerings. Such a strategy is probably the most effective way to utilise the knowledge of consumer behaviour. For example, a recent study advocates using a 'customer pyramid' where customers are grouped into four tiers:

1. the platinum tier includes heavy users who are not price sensitive and who are willing to try new offerings;
2. the gold tier consists of customers who are heavy users but not as profitable because they are more price sensitive than those in the higher tier, ask for more discounts and are likely to buy from several providers;
3. the iron tier consists of customers whose spending volume and profitability do not merit special treatment from the company;
4. the lead tier includes customers who actually cost the company money because they claim more attention than is merited by their spending, tie up company resources and spread negative word-of-mouth.

The authors of the study urge companies to develop distinct marketing responses for each group.[4] Methods for collecting the customer data needed to develop the kind of retention systems discussed here are described in Chapter 2. A corporate philosophy centred on customer value, satisfaction and retention evolves from the marketing concept and also unfolds new dimensions of marketing. Table 1-3 compares traditional marketing with perceived value and retention marketing. Applications of consumer behaviour concepts to value and retention-focused marketing are discussed throughout the book.

TABLE 1-3 The traditional marketing concept versus value- and retention-focused marketing

THE TRADITIONAL MARKETING CONCEPT	VALUE- AND RETENTION-FOCUSED MARKETING
Make only what you can sell instead of trying to sell what you make.	Use technology that enables customers to customize what you make.
Do not focus on the product; focus on the need that it satisfies.	Focus on the product's perceived value, as well as the need that it satisfies.
Market products and services that match customers' needs better than competitors' offerings.	Utilize an understanding of customer needs to develop offerings that customers perceive as more valuable than competitors' offerings.
Research consumer needs and characteristics.	Research the levels of profit associated with various consumer needs and characteristics.
Understand the purchase behavior process and the influences on consumer behavior.	Understand consumer behavior in relation to the company's product.
Realize that each customer transaction is a discrete sale.	Make each customer transaction part of an ongoing relationship with the customer.
Segment the market based on customers' geographic, demographic, psychological, sociocultural, lifestyle, and product-usage related characteristics.	Use hybrid segmentation that combines the traditional segmentation bases with data on the customer's purchase levels and patterns of use of the company's products.
Target large groups of customers that share common characteristics with messages transmitted through mass media.	Invest in technologies that enable you to send one-to-one promotional messages via digital channels.
Use one-way promotions whose effectiveness is measured through sales data or marketing surveys.	Use interactive communications in which messages to customers are tailored according to their responses to previous communications.
Create loyalty programs based on the volume purchased.	Create customer tiers based on both volume and consumption patterns.
Encourage customers to stay with the company and buy more.	Make it very unattractive for your customers to switch to a competitor and encourage them to purchase 'better' – in a manner that will raise the company's profitability levels.
Determine marketing budgets on the basis of the numbers of customers you are trying to reach.	Base your marketing budget on the 'lifetime value' of typical customers in each of the targeted segments compared with the resources needed to acquire them as customers.
Conduct customer satisfaction surveys and present the results to management.	Conduct customer satisfaction surveys that include a component that studies the customer's word-of-mouth about the company, and use the results immediately to enhance customer relationships.
Create customer trust and loyalty to the company and high levels of customer satisfaction.	Create customer intimacy and bonds with completely satisfied, 'delighted' customers.

Source: Adapted from Joseph Wisenblit, 'Beyond the Marketing Concept: From "Make Only What You Can Sell" to "Let Customers Customize What You Make"', The Stillman School of Business, Seton Hall University, South Orange, NJ.

THE IMPACT OF DIGITAL TECHNOLOGIES ON MARKETING STRATEGIES

Digital technologies allow much greater customisation of products, services and promotional messages than older marketing tools. They enable marketers to adapt the elements of the marketing mix to consumers' needs more quickly and efficiently, and to build and maintain relationships with customers on a much greater scale. By using new technologies, marketers can collect and analyse increasingly complex data on consumers' buying patterns and personal characteristics, and quickly analyse and use this information for targeting smaller and increasingly more focused groups of consumers. On the other hand, the same technologies enable consumers to find more information about products and services (including prices) more easily, efficiently and, for the most part, from the comfort of their own homes. Therefore, more than ever before, marketers must ensure that their products and services provide the right benefits and value and are positioned effectively to reach consumers.

Online communication and emerging digital technologies have introduced several dramatic changes into the business environment:

- Consumers have more power than ever before. They can use 'intelligent agents' to locate the best prices for products or services, bid on various marketing offerings, bypass distribution outlets and intermediaries, and shop for goods around the globe and around the clock from the convenience of their homes. Therefore, marketers must offer more competitively priced products and more options.
- Consumers have access to more information than ever before. They can easily find reviews for products they are considering buying that have been posted by previous buyers, click a button to compare the features of different product models at the sites of online retailers, and subscribe to 'virtual communities' of people who share the same interests as they do. In turn, marketers must be aware of the limits of their promotional messages and assume that consumers know all of their buying options.

Marketers can and must offer more services and products than ever before. The digitisation of information enables sellers to customise the products and services they are selling and still sell them at reasonable prices. It also allows marketers to customise the promotional messages directed at many customers. For example, www.amazon.com sends personalised emails to previous book purchasers announcing newly published books; these suggestions are based on a determination of the interests of the targeted consumers derived from their past purchases. Similarly, an online chemist may vary the initial display returning buyers see when they revisit its website. Buyers whose past purchases indicate that they tend to buy national brands will see a display arranged by brand. Past purchasers who bought mostly products that were on sale or generic brands will see a display categorised by price and discounted products.

The exchange between marketers and customers is increasingly interactive and instantaneous. Traditional advertising is a one-way street where the marketer pays a large sum of money to reach a large number of potential buyers via a mass medium, and then assesses (usually after the fact) whether or not the message was effective on the basis of future sales or market studies. On the other hand, digital communication enables a two-way interactive exchange in which consumers can instantly react to the marketer's message by, say, clicking on links within a given website or even by leaving the site. Thus, marketers can quickly gauge the effectiveness of their promotional messages rather than rely on delayed feedback through sales information that is collected after the fact.

Marketers can gather more information about consumers more quickly and easily. Marketers can track consumers' online behaviour and also gather information by requiring visitors to websites to register and provide some information about themselves before they get access to the site's features. Thus, marketers can construct and update their consumer databases efficiently and inexpensively. As a result, many marketers now employ *narrowcasting* – a method that enables them to develop and deliver more customised messages to increasingly smaller markets on an ongoing basis.

Impact reaches beyond the PC-based connection to the Web. Currently, most of the digital communications between consumers and marketers take place via a PC connected to the Web through a broadband connection, or wireless technology. However, the digital revolution also gave us cellphones that are rapidly becoming connected to the Web. In most European countries, consumers can already purchase products via their mobile phones. Mobile phones with built-in GPS systems are likely to become a medium that will deliver customised promotional messages to consumers everywhere. In addition, an increasing number of homes now have television cable boxes that enable interactive communication with broadcasters; as we switch to high-definition television, all cable subscribers will have such boxes. Also, as we receive more and more television programming on PCs, some companies are merging the television and the PC into a single device that provides households with hundreds of cable channels, interactive capabilities and high-speed, wireless access to the Web. Supermarket scanners that keep track of purchases and instantly provide personalised coupons at the checkout, and telephone devices that enable us to identify callers without picking up the phone, are two of the many additional products made possible by recently developed technologies.

Challenges marketers face

The digital revolution in the marketplace, and its impact on consumer behaviour, presents many challenges for today's marketers. For example, the specialised digital recorders allow viewers to control what they watch on television, when they watch it and whether or not to view the advertisements on which marketers spend billions a year. The recorders download programming information and allow users to record many hours of television programming onto a hard drive without the hassle of tapes. Users can programme the recorder by topic or keyword, easily play back selected segments, and, to the delight of many viewers, use a single button to skip commercial breaks. Since these devices are shifting the power over viewing behaviour from the broadcaster to the viewer, broadcasters are facing a new set of challenges. Should they develop their own systems? Should they try to block the sales of such devices legally on the grounds that they contribute to copyright infringement? Or should they develop business models centred on viewers paying for content? These questions are no longer hypothetical and will have to be addressed relatively soon. As consumers spend more time online and have more technological tools that enable them to avoid exposure to television advertisements, some marketers have begun reducing their advertising expenditures on the major networks and investing their advertising budget in the newer media, such as the Web or email.

Marketers have begun to insist that broadcasters develop new measurement systems to estimate more accurately the number and demographics of their viewers. Some marketers are considering investing in technologies that embed electronic tags of advertisements visible only to digital video recorder users, as some advertisers are already doing.

At Nike's website, buyers can now choose among many models of trainers in different price ranges, customise the selected shoe using several colours and features (some models even allow buyers to choose the colours of the Nike Swoosh and the laces), put a personal ID on each shoe, pay for the product and have it sent directly to them. Should Nike and other companies that produce non-durable consumer goods begin shifting resources away from building consumer demand by advertising products carried by independently owned retailers, and into direct distribution systems based on customised offerings?

Some suggest that because virtual competition eliminates distance and location-based benefits (such as a desirable shop location), online sellers will compete almost exclusively on the basis of price for branded merchandise. Does this mean that competitive differentiation – a key feature of modern marketing – will become meaningless in the virtual marketplace? These are only some of the many challenges marketers face as our technologies continue to evolve and change our daily lives and consumption patterns.

MARKETING ETHICS AND SOCIAL RESPONSIBILITY

The marketing concept as we know it – fulfilling the needs of target audiences – is sometimes inappropriate. This is particularly true in situations in which the means for need satisfaction, the product or service provided to fulfil customer 'needs', can be harmful to the individual or to society (e.g. drugs, tobacco) or cause environmental deterioration. Given the fact that all companies prosper when society prospers, many people believe that all of us, companies as well as individuals, would be better off if social responsibility were an integral component of every marketing decision. A reassessment of the traditional marketing concept suggests that a more appropriate conceptualisation for the times in which we live would balance the needs of society with the needs of the individual and the organisation. The **societal marketing concept** requires that all marketers adhere to principles of social responsibility in the marketing of their goods and services: that is, they should endeavour to satisfy the needs and wants of their target markets in ways that preserve and enhance the well-being of consumers and society as a whole. Thus, a restructured definition of the marketing concept calls on marketers to fulfil the needs of the target audience in ways that improve society as a whole, while fulfilling the objectives of the organisation. According to the societal marketing concept, fast-food restaurants should develop foods that contain less fat and starch and more nutrients, and marketers should not advertise alcohol or cigarettes to young people, or use young models or professional athletes in alcohol or tobacco advertisements, because celebrities so often serve as role models for the young.

A serious deterrent to widespread implementation of the societal marketing concept is the short-term orientation embraced by most business executives in their drive for increased market share and quick profits. This short-term orientation derives from the fact that managerial performance is usually evaluated on the basis of short-term results. Thus, a young and ambitious advertising executive may create a striking advertising campaign using unreasonably slim females with pale faces and withdrawn expressions in order dramatically to increase the sales of the advertised product, without considering the negative impact of the campaign, such as an increase in eating disorders among young women or the implicit approval of drug-taking reflected in the models' appearances. The societal marketing concept, however, advocates a long-term perspective. It recognises that all companies would be better off in a stronger, healthier society, and that companies that incorporate ethical behaviour and social responsibility in all of their business dealings attract and maintain loyal consumer support over the long term.

The primary purpose for studying consumer behaviour as part of a marketing curriculum is to understand why and how consumers make their purchase decisions. These insights enable marketers to design more effective marketing strategies, especially today when advanced technologies enable marketers to collect more data about consumers and target them more precisely. Some critics are concerned that an in-depth understanding of consumer behaviour makes it possible for unethical marketers to exploit human vulnerabilities in the marketplace and engage in other unethical marketing practices in order to achieve individual business objectives. As a result, many trade associations have developed industry-wide codes of ethics, because they recognise that industry-wide self-regulation is in every member's best interests in that it deters government from imposing its own regulations on the industry. A number of companies have incorporated specific social goals into their mission statements and include programmes in support of these goals as integral components of their strategic planning. They believe that **marketing ethics** and social responsibility are important components of organisational effectiveness. Most companies recognise that socially responsible activities improve their image among consumers, shareholders, the financial community and other relevant public bodies. They have found that ethical and socially responsible practices are simply good business, resulting not only in a favourable image, but ultimately in increased sales. The converse is also true: perceptions of a company's lack of social responsibility or unethical marketing strategies negatively affect consumer purchase decisions. Applicable marketing ethics and social responsibility issues are discussed throughout the book.

CONSUMER BEHAVIOUR AND DECISION-MAKING ARE INTERDISCIPLINARY

Consumer behaviour was a relatively new field of study in the mid- to late 1960s. Because it had no history or body of research of its own, marketing theorists borrowed heavily from concepts developed in other scientific disciplines, such as psychology (the study of the individual), sociology (the study of groups), social psychology (the study of how an individual operates in a group), anthropology (the influence of society on the individual) and economics, to form the basis of this new marketing discipline. Many early theories concerning consumer behaviour were based on economic theory, on the notion that individuals act rationally to maximise their benefits (satisfactions) in the purchase of goods and services. Later research discovered that consumers are just as likely to purchase impulsively and to be influenced not only by family and friends, by advertisers and role models, but also by mood, situation and emotion. All of these factors combine to form a comprehensive model of consumer behaviour that reflects both the cognitive and emotional aspects of **consumer decision-making**.

A simplified model of consumer decision-making

The process of consumer decision-making can be viewed as three distinct but interlocking stages: the input stage, the process stage and the output stage. These stages are depicted in the simplified model of consumer decision-making in Figure 1-1.

The *input stage* influences the consumer's recognition of a product need and consists of two major sources of information: the firm's marketing efforts (the product itself, its price, its promotion and where it is sold) and the external sociological influences on the consumer (family, friends, neighbours, other informal and non-commercial sources, social class and cultural and subcultural memberships). The cumulative impact of each firm's marketing efforts, the influence of family, friends and neighbours, and society's existing code of behaviour, are all inputs that are likely to affect what consumers purchase and how they use what they buy.

The *process stage* of the model focuses on how consumers make decisions. The psychological factors inherent in each individual (motivation, perception, learning, personality and attitudes) affect how the external inputs from the input stage influence the consumer's recognition of a need, pre-purchase search for information and evaluation of alternatives. The experience gained through evaluation of alternatives, in turn, affects the consumer's existing psychological attributes.

The *output stage* of the consumer decision-making model consists of two closely related post-decision activities: purchase behaviour and post-purchase evaluation. Purchase behaviour for a low-cost, non-durable product (e.g. a new shampoo) may be influenced by a manufacturer's extensive sales promotion (e.g. price cuts) and may actually be a trial purchase; if the consumer is satisfied, he or she may repeat the purchase. The trial is the exploratory phase of purchase behaviour in which the consumer evaluates the product through direct use. A repeat purchase usually signifies product adoption. For a relatively durable product such as a laptop ('relatively' durable because of the rapid rate of obsolescence), the purchase is more likely to signify adoption. Marketing to consumers has one overarching goal – that consumers choose to buy your product instead of alternative products offered by your competitors. Drawing from this, the consumer decision-making model is examined in greater depth in Chapter 4, as all psychological and sociocultural concepts explored throughout the book ultimately influence the decision-making process in one way or the other.

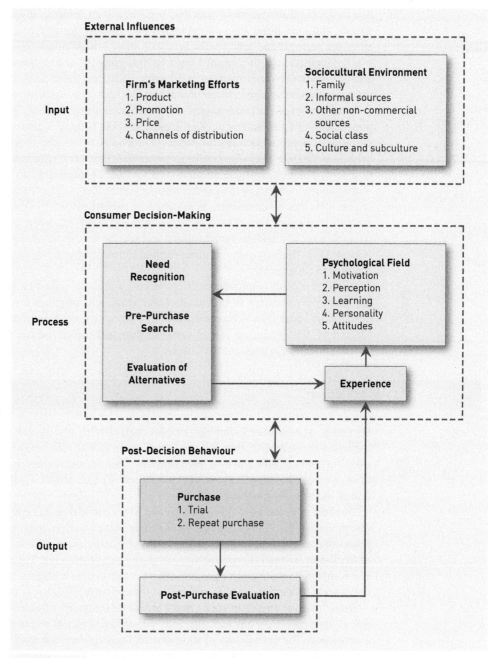

FIGURE 1-1 A simple model of consumer decision-making

THE PLAN OF THIS BOOK

In an effort to build a useful conceptual framework that both enhances understanding and permits practical application of consumer behaviour principles to marketing strategy, this book is divided into four parts: Part 1 gives an introduction to the study of consumer behaviour, Part 2 discusses the consumer as an individual, starting with how consumers make decisions, Part 3 examines consumers in their social and cultural settings and Part 4 synthesises all of the variables discussed earlier into the consumer decision-making process.

Chapter 1 introduced the reader to the study of consumer behaviour as an interdisciplinary science that investigates the consumption-related activities of individuals. It described the reasons for the development of consumer behaviour as an academic discipline and as an applied science, and introduced a simplified model of consumer decision-making that links together all of the personal and group influences that affect consumption decisions. Chapter 2 examines the methodology of consumer research, including the assumptions underlying qualitative and quantitative research approaches. Chapter 3 discusses the process of market segmentation, including the demographic, sociocultural and psychographic bases for segmenting markets.

Part 2 focuses on the psychological characteristics of the consumer. Chapter 4 gives a detailed presentation of the consumer decision-making process, Chapter 5 discusses how individuals are motivated, Chapter 6 examines the impact of individual personality characteristics on consumer behaviour, Chapter 7 explores consumer perception, Chapter 8 examines how consumers learn, Chapter 9 discusses consumer attitudes, and Chapter 10 concludes Part 2 with an examination of the communications process and consumer persuasion.

Part 3 focuses on consumers as members of society, subject to varying external influences on their buying behaviour, such as their group and family memberships (Chapter 11), social class (Chapter 12), and the broad cultural and specific subcultural groups to which they belong (Chapter 13). The importance of cross-cultural consumer research to international marketing is explored in Chapter 14.

Part 4 extends the topics on decision-making and social influence as Chapter 15 discusses the consumer's reactions to innovation and change, and describes the process by which new products are adopted and become diffused throughout society. Finally, the book concludes with Chapter 16, which summarises the variables discussed earlier and ties them back to the decision-making process presented in Chapter 4.

SUMMARY

The study of consumer behaviour enables marketers to understand and predict consumer behaviour in the marketplace; it is concerned not only with what consumers buy but also with why, when, where, how and how often they buy it. Consumer research is the methodology used to study consumer behaviour and takes place at every phase of the consumption process: before, during and after the purchase.

The field of consumer behaviour is rooted in the marketing concept, a business orientation that evolved in the 1950s through several alternative approaches, referred to, respectively, as the production concept, the product concept and the selling concept. The three major strategic tools of marketing are market segmentation, targeting and positioning. The marketing mix consists of a company's service and/or product offerings to consumers and the pricing, promotion and distribution methods needed to accomplish the exchange.

Skilled marketers make the customer the core of the company's organisational culture and ensure that all employees view any exchange with a customer as part of a customer relationship, not as a transaction. The three drivers of successful relationships between marketers and customers are customer value, high levels of customer satisfaction and building a structure for customer retention.

Digital technologies allow much greater customisation of products, services and promotional messages than do older marketing tools. They enable marketers to adapt the elements of the marketing mix to consumers' needs more quickly and efficiently, and to build and maintain relationships with customers on a much greater scale. However, these technologies also represent significant challenges to marketers and to business models that have been used for decades.

Consumer behaviour is interdisciplinary: that is, it is based on concepts and theories about people that have been developed by scientists in such diverse disciplines as psychology, sociology, social psychology, cultural anthropology and economics.

Consumer behaviour has become an integral part of strategic market planning. The belief that ethics and social responsibility should also be integral components of every marketing decision is embodied in a revised marketing concept – the societal marketing concept – that calls on marketers to fulfil the needs of their target markets in ways that improve society as a whole.

DISCUSSION QUESTIONS

1. Describe the interrelationship between consumer behaviour as an academic discipline and the marketing concept.
2. Describe the interrelationships between consumer research, market segmentation and targeting, and the development of the marketing mix for a manufacturer of high-definition television sets.
3. Define the societal marketing concept and discuss the importance of integrating marketing ethics into the company's philosophy and operations.
4. Discuss the interrelationships among customer expectations and satisfaction, perceived value and customer retention. Why is customer retention essential?
5. Discuss the role of the social and behavioural sciences in developing the consumer decision-making model.
6. Apply each of the two models depicted in Table 1-3 (i.e. traditional marketing and value and retention marketing) to the marketing of mobile phone services. You may want to incorporate into your answer your own and your peers' experiences in selecting network providers.

EXERCISES

1. You are the marketing manager of a bank's online banking division. How would you apply the concepts of providing value and customer satisfaction and retention to designing and marketing effective online banking?
2. Find two examples (e.g. advertisements, articles, etc.) depicting practices that are consistent with the societal marketing concept and two examples of business practices that contradict this concept. Explain your choices.
3. Apply each of the concepts featured in the section describing the development of the marketing concept to manufacturing and marketing cars.

NOTES

1. David Jobber, *Principles and Practice of Marketing*, 4th edn (Maidenhead, UK: McGraw-Hill Education, 2004).
2. Thomas O. Jones and W. Earl Sasser, Jr., 'Why Satisfied Customers Defect', *Harvard Business Review*, November–December 1995, 88–99.
3. Frederick F. Reichheld and W. Earl Sasser, Jr., 'Zero Defections: Quality Comes to Services', *Harvard Business Review*, September–October 1990, 105–11; Michael Treacy and Fred Wiersema, 'Customer Intimacy and Other Value Disciplines', *Harvard Business Review*, January–February 1993, 84–93.
4. Valerie A. Zeithaml, Roland T. Rust and Katherine N. Lemon, 'The Customer Pyramid: Creating and Serving Profitable Customers', *California Management Review*, Summer 2001, 118–42.

CHAPTER 2
CONSUMER RESEARCH

The marketing concept states that, to be successful, a company must understand the needs of specific groups of consumers (i.e. target markets) and then satisfy these needs more effectively than the competition. The satisfaction of consumer needs is delivered in the form of the marketing mix, which consists of the so-called '4 Ps': product, price, place and promotion. Marketers who have a thorough understanding of the consumer decision-making process are likely to design products, establish prices, select distribution outlets and design promotional messages that will favourably influence consumer purchase decisions.

The field of consumer research developed as an extension of the field of marketing research. Just as the findings of marketing research are used to improve managerial decision-making, so too are the findings of consumer research. Studying consumer behaviour, in all its ramifications, enables marketers to predict how consumers will react to promotional messages and to understand why they make the purchase decisions they do. Marketers realise that the more they know about their target consumers' decision-making process, the more likely they are to design marketing strategies and promotional messages that will favourably influence these consumers. Shrewd marketers recognise that consumer research is a unique subset of marketing research, which merits the use of specialised research methods to collect customer data. Consumer research enables marketers to study and understand consumers' needs and wants, and how they make consumption decisions. Table 2-1 details comparisons between customer research and marketing research.

TABLE 2-1 Comparisons between customer research and marketing research

	CUSTOMER RESEARCH	MARKETING RESEARCH
Study purpose	Data collection and, potentially, strengthening the relationship between the customers and the company. Contacted customers are told the identity of the survey's sponsor.	Data collection only. Respondents are not told the research sponsor's identity. Respondents cooperate because they are asked and sometimes paid.
Respondents' level of involvement and expectations	Increase respondents' involvement by indicating that the data collected will be used to improve the company's offerings. Respondents who tell the researcher about problems expect corrective action.	The respondents' level of involvement is generally low.
The sample size and the researcher's attitude toward the respondents	Since the survey is an opportunity to build relationships with customers, as many as possible are contacted. Respondents expect the researcher to know their usage habits concerning the company's offerings.	A sufficient number of respondents are contacted to achieve statistical validity at a given confidence level. When approached, respondents do not expect the researcher to know anything about them.
How the data are collected and analyzed	The data collected can be linked to specific respondents and analyzed at the respondent level.	The data are collected anonymously and aggregated. Typically, comparisons among sample averages are used in the analysis.
End result	Appropriate data are identified to fix product and service problems and to correct individual participant's problems.	Product and service problems are identified.
Follow-up surveys	Follow-up is encouraged. Customers who report problems expect some feedback. The follow-up may be linked to information collected previously from the same respondent.	Linking data collected to specific respondents and using the data in follow-up contacts is considered unethical.

Source: Adapted from Douglas R. Pruden and Terry G. Vavra, 'Customer Research, Not Marketing Research', *Marketing Research*, Summer 2000, 14–19.

CONSUMER RESEARCH PARADIGMS

The early consumer researchers gave little thought to the impact of mood, emotion or situation on consumer decisions. They believed that marketing was simply applied economics, and that consumers were rational decision makers who objectively evaluated the goods and services available to them and selected those that gave them the highest utility (satisfaction) at the lowest cost.

Despite their assumptions that consumers were logical problem solvers who engaged in careful thought processing (i.e. information processing) to arrive at their consumption decisions, researchers soon realised that consumers were not always consciously aware of why they made the decisions they did. Even when they were aware of their basic motivations, consumers were not always willing to reveal those reasons. In 1939, a Viennese psychoanalyst named Ernest Dichter began to use Freudian psychoanalytic techniques to uncover the hidden motivations of consumers. By the late 1950s, his research methodology (called **motivational research**), which was essentially qualitative in approach, was widely adopted by consumer researchers. As a result of Dichter's work and subsequent research designed to search deep within the consumer's psyche, consumer researchers today use two different types of research methodology to study consumer behaviour – **quantitative research** and **qualitative research**.

Quantitative research

Quantitative research is descriptive in nature and is used by researchers to understand the effects of various promotional inputs on the consumer, thus enabling marketers to 'predict' consumer behaviour. This research approach is known as *positivism*, and consumer researchers primarily concerned with predicting consumer behaviour are known as *positivists*. The research methods used in positivist research are borrowed primarily from the natural sciences and consist of experiments, survey techniques and observation. The findings are descriptive, empirical, and, if collected randomly (i.e. using a probability sample), can be generalised to larger populations. Because the data collected are quantitative, they lend themselves to sophisticated statistical analysis.

Qualitative research

Qualitative research methods consist of depth interviews, focus groups, metaphor analysis, collage research and projective techniques (discussed later in the chapter). These techniques are administered by a highly trained interviewer-analyst who also analyses the findings; thus, the findings tend to be somewhat subjective. Because sample sizes are necessarily small, findings cannot be generalised to larger populations. They are primarily used to obtain new ideas for promotional campaigns and products that can be tested more thoroughly in larger, more comprehensive studies.

A number of academics from the field of consumer behaviour, as well as from related social science disciplines, have become more interested in the act of *consumption* rather than in the act of *buying* (i.e. decision-making). They view consumer behaviour as a subset of human behaviour, and increased understanding as key to reducing negative aspects of consumer behaviour (the so-called 'dark side' of consumer behaviour), such as drug addiction, shoplifting, alcoholism and compulsive buying. Interest in understanding consumer experiences has led to the term *interpretivism*, and the researchers who adopt this paradigm are known as interpretivists.

Interpretivists engage in qualitative research. Among the research methodologies they use are depth interviews, projective techniques and other methods borrowed from cultural anthropology to study the meanings of cultural practices and symbols. Broadly speaking, the findings of qualitative research cannot be generalised to large populations but, as discussed in the following section, qualitative research nevertheless has an important role in managerial decision-making. Table 2-2 compares the purposes and assumptions of positivist research and interpretivist research.

Combining qualitative and quantitative research findings

Marketers often use a combination of quantitative and qualitative research to help make strategic marketing decisions. For example, they use qualitative research findings to discover new ideas and to develop promotional strategy, and quantitative research findings to predict consumer reactions to various promotional inputs. Frequently, ideas stemming from qualitative research are tested empirically and become the basis for the design of quantitative studies.

Marketers have discovered that these two research paradigms are really complementary in nature. The prediction made possible by quantitative (positivist) research and the understanding provided by qualitative (interpretivist) research together produce a richer and more robust profile of consumer behaviour than either research approach used alone. The combined findings enable marketers to design more meaningful and effective marketing strategies.

TABLE 2-2 Comparisons between positivism and interpretivism

	POSITIVISM	**INTERPRETIVISM**
Purpose	Prediction of consumer actions	Understanding consumption practices
Other descriptive terms	Positivism is also known as modernism, logical empiricism, operationalism and objectivism	Interpretivists are also known as experientialists and postmodernists; interpretivism is also known as naturalism, humanism and postpositivism
Methodology and research tools	*Quantitative research:* surveys, experiments and observations	*Qualitative research:* depth interviews and projective techniques *Ethnography:* a technique borrowed from cultural anthropology in which the researchers place themselves (participate) in the society under study in an effort to absorb the meaning of various cultural practices *Semiotics:* the study of symbols and the meanings they convey
Assumptions	• Rationality: consumers make decisions after weighing alternatives • The causes and effects of behaviour can be identified and isolated • Individuals are problem solvers who engage in information processing • A single reality exists • Events can be objectively measured • Causes of behaviour can be identified; by manipulating causes (i.e., inputs), the marketer can influence behaviour (i.e., outcomes) • Findings can be generalised to larger populations	• There is no single objective truth • Reality is subjective • Cause and effect cannot be isolated • Each consumption experience is unique • Researcher–respondent interactions affect research findings • Often findings are not generalisable to larger populations

Note: Not all researchers agree that interpretive research enhances traditional quantitative and qualitative market research. There is also disagreement regarding the alternative terms used to describe each research approach. The following sources illustrate the various conceptualisations of positivism and interpretivism.

Sources: Richard Lutz, 'Positivism, Naturalism, and Pluralism in Consumer Research: Paradigms in Paradise', *Advances in Consumer Research*, 16 (Provo, UT: Association for Consumer Research, 1989), 17; John Sherry, 'Postmodern Alternatives: The Interpretive Turn in Consumer Research', in *Handbook of Consumer Behavior*, eds. H. Kassarjian and T. Robertson (Upper Saddle River, NJ: Prentice Hall, 1991); Morris B. Holbrook and John O'Shaughnessy, 'On the Scientific Status of Consumer Research and the Need for an Interpretive Approach to Studying Consumption Behavior', *Journal of Consumer Research*, 15, December 1988, 398–402; and Morris Holbrook and Elizabeth C. Hirschman, 'The Experiential Aspects of Consumption: Consumer Fantasies, Feelings, and Fun', *Journal of Consumer Research*, 9, 2, 1982, 132–4.

THE CONSUMER RESEARCH PROCESS

The major steps in the consumer research process include:

1. defining the objectives of the research,
2. collecting and evaluating secondary data,

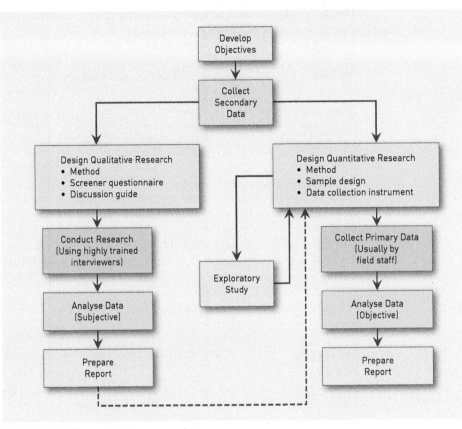

FIGURE 2-1 The consumer research process

3. designing a primary research study,
4. collecting primary data,
5. analysing the data, and
6. preparing a report on the findings.

Figure 2-1 depicts a model of the consumer research process.

Developing research objectives

The first step in the consumer research process is to define carefully the **objectives** of the study. Is it to segment the market for plasma television sets? To find out consumer attitudes about online shopping? To determine what percentage of households use email? It is important for the marketing manager and the researcher to agree at the outset on the purposes and objectives of the study to ensure that the research design is appropriate. A carefully thought-out statement of objectives helps to define the type and level of information needed.

For example, if the purpose of the study is to come up with new ideas for products or promotional campaigns, then a qualitative study is usually undertaken, in which respondents spend a significant amount of time face to face with a highly trained professional interviewer-analyst who also does the analysis. Because of the high costs of each interview, a fairly small sample of respondents is studied; thus, the findings are not projectable to the marketplace. If the purpose of the study is to find out how many people in the population (i.e. what percentage) use certain products and how frequently they use them, then a quantitative study that can be computer analysed is undertaken. Sometimes, in designing a quantitative study, the researcher may not know what questions to ask. In such cases, before undertaking a full-scale study, the researcher is likely to conduct a small-scale exploratory study to identify the critical issues to include in the data collection instrument (e.g. questionnaire).

Collecting secondary data

A search for **secondary data** generally follows the statement of objectives. Secondary information is any data originally generated for some purpose other than the present research objectives. It includes findings based on research done by outside organisations, data generated in-house for earlier studies, and even customer information collected by the firm's sales or credit departments. Locating secondary data is called **secondary research**. (Original research performed by individual researchers or organisations to meet specific objectives is called **primary research**.) Secondary research findings sometimes provide sufficient insight into the problem at hand to eliminate the need for primary research. Most often, they provide clues and direction for the design of primary research. Government agencies, private population data firms, marketing research companies and advertising agencies are all important sources of secondary market data. For example, in France the Institut National de la Statistique et des Etudes Economiques (l'INSEE) collects data on the age, education, employment and households of French residents, to name a few examples. The institute further offers a variety of statistical information on aspects of French society, including a monthly consumer confidence survey. In most countries similar government agencies offer this kind of information. Any firm operating globally may find key statistics about any country in the world in the CIA's electronic World Factbook published on the Web. For example, a company interested in Romanian consumers will easily find that the estimated population of the country was 22,215,421 as of July 2009, and that the population growth rate is actually negative with a decline of 0.147 per cent annually. Moreover, there were 2,188 Internet hosts in Romania in 2009, the life expectancy is 72.45 years, and the inhabitants can listen to 698 radio stations. If more detailed information on purchasing patterns or product usage is needed or if psychological or sociocultural consumer information is sought, then primary data must be collected. Research to secure such information is more costly and more time-consuming than secondary research but is likely to yield a more accurate picture than studies based on secondary data alone.

Syndicated Data

Because it is often very costly to collect primary data, many companies routinely purchase syndicated data on consumption patterns. Syndicated data are data of interest to a large number of users that are collected periodically and compiled and analysed according to a standard procedure, then sold to interested buyers. For example, AC Nielsen Consumer Panel Services provide marketers with consumer insights in over 20 countries around the world, capturing actual consumer purchase information for almost 125,000 households. AC Nielsen provide insights into buying behaviour across every outlet, from warehouse clubs to convenience shops and from supermarkets to independent chemists and mass merchandisers. Using in-home scanning technology or, in some markets, more traditional purchase diaries, AC Nielsen Homescan and Homepanel collect detailed information on consumer shopping behaviour, and companies who find these insights valuable can subscribe to the results of the panels.

Customer Profitability and Lifetime Value Data

The widely cited '80/20 rule' states that, generally, a relatively small percentage of all customers (20 per cent) accounts for a disproportionately large portion of the company's sales and profits (80 per cent). With the increased focus on building and maintaining long-term relationships with customers, many companies are now developing systems that will identify highly profitable customers as quickly as possible and are targeting those customers with special offers to buy even more of the company's products and services. Such systems stem from the collection and analysis

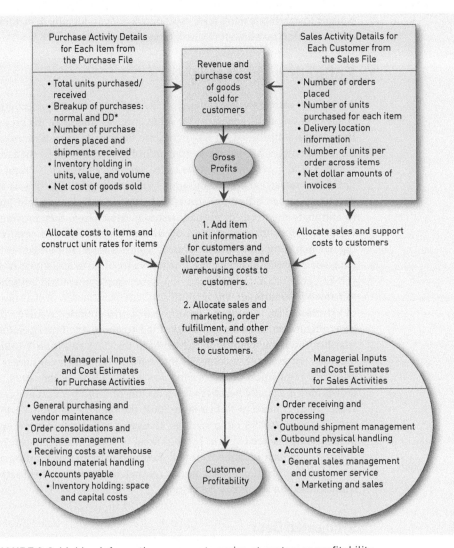

FIGURE 2-2 Linking information sources to arrive at customer profitability
*DD = direct delivery.
Source: Adapted from Rakesh Niraj, Mahendra Gupta and Chakravarthi Narasimhan, 'Customer Profitability in a Supply Chain', *Journal of Marketing*, July 2001.

of internal secondary data, such as past customer transactions, letters from customers, sales-call reports, warranty cards, and data on the frequency and duration of customer interactions. Based on these data, knowledgeable marketers compute **customer lifetime value** (CLV) profiles for various customer segments. The CLV can be computed from customer acquisition costs (the resources needed to establish a relationship with the customer), the profits generated from individual sales to each customer, the costs of handling customers and their orders (some customers may place more complex and variable orders that cost more to handle), and the expected duration of the relationship. A model depicting the linkage of internal data to customer profitability is shown in Figure 2-2.

Designing primary research

The design of a research study is based on the purposes of the study. If descriptive information is needed, then a quantitative study is likely to be undertaken; if the purpose is to get new ideas (e.g. for repositioning a product), then a qualitative study is undertaken. Because the approach for each type of research differs in terms of method of data collection, sample design and type of data collection instrument used, each research approach is discussed separately below.

Quantitative Research Designs

A quantitative research study consists of a research design, the data collection methods and instruments to be used and the sample design. Three basic designs are used in quantitative research: observation, experimentation (in a laboratory or in the field, such as in a retail outlet), or survey (i.e. by questioning people).

Observational Research

Observational research is an important method of consumer research because marketers recognise that the best way to gain an in-depth understanding of the relationship between people and products is by watching them in the process of buying and using products. Many large corporations and advertising agencies use trained researchers/observers to watch, note and sometimes videotape consumers in stores, shopping centres or their own homes. By watching people interact with products, observational researchers gain a better understanding of what the product symbolises to a consumer and greater insight into the bond between people and products that is the essence of brand loyalty.

Mechanical observation uses a mechanical or electronic device to record customer behaviour or response to a particular marketing stimulus. For example, a retailer may use a traffic counter to determine the business viability of a new shop location, government planners may use data collected from electronic pass devices in passenger cars to decide which roads should be expanded, and banks can use security cameras to observe problems customers may have in using ATMs.

Consumers are increasingly making use of technology in order to buy because such means generally reduce the need for cash or sales assistance and often provide rewards for using them. For example, film-goers who order tickets online can pick them up at ATM-like devices at cinemas and avoid queuing at the box office. Of course, as consumers use more and more highly convenient technologies, such as credit and ATM cards, frequency and loyalty cards, automated phone systems and online shopping, so the electronic records of their consumption patterns expand. These records are not anonymous, and sophisticated marketers are beginning to collect them and use them, sometimes almost instantly, to influence consumption behaviour. The debate about the ethical and privacy issues stemming from using technology to collect data that are not anonymous is growing.

Marketers also use **physiological observation** devices that monitor respondents' patterns of information processing. For example, an electronic eye camera may be used to monitor the eye movements of subjects looking at a series of advertisements for various products, and electronic sensors placed on the subjects' heads can monitor the brain activity and attentiveness levels involved in viewing each advertisement.

Experimentation

It is possible to test the relative sales appeal of many types of variables such as package designs, prices, promotional offers, or copy themes through experiments designed to identify cause and effect. In such experiments (called causal research), only some variables are manipulated (the independent variables), while all other elements are kept constant. A *controlled experiment* of this type ensures that any difference in the outcome (the dependent variable) is due to different treatments of the variable under study and not to extraneous factors. For example, one study tested the effectiveness of using an attractive versus unattractive endorser in promoting two types of products: products that are used to enhance one's attractiveness (e.g. a men's cologne) and products that are not (e.g. a pen). The endorser used was a fictitious character named Phil Johnson who was described as a member of the Olympic water polo team. The photograph depicting the attractive endorser was a scanned image of an attractive athletic man, whereas the picture depicting the unattractive endorser was the same image graphically modified to reduce attractiveness. The subjects viewed each endorser-product combination for 15 seconds (simulating the viewing of an actual print advertisement) and then filled out a questionnaire that measured their attitudes and purchase intentions towards the products advertised. In this study, the combinations of the product (used/not used to enhance one's attractiveness) and the endorser's attractiveness (attractive/unattractive endorser) were the manipulated treatments (the independent variables) and the combination of the attitudes and purchase intentions towards the product was the dependent variable. The study discovered that the attractive endorser was more effective in promoting both types of products.[1]

THE ROLE OF CONSUMER RESEARCH IN NEW PRODUCT DEVELOPMENT: THE STARSHIP AIRPLANE

The Starship was supposed to be a breathtaking airplane, sleek and fancy, and made from carbon-plastic rather than metal. It was designed with startling L-shaped wings, and by the power of two turbo prop engines mounted aft it was pushed forward rather than pulled. Raytheon Company invested a decade and a fortune-like amount of money on this new airplane, and it was to be their flashy but fuel-efficient alternative to the corporate jet.

However, the Starship made a rather hard landing, and became one of the most expensive flops in commercial aviation. Raytheon quietly wrote off much of the plane's development costs, which some analysts estimated to approach €375 million. A year after its first sale 23 Starship airplanes had been sold, substantially fewer than the 50 Raytheon hoped to sell. In other words, the Starship was far from the success its developers had expected. And an important question, then, is why not?

The Starship airplane won some plaudits from pilots, who praised the plane's stability, handling, avionics and roomy interior. According to airplane experts, the plane had everything needed to satisfy both pilots and passengers. However, as the sales manager of an air service company put it: 'for the money, the performance just isn't there'.

According to the experts, the Starship was an expensive plane, and one of its major competitive advantages was its fuel efficiency. Moreover, the space age design was intended to attract corporate managers. However, while the plane was being developed energy prices fell and became less of an issue. Starship was a turboprop airplane, and its relative slowness became a problem since speed is important to business customers. And as for the catchy design, older-generation CEO-level managers are (or at least were at the time) pretty conservative, and did not necessarily want people pointing at them when they landed. Hence, both the fuel-efficient but slow engines and the sleek design became drawbacks instead of the competitive advantages they were intended to be.

After the initial and not so successful launch, Raytheon Company targeted a customer segment different from the one they originally had in mind. They now aimed for the successful, independent-minded entrepreneur who wanted to make a statement when landing, and who appreciates having bystanders turn their heads as his plane taxies down the runway. Unfortunately, this new customer segment is fairly limited in comparison to the general corporate airplane segment.

The Starship case has some important learning points as to the role of marketing research, and consumer research, in new product development. First, trusting executive intuition that is focused on what the company is able to develop and provide is probably not as fruitful as asking what customers actually want. And, as seen here, it is often a more costly way too. Spending €200,000 on marketing research probably could have saved the Raytheon Company €375 million. Secondly, the longer that marketing research is postponed in a product development process, the more expensive it will be to fix or resolve problems that arise. In fact, few but the absolute largest companies would have survived a fiasco such as the Starship.

Source: This text is a rewritten version of a story presented by Carl McDaniel Jr. and Roger Gates in their superb book, *Contemporary Marketing Research*, 3rd edn (New York: West Publishing Company, 1996).

TABLE 2-3 Comparative advantages and disadvantages of postal, telephone, personal interview and online surveys

	POST	TELEPHONE	PERSONAL INTERVIEW	ONLINE
Cost	Low	Moderate	High	Low
Speed	Slow	Immediate	Slow	Fast
Response rate	Low	Moderate	High	Self-selected
Geographic flexibility	Excellent	Good	Difficult	Excellent
Interviewer bias	N/A	Moderate	Problematic	N/A
Interviewer supervision	N/A	Easy	Difficult	N/A
Quality of response	Limited	Limited	Excellent	Excellent

A major application of causal research is test marketing in which, prior to launching a new product, elements such as package, price and promotion are manipulated in a controlled setting in order to predict sales or gauge the possible responses to the product. Today some researchers employ virtual reality methods. For example, in a market test respondents can view supermarket shelves stocked with many products, including different versions of the same product, on computer screens, 'pick up' an item by touching the image, examine it by rotating the image with a track ball, and place it in a shopping basket if they decide to buy it. The researchers observe how long the respondents spend looking at the product, the time spent in examining each side of the package, the products purchased and the order of the purchases.[2]

Surveys

If researchers wish to ask consumers about their purchase preferences and consumption experiences they can do so in person, by telephone, by post or online. Each of these survey methods has certain advantages and certain disadvantages that the researcher must weigh when selecting the method of contact (see Table 2-3).

Personal interview surveys most often take place in the home or in retail shopping areas. The latter, referred to as mall intercepts, are used more frequently than home interviews because of the high incidence of working women who are not at home, and the reluctance of many people today to allow a stranger into their home.

Telephone surveys are also used to collect consumer data; however, evenings and weekends are often the only times to reach telephone respondents, who tend to be less responsive – even hostile – to calls that interrupt dinner, television viewing or general relaxation. The difficulties of reaching people with unlisted telephone numbers have been solved through random-digit dialling, and the costs of a widespread telephone survey are often minimised by using toll-free telephone lines. Other problems arise, however, from the increased use of answering machines and caller ID to screen calls. Some market research companies have tried to automate telephone surveys, but many respondents are even less willing to interact with an electronic voice than with a live interviewer. Lately, the widespread use at home of mobile phones instead of the traditional home telephone has made it even more difficult to persuade consumers to participate in telephone surveys. This is due to the fact that they are often interrupted at times and in places where they would not be reached if the marketing researcher called their home phone number. Instead, the calls now come while consumers are at the cinema, on a date or at the gym. While they may answer the call at the gym, for example, they are not willing to participate in a survey.

Postal surveys are conducted by sending questionnaires directly to individuals at their homes. One of the major problems of postal questionnaires is a low response rate, but researchers have developed a number of techniques to increase returns, such as enclosing a stamped, self-addressed envelope, using a provocative questionnaire, and sending pre-notification letters as well as follow-up letters. A number of commercial research firms that specialise in consumer surveys have set up panels of consumers who, for a token fee, agree to complete the research company's questionnaires on a regular basis. Sometimes panel members are also asked to keep diaries of their purchases.

Email surveys are an increasingly popular alternative to using the postal service as a means of distributing questionnaires to target consumers. One of the key attractions of using email is that it is as easy and quick to distribute a survey around the world as it is to distribute it down the block. Moreover, with an accurate list of email addresses, it is very inexpensive to distribute even a large number of questionnaires. We can expect that as the world increasingly turns to the Web for many types of social communications, we will see continued growth of emailing as a way to distribute surveys.[3]

Furthermore, there has been a rapid increase in the number of consumers who are interested in participating in online or Internet-based surveys. Potential respondents are directed to the marketer's (or researcher company's) website by online ads or targeted email invitations. Often, responses to online surveys are from consumer respondents who are self-selected, and therefore the results cannot be projected to the larger population. Most computer polls ask respondents to complete a profile consisting of demographic questions that enable the researchers to classify the responses to the substantive product or service questions.

Another online option is established online research companies that maintain a database of potential consumers who are willing (for a fee) to participate in online consumer research projects. The advantage of established online survey research firms is their substantial databases and comprehensive profiles of each potential participant. These act as significant safeguards in that only individuals who qualify are invited to participate in the particular online survey. Since members of the database desire to continue earning money for their participation, there is a very good chance that they will be reliable and will actually complete those surveys that they have been invited to complete; otherwise they will eventually be dropped for not participating.

Research firms that conduct computer surveys believe that the anonymity of the Internet encourages respondents to be more forthright and honest than they would be if asked the same questions in person or by mail. Still further, online survey research organisations cite the inherent advantages of their geographically wide reach and the affordability of online consumer surveys. However, in contrast, there are other marketers who are largely sceptical about online research because they fear that the data collected may be suspect because some respondents may create false online personalities that do not reflect their own beliefs or behaviours.

Quantitative Research Data Collection Instruments

Data collection instruments are developed as part of a study's total research design to systematise the collection of data and to ensure that all respondents are asked the same questions in the same order. Data collection instruments include questionnaires, personal inventories, attitude scales and, for qualitative data, discussion guides. Data collection instruments are usually pre-tested and 'debugged' to ensure the validity and reliability of the research study. A study is said to have **validity** if it does, in fact, collect the appropriate data needed to answer the questions or objectives stated in the first (objectives) stage of the research process. A study is said to have **reliability** if the same questions, asked of a similar sample, produce the same findings. Often a sample is systematically divided in two, and each half is given the same questionnaire to complete. If the results from each half are similar, the questionnaire is said to have **split-half reliability**.

Questionnaires

For quantitative research, the primary data collection instrument is the questionnaire, which can be sent through the post to selected respondents for self-administration or can be administered by field interviewers in person or by telephone. In order to motivate respondents to take the time to respond to surveys, researchers have found that questionnaires must be interesting, objective, unambiguous, easy to complete, and generally not burdensome. To enhance the analysis and facilitate the classification of responses into meaningful categories, questionnaires include both substantive questions that are relevant to the purposes of the study and pertinent demographic questions.

The questionnaire itself can be disguised or undisguised as to its true purpose; a disguised questionnaire sometimes yields more truthful answers and avoids responses that respondents may think are expected or sought. Questions can be *open-ended* (requiring answers in the respondent's own words) or *closed-ended* (the respondent merely ticks the appropriate answer from a list of options). Open-ended questions yield more insightful information but are more difficult to code and to analyse; closed-ended questions are relatively simple to tabulate and analyse, but the answers are limited to the alternative responses provided (i.e. to the existing insights of the questionnaire designer). Great care must be taken in wording each question to avoid biasing the responses. The sequence of questions is also important: the opening questions must be interesting enough to 'draw' the respondent into participating, they must proceed in a logical order, and demographic (classification) questions should be placed at the end where they are more likely to be answered. The format of the questionnaire and the wording and sequence of the questions affect the validity of the responses and, in the case of postal questionnaires, the number (rate) of responses received. Questionnaires usually offer respondents confidentiality or anonymity to dispel any reluctance about self-disclosure.

Attitude Scales

Researchers often present respondents with a list of products or product attributes for which they are asked to indicate their relative feelings or evaluations. The instruments most frequently used to capture this evaluative data are called **attitude scales**. The most frequently used attitude scales are Likert scales, semantic differential scales, behaviour intention scales and rank-order scales.

The *Likert scale* is the most popular form of attitude scale because it is easy for researchers to prepare and to interpret, and simple for consumers to answer. They tick or write the number corresponding to their level of 'agreement' or 'disagreement' with each of a series of statements that describes the attitude object under investigation. The scale consists of an equal number of agreement/disagreement choices on either side of a neutral choice. A principal benefit of the Likert scale is that it gives the researcher the option of considering the responses to each statement separately or of combining the responses to produce an overall score.

The *semantic differential scale*, like the Likert scale, is relatively easy to construct and administer. The scale typically consists of a series of bipolar adjectives (such as good/bad, hot/cold, like/dislike, or expensive/inexpensive) anchored at the ends of an odd-numbered (e.g. five- or seven-point) continuum. Respondents are asked to evaluate a concept (or a product or company) on the basis of each attribute by ticking the point on the continuum that best reflects their feelings or beliefs. Care must be taken to vary the location of positive and negative terms from the left side of the continuum to the right side to avoid consumer response bias. Sometimes an even-numbered scale is used to eliminate the option of a neutral answer. An important feature of the semantic differential scale is that it can be used to develop graphic consumer profiles of the concept under study. Semantic differential profiles are also used to compare consumer perceptions of competitive products and to indicate areas for product improvement when perceptions of the existing product are measured against perceptions of the 'ideal' product.

The *behaviour intention scale* measures the likelihood that consumers will act in a certain way in the future, such as buying the product again or recommending it to a friend. These scales are easy to construct, and consumers are asked to make subjective judgements regarding their future behaviour.

With *rank-order scales*, subjects are asked to rank items such as products (or retailers or websites) in order of preference in terms of some criterion, such as overall quality or value for money. Rank-order scaling procedures provide important competitive information and enable marketers to identify needed areas of improvement in product design and product positioning. Figure 2-3 provides examples of the attitude scales that are frequently utilised in consumer research.

LIKERT SCALE

For each of the following statements, please tick the response that best describes the extent to which you agree or disagree with each statement.

	Strongly Agree	Somewhat Agree	Neither Agree nor Disagree	Somewhat Disagree	Strongly Disagree
It's fun to shop online.					
I am afraid to give my credit card number online.					

Two widely used applications of the Likert Scale to measure consumer attitudes are:

SATISFACTION MEASURES

Overall, how satisfied are you with Bank X's online banking?

Very Satisfied	Somewhat Satisfied	Neither Satisfied nor Dissatisfied	Somewhat Dissatisfied	Very Dissatisfied

IMPORTANCE SCALES

The following features are associated with shopping on the Internet. For each feature, please tick the one alternative that best expresses how important or unimportant that feature is to you.

	Extremely Important	Somewhat Important	Neither Important nor Unimportant	Somewhat Unimportant	Not at All Important
Speed of downloading the order form					
Being able to register with the site					

SEMANTIC DIFFERENTIAL SCALE

For each of the following features, please tick one alternative that best expresses your impression of how that feature applies to online banking:

Competitive rates |—+—+—+—+—+—+—| Non-competitive rates

Reliable |—+—+—+—+—+—+—| Unreliable

Note: The same semantic differential scale can be applied to two competitive offerings, such as online banking and regular banking, and a graphic representation of the profiles of the two alternatives, along with the bipolar adjectives included in the scale, can be easily constructed.

BEHAVIOUR INTENTION SCALES

How likely are you to continue using Bank X's online banking for the next six months?

Definitely Will Continue	Probably Will Continue	Might or Might Not Continue	Probably Will Not Continue	Definitely Will Not Continue

How likely are you to recommend Bank X's online banking to a friend?

Definitely Will Recommend	Probably Will Recommend	Might or Might Not Recommend	Probably Will Not Recommend	Definitely Will Not Recommend

RANK-ORDER SCALE

We would like to find out about your preferences regarding banking methods. Please rank the following banking methods by placing a '1' in front of the method that you prefer most, a '2' next to your second preference, and continuing until you have ranked all of the methods.

_____ Inside the bank	_____ Online banking	_____ Banking by telephone
_____ ATM	_____ Banking by post	

FIGURE 2-3 Attitude scales

Qualitative Research Designs and Data Collection Methods

In selecting the appropriate research format for a qualitative study, the researcher has to take into consideration the purpose of the study and the types of data needed. Although the research methods used may differ in composition, they all have roots in psychoanalytical and clinical aspects of psychology, and they stress open-ended and free-response types of questions to stimulate respondents to reveal their innermost thoughts and beliefs.

The key data collection techniques for qualitative studies are depth interviews, focus groups, projective techniques and metaphor analysis. These techniques are regularly used in the early stages of attitude research to pinpoint relevant product-related beliefs or attributes and to develop an initial picture of consumer attitudes (especially the beliefs and attributes consumers associate with particular products and services).

Depth Interviews

A **depth interview** is a lengthy (generally 30 minutes to an hour), non-structured interview between a respondent and a highly trained interviewer, who minimises his or her own participation in the discussion after establishing the general subject to be discussed. (However, as noted earlier, interpretivist researchers often take a more active role in the discussion.) Respondents are encouraged to talk freely about their activities, attitudes and interests in addition to the product category or brand under study. Transcripts, videotapes or audiotape recordings of interviews are then carefully studied, together with reports of respondents' moods and any gestures or 'body language' they may have used to convey attitudes or motives. Such studies provide marketers with valuable ideas about product design or redesign and provide insights for positioning or repositioning the product. For purposes of copytesting, respondents might be asked to describe in depth various advertisements they are shown. Other techniques include *autodriving* in which researchers show respondents photos, videos and audiotapes of their own shopping behaviour and ask them to comment explicitly on their consumption actions.[4]

Focus Groups

A **focus group** consists of 8 to 10 respondents who meet with a moderator-analyst for a group discussion 'focused' on a particular product or product category (or any other subject of research interest). Respondents are encouraged to discuss their interests, attitudes, reactions, motives, lifestyles, feelings about the product or product category, usage experience and so forth.

Because a focus group takes about two hours to complete, a researcher can easily conduct two or three focus groups (with a total of 30 respondents) in one day, while it might take that same researcher five or six days to conduct 30 individual depth interviews. Analysis of responses in both depth interviews and focus groups requires a great deal of skill on the part of the researcher. Focus group sessions are invariably taped, and sometimes videotaped, to assist in the analysis. Interviews are usually held in specially designed conference rooms with one-way mirrors that enable marketers and advertising agency staff to observe the sessions without disrupting or inhibiting the responses.

Respondents are recruited on the basis of a carefully drawn consumer profile (called a *screener questionnaire*) based on specifications defined by marketing management and are usually paid a fee for their participation. Sometimes users of the company's brands are clustered in one or more groups, and their responses are compared to those of non-users interviewed in other groups.

Some marketers prefer focus groups to individual depth interviews because it takes less time overall to complete the study, and they feel that the freewheeling group discussions and group dynamics tend to yield a greater number of new ideas and insights than depth interviews. Other marketers prefer individual depth interviews because they feel that respondents are free of group pressure and thus are less likely to give socially acceptable (and not necessarily truthful) responses, are more likely to remain attentive during the entire interview, and – because of the greater personal attention received – are more likely to reveal private thoughts. Figure 2-4 presents a portion of a discussion guide that might be used in a focus group session to gain insights into the attitudes of consumers toward various mobile phone service providers. The findings would be equally relevant to the positioning of a new service provider or the repositioning of an existing provider.

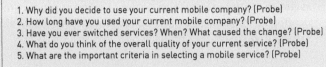

1. Why did you decide to use your current mobile company? (Probe)
2. How long have you used your current mobile company? (Probe)
3. Have you ever switched services? When? What caused the change? (Probe)
4. What do you think of the overall quality of your current service? (Probe)
5. What are the important criteria in selecting a mobile service? (Probe)

Examples of Probe questions:
a. Tell me more about that . . .
b. Share your thinking on this . . .
c. Does anyone see it differently . . .

FIGURE 2-4 Selected portions of a discussion guide

Projective Techniques

Projective techniques are designed to tap the underlying motives of individuals despite their unconscious rationalisations or efforts at conscious concealment. They consist of a variety of disguised 'tests' that contain ambiguous stimuli, such as incomplete sentences, untitled pictures or cartoons, ink blots, word-association tests and other-person characterisations. Projective techniques are sometimes administered as part of a focus group but more often are used during depth interviews. Because projective methods are closely associated with researching consumer needs and motivation, they are more fully discussed in Chapter 5.

Metaphor Analysis

In the 1990s, a stream of consumer research emerged suggesting that most communication is non-verbal and that people do not think in words but in images. If consumers' thought processes consist of a series of images, or pictures in their mind, then it is likely that many respondents cannot adequately convey their feelings and attitudes about the research subject (such as a product or brand) through the use of words alone. Therefore, it is important to enable consumers to represent their images in an alternative, non-verbal form – through the use, say, of sounds, music, drawings or pictures. The use of one form of expression to describe or represent feelings about another is called a metaphor. A number of consumer theorists have come to believe that people use metaphors as the most basic method of thought and communication.

The *Zaltman Metaphor Elicitation Technique* (ZMET) relies on visual images to assess consumers' deep and subconscious thoughts about products, services and marketing strategies. In one study about consumer perceptions of advertising, pre-screened respondents were asked to bring in to a depth interview pictures that illustrated their perceptions of the value of advertising. They were asked to bring pictures from magazines, newspapers, artwork, photos they took especially for the study or from existing collections, but not actual print advertisements. Each respondent participated in a two-hour videotaped interview (on average, each respondent brought in 13 images representing his or her impressions of the value of advertising). The interview used several methods that are part of the ZMET technique to elicit key metaphors and the interrelationships among them from the respondents. The interviews were then analysed by qualified researchers according to the ZMET criteria. The findings revealed that the ambivalent respondents had both favourable (e.g. information and entertainment values) and unfavourable (e.g. misrepresentation of reality) impressions of advertising; sceptics had mostly negative, but some positive impressions of advertising; and hostile respondents viewed advertising as an all-negative force.[5] Another application of ZMET is using the instrument to get consumers' reactions to film scripts.[6]

Customer Satisfaction Measurement

Gauging the level of customer satisfaction and its determinants is critical for every company. Marketers can use such data to retain customers, sell more products and services, improve the quality and value of their offerings and operate more effectively and efficiently. **Customer satisfaction measurement** includes quantitative and qualitative measures, as well as a variety of contact methods with customers. These methods and instruments and examples of their application to business situations are detailed in Table 2-4.

TABLE 2-4 Customer satisfaction data collection instruments

Customer satisfaction surveys	Generally, customer satisfaction surveys use 5-point semantic differential scales ranging from 'very dissatisfied' to 'very satisfied'. These surveys measure how satisfied the customers are along relevant attributes of the product or service and the relative importance of the attributes (using an importance scale). Research shows that customers who indicate they are 'very satisfied' (typically a score of 5 on the satisfaction scale) are much more profitable and loyal than customers who indicate that they are 'satisfied' (a score of 4). Therefore, companies that merely strive to have 'satisfied' customers are making a crucial error.[a]
Customers' expectations versus their perceptions of the product or service delivered	This approach states that customers' satisfaction or dissatisfaction is a function of the difference between what they had *expected* to get from the product or service purchased and their perceptions of what they *received*. A group of researchers developed a scale that measures the performance of the service received against two expectations levels: *adequate* service and *desired* service, and also measures the customers' future intentions regarding purchasing the service.[b] This approach is more sophisticated than standard customer satisfaction surveys and more likely to yield results that can be used to develop corrective measures for products and services that fall short of customers' expectations.
Mystery shoppers	This method consists of employing professional observers, posing as customers, to survey and provide an unbiased evaluation of the operation's service against the company's service standards in order to identify opportunities for improving productivity and efficiency. For example, one bank used mystery shoppers who, while dealing with a bank employee on another matter, dropped hints about buying a house or seeking to borrow college funds. Employees were scored on how quickly and effectively they provided information about the bank's pertinent product or service.[c]
Critical incident method	This method consists of asking customers to think back and describe interactions that they had with employees in a particular industry, such as hotels or airlines, that they recall as particularly satisfying or dissatisfying. This qualitative tool can yield important insights that can be used to train employees better. One study discovered that, somewhat surprisingly, many experiences cited as particularly satisfying were incidents where the service provided initially failed but, because it was 'recovered' well by the service employee, the customer remembered it as a particularly satisfactory experience.[d] Some argue that this method, if used by itself, is insufficient, but should only be used in the context of additional data on the customer–marketer relationship.[e]
Analysing customer complaints	Research indicates that only a few unsatisfied customers actually complain. Most unsatisfied customers say nothing but switch to competitors. A good complaint analysis system should: 1. Encourage customers to complain and provide suggestions for improvements by having adequate forms (with sufficient space to write comments) and mechanisms beyond the routine 'how was everything?' questions. A good approach is to include examples on the suggestions and complaint forms of how past customer input helped improve service. 2. Establish 'listening posts' where specially designated employees either listen to customers' comments or actively solicit input from them (e.g. in a hotel lobby or on checkout lines). 3. Each complaint, by itself, provides little information. The company must have a system in which complaints are categorized and then analyzed. 4. Use software to speed up complaint analysis and handling. eBay uses software on its Web site to track customers' opinions, capture complaints, and follow up on them very quickly. The company says it has reduced customer dissatisfaction by nearly 30% after one year of using this tool.[f]

(Continued)

TABLE 2-4 (*Continued*)

Analysing customer defections	Because high customer loyalty rates are an important competitive advantage, and because it is generally much cheaper to retain customers than to get new ones, companies must find out *why* customers leave (e.g. through exit interviews) and also *intervene* when customers' behaviors show that they may be considering leaving. For example, one bank that was losing about 20% of its customers every year discovered that segmenting defecting customers along demographic and family life cycle characteristics was ineffective in reducing defection rates. The bank then compared 500 transaction records of loyal customers with 500 transaction records of defectors, along such dimensions as number of transactions, frequency of transactions, and fluctuations in average balances. The bank then identified transaction patterns that may indicate future defection and started targeting potential defectors and encouraging them to stay.[g]

[a] Thomas O. Jones and W. Earl Sasser, Jr., 'Why Satisfied Customers Defect', *Harvard Business Review*, November–December 1995, 88–99.

[b] A. Parasuraman, Valarie A. Zeithaml, and Leonard L. Berry, 'Moving Forward in Service Quality Research: Measuring Different Customer-Expectation Levels, Comparing Alternative Scales, and Examining the Performance-Behavioral Intentions Link', Report No. 94–114, Marketing Science Institute, 1994.

[c] Cynthia Vinarsky, 'Mystery Shoppers Monitor Warren, Ohio, Credit Union's Customer Service', *Knight Ridder Business News*, 19 March 2002, 1.

[d] Mary Jo Bitner and Bernard H. Booms, 'The Service Encounter: Diagnosing Favorable and Unfavorable Incidents', *Journal of Marketing*, January 1990, 71–84.

[e] Bo Edvardsson and Tore Strandvik, 'Is a Critical Incident Critical for a Customer Relationship?', *Managing Service Quality*, 2000, 82–91.

[f] L. Biff Motley, 'Speeding Up Handling of Satisfaction Problems', *Bank Marketing*, September 2001, 35.

[g] Michael M. Pearson and Guy H. Gessner, 'Transactional Segmentation to Slow Customer Defections', *Marketing Management*, Summer 1999, 16–23.

Sampling and Data Collection

An integral component of a research design is the sampling plan. Specifically, the sampling plan addresses three questions: who to survey (the sampling unit), how many to survey (the sample size) and how to select them (the sampling procedure). Deciding who to survey requires explicit definition of the universe or boundaries of the market from which data are sought so that an appropriate sample can be selected (such as working mothers). Interviewing the correct target market or potential target market is basic to the validity of the study.

The size of the sample is dependent both on the size of the budget and on the degree of confidence that the marketer wants to place in the findings. The larger the sample, the more likely it is that the responses will reflect the total universe under study. It is interesting to note, however, that a small sample can often provide highly reliable findings, depending on the sampling procedure adopted. (The exact number needed to achieve a specific level of confidence in the accuracy of the findings can be computed with a mathematical formula that is beyond the scope of this discussion.)

If the researcher wants the findings to be projectable to the total population, then a **probability sample** should be chosen; if it is sufficient to have the findings 'representative' of the population, then a **non-probability sample** can be selected. Table 2-5 summarises the features of various types of probability and non-probability designs.

As indicated earlier, qualitative studies usually require highly trained social scientists to collect data. A quantitative study generally uses field staff that are either recruited and trained directly by the researcher or contracted from a company that specialises in conducting field interviews. In either case, it is often necessary to verify whether the interviews have, in fact, taken place. This is sometimes done by a postcard mailing to respondents asking them to verify that they participated in an interview on the date recorded on the questionnaire form. Completed questionnaires are reviewed on a regular basis as the research study progresses to ensure that the recorded responses are clear, complete and legible.

Data analysis and reporting research findings

In qualitative research, the moderator or test administrator usually analyses the responses received. In quantitative research, the researcher supervises the analysis. Open-ended responses

TABLE 2-5 Sampling

PROBABILITY SAMPLE	
Simple random sample	Every member of the population has a known and equal chance of being selected.
Systematic random sample	A member of the population is selected at random and then every 'nth' person is selected.
Stratified random sample	The population is divided into mutually exclusive groups (such as age groups), and random samples are drawn from each group.
Cluster (area) sample	The population is divided into mutually exclusive groups (such as streets), and the researcher draws a sample of the groups to interview.
NON-PROBABILITY SAMPLE	
Convenience sample	The researcher selects the most accessible population members from whom to obtain information (e.g. students in a classroom).
Judgement sample	The researcher uses his or her judgement to select population members who are good sources for accurate information (e.g. experts in the relevant field of study).
Quota sample	The researcher interviews a prescribed number of people in each of several categories (e.g. 50 men and 50 women).

are first coded and quantified (i.e. converted into numerical scores); then all of the responses are tabulated and analysed using sophisticated analytical programs that correlate the data by selected variables and cluster the data by selected demographic characteristics.

In both qualitative and quantitative research, the research report includes a brief executive summary of the findings. Depending on the assignment from marketing management, the research report may or may not include recommendations for marketing action. The body of the report includes a full description of the methodology used and, for quantitative research, also includes tables and graphics to support the findings. A sample of the questionnaire is usually included in the appendix to enable management to evaluate the objectivity of the findings.

Conducting a research study

In designing a research study, researchers adapt the research process described in the previous sections to the special needs of the study. For example, if a researcher is told that the purpose of the study is to develop a segmentation strategy for a new online dating service, he or she would first collect secondary data, such as population statistics (the number of men and women online in selected metropolitan areas within a certain age range, their marital status and occupations). Then, together with the marketing manager, the researcher would specify the parameters (define the sampling unit) of the population to be studied (e.g. single, university-educated men and women between the ages of 20 and 45 who live or work within the London metropolitan area). A qualitative study (e.g. focus groups) might be undertaken first to gather information about the target population's attitudes and concerns about meeting people online, their special interests, and the specific services and precautions they would like an online dating service to provide. This phase of the research should result in tentative generalisations about the specific age group(s) to target and the services to offer.

The marketing manager might then instruct the researcher to conduct a quantitative study to confirm and attach 'hard' numbers (percentages) to the findings that emerged from the focus groups. The first-phase study should have provided sufficient insights to develop a research design and to launch directly into a large-scale survey. If, however, there is still doubt about any element of the research design, such as question wording or format, they might decide first to do a small-scale **exploratory study**. Then, after refining the questionnaire and any other needed elements of the research design, they would launch a full-scale quantitative survey, using a probability sample that would allow them to project the findings to the total population of singles (as originally defined). The analysis should cluster prospective consumers of the online dating service into segments based on relevant sociocultural or lifestyle characteristics and on media habits, attitudes, perceptions and geodemographic characteristics.

SUMMARY

The field of consumer research developed as an extension of the field of marketing research to enable marketers to predict how consumers would react in the marketplace and to understand the reasons why they made the purchase decisions they did. Consumer research undertaken from a managerial perspective to improve strategic marketing decisions is known as positivism. Positivist research is quantitative and empirical and tries to identify cause-and-effect relationships in buying situations. It is often supplemented with qualitative research.

Qualitative research is concerned with probing deep within the consumer's psyche to understand the motivations, feelings and emotions that drive consumer behaviour. Qualitative research findings cannot be projected to larger populations but are used primarily to provide new ideas and insights for the development of positioning strategies. Interpretivism, a qualitative research perspective, is generally more concerned with understanding the act of consuming rather than the act of buying (consumer decision-making). Interpretivists view consumer behaviour as a subset of human behaviour, and increased understanding as a key to eliminating some of the ills associated with destructive consumer behaviour.

Each theoretical research perspective is based on its own specific assumptions and uses its own research techniques. Positivists typically use probability studies that can be generalised to larger populations. Interpretivists tend to view consumption experiences as unique situations that occur at specific moments in time; therefore, they cannot be generalised to larger populations. The two theoretical research orientations are highly complementary and, when used together, provide a deeper and more insightful understanding of consumer behaviour than either approach used alone.

The consumer research process – whether quantitative or qualitative in approach – generally consists of six steps: defining objectives, collecting secondary data, developing a research design, collecting primary data, analysing the data and preparing a report of the findings. The researcher must make every effort to ensure that the research findings are reliable (that a replication of the study would provide the same results) and valid (that they answer the specific questions for which the study was originally undertaken).

DISCUSSION QUESTIONS

1. Have you ever been selected as a respondent in a marketing research survey? If yes, how were you contacted? Why do you think you, in particular, were selected? Did you know or could you guess the purpose of the survey? Do you know the name of the company or brand involved in the survey?

2. Identify a purchase you have made that was motivated primarily by your desire to obtain a special 'feeling' or an 'experience'. Would the positivist or interpretivist research paradigm be a more appropriate way to study your consumption behaviour? Explain your answer.

3. What is the difference between primary and secondary research? Under what circumstances might the availability of secondary data make primary research unnecessary? What are some major sources of secondary data?

4. A manufacturer of powdered fruit drinks would like to investigate the effects of food colour and label information on consumers' perceptions of flavour and product preferences. Would you advise the manufacturer to use observational research, experimentation or a survey? Explain your choice.

5. Why might a researcher prefer to use focus groups rather than depth interviews? When might depth interviews be preferable?

6. Compare the advantages and disadvantages of postal, telephone, personal and online surveys.

7. How would the interpretation of survey results change if the researcher used a probability sample rather than a non-probability sample? Explain your answer.

8. Why is customer satisfaction measurement an important part of marketing research? Apply one of the methods in Table 2-4 to measure your fellow students' satisfaction with the services provided by the bookshop at your university.

9. Why is observation becoming a more important component of consumer research? Describe two new technologies that can be used to observe consumption behaviour and explain why they are better to use than questioning consumers about the behaviour being observed.

EXERCISES

1. Nivea is a manufacturer of personal care products, and offers products ranging from sun care to deodorants. The company would like to extend its facial care product line. Design (1) a qualitative and (2) a quantitative research design for the company focused on this objective.

2. How would you design an experiment able to test the effect of time pressure on consumers' ability to solve mathematical puzzles?

3. Using one of the customer satisfaction measures, construct an instrument to assess your fellow students' satisfaction with the technological support services provided by your university.

4. Develop a questionnaire to measure students' attitudes toward the instructor on this course.
   a. Prepare five statements measuring students' attitudes via a Likert scale.
   b. Prepare five semantic differential scales to measure student attitudes. Can the same dimensions be measured by using either scaling technique? Explain your answer.

NOTES

1. Brian D. Till and Michael Busler, 'The Match-Up Hypothesis: Physical Attractiveness, Expertise, and the Role of Fit on Brand Attitude, Purchase Intent and Brand Beliefs', *Journal of Advertising*, Fall 2000, 1–13.

2. Joseph F. Hair, Robert P. Bush and David J. Ortinau, *Marketing Research*, 2nd edn (New York: McGraw Hill Irwin, 2003), Chapter 10.

3. Nina Michaelidou and Sally Dibb, 'Using Email Questionnaires for Research: Good Practice in Tackling Non-Response', *Journal of Targeting, Measurement and Analysis for Marketing*, 14, July 2006, 289–96.

4. Deborah D. Heisley and Sidney J. Levy, 'Autodriving: A Photoelicitation Technique', *Journal of Consumer Research*, December 1991, 257–72.

5. Robin A. Coutler, Gerald Zaltman and Keith S. Coutler, 'Interpreting Consumer Perceptions of Advertising: An Application of the Zaltman Metaphor Elicitation Technique', *Journal of Advertising*, Winter 2001, 1–21.

6. Emily Eakin, 'Penetrating the Mind by Metaphor', *New York Times*, 23 February 2002, B9, B11.

CHAPTER 3
MARKET SEGMENTATION

Market segmentation and diversity are complementary concepts. Without a diverse marketplace composed of many different peoples with different backgrounds, countries of origin, interests, needs and wants, and perceptions, there would be little reason to segment markets. Diversity in the global marketplace makes market segmentation an attractive, viable, and potentially highly profitable strategy. The necessary conditions for successful segmentation of any market are a large enough population with sufficient money to spend (general affluence) and sufficient diversity to lend itself to partitioning the market into sizeable segments on the basis of demographic, psychological or other strategic variables. The presence of these conditions in most industrialised nations makes these marketplaces extremely attractive to global marketers.

When marketers provide a range of product or service choices to meet diverse consumer interests, consumers are better satisfied, and their overall happiness, satisfaction and quality of life are ultimately enhanced. Thus, market segmentation is a positive force for both consumers and marketers alike.

WHAT IS MARKET SEGMENTATION?

Market segmentation can be defined as the process of dividing a market into distinct subsets of consumers with common needs or characteristics and selecting one or more segments to target with a distinct marketing mix. Before the widespread acceptance of market segmentation, the prevailing way of doing business with consumers was through **mass marketing** – that is, offering the same product and marketing mix to all consumers. The essence of this strategy was summed up by the entrepreneur Henry Ford, who offered the Model T motor car to the public 'in any color they wanted, as long as it was black'.

If all consumers were alike – if they all had the same needs, wants and desires, and the same background, education and experience – mass (undifferentiated) marketing would be a logical strategy. Its primary advantage is that it costs less: only one advertising campaign is needed, only one marketing strategy is developed, and usually only one standardised product is offered. Some companies, primarily those that deal in agricultural products or very basic manufactured goods, successfully follow a mass-marketing strategy. Other marketers, however, see major draw-backs in an undifferentiated marketing approach. When trying to sell the same product to every prospective customer with a single advertising campaign, the marketer must portray its product as a means for satisfying a common or generic need and, therefore, it often ends up appealing to no one. A standard size station wagon or estate car may fulfil a widespread need to transport its owner between his or her home and the office, but it may be too big a car for the young person who lives alone, and too small for a family of six where a parent is dropping the four children off at school every morning. Without market differentiation, both the young person and the family of six would have to make do with the very same model and, as we all know, 'making do' is a far cry from being satisfied.

The strategy of segmentation allows producers to avoid head-on competition in the marketplace by differentiating their offerings, not only on the basis of price but also through styling, packaging, promotional appeal, method of distribution and superior service. Marketers have found that the costs of consumer segmentation research, shorter production runs and differentiated promotional campaigns are usually more than offset by increased sales. In most cases, consumers readily accept the passed-on cost increases for products that more closely satisfy their specific needs.

Market segmentation is just the first step in a three-phase marketing strategy. After segmenting the market into homogeneous clusters, the marketer then must select one or more segments to target. To accomplish this, the marketer must decide on a specific marketing mix – that is, a specific product, price, channel, and/or promotional appeal for each distinct segment. The third step is **positioning** the product so that it is perceived by the consumers in each target segment as satisfying their needs better than other competitive offerings.

Who uses market segmentation?

Because the strategy of market segmentation benefits both the consumer and the marketer, marketers of both goods and services are eager practitioners. For example, hotels segment their markets and target different products to different market segments. The Norwegian-based hotel chain Thon Hotels (www.thonhotels.com) has divided its hotels into three different categories based on the segment they aim to attract. Thon Budget is positioned as smart and basic, which is appealing to those interested in price-conscious short stays. Thon City focuses on comfort and location in the centre of town, while Thon Conference is the professional meeting place, and hotels in this category have dedicated conference personnel and a business centre.

Industrial firms also segment their markets, as do charities and the media. For example, Mercedes-Benz (www.mercedes-benz.com) produces different models of lorries to meet the needs of long-distance hauliers, waste-disposal firms, airport services and so on. The firm also offer buses designed especially for urban public transport, more rural bus services and an entire fleet of tour buses. The company's website offers a listing of its various vehicles by segment type.

Charities such as UNICEF (www.unicef.org) frequently focus their fund-raising efforts on 'heavy givers'. Some performing arts centres segment their subscribers on the basis of benefits sought and have succeeded in increasing attendance through specialised promotional appeals.

Segmentation studies are designed to discover the needs and wants of specific groups of consumers, so that specialised goods and services can be developed and promoted to satisfy each group's needs. Many new products have been developed to fill gaps in the marketplace revealed by segmentation research. Segmentation studies are also used to guide the redesign or repositioning of a product or the addition of a new market segment. For example, Nintendo (www.nintendo.com) has expanded its vision for its electronic games to include adult users (promising adult game players 'kid-like' fun).

In addition to filling product gaps, segmentation research is regularly used by marketers to identify the most appropriate media in which to place advertisements. Almost all media vehicles – from television and radio stations to newspapers and magazines – use segmentation research to determine the characteristics of their audience and to publicise their findings in order to attract advertisers seeking a similar audience.

In some cases if segments of customers are large enough and can attract enough advertising, the media will spin off separate programmes or publications targeted to the specific segments. For example, *TIME* (www.time.com) targets different segments with special editions of its magazine. Not only does an advertiser have the choice of placing an advertisement in geographically based editions (e.g. the Europe, Middle East and Africa edition or the South Pacific edition), but some of the other editions offered by the magazine include a 'Gold' edition for upscale mature adults, an 'Inside Business' edition for top, middle and technical management, and a 'Women's' edition for affluent professional women. On the company's website advertisers can find a Global Edit Calendar presenting the different future editions, their booking deadlines, material deadlines, issue date and the editorial feature of the edition (e.g. 'Inside the Olympics', 'Global warming' or 'Coolest inventions'). This enables advertisers to choose the edition(s) that their target segments are most likely to read, and to plan the advertisements in good time.

CRITERIA FOR EFFECTIVE TARGETING OF SEGMENTS

Before turning to how marketers identify attractive marketing segments, it is important to point out that a difficult part of the segmentation process is to choose which segment(s) to target. Not all identifiable segments are profitable, and the marketer's challenge is to select one or more segments to target with an appropriate marketing mix. To be an effective target, a market segment should be:

1. identifiable,
2. sufficient (in terms of size),
3. stable or growing,
4. accessible (reachable) in terms of both media and cost, and
5. congruent with the firm's objectives and resources.

Identification

To divide the market into separate segments on the basis of a series of common or shared needs or characteristics that are relevant to the product or service, a marketer must be able to identify these relevant characteristics. Some segmentation variables, such as geography (location) or demographics (age, gender, occupation, race), are relatively easy to identify or are even observable. Others, such as education, income or marital status, can be determined through questionnaires. However, other characteristics, such as benefits sought or lifestyle, are more difficult to identify.

A knowledge of consumer behaviour is especially useful to marketers who use such intangible consumer characteristics as the basis for market segmentation.

Sufficiency

For a market segment to be a worthwhile target, it must consist of a sufficient number of people to warrant tailoring a product or promotional campaign to its specific needs or interests. To estimate the size of each segment under consideration, marketers often use secondary demographic data, such as that provided by national census bureaux (available at many libraries and online via the Internet), or they undertake a probability survey whose findings can be projected to the total market. (Consumer research methodology was described in Chapter 2.)

Stability

Most marketers prefer to target consumer segments that are relatively stable in terms of demographic and psychological factors and needs and that are likely to grow larger over time. They prefer to avoid 'fickle' segments that are unpredictable in embracing fads. For example, teens are a sizeable and easily identifiable market segment, eager to buy, able to spend and easily reached. Yet, by the time a marketer produces merchandise for a popular teenage fad, interest in it may have waned.

Accessibility

A fourth requirement for effective targeting is accessibility, which means that marketers must be able to reach the market segments they want to target in an economical way. Despite the wide availability of special-interest magazines and cable television programmes, marketers are constantly looking for new media that will enable them to reach their target markets with minimum waste of circulation and competition. One way this can be accomplished is via the Internet. Upon the request of the consumer, a growing number of websites periodically send email messages concerning a subject of special interest to the computer user. For example, a native Russian studying at the university in Leuven, Belgium might have an airline company email him with all the coming special deals on tickets to his home town in Russia.

Congruent with the firm's objectives and resources

Not every firm is interested or has the resources to reach or serve all the market segments available, even if these segments meet the first four criteria mentioned previously. For example, some fitness centres have chosen to tailor their services to women only, due to limited space in their centres, limited access to certified instructors and limited marketing budgets. Although men are an equally attractive segment for many of these centres, they have chosen to use their limited resources to serve a more specialised segment as well as possible.

Other firms choose not to serve one or more segments because they do not fit the long-term objectives of the firm. Choosing what a company should be and do also implies a choice of what not to do, and this sometimes results in constraining the number of segments to target.

BASES FOR SEGMENTATION

The first step in developing a segmentation strategy is to select the most appropriate base(s) on which to segment the market. Nine major categories of consumer characteristics provide the most popular bases for market segmentation. They include geographic factors, demographic factors, psychological factors, psychographic (lifestyle) characteristics, sociocultural variables, use-related characteristics, use-situation factors, benefits sought and forms of **hybrid segmentation** – such as demographic-psychographic profiles and geodemographic factors. Hybrid segmentation formats each use a combination of several segmentation bases to create rich and comprehensive profiles of particular consumer segments (e.g. a combination of a specific age range, income range, lifestyle and profession). Table 3-1 lists the nine segmentation bases, divided into specific variables with examples of each. The following section discusses each of the nine segmentation bases. (Various psychological and sociocultural segmentation variables are examined in greater depth in later chapters.)

TABLE 3-1 Market segmentation categories and selected variables

SEGMENTATION BASE	SELECTED SEGMENTATION VARIABLES
GEOGRAPHIC SEGMENTATION	
Region	Scandinavia, Benelux, Middle East
City size	Major metropolitan areas, small cities, towns
Density of area	Urban, suburban, exurban, rural
Climate	Temperate, hot, humid, rainy
DEMOGRAPHIC SEGMENTATION	
Age	Under 12, 12–17, 18–34, 35–49, 50–64, 65–74, 75–99, 100+
Sex	Male, female
Marital status	Single, married, divorced, living together, widowed
Income	Under €25,000, €25,000–€34,999, €35,000–€49,999, €50,000–€74,999, €75,000–€99,999, €100,000 and over
Education	Some high school, high school graduate, some university, university graduate, postgraduate
Occupation	Professional, blue-collar, white-collar, agricultural, military
PSYCHOLOGICAL SEGMENTATION	
Needs-motivation	Shelter, safety, security, affection, sense of self-worth
Personality	Extroverts, novelty seekers, aggressives, low dogmatics
Perception	Low-risk, moderate-risk, high-risk
Learning-involvement	Low-involvement, high-involvement
Attitudes	Positive attitude, negative attitude
PSYCHOGRAPHIC SEGMENTATION	
Combines psychology and demographics, hence psychodemographics (Lifestyle) Segmentation	Economy-minded, couch potatoes, outdoors enthusiasts, status seekers
VALS™	Innovator, Thinker, Believer, Achiever, Striver, Experiencer, Maker, Survivor
SOCIOCULTURAL SEGMENTATION	
Cultures	Danish, Italian, Chinese, Australian, French, Pakistani
Religion	Catholic, Protestant, Moslem, Jewish, other

TABLE 3-1 *(Continued)*

Subcultures (race/ethnic)	African, American, Caucasian, Asian, Hispanic
Social class	Lower, middle, upper
Family life cycle	Bachelors, young marrieds, full nesters, empty nesters
USE-RELATED SEGMENTATION	
Usage rate	Heavy users, medium users, light users, non-users
Awareness status	Unaware, aware, interested, enthusiastic
Brand loyalty	None, some, strong
USAGE-SITUATION SEGMENTATION	
Time	Leisure, work, rush, morning, night
Objective	Personal, gift, snack, fun, achievement
Location	Home, work, friend's home, in-store
Person	Self, family members, friends, boss, peer
BENEFIT SEGMENTATION	
	Convenience, social acceptance, long lasting, economy, value-for-money
HYBRID SEGMENTATION	
Geodemographics	'New empty nests', 'Boomtown singles', 'Movers and Shakers'

Note: VALS™ is an example of a psychographic/demographic profile.

Source: Reprinted with permission of *Strategic Business Insights* (SBI); www.strategicbusinessinsights.com/VALS.

Geographic segmentation

In **geographic segmentation** the market is divided by location. The theory behind this strategy is that people who live in the same area share some similar needs and wants and that these needs and wants differ from those of people living in other areas. For example, certain food products and/or varieties sell better in one region than in others, or are used differently in different geographic areas. More specifically, mayonnaise is frequently used with chips in Belgium, whereas this combination is seldom seen in Norway. Furthermore, while curry-flavoured ketchup has been a well-known product in Belgium for years, the same product has until recently been difficult to find in Norwegian supermarkets.

Some marketing scholars have argued that direct-mail merchandise catalogues, national toll-free telephone numbers, satellite television transmission, global communication networks, and especially the Internet have erased all regional boundaries and that geographic segmentation should be replaced by a single global marketing strategy. Clearly, any company that decides to put its catalogue on the Internet enables individuals all over the world to browse its site and become customers. For example, shops offering collectables like first editions of old books may increase their target segment substantially by making their inventory searchable on the Internet. A shop in Greece may find that orders start coming in from Sweden, Japan, New Zealand and Ireland not long after posting its offer on the Internet.

Other marketers have, for a number of reasons, been moving in the opposite direction and developing highly regionalised marketing strategies. For example, due to the variety of consumer preferences, government regulations and brand images, General Motors segments

TABLE 3-3 Examples of country-specific or region-specific cohort-defining moments

EVENT*	DATE	COUNTRY AFFECTED
John Profumo scandal	1963	UK
Nelson Mandela's imprisonment and release	1964 and 1990	South Africa
Cultural Revolution	1966–1976	China
Six Days War	1967	Jordan, Israel and Egypt
Khmer Rouge Rule	1975–1979	Cambodia and South East Asia
Assassination of Anwar Sadat	1981	Egypt
Falklands War	1982	UK and Argentina
Assassination of Olof Palme	1986	Sweden
Tiananmen Square massacre	1989	China
Manuel Noriega's arrest and extradition to USA	1989	Panama
Japanese Economic 'bubble' bursts	1991	Japan
Irish legalisation of divorce	1995	Ireland

*These events are not ranked in order of importance, but by date.
Source: Adapted from Charles D. Schewe and Geoffrey Meredith, 'Segmenting Global Markets by Generational Cohorts: Determining Motivations by Age', *Journal of Consumer Behavior*, 4, October 2004, 56. Copyright 2004. Copyright John Wiley & Sons Limited. Reproduced with permission.

2010, may all be more recent examples of such defining moments for those who were affected. We must remember that cohort effects are ongoing and lifelong.

The selected age segments will receive more attention in our discussion of age as a subculture in Chapter 13.

Sex

Gender is quite frequently a distinguishing segmentation variable. Women have traditionally been the main users of such products as hair colouring and cosmetics, and men have been the main users of tools and shaving preparations. However, sex roles have blurred, and gender is no longer an accurate way to distinguish consumers in some product categories. For example, women are buying household repair tools and men have become significant users of skin care and hair products. It is becoming increasingly common to see magazine advertisements and television commercials that depict men and women in roles traditionally occupied by the opposite sex. For example, many advertisements reflect the expanded child-nurturing roles of young fathers in today's society.

Much of the change in sex roles has occurred because of the continued impact of dual-income households. One consequence for marketers is that women are not so readily accessible through traditional media as they once were. Because working women do not have much time to watch television or listen to the radio, many advertisers now emphasise magazines in their media schedules, especially those specifically aimed at working women. Direct marketers have also been targeting time-pressured working women who use mail-order catalogues, convenient toll-free numbers and Internet sites as ways of shopping for personal clothing and accessories, as well as many household and family needs. Recent research has shown that men and women differ in terms of the way they look at their Internet usage. Specifically, men tend to click on a website because they are 'information hungry', whereas women click on because 'they expect communications media to entertain and educate'.[6]

Marital Status

Traditionally, the family has been the focus of most marketing efforts, and for many products and services the household continues to be the relevant consuming unit. Marketers are interested in the number and kinds of households that buy and/or own certain products. They also are interested in determining the demographic and media profiles of household decision makers (those involved in the actual selection of the product) to develop appropriate marketing strategies.

Marketers have discovered the benefits of targeting specific marital status groupings, such as singles, divorced individuals, single parents and dual-income married couples. For instance, singles, especially one-person households with incomes greater than €50,000, comprise a market segment that tends to be above average in the use of products not traditionally associated with supermarkets (e.g. cognac, books, loose tea) and below average in their consumption of traditional supermarket products (e.g. ketchup, peanut butter, mayonnaise). Such insights can be particularly useful to a supermarket manager operating in a neighbourhood of one-person households when deciding on the merchandise mix for the store. Some marketers target one-person households with single-serving prepared foods and others with mini-appliances such as small microwave ovens and two-cup coffee makers. (The family as a consuming unit is discussed in greater detail in Chapter 11.)

Income, Education and Occupation

Income has long been an important variable for distinguishing between market segments. Marketers commonly segment markets on the basis of income because they feel that it is a strong indicator of the ability (or inability) to pay for a product or a specific model of the product. For instance, initially marketers of home computers under €1,000 felt that such products would be particularly attractive to homes with modest family incomes. However, low-priced PCs also proved to be quite popular with higher-income families who wanted additional computers for younger family members.

Income is often combined with other demographic variables to define target markets more accurately. To illustrate, high income has been combined with age to identify the important affluent elderly segment. It also has been combined with both age and occupational status to produce the so-called yuppie segment, a sought-after sub-group of the baby boomer market.

Education, occupation and income tend to be closely correlated in almost a cause-and-effect relationship. High-level occupations that produce high incomes usually require advanced educational training. Individuals with little education rarely qualify for high-level jobs. Insights on Internet usage preferences tend to support the close relationship among income, occupation and education. Research reveals that consumers with lower incomes, lower education and blue-collar occupations tend to spend more time online at home than those with higher incomes, higher education and white-collar occupations.[7] One possible reason for this difference is that those in blue-collar jobs often do not have access to the Internet during the course of the working day.

Psychological segmentation

Psychological characteristics refer to the inner or intrinsic qualities of the individual consumer. Consumer segmentation strategies are often based on specific psychological variables. For instance, consumers may be segmented in terms of their motivations, personality, perceptions, learning and attitudes. (Part 2 examines in detail the wide range of psychological variables that influence consumer decision-making and consumption behaviour.)

Psychographic segmentation

Marketing practitioners have heartily embraced psychographic research, which is closely aligned with psychological research, especially personality and attitude measurement. This form of applied consumer research (commonly referred to as lifestyle analysis) has proved to be a valuable marketing tool that helps identify promising consumer segments likely to be responsive to specific marketing messages.

The psychographic profile of a consumer segment can be thought of as a composite of consumers' measured **activities, interests and opinions (AIOs)**. As an approach to constructing consumer psychographic profiles, AIO research seeks consumers' responses to a large number of statements that measure activities (how the consumer or family spends time, e.g. golfing, gardening), interests (the consumer's or family's preferences and priorities, e.g. home, fashion, food) and opinions (how the consumer feels about a wide variety of events and political issues, social issues, the state of the economy, ecology). In their most common form, AIO-psychographic studies use a battery of statements (a **psychographic inventory**) designed to identify relevant aspects of a consumer's personality, buying motives, interests, attitudes, beliefs and values. Table 3-4 presents a portion of a psychographic inventory designed to gauge 'techno-road-warriors', business people who spend a high percentage of their working week travelling, equipped with laptop computers, mobile phones with broadband network connection and electronic organisers. Table 3-5 presents a hypothetical psychographic profile of a techno-road-warrior. The appeal of psychographic research lies in the frequently vivid and practical profiles of consumer segments that it can produce (which will be illustrated later in this chapter).

TABLE 3-4 A portion of an AIO inventory used to identify techno-road-warriors

*Instructions: Please read each statement and place an 'x' in the box that **best** indicates how strongly you 'agree' or 'disagree' with the statement.*

	AGREE COMPLETELY						DISAGREE COMPLETELY
I feel that my life is moving faster and faster, sometimes just too fast	[1]	[2]	[3]	[4]	[5]	[6]	[7]
If I could consider the 'pluses' and 'minuses', technology has been good for me	[1]	[2]	[3]	[4]	[5]	[6]	[7]
I find that I have to pull myself away from email	[1]	[2]	[3]	[4]	[5]	[6]	[7]
Given my lifestyle, I have more of a shortage of time than money	[1]	[2]	[3]	[4]	[5]	[6]	[7]
I like the benefits of the Internet, but I often don't have the time to take advantage of them	[1]	[2]	[3]	[4]	[5]	[6]	[7]
I am generally open to considering new practices and new technology	[1]	[2]	[3]	[4]	[5]	[6]	[7]

TABLE 3-5 A hypothetical psychographic profile of the techno-road-warrior

- Goes on the Internet more than 20 times a week
- Sends and/or receives 50 or more email messages a week
- Regularly visits websites to gather information and/or to comparison shop
- Often buys personal items via 800 numbers and/or over the Internet
- May trade stocks and/or make travel reservations over the Internet
- Earns €75,000 or more a year
- Belongs to several rewards programmes (e.g. frequent flyer, hotel and hire-car programmes)

AIO research has even been employed to explore pet ownership as a segmentation base. One study has found that people who do *not* have pets are more conservative in nature, more brand loyal, and more likely to agree with statements such as 'I am very good at managing money' and 'It is important for me to look well dressed'. Such findings can be used by marketers when developing promotional messages for their products and services.[8]

The results of psychographic segmentation efforts are frequently reflected in firms' marketing messages. **Psychographic segmentation** is further discussed later in the chapter, where we consider hybrid segmentation strategies that combine psychographic and demographic variables to create rich descriptive profiles of consumer segments.

Sociocultural segmentation

Sociological (group) and anthropological (cultural) variables – that is, **sociocultural variables** – provide further bases for market segmentation. For example, consumer markets have been successfully subdivided into segments on the basis of stage in the family life cycle, social class, core cultural values, subcultural memberships and cross-cultural affiliation.

Family Life Cycle

Family life-cycle segmentation is based on the premise that many families pass through similar phases in their formation, growth and final dissolution. At each phase, the family unit needs different products and services. Young single people, for example, need basic furniture for their first apartment, whereas their parents, finally free of child rearing, often refurnish their homes with more elaborate pieces. Family life cycle is a composite variable based explicitly on marital and family status but implicitly reflects relative age, income and employment status. Each of the stages in the traditional family life cycle (bachelorhood, honeymooners, parenthood, post-parenthood and dissolution) represents an important target segment to a variety of marketers. For example, the financial services industry segments customers in terms of family life-cycle stages because it has been found that families' financial needs tend to shift as they progress through the various stages of life.[9] (Chapter 11 discusses the family life cycle in greater depth and shows how marketers cater to the needs and wishes of consumers in each stage of the life cycle.)

Social Class

Social class (or relative status in the community) can be used as a base for market segmentation and is usually measured by a weighted index of several demographic variables, such as education, occupation and income. The concept of social class implies a hierarchy in which individuals in the same class generally have the same degree of status, whereas members of other classes have either higher or lower status. Studies have shown that consumers in different social classes vary in terms of values, product preferences and buying habits. Many major banks and investment companies, for example, offer a variety of different levels of service to people of different social classes (e.g. private banking services to the upper classes). Some investment companies appeal to upper-class customers by offering them options that correspond to their wealthy status. In contrast, a financial programme targeted to a lower social class might talk instead about savings accounts. (Chapter 12 discusses in depth the use of social class as a segmentation variable.)

Culture and Subculture

Some marketers have found it useful to segment their markets on the basis of cultural heritage because members of the same culture tend to share the same values, beliefs and customs. Marketers who use cultural segmentation stress specific, widely held cultural values with which they hope consumers will identify. Cultural segmentation is particularly successful in international marketing, but it is important for the marketer to understand fully the target country's beliefs, values and customs (the cross-cultural context).

Within the larger culture, distinct subgroups (subcultures) are often united by certain experiences, values or beliefs that make effective market segments. These groupings could be based on a specific demographic characteristic (such as race, religion, ethnicity or age) or lifestyle characteristic (teachers, joggers). Research on subcultural differences, which will be discussed more fully in Chapter 13, tends to reveal that consumers are more responsive to promotional messages that they perceive relate to their own ethnicity.

Culturally distinct segments can be prospects for the same product but are often targeted more efficiently with different promotional appeals. For example, a bicycle might be promoted as an efficient means of transport in Asia and as a health-and-fitness product in Finland. Similarly, a fishing rod or shotgun could be advertised in many parts of the world as a way to put food on the dinner table but might be promoted in the UK as leisure-time sporting equipment. In a study that divided China's urban consumers into four segments ('working poor', 'salary class', 'little rich', and 'yuppies'), the researchers found that for all four groups television was the most popular medium of entertainment and information. However, the working poor spent the most time listening to radio, while yuppies and the little rich spent the most time reading newspapers and magazines.[10] (Chapters 13 and 14 examine cultural, subcultural and cross-cultural bases of market segmentation in greater detail.)

Cross-cultural or Global Marketing Segmentation

As the world has become smaller, a true global marketplace has developed. For example, as you read this you may be sitting on an IKEA chair or sofa (Sweden), drinking Earl Grey tea (England), wearing a Swatch watch (Switzerland), Nike trainers (China), a Polo golf shirt (Mexico) and Dockers trousers (Dominican Republic). Some global market segments, such as teenagers, appear to want the same types of products, regardless of which nation they call home – products that are trendy, entertaining and image-oriented. This global 'sameness' allowed Reebok, for example, to launch its Instapump line of trainers using the same global advertising campaign in approximately 140 countries.[11] (The issue of global or international marketing segmentation will be more fully discussed in Chapter 14.)

Use-related segmentation

An extremely popular and effective form of segmentation categorises consumers in terms of product, service or brand usage characteristics, such as level of usage, level of awareness and degree of brand loyalty.

Rate of usage segmentation differentiates among heavy users, medium users, light users and non-users of a specific product, service or brand. For example, research has consistently indicated that between 25 and 35 per cent of beer drinkers account for more than 70 per cent of all beer consumed. For this reason, most marketers prefer to target their advertising campaigns to heavy users rather than spend considerably more money trying to attract light users. This also explains the successful targeting of light beer to heavy drinkers on the basis that it is less filling (and, thus, can be consumed in greater quantities) than regular beer. Recent studies have found that heavy soup consumers were more socially active, creative, optimistic, witty and less stubborn than light consumers and non-consumers, and they were also less likely to read entertainment and sports magazines and more likely to read family and home magazines. Likewise, heavy users of travel agents in Singapore were more involved with and more enthusiastic about holiday travel, more innovative with regard to their selection of holiday travel products, more likely to travel for pleasure, and more widely exposed to travel information from the mass media.[12]

Marketers of a host of other products have also found that a relatively small group of heavy users accounts for a disproportionately large percentage of product use; targeting these heavy users has become the basis of their marketing strategies. Other marketers take note of the gaps in market coverage for light and medium users and profitably target those segments. Table 3-6 presents an overview of a segmentation strategy especially suitable for marketers seeking to organise their

TABLE 3-6 A framework for segmenting a firm's database of customers

SEGMENT NAME	SEGMENT CHARACTERISTIC	COMPANY ACTION
LoLows	Low current share, low-consumption customers	Starve
HiLows	High current share, low-consumption customers	Tickle
LowHighs	Low current share, high-consumption customers	Chase
HiHighs	High current share, high-consumption customers	Stroke

Source: Adapted from Richard G. Barlow, 'How to Court Various Target Markets', *Marketing News*, 9 October 2000, 22.

database of customers into an action-oriented framework. The framework proposes a way to identify a firm's best customers by dividing the database into the following segments:

1. *LoLows* (low current share, low-consumption customers),
2. *HiLows* (high current share, low-consumption customers),
3. *LowHighs* (low current share, high-consumption customers), and
4. *HiHighs* (high current share, high-consumption customers).

Moreover, the framework suggests the following specific strategies for each of the four segments: 'starve' the *LoLows*, 'tickle' the *HiLows*, 'chase' the *LowHighs*, and 'stroke' the *HiHighs*.[13]

In addition to segmenting customers in terms of rate of usage or other usage patterns, consumers can also be segmented in terms of their *awareness status*. In particular, the notion of consumer awareness of the product, interest level in the product, readiness to buy the product or whether consumers need to be informed about the product are all aspects of awareness.

Sometimes brand loyalty is used as the basis for segmentation. Marketers often try to identify the characteristics of their brand-loyal consumers so that they can direct their promotional efforts to people with similar characteristics in the larger population. Other marketers target consumers who show no brand loyalty ('brand switchers') in the belief that such people represent greater market potential than consumers who are loyal to competing brands. Also, almost by definition, consumer innovators – often a prime target for new products – tend not to be brand loyal. (Chapter 15 discusses the characteristics of consumer innovators.)

Increasingly, marketers stimulate and reward brand loyalty by offering special benefits to consistent or frequent customers. Such frequent usage or relationship programmes often take the form of a membership club (e.g. Hertz Number 1 Club Gold, KLM and Air France's joint programme 'Flying Blue', or the Hilton HHonors). Relationship programmes tend to provide special accommodation and services, as well as free extras, to keep these frequent customers loyal and happy.

Usage-situation segmentation

Marketers recognise that the occasion or situation often determines what consumers will purchase or consume. For this reason, they sometimes focus on **usage-situation segmentation** as a variable.

The following three statements reveal the potential of situation segmentation: 'Whenever our daughter Jamie gets a rise or a promotion, we always take her out to dinner'; 'When I'm away on business for a week or more, I try to stay at a Radisson hotel'; 'I always buy my wife flowers on her birthday'. Under other circumstances, in other situations and on other occasions, the same consumer might make other choices. Some situational factors that might influence a purchase or consumption choice include whether it is a weekday or weekend (e.g. going to the cinema); whether there is sufficient time (e.g. use of regular mail or express mail); whether it is a gift for a girlfriend, a parent or a self-gift (a reward to one's self).

Many products are promoted for special usage occasions. The greetings card industry, for example, stresses special cards for a variety of occasions that seem to be increasing almost daily (Grandparents' Day, Secretaries' Day, etc.). The florist and confectionery industries promote their products for Valentine's Day and Mother's Day, the diamond industry promotes diamond rings as an engagement symbol, and the wristwatch industry promotes its products as graduation gifts. The Volvo car advertisement in Figure 3-1 is based on situational, special usage segmentation. It appeared in Norwegian newspapers prior to Christmas, covering two consecutive pages. The first picture portrays Rudolph the Reindeer pulling an empty sleigh, with both Santa Claus and the Christmas presents obviously missing. The second picture shows a Volvo XC90

FIGURE 3-1 A Volvo occasion-specific advertising campaign telling consumers that Santa Claus has replaced Rudolph the Reindeer with a Volvo XC90
Source: Volvo Personbiler Norge AS/TWBA.

speeding through the snow-covered landscape with someone that might be Santa Claus sitting behind the wheel. The text, which can't be misunderstood, simply says 'Sorry Rudolf'.

Benefit segmentation

Marketing and advertising executives constantly attempt to identify the one most important benefit of their product or service that will be most meaningful to consumers. Examples of benefits that are commonly used include financial security, data protection, good health, fresh breath and peace of mind.

In an article dealing with brand strategies in India, the point is made that 'nothing is as effective as segmentation based on the benefits a group of customers seek from your brand'. To illustrate, the article points out that in India Dettol soap is targeted at the hygiene-conscious consumer – the individual seeking protection from germs and contamination – rather than the consumer looking for beauty, fragrance, freshness or economy.[14]

Changing lifestyles also play a major role in determining the product benefits that are important to consumers and provide marketers with opportunities for new products and services. For example, the microwave oven was the perfect solution to the needs of dual-income households, where neither the husband nor the wife has the time for lengthy meal preparation. Food marketers offer busy families the benefit of breakfast products that require only seconds to prepare.

Benefit segmentation can be used to position various brands within the same product category.[15] The classic case of successful benefit segmentation is the market for toothpaste, and one article suggested that if consumers are socially active, they want a toothpaste that can deliver white teeth and fresh breath; if they smoke, they want a toothpaste to fight stains; if disease prevention is their major focus, then they want a toothpaste that will fight germs; and if they have children, they want to lower their dental bills.[16]

Hybrid segmentation

Marketers commonly segment markets by combining several segmentation variables rather than relying on a single segmentation base. This section examines three hybrid segmentation approaches that provide marketers with richer and more accurately defined consumer segments than can be derived from using a single segmentation variable. These include psychographic–demographic profiles, geodemographics and VALS.

Psychographic–Demographic Profiles

Psychographic and demographic profiles are highly complementary approaches that work best when used together. By combining the knowledge gained from both demographic and psychographic studies, marketers are provided with powerful information about their target markets.

Demographic–psychographic profiling has been widely used in the development of advertising campaigns to answer three questions: 'Who should we target?'; 'What should we say?'; 'Where should we say it?' To help advertisers answer the third question, many advertising media vehicles sponsor demographic–psychographic research on which they base very detailed audience profiles. By offering media buyers such carefully defined dual profiles of their audiences, mass media publishers and broadcasters make it possible for advertisers to select media whose audiences most closely resemble their target markets.

Morever, advertisers are increasingly designing advertisements that depict in words and/or pictures the essence of a particular target-market lifestyle or segment that they want to reach. For example, Bavac has several advertisements that appeals to specific active and outdoor lifestyles, and the advertisement presented in Figure 3-2 is one example.

FIGURE 3-2 This advertisement targets an active outdoor lifestyle
Source: Jagged Globe.

Geodemographic Segmentation

This type of hybrid segmentation scheme is based on the notion that people who live close to one another are likely to have similar financial means, tastes, preferences, lifestyles and consumption habits (similar to the old adage, 'Birds of a feather flock together'). This segmentation approach uses computers to generate geodemographic market clusters of like consumers.

Specifically, computer software clusters a region or nation's neighbourhoods into lifestyle groupings based on postal area codes. Clusters are created based on consumer lifestyles, and a specific cluster includes area codes that are composed of people with similar lifestyles widely scattered throughout the country. Marketers use the cluster data for direct-mail campaigns, to select retail sites and appropriate merchandise mixes, to locate banks and restaurants and to design marketing strategies for specific market segments.

Geodemographic segmentation is most useful when an advertiser's or marketer's best prospects (in terms of consumer personalities, goals and interests) can be isolated in terms of where they live. However, for products and services used by a broad cross-section of the public, other segmentation schemes may be more productive.

Strategic Business Insights VALS™ System

Drawing on Maslow's need hierarchy (see Chapter 5) and the concept of social character, in the late 1970s researchers at SRI International developed a generalised segmentation scheme known as Values and Lifestyles (**VALS™**). This original system was designed to explain the dynamics of societal change and was quickly adapted as a marketing tool.

Over the years the VALS™ system (currently owned and operated by Strategic Business Insights (SBI), a spin-out of SRI International) was revised to focus more explicitly on explaining consumer purchase behaviour. The current US VALS™ typology classifies the population into eight distinctive subgroups (segments) based on consumer responses to 35 attitudinal and four demographic questions.[17] Figure 3-3 depicts the VALS™ classification scheme and offers a brief profile of the consumer traits of each of the VALS™ segments. The major groupings are defined in terms of three primary motivations and a new definition of resources: the ideals-motivated (consumers whose choices are motivated by their beliefs rather than by desires for approval), the achievement-motivated (consumers whose choices are guided by the actions, approval and opinions of others) and the self-expression-motivated (consumers who are motivated by a desire for social or physical activity, variety and risk-taking). Resources (from most to least) include the range of psychological, physical, demographic and material means and capacities consumers have to draw upon, including education, income, self-confidence, health, eagerness to buy and energy level.

Members of each of the eight VALS™ segments have different mindsets that drive different consumption patterns – lifestyles, decision-making styles, communication styles, etc. For instance, Believers are slow to alter their consumption-related habits, whereas Innovators are drawn to top-of-the-range and new products, especially innovative technologies. Therefore, it is not surprising that marketers of intelligent in-vehicle technologies (e.g. global positioning devices) must first target Innovators, because they are early adopters of new products.[18]

IMPLEMENTING SEGMENTATION STRATEGIES

Firms that use market segmentation can pursue a concentrated marketing strategy or a differentiated marketing strategy. In certain instances, they might use a counter-segmentation strategy.

Concentrated versus differentiated marketing

Once an organisation has identified its most promising market segments, it must decide whether to target one segment or several segments. The premise behind market segmentation is that each targeted segment receives a specially designed marketing mix, that is, a specially tailored product, price, distribution network, and/or promotional campaign. Targeting several segments using individual marketing mixes is called **differentiated marketing**; targeting just one segment with a unique marketing mix is called **concentrated marketing**.

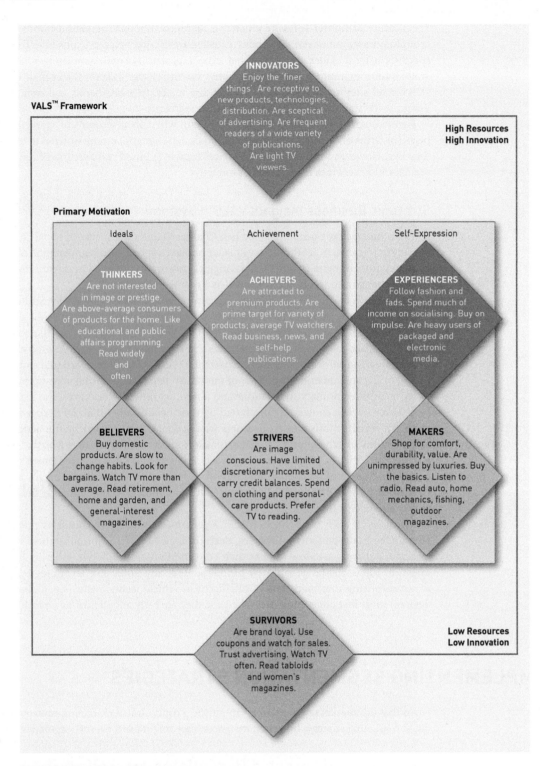

FIGURE 3-3 SRI VALS™ segments

Source: © 2007 by SRI Consulting Business Intelligence. All rights reserved. Reprinted with permission of SRI Consulting Business Intelligence (SRIC-BI); www.sric-bi.com/VALS.

Differentiated marketing is a highly appropriate segmentation strategy for financially strong companies that are well established in a product category and competitive with other firms that are also strong in the category (e.g. soft drinks, motor cars or detergents). However, if a company is small or new to the field, concentrated marketing is probably a better prospect. A company can survive and prosper by filling a niche not occupied by stronger companies.

Counter-segmentation

Sometimes companies find that they must reconsider the extent to which they are segmenting their markets. They might find that some segments have contracted over time to the point where they do not warrant an individually designed marketing programme. In such cases, the company seeks to discover a more generic need or consumer characteristic that would apply to the members of two or more segments and recombine those segments into a larger single segment that could be targeted with an individually tailored product or promotional campaign. This is called a **counter-segmentation strategy**. Some business schools with wide course offerings in each department were forced to adopt a counter-segmentation strategy when they discovered that students simply did not have enough available credits to take a full spectrum of in-depth courses in their major area of study. As a result, some courses had to be cancelled each term because of inadequate registration. For some schools, a counter-segmentation strategy effectively solved the problem (e.g. by combining advertising, publicity, sales promotion and personal selling courses into a single course called Promotion).

SUMMARY

Market segmentation and diversity are complementary concepts. Without a diverse marketplace, composed of many different people, with different backgrounds, countries of origin, interests, needs and wants, there really would be little reason to segment markets.

Before the widespread adoption of the marketing concept, mass marketing (offering the same product or marketing mix to everyone) was the marketing strategy most widely used. Market segmentation followed as a more logical way to meet consumer needs. Segmentation is defined as the process of dividing a potential market into distinct subsets of consumers with a common need or characteristic and selecting one or more segments to target with a specially designed marketing mix. Besides aiding in the development of new products, segmentation studies assist in the redesign and repositioning of existing products, in the creation of promotional appeals and the selection of advertising media.

Because segmentation strategies benefit both marketers and consumers, they have received wide support from both sides of the marketplace. Market segmentation is now widely used by manufacturers, retailers and the charity sector.

Nine major classes of consumer characteristics serve as the most common bases for market segmentation. These include geographic factors, demographic factors, psychological factors, psychographic characteristics, sociocultural variables, use-related characteristics, use-situation factors, benefits sought and hybrid forms of segmentation. Important criteria for segmenting markets include identification, sufficiency, stability and accessibility. Once an organisation has identified promising target markets, it must decide whether to target several segments (differentiated marketing) or just one segment (concentrated marketing). It then develops a positioning strategy for each targeted segment. In certain instances, a company might decide to follow a counter-segmentation strategy and recombine two or more segments into one larger segment.

DISCUSSION QUESTIONS

1. What is market segmentation? How is the practice of market segmentation related to the marketing concept?
2. How are market segmentation, targeting and positioning interrelated? Illustrate how these three concepts can be used to develop a marketing strategy for a product of your choice.
3. Discuss the advantages and disadvantages of using demographics as a basis for segmentation. Can demographics and psychographics be used together to segment markets? Illustrate your answer with a specific example.
4. Many marketers have found that a relatively small group of heavy users accounts for a disproportionately large amount of the total product consumed. What are the advantages and disadvantages of targeting these heavy users?
5. Under which circumstances and for what types of products should a marketer segment the market on the basis of (a) awareness status, (b) brand loyalty and (c) usage situation?
6. Some marketers consider benefit segmentation as the segmentation approach most consistent with the marketing concept. Do you agree or disagree with this view? Why?
7. Scandinavian Airlines Systems (SAS) is a prominent company in the airline and hotel industry. Describe how the company can use demographics and psychographics to identify television shows and magazines in which to place its advertisements.
8. How can a marketer for a chain of health clubs use the VALS™ segmentation profiles to develop an advertising campaign? Which segments should be targeted? How should the health club be positioned in each of these segments?
9. For each of the following products, identify the segmentation base that you consider best for targeting consumers: (a) coffee, (b) soup, (c) home exercise equipment, (d) cordless telephones and (e) fat-free frozen yogurt. Explain your choices.
10. Apply the criteria for effective segmentation to marketing a product of your choice to college students.

EXERCISES

1. Select a product and brand that you use frequently and list the benefits you receive from using it. Without disclosing your list, ask a fellow student who uses a different brand in this product category (preferably a friend of the opposite sex) to make a similar list for his or her brand. Compare the two lists and identify the implications for using benefit segmentation to market the two brands.
2. Does your lifestyle differ significantly from your parents' lifestyle? If so, how are the two lifestyles different? What factors cause these differences?
3. Do you anticipate any major changes in your lifestyle in the next five years? If so, to which VALS™ segment are you likely to belong five years from now? Explain.
4. The owners of a local health-food restaurant have asked you to prepare a psychographic profile of families living in the community surrounding the restaurant's location. Construct a 10-question psychographic inventory appropriate for segmenting families on the basis of their dining-out preferences.
5. Find three print advertisements that you believe are targeted at a particular psychographic segment. How effective do you think each advertisement is in terms of achieving its objective? Why?

NOTES

1. Linda P. Morton, 'Segmenting to Target Investors', *Public Relations Quarterly*, Summer 2000, 45–6.
2. Stephanie Thompson, 'Minute Maid Line Takes Cooler Tack to Attract Tweens', *Advertising Age*, 14 August 2000, 43.
3. 'Superstars of Spending', *Advertising Age*, 12 February 2001, S1, S10.
4. Ellen Neuborne, 'Pepsi's Aim Is True', *Business Week E. Biz*, 22 January 2001, EB 52.
5. Linda Morton, 'Segmenting Publics by Life Development Stages', *Public Relations Quarterly*, Spring 1999, 46.
6. Scott Smith and David Whitlark, 'Men and Women Online: What Makes Them Click?', *Marketing Research*, Summer 2001, 20–25.
7. 'Less Well-To-Do Web Surfers Spend More Time Online Than More Affluent People, According to Nielsen//NetRatings', *Business Wire*, 21 September 2000, 1.
8. William James, Charles A. McMellon and Gladys Torres-Baumgarten, 'Dogs and Cats Rule: A New Insight into Segmentation', *Journal of Targeting, Measurement and Analysis for Marketing*, 13, October 2004, 70–77.
9. Patrick Dalton, 'Pick Your Targets', *Bankers News*, 9 March 1999, 1, 3.
10. Geng Cui and Quiming Liu, 'Emerging Market Segments in a Transitional Economy: A Study of Urban Consumers in China', *Journal of International Marketing*, 9, 1, 2001, 84–106.
11. V. Kumar and Anish Nagpal, 'Segmenting Global Markets: Look Before You Leap', *Marketing Research*, Spring 2001, 8–13.
12. Brian Wansink and Sea Bum Park, 'Methods and Measures That Profile Heavy Users', *Journal of Advertising Research*, July–August 2000, 61–72; Ronald E. Goldsmith and Stephen W. Litvin, 'Heavy Users of Travel Agents: A Segmentation Analysis of Vacation Travelers', *Journal of Travel Research*, November 1999, 127–33.
13. Richard G. Barlow, 'How to Court Various Target Markets', *Marketing News*, 9 October 2000, 22.
14. 'India: Mantras to Work Brand Magic', *Businessline*, 26 April 2001, 1–4.
15. Russell Haley, 'Benefit Segmentation: A Decision-Oriented Research Tool', *Marketing Management*, 4, Summer 1995, 59–62; Dianne Cermak, Karen Maru File and Russ Alan Prince, 'A Benefit Segmentation of the Major Donor Market', *Journal of Business Research*, February 1994, 121–30; Elisabeth Kastenholz, Duane Davis and Gordon Paul, 'Segmenting Tourism in Rural Areas: The Case of North and Central Portugal', *Journal of Travel Research*, 37, May 1999, 353–63.
16. William Trombetta, 'A Strategic Overview', *Pharmaceutical Executive Supplement*, May 2001, 8–16.
17. 'Mediamark Research Inc. Enhances Data with Segmentation Analysis from VALS™ and Forrester', *PR Newswire*, 22 August 2001, 1; Linda P. Morton, 'Segmenting Publics by Lifestyles', *Public Relations Quarterly*, Fall 1999, 46–7.
18. 'Who Will Buy Intelligent In-Vehicle Products? New Report Assesses Consumer Perceptions and Acceptance of Intelligent Transportation Systems Products', *Business Wire*, 2 November 1999, 1.

PART 2
THE CONSUMER AS AN INDIVIDUAL

PART 2 DISCUSSES THE CONSUMER AS AN INDIVIDUAL

Chapters 4 to 9 provide the reader with a comprehensive picture of consumer psychology. These chapters explain the basic psychological concepts that account for individual behaviour and demonstrate how these concepts influence the individual's consumption-related behaviour. Chapter 10 shows how communication links consumers as individuals to the world and the people around them.

CHAPTER 4
CONSUMER DECISION-MAKING

This chapter draws together many of the psychological, social and cultural concepts applied in the study of consumer behaviour into an overview framework for understanding how consumers make decisions. The chapter takes a broad perspective and examines **consumer decision-making** in the context of all types of consumption choices, ranging from the consumption of new products to the use of old and established products. It also considers consumers' decisions not as the end point but rather as the beginning point of a **consumption process**.

WHAT IS A DECISION?

Every day, each of us makes numerous decisions concerning every aspect of our daily lives. However, we generally make these decisions without stopping to think about how we make them and what is involved in the particular decision-making process itself. In the most general terms, a decision is the selection of an option from two or more alternative choices. In other words, for a person to make a decision, a number of alternatives to choose from must be available. When a person has a choice between making a purchase and not making a purchase, a choice between brand X and brand Y, or a choice of spending time doing A or B, that person is in a position to make a decision. On the other hand, if the consumer has no alternatives from which to choose and is literally forced to make a particular purchase or take a particular action (e.g. use a prescribed medication), then this single 'no-choice' instance does not constitute a decision; such a no-choice decision is commonly referred to as 'Hobson's choice'.

In reality, no-choice purchase or consumption situations are fairly rare. In most industrialised countries of today, freedom is often expressed in terms of a wide range of product choices. Thus, if there is almost always a choice then there is almost always an opportunity for consumers to make decisions. Moreover, experimental research reveals that providing consumers with a choice when there was originally none can be a very good business strategy, one that can substantially increase sales.[1] For instance, when a direct-mail electrical appliance catalogue displayed two coffee-makers instead of just one, the addition of the second coffee-maker for comparison seemed to stimulate consumer evaluation that significantly increased the sales of the original coffee-maker.

Table 4-1 summarises various types of consumption and purchase-related decisions. Although not exhaustive, this list does serve to demonstrate that the scope of consumer decision-making is far broader than the mere selection of one brand from a number of brands.

TABLE 4-1 Types of purchase or consumption decisions

DECISION CATEGORY	ALTERNATIVE A	ALTERNATIVE B
Basic Purchase or Consumption Decision	To purchase or consume a product (or service)	Not to purchase or consume a product (or service)
Brand Purchase or Consumption Decision	To purchase or consume a specific brand	To purchase or consume another brand
	To purchase or consume one's usual brand	To purchase or consume another established brand (possibly with special features)
	To purchase or consume a basic model	To purchase or consume a luxury or status model
	To purchase or consume a new brand	To purchase or consume one's usual brand or some other established brand
	To purchase or consume a standard quantity	To purchase or consume more or less than a standard quantity
	To purchase or consume an on-sale brand	To purchase or consume a non-sale brand
	To purchase or consume a national brand	To purchase or consume a store brand
Channel Purchase Decisions	To purchase from a specific type of store (e.g. a department store)	To purchase from some other type of store (e.g. a discount store)
	To purchase from one's usual store	To purchase from some other store
	To purchase in-home (by phone or catalogue or Internet)	To purchase in-store merchandise
	To purchase from a local store	To purchase from a store requiring some travel (outshopping)
Payment Purchase Decisions	To pay for the purchase with cash	To pay for the purchase with a credit card
	To pay the bill in full when it arrives	To pay for the purchase in instalments

LEVELS OF CONSUMER DECISION-MAKING

The choices we make as consumers all have some kind of consequence, and some will say that when making a decision we are actually choosing between consequences, or outcomes. As such outcomes differ in their level of importance, not all consumer decision-making situations receive (or require) the same degree of information search. If all purchase decisions required extensive effort, then consumer decision-making would be an exhausting process that left little time for anything else. On the other hand, if all purchases were routine, then they would tend to be monotonous and would provide little pleasure or novelty. On a continuum of effort ranging from very high to very low, we can distinguish three specific levels of consumer decision-making: extensive problem-solving, limited problem-solving, and routinised response behaviour.[2] As a rule of thumb, decisions can be grouped into these categories depending on the importance of the outcome, and thus the importance of not choosing the wrong alternative.

Extensive problem-solving

When consumers have no established criteria for evaluating a product category or specific brands in that category or have not narrowed the number of brands they will consider to a small, manageable subset, their decision-making efforts can be classified as **extensive problem-solving**. At this level, the consumer needs a great deal of information to establish a set of criteria on which to judge specific brands and a correspondingly large amount of information concerning each of the brands to be considered. Extensive problem-solving usually occurs when buying products that are expensive, important and technically complicated, and implies long time commitments (e.g. a car, an apartment, a high-definition television).

Limited problem-solving

At the **limited problem-solving level**, consumers have already established the basic criteria for evaluating the product category and the various brands in the category. However, they have not fully established preferences concerning a select group of brands. Their search for additional information is more like 'fine-tuning'; they must gather additional brand information to discriminate among the various brands. This level of problem-solving commonly occurs when purchasing an updated version of a product the consumer has bought before, such as replacing a mobile phone with a new one, buying a food processor or replacing an old laptop with a new one.

Routinised response behaviour

At this level, consumers have experience with the product category and a well-established set of criteria with which to evaluate the brands they are considering. In some situations, they may search for a small amount of additional information; in others, they simply review what they already know. Buying a refill of laundry detergent, toothpaste or hand soap are all examples of products consumers purchase more or less based on routine.

Just how extensive a consumer's problem-solving task is depends on how well established his or her criteria for selection are, how much information he or she has about each brand being considered, and how narrow the set of brands is from which the choice will be made. Clearly, extensive problem-solving implies that the consumer must seek more information to make a choice, whereas **routinised response behaviour** hardly ever implies a need for additional information.

All decisions in our lives cannot be complex and require extensive search and consideration – we just cannot exert the level of effort required. Some decisions have to be 'easy ones'.

MODELS OF CONSUMERS: FOUR VIEWS OF CONSUMER DECISION-MAKING

Before presenting an overview model of how consumers make decisions, we will consider several schools of thought that depict consumer decision-making in distinctly different ways. The term *models of consumers* refers to a general view or perspective as to how (and why) individuals behave as they do. Specifically, we will examine models of consumers in terms of the following four views:

1. an economic view,
2. a passive view,
3. an emotional view, and
4. a cognitive view.

An economic view

In the field of theoretical economics, which portrays a world of perfect competition, the consumer has often been characterised as making rational decisions. This model, called the *economic man theory*, has been criticised by consumer researchers for a number of reasons. To behave rationally in the economic sense, a consumer would have to

1. be aware of all available product alternatives,
2. be capable of correctly ranking each alternative in terms of its benefits and disadvantages, and
3. be able to identify the one best alternative.

Realistically, however, consumers rarely have all of the information or sufficiently accurate information or even an adequate degree of involvement or motivation to make the so-called 'perfect' decision.

It has been argued that the classical economic model of an all-rational consumer is unrealistic for the following reasons:

a. people are limited by their existing skills, habits and reflexes;
b. people are limited by their existing values and goals; and
c. people are limited by the extent of their knowledge.[3]

Consumers operate in an imperfect world in which they do not maximise their decisions in terms of economic considerations, such as price–quantity relationships, marginal utility or indifference curves. Indeed, the consumer generally is unwilling to engage in extensive decision-making activities and will settle instead for a 'satisfactory' decision, one that is 'good enough'.[4] For this reason, the economic model is often rejected as too idealistic and simplistic. As an example, recent research has found that consumers' primary motivation for price haggling, which was long thought to be the desire to obtain a better price (i.e. better money value for the purchase), may instead be related to the need for achievement, affiliation and dominance.[5]

A passive view

Quite the opposite of the rational economic view of consumers is the *passive* view that depicts the consumer as basically submissive to the self-serving interests and promotional efforts of marketers. In the passive view, consumers are perceived as impulsive and irrational purchasers, ready to yield to the aims and into the arms of marketers. At least to some degree, the hard-driving supersalespeople of old, who were trained to regard the consumer as an object to be manipulated, subscribed to the passive model of the consumer.

The principal limitation of the passive model is that it fails to recognise that the consumer plays an equal, if not dominant, role in many buying situations – sometimes by seeking information about product alternatives and selecting the product that appears to offer the greatest satisfaction and at other times by impulsively selecting a product that satisfies the mood or emotion of the moment. All that we shall later study about motivation (see Chapter 5), selective perception (Chapter 7), learning (Chapter 8), attitudes (Chapter 9), communication (Chapter 10) and opinion leadership (Chapter 15) serves to support the proposition that consumers are rarely objects of manipulation. Therefore, this simple and single-minded view is arguably also unrealistic.

An emotional view

Although long aware of the *emotional* or *impulsive* model of consumer decision-making, marketers frequently prefer to think of consumers in terms of either economic or passive models. In reality, however, each of us is likely to associate deep feelings or emotions, such as joy, fear, love, hope, sexuality, fantasy and even a little 'magic', with certain purchases or possessions. These feelings or emotions are likely to be highly involving. For instance, a person who misplaces a favourite fountain pen might go to great lengths to look for it, despite the fact that he or she has six others at hand.

If we were to reflect on the nature of our recent purchases, we might be surprised to realise just how impulsive some of them were. Rather than carefully searching, deliberating and evaluating alternatives before buying, we are just as likely to have made many of these purchases on impulse, on a whim, or because we were emotionally driven.

When a consumer makes what is basically an emotional purchase decision, less emphasis is placed on the search for pre-purchase information. Instead, more emphasis is placed on current mood and feelings ('Go for it!'). This is not to say that emotional decisions are not rational. Some emotional decisions are expressions like 'you deserve it' or 'treat yourself'. For instance, many consumers buy designer-label clothing, not because they look any better in it, but because status labels make them feel better. This is a rational decision, although not in strict economic terms. Of course, if a man with a wife and three children purchases a two-seat sports car for himself, the neighbours might wonder about his level of rationality (although some might think it was deviously high). No such question would arise if the same man selected a can of Carlsberg lager, instead of a Heineken, although in both instances each might be an impulsive, emotional purchase decision.

Consumers' **moods** are also important to decision-making. Mood can be defined as a 'feeling state' or state of mind.[6] Unlike an emotion, which is a response to a particular environment, a mood is more typically an unfocused, pre-existing state – already present at the time a consumer 'experiences' an advertisement, a retail environment, a brand or a product.[7] Compared to emotions, moods are generally lower in intensity and longer lasting and are not as directly coupled with action tendencies and explicit actions as emotions.[8]

Mood appears to be important to consumer decision-making because it impacts when consumers shop, where they shop, and whether they shop alone or with others. It is also likely to influence how the consumer responds to actual shopping environments (i.e. at point of purchase). Some retailers attempt to create a mood for shoppers, even though shoppers enter the store with a pre-existing mood. Research suggests that a store's image or atmosphere can affect shoppers' moods; in turn, shoppers' moods can influence how long they stay in the store, as well as other behaviour that retailers wish to encourage.[9] In general, individuals in a positive mood recall more information about a product than those in a negative mood. As the results of one study suggest, however, inducing a positive mood at the point-of-purchase decision (as through background music, point-of-purchase displays, etc.) is unlikely to have a meaningful impact on specific brand choice unless a previously stored brand evaluation already exists.[10] Additionally, consumers in a positive mood typically employ a mood maintenance strategy designed to avoid investing cognitive effort in any task unless it promises to maintain or enhance the positive mood.[11]

A cognitive view

The fourth model portrays the consumer as a *thinking problem solver*. Within this framework, consumers are frequently pictured as either receptive to or actively searching for products and services that fulfil their needs and enrich their lives. The cognitive model focuses on the processes by which consumers seek and evaluate information about selected brands and retail outlets.

Within the context of the cognitive model, consumers are viewed as information processors. Information processing leads to the formation of preferences and, ultimately, to purchase intentions. The cognitive view also recognises that the consumer is unlikely even to attempt to obtain all available information about every choice. Instead, consumers are likely to cease their information-seeking efforts when they perceive that they have sufficient information about some of the alternatives to make a 'satisfactory' decision. As this information-processing viewpoint suggests, consumers often develop short-cut decision rules (called **heuristics**) to facilitate the decision-making process. They also use decision rules to cope with exposure to too much information (i.e. information overload).

The cognitive, or problem-solving, view describes a consumer who falls somewhere between the extremes of the economic and passive views, who does not (or cannot) have total knowledge about available product alternatives and, therefore, cannot make perfect decisions, but who nonetheless actively seeks information and attempts to make satisfactory decisions.

Consistent with the problem-solving view is the notion that a great deal of consumer behaviour is goal directed. For example, a consumer might purchase a computer in order to manage finances or look for a laundry detergent that will be gentle on fabrics. Goal setting is especially important when it comes to the adoption of new products because the greater the degree of 'newness', the more difficult it would be for the consumer to evaluate the product and relate it to his or her need (because of a lack of experience with the product).[12] Figure 4-1 shows goal setting and goal pursuit in consumer behaviour.

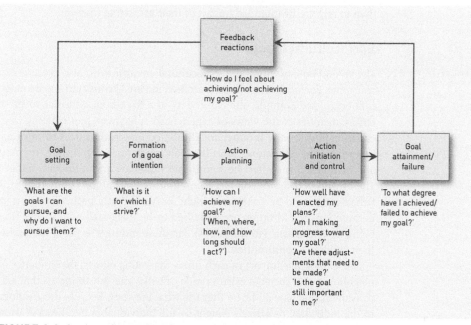

FIGURE 4-1 Goal setting and goal pursuit in consumer behaviour

Source: Adapted from Richard P. Bagozzi and Utpal Dholakia, 'Goal Setting and Goal Striving in Consumer Behavior', *Journal of Marketing*, 63, 1999, 21.

A MODEL OF CONSUMER DECISION-MAKING

This section presents an overview model of consumer decision-making (briefly introduced in Chapter 1) that reflects the cognitive (or problem-solving) consumer and, to some degree, the emotional consumer. The model is designed to tie together many of the ideas on consumer decision-making and consumption behaviour discussed throughout the book. It does not presume to provide an exhaustive picture of the complexities of consumer decision-making. Rather, it is designed to synthesise and coordinate relevant concepts into a significant whole. The model, presented in Figure 4-2, has three major components: input, process and output.

Input

The input component of our consumer decision-making model draws on external influences that serve as sources of information about a particular product and influence a consumer's product-related values, attitudes and behaviour. Chief among these input factors are the marketing mix activities of organisations that attempt to communicate the benefits of their products and services to potential consumers and the non-marketing sociocultural influences, which, when internalised, affect the consumer's purchase decisions.

Marketing Inputs

The firm's marketing activities are a direct attempt to reach, inform and persuade consumers to buy and use its products. These inputs to the consumer's decision-making process take the form of specific marketing mix strategies that consist of the product itself (including its package, size and guarantees); mass-media advertising, direct marketing, personal selling and other promotional efforts; pricing policy; and the selection of distribution channels to move the product from the manufacturer to the consumer. Ultimately, the impact of a firm's marketing efforts in large measure is governed by the consumer's perception of these efforts. Thus, marketers do well to remain diligently alert to consumer perceptions by sponsoring consumer research, rather than to rely on the intended impact of their marketing messages.

Sociocultural Inputs

The second type of input, the sociocultural environment, also exerts a major influence on the consumer. Sociocultural inputs (examined in Part 3) consist of a wide range of non-commercial influences. For example, the comments of a friend, an editorial in the newspaper, use by a family member or the views of experienced consumers participating in a special-interest discussion group on the Internet are all non-commercial sources of information. The influences of social class, culture and subculture, although less tangible, are important input factors that are internalised and affect how consumers evaluate and ultimately adopt (or reject) products. The unwritten codes of conduct communicated by culture subtly indicate which consumption behaviour should be considered 'right' or 'wrong' at a particular point in time. For example, because Japanese children are socialised to be integrated with others (to stand in) instead of being individualistic (to stand out), Japanese mothers seem to maintain higher control over their children's consumption.[13]

The cumulative impact of each firm's marketing efforts, the influence of family, friends and neighbours, and society's existing code of behaviour are all inputs that are likely to affect what consumers purchase and how they use what they buy. Because these influences may be directed to the individual or actively sought by the individual, a two-headed arrow is used to link the input and process segments of the model (Figure 4-2).

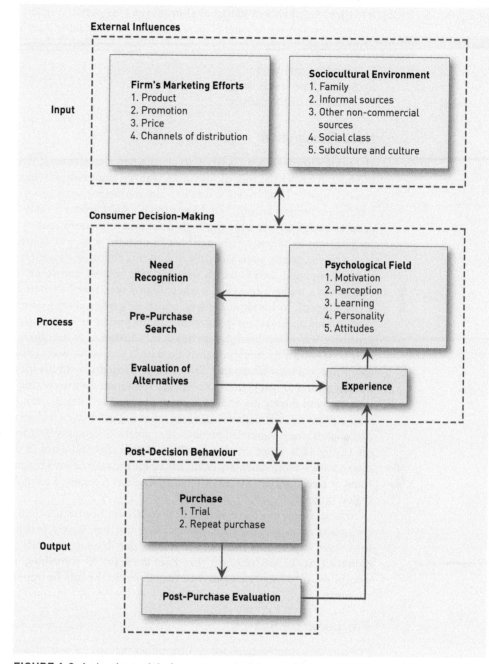

FIGURE 4-2 A simple model of consumer decision-making

Process

The process component of the model is concerned with how consumers make decisions. The psychological field represents the internal influences (motivation, perception, learning, personality and attitudes) that affect consumers' decision-making processes (what they need or want, their awareness of various product choices, their information-gathering activities, and their **evaluation of alternatives**). As pictured in the process component of the overview decision model (Figure 4-2), the act of making a consumer decision consists of three stages:

1. need recognition,
2. pre-purchase search, and
3. evaluation of alternatives.

Need Recognition

The recognition of a need is likely to occur when a consumer is faced with a 'problem'. For example, consider the case of Eric, a 25-year-old university graduate working for an equity research firm in London. He is totally computer literate, having had computers in the classroom since primary school, and, like others his age, knows a great deal about other high-tech gadgets, such as iPads, Blue-ray, high-definition televisions and mobile phones. In fact, in his bedroom he recently exchanged his 23-inch flat screen TV for its 42-inch HDTV equivalent. Eric frequently visits websites to find out about new state-of-the-art digital and electronic equipment, knows which websites offer reviews and comparisons of high-tech gear and knows a number of websites where highly specialised e-tailers are offering state-of-the-art equipment. In his shoulder bag, which he carries almost everywhere, is both his new iPad and his personal laptop computer. In his pocket he has his 64GB iPod Touch, with the expensive Sennheiser headphones he got for Christmas. In his other pocket is his HTC Desire cellphone, which he bought mainly because it was rated 'best cellphone in the world' by a columnist in a local newspaper. Eric often gets together with his friends for birthday parties, holiday parties or just plain 'let's meet at a restaurant for the evening' gatherings, and he also likes to travel during his annual holiday. He has been taking photos for the past few years with a 10 megapixels digital single lens reflex (dSLR) camera that was a gift from his parents. Although taking magnificent pictures, the camera is somewhat big and bulky to carry around on a daily basis. Since Eric is part of the 'digital age' and a hobby photographer, he would like to have a complementary camera that, for the sake of convenience, can fit easily into his jeans or jacket pocket. Stated differently, Eric has recognised a need for a small and handy digital camera.

Among consumers, there seem to be two different need or problem recognition styles. Some consumers are *actual state types*, who perceive that they have a problem when a product fails to perform satisfactorily (such as a telephone that develops constant static). In contrast, other consumers are *desired state types*, for whom the desire for something new may trigger the decision process.[14] Since Eric's current camera can do the job, he appears to be a desired state consumer.

Pre-purchase Search

Pre-purchase search begins when a consumer perceives a need that might be satisfied by the purchase and consumption of a product. The recollection of past experiences (drawn from storage in long-term memory) might provide the consumer with adequate information to make the present choice. On the other hand, when the consumer has had no prior experience, he or she may have to engage in an extensive search of the outside environment for useful information on which to base a choice.

The consumer usually searches his or her memory (the *psychological field* depicted in the model) before seeking external sources of information regarding a given consumption-related need. Past experience is considered an internal source of information. The greater the relevant past experience, the less external information the consumer is likely to need to reach a decision. Many consumer decisions are based on a combination of past experience (internal sources) and marketing and non-commercial information (external sources). The degree of perceived risk can also influence this stage of the decision process (see Chapter 7).

In high-risk situations, consumers are likely to engage in complex and extensive information search and evaluation; in low-risk situations, they are likely to use very simple or limited search and evaluation tactics.

The act of shopping is an important form of external information. According to one consumer study, there is a big difference between men and women in terms of their response to shopping. Whereas most men do not like to shop, most women claim to like the experience of shopping; and although the majority of women found shopping to be relaxing and enjoyable, the majority of men did not feel that way.[15]

An examination of the external search effort associated with the purchase of different product categories (TVs, DVD players or personal computers) found that as the amount of total search effort increased consumer attitudes towards shopping became more positive, and more time was made available for shopping. Not surprisingly, the external search effort was greatest for consumers who had the least amount of product category knowledge.[16] It follows that the less consumers know about a product category and the more important the purchase is to them, the more time they will make available and the more extensive their pre-purchase search activity is likely to be. Conversely, research studies have indicated that consumers high in subjective knowledge (a self-assessment of how much they know about the product category) rely more on their own evaluations than on dealer recommendations.[17]

It is also important to point out that the Internet has had a great impact on pre-purchase search. Rather than visiting a shop to find out about a product or calling the manufacturer and asking for a brochure, consumers find that manufacturers' websites can provide much of the information they need about the products and services they are considering. For example, many motor vehicle websites provide product specifications, prices and dealer cost information, reviews, and even comparisons with competing vehicles. Jaguar's website (www.jaguar.com) lets you 'build' your own Jaguar and see how it would look, for example, in different colours. Some websites will even list a particular dealer's new and used car inventory.

With respect to surfing the Internet for information, consider one consumer's comments drawn from a research study: 'I like to use the Web because it's so easy to find information, and it's really easy to use. The information is at my finger-tips and I don't have to search books in libraries.'[18]

But what happens if the search is a failure? A recent article examined the issue of 'search regret', which it identified as 'a post search dissonance that results from an unsuccessful pre-purchase search'.[19] Search regret can have a damaging effect on retailers, because in this pilot study store blame and self-blame were not significantly correlated with each other. The study noted that retailers can help eliminate or reduce search regret by providing ample information, trying to reduce out-of-stock situations and proper training of salespeople.[20] Figure 4-3 presents a model of search regret. Note how this negative outcome can lead to blaming the product, the store, oneself or others, or coping (where the consumer actively tries to resolve the issue).

How much information a consumer will gather also depends on various situational factors. Getting back to Eric, while he works long hours in London, he is willing to spend time researching his desired purchase. He starts by sitting at his office desk with his office computer connected to the firm's network broadband connection. He visits the websites of digital camera manufacturers such as Nikon (www.nikon.com), Canon (www.canon.com), Sony (www.sony.co.uk), Pentax (www.pentax.co.uk) and Casio (www.casio.co.uk), as well as e-tailer websites like Amazon (www.amazon.co.uk) to see which brands and models of digital cameras are small and lightweight.

Eric also talks to some of his friends and colleagues who are more into digital cameras than he is. One suggests that he try to find product reviews of any camera that he considers to be a possibility on such websites as CNET (www.cnet.com), Digital Photograph Review (www.dpreview.com) and Digital Camera Resource (www.dcresource.com).

As Table 4-2 indicates, a number of factors are likely to increase consumers' pre-purchase search. For some products and services, the consumer may have ongoing experience on which

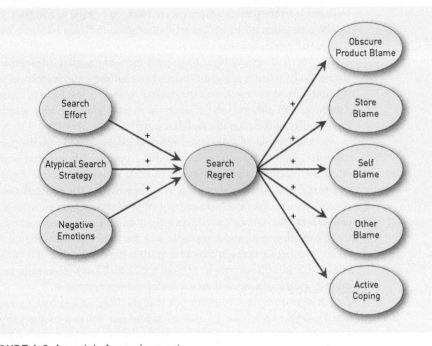

FIGURE 4-3 A model of search regret

Source: Kristy E. Reynolds, Judith Anne Garretson Folse, and Michael A. Jones, 'Search Regret: Antecedents and Consequences,' *Journal of Retailing*, 82, no. 4 (2006): 342. Copyright 2006 with permission from Elsevier.

to draw (such as a skier purchasing a better pair of skis), or the purchase may essentially be discretionary in nature (rather than a necessity), so there is no rush to make a decision. In the case of Eric, our equity researcher, while there is no particular need to rush into the purchase of the digital camera, he would like to have it in a month, when he is planning to take a week's holiday.

Let's consider several of the pre-purchase search alternatives open to a computer buyer. At the most fundamental level, search alternatives can be classified as either personal or impersonal. Personal search alternatives include more than a consumer's past experience with the product or service. They also include asking for information and advice from friends, relatives, colleagues and sales representatives. For instance, Eric spoke with a few friends and colleagues and asked them what they knew about digital cameras. Eric also investigated whether photography magazines, such as *Popular Photography*, or computer magazines such as *Computer Shopper*, might have rated the various brands or models of digital cameras. Table 4-3 presents some of the sources of information that Eric might use as part of his pre-purchase search. Any or all of these sources might be used as part of a consumer's search process.

Evaluation of Alternatives

When evaluating potential alternatives, consumers tend to use two types of information:

1. a list of brands (or models) from which they plan to make their selection (the evoked set), and
2. the criteria they will use to evaluate each brand (or model).

Making a selection from a sample of all possible brands (or models) is a human characteristic that helps simplify the decision-making process.

TABLE 4-2 Factors that are likely to increase pre-purchase search

PRODUCT FACTORS

Long interpurchase time (a long-lasting or infrequently used product)
Frequent changes in product styling
Frequent price changes
Volume purchasing (large number of units)
High price
Many alternative brands
Much variation in features

SITUATIONAL FACTORS

Experience

First-time purchase
No past experience because the product is new
Unsatisfactory past experience within the product category

Social Acceptability

The purchase is for a gift
The product is socially visible

Value-Related Considerations

Purchase is discretionary rather than necessary
All alternatives have both desirable and undesirable consequences
Family members disagree on product requirements or evaluation of alternatives
Product usage deviates from important reference groups
The purchase involves ecological considerations
Many sources of conflicting information

PRODUCT FACTORS

Demographic Characteristics of Consumer

Well educated
High income
White-collar occupation
Under 35 years of age

Personality

Low dogmatic
Low-risk perceiver (broad categoriser)
Other personal factors such as high product involvement and enjoyment of shopping and search

TABLE 4-3 Alternative pre-purchase information sources

PERSONAL	IMPERSONAL
Friends	Newspaper articles
Neighbours	Magazine articles
Relatives	Internal websites
Colleagues	Direct-mail brochures
Computer salespeople	Information from product advertisements

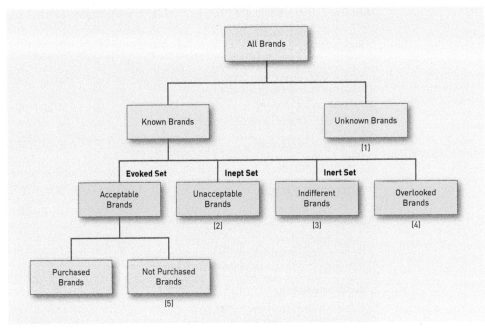

FIGURE 4-4 The evoked set as a subset of all brands in a product class

Evoked Set

Within the context of consumer decision-making, the **evoked set** refers to the specific brands (or models) a consumer considers in making a purchase within a particular product category. (The evoked set is also called the consideration set.) A consumer's evoked set is distinguished from his or her **inept set**, which consists of brands (or models) the consumer excludes from purchase consideration because they are felt to be unacceptable (or they are seen as inferior), and from the **inert set**, which consists of brands (or models) the consumer is indifferent towards because they are perceived as not having any particular advantages. Regardless of the total number of brands (or models) in a product category, a consumer's evoked set tends to be quite small on average, often consisting of only three to five brands (or models). However, research indicates that a consumer's consideration set increases in size as experience with a product category grows.[21]

The evoked set consists of the small number of brands the consumer is familiar with, remembers and finds acceptable. Figure 4-4 depicts the evoked set as a subset of all available brands in a product category. As the figure indicates, it is essential that a product be part of a consumer's evoked set if it is to be considered at all. The five terminal positions in the model that do not end in purchase would appear to have perceptual problems. For example:

1. brands or models may be unknown because of the consumer's selective exposure to advertising media and selective perception of advertising stimuli (see Chapter 7);
2. brands or models may be unacceptable because of poor qualities or attributes or inappropriate positioning in either advertising or product characteristics;
3. brands or models may be perceived as not having any special benefits and are regarded indifferently by the consumer;
4. brands or models may be overlooked because they have not been clearly positioned or sharply targeted at the consumer market segment under study; and
5. brands or models may not be selected because they are perceived by consumers as unable to satisfy perceived needs as fully as the brand that is chosen.

In each of these instances, the implication for marketers is that promotional techniques should be designed to impart a more favourable, perhaps more relevant, product image to the target consumer. This may also require a change in product features or attributes (more or better features). An alternative strategy is to invite consumers in a particular target segment to consider a specific offering and possibly put it in their evoked set.

Research also suggests that the use of white space and choice of typeface in advertisements may influence the consumer's image of the product. For example, quality, prestige, trust, attitude towards the brand and purchase intention have been shown to be positively conveyed by white space and typefaces that were perceived as being attractive, warm and liked when they were simple, more natural and included a typefont with serifs.[22]

It has also been suggested that consumers may not, all at once, reduce the number of possible choices into their evoked set, but instead may make several decisions within a single decision process. These screening decisions, or decision waves, are used to eliminate unsuitable alternatives before gathering information or comparing options, and help reduce decision complexity to a more manageable level.[23]

Criteria Used for Evaluating Brands

The criteria consumers use to evaluate the alternative products that constitute their evoked sets are usually expressed in terms of important product attributes. Examples of product attributes that consumers have used as criteria in evaluating eight product categories are listed in Table 4-4.

When a company knows that consumers will be evaluating alternatives, it sometimes advertises in a way that recommends the criteria that consumers should use in assessing

TABLE 4-4 Possible product attributes used as purchase criteria for eight product categories

PERSONAL COMPUTERS	CD PLAYERS	WRISTWATCHES
Processing speed	Mega bass	Watchband
Price	Electronic shock protection	Alarm feature
Type of display	Length of play on batteries	Price
Hard-disk size	Random play feature	Water resistant
Amount of memory	Water resistant	Quartz movement
Laptop or desktop		Size of dial

COLOUR INKJET PRINTERS	COLOUR TVS	FROZEN DINNERS
Output speed	Picture quality	Taste
Number of ink colours	Length of warranty	Type of main course
Resolution (DPI)	Cable ready	Type of side dishes
Length of warranty	Price	Price
USB capability	Size of screen	Preparation requirements

DIGITAL CAMERAS	FOUNTAIN PENS	
Autofocus	Balance	
Built-in flash	Price	
Battery capacity	Gold nib	
Lens type	Smoothness	
Size and weight	Ink reserve	

product or service options. We have probably all had the experience of comparing or evaluating different brands or models of a product and finding the one that just feels, looks, and/or performs 'right'. Interestingly, research shows that when consumers discuss such 'right products', there is little or no mention of price; brand names are not often uppermost in consumers' minds; items often reflect personality characteristics or childhood experiences and it is often 'love at first sight'. In one study, the products claimed by research participants to 'just feel right' included old leather briefcases, Post-it notes and the Honda Accord.[24] And a product's country of origin can also play a role in how a consumer evaluates a brand (see Chapter 14).

Research has explored the role of brand credibility (which consists of trustworthiness and expertise) on brand choice and has found that brand credibility improves the chances that a brand will be included in the consideration set. Three factors that impact a brand's credibility are: the perceived quality of the brand, the perceived risk associated with the brand and the information costs saved with that brand (due to the time and effort saved by not having to shop around).[25] Still further, the study indicates that trustworthiness is more important than expertise when it comes to making a choice.

Let's return for a moment to Eric and his search for a small, lightweight digital camera. As part of his search process, he has acquired information about a number of relevant issues (or attributes) that could influence his final choice. For example, Eric has learned that the overall size of a digital camera is very much a function of the features that it contains, such as whether or not the camera has a viewfinder, how powerful its flash is, whether it offers manual control of functions such as shutter speed and aperture, and the size of its camera-back LCD screen. Still further, Eric realises that the higher the megapixel count of the pictures the camera takes, the higher the camera's price is going to be. He reasoned that for the types of photos that he takes, 10 megapixels is plenty. As part of his search process, Eric has also acquired information about other relevant issues (or attributes) that could influence his final choice (see Table 4-5). For example, he has learned that some digital camera zoom lenses have less of a zoom range than others, and that all LCD screens are not equally sharp because some have only half or two-thirds the number of pixels of others (the greater the number of pixels, the sharper the image on the camera-back LCD screen). On the basis of his information search, Eric realises

TABLE 4-5 Comparison of selected characteristics of digital cameras

FEATURE	FUJIFILM	CANON	PANASONIC
Megapixels	12	10	14
Picture stabiliser	Optic & digital	Optic	Optic
Dimensions (cm)	$5.9 \times 9.9 \times 2.8$	$5.4 \times 10 \times 2.36$	$5.5 \times 10.2 \times 2.28$
Lens focal length	27–270	28–105	24–120
LCD screen size	3''	3''	3''
Weight	183 g	175 g	165 g
Media	SD/SDHC	SD/SDHC/SDXC/ MMC/MMCplus/ HC MMCplus	SD/SDXC
No of pictures	300/230 with/without blitz	250/250	Not reported by manufacturer
Price	€289	€318	€339

Source: www.elkjop.no.

TABLE 4-6 Hypothetical ratings for digital cameras

FEATURE	FUJIFILM	CANON	PANASONIC
Megapixels	7	5	9
Weight	4	6	8
Dimensions	3	6	6
Lens focal length	8	4	5
LCD screen size	4	4	4
Media	5	10	7
Price	8	6	5
Total	39	41	44

that he is going to have to make a decision regarding what he really wants from this new digital camera. Does he want just a miniature version of his other camera, or is he willing to sacrifice some features for a camera that is substantially smaller and lighter? He comes to realise that he always has his current camera set to 'auto' when he takes pictures, and that the only features he really wants, in addition to small size, are autofocus (which all the digital cameras he's investigated have) and a zoom lens. Thus, Eric realises that he is willing to give up some functionality (such as manual control of shutter speed) in exchange for reduced size and weight.

Consumer Decision Rules

Consumer decision rules, often referred to as *heuristics*, *decision strategies* and *information-processing strategies*, are procedures used by consumers to facilitate brand (or other consumption-related) choices. These rules reduce the burden of making complex decisions by providing guidelines or routines that make the process less taxing.

Consumer decision rules have been broadly classified into two major categories: compensatory and non-compensatory decision rules. In following a **compensatory decision rule**, a consumer evaluates brand or model options in terms of each relevant attribute and computes a weighted or summated score for each brand. The computed score reflects the brand's relative merit as a potential purchase choice. The assumption is that the consumer will select the brand that scores highest among the alternatives evaluated. Referring to Table 4-6, it is clear that when using a compensatory decision rule, the Panasonic digital camera scores highest.

A unique feature of a compensatory decision rule is that it allows a positive evaluation of a brand on one attribute to balance out a negative evaluation on some other attribute. For example, a positive assessment of the energy savings made possible by a particular brand or type of light bulb may offset an unacceptable assessment in terms of the bulb's diminished light output.

In the example in Table 4-6, the attribute ratings for the three cameras are summarised to arrive at a total score for each camera. This is called a *summarised* score. However, in most product choices, consumers will emphasise the various attributes differently. This implies that the summarised score treats all attributes as equally important to the consumer, while in real choices we often put more weight on some attributes and less on others. When so doing, we apply a *weighted score*. To arrive at a weighted score, consumers establish an importance weight for each attribute, and multiply the attribute score and the weight to arrive at a weighted attributes score for each attribute. These are then summarised, just as in Table 4-6, and give you a total, weighted score for the product in question. The same procedure is then applied to the next product.

In contrast, **non-compensatory decision rules** do not allow consumers to balance positive evaluations of a brand on one attribute against a negative evaluation on some other attribute. For instance, in the case of an energy-saving light bulb, the product's negative (unacceptable) rating on its light output would not be offset by a positive evaluation of its energy savings. Instead, this particular light bulb would be disqualified from further consideration. If Eric's choice of a digital camera was based on the desire to have more media choices than just SD and SDHC (refer again to Table 4-5), a non-compensatory decision rule would have eliminated the Fujifilm camera.

Three non-compensatory rules are considered briefly here: the *conjunctive decision rule*, the *disjunctive rule* and the *lexicographic decision rule*.

In following a **conjunctive decision rule**, the consumer establishes a separate, minimally acceptable level as a cut-off point for each attribute. To be found acceptable, a particular brand or model cannot be judged to perform below the cut-off point on any one attribute. Thus, even if the evaluation falls below the cut-off point on one attribute only, that product alternative will be eliminated from further consideration. Because the conjunctive rule can result in several acceptable alternatives, it becomes necessary in such cases for the consumer to apply an additional decision rule to arrive at a final selection. For example, the consumer can decide to accept the first satisfactory brand or to increase the level of the cut-off points to reduce the number of acceptable alternatives. The conjunctive rule is particularly useful in quickly reducing the number of alternatives to be considered. The consumer can then apply another more refined decision rule to arrive at a final choice.

The **disjunctive rule** is the 'mirror image' of the conjunctive rule. In applying this decision rule, the consumer establishes a separate, minimally acceptable cut-off level for each attribute (which may be higher than the one normally established for a conjunctive rule). In this case, if an option meets or exceeds the cut-off established for any one attribute, it is accepted. Here again, a number of brands (or models) might exceed the cut-off point, producing a situation in which another decision rule is required. When this occurs, the consumer may accept the first satisfactory alternative as the final choice or apply another decision rule that is perhaps more suitable.

In following a **lexicographic decision rule**, the consumer first ranks the attributes in terms of perceived relevance or importance. The consumer then compares the various alternatives in terms of the single attribute that is considered most important. If one option scores sufficiently high on this top-ranked attribute (regardless of the score on any of the other attributes), it is selected and the process ends. When there are two or more surviving alternatives, the process is repeated with the second highest-ranked attribute (and so on), until the point is reached where one of the options is selected because it exceeds the others on a particular attribute.

With the lexicographic rule, the highest-ranked attribute (the one applied first) may reveal something about the individual's basic consumer (or shopping) orientation. For instance, a 'buy the best' rule might indicate that the consumer is quality-oriented; a 'buy the most prestigious brand' rule might indicate that the consumer is status-oriented; a 'buy the least expensive' rule might reveal that the consumer is economy-minded.

A variety of decision rules appear quite commonplace. According to a consumer survey, nine out of ten shoppers possess a specific shopping strategy for saving money on frequently purchased items. The consumer segment and the specific shopping rules that these segments employ are:[26]

1. Practical loyalists – those who look for ways to save on the brands and products they would buy anyway.
2. Bottom-line price shoppers – those who buy the lowest-priced item with little or no regard for brand.

TABLE 4-7 Hypothetical use of popular decision rules in making a decision to purchase a digital camera

DECISION RULE	MENTAL STATEMENT
Compensatory rule	'I selected the camera that came out best when I balanced the good ratings against the bad ratings.'
Conjunctive rule	'I selected the camera that had no bad features.'
Disjunctive rule	'I picked the camera that excelled in at least one attribute.'
Lexicographic rule	'I looked at the feature that was most important to me and chose the camera that ranked highest on that attribute.'
Affect referral rule	'I bought the brand with the highest overall rating.'

3. Opportunistic switchers – those who use coupons or sales to decide among brands and products that fall within their evoked set.
4. Deal hunters – those who look for the best bargain and are not brand loyal.

We have considered only the most basic of an almost infinite number of consumer decision rules. Most of the decision rules described here can be combined to form new variations, such as conjunctive–compensatory, conjunctive–disjunctive and disjunctive–conjunctive rules. It is likely that for many purchase decisions, consumers maintain in their long-term memory over-all evaluations of the brands in their evoked sets. This would make assessment by individual attributes unnecessary. Instead, the consumer would simply select the brand with the highest perceived overall rating. This type of synthesised decision rule is known as the **affect referral decision rule** and may represent the simplest of all rules.

Table 4-7 summarises the essence of many of the decision rules considered in this chapter in terms of the kind of mental statements that Eric might make in selecting a digital camera.

How Do Functionally Illiterate Consumers Decide?

Research has found that functionally illiterate consumers do make decisions differently, in terms of cognitive predilections, decision rules and trade-offs, and coping behaviours (see Figure 4-5). For example, they use concrete reasoning and non-compensatory decision rules, meaning that they base the purchase decision on a single piece of information, without regard to other product attributes (e.g. 'I just look at the price tag and see what's cheapest. I don't look at their sizes'). Such consumers, if confronted with two boxes of a product at the same price, would tend to purchase the one in the physically larger box, even if the label on the smaller sized package indicated a higher weight or greater volume. And through what might be referred to as 'sight reading', they recognise brand logos in the same way as they might recognise people in a photograph. In fact, functionally illit-erate consumers treat all words and numbers as pictorial elements. They also become anxious when shopping in a new store (they prefer to shop in the same store, especially if they have established a rapport with a friendly and helpful employee), and often give all their money to the cashier expecting him or her to return the proper change.[27] Table 4-8 presents the coping strategies used by functionally illiterate consumers. Note how such consumers avoid purchasing unknown brands and try to carry limited amounts of cash to the shop.

Lifestyles as a Consumer Decision Strategy

An individual's or a family's decision to be committed to a particular lifestyle (e.g. devoted followers of a particular religion) impacts a wide range of specific everyday consumer

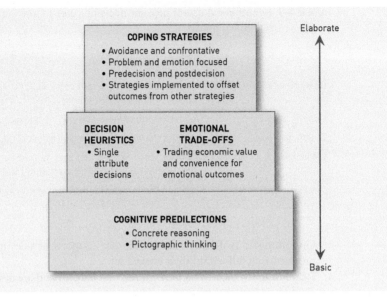

FIGURE 4-5 The decision process for functionally illiterate consumers

Source: Adapted from Madhubalan Viswanathan, José Antonio Rosa and James Edwin Harris, 'Decision Making and Coping of Functionally Illiterate Consumers and Some Implications for Marketing Management', *Journal of Marketing*, 69, January 2005, 19.

behaviour. For instance, the Trends Research Institute has identified 'voluntary simplicity' as one of the top ten lifestyle trends.[28] Researchers there estimate that 15 per cent of all 'boomers' seek a simpler lifestyle with reduced emphasis on ownership and possessions. Voluntary simplifiers are making do with less clothing and fewer credit cards (with no outstanding balances) and moving to smaller, yet still adequate, homes or apartments in less densely populated communities. Most importantly, it is not that these consumers can no longer afford their affluence or 'lifestyle of abundance'; rather, they are seeking new, 'reduced', less extravagant lifestyles. As part of this new lifestyle commitment, some individuals are seeking less stressful and lower-salary careers or jobs. In a telephone survey, for example, 33 per cent of those contacted claimed that they would be willing to take a 20 per cent pay cut in return for working fewer hours.[29] Time pressure may also play a role in the consumer's decision process, as research has positively associated this factor with both sale proneness (responding positively to special offers) and display proneness (responding positively to in-store displays offering a special price).[30]

As another lifestyle issue, consider the huge success of the Apple iPod. Especially among teenagers and young adults, the iPod is overwhelmingly the portable music player of choice. While some might argue that the introduction of the iPod Shuffle cheapens the product's image, it could also be a way for Apple to offer a product that allows more parents with modest incomes to placate their teenagers. One industry analyst has commented, 'The cachet is not in the price, it's in the brand. iPod is an affordable luxury item, and they're simply bringing it to another level of buyers. People who want an iPod will forgo buying an MP3 player at all saying "If I buy, I will buy an iPod"'.[31]

Incomplete Information and Non-comparable Alternatives

In many choice situations, consumers face incomplete information on which to base decisions and must use alternative strategies to cope with the missing elements. Missing information

TABLE 4-8 Coping strategies of functionally illiterate consumers

COPING STRATEGIES	CLASSIFICATIONS
AVOIDANCE	
Shop at the same store: avoids stress of unfamiliar environment	Problem focused: shops effectively Predecision: habitual choice about store helps with choices about products
Shop at smaller stores: avoids cognitive demands from product variety	Emotion focused: reduces stress Predecision: requires advance planning
Single-attribute decisions: avoids stressful and complex product comparisons	Problem focused: makes decisions manageable Emotion focused: preserves image of competence Predecision: requires advance planning
Avoid percentage- and fraction-off discounted items: avoids difficult numerical tasks	Emotion focused: reduces stress Problem focused: less chance of mistakes Predecision: implements habitually
Buy only known brands (loyalty): avoids risks from unknown brands	Problem focused: facilitates shopping Predecision: implements habitually
Rationalize outcomes to shift responsibility: avoids responsibility for outcomes	Emotion focused: protects self esteem Postdecision: implements after outcome is clear
Carry limited amounts of cash: avoids risks of overspending and being cheated	Problem focused: controls transactions Predecision: requires advance planning
Buy small amounts more often: avoids risk of large scale cheating	Problem focused: controls transactions Predecision: requires advance planning
Pretend disability: avoids revealing deficiencies and embarrassment	Problem focused: obtains assistance Emotion focused: preserves public image Predecision: requires advance planning
Pretend to evaluate products and prices: avoids revealing deficiencies indirectly	Emotion focused: preserves public image Predecision: requires advance planning
CONFRONTATIVE	
Shop with family members and friends: enables others to know deficiencies	Problem focused: helps shop on a budget Predecision: involves advance planning
Establish relationships with store personnel: enables others to know deficiencies	Emotion focused: avoids embarrassment and stress Predecision: involves advance planning
Seek help in the store: enables others to know deficiencies	Problem focused: facilitates final decision Predecision: leads to a purchase decision
Give all money in pockets to cashier: admits deficiencies, plays on honesty standards	Problem focused: avoids not being able to count Predecision: implements habitually
Buy one item at a time: addresses the problem of loss of control when turning over cash	Problem focused: controls pace of transactions and flow of funds Predecision: requires advance planning
Confront store personnel and demand different treatment: focuses on responses and behaviors of others	Emotion focused: seeks to minimize or eliminate embarrassment and to preserve or restore public image Postdecision: implements in response to others
Plan expenditures with assistance from others: enables others to know deficiencies	Problem focused: facilitates a budget Predecision: involves advance planning

Source: Adapted from Madhubalan Viswanathan, José Antonio Rosa and James Edwin Harris, 'Decision Making and Coping of Functionally Illiterate Consumers and Some Implications for Marketing Management', *Journal of Marketing*, 69, January 2005, 25.

may result from advertisements or packaging that mention only certain attributes or the consumer's own imperfect memory of attributes for alternatives that are not present, or because some attributes are experiential and can only be evaluated after product use.[32] There are at least four alternative strategies that consumers can adopt for coping with missing information:[33]

1. Consumers may delay the decision until missing information is obtained. This strategy is likely to be used for high-risk decisions.
2. Consumers may ignore missing information and decide to continue with the current decision rule (e.g. compensatory or non-compensatory), using the available attribute information.
3. Consumers may change the customarily used decision strategy to one that better accommodates missing information.
4. Consumers may infer ('construct') the missing information.

Research has demonstrated that consumers tend to deal with missing information by purchasing the option that is deemed to be superior on the common attribute (i.e. basing the decision on the information that is available for all of the options or brands being considered). For marketers, therefore, the decision as to what information to provide or not to provide can help determine the product's success or failure in the marketplace.[34]

In discussing consumer decision rules, we have assumed that a choice is made from among the brands (or models) evaluated. Of course, a consumer also may conclude that none of the alternatives offers sufficient benefits to warrant purchase. If this were to occur with a necessity, such as a refrigerator, the consumer would probably either lower his or her expectations and settle for the best of the available alternatives or seek information about additional brands, hoping to find one that more closely meets predetermined criteria. On the other hand, if the purchase were more discretionary (a second or third pair of trainers), the consumer would probably postpone the purchase. In this case, information gained from the search up to that point would be transferred to long-term storage (in the psychological field) and retrieved and reintroduced as input if and when the consumer regains interest in making such a purchase.

Applying Decision Rules

It should be noted that, in applying decision rules, consumers may at times attempt to compare dissimilar (non-comparable) alternatives. For example, a consumer may be undecided about whether to buy a large-screen, high-definition television set or a new set of diving gear, because the individual can afford one or the other but not both. Another example: a consumer may try to decide between buying a new sweater or a new raincoat. When there is great dissimilarity in the alternative ways of allocating available funds, consumers abstract the products to a level in which comparisons are possible. In the foregoing examples, a consumer might weigh the alternatives (television set versus diving gear or sweater versus raincoat) in terms of which alternative would offer more pleasure or which, if either, is more of a 'necessity'.

A Series of Decisions

Although we have discussed the purchase decision as if it were a single decision, in reality, a purchase can involve a number of decisions. For example, when purchasing a car, consumers are involved in multiple decisions such as choosing the make or country of origin of the car (foreign versus domestic), the dealer, the financing and particular options. In the case of a replacement car, these decisions must be preceded by a decision as to whether or not to trade in one's current car. A study found that the attitudes and search behaviour of consumers who replace their cars after only a few years (early replacement buyers) differ greatly from those who replace their cars after many years (late replacement buyers). In particular, early car replacement buyers were more concerned with the car's styling and image or status and were less concerned with cost. In contrast, late car replacement buyers undertook a greater amount of information and dealer search and were greatly influenced by friends.[35]

Decision Rules and Marketing Strategy

An understanding of which decision rules consumers apply in selecting a particular product or service is useful to marketers concerned with formulating a promotional programme. A marketer familiar with the prevailing decision rule can prepare a promotional message in a format that would facilitate consumer information processing. The promotional message might even suggest how potential consumers should make a decision. For instance, a direct-mail piece for a desktop computer might tell potential consumers 'what to look for in a new PC'. This mail piece might specifically ask consumers to consider the attributes of hard disk size, amount of memory, processor speed, monitor size and maximum resolution, video card memory and CD burner speed.

Output

The output portion of the consumer decision-making model concerns two closely associated kinds of post-decision activity: purchase behaviour and post-purchase evaluation. The objective of both activities is to increase the consumer's satisfaction with his or her purchase.

Purchase Behaviour

Consumers make three types of purchase: trial purchases, repeat purchases and long-term commitment purchases. When a consumer purchases a product (or brand) for the first time and buys a smaller quantity than usual, this purchase would be considered a trial. Thus, a trial is the exploratory phase of **purchase behaviour** in which consumers attempt to evaluate a product through direct use. For instance, when consumers purchase a new brand of laundry detergent about which they may be uncertain, they are likely to purchase smaller trial quantities than if it were a familiar brand. Consumers can also be encouraged to try a new product through such promotional tactics as free samples and/or sale prices.

When a new brand in an established product category (toothpaste, chewing gum or cola) is found by trial to be more satisfactory or better than other brands, consumers are likely to repeat the purchase. Repeat purchase behaviour is closely related to the concept of brand loyalty, which most firms try to encourage because it contributes to greater stability in the marketplace (see Chapter 8). Unlike a trial, in which the consumer uses the product on a small scale and without any commitment, a repeat purchase usually signifies that the product meets with the consumer's approval and that he or she is willing to use it again and in larger quantities.

Trial, of course, is not always feasible. For example, with most durable goods (refrigerators, washing machines or electric cookers), a consumer usually moves directly from evaluation to a long-term commitment (through purchase) without the opportunity for an actual trial. While purchasers of the new Volkswagen Beetle were awaiting delivery of their newly purchased cars, they were kept 'warm' by being sent a mailing that included a psychographic tool called 'Total Visual Imagery' that was personalised to the point that it showed them the precise model and colour they had ordered.[36]

Consider Eric and his decision concerning the selection of a digital camera. Since he lives and works in London, it was easy for him to visit several of the large camera shops. His first stop was a shop where all three of the cameras he was considering were on display. He was able to hold each one, play with all of the camera controls and, since the shop keeps batteries in its demo models, Eric was able to take pictures with each one. The salesperson was neutral in his opinion, feeling that all three cameras were essentially equivalent, and all took excellent pictures. A few days later, Eric stopped at another shop on his way home from the office. Again, he was able to handle all three cameras and take pictures with them. It seemed to him that the Canon felt better in his hands than the other two, and the controls seemed to fall right where he placed his fingers when holding the camera (a positive). Also, the Canon had an optical finder, which was the way Eric was used to taking pictures. Next, Eric again went to the Internet. A colleague had told him that there were many digital camera discussion groups on the Internet, and that many of them were camera-model specific. So he spent one evening at home reading owner/user comments on the forums of *Digital Photography Review* and *Digital Camera Resource*. He learned what some owners liked and disliked about each of the three cameras he was considering. He also learned that the capacity of the memory cards packaged with each camera was too small to be of any use, and that along with purchasing a memory card with greater capacity he should also purchase a spare battery for whichever camera he bought. He also posted a message on the www.dpreview.com forum, asking which of the three cameras might be best for him, and within a day he had received five responses. The general sense was that all three cameras were excellent, but that the Canon, with its many possibilities for memory cards, might be the best of the three. Eric is now convinced that the Canon is the digital camera he should purchase. It has a viewfinder, which is a feature that he likes and is used to, it is small and light in weight, and he considers its appearance to be very stylish. Also, he feels that he will have no difficulty carrying the camera by slipping it into his jeans or jacket pocket. So he checks the prices for this camera both at the retailers in London that he visited, and at several e-tailers. He finds that the lowest price for the camera is at www.amazon.co.uk, which includes free delivery, and he orders it. He had been told by friends that he can use any brand of SD memory card in the camera, and that rather than pay a lot of money for a Canon battery (in order to have a spare), he should go online where he should be able to find a comparable spare battery at less than half the cost of the Canon one. Eric goes to several e-tailer websites, and is able to find a 5GB SD card for €25 (after discount), and a spare battery for €13 – he orders both. Within the next week, UPS delivers his new Canon digital camera, as well as his SD memory card and spare battery.

Post-purchase Evaluation

As consumers use a product, particularly during a trial purchase, they evaluate its performance in the light of their own expectations. There are three possible outcomes of these evaluations:

1. actual performance matches expectations, leading to a neutral feeling;
2. performance exceeds expectations, causing what is known as positive disconfirmation of expectations (which leads to satisfaction); and
3. performance is below expectations, causing negative disconfirmation of expectations and dissatisfaction.[37]

For each of these three outcomes, consumers' expectations and satisfaction are closely linked: that is, consumers tend to judge their experience against their expectations when performing a **post-purchase evaluation**.

An important component of post-purchase evaluation is the reduction of any uncertainty or doubt that the consumer might have had about the selection. As part of their post-purchase analyses, consumers try to reassure themselves that their choice was a wise one: that is, they attempt to reduce post-purchase cognitive dissonance. As will be further discussed in Chapter 9, they do this by adopting one of the following strategies: they may rationalise the decision as being wise; they may seek advertisements that support their choice and avoid those of competitive brands; they may attempt to persuade friends or neighbours to buy the same brand (and thus confirm their own choice); or they may turn to other satisfied owners for reassurance.

The degree of post-purchase analysis that consumers undertake depends on the importance of the product decision and the experience acquired in using the product. When the product lives up to expectations, they probably will buy it again. When the product's performance is disappointing or does not meet expectations, however, they will search for more suitable alternatives. Thus, the consumer's post-purchase evaluation feeds back as experience to the consumer's psychological field and serves to influence future related decisions. Although it would be logical to assume that customer satisfaction is related to customer retention (i.e. if a consumer is satisfied with his adidas shoes he will buy other adidas products), a recent study found no direct relationship between satisfaction and retention. The findings show that customer retention may be more a matter of the brand's reputation – especially for products consumers find difficult to evaluate.[38]

What was Eric's post-purchase evaluation of his new digital camera? He absolutely loves it! First of all, because it is so small in size, he can carry it in his trouser pocket anywhere he goes, and is therefore always ready to take pictures, which is something he very much enjoys doing. His 5GB secure digital card allows him to take over 1,000 photos before replacing it, even using the camera's 'best picture' setting. After coming back from a friend's party, where he took about 25 pictures, he quickly transferred the photos from his camera to his laptop (using the software and lead supplied with the camera), easily cropped a few of the photos and eliminated 'red eye' in others, and then uploaded the 15 photos he really liked to his Facebook profile. He was absolutely thrilled with how sharp and colourful his pictures were, and couldn't wait to share these photos with his friends.

CONSUMER GIFTING BEHAVIOUR

In terms of both the amount of money spent each year and how they make givers and receivers feel, gifts are a particularly interesting part of consumer behaviour. Products and services chosen as gifts represent more than ordinary 'everyday' purchases. Because of their symbolic meaning, they are associated with such important events as Mother's Day, births and birthdays, engagements, weddings, graduations and many other accomplishments and milestones.

Gifting behaviour has been defined as 'the process of gift exchange that takes place between a giver and a recipient'.[39] The definition is broad in nature and embraces gifts given voluntarily ('Just to let you know I'm thinking of you'), as well as gifts that are an obligation ('I had to get him a gift').[40] It includes gifts given to (and received from) others and gifts to one's self, or **self-gifts**.

Gifting is an act of symbolic communication, with explicit and implicit meanings ranging from congratulations, love and regret to obligation and dominance. The nature of the relationship between gift giver and gift receiver is an important consideration in choosing a gift. Indeed, gifting often impacts the relationship between the giver and the recipient.[41] Table 4-9 presents an enumeration of the relationships between various combinations of gift givers and gift receivers in the consumer gifting process. The model reveals the following five gifting subdivisions:

1. intergroup gifting,
2. intercategory gifting,
3. intragroup gifting,
4. interpersonal gifting, and
5. intrapersonal gifting.

Intergroup gifting behaviour occurs whenever one group exchanges gifts with another group (such as one family and another). You will see in Chapter 11 that the process and

TABLE 4-9 Five giver–receiver gifting subdivisions

GIVERS	INDIVIDUAL	RECEIVERS 'OTHER' GROUP	SELF*
Individual	Interpersonal gifting	Intercategory gifting	Intrapersonal gifting
Group	Intercategory gifting	Intergroup gifting	Intragroup gifting

*This 'SELF' is either singular self ('me') or plural ('us').
Source: Based on Deborah Y. Cohn and Leon G. Schiffman, 'Gifting: A Taxonomy of Private Realm Giver and Recipient Relationships', Working Paper, City University of New York, Baruch College, 1996, 2–7.

outcome of family decision-making is different from individual decision-making. Similarly, gifts given to families will be different from those given to individual family members. For example, a joint wedding gift for a bride and a groom may include products for setting up a household rather than a gift that would be used personally by either the bride or the groom. When it comes to *intercategory gifting*, either an individual is giving a gift to a group (a single friend is giving a couple an anniversary gift) or a group is giving an individual a gift (friends chip in and give another friend a joint birthday gift). The gift selection strategies 'buy for joint recipients' or 'buy with someone' (creating intercategory gifting) are especially useful when it comes to a difficult recipient situation (when 'nothing seems to satisfy her').[42] These strategies can also be applied to reduce some of the time pressure associated with shopping for the great number of gifts exchanged during the Christmas season gift-giving ritual. For example, a consumer may choose to purchase five intercategory gifts for five aunt and uncle pairs (intercategory gifting), instead of buying ten personal gifts for five aunts and five uncles (interpersonal gifting). In this way, less time, money and effort may be expended.

An *intragroup gift* can be characterised by the sentiment 'we gave this to ourselves': that is, a group gives a gift to itself or its members. For example, a dual-income couple may find that their demanding work schedules limit leisure time spent together as husband and wife. Therefore, an anniversary gift ('to us') of a Caribbean holiday would be an example of an intragroup gift. It would also remedy the couple's problem of not spending enough time together. In contrast, *interpersonal gifting* occurs between just two individuals, a gift giver and gift receiver. By their very nature, interpersonal gifts are 'intimate' because they provide an opportunity for a gift giver to reveal what he or she thinks of the gift receiver. Successful gifts are those that communicate that the giver knows and understands the receiver and their relationship. For example, a pair of earrings given to a friend in just the right shape and size can be viewed as 'he really knows me'. In contrast, a toaster given as a Valentine's Day gift when the recipient is expecting a more intimate gift can mean the deterioration of a relationship.[43] Still further, researchers who have explored the gender of gift givers and their feelings about same-sex gifting (female to female or male to male) and opposite-sex gifting (male to female or female to male) have found that both male and female gift givers feel more comfortable in giving gifts to the same sex; however, they also reported that they felt more intense feeling with respect to gifts given to members of the opposite sex.[44] Additionally, although females get more pleasure than males from giving gifts and generally play the dominant role in gift exchanges, both sexes are strongly motivated by feelings of obligation.[45] Other research has also found that interpersonal gifting can be the cause of 'gifting anxiety' (which is related to social anxiety) on the part of the givers and the recipients and in the gifting situations themselves.[46] Knowledge of such gender differences is useful for marketers because it implies that additional support might be appreciated at the point of purchase (while in a store) when a consumer is considering a gift for an opposite-sex recipient. Table 4-10 presents a picture of the dynamics of the gift continuum in Hong Kong. Note how a number of issues associated with the gift, such as risk, emotional expectations and the 'why', vary across the four categories of gifts. For example, a gift given to a 'romantic

TABLE 4-10 The dynamics of the gift continuum in Hong Kong

WHO	ROMANTIC OTHER	CLOSE FRIENDS	JUST FRIENDS	HI/BYE FRIENDS
Chinese Terminology	*Sui láih math*	*Yihhei*	*Renqing*	*Guanxi*
When (examples)	(1) Birthday Gift	(1) Birthday Gift	(1) Birthday Gift	(1) Birthday Gift
	(2) Special Occasions (e.g., Valentine's Day)	(2) Special Occasions (e.g., leaving on a trip)	(2) Maintenance Gift (e.g., souvenir from a trip)	
	(3) Spontaneous (e.g., small gifts)	(3) Spontaneous (e.g., special awards)		
	(4) Formal/Ceremonial (e.g., Mid-Autumn Festival)	(4) Formal/Ceremonial (e.g., New Year)		
Type of Gift	Expressive	Expressive	Expressive/ Instrumental	Instrumental
Emotional Expectations	High	High	Medium	Low
Selection Criteria	Inexpensive (early) Expensive (later) No Gift (family)	Mostly Expensive	Somewhat Expensive	Inexpensive
Effort in Selection	Match Needs (e.g., jewellery)	Match Needs (e.g., desired clothing)	Typical Gift (e.g., having meal)	Typical Gift (e.g., birthday card)
Token Gift (Interim)	Often	Often	Occasionally	Occasionally
Why	Win Hearts	Care	Care/Build Network	Build Network
Face	Social (early) Moral (later)	Moral	Mostly Social	Social
Risks	Guilt/Shame	Guilt/Shame	Loss of Face	Loss of Face

Source: Adapted from Annamma Joy, 'Gift Giving in Hong Kong and the Continuum of Social Ties', *Journal of Consumer Research*, 28, September 2001, 244. Reprinted by permission of The University of Chicago Press. Copyright © 2001, JCR, Inc.

other' involves a high emotional expectation, but one given to a friend has a low emotional expectation.[47]

One study examined mothers giving gifts to their children (interpersonal gifting) across three different cultures:

1. Anglo-Celtic (mothers born in Australia),
2. Sino-Vietnamese (mothers born in Vietnam), and
3. Israeli (mothers born in Israel).[48]

Whereas in all three of these cultures the mother plays a central role in family gift giving, Table 4-11 presents the major differences among these groups. For instance, when it comes to gift giving, Anglo-Celtic mothers were found to be motivated to select status or prestige gifts, whereas Sino-Vietnamese mothers were likely to pick practical gifts, and Israeli mothers tended to select gifts that they felt would be important to the recipient. Examine the table for other differences.

Intrapersonal gifting, or a self-gift (also called 'monadic giving'), occurs when the giver and the receiver are the same individual.[49] To some extent a self-gift is a 'state of mind'. If a consumer sees a purchase as 'buying something I need', then it is simply a purchase. On the other hand, if the same consumer sees the same purchase as a 'self-gift', then it is something special, with special meaning. Consumers may treat themselves to self-gifts that are products (clothing, CDs

TABLE 4-11 Major differences between gift-giving behaviour of Anglo-Celtic, Sino-Vietnamese and Israeli mothers

GIFT-GIVING ELEMENTS	ANGLO-CELTIC MOTHERS	SINO-VIETNAMESE MOTHERS	ISRAELI MOTHERS
1. Motivation			
Justification	Short-term goals	Long-term goals	Long-term/short-term goals
Significance	Prestige gifts Birthday gifts	Practical gifts Lucky money	Importance to recipient
Timing	Special occasions (e.g., birthdays, Christmas)	Chinese New Year and academic reward	Birthdays and general needs
2. Selection			
Involvement	High priority Social and psychological risks	Low priority Financial risks	Low priority
Family Influences	Children	Mother	Mother dominant with younger children and influenced by older children
Promotional Influences	Status symbols	Sale items	Sale items
Gift Attributes	Quality Money unsuitable	Price Money suitable	Price Money suitable
3. Presentation			
Presentation Messages	Immediate self-gratification	Delayed self-gratification	Immediate self-gratification
Allocation Messages	Multiple gifts Mothers favoured	Single gifts Eldest child favoured	Single gifts
Understanding of Messages	Always	Not always	Never
4. Reaction			
Achievement	Often	Most of the time	Never
Feedback	More expressive	Less expressive	Least expressive
Usage	Often private	Often shared	Never shared

Source: Adapted from Constance Hill and Celia T. Romm, 'The Role of Mothers as Gift Givers: A Comparison Across Three Cultures', in *Advances in Consumer Research*, 23, ed. Kim P. Corfman and John G. Lynch, Jr. (Provo, UT: Association for Consumer Research, 1996), 26. Reproduced with permission of Association for Consumer Research; permission conveyed through Copyright Clearance Center, Inc.

or jewellery), services (hair styling, restaurant meals, spa membership), or experiences (socialising with friends).[50] For example, while purchasing holiday gifts for others, some consumers find themselves in shops that they might not otherwise visit or find themselves looking at merchandise (such as a scarf) that they want but would not ordinarily buy.[51] Such intrapersonal gifts have their own special range of meaning and context. Table 4-12 illustrates specific circumstances and motivations that might lead a consumer to engage in self-gift behaviour. Research focusing on college students' self-gifting behaviour found that when they had the money to spend and when they either felt good or wished to cheer themselves up, they were particularly likely to purchase self-gifts.[52]

Finally, Table 4-13 summarises the five gifting behaviour subdivisions explored earlier.

TABLE 4-12 Reported circumstances and motivations for self-gift behaviour

CIRCUMSTANCES	MOTIVATIONS
Personal accomplishment	To reward oneself
Feeling down	To be nice to oneself
Holiday	To cheer oneself up
Feeling stressed	To fulfil a need
Have some extra money	To celebrate
Need	To relieve stress
Had not bought for self in a while	To maintain a good feeling
Attainment of a desired goal	To provide an incentive toward a goal
Others	Others

Source: Adapted from David Glen Mick and Mitchelle DeMoss, 'To Me from Me: A Descriptive Phenomenology of Self-Gifts', in *Advances in Consumer Research*, 23, eds Marvin E. Goldberg, Gerald Gorn and Richard W. Pollay (Provo, UT: Association for Consumer Research, 1990), 677–82. Reproduced with permission of Association for Consumer Research; permission conveyed through Copyright Clearance Center Inc.

TABLE 4-13 Gifting relationship categories: Definitions and examples

GIFTING RELATIONSHIP	DEFINITION	EXAMPLE
Intergroup	A group giving a gift to another group	A Christmas gift from one family to another family
Intercategory	An individual giving a gift to a group or a group giving a gift to an individual	A group of friends chips in to buy a new mother a baby gift
Intragroup	A group giving a gift to itself or its members	A family buys a DVD player for itself as a Christmas gift
Interpersonal	An individual giving a gift to another individual	Valentine's Day chocolates presented from a boyfriend to a girlfriend
Intrapersonal	Self-gift	A woman buys herself jewelry to cheer herself up

Source: Adapted from Deborah Y. Cohn and Leon G. Schiffman, 'Gifting: A Taxonomy of Private Realm Giver and Recipient Relationships', Working Paper, City University of New York, Baruch College, 1996, 2.

BEYOND THE DECISION: CONSUMING AND POSSESSING

Historically, the emphasis in consumer behaviour studies has been on product, service and brand choice decisions. As will be shown throughout this book, however, there are many more facets to consumer behaviour. The experience of using products and services, as well as the sense of pleasure derived from possessing, collecting or consuming 'things' and 'experiences' (mechanical watches, old fountain pens or a stamp collection) contribute to consumer satisfaction and over-all quality of life. These consumption outcomes or experiences, in turn, affect consumers' future decision processes.

Thus, given the importance of possessions and experiences, a broader perspective of con-sumer behaviour might view consumer choices as the beginning of a consumption process, not merely the end of a consumer decision-making effort. In this context, the choice or pur-chase decision is an input into a process of consumption. The input stage includes the estab-lishment of a consumption set (an assortment or portfolio of products and their attributes) and a consuming style (the 'rules' by which the individual or household fulfils consumption requirements). The process stage of a simple model of consumption might include (from the consumer's perspective) the using, possessing (or having), collecting and disposing of things and experiences. The output stage of this process would include changes in a wide range of feelings, moods, attitudes and behaviour, as well as reinforcement (positive or negative) of a particular lifestyle (e.g. a devotion to physical fitness), enhancement of a sense of self, and the level of consumer satisfaction and quality of life.[53] Figure 4-6 presents a simple model of consumption that reflects the ideas discussed here and throughout the book.

Products have special meaning and memories

Consuming is a diverse and complex concept.[54] It includes the simple utility derived from the continued use of a superior toothpaste, the stress reduction of an island holiday, the stored memories of a video reflecting one's childhood, the 'sacred' meaning or 'magic' of a grand-parent's wristwatch, the symbol of membership gained from wearing a school tie, the pleasure and sense of accomplishment that comes from building a model aeroplane and the fun and even financial reward that come from collecting almost anything (even jokers from decks of cards). There are special possessions that consumers resist replacing, even with an exact replica, because the replica cannot possibly hold the same meaning as the original. Such possessions are often tied, in the consumer's mind, to a specific physical time or person.[55]

Consider how some consumers have a fascination with Swatch watches. For example, there is the story of how one woman hid in a department store for the lunch shift, so that the person filling in at the Swatch counter would sell her a second Swatch watch. Such collecting can

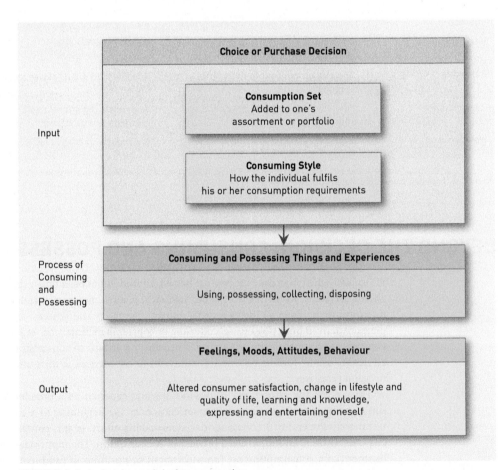

FIGURE 4-6 A simple model of consumption

be 'both rational and irrational, deliberate and uncontrollable, cooperative and competitive, passive and aggressive, and tension producing and tension reducing'.[56] In fact, with respect to Swatch watches, the company has changed its 'limited-edition' strategy from offering 30,000 pieces worldwide to offering certain designs now in only a single outlet.[57]

Some possessions (such as photographs, souvenirs, trophies and everyday objects) serve to assist consumers in their effort to create 'personal meaning' and to maintain a sense of the past, which is essential to having a sense of self.[58] For instance, objects of the past are often acquired and retained intentionally (some become antiques or even heirlooms) to memorialise pleasant or momentous times and people in one's past.

Why are some consumers so interested in the past? It has been suggested that nostalgia permits people to maintain their identity after some major change in their life. This nostalgia can be based on family and friends; on objects such as toys, books, jewellery and cars; or on special events, such as graduations, weddings and holidays.[59] Providing the triple benefits of a sense of nostalgia, the fun of collecting and the attraction of a potential return on investment, there is a strong interest in collecting Barbie dolls. It is estimated that there are currently more than 100,000 Barbie doll collectors, who are dedicated to hunting down rare and valuable Barbie dolls to add to their collections.

Older consumers are often faced with the issue of how they should dispose of such special possessions. Indeed, a number of researchers have examined this subject area. Sometimes it is some precipitating event, such as the death of a spouse, illness or moving out of one's home (to a nursing home or retirement community), that gets the consumer thinking about the disposal of his or her possessions. Often the older person wants to pass a family legacy on to a child, ensure a good home for a cherished collection and/or influence the lives of others. The aim is not to 'sell' the items, because they could do that themselves.[60]

SUMMARY

The consumer's decision to purchase or not to purchase a product or service is an important moment for most marketers. It can signify whether a marketing strategy has been wise, insightful and effective, or whether it was poorly planned and missed the mark. Thus, marketers are particularly interested in the consumer's decision-making process. For a consumer to make a decision, more than one alternative must be available. (The decision not to buy is also an alternative.)

Theories of consumer decision-making vary, depending on the researcher's assumptions about the nature of humankind. The various models of consumers (economic view, passive view, cognitive view and emotional view) depict consumers and their decision-making processes in distinctly different ways. An overview consumer decision-making model ties together the psychological, social and cultural concepts examined later in Part 2 and in Part 3 into an easily understood framework. This decision model has three sets of variables: input, process and output.

Input variables that affect the decision-making process include commercial marketing efforts, as well as non-commercial influences from the consumer's sociocultural environment. The decision process variables are influenced by the consumer's psychological field, including the evoked set (or the brands in a particular product category considered in making a purchase choice). Taken as a whole, the psychological field influences the consumer's recognition of a need, pre-purchase search for information and evaluation of alternatives.

The output phase of the model includes the actual purchase (either trial or repeat purchase) and post-purchase evaluation. Both pre-purchase and post-purchase evaluation feeds back in the form of experience into the consumer's psychological field and serves to influence future decision processing.

The process of gift exchange is an important part of consumer behaviour. Various gift-giving and gift-receiving relationships are captured by the following five specific categories in the gifting classification scheme:

1. intergroup gifting (a group gives a gift to another group);
2. intercategory gifting (an individual gives a gift to a group or a group gives a gift to an individual);
3. intragroup gifting (a group gives a gift to itself or its members);
4. interpersonal gifting (an individual gives a gift to another individual); and
5. intrapersonal gifting (a self-gift).

Consumer behaviour is not just making a purchase decision or the act of purchasing; it also includes the full range of experiences associated with using or consuming products and services. It also includes the sense of pleasure and satisfaction derived from possessing or collecting 'things'. The outputs of consumption are changes in feelings, moods or attitudes; reinforcement of lifestyles; an enhanced sense of self; satisfaction of a consumer-related need; belonging to groups; and expressing and entertaining oneself.

Among other things, consuming includes the simple utility of using a superior product, the stress reduction of a holiday, the sense of having a 'sacred' possession and the pleasures of a hobby or a collection. Some possessions serve to assist consumers in their effort to create personal meaning and to maintain a sense of the past.

DISCUSSION QUESTIONS

1. Compare and contrast the economic, passive, cognitive and emotional models of consumer decision-making.
2. What kinds of marketing and sociocultural inputs would influence the purchase of (a) a high-definition TV, (b) a concentrated liquid laundry detergent, and (c) fat-free ice cream? Explain your answers.
3. Define extensive problem-solving, limited problem-solving and routinised response behaviour. What are the differences among the three decision-making approaches? What type of decision process would you expect most consumers to follow in their first purchase of a new product or brand in each of the following areas: (a) chewing gum, (b) sugar, (c) men's aftershave, (d) carpeting, (e) a mobile phone, and (f) a luxury car? Explain your answers.
4. a. Identify three different products that you believe require a reasonably intensive pre-purchase search by a consumer. Then, using Table 4-2 as a guide, identify the specific characteristics of these products that make an intensive pre-purchase search likely.
   b. For each of the products you listed, identify the perceived risks that a consumer is likely to experience before a purchase. Discuss how the marketers of these products can reduce these perceived risks.
5. Let's assume that this coming summer you are planning to spend a month touring Europe and are, therefore, in need of a good digital camera. (a) Develop a list of product attributes that you will use as the purchase criteria in evaluating various cameras. (b) Distinguish the differences that would occur in your decision process if you were to use compensatory versus non-compensatory decision rules.
6. How can a marketer of very light, very powerful laptops use its knowledge of customers' expectations in designing a marketing strategy?
7. How do consumers reduce post-purchase dissonance? How can marketers provide positive reinforcement to consumers after the purchase to reduce their dissonance?
8. The Gillette Company, which produces the highly successful MACH3 shaving blade, also offers a clear gel antiperspirant and deodorant for men. Identify the perceived risks associated with the purchase of this new product and outline a strategy designed to reduce these perceived risks during the product's introduction.

9. Albert Einstein once wrote that 'the whole of science is nothing more than a refinement of everyday thinking'. Do you think that this quote applies to the development of the consumer decision-making model presented in Figure 4-2?

EXERCISES

1. Find two print advertisements, one that illustrates the cognitive model of consumer decision-making and one that illustrates the emotional model. Explain your choices. In your view, why did the marketers choose the approaches depicted in the advertisements?

2. Describe the need recognition process that took place before you purchased your last can of soft drink. How did it differ from the process that preceded the purchase of a new pair of trainers? What role, if any, did advertising play in your need recognition?

3. List the alternatives that you considered when choosing which university or business school to attend and the criteria that you used to evaluate them. Describe how you acquired information on the different schools along the different attributes that were important to you and how you made your decision. Be sure to specify whether you used compensatory or non-compensatory decision rules.

4. Select one of the following product categories: (a) CD players, (b) fast-food restaurants or (c) shampoo, and: (1) write down the brands that constitute your evoked set, (2) identify brands that are not part of your evoked set and (3) discuss how the brands included in your evoked set differ from those that are not included in terms of important attributes.

5. Select a newspaper or magazine advertisement that attempts (a) to provide the consumer with a decision strategy to follow in making a purchase decision or (b) to reduce the perceived risk(s) associated with a purchase. Evaluate the effectiveness of the advertisement you selected.

NOTES

1. Itamar Simonson, 'Shoppers' Easily Influenced Choices', *New York Times*, 6 November 1994, 11.
2. John A. Howard and Jagdish N. Sheth, *The Theory of Buyer Behavior* (New York: Wiley, 1969), 46–7; see also John Howard, *Consumer Behavior in Marketing Strategy* (Upper Saddle River, NJ: Prentice Hall, 1989).
3. Herbert A. Simon, *Administrative Behavior*, 2nd edn (New York: Free Press, 1965), 40.
4. James G. March and Herbert A. Simon, *Organizations* (New York: Wiley, 1958), 140–241.
5. Michael A. Jones, Philip J. Trocchia and David L. Mothersbaugh, 'Noneconomic Motivations for Price Haggling: An Exploratory Study', in *Advances in Consumer Research*, 24, eds Merrie Brucks and Deborah J. MacInnis (Provo, UT: Association for Consumer Research, 1997), 388–91.
6. Meryl Paula Gardner, 'Mood States and Consumer Behavior: A Critical Review', *Journal of Consumer Research*, 12, December 1985, 281–300; and Robert A. Peterson and Matthew Sauber, 'A Mood Scale for Survey Research', in *1983 AMA Educators' Proceedings*, eds Patrick E. Murphy *et al.* (Chicago: American Marketing Association, 1983), 409–14.
7. Barry J. Babin, William R. Darden and Mitch Griffin, 'Some Comments on the Role of Emotions in Consumer Behavior', in *1992 AMA Educators' Proceedings*, ed. Robert P. Leone and V. Kumor *et al.* (Chicago: American Marketing Association, 1992), 30–39; and Patricia A. Knowles, Stephen J. Grove and W. Jeffrey Burroughs, 'An Experimental Examination of Mood Effects on Retrieval and Evaluation of Advertisement and Brand Information', *Journal of the Academy of Marketing Science*, 21, Spring 1993, 135–42.
8. Richard P. Bagozzi, Mahesh Gopinath and Prashanth U. Nyer, 'The Role of Emotions in Marketing', *Academy of Marketing Science Journal*, 27, 2, Spring 1999, 184–206; and Gardner, 'Mood States and Consumer Behavior'.

9. Ruth Belk Smith and Elaine Sherman, 'Effects of Store Image and Mood on Consumer Behavior: A Theoretical and Empirical Analysis', in *Advances in Consumer Research*, 20, eds Leigh McAlister and Michael L. Rothschild (Provo, UT: Association for Consumer Research, 1993), 631.

10. Knowles, Grove and Burroughs, 'An Experimental Examination'.

11. Bagozzi *et al.*, 'The Role of Emotions in Marketing'.

12. Richard P. Bagozzi and Utpal Dholakia, 'Goal Setting and Goal Striving in Consumer Behavior', *Journal of Marketing*, 63, 1999, 19–32.

13. Gregory M. Rose, 'Consumer Socialization, Parental Style, and Developmental Timetables in the United States and Japan', *Journal of Marketing*, 63, 3, July 1999, 105–19.

14. Gordon C. Bruner, II, 'The Effect of Problem-Recognition Style on Information Seeking', *Journal of the Academy of Marketing Science*, 15, Winter 1987, 33–41.

15. Matthew Klein, 'He Shops, She Shops', *American Demographics*, March 1998, 34–5.

16. Sharon E. Beatty and Scott M. Smith, 'External Search Effort: An Investigation Across Several Product Categories', *Journal of Consumer Research*, 14, June 1987, 83–95.

17. Richard A. Spreng, Richard L. Divine and Thomas J. Page, Jr., 'An Empirical Examination of the Differential Effects of Objective and Subjective Knowledge on Information Processing', in *2001 AMA Educators' Proceedings*, 12, eds Greg W. Marshall and Stephen J. Grove (Chicago: American Marketing Association, 2001), 329.

18. Niranjan V. Raman, 'A Qualitative Investigation of Web-Browsing Behavior', in *Advances in Consumer Research*, 24, eds Brucks and MacInnis, 511–16.

19. Kristy E. Reynolds, Judith Anne Garretson Folse and Michael A. Jones, 'Search Regret: Antecedents and Consequences', *Journal of Retailing*, 82 (4), 2006, 339.

20. Ibid, 339–48.

21. Michael D. Johnson and Donald R. Lehmann, 'Consumer Experience and Consideration Sets for Brands and Product Categories', in *Advances in Consumer Research*, 24, eds Brucks and MacInnis, 295–300.

22. John W. Pracejus, G. Douglas Olsen and Thomas C. O'Guinn, 'Nothing Is Something: The Production and Reception of Advertising Meaning Through the Use of White Space', *Advances in Consumer Research*, 30, eds Punam Anand Keller and Dennis W. Rook (Valdosta, GA: Association for Consumer Research, 2003), 174; and Pamela Henderson, Joan Giese and Joseph A. Cote, 'Typeface Design and Meaning: The Three Faces of Typefaces', *Advances in Consumer Research*, 30, eds Keller and Rook, 175.

23. Ashley Lye, Wei Shao and Sharyn Rundle-Thiele, 'Decision Waves: Consumer Decisions in Today's Complex World', *European Journal of Marketing*, 39 (1/2), 2005, 216–30.

24. Jeffrey F. Durgee, 'Why Some Products "Just Feel Right", or, the Phenomenology of Product Rightness', in *Advances in Consumer Research*, 22, eds Frank R. Kardes and Mita Sujan (Provo, UT: Association for Consumer Research, 1995), 650–52.

25. Tulin Erdem and Joffre Swait, 'Brand Credibility, Brand Consideration, and Choice', *Journal of Consumer Research*, 31, June 2004, 191–8.

26. Laurie Peterson, 'The Strategic Shopper', *Adweek's Marketing Week*, 30 March 1992, 18–20.

27. Madhubalan Viswanathan, José Antonio Rosa and James Edwin Harris, 'Decision Making and Coping of Functionally Illiterate Consumers and Some Implications for Marketing Management', *Journal of Marketing*, 69, January 2005, 15–31.

28. Carey Goldberg, 'Choosing the Joys of a Simplified Life', *New York Times*, 21 September 1995, C1, C9.

29. Ibid.

30. Nancy Spears, 'The Time Pressured Consumer and Deal Proneness: Theoretical Framework and Empirical Evidence', in *2000 AMA Winter Educators' Conference*, 11, eds John P. Workman and William D. Perreault (Chicago: American Marketing Association, 2000), 35–40.

31. Beth Snyder Bulik, 'Apple Puts iPod Halo to Test with Shuffle and Mini', *Advertising Age*, 17 January 2005, 33, 28; and Walter S. Mossberg, 'The Newest iPod mini Rival: iRiver's $280 H10', *The Wall Street Journal*, February 23, 2005, D4.

32. Sandra J. Burke, 'The Effects of Missing Information on Decision Strategy Selection', in *Advances in Consumer Research*, 17, eds Marvin E. Goldberg, Gerald Gorn and Richard W. Pollay (Provo, UT: Association for Consumer Research, 1990), 250–56.

33. Sarah Fisher Gardial and David W. Schumann, 'In Search of the Elusive Consumer Inference', in *Advances in Consumer Research*, 17, eds Goldberg, Gorn and Pollay, 283–7; see also Burke, 'The Effects of Missing Information'.

34. Ran Kivetz and Itamar Simonson, 'The Effects of Incomplete Information on Consumer Choice', *Journal of Marketing Research*, 37, 4, November 2000, 427–48.

35. Barry L. Bayus, 'The Consumer Durable Replacement Buyer', *Journal of Marketing*, 55, January 1991, 42–51.

36. Emily Booth, 'Getting Inside a Shopper's Mind', *Marketing* (UK), 3 June 1999, 33.

37. Ernest R. Cadotte, Robert B. Woodruff and Roger L. Jenkins, 'Expectations and Norms in Models of Consumer Satisfaction', *Journal of Marketing Research*, 24, August 1987, 305–14.

38. Kare Sandvik, Kjell Gronhaug and Frank Lindberg, 'Routes to Customer Retention: The Importance of Customer Satisfaction, Performance Quality, Brand Reputation and Customer Knowledge', in *AMA Winter Conference*, eds Debbie Thorne LeClair and Michael Hartline (Chicago: American Marketing Association, 1997), 211–17.

39. Deborah Y. Cohn and Leon G. Schiffman, 'Gifting: A Taxonomy of Private Realm Giver and Recipient Relationships', Working Paper, City University of New York, Baruch College, 1996, 2.

40. Russell W. Belk and Gregory S. Coon, 'Gift Giving as Agapic Love: An Alternative to the Exchange Paradigm Based on Dating Experiences', *Journal of Consumer Research*, 20, December 1993, 393–417.

41. Julie A. Ruth, Cele C. Otnes and Frédéric F. Brunel, 'Gift Receipt and the Reformulation of Interpersonal Relationships', *Journal of Consumer Research*, 25, March 1999, 385–402.

42. Cele Otnes, Tina M. Lowrey and Young Chan Kim, 'Gift Selection for Easy and Difficult Recipients: A Social Roles Interpretation', *Journal of Consumer Research*, 20, September 1993, 229–44.

43. John F. Sherry, 'Reflections on Giftware and Giftcare: Whither Consumer Research?' in *Gift Giving: An Interdisciplinary Anthology*, eds Cele Otnes and Richard F. Beltramini (Bowling Green, KY: Popular Press, 1996), 220.

44. Stephen J. Gould and Claudia E. Weil, 'Gift-Giving and Gender Self-Concepts', *Gender Role*, 24, 1991, 617–37.

45. Cynthia Webster and Linda Nottingham, 'Gender Differences in the Motivations for Gift Giving', in *2000 AMA Educators' Proceedings*, 11, eds Gregory T. Gundlach and Patrick E. Murphy (Chicago: American Marketing Association, 2000), 272.

46. David B. Wooten, 'Qualitative Steps Toward an Expanded Model of Anxiety in Gift-Giving', *Journal of Consumer Research*, 27, 1, June 2000, 84–95.

47. Annamma Joy, 'Gift Giving in Hong Kong and the Continuum of Social Ties', *Journal of Consumer Research*, 28, 2, September 2001, 239–56.

48. Constance Hill and Celia T. Romm, 'The Role of Mothers as Gift Givers: A Comparison Across Three Cultures', in *Advances in Consumer Research*, 23, eds Kim P. Corfman and John G. Lynch, Jr. (Provo, UT: Association for Consumer Research, 1996), 21–7.

49. For a really interesting article on self-gifts, see John F. Sherry, Jr., Mary Ann McGrath and Sidney J. Levy, 'Monadic Gifting: Anatomy of Gifts Given to the Self', in *Contemporary Marketing and Consumer Behavior*, ed. John F. Sherry, Jr. (Thousand Oaks, CA: Sage, 1995), 399–432.

50. David Glen Mick and Mitchelle DeMoss, 'To Me from Me: A Descriptive Phenomenology of Self-Gifts', in *Advances in Consumer Research*, 23, eds Goldberg, Gorn and Pollay, 677–82; and Shay Sayre and David Horne, 'I Shop, Therefore I Am: The Role of Possessions for Self-Definition', in *Advances in Consumer Research*, 23, eds Corfman and Lynch, 323–8.

51. Cynthia Crossen, '"Merry Christmas to Moi", Shoppers Say', *Wall Street Journal*, 11 December 1997, B1, B10.

52. Kim K. R. McKeage, Marsha L. Richins and Kathleen Debevec, 'Self-Gifts and the Manifestation of Material Values', in *Advances in Consumer Research*, 20, eds McAlister and Rothschild, 359–64.
53. Kathleen M. Rassuli and Gilbert D. Harrell, 'A New Perspective on Choice', in *Advances in Consumer Research*, 17, eds Goldberg, Gorn and Pollay, 737–44.
54. For an interesting article on 'consumption practices', see Douglas B. Holt, 'How Consumers Consume: A Typology of Consumer Practices', *Journal of Consumer Research*, 22, June 1995, 1–16.
55. Kent Grayson and David Shulman, 'Indexicality and the Verification of Irreplaceable Possessions: A Semiotic Analysis', *Journal of Consumer Research*, 27, 1, 17–30.
56. Mary M. Long and Leon G. Schiffman, 'Swatch Fever: An Allegory for Understanding the Paradox of Collecting', *Psychology and Marketing*, 14, August 1997, 495–509.
57. 'Nicholas Hayek Sees Affinities in Making Movies and Watches, David Evans Finds Swatch Head Stages Timely Job Switch', *The South China Morning Post* (Hong Kong), 3 April 2000, 10.
58. Russell W. Belk, 'The Role of Possessions in Constructing and Maintaining a Sense of Past', in *Advances in Consumer Research*, 17, eds Goldberg, Gorn and Pollay, 669–76.
59. Stacey Menzel Baker and Patricia F. Kennedy, 'Death by Nostalgia: A Diagnosis of Context-Specific Cases', in *Advances in Consumer Research*, 21, eds Chris T. Allen and Deborah Roedder John (Provo, UT: Association for Consumer Research, 1994), 169–74.
60. Linda L. Price, Eric J. Arnould and Carolyn Folkman Curasi, 'Older Consumers' Disposition of Special Possessions', *Journal of Consumer Research*, 27, September 2001, 2, 179–201.

CHAPTER 5
CONSUMER MOTIVATION

Human needs – consumer needs – are the basis of all modern marketing. Needs are the essence of the marketing concept. The key to a company's survival, profitability and growth in a highly competitive marketplace is its ability to identify and satisfy unfulfilled consumer needs better and sooner than the competition.

Marketers do not create needs, though in some instances they may make consumers more keenly aware of unfelt needs. Successful marketers define their markets in terms of the needs they presume to satisfy, not in terms of the products they sell. This is a market-oriented, rather than a production-oriented, approach to marketing. A marketing orientation focuses on the needs of the buyer; a production orientation focuses on the needs of the seller. The marketing concept implies that the manufacturer will make only what it knows people will buy; a production orientation implies that the manufacturer will try to sell whatever it decides to make.

The philosophy and marketing strategy of Charles Revson, the builder of the Revlon cosmetics empire, depict an insightful understanding of consumer needs. Charles Revson started by manufacturing nail polish, but he defined nail polish as a fashion accessory and not merely a nail covering. His strategy was designed to induce women to use different shades of nail polish to match different outfits, moods and occasions. This approach vastly broadened the market for the product, because it persuaded women to buy and use many different colours of nail polish in the same season rather than wait to finish one bottle before buying another one. And Revson ensured that women would buy more and more bottles of nail polish by introducing new nail colour fashions every season. Emulating GM's strategy of planned obsolescence (i.e. introducing new car models every year), Revlon would introduce new nail colours every autumn and spring and, through heavy and effective advertising, would persuade women that buying the new colours would satisfy their need to appear fashionable and attractive.[1]

Using an approach similar to GM's segmentation strategy, Revson developed separate cosmetic lines targeting different consumer segments, such as the popularly priced Revlon (which Revson equated with the positioning of the Pontiac), Natural Wonder (targeting the youth market), and Marcella Borghese (positioned as the high-class line with international 'flavour'). Most importantly, Revson understood that he was not selling women the physical product (e.g. nail lacquer to cover their nails) but the fantasy that the nail polish would attract attention and bestow class and glamour on the user. Thus, Revson did not sell deep red polish; he sold Fire and Ice. He did not sell dark red polish; he sold Berry Bon Bon. Charles Revson summed up his philosophy by saying, 'In the factory, we make cosmetics; in the store, we sell hope.' And selling hope, rather than the physical product known as cosmetics, allowed Revson to charge much more for his products. Rather than compete with other manufacturers on the basis of price, Revson competed on the basis of perceived quality and greater satisfaction of women's needs for fantasy and attention.[2]

Perceptive savvy companies define their missions in terms of the consumer needs they satisfy rather than the products they produce and sell. Because consumers' basic needs do not change but the products that satisfy them do, a corporate focus on making products that will satisfy consumers' needs ensures that the company stays in the forefront of the search for new and effective solutions. By doing so, such companies are likely to survive and grow despite strong competition or adverse economic conditions. On the other hand, companies that define themselves in terms of the products they make may suffer or even go out of business when their products are replaced by competitive offerings that better satisfy the same need. Table 5-1 includes examples of companies that define themselves as need rather than product-oriented.

This chapter discusses basic needs that operate in most people to motivate behaviour. It explores the influence that such needs have on consumption behaviour. Later chapters in Part 2 explain why and how these basic human needs, or motives, are expressed in so many diverse ways.

TABLE 5-1 Product-oriented versus need-oriented definitions

	PRODUCT-ORIENTED	CONSUMER NEED-ORIENTED DEFINITIONS
Pfizer	We make pharmaceuticals.	'Pfizer Inc. is a research-based, global pharmaceutical company. We discover and develop innovative, value-added products that improve the quality of life of people around the world and help them enjoy longer, healthier, and more productive lives.'[a]
Ritz-Carlton	We rent rooms and provide facilities for meetings and events.	The company's credo stresses the genuine care and comfort of the guests, the finest personal service and facilities, a warm yet refined ambience, and an experience that fulfills even the unexpressed needs and wishes of the guests.[b]
Sony	We make electronics, movies, and recorded CDs.	Sony is adopting a new marketing concept called 'segment solutions'. Accordingly, Sony will no longer offer products for the mass market, but will offer consumers in different lifestyle segments a variety of solutions that meet virtually every lifestyle need. For example, Sony's Walkman and S-2 lines target 'active lifestyle enthusiasts' by offering them the benefits of water and impact resistance, active control, and high visibility. The new products include features that allow users to carry, listen to, and manipulate many forms of recorded sounds.[c]
Unilever	We make food and personal care products.	'At Unilever we aim to help people in their daily lives. We meet everyday needs for nutrition, hygiene and personal care with brands that help people feel good, look good and get more out of life.'[d]

Sources: [a]www.pfizer.com; [b]www.ritzcarlton.com; [c]Tobi Elkin, 'Sony Marketing Aims at Lifestyle Segments', *Advertising Age*, 18 March 2002, 3, 72; [d]www.unilever.com.

MOTIVATION AS A PSYCHOLOGICAL FORCE

Motivation is the driving force within individuals that impels them to action. This driving force is produced by a state of tension, which exists as the result of an unfulfilled need. Individuals strive both consciously and subconsciously to reduce this tension through behaviour that they anticipate will fulfil their needs and thus relieve them of the stress they feel. The specific goals they select and the patterns of action they undertake to achieve their goals are the results of individual thinking and learning. Figure 5-1 presents a model of the motivational process. It portrays motivation as a state of need-induced tension that 'drives' the individual to engage in behaviour that he or she believes will satisfy the need and thus reduce the tension. Whether gratification is actually achieved depends on the course of action pursued. The specific goals that consumers wish to achieve and the courses of action they take to attain these goals are selected on the basis of their thinking processes (cognition) and previous learning. Therefore, marketers must view motivation as the force that induces consumption and, through consumption experiences, the process of consumer learning (discussed in Chapter 8).

Needs

Every individual has needs: some are innate, others are acquired. **Innate needs** are physiological (i.e. biogenic); they include the needs for food, water, air, clothing, shelter and sex. Because they are needed to sustain biological life, the biogenic needs are considered primary needs or motives.

Acquired needs are needs that we learn in response to our culture or environment. These may include needs for self-esteem, prestige, affection, power and learning. Because acquired needs are generally psychological (i.e. psychogenic), they are considered **secondary needs** or motives. They result from the individual's subjective psychological state and from relationships with others. For example, all individuals need shelter from the elements; thus, finding a place to live fulfils an important primary need for a newly transferred executive. However, the kind of home she rents or buys may be the result of secondary needs. She may seek a place in which she and her husband can

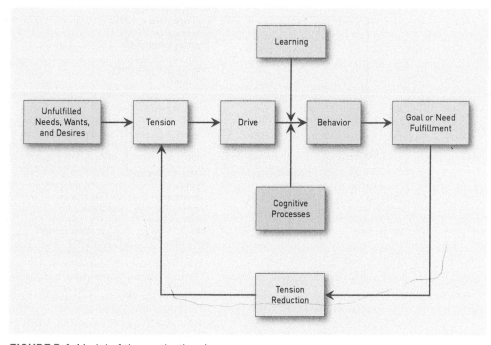

FIGURE 5-1 Model of the motivational process

Source: Adapted from Jeffrey F. Dugree *et al.*, 'Observations: Translating Values into Product Wants', *Journal of Advertising Research*, 36, 6, November 1996. With permission of Warc.

entertain large groups of people (and fulfil social needs); she may want to live in an exclusive community to impress her friends and family (and fulfil ego needs). The place where an individual ultimately chooses to live may thus serve to fulfil both primary and secondary needs.

Goals

Goals are the sought-after results of motivated behaviour. As Figure 5-1 indicated, all behaviour is goal-oriented. Our discussion of motivation in this chapter is in part concerned with **generic goals**, that is, the general classes or categories of goals that consumers see as a way to fulfil their needs. If a person tells his parents that he wants to get a graduate degree, he has stated a generic goal. If he says he wants to get a Masters degree in Marketing from the Catholic University of Leuven, Belgium, he has expressed a **product-specific goal**. Marketers are particularly concerned with product-specific goals, that is, the specifically branded products and services that consumers select for goal fulfilment.

Individuals set goals on the basis of their personal values, and they select means (or behaviours) that they believe will help them achieve their desired goals. Figure 5-2 depicts a framework of the goal structure behind losing weight, maintaining weight loss and the results of a study based on this model. Figure 5-2(A) depicts an overall framework for pursuing consumption-related goals. Figure 5-2(B) depicts the interrelationship among the needs driving the goal of losing weight (e.g. increased self-confidence, looking and feeling better and living longer) and the behaviours required to achieve the goal (i.e. exercising and/or dieting). Figure 5-2(C) depicts the complex nature of goal setting based on subjects' responses to questions regarding their reasons for selecting weight loss as a goal, providing justification for each reason and explaining each justification.[3] The three diagrams together depict the complexity of goal setting and the difficulties in understanding this process through a set theoretical model.

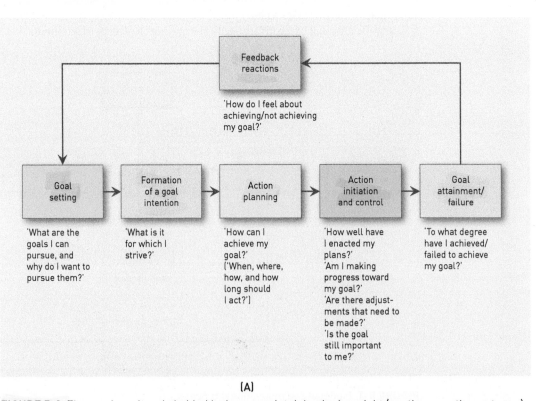

(A)

FIGURE 5-2 The needs and goals behind losing or maintaining body weight (*continues on the next page*)

Source: Adapted from 'Goal Setting and Goal Pursuit in the Regulation of Body Weight', by Richard Bagozzi and Elizabeth Edwards, originally published in *Psychology and Health*, 13, 1998. Reprinted by permission of Taylor & Francis Ltd.

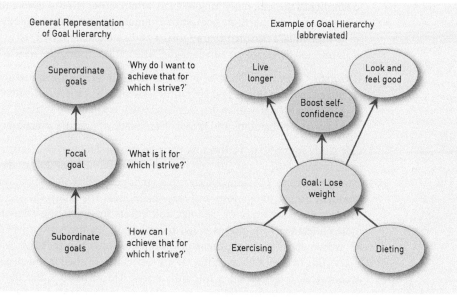

(B)

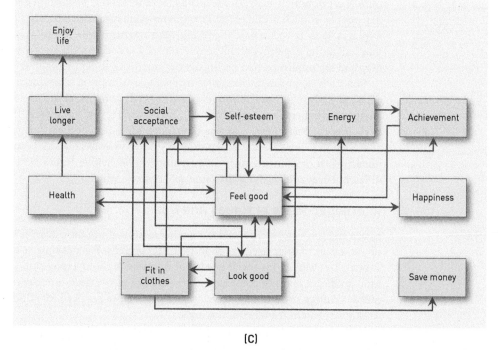

(C)

FIGURE 5-2 The needs and goals behind losing or maintaining body weight (*continued*)

The Selection of Goals

For any given need there are many different and appropriate goals. The goals selected by individuals depend on their personal experiences, physical capacity, prevailing cultural norms and values, and the goal's accessibility in the physical and social environment. For example, a young woman may wish to get a deep and even tan and may envision spending time in the sun as a way to achieve her goal. However, if her dermatologist advises her to avoid direct exposure to the sun, she may settle for a self-tanning product instead. The goal object has to be both socially acceptable and physically accessible. If cosmetics companies did not offer effective alternatives to tanning in the sun, our young woman would either have to ignore the advice of her dermatologist or select a substitute goal, such as untanned (but undamaged) youthful-looking skin.

An individual's personal characteristics and own perception of self also influence the specific goals selected. Research on personal goal orientation distinguished two types of people:

1. persons with a *promotion focus* are interested in their growth and development, have more hopes and aspirations and favour the presence of positive outcomes;
2. persons with a *prevention focus* are interested in safety and security, are more concerned with duties and obligations and favour the absence of negative outcomes.

One study found that, in forming consumption-related goals, consumers with a prevention focus favoured the status quo and inaction over action.[4] Another study distinguished between two types of goals: (1) *ideals*, which represent hopes, wishes and aspirations; and (2) *oughts*, which represent duties, obligations and responsibilities. The study showed that people concerned with ideals relied more on feelings and affects in evaluating advertisements, while people more concerned with oughts relied more heavily on the substantive and factual contents of advertisements.[5] In yet another study, some consumers were led to believe that they obtained a discount in the purchase price of a PC because of their good negotiating skills and were encouraged to feel proud, while others were led to believe that they received the discount because the computer was on sale and were not encouraged to feel proud. In addition, the goals that the consumers were encouraged to believe they had obtained were stated as either gains (i.e. promotion goals) or the avoidance of losses (i.e. prevention goals). The study showed that people who felt proud of their negotiating skills and also believed that they avoided losses were less likely to repurchase the product than persons who felt proud and also believed that they had achieved gains. For the people who did not feel proud, the type of goals they believed they had accomplished had no impact on intentions to repurchase the product.[6]

Goals are also related to negative forms of consumption behaviour. One study found that personal goals that focus on *extrinsic benefits* (such as financial success, social status and being attractive to others) are associated with higher degrees of compulsive buying than goals that stress *intrinsic benefits* (such as self-acceptance, affiliation and connection with community).[7] These studies illustrate the complexity of the ways consumers conceptualise goals and the impact of set or achieved goals on consumption behaviour. Figure 5-3 shows appeals to three different target audiences for the same goal object – wine.

Interdependence of Needs and Goals

Needs and goals are interdependent; neither exists without the other. However, people are often not as aware of their needs as they are of their goals. For example, a teenager may not consciously be aware of his social needs but may join a photography club to meet new friends. A local politician may not consciously be aware of a power need but may regularly run for public office. A college student may not consciously recognise her need for achievement but may strive to attain a straight A grade point average.

Individuals are usually somewhat more aware of their *physiological* needs than they are of their *psychological* needs. Most people know when they are hungry, thirsty or cold, and they take appropriate steps to satisfy these needs. The same people may not consciously be aware of their needs for acceptance, self-esteem or status. They may, however, subconsciously engage in behaviour that satisfies their psychological (acquired) needs.

Positive and negative motivation

Motivation can be **positive** or **negative** in direction. We may feel a driving force towards some object or condition or a driving force away from some object or condition. For example, a person may be impelled towards a restaurant to fulfil a hunger need, and away from mountaineering to fulfil a safety need.

(A)

FIGURE 5-3 Different appeals for the same goal object (*continues on the next page*)
Source: Branded Wines AS. www.sonadorwines.com.

FIGURE 5-3 Different appeals for the same goal object (*continued*)
Source: Branded Wines AS. www.sonadorwines.com.

(C)

FIGURE 5-3 Different appeals for the same goal object (*continued*)

Source: Branded Wines AS. www.sonadorwines.com.

FIGURE 5-4 Positive versus negative motivation
Source: © Neutrogena Corporation.

Some psychologists refer to positive drives as needs, wants or desires and to negative drives as fears or aversions. However, although positive and negative motivational forces seem to differ dramatically in terms of physical (and sometimes emotional) activity, they are basically similar in that both serve to initiate and sustain human behaviour. For this reason, researchers often refer to both kinds of drives or motives as needs, wants and desires. Some theorists distinguish wants from needs by defining wants as product-specific needs. Others differentiate between desires, on the one hand, and needs and wants on the other. Thus, there is no uniformly accepted distinction among needs, wants and desires.

Needs, wants or desires may create goals that can be positive or negative. A positive goal is one towards which behaviour is directed; thus, it is often referred to as an **approach object**. A negative goal is one from which behaviour is directed away and is referred to as an **avoidance object**. Because both approach and avoidance goals are the results of motivated behaviour, most researchers refer to both simply as goals. Consider this example: a middle-aged woman may have a positive goal of fitness and join a health club to work out regularly. Her husband may view getting fat as a negative goal, and so he starts exercising as well. In the former case, the wife's actions are designed to achieve the positive goal of health and fitness; in the latter case, her husband's actions are designed to avoid a negative goal – a flabby physique. Figure 5-4 shows two advertisements for Neutrogena sun lotion, one stressing positive motivation and the other negative motivation.

Sometimes people become motivationally aroused by a threat to or elimination of a behavioural freedom, such as the freedom to make a product choice. This motivational state is called **psychological reactance**. A classic example occurred in 1985 when the Coca-Cola Company changed its traditional formula and introduced 'New Coke'. Many people reacted negatively to the notion that their 'freedom to choose' had been taken away, and they refused to buy New Coke. Company management responded to this unexpected psychological reaction by reintroducing the original formula as Classic Coke and gradually developing additional versions of Coke.

Rational versus emotional motives

Some consumer behaviourists distinguish between so-called **rational motives** and **emotional motives**. They use the term rationality in the traditional economic sense, which assumes that consumers behave rationally by carefully considering all alternatives and choosing those that give them the greatest utility. In a marketing context, the term rationality implies that consumers select goals based on totally objective criteria, such as size, weight, price or miles per gallon. Emotional motives imply the selection of goals according to personal or subjective criteria (e.g. pride, fear, affection or status).

The assumption underlying this distinction is that subjective or emotional criteria do not maximise utility or satisfaction. However, it is reasonable to assume that consumers always attempt to select alternatives that, in their view, serve to maximise their satisfaction. Obviously, the assessment of satisfaction is a very personal process, based on the individual's own need structure, as well as on past behavioural and social (or learned) experiences. What may appear irrational to an outside observer may be perfectly rational in the context of the consumer's own psychological field. For example, a person who pursues extensive facial plastic surgery in order to appear younger is using significant economic resources, such as the surgical fees, time lost in recovery, inconvenience and the risk that something may go wrong. To that person, the pursuit of the goal of looking younger and utilisation of the resources involved are perfectly rational choices. However, to many other people within the same culture who are less concerned with ageing, and certainly to people from other cultures that are not as preoccupied with personal appearance as Westerners are, these choices appear completely irrational.

THE DYNAMICS OF MOTIVATION

Motivation is a highly dynamic construct that is constantly changing in reaction to life experiences. Needs and goals change and grow in response to an individual's physical condition, environment, interactions with others and experiences. As individuals attain their goals, they develop new ones. If they do not attain their goals, they continue to strive for old goals or they develop substitute goals. Some of the reasons why need-driven human activity never ceases include the following:

1. Many needs are never fully satisfied; they continually impel actions designed to attain or maintain satisfaction.
2. As needs become satisfied, new and higher-order needs emerge that cause tension and induce activity.
3. People who achieve their goals set new and higher goals for themselves.

The appeal of the advertisement in Figure 5-5 stems from the need to achieve and satisfy new and higher goals.

Needs are never fully satisfied

Most human needs are never fully or permanently satisfied. For example, at fairly regular intervals throughout the day individuals experience hunger needs that must be satisfied. Most people regularly seek companionship and approval from others to satisfy their social needs. Even more complex psychological needs are rarely fully satisfied. For example, a person may partially satisfy a power need by working as administrative assistant to a local politician, but this vicarious taste of power may not sufficiently satisfy her need; thus, she may strive to work for a national politician or even to run for political office herself. In this instance, temporary goal achievement does not adequately satisfy the need for power, and the individual strives harder in an effort to satisfy her need more fully.

New needs emerge as old needs are satisfied

Some motivational theorists believe that a hierarchy of needs exists and that new, higher-order needs emerge as lower-order needs are fulfilled.[8] For example, a man who has largely satisfied his basic physiological needs (food, housing, etc.) may turn his efforts to achieving acceptance among his new neighbours by joining their political clubs and supporting their candidates. Once he is confident that he has achieved acceptance, he may then seek recognition by giving lavish parties or building a larger house. Hence, it is important that marketers are attuned to changing needs.

FIGURE 5-5 New and higher goals motivate behaviour
Source: www.super-collider.com.

Success and failure influence goals

A number of researchers have explored the nature of the goals that individuals set for them-selves. Broadly speaking, they have concluded that individuals who successfully achieve their goals usually set new and higher goals; that is, they raise their **level of aspiration**. This may be due to the fact that their success in reaching lower goals makes them more confident of their ability to reach higher goals. Conversely, those who do not reach their goals sometimes lower their levels of aspiration.[9] Thus, goal selection is often a function of success and failure. For example, a student who is not accepted into medical school may try instead to become a dentist or a nurse.

The nature and persistence of an individual's behaviour are often influenced by expectations of success or failure in reaching certain goals. Those expectations, in turn, are often based on past experience. A person who takes good snapshots with an inexpensive camera may be motivated to buy a more sophisticated camera in the belief that it will enable her to take even better photographs. In this way, she eventually may upgrade her camera by spending several hundred euros. On the other hand, a person who has not been able to take good photographs is just as likely to keep the same camera or even to lose all interest in photography.

These effects of success and failure on goal selection have strategy implications for marketers. Goals should be reasonably attainable. Advertisements should not promise more than the product will deliver. Products and services are often evaluated by the size and direction of the gap between consumer expectations and objective performance. Thus, even a good product will not be repurchased if it fails to live up to unrealistic expectations created by advertisements that over-promise. Similarly, a consumer is likely to regard a mediocre product with greater satisfaction than it warrants if its performance exceeds his or her expectations.

Substitute Goals

When an individual cannot attain a specific goal or type of goal that he or she anticipates will satisfy certain needs, behaviour may be directed to a **substitute goal**. Although the substitute goal may not be as satisfactory as the primary goal, it may be sufficient to dispel uncomfortable tension. Continued deprivation of a primary goal may result in the substitute goal assuming primary-goal status. For example, a woman who has stopped drinking whole milk because she is dieting may actually begin to prefer skimmed milk. A man who cannot afford a BMW may convince himself that a new Mazda has an image he clearly prefers.

Frustration

Failure to achieve a goal often results in feelings of frustration. At one time or another, everyone has experienced the frustration that comes from the inability to attain a goal. The barrier that prevents attainment of a goal may be personal to the individual (e.g. limited physical or financial resources) or an obstacle in the physical or social environment (e.g. a volcano ash cloud that causes the postponement of a long-awaited holiday). Regardless of the cause, individuals react differently to frustrating situations. Some people manage to cope by finding their way around the obstacle or, if that fails, by selecting a substitute goal. Others are less adaptive and may regard their inability to achieve a goal as a personal failure. Such people are likely to adopt a defence mechanism to protect their egos from feelings of inadequacy. The creation of a new type of children's board game represents a creative response to the concept of frustration. Unlike most board games, where a child who has lost may be frustrated and subject to the ridicule of other children, the new game is centred on skill-building activities and provides every child with a chance to shine. While the game is built on a 'nobody loses' concept, the designers have carefully built in an element of competition because a complete lack of competition may make a game seem boring.[10]

Defence Mechanisms

People who cannot cope with frustration often mentally redefine their frustrating situations in order to protect their self-images and defend their self-esteem. For example, a man living in

TABLE 5-2 Defence mechanisms

DEFENCE MECHANISM	DESCRIPTION AND ILLUSTRATIONS
Aggression	In response to frustration, individuals may resort to aggressive behaviour in attempting to protect their self-esteem. The tennis pro who slams his tennis racket to the ground when disappointed with his game or the football player who kicks the ball away when disagreeing with the referee are examples of such conduct. So are consumer boycotts of companies or stores.
Rationalisation	People sometimes resolve frustration by inventing plausible reasons for being unable to attain their goals (e.g. not having enough time to practise) or deciding that the goal is not really worth pursuing (e.g. how important is it to achieve a high bowling score?).
Regression	An individual may react to a frustrating situation with childish or immature behaviour. A shopper attending a bargain sale, for example, may fight over merchandise and even rip a garment that another shopper will not relinquish rather than allow the other person to have it.
Withdrawal	Frustration may be resolved by simply withdrawing from the situation. For instance, a person who has difficulty achieving officer status in an organisation may decide he can use his time more constructively in other activities and simply resign from that organisation.
Projection	An individual may redefine a frustrating situation by projecting blame for his or her own failures and inabilities on other objects or persons. Thus, the golfer who misses a stroke may blame his golf clubs or his caddy.
Autism	Autistic thinking is thinking dominated by needs and emotions, with little effort made to relate to reality. Such daydreaming, or fantasising, enables the individual to attain imaginary gratification of unfulfilled needs. A person who is shy and lonely, for example, may daydream about a romantic love affair.
Identification	People resolve feelings of frustration by subconsciously identifying with other persons or situations that they consider relevant. For example, slice-of-life commercials often portray a stereotypical situation in which an individual experiences a frustration and then overcomes the problem by using the advertised product. If the viewer can identify with the frustrating situation, he or she may very likely adopt the proposed solution and buy the product advertised.
Repression	Another way that individuals avoid the tension arising from frustration is by repressing the unsatisfied need. Thus, individuals may 'force' the need out of their conscious awareness. Sometimes repressed needs manifest themselves indirectly. The wife who is unable to bear children may teach in a school or work in a library; her husband may do volunteer work in a boys' club. The manifestation of repressed needs in a socially acceptable form is called *sublimation*, another type of defence mechanism.

Helsinki, Finland, may want to take his family on an Australian holiday he cannot afford. The coping individual may select a less expensive trip to Disneyland Resort, Paris or to Legoland in Denmark. The person who cannot cope may react with anger towards his boss for not paying him enough money to afford the holiday he prefers, or he may persuade himself that Australia is unseasonably warm this year. These last two possibilities are examples, respectively, of aggression and rationalisation, **defence mechanisms** that people sometimes adopt to protect their egos from feelings of failure when they do not attain their goals. Other defence mechanisms include regression, withdrawal, projection, autism, identification and repression. These defence mechanisms are described in Table 5-2. This listing of defence mechanisms is far from exhaustive, because individuals tend to develop their own ways of redefining frustrating situations to protect their self-esteem from the anxieties that result from experiencing failure. Marketers often consider this fact in their selection of advertising appeals and construct advertisements that portray a person resolving a particular frustration through the use of the advertised product.

Multiplicity of needs

A consumer's behaviour often fulfils more than one need. In fact, it is likely that specific goals are selected because they fulfil several needs. We buy clothing for protection and for a certain degree of modesty; in addition, our clothing fulfils a wide range of personal and social needs, such as acceptance or ego needs.

One cannot accurately infer motives from behaviour. People with different needs may seek fulfilment through selection of the same goal; people with the same needs may seek fulfilment through different goals. Consider the following examples. Five people who are active in a consumer advocacy organisation may each belong for a different reason. The first may be genuinely concerned with protecting consumer interests; the second may be concerned about an increase in counterfeit merchandise; the third may seek social contacts from organisational meetings; the fourth may enjoy the power of directing a large group; and the fifth may enjoy the status provided by membership in an attention-getting organisation.

Similarly, five people may be driven by the same need (e.g. an ego need) to seek fulfilment in different ways. The first may seek advancement and recognition through a professional career; the second may become active in a political organisation; the third may run in regional marathons; the fourth may take professional dance lessons; and the fifth may seek attention by monopolising classroom discussions.

Arousal of motives

Most of an individual's specific needs are dormant much of the time. The arousal of any particular set of needs at a specific moment in time may be caused by internal stimuli found in the individual's physiological condition, by emotional or cognitive processes, or by stimuli in the outside environment.

Physiological Arousal

Bodily needs at any one specific moment in time are based on the individual's physiological condition at that moment. A drop in blood sugar level or stomach contractions will trigger awareness of a hunger need. Secretion of sex hormones will awaken the sex need. A decrease in body temperature will induce shivering, which makes the individual aware of the need for warmth. Most of these physiological cues are involuntary; however, they arouse related needs that cause uncomfortable tensions until they are satisfied. For example, a person who is cold may turn up the heat in his bedroom and also make a mental note to buy a warm sweater to wear around the house. Figure 5-6 depicts arousal of a physiological need.

Emotional Arousal

Sometimes daydreaming results in the arousal or stimulation of latent needs. People who are bored or who are frustrated in trying to achieve their goals often engage in daydreaming (autistic thinking), in which they imagine themselves in all sorts of desirable situations. These thoughts tend to arouse dormant needs, which may produce uncomfortable tensions that drive them into goal-oriented behaviour. A young woman who daydreams of a torrid romance may spend her free time in Internet single chat rooms; a young man who dreams of being a famous novelist may enrol in a writing workshop.

Cognitive Arousal

Sometimes random thoughts can lead to a cognitive awareness of needs. An advertisement that provides reminders of home might trigger instant yearning to speak with one's parents. This is

FIGURE 5-6 Physiological need
Source: Courtesy of The Advertising Archives.

the basis for many long-distance telephone company campaigns that stress the low cost of international long-distance rates. Figure 5-7 portrays an advertisement directed at cognitive arousal of the need for a holiday.

Environmental (or Situational) Arousal

The set of needs an individual experiences at a particular time is often activated by specific cues in the environment. Without these cues, the needs might remain dormant. For example, the 6 o'clock news, the sight or smell of bakery goods, fast-food commercials on television, the end of the school day – all of these may arouse the 'need' for food. In such cases, modification of the environment may be necessary to reduce the arousal of hunger.

A most potent form of situational cue is the goal object itself. A man who wants to take his family on holiday in New Zealand may experience an overwhelming desire to visit New Zealand when he is drawn to the scene depicted in Figure 5-8. Sometimes an advertisement or other environmental cue produces a psychological imbalance in the viewer's mind. For example, a young university student who constantly uses his mobile phone may see a new, cool-looking model with more features displayed in a store window. The exposure may make him unhappy with his old phone and cause him to experience tension that will be reduced only when he buys himself the new model.

When people live in a complex and highly varied environment, they experience many opportunities for need arousal. Conversely, when their environment is poor or deprived, fewer needs are activated. This explains why television has had such a mixed effect on the lives of people in underdeveloped countries. It exposes them to various lifestyles and expensive products that they would not otherwise see, and it awakens wants and desires that they have little opportunity or even hope of satisfying. Thus, while television enriches many lives, it also serves to frustrate people with little money or education or hope, and may result in the adoption of such aggressive defence mechanisms as robbery, boycotts or even revolts.

FIGURE 5-7 Cognitive need arousal
Source: Courtesy of The Advertising Archives.

There are two opposing philosophies concerned with the arousal of human motives. The *behaviourist school* considers motivation to be a mechanical process; behaviour is seen as the response to a stimulus, and elements of conscious thought are ignored. An extreme example of the stimulus–response theory of motivation is the impulse buyer who reacts largely to external stimuli in the buying situation. According to this theory, the consumer's cognitive control is limited; he or she does not act but reacts to stimuli in the marketplace. The *cognitive school* believes that all behaviour is directed at goal achievement. Needs and past experiences are reasoned, categorised, and transformed into attitudes and beliefs that act as predispositions to behaviour. These predispositions are focused on helping the individual satisfy needs, and they determine the actions that he or she takes to achieve this satisfaction.

FIGURE 5-8 Environmental arousal
Source: Courtesy of The Advertising Archives.

TYPES AND SYSTEMS OF NEEDS

For many years, psychologists and others interested in human behaviour have attempted to develop exhaustive lists of human needs. Most lists of human needs tend to be diverse in content as well as in length. Although there is little disagreement about specific physiological needs, there is considerable disagreement about specific psychological (i.e. psychogenic) needs.

TABLE 5-3 Murray's list of psychogenic needs

NEEDS ASSOCIATED WITH INANIMATE OBJECTS
Acquisition
Conservancy
Order
Retention
Construction

NEEDS THAT REFLECT AMBITION, POWER, ACCOMPLISHMENT, AND PRESTIGE
Superiority
Achievement
Recognition
Exhibition
Inviolacy (inviolate attitude)
Inavoidance (to avoid shame, failure, humiliation, ridicule)
Defendance (defensive attitude)
Counteraction (counteractive attitude)

NEEDS CONCERNED WITH HUMAN POWER
Dominance
Deferrence
Similance (suggestible attitude)
Autonomy
Contrariance (to act differently from others)

SADOMASOCHISTIC NEEDS
Aggression
Abasement

NEEDS CONCERNED WITH AFFECTION BETWEEN PEOPLE
Affiliation
Rejection
Nurturance (to nourish, aid, or protect the helpless)
Succorance (to seek aid, protection, or sympathy)
Play

NEEDS CONCERNED WITH SOCIAL INTERCOURSE (THE NEEDS TO ASK AND TELL)
Cognizance (inquiring attitude)
Exposition (expositive attitude)

Source: Adapted from Henry A. Murray, 'Types of Human Needs', in David C. McClelland, *Studies in Motivation* (New York: Appleton-Century-Crofts,1955), 63–6. By permission of Ardent Media, Inc.

In 1938, the psychologist Henry Murray prepared a detailed list of psychogenic needs. This research was probably the first systematic approach to the understanding of non-biological human needs. Murray believed that everyone has the same basic set of needs but that individuals differ in their priority ranking of these needs. Murray's basic needs include many motives that are assumed to play an important role in consumer behaviour, such as acquisition, achievement, recognition and exhibition (see Table 5-3).

Hierarchy of needs

Dr Abraham Maslow, a clinical psychologist, formulated a widely accepted theory of human motivation based on the notion of a universal hierarchy of human needs.[11] Maslow's theory identifies five basic levels of human needs, which rank in order of importance from lower-level (biogenic) needs to higher-level (psychogenic) needs. The theory postulates that individuals

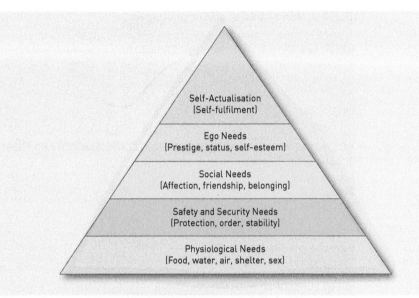

FIGURE 5-9 Maslow's hierarchy of needs

seek to satisfy lower-level needs before higher-level needs emerge. The lowest level of chronically unsatisfied need that an individual experiences serves to motivate his or her behaviour. When that need is 'fairly well' satisfied, a new (and higher) need emerges that the individual is motivated to fulfil. When this need is satisfied, a new (and still higher) need emerges, and so on. Of course, if a lower-level need experiences some renewed deprivation (e.g. thirst), it may temporarily become dominant again.

Figure 5-9 presents a diagram of **Maslow's hierarchy of needs**. For clarity, each level is depicted as mutually exclusive. According to the theory, however, there is some overlap between the levels, as no need is ever completely satisfied. For this reason, although all levels of need below the level that is currently dominant continue to motivate behaviour to some extent, the prime motivator – the major driving force within the individual – is the lowest level of need that remains largely unsatisfied.

Physiological Needs

In the hierarchy-of-needs theory, physiological needs are the first and most basic level of human needs. These needs, which are required to sustain biological life, include food, water, air, shelter, clothing, sex – all the biogenic needs, in fact, that were listed as primary needs earlier.

According to Maslow, physiological needs are dominant when they are chronically unsatisfied: 'For the man who is extremely and dangerously hungry, no other interest exists but food. He dreams food, he remembers food, he thinks about food, he emotes only about food, he perceives only food, and he wants only food.'[12] For people living in industrialised countries, the biogenic needs are generally satisfied and higher-level needs are dominant. Unfortunately, however, the lives of many people living in developing countries or in physically devastated areas are focused almost entirely on satisfying their biogenic needs, such as the needs for food, clothing and shelter.

Safety and Security Needs

After the first level of need is satisfied, safety and security needs become the driving force behind an individual's behaviour. These needs are concerned not only with physical safety but also include order, stability, routine, familiarity and control over one's life and environment. Health and the availability of health care are important safety concerns. Savings accounts, insurance policies, education and vocational training are all means by which individuals satisfy the need for security.

FIGURE 5-10 Appeal to social needs
Source: Courtesy of The Advertising Archives.

Social Needs

The third level of Maslow's hierarchy includes such needs as love, affection, belonging and acceptance. People seek warm and satisfying human relationships with other people and are motivated by love for their families. Because of the importance of social motives in our society, advertisers of many product categories emphasise this appeal in their advertisements, for example as shown in Figure 5-10.

Egoistic Needs

When social needs are more or less satisfied, the fourth level of Maslow's hierarchy becomes operative. This level is concerned with egoistic needs. These needs can take either an inward or an outward orientation, or both. Inwardly-directed ego needs reflect an individual's need for self-acceptance, self-esteem, success, independence and personal satisfaction with a job well done. Outwardly-directed ego needs include the needs for prestige, reputation, status and recognition from others. The presumed desire to 'show off' one's success and achievement through material possessions is a reflection of an outwardly-oriented ego need.

Need for Self-Actualisation

According to Maslow, most people do not satisfy their ego needs sufficiently ever to move to the fifth level – the need for self-actualisation (self-fulfilment). This need refers to an individual's desire to fulfil his or her potential – to become everything he or she is capable of becoming. In Maslow's words, 'What a man can be, he must be.'[13] This need is expressed in different ways by different people. A young man may desire to be an Olympic star and work single-mindedly for years to become the best in his sport. An artist may need to express herself on canvas; a research scientist may strive to find a new drug that eradicates cancer. Maslow noted that the self-actualisation need is not necessarily a creative urge but that it is likely to take that form in people with some capacity for creativity. Some large companies use motivation-based promotion to encourage their highly paid employees to look beyond their salaries to find gratification and self-fulfilment in the workplace – to view their jobs as the way to become 'all they can be'.

An evaluation of the need hierarchy and marketing applications

Maslow's hierarchy-of-needs theory postulates a five-level hierarchy of **prepotent human needs**. Higher-order needs become the driving force behind human behaviour as lower-level needs are satisfied. The theory says, in effect, that dissatisfaction, not satisfaction, motivates behaviour.

The need hierarchy has received wide acceptance in many social disciplines because it appears to reflect the assumed or inferred motivations. The five levels of need postulated by the hierarchy are sufficiently generic to encompass most lists of individual needs. The major problem with the theory is that it cannot be tested empirically; there is no way to measure precisely how satisfied one level of need must be before the next higher need becomes operative. The need hierarchy also appears to be very closely bound to contemporary culture (i.e. it appears to be both culture- and time-bound).

Despite these limitations, the hierarchy offers a highly useful framework for marketers trying to develop appropriate advertising appeals for their products. It is adaptable in two ways: first, it enables marketers to focus their advertising appeals on a need level that is likely to be shared by a large segment of the target audience; secondly, it facilitates product positioning or repositioning.

Segmentation and Promotional Applications

Maslow's need hierarchy is readily adaptable to market segmentation and the development of advertising appeals because there are consumer goods designed to satisfy each of the need levels and because most needs are shared by large segments of consumers. For example, individuals buy health foods, medicines, and low-fat and diet products to satisfy physiological needs. They buy insurance, preventive medical services, and home security systems to satisfy safety and security needs. Almost all personal care and grooming products (e.g. cosmetics, mouthwash, shaving cream), as well as most clothes, are bought to satisfy social needs. High-tech products such as computers or sound systems and luxury products such as furs, big cars or expensive furniture are often bought to fulfil ego and esteem needs. Postgraduate college education, hobby-related products, exotic and physically challenging adventure trips are sold as ways of achieving self-fulfilment.

The need hierarchy is often used as the basis for market segmentation with specific advertising appeals directed to one or more need-segment levels. For example, an advertisement for a very expensive sports car may use a self-actualisation appeal such as 'you deserve the very best'.

Advertisers may use the need hierarchy for positioning products – that is, deciding how the product should be perceived by prospective consumers. The key to positioning is to find a niche – an unsatisfied need – that is not occupied by a competing product or brand. The need hierarchy is a very versatile tool for developing positioning strategies because different appeals for the same product can be based on different needs included in this framework. For example, many advertisements for soft drinks stress social appeal by showing a group of young people enjoying themselves and the advertised product. Others for nutritional drinks stress refreshment (a physiological need); still others may focus on a low calorie content (thus indirectly appealing to the ego need).

A trio of needs

Some psychologists believe in the existence of a trio of basic needs: the needs for power, for affiliation and for achievement. These needs can each be subsumed within Maslow's need hierarchy; considered individually, however, each has a unique relevance to consumer motivation.

Power

The power need relates to an individual's desire to control his or her environment. It includes the need to control other persons and various objects. This need appears to be closely related to the ego need, in that many individuals experience increased self-esteem when they exercise power over objects or people.

Affiliation

Affiliation is a well-known and well-researched social motive that has far-reaching influence on consumer behaviour. The affiliation need suggests that behaviour is strongly influenced by the desire for friendship, for acceptance, for belonging. People with high affiliation needs tend to be socially dependent on others. They often select goods they feel will meet with the approval of friends. Teenagers who hang out at fast-food stores or techies who congregate at computer shows often do so more for the satisfaction of being with others than for making a purchase. An appeal to the affiliation needs of young adults is shown in Figure 5-11. The affiliation need is very similar to Maslow's social need.

Achievement

A considerable number of research studies have focused on the achievement need.[14] Individuals with a strong need for achievement often regard personal accomplishment as an end in itself. The achievement need is closely related to both the egoistic need and the self-actualisation need. People with a high need for achievement tend to be more self-confident, enjoy taking calculated risks, actively research their environments and value feedback. Monetary rewards provide an important type of feedback as to how they are doing. People with high achievement needs prefer situations in which they can take personal responsibility for finding solutions. High achievement is a useful promotional strategy for many products and services targeted to educated and affluent consumers.

In summary, individuals with specific psychological needs tend to be receptive to advertising appeals directed at those needs. They also tend to be receptive to certain kinds of products. Thus, a knowledge of motivational theory provides marketers with key bases for segmenting markets and developing promotional strategies.

MOTIVATIONAL RESEARCH

The term **motivational research**, which should logically include all types of research into human motives, has become a 'term of art' used to refer to qualitative research designed to uncover the consumer's subconscious or hidden motivations. Based on the premise that consumers are not always aware of the reasons for their actions, motivational research attempts to discover underlying feelings, attitudes and emotions concerning product, service or brand use.

The development of motivational research

Sigmund Freud's psychoanalytic theory of personality (discussed in Chapter 6) provided the foundation for the development of motivational research. This theory was built on the premise that unconscious needs or drives – especially biological and sexual drives – are at the heart of human motivation and personality. Freud constructed his theory from patients' recollections of early childhood experiences, analysis of their dreams, and the specific nature of their mental and physical adjustment problems.

Dr Ernest Dichter, formerly a psychoanalyst in Vienna, adapted Freud's psychoanalytical techniques to the study of consumer buying habits. Up to this time, marketing research had focused on what consumers did (i.e. quantitative, descriptive studies). Dichter used qualitative research methods to find out why they did it. Marketers were quickly fascinated by the glib, entertaining and usually surprising explanations offered for consumer behaviour, especially since many of these explanations were grounded in sex. For example, marketers were told that cigarettes were bought because of their sexual symbolism, that men regarded convertible cars as surrogate mistresses and that women baked cakes to fulfil their reproductive yearnings. Before long, almost every major advertising agency had a psychologist on the staff to conduct motivational research studies. Three product profiles developed by Dichter and their applications to contemporary products are presented in Table 5-4.

By the early 1960s, however, marketers realised that motivational research had a number of drawbacks. Because of the intensive nature of qualitative research, samples necessarily were small; thus, there was concern about generalising findings to the total market. Also, marketers soon realised that the analysis of projective tests and depth interviews was highly subjective. The same data given to three different analysts could produce three different reports, each offering its own explanation of the consumer behaviour examined. Critics noted that many of the projective tests that were used had originally been developed for clinical purposes rather than for studies of marketing or consumer behaviour. (One of the basic criteria for test development is that the test be developed and validated for the specific purpose and on the specific audience profile from which information is desired.)

Other consumer theorists noted additional inconsistencies in applying Freudian theory to the study of consumer behaviour. First, psychoanalytic theory was structured specifically for use with disturbed people, whereas consumer behaviourists were interested in explaining the behaviour of 'typical' consumers. Secondly, Freudian theory was developed in an entirely different social context (nineteenth-century Vienna), whereas motivational research was introduced in the 1950s in post-war America. Finally, too many motivational researchers imputed highly exotic (usually sexual) reasons to rather prosaic consumer purchases. Marketers began to question their recommendations (e.g. Is it better to sell a man a pair of braces as a means of holding up his trousers or as a 'reaction to castration anxiety'? Is it easier to persuade a woman to buy a garden hose to water her lawn or as a symbol of 'genital competition with males'?).

TABLE 5-4 Dichter's research: selected product personality profiles and current applications

AUTOMOBILES

According to Dichter, the car allows consumers to convert their subconscious urges to destroy and their fear of death – two key forces in the human psyche – into reality. For example, the expression 'step on it' stems from the desire to feel power, and the phrase 'I just missed that car by inches' reflects the desire to play with danger. Based on this view, Dichter advised Esso (now Exxon) to tap into consumers' aggressive motives for driving cars in promoting the superiority of its gasoline product. The slogan 'Put a tiger in your tank' was developed as a result of his advice.[a]

Dichter also maintained that cars have personalities, and that people become attached to their cars and view them as companions rather than objects. This notion stands behind his views that a man views a convertible as a mistress and a sedan as his wife.

DOLLS

Dolls play an important part in the socialization of children and are universally accepted as an essential toy for girls. Parents choose dolls that have the kind of characteristics they want their children to have, and the doll is an object for both the parents and the children to enjoy. When Mattel introduced Barbie in 1959, the company hired Dichter as a consultant. His research indicated that while girls liked the doll, their mothers detested the doll's perfect bodily proportions and Teutonic appearance. Dichter advised Mattel to market the doll as a teenage fashion model, reflecting the mother's desire for a daughter's proper and fashionable appearance. The advertising themes used subtly told mothers that it is better for their daughters to appear attractive to men rather than nondescript.[b]

ICE CREAM

Dichter described ice cream as an effortless food that does not have to be chewed and that melts in your mouth, a sign of abundance, an almost orgiastic kind of food that people eat as if they want it to run down their chins. Accordingly, he recommended that ice cream packaging should be round, with illustrations that run around the box panel, suggesting unlimited quantity.

Sources: [a]Phil Patton, 'Car Shrinks', *Fortune*, 18 March 2002, 6. [b]Barbara Lippert, 'B-Ball Barbie', *Adweek*, 9 November 1998, 39.

Evaluation of motivational research

Despite its criticisms, motivational research is still regarded as an important tool by marketers who want to gain deeper insights into the whys of consumer behaviour than conventional marketing research techniques can yield. Since motivational research often reveals unsuspected consumer motivations concerning product or brand usage, its principal use today is in the development of new ideas for promotional campaigns, ideas that can penetrate the consumer's conscious awareness by appealing to unrecognised needs.

Motivational research also provides marketers with a basic orientation for new product categories and enables them to explore consumer reactions to ideas and advertising copy at an early stage to avoid costly errors. Furthermore, as with all qualitative research techniques, motivational research findings provide consumer researchers with basic insights that enable them to design structured, quantitative marketing research studies to be conducted on larger, more representative samples of consumers.

SUMMARY

Motivation is the driving force within individuals that impels them to action. This driving force is produced by a state of uncomfortable tension, which exists as the result of an unsatisfied need. All individuals have needs, wants and desires. The individual's subconscious drive to reduce need-induced tension results in behaviour that he or she anticipates will satisfy needs and thus bring about a more comfortable internal state.

All behaviour is goal-oriented. Goals are the sought-after results of motivated behaviour. The form or direction that behaviour takes – the goal that is selected – is a result of thinking processes (cognition) and previous learning. There are two types of goal: generic goals and product-specific goals. A generic goal is a general category of goal that may fulfil a certain need; a product-specific goal is a specifically branded or labelled product that the individual sees as a way to fulfil a need. Product-specific needs are sometimes referred to as wants.

Innate needs – those an individual is born with – are physiological (biogenic) in nature; they include all the factors required to sustain physical life (e.g. food, water, clothing, shelter, sex and physical safety). Acquired needs – those an individual develops after birth – are primarily psychological (psychogenic); they include love, acceptance, esteem and self-fulfilment. For any given need there are many different and appropriate goals. The specific goal selected depends on the individual's experiences, physical capacity, prevailing cultural norms and values and the goal's accessibility in the physical and social environment.

Needs and goals are interdependent and change in response to the individual's physical condition, environment, interaction with other people and experiences. As needs become satisfied, new, higher-order needs emerge that must be fulfilled.

Failure to achieve a goal often results in feelings of frustration. Individuals react to frustration in two ways: 'fight' or 'flight'. They may cope by finding a way around the obstacle that prohibits goal attainment or by adopting a substitute goal (fight); or they may adopt a defence mechanism that enables them to protect their self-esteem (flight). Defence mechanisms include aggression, regression, rationalisation, withdrawal, projection, autism, identification and repression.

Motives cannot easily be inferred from consumer behaviour. People with different needs may seek fulfilment through selection of the same goals; people with the same needs may seek fulfilment through different goals. Although some psychologists have suggested that individuals have different need priorities, others believe that most human beings experience the same basic needs, to which they assign a similar priority ranking. Maslow's hierarchy-of-needs theory proposes five levels of prepotent human needs: physiological needs, safety needs, social needs, egoistic needs and self-actualisation needs. Other needs widely integrated into consumer advertising include the needs for power, affiliation and achievement.

Motivational research is qualitative research designed to delve below the consumer's level of conscious awareness. Despite some shortcomings, motivational research has proved to be of great value to marketers concerned with developing new ideas and new copy appeals.

DISCUSSION QUESTIONS

1. a. 'Marketers don't create needs; needs pre-exist marketers.' Discuss this statement.
   b. Can marketing efforts change consumers' needs? Why or why not?
2. Consumers have both innate and acquired needs. Give examples of each kind of need and show how the same purchase can serve to fulfil either or both kinds of need.
3. Specify both innate and acquired needs that would be useful bases for developing promotional strategies for:
   a. global positioning systems,
   b. sunglasses with built-in earphones and MP3 player,
   c. a holiday to Australia,
   d. a new super-compact and powerful digital camera.

4. Why are consumers' needs and goals constantly changing? What factors influence the formation of new goals?
5. How can marketers use consumers' failures at achieving goals in developing promotional appeals for specific products and services? Give examples.
6. Most human needs are dormant much of the time. What factors cause their arousal? Give examples of advertisements for TV equipment that are designed to arouse latent consumer needs.
7. For each of the situations listed in Question 3, select one level from Maslow's hierarchy of human needs that can be used to segment the market and position the product (or the organisation). Explain your choices. What are the advantages and disadvantages of using Maslow's need hierarchy for segmentation and positioning applications?

EXERCISES

1. You are a member of an advertising team assembled to develop a promotional campaign for a new digital camera. Develop three headlines for this campaign, each based on one of the levels in Maslow's need hierarchy.
2. Find two advertisements that depict two different defence mechanisms and discuss their effectiveness.
3. Find three advertisements that are designed to appeal to the needs for power, affiliation and achievement, and discuss their effectiveness.

NOTES

1. Andrew Tobias, *Fire and Ice* (New York: William Morrow and Company, 1976), Chapter 8.
2. Ibid.
3. Richard P. Bagozzi and Utpal Dholakia, 'Goal Setting and Goal Striving in Consumer Behavior', *Journal of Marketing*, 1999, 19–32.
4. Alexander Chernev, 'Goal Orientation and Consumer Preference for the Status Quo', *Journal of Consumer Research*, December 2004, 557–65.
5. Michel Tuan Pham and Tamar Avnet, 'Ideals and Oughts and the Reliance on Affect versus Substance in Persuasion', *Journal of Consumer Research*, March 2004, 503–19.
6. Maria J. Louro, Rik Pieters and Marcel Zeelenberg, 'Negative Returns on Positive Emotions: The Influence of Pride and Self-Regulatory Goals on Repurchase Decisions', *Journal of Consumer Research*, March 2005, 833–41.
7. James A. Roberts and Stephen F. Pirog, III, 'Personal Goals and Their Role in Consumer Behavior: The Case of Compulsive Buying', *Journal of Marketing Theory and Practice*, Summer 2004, 61–73.
8. See Abraham H. Maslow, 'A Theory of Human Motivation', *Psychological Review*, 50, 1943, 370–96; Abraham H. Maslow, *Motivation and Personality* (New York: Harper & Row, 1954); and Abraham H. Maslow, *Toward a Psychology of Being* (New York: Van Nostrand Reinhold, 1968), 189–215.
9. A number of studies have focused on human levels of aspiration. See, for example, Kurt Lewin *et al.*, 'Level of Aspiration', in *Personality and Behavior Disorders*, ed. J. McV. Hunt (New York: Ronald Press, 1944); Howard Garland, 'Goal Levels and Task Performance, a Compelling Replication of Some Compelling Results', *Journal of Applied Psychology*, 67, 1982, 245–8; Edwin A. Locke, Elizabeth Frederick, Cynthia Lee and Philip Bobko, 'Effect of

Self Efficacy, Goals and Task Strategies on Task Performance', *Journal of Applied Psychology*, 69, 2, 1984, 241–51; Edwin A. Locke, Elizabeth Frederick, Elizabeth Buckner and Philip Bobko, 'Effect of Previously Assigned Goals on Self Set Goals and Performance', *Journal of Applied Psychology*, 72, 2, 1987, 204–11; and John R. Hollenbeck and Howard J. Klein, 'Goal Commitment and the Goal Setting Process: Problems, Prospects and Proposals for Future Research', *Journal of Applied Psychology*, 2, 1987, 212–20.

10. Clive Thompson, 'The Play's the Thing', *New York Times Magazine*, 11 November 2004, 49ff.
11. Maslow, 'A Theory of Human Motivation', 380.
12. Ibid.
13. Ibid.
14. See, for example, David C. McClelland, *Studies in Motivation* (New York: Appleton Century Crofts, 1955); David C. McClelland, 'Business Drive and National Achievement', *Harvard Business Review*, July–August 1962; 'Achievement Motivation Can Be Developed', *Harvard Business Review*, 5, 24, November–December 1965; and Abraham K. Korman, *The Psychology of Motivation* (Upper Saddle River, NJ: Prentice Hall, 1974).

CHAPTER 6
PERSONALITY AND CONSUMER BEHAVIOUR

Marketers have long tried to appeal to consumers in terms of their personality characteristics. They have intuitively felt that what consumers purchase and when and how they consume are likely to be influenced by personality factors. For this reason, advertising and marketing people have frequently depicted (or incorporated) specific personality traits or characteristics in their marketing and advertising messages. A recent example is an appeal to individuality for the Harley-Davidson motorcycle where the headline says, 'We're all created equal. But after that, it's up to you.'

This chapter is designed to provide the reader with an understanding of how personality and self-concept are related to various aspects of consumer behaviour. It examines what personality is, reviews several major personality theories, and describes how these theories have stimulated marketing interest in the study of consumer personality. The chapter considers the important topics of brand personality, how the related concepts of self and self-image influence consumer attitudes and behaviour and concludes with an exploration of virtual personality or self.

WHAT IS PERSONALITY?

The study of **personality** has been approached by theorists in a variety of ways. Some have emphasised the dual influence of heredity and early childhood experiences on personality development; others have stressed broader social and environmental influences and the fact that personalities develop continuously over time. Some theorists prefer to view personality as a unified whole; others focus on specific traits. The wide variation in viewpoints makes it difficult to arrive at a single definition. However, we propose that personality be defined as those inner psychological characteristics that both determine and reflect how a person responds to his or her environment.

The emphasis in this definition is on inner characteristics – those specific qualities, attributes, traits, factors and mannerisms that distinguish one individual from other individuals. As discussed later in the chapter, the deeply ingrained characteristics that we call personality are likely to influence the individual's product choices: they affect the way consumers respond to marketers' promotional efforts, and when, where and how they consume particular products or services. Therefore, the identification of specific personality characteristics associated with consumer behaviour has proved to be highly useful in the development of a firm's market segmentation strategies.

The nature of personality

In the study of personality, three distinct properties are of central importance:

1. personality reflects individual differences;
2. personality is consistent and enduring; and
3. personality can change.

Personality Reflects Individual Differences

Because the inner characteristics that constitute an individual's personality are a unique combination of factors, no two individuals are exactly alike. Nevertheless, many individuals may be similar in terms of a single personality characteristic but not in terms of others. For instance, some people can be described as 'high' in venturesomeness (e.g. willing to accept the risk of doing something new or different, such as skydiving or mountain climbing), whereas others can be described as 'low' in venturesomeness (e.g. afraid to buy a recently introduced product). Personality is a useful concept because it enables us to categorise consumers into different groups on the basis of one or even several traits. If each person were different in terms of all personality traits, it would be impossible to group consumers into segments, and there would be little reason for marketers to develop products and promotional campaigns targeted to particular segments.

Personality Is Consistent and Enduring

An individual's personality tends to be both consistent and enduring. Indeed, the mother who comments that her child 'has been impulsive from the day he was born' is supporting the contention that personality has both consistency and endurance. Both qualities are essential if marketers are to explain or predict consumer behaviour in terms of personality.

Although marketers cannot change consumers' personalities to conform to their products, if they know which personality characteristics influence specific consumer responses they can attempt to appeal to the relevant traits inherent in their target group of consumers.

Even though consumers' personalities may be consistent, their consumption behaviour often varies considerably because of the various psychological, sociocultural, environmental and situational factors that affect behaviour. For instance, although an individual's personality may be relatively stable, specific needs or motives, attitudes, reactions to group pressures, and even responses to newly available brands may cause a change in the person's behaviour. Personality is only one of a combination of factors that influence how a consumer behaves.

Personality Can Change

Under certain circumstances personalities change. For instance, an individual's personality may be altered by major life events, such as the birth of a child, the death of a loved one, a divorce or a significant career promotion. An individual's personality changes not only in response to abrupt events but also as part of a gradual maturing process – 'She's growing up, she is much calmer,' says an aunt after not seeing her niece for five years.

There is also evidence that personality stereotypes may change over time. More specifically, although it is felt that men's personality has generally remained relatively constant over the past 50 years, women's personality has seemed to become increasingly more masculine and should continue to do so over the next 50 years. This prediction indicates a convergence in the personality characteristics of men and women.[1] The reason for this shift is that women have been moving into occupations that have traditionally been dominated by men and, therefore, are being increasingly associated with masculine personality attributes.

THEORIES OF PERSONALITY

This section briefly reviews three major theories of personality:

1. **Freudian theory**.
2. **neo-Freudian theory**, and
3. **trait theory**.

These theories have been chosen for discussion from among many theories of personality because each has played a prominent role in the study of the relationship between consumer behaviour and personality.

Freudian theory

Sigmund Freud's **psychoanalytic theory** of personality is a cornerstone of modern psychology. This theory was built on the premise that unconscious needs or drives, especially sexual and other biological drives, are at the heart of human motivation and personality. Freud constructed his theory on the basis of patients' recollections of early childhood experiences, analysis of their dreams and the specific nature of their mental and physical adjustment problems.

Id, Superego and Ego

Based on his analyses, Freud proposed that the human personality consists of three interacting systems: the id, the superego and the ego. The *id* is conceptualised as a 'warehouse' of primitive and impulsive drives – basic physiological needs such as thirst, hunger and sex – for which the individual seeks immediate satisfaction without concern for the specific means of satisfaction.

In contrast to the id, the *superego* is conceptualised as the individual's internal expression of society's moral and ethical codes of conduct. The superego's role is to see that the individual satisfies needs in a socially acceptable fashion. Thus, the superego is a kind of brake that restrains or inhibits the impulsive forces of the id.

Finally, the *ego* is the individual's conscious control. It functions as an internal monitor that attempts to balance the impulsive demands of the id and the sociocultural constraints of the superego. Figure 6-1 represents the interrelationships among the three interacting systems. In addition to specifying a structure for personality, Freud emphasised that an individual's

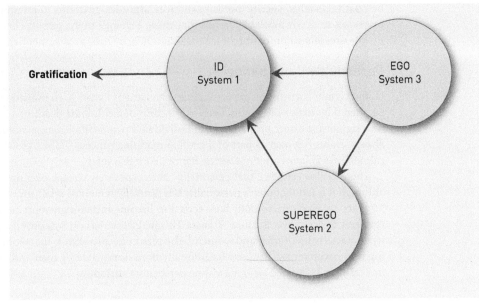

FIGURE 6-1 A representation of the relationships among the id, ego and superego

personality is formed as he or she passes through a number of distinct stages of infant and childhood development. These are the oral, anal, phallic, latent and genital stages. Freud labelled four of these stages of development to conform to the area of the body on which he believed the child's sexual instincts are focused at the time.

According to Freudian theory, an adult's personality is determined by how well he or she deals with the crises that are experienced while passing through each of these stages (particularly the first three). For instance, if a child's oral needs are not adequately satisfied at the first stage of development, the person may become fixated at this stage and as an adult display a personality that includes such traits as dependence and excessive oral activity (e.g. gum chewing and smoking). When an individual is fixated at the anal stage, the adult personality may display other traits, such as an excessive need for neatness.

Freudian Theory and 'Product Personality'

Researchers who apply Freud's psychoanalytic theory to the study of consumer personality believe that human drives are largely unconscious and that consumers are primarily unaware of their true reasons for buying what they buy. These researchers tend to see consumer purchases and/or consumption situations as a reflection and an extension of the consumer's own personality. In other words, they consider the consumer's appearance and possessions – grooming, clothing, jewellery and so forth – as reflections of the individual's personality. Table 6-1 presents the results of a study of 19,000 consumers that examines the link between snack food perceptions and selected personality traits.[2] The findings of the research, for example, reveal that potato chips (crisps) are associated with being ambitious, successful, a high achiever and impatient with less than the best, whereas popcorn seems to be related to a personality that takes charge, pitches in often, is modest and self-confident but not a show-off. (The related topics of brand personality, and the self and self-images are considered later in the chapter.)

Neo-freudian theory

Several of Freud's colleagues disagreed with his contention that personality is primarily instinctual and sexual in nature. Instead, these neo-Freudians believed that social relationships are

TABLE 6-1 Snack foods and personality traits

SNACK FOOD	PERSONALITY TRAITS
Potato chips	Ambitious, successful, high achiever, impatient with less than the best.
Tortilla chips	Perfectionist, high expectations, punctual, conservative, responsible.
Pretzels	Lively, easily bored with same old routine, flirtatious, intuitive, may overcommit to projects.
Snack crackers	Rational, logical, contemplative, shy, prefers time alone.
Cheese curls	Conscientious, principled, proper, fair, may appear rigid but has great integrity, plans ahead, loves order.
Nuts	Easygoing, empathetic, understanding, calm, even-tempered.
Popcorn	Takes charge, pitches in often, modest, self-confident but not a show-off.
Meat snacks	Gregarious, generous, trustworthy, tends to be overly trusting.

Source: Adapted from *What Flavor is Your Personality? Discover Who You Are by Looking at What You Eat.* by Alan Hirsch, MD, Naperville, Il, Sourcebooks, 2001.

fundamental to the formation and development of personality. For instance, Alfred Adler viewed human beings as seeking to attain various rational goals, which he called style of life. He also placed much emphasis on the individual's efforts to overcome feelings of inferiority (i.e. by striving for superiority). Harry Stack Sullivan, another neo-Freudian, stressed that people continuously attempt to establish significant and rewarding relationships with others. He was particularly concerned with the individual's efforts to reduce tensions, such as anxiety.

Like Sullivan, Karen Horney was also interested in anxiety. She focused on the impact of child–parent relationships and the individual's desire to conquer feelings of anxiety. Horney proposed that individuals be classified into three personality groups: compliant, aggressive and detached (CAD).[3]

1. Compliant individuals are those who move towards others (they desire to be loved, wanted and appreciated).
2. Aggressive individuals are those who move against others (they desire to excel and win admiration).
3. Detached individuals are those who move away from others (they desire independence, self-reliance, self-sufficiency, and individualism or freedom from obligations).

A personality test based on Horney's CAD theory has been developed and tested within the context of consumer behaviour.[4] The initial CAD research uncovered a number of tentative relationships between college students' scores and their product and brand usage patterns. More recent research has found that children who scored high in self-reliance – who preferred to do things independently of others (i.e. detached personalities) – were less likely to be brand loyal and were more likely to try different brands.[5]

Many marketers use some of these neo-Freudian theories intuitively. For example, marketers who position their products or services as providing an opportunity to belong or to be appreciated by others in a group or social setting would seem to be guided by Horney's characterisation of the compliant individual.

Trait theory

Trait theory constitutes a major departure from the qualitative measures that typify the Freudian and neo-Freudian movements (e.g. personal observation, self-reported experiences, dream analysis, projective techniques).

The orientation of trait theory is primarily quantitative or empirical; it focuses on the measurement of personality in terms of specific psychological characteristics, called traits. A trait is defined as 'any distinguishing, relatively enduring way in which one individual differs from another'.[6] Trait theorists are concerned with the construction of personality tests (or inventories) that enable them to pinpoint individual differences in terms of specific traits.

Selected single-trait personality tests (which measure just one trait, such as self-confidence) are often developed specifically for use in consumer behaviour studies. These tailor-made personality tests measure such traits as **consumer innovativeness** (how receptive a person is to new experiences), **consumer materialism** (the degree of the consumer's attachment to 'worldly possessions') and **consumer ethnocentrism** (the consumer's likelihood to accept or reject foreign-made products).

Trait researchers have found that it is generally more realistic to expect personality to be linked to how consumers make their choices and to the purchase or consumption of a broad product category rather than a specific brand. For example, there is more likely to be a relationship between a personality trait and whether or not an individual owns a convertible sports car than between a personality trait and the brand of convertible sports car purchased.

The next section shows how trait measures of personality are used to expand our understanding of consumer behaviour.

PERSONALITY AND UNDERSTANDING CONSUMER DIVERSITY

Marketers are interested in understanding how personality influences consumption behaviour because such knowledge enables them to understand consumers better and to segment and target those consumers who are likely to respond positively to their product or service communications. Several specific personality traits that provide insights about consumer behaviour are examined next.

Consumer innovativeness and related personality traits

Marketing practitioners try to learn all they can about **consumer innovators** – those who are likely to be the first to try new products, services or practices – for the market response of such innovators is often a critical indication of the eventual success or failure of a new product or service.

Personality traits that have been useful in differentiating between consumer innovators and non-innovators include consumer innovativeness, dogmatism, social character, need for uniqueness, optimum stimulation level, sensation seeking, and variety or novelty seeking. (Chapter 15 examines non-personality characteristics that distinguish between consumer innovators and non-innovators.)

Consumer Innovativeness

Consumer researchers have endeavoured to develop measurement instruments to gauge the level of consumer innovativeness, because such personality trait measures provide important insights into the nature and boundaries of a consumer's willingness to innovate.[7] Over the years, the trait of consumer innovativeness has been linked to the need for stimulation, novelty seeking and the need for uniqueness – three other traits that will be discussed later in this chapter.[8] Table 6-2 presents two alternative scales for measuring consumer innovativeness, the first measuring general innovativeness and the second measuring domain-specific (i.e. product-specific) innovativeness.

Available consumer research indicates a positive relationship between innovative use of the Internet and buying online.[9] Other research exploring the association between personality traits and innovative Internet behaviour has reported that Internet shoppers tend to see themselves as being able to control their own future, using the Internet to seek out information, enjoying change and not being afraid of uncertainty.[10]

TABLE 6-2 Two consumer innovativeness measurement scales

A 'GENERAL' CONSUMER INNOVATIVENESS SCALE

1. I would rather stick to a brand I usually buy than try something I am not very sure of.
2. When I go to a restaurant, I feel it is safer to order dishes I am familiar with.
3. If I like a brand, I rarely switch from it just to try something different.
4. I enjoy taking chances in buying unfamiliar brands just to get some variety in my purchase.
5. When I see a new brand on the shelf, I'm not afraid of giving it a try.

A DOMAIN-SPECIFIC CONSUMER INNOVATIVENESS SCALE

1. Compared to my friends, I own few rock albums.
2. In general, I am the last in my circle of friends to know the titles of the latest rock albums.
3. In general, I am among the first in my circle of friends to buy a new rock album when it appears.
4. If I heard that a new rock album was available in the store, I would be interested enough to buy it.
5. I will buy a new rock album, even if I haven't heard it yet.
6. I know the names of new rock acts before other people do.

Source: Adapted from Gilles Roehrich, 'Consumer Innovativeness: Concepts and Measurements', *Journal of Business Research*, 57, June 2004, 674.

Dogmatism

Consumer responses to distinctively unfamiliar products or product features (i.e. level of dogmatism – a personality-linked behaviour) is of keen interest to many marketers, especially marketers of technologically rich products. **Dogmatism** is a personality trait that measures the degree of rigidity (versus openness) that individuals display towards the unfamiliar and towards information that is contrary to their own established beliefs.[11] A person who is highly dogmatic approaches the unfamiliar defensively and with considerable discomfort and uncertainty. At the other end of the spectrum, a person who is low in dogmatism will readily consider unfamiliar or opposing beliefs.

Consumers who are low in dogmatism (open-minded) are more likely to prefer innovative products to established or traditional alternatives. In contrast, highly dogmatic (closed-minded) consumers are more likely to choose established, rather than innovative, product alternatives.

Highly dogmatic consumers tend to be more receptive to advertisements for new products or services that contain an appeal from an authoritative figure. To this end, marketers have used celebrities and experts in their new-product advertising to make it easier for potentially reluctant consumers (non-innovators) to accept the innovation. In contrast, low-dogmatic consumers (who are frequently high in innovativeness) seem to be more receptive to messages that stress factual differences, product benefits and other forms of product-usage information.

Social Character

The personality trait known as social character has its origins in sociological research, which focuses on the identification and classification of individuals into distinct sociocultural types. As used in consumer psychology, social character is a personality trait that ranges on a continuum from **inner-directedness** to **other-directedness**. Inner-directed consumers tend to rely on their own inner values or standards in evaluating new products and are likely to be consumer innovators. Conversely, other-directed consumers tend to look to others for direction on what is right or wrong; thus, they are less likely to be consumer innovators.

Inner- and other-directed consumers are attracted to different types of promotional messages. Inner-directed people seem to prefer advertisements that stress product features and personal benefits (enabling them to use their own values and standards in evaluating products),

TABLE 6-3 Sample items from a consumers' need for uniqueness scale[a]

I collect unusual products as a way of telling people I'm different.
When dressing, I have sometimes dared to be different in ways that others are likely to disapprove.
When products or brands I like become extremely popular, I lose interest in them.
As far as I'm concerned, when it comes to the products I buy and the situations in which I use them, customs and rules are made to be broken.
I have sometimes purchased unusual products or brands as a way to create a more distinctive personal image.
I sometimes look for one-of-a-kind products or brands so that I create a style that is all my own.
I avoid products or brands that have already been accepted and purchased by the average consumer.

[a]This inventory is measured on a 5-point Likert scale ranging from 'strongly agree' to 'strongly disagree'.
Source: Adapted from Kelly Tepper Tian, William O. Bearden and Gary L. Hunter, 'Consumers' Need for Uniqueness: Scale Development and Validation', *Journal of Consumer Research*, 28, June 2001, 50–66, published by The University of Chicago Press. Copyright © 2001, JCR, Inc.

whereas other-directed people prefer advertisements that feature an approving social environment or social acceptance (in keeping with their tendency to look to others for direction). Thus, other-directed individuals may be more easily influenced because of their natural inclination to go beyond the content of an advertisement and think in terms of likely social approval of a potential purchase.

Need for Uniqueness

We all know people who seek to be unique. For these people conformity to others' expectations or standards, either in appearance or in their possessions, is something to be avoided. Moreover, we would expect that it is easier to express or act uniquely if one does not have to pay a price in the form of others' criticism. Supporting this perspective, a recent study of consumers' need for uniqueness (NFU) explored the circumstances under which high NFU individuals do (and do not) make unconventional (i.e. unique) choices. The research revealed that when consumers are asked to explain their choices, but are not concerned about being criticised by others, they are more receptive to making unique choices.[12] Seeing the importance of NFU, other consumer researchers have developed an inventory to measure the trait within the context of consumer behaviour. Table 6-3 presents a sample of items drawn from the inventory.

Optimum Stimulation Level

Some people seem to prefer a simple, uncluttered and calm existence, whereas others prefer an environment crammed with novel, complex and unusual experiences. Consumer research has examined how such variations in individual needs for stimulation may be related to consumer behaviour. Research has found that high **optimum stimulation levels (OSLs)** are linked with greater willingness to take risks, to try new products, to be innovative, to seek purchase-related information and to accept new retail facilities than low OSLs. One recent study investigating students' willingness to select mass customisation of fashion items (e.g. a pair of jeans that are especially measured, cut and sewn so they offer a better fit or appearance), found that OSL predicted two factors – students' openness to experimentation with appearance (e.g. 'I try on some of the newest clothes each season to see how I look in the styles') and enhancement of individuality (e.g. 'I try to buy clothes that are very unusual').[13]

OSL scores also seem to reflect a person's desired level of lifestyle stimulation.[14] For instance, consumers whose actual lifestyles are equivalent to their OSL scores appear to be quite satisfied, whereas those whose lifestyles are understimulated (their OSL scores are greater than the lifestyle they are currently living) are likely to be bored. Those whose lifestyles are overstimulated (their OSLs are lower than current reality) are likely to seek rest or relief. This suggests that the relationship between consumers' lifestyles and their OSLs is likely to influence their choices of products or services and how they manage and spend their time. For instance, a person who feels bored (an understimulated consumer) is likely to be attracted to a holiday that offers a great deal of activity and excitement. In contrast, a person who feels overwhelmed (an over-stimulated consumer) is likely to seek a quiet, isolated, relaxing and rejuvenating holiday.

Sensation Seeking

Closely related to the OSL concept is **sensation seeking (SS)**, which has been defined as 'a trait characterised by the need for varied, novel, and complex sensations and experience, and the willingness to take physical and social risks for the sake of such experience'. Research evidence shows that teenage males with higher SS scores are more likely than other teenagers to prefer listening to heavy metal music and to engage in reckless or even dangerous behaviour.[15]

Variety or Novelty Seeking

Still another personality-driven trait quite similar to and related to OSL is **variety or novelty seeking**.[16] There appear to be many different types of consumer variety seeking: exploratory purchase behaviour (switching brands to experience new and possibly better alternatives), vicarious exploration (securing information about a new or different alternative and then contemplating or even daydreaming about the option), and use innovativeness (using an already adopted product in a new or novel way).[17] The use innovativeness trait is particularly relevant to technological products (such as home electronics products), in which some models offer an abundance of features and functions, whereas others contain just a few essential features or functions. For example, a consumer with a high variety-seeking score might purchase a mobile phone with more features than a consumer with a lower variety-seeking score. Consumers with high variety-seeking scores are also more likely to be attracted to brands that claim to have novel features or multiple uses or applications. Still further, there appears to be a relationship between variety seeking and time of day, with greater variety-seeking behaviour occurring when the consumer is experiencing arousal lows (as opposed to arousal peaks). And during the time of day when arousal seeking is relatively minimal, leader brands fare better, while follower brands do better during periods of the day when variety seeking is heightened.[18]

Marketers, up to a point, benefit by offering additional options to consumers seeking more product variety because consumers with a high need for variety tend to search for marketers that provide a diverse product line (offering much choice).[19] However, a point may be reached where a marketer might offer too many products with too many features. In such a case, the consumer may be turned off and avoid a product line with too much variety. Ultimately, in searching for the 'just right', marketers must walk the fine line between offering consumers too little and too much choice. Additionally, research has shown that variety seekers often use price promotions as a low-cost way to try different brands over time – high-variety seekers tend to pay lower prices for the same item than do low-variety seekers.[20]

The stream of research examined here indicates that the consumer innovator differs from the non-innovator in terms of personality orientation. A knowledge of such personality differences should help marketers select target segments for new products and then to design distinctive promotional strategies for specific segments.

Cognitive personality factors

Consumer researchers have been increasingly interested in how **cognitive personality** factors influence various aspects of consumer behaviour. In particular, two cognitive personality traits – **need for cognition** and **visualisers** versus **verbalisers** – have been useful in understanding selected aspects of consumer behaviour.

Need for Cognition

A promising cognitive personality characteristic is need for cognition (NC). It measures a person's craving for or enjoyment of thinking. Available research indicates that consumers who are high in NC are more likely to be responsive to the part of an advertisement that is rich in product-related information or description; consumers who are relatively low in NC are more likely to be attracted to the background or peripheral aspects of an advertisement, such as an attractive model or well-known celebrity.[21] In this realm, research among adolescents compared the effectiveness of a cartoon message and a written message. As expected, for low-NC subjects, the cartoon message was more effective in changing attitudes and subjective norms, whereas the written message was more effective for high-NC adolescents.[22] In still another study, it was found that message framing (e.g. positively emphasising a brand's advantages) has more impact on low-NC individuals than it has on high-NC individuals.[23] Furthermore, research suggests that consumers who are high in NC are likely to spend more time processing print advertisements, which results in superior brand and advertisement claim recall.[24]

Need for cognition seems to play a role in an individual's use of the Internet. More precisely, NC has been positively related to Internet use for product information, current events and news, and learning and education – all activities that incorporate a cognitive element.[25] One study examined both need for cognition and sensation seeking (discussed earlier in this chapter) with regard to website complexity. The research discovered that the subjects preferred websites with a medium level of complexity (rather than high or low complexity). Still further, those with a high need for cognition tended to evaluate websites with low visual complexity and high verbal complexity more favourably. In contrast, those who were high sensation seekers tended to prefer complex visual designs, whereas those who were low sensation seekers preferred simple visual designs.[26]

Such research insights provide advertisers with valuable guidelines for creating advertising messages (including supporting art) that appeal to a particular target audience grouping's need for cognition.

Visualisers versus Verbalisers

It is fairly well established that some people seem to be more open to and prefer the written word as a way of securing information, whereas others are more likely to respond to and prefer visual images or messages as sources of information. Consistent with such individual differences, cognitive personality research classifies consumers into two groups: *visualisers* (consumers who prefer visual information and products that stress the visual, such as membership in a video club) or *verbalisers* (consumers who prefer written or verbal information and products, such as membership in book clubs). Some marketers stress strong visual dimensions in order to attract visualisers; others raise a question and provide the answer, or feature a detailed description or point-by-point explanation to attract verbalisers (see Figure 6-2).

From consumer materialism to compulsive consumption

Consumer researchers have become increasingly interested in exploring various consumption and possession traits. These traits range from consumer materialism to fixated consumption behaviour to compulsive consumption behaviour.

Consumer Materialism

Materialism (the extent to which a person is considered materialistic) is a topic frequently discussed in newspapers, in magazines and on television (e.g. 'Americans are very materialistic') and in everyday conversations between friends ('He's so materialistic!').

FIGURE 6-2 IKEA targets verbalisers

Source: Tillsammans together with IKEA, illustrator Lotta Kühlhorn, with agency Agent Bauer. Used with the permission of Inter IKEA Systems BV.

Materialism, as a personality-like trait, distinguishes between individuals who regard possessions as essential to their identities and their lives and those for whom possessions are secondary.[27] Researchers have found some general support for the following characteristics of materialistic people:

1. they especially value acquiring and showing off possessions;
2. they are particularly self-centred and selfish;

TABLE 6-4 Sample items from a materialism scale

SUCCESS
The things I own say a lot about how well I'm doing in life.
I don't place much emphasis on the amount of material objects people own as a sign of success.[a]
I like to own things that impress people.

CENTRALITY
I enjoy spending money on things that aren't practical.
I try to keep my life simple, as far as possessions are concerned.[a]
Buying things gives me a lot of pleasure.

HAPPINESS
I'd be happier if I could afford to buy more things.
I have all the things I really need to enjoy life.[a]
It sometimes bothers me quite a bit that I can't afford to buy all the things I'd like.

Note: Measured on a 5-point 'agreement' scale.
[a]Items are negatively worded and are scored inversely.
Source: Adapted from Marsha L. Richins and Scott Dawson, 'A Consumer Values Orientation for Materialism and Its Measurement: Scale Development and Validation', *Journal of Consumer Research*, 19, December 1992, 310. Reprinted by permission of The University of Chicago Press as publisher. Copyright © 1992, JCR, Inc.

3. they seek lifestyles full of possessions (e.g. they desire to have lots of 'things', rather than a simple, uncluttered lifestyle); and

4. their many possessions do not give them greater personal satisfaction (i.e. their possessions do not lead to greater happiness).[28]

Table 6-4 presents sample items from a materialism scale.

Fixated Consumption Behaviour

Somewhere between materialism and compulsion, with respect to buying or possessing objects, is the notion of being fixated with regard to consuming or possessing. Like materialism, fixated consumption behaviour is in the realm of normal and socially acceptable behaviour. Fixated consumers do not keep their objects or purchases of interest a secret; rather, they frequently display them, and their involvement is openly shared with others who have a similar interest. In the world of serious collectors (Barbie dolls, rare antique teddy bears or almost anything else that has drawn collectors), there are countless millions of fixated consumers pursuing their interests and trying to add to their collections.

Fixated consumers typically possess the following characteristics:

1. a deep (possibly passionate) interest in a particular object or product category,
2. a willingness to go to considerable lengths to secure additional examples of the object or product category of interest, and
3. the dedication of a considerable amount of discretionary time and money to searching out the object or product.[29]

This profile of the fixated consumer describes many collectors or hobbyists (e.g. collectors of coins, stamps, antiques, vintage wristwatches or fountain pens). Research exploring the dynamics of the fixated consumer (in this case, coin collectors) revealed that, for fixated consumers, there is not only an enduring involvement in the object category itself but also a considerable amount of involvement in the process of acquiring the object (sometimes referred to as the 'hunt').[30]

TABLE 6-5 Sample items from scales to measure compulsive buying

---

VALENCE, D'ASTOUS, AND FORTIER COMPULSIVE BUYING SCALE

1. When I have money, I cannot help but spend part or the whole of it.
2. I am often impulsive in my buying behavior.
3. As soon as I enter a shopping center, I have an irresistible urge to go into a shop to buy something.
4. I am one of those people who often responds to direct-mail offers (e.g., books or compact discs).
5. I have often bought a product that I did not need, while knowing I had very little money left.

FABER AND O'GUINN COMPULSIVE BUYING SCALE

1. If I have any money left at the end of the pay period, I just have to spend it.
2. I felt others would be horrified if they knew my spending habits.
3. I have bought things even though I couldn't afford them.
4. I wrote a check when I knew I didn't have enough money in the bank to cover it.
5. I bought something in order to make myself feel better.

Source: Gilles Valence, Alain d'Astous and Louis Fortier, 'Compulsive Buying: Concept and Measurement', *Journal of Consumer Policy*, 11, 1988, 419–33; Ronald J. Faber and Thomas C. O'Guinn, 'A Clinical Screener for Compulsive Buying', *Journal of Consumer Research*, 19, December 1992, 459–69; and Leslie Cole and Dan Sherrell, 'Comparing Scales to Measure Compulsive Buying: An Exploration of Their Dimensionality', in *Advances in Consumer Research*, 22, eds. Frank R. Kardes and Mita Sujan (Provo, UT: Association for Consumer Research, 1995), 419–27.

Compulsive Consumption Behaviour

Unlike materialism and fixated consumption, **compulsive consumption** is in the realm of abnormal behaviour – an example of the dark side of consumption. Consumers who are compulsive have an addiction; in some respects they are out of control, and their actions may have damaging consequences for them and those around them. Examples of compulsive consumption problems are uncontrollable shopping, gambling, drug addiction, alcoholism and various food and eating disorders.[31] For instance, there are many women and a small number of men who are chocoholics – they have an intense craving (also termed an addiction) for chocolate.[32] From a marketing and consumer behaviour perspective, compulsive buying can also be included in any list of compulsive activities. To control or possibly eliminate such compulsive problems generally requires some type of therapy or clinical treatment. There have been some research efforts to develop a screener inventory to pinpoint compulsive buying behaviour. Table 6-5 presents sample items from several of these scales. Evidence suggests that some consumers use self-gifting, impulse buying and compulsive buying as a way to influence or manage their moods; that is, the act of purchasing may convert a negative mood to a more positive one ('I'm depressed, I'll go out shopping and I'll feel better').[33]

Consumer ethnocentrism: responses to foreign-made products

In an effort to distinguish between consumer segments that are likely to be receptive to foreign-made products and those that are not, researchers have developed and tested the consumer ethnocentrism scale, called CETSCALE (see Table 6-6).[34] The CETSCALE has been successful in identifying consumers with a predisposition to accept (or reject) foreign-made products.

TABLE 6-6 The consumer ethnocentrism scale – CETSCALE

1. Italian people should always buy Italian-made products instead of imports.
2. Only those products that are unavailable in Italy should be imported.
3. Buy Italian-made products. Keep Italy working.
4. Italian products, first, last, and foremost.
5. Purchasing foreign-made products is un-Italian.
6. It is not right to purchase foreign products, because it puts Italians out of jobs.
7. A real Italian should always buy Italian-made products.
8. We should purchase products manufactured in Italy instead of letting other countries get rich off us.
9. It is always best to purchase Italian products.
10. There should be very little trading or purchasing of goods from other countries unless out of necessity.
11. Italians should not buy foreign products, because this hurts Italian business and causes unemployment.
12. Curbs should be put on all imports.
13. It may cost me in the long run but I prefer to support Italian products.
14. Foreigners should not be allowed to put their products on our markets.
15. Foreign products should be taxed heavily to reduce their entry into Italy.
16. We should buy from foreign countries only those products that we cannot obtain within our own country.
17. Italian consumers who purchase products made in other countries are responsible for putting their fellow Italians out of work.

Notes: Response format is a 7-point Likert-type scale (strongly agree 7, strongly disagree 1). Range of scores is from 17 to 119. Calculated from confirmatory factor analysis of data from a four-area study.

Source: Adapted from Terence A. Shimp and Subhash Sharma, 'Consumer Ethnocentrism: Construction and Validation of the CETSCALE', *Journal of Marketing Research*, 24, August 1987, 282. Reprinted by permission.

Consumers who are highly ethnocentric are likely to feel that it is inappropriate or wrong to purchase foreign-made products because of the resulting economic impact on the domestic economy, whereas non-ethnocentric consumers tend to evaluate foreign-made products – ostensibly more objectively – for their extrinsic characteristics (e.g. 'how good are they?'). A portion of the consumers who would score low on an ethnocentric scale are actually likely to be quite receptive to products made in foreign countries.

Ethnocentrism has been found to vary by country and product. Mexican consumers, for example, are more ethnocentric than their French counterparts; and Malaysian consumers, while preferring to purchase trousers, shirts, undergarments and belts that are manufactured locally, want to buy imported sunglasses and watches.[35]

Marketers successfully target ethnocentric consumers in any national market by stressing a nationalistic theme in their promotional appeals (e.g. 'Made in Finland' or 'Made in France') because this segment is predisposed to buy products made in their native land. In trying to appeal to both ethnocentric Norwegians and non-ethnocentric tourists, the producer of wool underwear, Devold, claims that their products have been 'worn by Norwegians since 1853' (see Figure 6-3).

One study examining the preferences of UK consumers across eight product categories found that domestic country bias (a preference for products manufactured in a consumer's country of residence) varied among product categories. This means that a domestic

FIGURE 6-3 Devold appeals to ethnocentric Norwegians and non-ethnocentric tourists (who experience the cold temperatures in Norway)
Source: Devold of Norway AS.

manufacturer cannot expect that local consumers will automatically prefer their offerings over imported ones.[36] Still further, one research study found that the product attitude of consumers with little knowledge about the product is more strongly influenced by country-of-origin perceptions than the product attitude of consumers with high knowledge.[37] Table 6-7 presents a marketing mix strategy that can be used to manage country-of-origin

TABLE 6-7 Strategies for managing country-of-origin effects

| MARKETING MIX | COUNTRY IMAGE | |
	POSITIVE	NEGATIVE
Product	Emphasise 'Made In'	Emphasise Brand Name
Price	Premium Price	Low Price to Attract Value Conscious
Place (Channel of Distribution)	Exclusive Locations	Establish Supply Chain Partners
Promotion	Country Image Nation Sponsored	Brand Image Manufacturer Sponsored

Source: Adapted from Osman Mohamad, Zafar U. Ahmed, Earl D. Honeycutt, Jr. and Taizoon Hyder Tyebkhan, 'Does "Made In . . ." Matter to Consumers? A Malaysian Study of Country of Origin Effect', *Multinational Business Review*, Fall 2000, 73.

effects. Specifically, if marketers determine that the potential customers in a particular country possess a positive image of products made in the country in which their products originate, the marketers may be able to create a marketing mix strategy that follows options in the Positive column. In contrast, if marketers assess that the potential customers in a particular country possess a negative image of products made in the country in which their products originate, the marketers might be wise to elect a marketing mix strategy that follows options in the Negative column of Table 6-7.

BRAND PERSONALITY

Earlier in this chapter, as part of our discussion of Freudian theory, we introduced the notion of product personality. Consumers also subscribe to the notion of brand personality; that is, they attribute various descriptive personality-like traits or characteristics to different brands in a wide variety of product categories. For instance, with some help from frequent advertising, consumers tend to see Volvo as representing safety, Nike as the athlete in all of us, and BMW as performance driven.[38] In a similar fashion, the brand personality for Levi's 501 jeans is 'dependable and rugged', 'real and authentic' and 'American and Western'. Such personality-like images of brands reflect consumers' visions of the inner core of many strong brands of consumer products. As these examples reveal, a brand's personality can either be functional ('provides safety') or symbolic ('the athlete in all of us').[39] There is common sense and research evidence to conclude that any brand personality, as long as it is strong and favourable, will strengthen a brand.[40] However, it is not clear, for example, how many consumers would be willing to pay a 10 to 15 per cent premium for a brand-name diamond.[41]

One of the fast-food chains that many readers of this textbook may patronise with some frequency, McDonald's, can exemplify companies that have built distinctive brand personalities for themselves. The McDonald's brand personality, through Ronald McDonald and other cartoon characters, has always been associated with fun.[42]

Marketers have even provided an instant personality or heritage for a new product by employing a symbolic or fictional historical branding strategy. For example, when Brown Forman entered the microbrewed beer market in 1996, it used the brand name '1886' for its new beer, which is the year that one of its other products, Jack Daniel's bourbon, was first distilled.[43] In another vein, marketers are increasingly interested in learning how the experience of consumers visiting their product's website impacts their brand's personality. An exploration of this issue reveals that, compared to non-visitors, visitors to a brand's website tend to perceive the brand to be a younger and more modern product, as well as more sincere and trustworthy.[44]

Brand personification

Some marketers find it useful to create a **brand personification**, which tries to recast consumers' perception of the attributes of a product or service into a human-like character. For instance, in focus group research, well-known brands of dishwashing liquid have been likened to 'demanding task masters' or 'high-energy people'. Many consumers express their inner feelings about products or brands in terms of their association with known personalities. Identifying consumers' current brand–personality links and creating personality links for new products are important marketing tasks. The M&M 'people' are a current 'fun' example of brand personification. It is based on the line of questioning that could ask the following: 'If an M&M (or a chocolate-coated peanut variety) was a person, what kind of person would it be?' Additional questioning would be likely to explore how the colour of the coating impacts consumers' perceived personality for the 'M&M people'.

Figure 6-4 presents a brand personality framework that reflects extensive consumer research designed to pinpoint the structure and nature of a brand's personality. The framework suggests that there are five defining dimensions of a brand's personality ('sincerity', 'excitement', 'competence', 'sophistication', 'ruggedness'), and 15 facets of personality that flow from the five dimensions (e.g. 'down-to-earth', 'daring', 'reliable', 'upper class', 'outdoors').[45] If we carefully review these brand personality dimensions and facets, it appears that this framework tends to accommodate the brand personalities pursued by many consumer products. Figure 6-5 portrays an advertisement that presents Tag Heuer as a brand with a certain personality (excitement and ruggedness are in focus here).

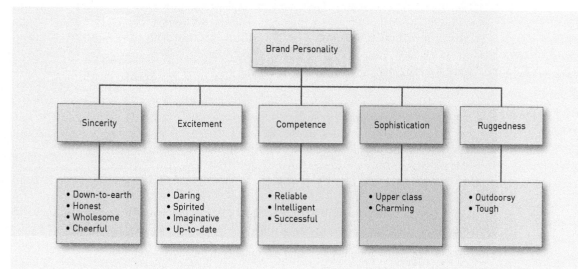

FIGURE 6-4 A brand personality framework

Source: Adapted from Jennifer L. Aaker, 'Dimensions of Brand Personality', *Journal of Marketing Research*, 35, August 1997, 352. Reprinted by permission of the American Marketing Association.

FIGURE 6-5 Tag Heuer emphasise brand personality in this advertisement
Source: Courtesy of The Advertising Archives.

It is important to point out that the consumer sometimes develops a relationship with a brand that is similar in certain respects to the relationships they have with others (e.g. friends, family, neighbours). Some consumers, for example, become 'brand zealots', and develop a relationship that goes beyond a functional need. An example of this would be VW Beetle owners who give their cars names and who can be seen talking to their vehicles and affectionately stroking them. Another would be the advertising executive who had the Apple Macintosh logo tattooed on his chest (near his heart), or the Harley-Davidson motorcycle owner with a Harley tattoo. While in an 'exchange relationship' the consumer gets something back in return, brand zealots develop a 'communal relationship' with the product and demonstrate a passion that is typically associated only with close friends and family.[46]

Product personality and gender

A product personality, or persona, frequently endows the product or brand with a gender. The assigning of gender as part of a product's personality description is fully consistent with the marketplace reality that products and services, in general, are viewed by consumers as having gender. A study that asked Chinese consumers to categorise various products in terms of gender, found that they perceived coffee and toothpaste to be masculine products, whereas bath soap and shampoo were seen as feminine products.[47]

Armed with knowledge of the perceived gender of a product or a specific brand, marketers are in a better position to select visuals and text copy for various marketing messages.

Product personality and geography

Marketers learned long ago that certain products, in the minds of consumers, possess a strong geographical association (e.g. French wine). Consequently, by employing geography in the product's name, the product's manufacturer creates a geographic personality for the product. Such a geographic personality can lead to geographic equity for the brand, meaning that in the consumer's memory the knowledge of the brand reflects a strong geographic association.

Interestingly, geographic brand names and brand names that evoke geographical associations can be either familiar or unfamiliar or even fictitious. For example, Putinoff Vodka, Boris Jeltzin Vodka and Vladivar Vodka all sound like Russian or Polish brand names, but these products are produced in Germany, France and Scotland, respectively. And the Kalashnikov Vodka is produced in the Netherlands. However, more important than whether the name is real or fictitious is whether the location and its image add to the product's brand equity.[48]

Personality and colour

Consumers not only ascribe personality traits to products and services, but they also tend to associate personality factors with specific colours. For instance, Coca-Cola is associated with red, which connotes excitement. Blue bottles are often used to sell wine because the colour blue appeals particularly to female consumers, and they buy the majority of wine.[49] Yellow is associated with novelty, and black frequently connotes sophistication.[50] For this reason, brands wishing to create a sophisticated persona or an upscale or premium image use labelling or packaging that is primarily black (see Figure 6-6). A combination of black and white communicates that a product is carefully engineered, high-tech and sophisticated in design. IBM has consistently used an all-black case with a few selected red buttons

FIGURE 6-6 Brands wishing to create a sophisticated persona or an upscale image primarily use black

Source: From LG Born to Shine advertisement, LG Electronics Nordic AB

TABLE 6-8 The personality-like associations of selected colours

COLOUR	PERSONALITY LINK	MARKETING INSIGHTS
Blue	Commands respect, authority	• IBM holds the title to blue • Associated with club soda • Men seek products packaged in blue • Houses painted blue are avoided • Low-calorie, skimmed milk • Coffee in a blue can perceived as 'mild'
Yellow	Caution, novelty, temporary, warmth	• Eyes register it fastest • Coffee in yellow can tasted 'weak' • Stops traffic • Sells a house
Green	Secure, natural, relaxed or easygoing, living things	• Good work environment • Associated with vegetables and chewing gum • Canada Dry ginger ale sales increased when it changed sugar-free package from red to green and white
Red	Human, exciting, hot, passionate, strong	• Makes food 'smell' better • Coffee in a red can perceived as 'rich' • Women have a preference for bluish red • Men have a preference for yellowish red • Coca-Cola 'owns' red
Orange	Powerful, affordable, informal	• Draws attention quickly
Brown	Informal and relaxed, masculine, nature	• Coffee in a dark-brown can was 'too strong' • Men seek products packaged in brown
White	Goodness, purity, chastity, cleanliness, delicacy, refinement, formality	• Suggests reduced calories • Pure and wholesome food • Clean, bath products, feminine
Black	Sophistication, power, authority, mystery	• Powerful clothing • High-tech electronics
Silver, Gold, Platinum	Regal, wealthy, stately	• Suggests premium price

Source: Adapted from Bernice Kanner, 'Colour Schemes', *New York Magazine*, 1989, 2 April, 22–3. Bernice Kanner/New York Magazine, New York Media.

and bars to house its very successful line of Thinkpad laptops. Nike has used black, white and a touch of red for selected models of its sports shoes. This colour combination seems to imply advanced-performance sports shoes. Although we all know that ketchup is red, Heinz developed its green ketchup after doing research with more than 1,000 children, who helped decide on the product's green colour and its packaging (e.g. the bottle designed to fit smaller hands).[51]

Many fast-food restaurants use combinations of bright colours, like red, yellow and blue, for their roadside signs and interior designs. These colours have come to be associated with fast service and inexpensive food. In contrast, fine dining restaurants tend to use sophisticated colours like grey, white, shades of tan or other soft, pale or muted colours to reflect the feeling of fine, leisurely service. Table 6-8 presents a list of various colours, their personality-like meanings, and associated marketing insights. As part of a research project on colours, consumers were asked to look over a palette of 44 colour shades and to indicate which one best reflects their nature. The six colour shades cited with the greatest frequency were Palace Blue (11 per cent), Fiery Red (9 per cent), Sunshine (7 per cent), Little Boy Blue (6 per cent), Sailor Blue (5 per cent) and Black Limo (4 per cent). Interestingly, while the top selection for males was Palace Blue (17 per cent), two top vote-getters among women were Fiery Red and Sunshine (9 per cent each).[52] Table 6-9 presents the associations made by consumers with their 'personal shade'. It is also important to point out that consumers' liking and disliking of specific colours can vary from one country to another. In one study, individuals in eight countries were asked to rate each of 10 colours on a 7-point scale, and Table 6-10 presents

TABLE 6-9 Consumers' associations with their personal shade

PALACE BLUE IS . . .	
'calming/peaceful'	27%
FIERY RED IS . . .	
'fiery/hot' & 'energetic'	24%
SUNSHINE IS . . .	
'happy/cheerful'	58%
'bright'	30%
'optimistic'	25%
'sunny'	19%
LITTLE BOY BLUE IS . . .	
'calming/peaceful'	28%
a 'favorite color'	21%
'easy going/laid back'	16%
'happy/cheerful'	16%
SAILOR BLUE IS . . .	
a 'favorite color'	19%
'strong/powerful'	18%
'calming/peaceful'	17%
BLACK LIMO IS . . .	
'dark'	19%
'matches everything/basic'	19%
'mysterious'	14%
'fits my mood'	14%
a 'favorite color'	13%
'strong/powerful'	12%

Source: Brandweek, 4 April 2005, 24.

TABLE 6-10 A cross-national study of colour ratings (measured on a 7-point scale)

AUSTRIA		BRAZIL		CANADA		COLOMBIA	
COLOUR	MEAN	COLOUR	MEAN	COLOUR	MEAN	COLOUR	MEAN
Blue	6.59	White	6.34	Black	5.52	Blue	6.23
Green	5.86	Blue	6.12	Blue	5.48	White	5.54
White	5.52	Green	5.35	White	5.41	Green	5.38
Black	5.21	Black	5.23	Red	5.24	Red	5.10
Red	4.34	Red	5.00	Green	5.21	Black	5.02
Orange	4.34	Brown	4.50	Purple	4.03	Purple	3.83
Brown	3.97	Yellow	4.31	Yellow	3.79	Yellow	3.63
Yellow	3.59	Purple	4.27	Orange	3.55	Gold	3.52
Purple	3.24	Gold	3.77	Gold	3.55	Brown	3.21
Gold	3.17	Orange	3.58	Brown	3.03	Orange	2.90

HONG KONG		PRC		TAIWAN		UNITED STATES	
COLOUR	MEAN	COLOUR	MEAN	COLOUR	MEAN	COLOUR	MEAN
White	5.84	Blue	5.81	Blue	6.27	Blue	5.90
Blue	5.37	White	5.65	White	6.23	Green	5.63
Black	5.21	Black	5.26	Purple	5.18	Black	5.31
Red	5.21	Red	5.16	Black	4.82	White	5.29
Yellow	5.05	Green	5.13	Green	4.82	Red	5.14
Purple	5.00	Gold	4.55	Yellow	4.64	Gold	3.94
Gold	4.84	Yellow	4.16	Brown	4.59	Purple	3.90
Green	4.58	Orange	4.13	Orange	4.36	Brown	3.80
Brown	4.11	Purple	3.87	Red	4.32	Orange	3.27
Orange	3.89	Brown	3.48	Gold	4.31	Yellow	3.26

Source: Adapted from Thomas J. Madden, Kelly Hewett and Martin S. Roth, 'Managing Images in Different Cultures: A Cross-National Study of Color Meanings and Preferences', Journal of International Marketing, 8, 4, 2000, 95.

these results.[53] To discover such insights, researchers used a variety of qualitative measurement techniques, such as observation, focus groups, depth interviews and projective techniques (discussed in Chapter 2).

SELF AND SELF-IMAGE

Consumers have a variety of enduring images of themselves. These self-images, or perceptions of self, are very closely associated with personality in that individuals tend to buy products and services and patronise retailers whose images or personalities relate in some meaningful way to their own self-images. In essence, consumers seek to depict themselves in their brand choices – they tend to approach products with images that could enhance their self-concept and avoid those products that do not.[54] In this final section, we examine the issue of one or multiple selves, explore the make-up of the self-image, the notion of extended self, and the possibilities or options of altering the self-image.

One or multiple selves

Historically, individuals have been thought to have a single self-image and to be interested, as consumers, in products and services that satisfy that single self. However, it is more accurate to think of consumers as having **multiple selves**.[55] This change in thinking reflects the understanding that a single consumer is likely to act quite differently with different people and in different situations. For instance, a person is likely to behave in different ways with parents, at school, at work, at a museum opening, or with friends at a nightclub. The healthy or normal person is likely to display a somewhat different personality in each of these different situations or social **roles**. In fact, acting exactly the same in all situations or roles and not adapting to the situation at hand may be considered a sign of an abnormal or unhealthy person.

In terms of consumer behaviour, the idea that an individual embodies a number of different 'selves' (i.e. has multiple self-images) suggests that marketers should target their products and services to consumers within the context of a particular 'self', and in certain cases, a choice of different products for different selves. (The notion of a consumer having multiple selves or playing multiple roles supports the application of usage situation as a segmentation base discussed in Chapter 3.)

The Make-up of the Self-Image

Consistent with the idea of multiple self-images, each individual has an image of himself or herself as a certain kind of person, with certain traits, skills, habits, possessions, relationships and ways of behaving. As with other types of images and personality, the individual's self-image is unique, the outgrowth of that person's background and experience. Individuals develop their self-images through interactions with other people – initially their parents, and then other individuals or groups with whom they relate over the years.

Products and brands have symbolic value for individuals, who evaluate them on the basis of their consistency (congruence) with their personal pictures or images of themselves. Some products seem to match one or more of an individual's self-images; others seem totally alien. It is generally believed that consumers attempt to preserve or enhance their self-images by selecting products and brands with 'images' or 'personalities' that they believe are congruent with their own self-images and avoiding products that are not.[56] This seems to be especially true for women; research reveals that more women than men (77 per cent versus 64 per cent) feel that the brands they select reflect their personalities.[57] Given this relationship between brand preference and consumers' self-images, it is natural that consumers use brands to help them in their task of defining themselves. Research indicates that consumers who have strong links to particular brands – a positive self–brand connection – see such brands as representing an aspect of themselves. For marketers, such connections are certainly an important step in the formation of consumer loyalty and a positive relationship with consumers.[58] Consider the two charts presented in Figure 6-7, which show purchase intent to be strongest when there is a good fit between brand image and self-image.[59]

A variety of different self-images have been recognised in the consumer behaviour literature for a long time. In particular, many researchers have depicted some or all of the following kinds of self-image:

1. **actual self-image** (how consumers in fact see themselves),
2. **ideal self-image** (how consumers would like to see themselves),
3. **social self-image** (how consumers feel others see them), and
4. **ideal social self-image** (how consumers would like others to see them).

It also seems useful to think in terms of two other types of self-images – **expected self** and the **'ought-to' self**. The expected self-image (how consumers expect to see themselves at some specified future time) is somewhere between the actual and ideal self-images. It is a future-oriented combination of what is (the actual self-image) and what consumers would like to be (the ideal self-image). As another interesting type of self-image, the 'ought-to' self consists of traits or characteristics that an individual believes it is his or her duty or obligation to possess.[60] Examples of this form of self-image might be the striving to achieve a deeper religious understanding or the seeking of a fair and just solution to a challenging ethical problem. Because the expected self and the ought-to self provide consumers with a realistic opportunity to change the self, they are both likely to be more valuable to marketers than the actual or ideal self-image as a guide for designing and promoting products.

In different contexts (i.e. in different situations and/or with respect to different products), consumers might select a different self-image to guide their attitudes or behaviour. For instance, with some everyday household products consumers might be guided by their actual self-image, whereas for some socially enhancing or socially conspicuous products they might be guided by their social self-image. When it comes to a so-called fantasy product, they might be guided by either their ideal self-image or ideal social self-image.

The concept of self-image has strategic implications for marketers. For example, marketers can segment their markets on the basis of relevant consumer self-images and then position their products or services as symbols of such self-images. Such a strategy is fully consistent with the marketing concept in that the marketer first assesses the needs of a consumer segment (with respect to both the product category and to an appropriate symbol of self-image) and then proceeds to develop and market a product or service that meets both criteria. The importance of marketing cannot be overstated, as brand equity theory (which focuses on the value inherent in a brand name) postulates that the power of a brand resides in the consumer's mind from both lived (purchase and usage) and mediated (advertising and promotion) experiences.[61]

The extended self

The interrelationship between consumers' self-images and their possessions (i.e. objects they call their own) is an exciting topic. Specifically, consumers' possessions can be seen to confirm or extend their self-images. For instance, acquiring a desired or sought-after pair of 'vintage' Nike trainers might serve to expand or enrich a teenager's image of self. The teenager might now see herself as being more desirable, more fashionable and more successful because she has a pair of the sought-after vintage trainers (often one of the previous year's hard-to-get styles). In a similar manner, if the bracelet that a college student (let's call her Andrea) received as a gift from her aunt is stolen, Andrea is likely to feel diminished in some way. Indeed, the loss of a prized possession may lead Andrea to 'grieve' and to experience a variety of emotions, such as frustration,

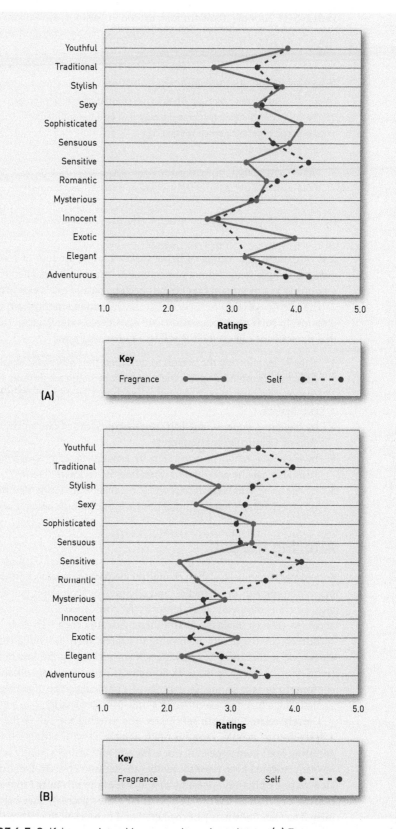

FIGURE 6-7 Self-image, brand image and purchase intent. (a) Fragrance commercial: Self-image and brand-image convergence among respondents with strong purchase intent. (b) Self-image and brand-image convergence among respondents with weak purchase intent.

Source: Adapted from Abhilasha Mehta, 'Using Self-Concept to Assess Advertising Effectiveness', *Journal of Advertising Research*, February 1999, 87.

TABLE 6-11 Sample items from an extended self-survey[a]

My _____ holds a special place in my life.

My _____ is central to my identity.

I feel emotionally attached to my _____ .

My _____ helps me narrow the gap between what I am and try to be.

If my _____ was stolen from me, I would feel as if part of me is missing.

I would be a different person without my _____.

I take good care of my _____ .

I trust my _____ .

[a]A 6-point agree–disagree scale was used.

Source: Adapted from Kimberly J. Dodson, 'Peak Experiences and Mountain Biking: Incorporating the Bike in the Extended Self', *Advances in Consumer Research*, 1996. Reprinted by permission.

loss of control, the feeling of being violated, even the loss of magical protection. Table 6-11 presents sample items from a measurement instrument designed to reflect how particular possessions (e.g. a mountain bike) might become part of one's **extended self**.

The previous examples suggest that much human emotion can be connected to valued possessions. In such cases, possessions are considered extensions of the self. It has been proposed that possessions can extend the self in a number of ways:

1. *actually*, by allowing the person to do things that otherwise would be very difficult or impossible to accomplish (e.g. problem-solving by using a computer);
2. *symbolically*, by making the person feel better or 'bigger' (receiving an employee award for excellence);
3. by *conferring status or rank* (e.g. among collectors of rare works of art because of the ownership of a particular masterpiece);
4. by *bestowing feelings of immortality* by leaving valued possessions to young family members (this also has the potential of extending the recipients' selves); and
5. by *endowing with magical powers* (e.g. a pocket watch inherited from one's grandfather might be perceived as a magic amulet bestowing good luck when it is worn).[62]

Altering the self

Sometimes consumers wish to change themselves to become a different or improved self. Clothing, grooming aids or cosmetics, and all kinds of accessories (such as sunglasses, jewellery, tattoos, or even coloured contact lenses) offer consumers the opportunity to modify their appearances (to create a 'makeover') and thereby to alter their 'selves'. In using self-altering products, consumers are frequently attempting to express their individualism or uniqueness by creating a new self, maintaining the existing self (or preventing the loss of self), and extending the self (modifying or changing the self). Sometimes consumers use self-altering products or services to conform to or take on the appearance of a particular type of person (such as a military person, a physician, a business executive or a university professor).

Closely related to both self-image and altering the self is the idea of personal vanity. As a descriptor of people, vanity is often associated with acting self-important, self-interested or admiring one's own appearance or achievements. Using a 'vanity scale' (Table 6-12), researchers have investigated both physical vanity (an excessive concern for and/or a positive – or inflated – view of one's physical appearance) and achievement vanity (an excessive concern for and/or a positive or inflated view of one's personal achievements). They have found both these ideas are related to materialism, use of cosmetics and concern with clothing.[63]

There is also research evidence to suggest that self-monitoring may serve as a moderating variable when it comes to how well a person is guided by situational cues regarding social

TABLE 6-12 Sample items from a vanity scale

PHYSICAL-CONCERN ITEMS

1. The way I look is extremely important to me.
2. I am very concerned with my appearance.
3. It is important that I always look good.

PHYSICAL-VIEW ITEMS

1. People notice how attractive I am.
2. People are envious of my good looks.
3. My body is sexually appealing.

ACHIEVEMENT-CONCERN ITEMS

1. Professional achievements are an obsession with me.
2. Achieving greater success than my peers is important to me.
3. I want my achievements to be recognized by others.

ACHIEVEMENT-VIEW ITEMS

1. My achievements are highly regarded by others.
2. I am a good example of professional success.
3. Others wish they were as successful as me.

Source: Adapted from Richard G. Netemeyer, Scot Burton and Donald R. Lichtenstein, 'Trait Aspects of Vanity: Measurement and Relevance to Consumer Behavior', *Journal of Consumer Research*, 21, March 1995, 624. Reprinted by permission of The University of Chicago Press as publisher.

appropriateness. Low self-monitors are individuals who are typically guided by their inner feelings, whereas high self-monitors claim that they act differently in different situations and with different people.[64] Consequently, high self-monitors might be more prone to employ a self-altering product in order to enhance their ideal social self-image.

Altering one's self, particularly one's appearance or body parts, can be accomplished by cosmetics, hair restyling or colouring, getting a tattoo, switching from spectacles to contact lenses (or the reverse), or undergoing cosmetic surgery.

VIRTUAL PERSONALITY OR SELF

With the widespread interest in using the Internet as a form of entertainment and as a social vehicle to meet new people with similar interests, there has been a tremendous growth in the use of online chat rooms. People who visit chat rooms are able to carry on real-time conversations about themselves and topics of mutual interest with people from all over the globe. Because most chats are actually text conversations rather than live video broadcasts, the participants usually never get to see each other. This creates an opportunity for chat room participants to try out new identities or to change their identities while online. For instance, one can change from male to female (known as 'gender swapping'), from old to young, from married to single, or from grossly overweight to svelte. In terms of personality, one can change from mild-mannered to aggressive, or from introvert to extrovert.

The notion of a **virtual personality or virtual self** provides an individual with the opportunity to try on different personalities or different identities, much like going to the shops and trying on different outfits in a department or speciality store. If the identity fits, or the personality can be enhanced, the individual may decide to keep the new personality in favour of his or her old personality. From a consumer behaviour point of view, it is likely that such opportunities to try out a new personality or alter the self may result in changes in selected forms of purchase behaviour. This may in turn offer marketers new opportunities to target various 'online selves'.

Want to find out about your personality online? One website, www.outofservice.com/bigfive, offers Internet users an online test called 'The Big Five Personality Test', which takes a few minutes to finish and measures five fundamental dimensions of personality. Give it a try.

SUMMARY

Personality can be described as the psychological characteristics that both determine and reflect how a person responds to his or her environment. Although personality tends to be consistent and enduring, it may change abruptly in response to major life events, as well as gradually over time.

Three theories of personality are prominent in the study of consumer behaviour: psychoanalytic theory, neo-Freudian theory and trait theory. Freud's psychoanalytic theory provides the foundation for the study of motivational research, which operates on the premise that human drives are largely unconscious in nature and serve to motivate many consumer actions. Neo-Freudian theory tends to emphasise the fundamental role of social relationships in the formation and development of personality. Alfred Adler viewed human beings as seeking to overcome feelings of inferiority. Harry Stack Sullivan believed that people attempt to establish significant and rewarding relationships with others. Karen Horney saw individuals as trying to overcome feelings of anxiety and categorised them as compliant, aggressive or detached.

Trait theory is a major departure from the qualitative (or subjective) approach to personality measurement. It postulates that individuals possess innate psychological traits (e.g. innovativeness, novelty seeking, need for cognition, materialism) to a greater or lesser degree, and that these traits can be measured by specially designed scales or inventories. Because they are simple to use and to score and can be self-administered, personality inventories are the preferred method for many researchers in the assessment of consumer personality. Product and brand personalities represent real opportunities for marketers to take advantage of consumers' connections to various brands they offer. Brands often have personalities – some include humanlike traits and even gender. These brand personalities help shape consumer responses, preferences and loyalties.

Each individual has a perceived self-image (or multiple self-images) as a certain kind of person with certain traits, habits, possessions, relationships and ways of behaving. Consumers frequently attempt to preserve, enhance, alter, or extend their self-images by purchasing products or services and shopping at stores they perceive as consistent with their relevant self-image(s) and by avoiding products and stores they perceive are not. With the growth of the Internet, there appear to be emerging virtual selves or virtual personalities. Consumer experiences with chat rooms sometimes provide an opportunity to explore new or alternative identities.

DISCUSSION QUESTIONS

1. How would you explain the fact that, although no two individuals have identical personalities, personality is sometimes used in consumer research to identify distinct and sizeable market segments?
2. Contrast the major characteristics of the following personality theories: (a) Freudian theory, (b) neo-Freudian theory, and (c) trait theory. In your answer, illustrate how each theory is applied to the understanding of consumer behaviour.
3. Describe personality trait theory. Give five examples of how personality traits can be used in consumer research.
4. How can a marketer of perfume use research findings that indicate a target market consists primarily of inner-directed or other-directed consumers? Or of consumers who are high (or low) on innovativeness?

5. Describe the type of promotional message that would be most suitable for each of the following personality market segments and give an example of each: (a) highly dogmatic consumers, (b) inner-directed consumers, (c) consumers with high optimum stimulation levels, (d) consumers with a high need for recognition, and (e) consumers who are visualisers versus consumers who are verbalisers.
6. Is there likely to be a difference in personality traits between Spanish individuals who readily purchase foreign-made products and those who prefer Spanish-made products? How can marketers use the consumer ethnocentrism scale to segment consumers?
7. A marketer of health foods is attempting to segment a certain market on the basis of consumer self-image. Describe the four types of consumer self-image and discuss which one(s) would be most effective for the stated purpose.

EXERCISES

1. How do your clothing preferences differ from those of your friends? What personality traits might explain why your preferences are different from those of other people?
2. Find three print advertisements based on Freudian personality theory. Discuss how Freudian concepts are used in these advertisements. Do any of them personify a brand? If so, how?
3. Administer the nine items from the materialism scale (listed in Table 6-4) to two of your friends. In your view, are their consumption behaviours consistent with their scores on the scale? Why or why not?

NOTES

1. Amanda B. Diekman and Alice H. Eagly, 'Stereotypes as Dynamic Constructs: Women and Men of the Past, Present, and Future', *Personality and Social Psychology Bulletin*, 26, 10, October 2000, 1171–88.
2. Ellen Creager, 'Do Snack Foods Such as Nuts and Popcorn Affect Romance?', *The Patriot-News*, Harrisburg, PA, 14 February 2001, E11.
3. For example, see Karen Horney, *The Neurotic Personality of Our Time* (New York: Norton, 1937).
4. Joel B. Cohen, 'An Interpersonal Orientation to the Study of Consumer Behavior', *Journal of Marketing Research*, 6, August 1967, 270–78; Arch G. Woodside and Ruth Andress, 'CAD Eight Years Later', *Journal of the Academy of Marketing Science*, 3, Summer–Fall 1975, 309–13; see also Jon P. Noerager, 'An Assessment of CAD: A Personality Instrument Developed Specifically for Marketing Research', *Journal of Marketing Research*, 16, February 1979, 53–9; and Pradeep K. Tyagi, 'Validation of the CAD Instrument: A Replication', *in Advances in Consumer Research*, 10, eds Richard P. Bagozzi and Alice M. Tybout (Ann Arbor, MI: Association for Consumer Research, 1983), 112–14.
5. Morton I. Jaffe, 'Brand-Loyalty/Variety-Seeking and the Consumer's Personality: Comparing Children and Young Adults', in *Proceedings of the Society for Consumer Psychology*, eds Scott B. MacKenzie and Douglas M. Stayman (La Jolla, CA: American Psychological Association, 1995), 144–51.
6. J. P. Guilford, *Personality* (New York: McGraw-Hill, 1959), 6.
7. Ronald E. Goldsmith and Charles F. Hofacker, 'Measuring Consumer Innovativeness', *Journal of the Academy of Marketing Science*, 19, 1991, 209–21; Suresh Subramanian and Robert A. Mittelstaedt, 'Conceptualizing Innovativeness as a Consumer Trait: Consequences and Alternatives', in *1991 AMA Educators' Proceedings*, eds Mary C. Gilly and F. Robert Dwyer *et al.* (Chicago: American Marketing Association, 1991), 352–60; and eid. 'Reconceptualizing and Measuring Consumer Innovativeness', in *1992 AMA Educators' Proceedings*, eds Robert P. Leone and V. Kumor *et al.* (Chicago: American Marketing Association, 1992), 300–7.

8. Gilles Roehrich, 'Consumer Innovativeness: Concepts and Measurements', *Journal of Business Research*, 57, June 2004, 671–7.

9. Alka Varma Citrin, David E. Sprott, Steven N. Silverman and Donald E. Stem, Jr., 'From Internet Use to Internet Adoption: Is General Innovativeness Enough?', in *1999 AMA Winter Educators' Conference*, 10, eds Anil Menon and Arun Sharma (Chicago: American Marketing Association, 1999), 232–3.

10. Angela D'Auria Stanton and Wilbur W. Stanton, 'To Click or Not to Click: Personality Characteristics of Internet Versus Non-Internet Purchasers', in *2001 AMA Winter Educators' Conference*, 12, eds Ram Krishnan and Madhu Viswanathan (Chicago: American Marketing Association, 2001), 161–2.

11. Milton Rokeach, *The Open and Closed Mind* (New York: Basic Books, 1960).

12. Itamar Simonson and Stephen M. Nowlis, 'The Role of Explanations and Need for Uniqueness in Consumer Decision Making: Unconventional Choices Based on Reasons', *Journal of Consumer Research*, 27, June 2000, 49–68.

13. Ann Marie Fiore, Leung-Eun Lee and Grace Kunz, 'Individual Differences, Motivations, and Willingness to Use a Mass Customization Option for Fashion Products', *European Journal of Marketing*, 38, 7, 2004, 835–49.

14. P. S. Raju, 'Optimum Stimulation Level: Its Relationship to Personality, Demographics, and Exploratory Behavior', *Journal of Consumer Research*, 7, December 1980, 272–82; Leigh McAlister and Edgar Pessemier, 'Variety Seeking Behavior: An Interdisciplinary Review', *Journal of Consumer Research*, 9, December 1982, 311–22; Jan-Benedict E. M. Steenkamp and Hans Baumgartner, 'The Role of Optimum Stimulation Level in Exploratory Consumer Behavior', *Journal of Consumer Research*, 19, December 1992, 434; Russell G. Wahlers and Michael J. Etzel, 'A Consumer Response to Incongruity between Optimal Stimulation and Life Style Satisfaction', in *Advances in Consumer Research*, 12, eds Elizabeth C. Hirschman and Morris B. Holbrook (Provo, UT: Association for Consumer Research, 1985), 97–101; and Jan-Benedict E. M. Steenkamp, Frenkel ter Hofstede and Michael Wedel, 'A Cross-National Investigation into the Individual and National Cultural Antecedents of Consumer Innovativeness', *Journal of Marketing*, 62, April 1999, 55–69.

15. Linda McNamara and Mary E. Ballard, 'Resting Arousal, Sensation Seeking, and Music Preference', *Genetic, Social, and General Psychology Monographs*, 125, 3, 1999, 229–50.

16. Satya Menon and Barbara E. Kahn, 'The Impact of Context on Variety Seeking in Product Choices', *Journal of Consumer Research*, 22, December 1995, 285–95.

17. Elizabeth C. Hirschman, 'Innovativeness, Novelty Seeking and Consumer Creativity', *Journal of Consumer Research*, 7, 1980, 283–95; Wayne Hoyer and Nancy M. Ridgway, 'Variety Seeking as an Explanation for Exploratory Purchase Behavior: A Theoretical Model', in *Advances in Consumer Research*, 11, eds Thomas C. Kinnear (Provo, UT: Association for Consumer Research, 1984), 114–19; and Minakshi Trivedi, 'Using Variety-Seeking-Based Segmentation to Study Promotional Response', *Journal of the Academy of Marketing Science*, 27, 1, Winter 1999, 37–49.

18. Harper A. Roehm, Jr. and Michelle L. Roehm, 'Variety-Seeking and Time of Day: Why Leader Brands Hope Young Adults Shop in the Afternoon, but Follower Brands Hope for Morning', *Marketing Letters*, Boston, 15, January 2005, 213–21.

19. Barbara E. Kahn, 'Dynamic Relationships with Customers: High-Variety Strategies', *Journal of the Academy of Marketing Science*, 26, Winter 1998, 47–53. Also see J. Jeffrey Inman, 'The Role of Sensory-Specific Satiety in Attribute-Level Variety Seeking', *Journal of Consumer Research*, 28, June 2001, 105–20.

20. Minakshi Trivedi and Michael S. Morgan, 'Promotional Evaluation and Response among Variety Seeking Segments', *Journal of Product and Brand Management*, 12, 6/7, 2003, 408–25.

21. Richard Petty *et al.*, 'Personality and Ad Effectiveness: Exploring the Utility of Need for Cognition', in *Advances in Consumer Research*, 15, ed. Michael Houston (Ann Arbor, MI: Association for Consumer Research, 1988), 209–12; and Susan Powell Mantel and Frank R. Kardes, 'The Role of Direction of Comparison, Attribute-Based Processing, and

Attitude-Based Processing in Consumer Preference', *Journal of Consumer Research*, 25, March 1999, 335–52.

22. Arnold B. Bakker, 'Persuasive Communication About AIDS Prevention: Need for Cognition Determines the Impact of Message Format', *AIDS Education and Prevention*, 11(2), 1999, 150–62.

23. Yong Zhang and Richard Buda, 'Moderating Effects of Need for Cognition on Responses to Positively versus Negatively Framed Advertising Messages', *Journal of Advertising*, 28, 2, Summer 1999, 1–15.

24. Ayn E. Crowley and Wayne D. Hoyer, 'The Relationship Between Need for Cognition and Other Individual Difference Variables: A Two-Dimensional Framework', in *Advances in Consumer Research*, 16, ed. Thomas K. Srull (Provo, UT: Association for Consumer Research, 1989), 37–43; and James W. Peltier and John A. Schibrowsky, 'Need for Cognition, Advertisement Viewing Time and Memory for Advertising Stimuli', *Advances in Consumer Research*, 21, eds Chris T. Allen and Deborah Roedder John (Provo, UT: Association for Consumer Research, 1994), 244–50.

25. Tracy L. Tuten and Michael Bosnjak, 'Understanding Differences in Web Usage: The Role of Need for Cognition and the Five Factor Model of Personality', *Social Behavior and Personality*, 29(4), 2001, 391–8.

26. Brett A. S. Martin, Michael J. Sherrard and Daniel Wentzel, 'The Role of Sensation Seeking and Need for Cognition on Web-site Evaluations: A Resource-Matching Perspective', *Psychology and Marketing*, 22, 15 December 2004, 109–26.

27. Russell W. Belk, 'Three Scales to Measure Constructs Related to Materialism' and 'Materialism: Trait Aspects of Living in the Material World', *Journal of Consumer Research*, 12, December 1985, 265–80.

28. Marsha L. Richins and Scott Dawson, 'A Consumer Values Orientation for Materialism and Its Measurement: Scale Development and Validation', *Journal of Consumer Research*, 19, December 1992, 303–16; and Jeff Tanner and Jim Roberts, 'Materialism Cometh', *Baylor Business Review*, Fall 2000, 8–9.

29. Ronald J. Faber and Thomas C. O'Guinn, 'A Clinical Screener for Compulsive Buying', *Journal of Consumer Research*, 19, December 1992, 459–69.

30. Ibid. See also Stacey Menzel Baker and Robert A. Mittelstaedt, 'The Meaning of the Search, Evaluation, and Selection of "Yesterday's Cast-Offs": A Phenomenological Study into the Acquisition of the Collection', in *1995 AMA Educators' Proceedings*, eds Barbara B. Stern and George M. Zinkan (Chicago: American Marketing Association, 1995), 152.

31. Elizabeth C. Hirschman, 'The Consciousness of Addiction: Toward a General Theory of Compulsive Consumption', *Journal of Consumer Research*, 19, September 1992, 155–79; and Seung-Hee Lee, Sharron J. Lennon and Nancy A. Rudd, 'Compulsive Consumption Tendencies Among Television Shoppers', *Family and Consumer Sciences Research Journal*, 28, 4, June 2000, 463–88, and Booth Moore, 'Shopping for a Defense – Consumer-Driven Culture Spills over into the Courtroom', *Houston Chronicle*, 11 July 2001, 8.

32. Kristen Bruinsma and Douglas L. Taren, 'Chocolate: Food or Drug?', *Journal of the American Dietetic Association*, 99, 10, October 1999, 1249–56.

33. Ronald J. Faber and Gary A. Christenson, 'Can You Buy Happiness?: A Comparison of the Antecedent and Concurrent Moods Associated with the Shopping of Compulsive and Non-Compulsive Buyers', in *1995 Winter Educators' Conference*, 6, eds David W. Stewart and Naufel J. Vilcassin (Chicago: American Marketing Association, 1995), 378–9.

34. Terence A. Shimp and Subhash Sharma, 'Consumer Ethnocentrism: Construction and Validation of the CETSCALE', *Journal of Marketing Research*, 24, August 1987, 280–89; Richard G. Netemeyer, Srinivas Durvaula and Donald R. Lichtenstein, 'A Cross-National Assessment of the Reliability and Validity of the CETSCALE', *Journal of Marketing Research*, 28, August 1991, 320–27.

35. Osman Mohamad, Zafar U. Ahmed, Earl D. Honeycutt, Jr. and Taizoon Hyder Tyebkhan, 'Does "Made In . . ." Matter to Consumers? A Malaysian Study of Country of Origin Effect',

Multinational Business Review, Fall 2000, 69–73; and Irvin Clarke, Mahesh N. Shankarmahesh and John B. Ford, 'Consumer Ethnocentrism, Materialism and Values: A Four Country Study', in *2000 AMA Winter Educators' Conference*, 11, eds John P. Workman and William D. Perreault (Chicago: American Marketing Association, 2000), 102–3.

36. George Balabanis and Adamantios Diamantopoulos, 'Domestic Country Bias, Country-of-Origin Effects, and Consumer Ethnocentrism: A Multidimensional Unfolding Approach', *Journal of the Academy of Marketing Science*, 32, Winter 2004, 80–95.

37. Byeong-Joon Moon, 'Effects of Consumer Ethnocentrism and Product Knowledge on Consumers' Utilization of Country-of-Origin Information', *Advances in Consumer Research*, 31, eds Barbara E. Kahn and Mary Frances Luce (Valdosta, GA: Association for Consumer Research, 2004), 667–73.

38. David Martin, 'Branding: Finding That "One Thing"', *Brandweek*, 16 February 1998, 18.

39. Subodh Bhat and Srinivas K. Reddy, 'Symbolic and Functional Positioning of Brands', *Journal of Consumer Marketing*, 15, 1998, 32–43.

40. Traci L. Haigood, 'The Brand Personality Effect: An Empirical Investigation', in *1999 AMA Winter Educators' Conference*, 10, eds Anil Menon and Arun Sharma (Chicago: American Marketing Association, 1999), 149–50; and Traci L. Haigood, 'Deconstructing Brand Personality', in *2001 AMA Educators' Proceedings*, 12, eds Greg W. Marshall and Stephen J. Grove (Chicago: American Marketing Association, 2001), 327–8.

41. Lauren Weber, 'The Diamond Game, Shedding Its Mystery', *New York Times*, 8 April 2001, P1.

42. Judy A. Siguaw, Anna Mattila and Jon R. Austin, 'The Brand-Personality Scale', *Hotel and Restaurant Administration Quarterly*, June 1999, 48–55.

43. Janice S. Griffiths, Mary Zimmer and Sheniqua K. Little, 'The Effect of Reality Engineering on Consumers' Brand Perceptions Using a Fictional Historical Branding Strategy', *American Marketing Association*, Winter 1999, 250–58.

44. Brigitte Muller and Jean-Louis Chandon, 'The Impact of Visiting a Brand Website on Brand Personality', *Electronic Markets*, 13, 3, 2003, 18–29.

45. Jennifer L. Aaker, 'Dimension of Brand Personality', *Journal of Marketing Research*, 35, August 1997, 351–2.

46. Pankaj Aggarwal, 'The Effects of Brand Relationship Norms on Consumer Attitudes and Behavior', *Journal of Consumer Research*, 31, June 2004, 87–101.

47. Laura M. Milner and Dale Fodness, 'Product Gender Perception: The Case of China', in *1995 Winter Educators' Conference*, 6, eds David W. Stewart and Naufel J. Vilcassin (Chicago: American Marketing Association, 1995), 331–6.

48. Max Blackston, 'Observations: Building Brand Equity by Managing the Brand's Relationships', *Journal of Advertising Research*, November/December 2000, 101–5.

49. Elizabeth Jensen, 'Blue Bottles, Gimmicky Labels Sell Wine', *Wall Street Journal*, 7 July 1997, B1.

50. Pamela S. Schindler, 'Color and Contrast in Magazine Advertising', *Psychology and Marketing*, 3, 1986, 69–78.

51. 'Heinz EZ Squirt™ Hits Store Shelves: Industry Watches Unusual Food Phenomenon Unfold', *PR Newswire*, 17 October 2000, 1.

52. Becky Ebenkamp (ed.), 'Living in Color', *Brandweek*, 4 April 2005, 22–4.

53. Thomas J. Madden, Kelly Hewett and Martin S. Roth, 'Managing Images in Different Cultures: A Cross-National Study of Color Meanings and Preferences', *Journal of International Marketing*, 8, 4, 2000, 90–107.

54. Kiran Karande, George M. Zinkhan and Alyssa Baird Lum, 'Brand Personality and Self Concept: A Replication and Extension', *AMA Summer 1997 Conference*, 165–71.

55. Hazel Markus and Paula Nurius, 'Possible Selves', *American Psychologist*, 1986, 954–69.

56. For a detailed discussion of self-images and congruence, see M. Joseph Sirgy, 'Self-Concept in Consumer Behavior: A Critical Review', *Journal of Consumer Research*, 9, December 1992, 287–300; C. B. Claiborne and M. Joseph Sirgy, 'Self-Image Congruence as a Model of

Consumer Attitude Formation and Behavior: A Conceptual Review and Guide for Future Research', in *Developments in Marketing Science*, 13, ed. B. J. Dunlap (Cullowhee, NC: Academy of Marketing Science, 1990), 1–7; and J. S. Johar and M. Joseph Sirgy, 'Value-Expressive versus Utilitarian Advertising Appeals: When and Why to Use Which Appeal', *Journal of Advertising*, 20, September 1991, 23–33.

57. 'Sex Appeal', *Brandweek*, 20 April 1998, 26.

58. Susan Fournier, 'Consumers and Their Brands: Developing Relationship Theory in Consumer Research', *Journal of Consumer Research*, 24, March 1998; and Kimberly J. Dodson, 'Peak Experiences and Mountain Biking: Incorporating the Bike in the Extended Self', in *Advances in Consumer Research*, 23, eds Kim P. Corfman and John G. Lynch, Jr. (Provo, UT: Association for Consumer Research, 1996), 317–22.

59. Abhilasha Mehta, 'Using Self-Concept to Assess Advertising Effectiveness', *Journal of Advertising Research*, February 1999, 81–9.

60. Marlene M. Moretti and E. Tory Higgens, 'Internal Representations of Others in Self-Regulation: A New Look at a Classic Issue', *Social Cognition*, 17, 2, 1999, 186–208.

61. Robert Underwood, Edward Bond and Robert Baer, 'Building Service Brands via Social Identity: Lessons from the Sports Marketplace', *Journal of Marketing Theory and Practice*, Winter 2001, 1–13.

62. Russell W. Belk, 'Possessions and the Extended Self', *Journal of Consumer Research*, 15, September 1988, 139–68; and Amy J. Morgan, 'The Evolving Self in Consumer Behavior: Exploring Possible Selves', in *Advances in Consumer Research*, 20, eds Leigh McAlister and Michael L. Rothschild (Provo, UT: Association for Consumer Research, 1993), 429–32.

63. Richard G. Netemeyer, Scot Burton and Donald R. Lichtenstein, 'Trait Aspects of Vanity: Measurement and Relevance to Consumer Behavior', *Journal of Consumer Research*, 21, March 1995, 613.

64. Jennifer L. Aaker, 'The Malleable Self: The Role of Self-Expression in Persuasion', *Journal of Marketing Research*, 36, February 1999, 45–57.

CHAPTER 7
CONSUMER PERCEPTION

Individuals act and react on the basis of their perceptions, not on the basis of objective reality. For each individual, reality is a totally personal phenomenon, based on that person's needs, wants, values and personal experiences. Thus, to the marketer, consumers' perceptions are much more important than their knowledge of objective reality. For if we think about it, it's not how things actually are, but how consumers think they are, that affects their actions, their buying habits, their leisure habits and so forth. And, because individuals make decisions and take actions based on what they perceive to be reality, it is important that marketers understand the whole notion of perception and its related concepts to determine more readily what factors influence consumers to buy.

This chapter examines the psychological and physiological bases of human perception and discusses the principles that influence our perception and interpretation of the world we see. Knowledge of these principles enables astute marketers to develop advertisements that have a better-than-average chance of being seen and remembered by their target consumers.

ELEMENTS OF PERCEPTION

Perception is defined as the process by which an individual selects, organises and interprets stimuli into a meaningful and coherent picture of the world. It can be described as 'how we see the world around us'. Two individuals may be exposed to the same stimuli under the same apparent conditions, but how each person recognises, selects, organises and interprets these stimuli is a highly individual process based on each person's own needs, values and expectations. The influence that each of these variables has on the perceptual process and its relevance to marketing will be explored later in the chapter. First, however, we will examine some of the basic concepts that underlie the perceptual process. These will be discussed within the framework of consumer behaviour.

Sensation

Sensation is the immediate and direct response of the sensory organs to stimuli. A stimulus is any unit of input to any of the senses. Examples of stimuli (i.e. sensory input) include products, packages, brand names, advertisements and commercials. **Sensory receptors** are the human organs (the eyes, ears, nose, mouth and skin) that receive sensory inputs. Their sensory functions are to see, hear, smell, taste and feel. All of these functions are called into play, either singly or in combination, in the evaluation and use of most consumer products. Human sensitivity refers to the experience of sensation. Sensitivity to stimuli varies with the quality of an individual's sensory receptors (e.g. eyesight or hearing) and the amount (or intensity) of the stimuli to which he or she is exposed. For example, a blind person may have a more highly developed sense of hearing than the average sighted person and may be able to hear sounds that the average person cannot.

Sensation itself depends on energy change within the environment where the perception occurs (i.e. on differentiation of input). A perfectly bland or unchanging environment, regardless of the strength of the sensory input, provides little or no sensation at all. Thus, a person who lives on a busy street in Copenhagen would probably receive little or no sensation from the inputs of such noisy stimuli as horns honking, tyres screeching and fire engines clanging, because such sounds are so commonplace in a large city. In situations in which there is a great deal of sensory input, the senses do not detect small changes or differences in input. Thus, one honking horn more or less would never be noticed on a street with heavy traffic.

As sensory input decreases, however, our ability to detect changes in input or intensity increases, to the point that we attain maximum sensitivity under conditions of minimal stimulation. This accounts for the statement, 'It was so quiet I could hear a pin drop.' The ability of the human organism to accommodate itself to varying levels of sensitivity as external conditions vary not only provides more sensitivity when it is needed but also serves to protect us from damaging, disruptive or irrelevant bombardment when the input level is high.

One researcher pointed out that 83 per cent of all communications today appeal to sight; also that smell, not sound, is the second most important sensory input. This study also reported that consumers preferred shoes and belts presented in a scented room rather than a non-scented room, and were also willing to pay higher prices for these products.[1] The importance of smell in communication was strongly supported by researchers who developed a scientific explanation as to how people associate memories with smells (and won the 2004 Nobel Prize in Physiology for this work) and other studies demonstrating the impact of fragrance on product and store choices.[2]

The absolute threshold

The lowest level at which an individual can experience a sensation is called the **absolute threshold**. The point at which a person can detect a difference between 'something' and 'nothing' is that person's absolute threshold for that stimulus. To illustrate, the distance at which a driver can note a specific hoarding beside a road is that individual's absolute threshold. Two people travelling together may first spot the hoarding at different times (i.e. at different distances); thus, they appear to have different absolute thresholds. Under conditions of constant stimulation, such as driving through a 'corridor' of hoardings, the absolute threshold increases (i.e. the senses tend to become increasingly dulled). After an hour of driving through hoardings, it is doubtful that any one hoarding will make an impression. Hence, we often speak of 'getting used to' a hot bath, a cold shower or the bright sun. As our exposure to the stimulus increases, we notice it less. In the field of perception, the term adaptation refers specifically to 'getting used to' certain sensations; that is, becoming accommodated to a certain level of stimulation.

Sensory adaptation is a problem that concerns many national advertisers, which is why they try to change their advertising campaigns regularly. They are concerned that consumers will get so used to their current print advertisements and television commercials that they will no longer 'see' them: the advertisements will no longer provide sufficient sensory input to be noted.

In an effort to cut through the advertising clutter and ensure that consumers note their advertisements, some marketers try to increase sensory input. For example, Apple Computer once bought all the advertising space in an issue of *Newsweek* magazine to ensure that readers would note its advertisements. Other advertisers try to attract attention by decreasing sensory input – some print advertisements include a lot of empty space in order to accentuate the brand name or product illustration, and some television advertisements use silence, the absence of audio sound, to generate attention. Figure 7-1 depicts the use of decreased sensory input to support the product's advertising claim.

Some marketers seek unusual or technological media in which to place their advertisements in an effort to gain attention. Examples of such media include small monitors attached to shopping trolleys that feature actual brands in television shows and in films, individual television screens (placed in the back of the seat in front) on aircraft, and monitors integrated into the floor indicators in lifts. Fragrance marketers often include fragrance samples in their direct-mail and magazine advertisements through sealed perfume inserts. Researchers have reported that the use of an ambient scent in a retail environment enhances the shopping experience for consumers and makes the time they spend examining merchandise, queuing and waiting for help seem shorter than it actually is.[3] Some marketers have invested in the development of specially engineered scents to enhance their products and entice consumers to buy. Marketers try to form stronger bonds between young, design-oriented consumers and brands, using the store image itself to give 'dimension' to their brands and present them as 'cool'. For example, in one store selling sports footwear, the shoes are integrated into a huge sound system in the shape of a wall; in another store selling advertised high-definition televisions, the screens show works of art inside the store.[4]

The differential threshold

The minimal difference that can be detected between two similar stimuli is called the **differential threshold**, or the **just noticeable difference (JND)**. A nineteenth-century German scientist named Ernst Weber discovered that the JND between two stimuli was not an absolute amount, but an amount relative to the intensity of the first stimulus. **Weber's law**, as it has come to be known, states that the stronger the initial stimulus, the greater the additional intensity needed for the second stimulus to be perceived as different. For example, if the price of a large container of premium, freshly squeezed orange juice is €6.50, most consumers will probably not notice an increase of 25 cents (i.e. the increment would fall below the JND), and it may take an increase of 50 cents or more before a differential in price would be noticed. However, a similar 25-cent increase in the price of a litre container of milk would be noticed very quickly by consumers because it is a significant percentage of the initial (base) cost of the milk.

According to Weber's law, an additional level of stimulus equivalent to the JND must be added for the majority of people to perceive a difference between the resulting stimulus and the initial stimulus. Imagine that a manufacturer of silver polishes wants to improve its

Mediterranean bluefin tuna are killed to make sushi and now stocks are on the verge of collapse. The EU must cut its fishing quota in half or the species may be lost from the Mediterranean forever.

If you care about seafood that doesn't destroy ocean life, go to: **www.panda.org/tuna**   **WWF** *for a living planet*®

FIGURE 7-1

Source: Photographer Piet Johnson, with kind permission from WWF and Ogilvy and Mather.

product sufficiently to claim that it retards tarnish longer than the leading competitive brand. In a series of experiments, the company determines that the JND for its present polish (which now gives a shine that lasts about 20 days) is 5 days, or one-quarter longer. That means that the shine given by the improved silver polish must last at least 25 days (or one-quarter longer) if the new polish is to be perceived by the majority of users as in fact improved. By finding this

JND of 5 days, the company has isolated the minimum amount of time necessary to make its claim of 'lasts longer' believable to the majority of consumers. If it had decided to make the polish effective for 23 days (just 3 extra days of product life), its claim of 'lasts longer' would not be perceived as true by most consumers and, from the marketer's point of view, would be wasted. On the other hand, if the company had decided to make the silver polish effective for 40 days, it would have sacrificed a good deal of repeat purchase frequency. Making the product improvement just equal to the JND thus becomes the most efficient decision that management can make.

An interesting application of the JND is the development of new food products. With the public alarm regarding the rapidly rising obesity rates, food marketers are looking for substances that can mimic the creamy and palate-coating food of fatty products such as puddings, cheese and chocolate.[5] The challenge is to create fat substitutes with taste that is below, or at least not significantly above, consumers' JND for the original, fatty foods. Another example of the use of JND is the reduction in salt use in manufactured food products. The manufacturers of bread have reduced the salt level several times, each time by just less than JND (taste). As a result there has been a significant reduction in salt use.

Marketing Applications of the JND

Weber's law has important applications in marketing. Manufacturers and marketers endeavour to determine the relevant JND for their products for two very different reasons: (1) so that negative changes (reductions in product size or quality, or increases in product price) are not readily discernible to the public (they remain below the JND) and (2) so that product improvements (such as improved or updated packaging, larger size or lower price) are very apparent to consumers without being wastefully extravagant (i.e. they are at or just above the JND). For example, what if our silver polish manufacturer, in an apparent misunderstanding of the JND, introduced an extension of its silver polish brand that prolonged the shine of the silver by months but raised its product price by pennies only? By doing so, the company would have decreased its sales revenue because the new version cannibalised the sales of the old product and, at the same time, was purchased much less frequently than the old version. Could the flaw have been corrected by doubling the price? For a non-durable consumer good, a product that has been improved dramatically but is doubled in price is inconsistent with the concept of the JND. A better strategy would have been to introduce several successive versions of the polish, each version with a shine that lasted longer than the previous version (and at or above the JND) and offered at a higher price (but a price that is lower than the JND).

When it comes to product improvements, marketers very much want to meet or exceed the consumer's differential threshold; that is, they want consumers readily to perceive any improvements made in the original product. Marketers use the JND to determine the amount of improvement they should make in their products. Less than the JND is wasted effort because the improvement will not be perceived; more than the JND is wasteful because it reduces the level of repeat sales. On the other hand, when it comes to price increases, less than the JND is desirable because consumers are unlikely to notice it. Since many routinely purchased consumer goods are relatively inexpensive, companies are reluctant to raise prices when their profit margins on these items are declining. Instead, many marketers decrease the product quantity included in the packages, while leaving the prices unchanged – thus, in effect, increasing the per unit price.

Marketers often want to update their existing package designs without losing the ready recognition of consumers who have been exposed to years of cumulative advertising impact. In such cases, they usually make a number of small changes, each carefully designed to fall below the JND, so that consumers will perceive minimal difference between succeeding versions.

When Lexmark International, Inc. bought the office supplies and equipment line from IBM in March 1991, it agreed to relinquish the IBM name by 1996. Recognising the need to build a brand image for Lexmark while moving away from the well-known IBM name, Lexmark officials conducted a four-stage campaign for phasing in the Lexmark name on products. Stage 1 carried only the IBM name, Stage 2 featured the IBM name and downplayed Lexmark, Stage 3 featured the Lexmark name and downplayed IBM, and Stage 4 features only the Lexmark name.

Subliminal perception

In Chapter 5 we spoke of people being motivated below their level of conscious awareness. People are also stimulated below their level of conscious awareness; that is, they can perceive stimuli without being consciously aware that they are doing so. Stimuli that are too weak or too brief to be consciously seen or heard may nevertheless be strong enough to be perceived by one or more receptor cells. This process is called **subliminal perception** because the stimulus is beneath the threshold, or 'limen', of conscious awareness, though obviously not beneath the absolute threshold of the receptors involved. (Perception of stimuli that are above the level of conscious awareness technically is called *supraliminal perception*, though it is usually referred to simply as perception.)

The effectiveness of so-called subliminal advertising was reportedly first tested at a drive-in cinema in New Jersey in 1957, where the words 'Eat popcorn' and 'Drink Coca-Cola' were flashed on the screen during the film. Exposure times were so short that viewers were unaware of seeing a message. It was reported that during the six-week test period, popcorn sales increased 58 per cent and Coca-Cola sales increased 18 per cent, but these findings were later reported to be false. Years later, a scientific study found that although the simple subliminal stimulus 'Coke' served to arouse thirst in subjects, the subliminal command 'Drink Coke' did not have a greater effect, nor did it have any behavioural consequences.[6]

Evaluating the Effectiveness of Subliminal Persuasion

Despite the many studies undertaken by academics and researchers since the 1950s, there is no evidence that subliminal advertising persuades people to buy goods or services. A review of the literature indicates that subliminal perception research has been based on two theoretical approaches. According to the first theory, constant repetition of very weak (i.e. sub-threshold) stimuli has an incremental effect that enables such stimuli to build response strength over many presentations. This would be the operative theory when weak stimuli are flashed repeatedly on a cinema screen or played on a soundtrack or MP3 player. The second approach is based on the theory that subliminal sexual stimuli arouse unconscious sexual motivations. This is the theory behind the use of sexual embeds in print advertising. But no studies have yet indicated that either of these theoretical approaches have been effectively used by advertisers to increase sales. However, there is some indication that subliminal advertising may provide new opportunities for modifying anti-social behaviour through public awareness campaigns that call for individuals to make generalised responses to suggestions that enhance their personal performance or improve their attitudes.[7] There is also some (though not definitive) evidence that subliminal methods can indirectly influence attitudes and feelings toward brands.[8]

In summary, although there is some evidence that subliminal stimuli may influence affective reactions, there is no evidence that subliminal stimulation can influence consumption motives or actions. There continues to be a big gap between perception and persuasion. A recent review of the evidence on subliminal persuasion indicates that the only way for subliminal techniques to have a significant persuasive effect would be through long-term repeated exposure under a limited set of circumstances, which would not be economically feasible or practical within an advertising context.[9]

As to sexual embeds, most researchers are of the opinion that 'what you see is what you get'; that is, a vivid imagination can see whatever it wants to see in just about any situation. And that really sums up the whole notion of perception: individuals see what they want to see (e.g. what they are motivated to see) and what they expect to see. Several studies concerned with public beliefs about subliminal advertising found that a large percentage of consumers know what sub-liminal advertising is, they believe it is used by advertisers, and that it is effective in persuading consumers to buy.[10] To correct any misperceptions among the public that subliminal advertising does, in fact, exist, the advertising community occasionally sponsors advertisements like the one depicted in Figure 7-2, which ridicules the notion that subliminal techniques are effective or

FIGURE 7-2 Subliminal embeds are in the eye of the beholder
Source: Courtesy of American Association of Advertising Agencies.

that they are used in advertising applications. The ethical issues related to subliminal advertising are discussed later in this chapter.

DYNAMICS OF PERCEPTION

The preceding section explained how the individual receives sensations from stimuli in the outside environment and how the human organism adapts to the level and intensity of sensory input. We now come to one of the major principles of perception: raw sensory input by itself does not produce or explain the coherent picture of the world that most adults possess. Indeed, the study of perception is largely the study of what we subconsciously add to or subtract from raw sensory inputs to produce our own private picture of the world.

Human beings are constantly bombarded with stimuli during every minute and every hour of every day. The sensory world is made up of an almost infinite number of discrete sensations that are constantly and subtly changing. According to the principles of sensation, intensive stimulation 'bounces off' most individuals, who subconsciously block (i.e. adapt to) the receipt of a heavy bombardment of stimuli. Otherwise, the billions of different stimuli to which we are constantly exposed might serve to confuse us totally and keep us perpetually disoriented in a constantly changing environment. However, neither of these consequences tends to occur, because perception is not a function of sensory input alone. Rather, perception is the result of two different kinds of inputs that interact to form the personal pictures – the perceptions – that each individual experiences.

One type of input is *physical stimuli* from the outside environment; the other type of input is provided by individuals themselves in the form of certain predispositions (expectations, motives and learning) based on *previous experience*. The combination of these two very different kinds of inputs produces for each of us a very private, very personal picture of the world. Because each person is a unique individual, with unique experiences, needs, wants, desires and expectations, it follows that each individual's perceptions are also unique. This explains why no two people see the world in precisely the same way.

Individuals are very selective as to which stimuli they 'recognise'; they subconsciously organise the stimuli they do recognise according to widely held psychological principles, and they interpret such stimuli (they give meaning to them) subjectively in accordance with their personal needs, expectations and experiences. Let us examine in some detail each of these three aspects of perception: the *selection*, *organisation* and *interpretation* of stimuli.

Perceptual selection

Consumers subconsciously exercise a great deal of selectivity as to which aspects of the environment (which stimuli) they perceive. An individual may look at some things, ignore others, and turn away from still others. In actuality, people receive (i.e. perceive) only a small fraction of the stimuli to which they are exposed. Consider, for example, a woman in a supermarket. She may be exposed to over 20,000 products of different colours, sizes and shapes; to perhaps 100 people (looking, walking, searching, talking); to smells (from fruit, meat, disinfectant, people); to sounds within the store (cash registers ringing, shopping trolleys rolling, air conditioners humming, and assistants sweeping, mopping aisles, stocking shelves); and to sounds from outside the store (planes passing, horns sounding, tyres screeching, children shouting, car doors slamming). Yet she manages on a regular basis to visit her local supermarket, select the items she needs, pay for them and leave, all within a relatively brief period of time, without losing her sanity or her personal orientation to the world around her. This is because she exercises selectivity in perception.

Which stimuli get selected depends on two major factors in addition to the nature of the stimulus itself:

1. consumers' previous experience as it affects their expectations (what they are prepared, or 'set', to see), and
2. their motives at the time (their needs, desires, interests and so on).

Each of these factors can serve to increase or decrease the probability that a stimulus will be perceived.

Nature of the Stimulus

Marketing stimuli include an enormous number of variables that affect the consumer's perception, such as the nature of the product, its physical attributes, the package design, the brand name, the advertisements and commercials (including copy claims, choice and sex of model, positioning of model, size of advertisement, typography), the position of a print advertisement or a commercial, and the editorial environment. In general, contrast is one of the most attention-compelling attributes of a stimulus. Advertisers often use extreme attention-getting devices to achieve maximum contrast and, thus, penetrate the consumer's perceptual 'screen'. For example, a number of magazines and newspapers carry advertisements that readers can unfold to reveal oversized, posterlike advertisements for products ranging from cosmetics to cars, because of the 'stopping power' of giant advertisements among more traditional sizes. However, advertising does not have to be unique to achieve a high degree of differentiation; it simply has to contrast with the environment in which it is run. The use of a dramatic image of the product against a white background with little copy in a print advertisement, the absence of sound in a television commercial's opening scene, a 60-second commercial within a string of 20-second spots – all offer sufficient contrast from their environments to achieve differentiation and merit the consumer's attention. Figure 7-3 illustrates the attention-getting nature of a dramatic image in an advertisement. In an effort to achieve contrast, advertisers are also using splashes of colour in black-and-white print advertisements to highlight the advertised product.

With respect to packaging, astute marketers usually try to differentiate their packages to ensure rapid consumer perception. Since the average package on the supermarket shelf has about one-tenth of a second to make an impression on the consumer, it is important that every aspect of the package – the name, shape, colour, label and copy – provide sufficient sensory stimulation to be noted and remembered.

Expectations

People usually see what they expect to see, and what they expect to see is usually based on familiarity, previous experience or preconditioned set (**expectations**). In a marketing context, people tend to perceive products and product attributes according to their own expectations. A student who has been told by his friends that a particular professor is interesting and dynamic will probably perceive the professor in that manner when the class begins; a teenager who attends a horror film that has been billed as terrifying will probably find it so. On the other hand, stimuli that conflict sharply with expectations often receive more attention than those that conform to expectations. For years, certain advertisers have used blatant sexuality in advertisements for products to which sex was not relevant, in the belief that such advertisements would attract a high degree of attention. However, advertisements with irrelevant sexuality often defeat the marketer's objectives because readers tend to remember the sexual aspects (e.g. the innuendo or the model), not the product or brand advertised. Nevertheless, some advertisers continue to use erotic appeals in promoting a wide variety of products, from office furniture to jeans. (The use of sex in advertising is discussed in Chapter 10.)

FIGURE 7-3 Dramatic image compels attention
Source: © Image courtesy of Peta (*www.peta.org*). Used with permission.

Motives

People tend to perceive the things they need or want: the stronger the need, the greater the tendency to ignore unrelated stimuli in the environment. A student who is looking for a new mobile phone provider is more likely to notice and read carefully advertisements for deals and special offers regarding such services than his room-mate, who may be satisfied with his present network service. In general, there is a heightened awareness of stimuli that are relevant to one's needs and interests and a decreased awareness of stimuli that are irrelevant to those needs. An individual's perceptual process simply attunes itself more closely to those elements in the environment that are important to that person. Someone who is hungry is more likely to notice advertisements for food; a sexually repressed person may perceive sexual symbolism where none exists.

Marketing managers recognise the efficiency of targeting their products to the perceived needs of consumers. For example, a marketer can determine through marketing research what consumers consider to be the ideal attributes of the product category or what consumers perceive their needs to be in relation to the product category. The marketer can then segment the market on the basis of those needs and vary the product advertising so that consumers in each segment will perceive the product as meeting their own special needs, wants and interests.

Selective Perception

As the preceding discussion illustrates, the consumer's 'selection' of stimuli from the environment is based on the interaction of expectations and motives with the stimulus itself. These factors give rise to four important concepts concerning perception.

Selective Exposure

Consumers actively seek out messages that they find pleasant or to which they are sympathetic, and they actively avoid painful or threatening ones. They also selectively expose themselves to advertisements that reassure them of the wisdom of their purchase decisions.

Selective Attention

Consumers exercise a great deal of selectivity in terms of the attention they give to commercial stimuli. They have a heightened awareness of stimuli that meet their needs or interests and minimal awareness of stimuli irrelevant to their needs. Thus, consumers are likely to note advertisements for products that would satisfy their needs and disregard those in which they have no interest. People also vary in terms of the kinds of information in which they are interested and the form of message and type of medium they prefer. Some people are more interested in price, some in appearance, and some in social acceptability. Some people like complex, sophisticated messages; others like simple graphics.

Perceptual Defence

Consumers subconsciously screen out stimuli that they find psychologically threatening, even though exposure has already taken place. Thus, threatening or otherwise damaging stimuli are less likely to be consciously perceived than are neutral stimuli at the same level of exposure. Furthermore, individuals sometimes unconsciously distort information that is not consistent with their needs, values and beliefs. One way to combat perceptual defence is to vary and increase the amount of sensory input. For example, since most smokers no longer pay attention to the written warning labels on cigarette packets, Canada now requires tobacco firms to feature graphic health warnings on cigarette packets; one such warning shows a damaged brain and warns about strokes, and another shows a limp cigarette and states that tobacco can cause impotence.[11] Politicians in some European countries have suggested that similar visualised warnings should be mandatory in their home countries.

Perceptual Blocking

Consumers protect themselves from being bombarded with stimuli by simply 'tuning out' – blocking such stimuli from conscious awareness. They do so out of self-protection because of the visually overwhelming nature of the world in which we live. The popularity of devices which enable viewers to skip over television commercials with great ease is, in part, a result of **perceptual blocking**.

Perceptual organisation

People do not experience the numerous stimuli they select from the environment as separate and discrete sensations; rather, they tend to organise them into groups and perceive them as unified wholes. Thus, the perceived characteristics of even the simplest stimulus are viewed as a function of the whole to which the stimulus appears to belong. This method of perceptual organisation simplifies life considerably for the individual.

The specific principles underlying perceptual organisation are often referred to by the name given to the school of psychology that first developed it: **Gestalt** psychology. (*Gestalt*, in German, means pattern or configuration.) Three of the most basic principles of perceptual organisation are *figure and ground*, *grouping* and *closure*.

Figure and Ground

As was noted earlier, stimuli that contrast with their environment are more likely to be noticed. A sound must be louder or softer, a colour brighter or paler. The simplest visual illustration consists of a figure on a ground (i.e. background). The figure is perceived more clearly because, in contrast to its ground, it appears to be well defined, solid and in the forefront. The ground is usually perceived as indefinite, hazy and continuous. The common line that separates the figure and the ground is generally attributed to the figure rather than to the ground, which helps give the figure greater definition. Consider the stimulus of music. People can either 'bathe' in music or listen to music. In the first case, music is simply background to other activities; in the second, it is figure. Figure is more clearly perceived because it appears to be dominant; in contrast, ground appears to be subordinate and, therefore, less important.

People have a tendency to organise their perceptions into **figure-and-ground** relationships. How a figure–ground pattern is perceived can be influenced by prior pleasant or painful associations with one or the other element in isolation. For example, a short time after the destruction of the World Trade Center on 11 September 2001 by aircraft hijacked by terrorists, a lecturer came across an advertisement for Lufthansa (Germany's national airline) that featured a flying jet, photographed from the ground up, between two glass-clad high-rise buildings. Rather than focusing on the brand and the jet (i.e. the 'figure'), all the viewer could think about was the two tall glass-clad towers in the background (i.e. the 'ground'), and the possibility of the jet crashing into them. When the professor presented the advertisement to his students, many expressed the same thoughts. Clearly, this figure–ground reversal was the outcome of the painful events that occurred in September 2001.

Advertisers have to plan their advertisements carefully to make sure that the stimulus they want noted is seen as figure and not as ground. The musical background must not overwhelm the jingle; the background of an advertisement must not detract from the product. Print advertisers often silhouette their products against an indistinct background to make sure that the features they want noted are clearly perceived. We are all familiar with figure–ground patterns, such as the picture of the woman in Figure 7-4. How old would you say she is? Look again very carefully. Depending on how you perceived figure and how you perceived ground, she can be either in her early twenties or her late seventies. This optically ambiguous picture, often called 'old woman and young woman' or 'My wife and my mother-in-law', is one of the most famous multiple images. In fact, it also appeared in an advertisement in the nineteenth century (see Figure 7-5).

Marketers sometimes run advertisements that confuse the consumer because there is no clear indication of which is figure and which is ground. Of course, in some cases, the blurring of figure and ground is deliberate. The well-known Absolut Vodka campaign, started over 25 years ago, often runs print advertisements in which the figure (the shape of the Absolut bottle) is poorly delineated against its ground, challenging readers to search for the bottle; the resulting audience 'participation' produces more intense scrutiny (for examples see Figure 8-3 in Chapter 8, page 202).

FIGURE 7-4 Figure-and-ground reversal

Grouping

Individuals tend to group stimuli so that they form a unified picture or impression. The perception of stimuli as groups or chunks of information, rather than as discrete bits of information, facilitates their memory and recall. **Grouping** can be used advantageously by marketers to imply certain desired meanings in connection with their products. For example, an advertisement for tea may show a young man and woman sipping tea in a beautifully appointed room before a blazing hearth. The overall mood implied by the grouping of stimuli leads the consumer to associate the drinking of tea with romance, fine living and winter warmth.

Most of us can remember and repeat our telephone numbers because we automatically group them into chunks, rather than try to remember all the separate numbers.

Closure

Individuals have a need for **closure**. They express this need by organising their perceptions so that they form a complete picture. If the pattern of stimuli to which they are exposed is

FIGURE 7-5 Nineteenth-century advertisement containing the same picture as in Figure 7-6
Source: © Swim Ink 2/Corbis.

incomplete, they tend to perceive it, nevertheless, as complete; that is, they consciously or subconsciously fill in the missing pieces. Thus, a circle with a section of its circumference missing is invariably perceived as a circle, not an arc.

Incomplete messages or tasks are better remembered than completed ones. One explanation for this phenomenon is that a person who hears the beginning of a message or who begins a task develops a need to complete it. If he or she is prevented from doing so, a state of tension is created that manifests itself in improved memory for the incomplete task. For example, hearing the beginning of a message leads to the need to hear the rest of it – like waiting for the second shoe to drop.

The need for closure has interesting implications for marketers. Promotional messages in which viewers are required to 'fill in' information beg for completion by consumers, and the very act of completion serves to involve them more deeply in the message (see Figure 7-6). In a related vein, advertisers have discovered that they can achieve excellent results by using the soundtrack of a frequently viewed television commercial on radio. Consumers who are familiar with the television commercial perceive the audio track alone as incomplete; in their need for completion, they mentally play back the visual content from memory.

In summary, it is clear that perceptions are not equivalent to the raw sensory input of discrete stimuli, nor to the sum total of discrete stimuli. Rather, people tend to add to or subtract from stimuli to which they are exposed on the basis of their expectations and motives, using generalised principles of organisation based on Gestalt theory.

Perceptual interpretation

The preceding discussion has emphasised that perception is a personal phenomenon. People exercise selectivity as to which stimuli they perceive, and they organise these stimuli on the basis of certain psychological principles. The interpretation of stimuli is also uniquely individual, because it is based on what individuals expect to see in the light of their previous experience, on the number of plausible explanations they can envision, and on their motives and interests at the time of perception.

Stimuli are often highly ambiguous. Some stimuli are weak because of such factors as poor visibility, brief exposure, high noise level or constant fluctuation. Even stimuli that are strong tend to fluctuate dramatically because of such factors as different angles of viewing, varying distances and changing levels of illumination. Consumers usually attribute the sensory input they receive to sources they consider most likely to have caused the specific pattern of stimuli. Past experiences and social interactions help to form certain expectations that provide categories (or alternative explanations) that individuals use in interpreting stimuli. The narrower the individual's experience, the more limited the access to alternative categories.

When stimuli are highly ambiguous, an individual will usually interpret them in such a way that they serve to fulfil personal needs, wishes, interests and so on. How close a person's interpretations are to reality, then, depends on the clarity of the stimulus, the past experiences of the perceiver, and his or her motives and interests at the time of perception.

Perceptual Distortion

Individuals are subject to a number of influences that tend to distort their perceptions, such as physical appearances, stereotypes, first impressions, jumping to conclusions and the halo effect.

Physical Appearances

People tend to attribute the qualities they associate with certain people to others who may resemble them, whether or not they consciously recognise the similarity. For this reason, the selection of models for print advertisements and for television commercials can be a key element in their ultimate persuasiveness. Studies have found that attractive models are more persuasive and have a more positive influence on consumer attitudes and behaviour than average-looking models;

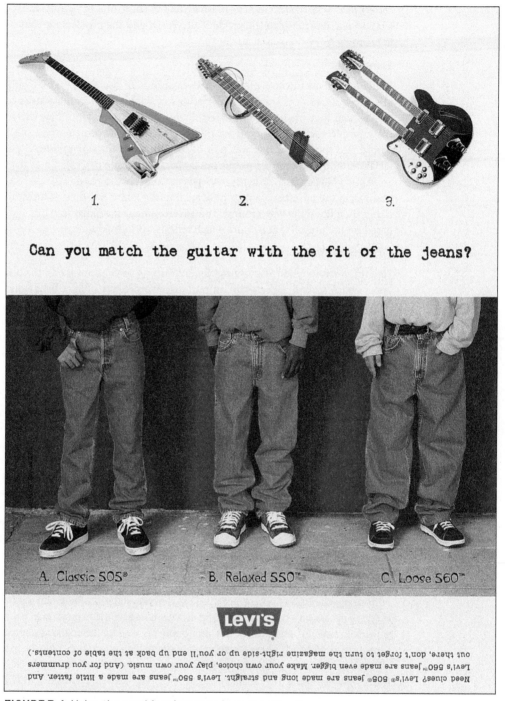

FIGURE 7-6 Using the need for closure to increase attention
Source: Courtesy of Levi Strauss and Co.

attractive men are perceived as more successful businessmen than average-looking men. Some research suggests that models influence consumers' perceptions of physical attractiveness and, through comparisons, their own self-perceptions.[12] Recent research indicates that merely choosing a highly attractive model may not increase message effectiveness. One study revealed that highly attractive models are perceived as having more expertise regarding enhancing products (e.g. jewellery, lipstick, perfume) but not regarding problem-solving products (e.g. products that correct beauty flaws such as acne or dandruff).[13] Therefore, advertisers must ensure that there is a rational match between the product advertised and the physical attributes of the model used to promote it.

Stereotypes

Individuals tend to carry pictures in their minds of the meanings of various kinds of stimuli. These stereotypes serve as expectations of what specific situations, people or events will be like, and they are important determinants of how such stimuli are subsequently perceived. For example, an advertisement for Benetton featuring two men – one black and one white – handcuffed together, which was part of the 'United Colors of Benetton' campaign promoting racial harmony, produced a public outcry because people perceived it as depicting a white man arresting a black man.[14] Clearly, this perception was the result of stereotypes, since there was nothing in the advertisement to indicate that the white person was arresting the black person rather than the other way around. The advertisement for Akteo watches shown in Figure 7-7 is based on the notion that a man's watch reflects his individuality.

First Impressions

First impressions tend to be lasting; yet, in forming such impressions, the perceiver does not yet know which stimuli are relevant, important, or predictive of later behaviour. A shampoo commercial effectively used the line, 'You'll never have a second chance to make a first impression.' Since first impressions are often lasting, introducing a new product before it has been perfected may prove fatal to its ultimate success; subsequent information about its advantages, even if true, will often be negated by the memory of its early performance.

Jumping to Conclusions

Many people tend to jump to conclusions before examining all the relevant evidence. For example, the consumer may hear just the beginning of a commercial message and draw conclusions regarding the product or service being advertised. For this reason, some copywriters are careful to give their most persuasive arguments first. One study showed that consumers who ate foods with elaborate names such as 'succulent Italian seafood filet' rated those foods as more tasty and appealing than those who ate the same foods with such regular names as 'seafood filet'.[15]

Many consumers do not read the volume information on food labels. One study found that consumers purchase packages that they believe contain greater volume, whether or not this is actually so, and that they perceive elongated packaging to contain more volume than round packaging.[16] Clearly, these findings have important implications for package design, advertising and pricing and also represent some ethical dilemmas that are discussed later on in this chapter.

Halo Effect

Historically, the halo effect has been used to describe situations in which the evaluation of a single object or person on a multitude of dimensions is based on the evaluation of just one or a few dimensions (e.g. a man is trustworthy, fine and noble because he looks you in the eye when he speaks). Consumer behaviourists broaden the notion of the halo effect to include the evaluation of multiple objects (e.g. a product line) on the basis of the evaluation of just one dimension (a brand name or a spokesperson). Using this broader definition, marketers take advantage of the halo effect when they extend a brand name associated with one line of products to another. The lucrative field of licensing is based on the halo effect. Manufacturers and retailers hope to acquire instant recognition and status for their products by associating them with a well-known name. (Chapter 8 discusses licensing in greater detail.) A recent study discovered that brands are judged more positively than warranted when evaluated alone than when evaluated within a group of other brands.[17] These findings have implications for the placement of brands in shops and the position of a given brand's advertisements in relation to competing ones within a magazine or a commercial break.

Despite the many subjective influences on perceptual interpretation, individuals usually resolve stimulus ambiguity somewhat 'realistically' on the basis of their previous experiences. Only in situations of unusual or changing stimulus conditions do expectations lead to wrong interpretations.

FIGURE 7-7 Advertisement depicting stereotypes
Source: Courtesy of Universal Watch Company.

CONSUMER IMAGERY

Consumers have a number of enduring perceptions, or images, that are particularly relevant to the study of consumer behaviour. Products and brands have symbolic value for individuals, who evaluate them on the basis of their consistency (congruence) with their personal pictures of themselves. Chapter 6 discussed consumer self-images and how consumers attempt to preserve or enhance their self-images by buying products and patronising services that they believe are congruent with their self-images and by avoiding those that are not. The following section examines consumers' perceived images of products, brands, services, prices, product quality, retail shops and manufacturers.

Product positioning

The essence of successful marketing is the image that a product has in the mind of the consumer – that is, its **positioning**. Positioning is more important to the ultimate success of a product than are its actual characteristics, although products that are poorly made will not succeed in the long run on the basis of image alone. The core of effective positioning is a unique position that the product occupies in the mind of the consumer. Most new products fail because they are perceived as 'me too' offerings that do not offer potential consumers any advantages or unique benefits over competitive products.

Marketers of different brands in the same category can effectively differentiate their offerings only if they stress the benefits that their brands provide rather than their products' physical features. The benefits featured in a product's positioning must reflect attributes that are important to and congruent with the perceptions of the targeted consumer segment.

Positioning strategy is the essence of the marketing mix; it complements the company's definition of the competition, its segmentation strategy and its selection of target markets.

Positioning conveys the concept, or meaning, of the product or service in terms of how it fulfils a consumer need. A good positioning strategy should have a two-pronged meaning: one that is congruent with the consumer's needs while, at the same time, featuring the brand against its competition. For example, the classic 7-Up slogan 'The Un-Cola' was designed to appeal to consumers' desire for an alternative to the most popular soft drink (by using the prefix un-), while also elevating the product by placing it in the same league as its giant competitor (by using the word cola). Similarly, Avis's slogan 'We are number 2, we try harder' reflects a long history of people supporting the underdog and, equally important, it sets Avis above its other competitors in the car hire industry (most people know that Hertz is number 1). Also, as demonstrated by 7-Up's change in positioning strategy to 'Caffeine – never had it, never will' to depict its core benefit, the same product (or service) can be positioned differently to different market segments or can be repositioned to the same audience, without being physically changed.

The result of a successful positioning strategy is a distinctive brand image on which consumers rely in making product choices. A positive brand image also leads to consumer loyalty, positive beliefs about brand value and a willingness to search for the brand. A positive brand image also promotes consumer interest in future brand promotions and inoculates consumers against competitors' marketing activities. Furthermore, research suggests that an advertiser's positioning strategy affects consumer beliefs about its brand's attributes and the prices consumers are willing to pay.[18]

In today's highly competitive environment, a distinctive product image is most important, but also very difficult to create and maintain. As products become more complex and the marketplace more crowded, consumers rely more on the product's image and claimed benefits than on its actual attributes in making purchase decisions.

Product repositioning

Regardless of how well positioned a product appears to be, the marketer may be forced to **reposition** it in response to market events, such as a competitor cutting into the brand's market share or too many competitors stressing the same attribute. For example, rather than trying to meet the lower prices of high-quality private-label competition, some premium brand marketers have repositioned their brands to justify their higher prices, playing up brand attributes that had previously been ignored.

Another reason to reposition a product or service is to satisfy changing consumer preferences. For example, when health-oriented consumers began to avoid high-fat foods, many fast-food chains acted swiftly to reposition their images by offering salad bars and other health-oriented foods. Kentucky Fried Chicken changed its well-known corporate name to KFC in order to omit the dreaded word 'fried' from its advertising.

Perceptual Mapping

The technique of **perceptual mapping** helps marketers to determine just how their products or services appear to consumers in relation to competitive brands on one or more relevant characteristics. It enables them to see gaps in the positioning of all brands in the product or service class and to identify areas in which consumer needs are not being adequately met. For example, if a magazine publisher wants to introduce a new magazine, it may use perceptual mapping to uncover a niche of consumers with a special set of interests that are not being adequately or equally addressed by other magazines targeted to the same demographic segment. This insight allows the publisher to position the new magazine as specifically focused on these interests. Or, a publisher may discover through perceptual mapping that consumers perceive its magazine (let's call it *Splash*) to be very similar in editorial content and format to its closest competitors, *Slash* and *Crash*. By changing the focus of its editorial features to appeal to a new market niche, the publisher can reposition the magazine (e.g. from *Splash* to *Fashion Splash*). Figure 7-8 presents this example in a perceptual map.

Positioning of services

Compared with manufacturing firms, service marketers face several unique problems in positioning and promoting their offerings. Because services are intangible, image becomes a key factor in differentiating a service from its competition. Thus, the marketing objective is to enable the consumer to link a specific image with a specific brand name. Many service marketers have developed strategies to provide customers with visual images and tangible reminders of their

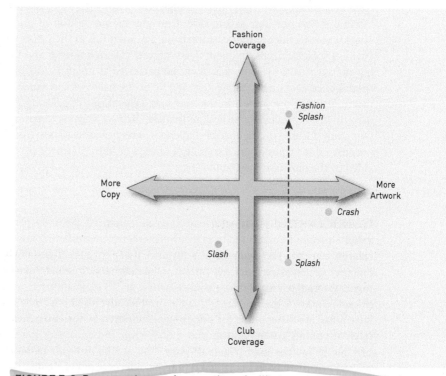

FIGURE 7-8 Perceptual map of competitors facilitates magazine repositioning

service offerings. These include delivery vehicles painted in distinct colours, restaurant matchbooks, packaged hotel soaps and shampoos, and a variety of other speciality items. Many service companies feature real service employees in their advertisements (as tangible cues) and some use people-focused themes to differentiate themselves.

Many service companies market several versions of their service to different market segments by using a differentiated positioning strategy. However, they must be careful to avoid perceptual confusion among their customers.

Although distinct brand names are important to all products or services, they are particularly crucial in marketing services due to the abstract and intangible nature of many services. For example, a name such as Federal Express (later abbreviated to FedEx) is an excellent name because it is distinctive, memorable and relevant to the services it features.

The design of the service environment is an important aspect of service positioning strategy and sharply influences consumer impressions and consumer and employee behaviour. The physical environment is particularly important in creating a favourable impression for such services as banks, shops and professional offices, because there are so few objective criteria by which consumers can judge the quality of the services they receive. The service environment conveys the image of the service provider with whom the service is so closely linked.

One study of service environments identified five environmental variables most important to bank customers:

1. privacy (both visually and verbally, with enclosed offices, transaction privacy, etc.);
2. efficiency/convenience (e.g. transaction areas that are easy to find, directional signs);
3. ambient background conditions (temperature, lighting, noise, music);
4. social conditions (the physical appearance of other people in the bank environment, such as bank customers and bank personnel); and
5. aesthetics (e.g. colour, style, use of materials and artwork).[19]

Perceived price

How a consumer perceives a price – as high, low or fair – has a strong influence on both purchase intentions and purchase satisfaction. Consider the perception of price fairness, for example. There is some evidence that customers do pay attention to the prices paid by other customers (such as senior citizens, frequent flyers, affinity club members), and that the differential pricing strategies used by some marketers are perceived as unfair by customers not eligible for the special prices. No one is happy knowing he or she paid twice as much for an airline ticket or a theatre ticket as the person in the next seat. Perceptions of price unfairness affect consumers' perceptions of product value and, ultimately, their willingness to patronise a shop or a service. One study, focused on the special challenges of service industries in pricing intangible products, proposed three types of pricing strategies based on the customer's perception of the value provided by the purchase (see Table 7-1).

Reference Prices

Products advertised as 'on sale' tend to create enhanced customer perceptions of savings and value. Different formats used in sales advertisements have differing impacts, based on consumer **reference prices**. A reference price is any price that a consumer uses as a basis for comparison in judging another price. Reference prices can be external or internal. An advertiser generally uses a higher external reference price ('sold elsewhere at ...') in an advertisement offering a lower sales price, to persuade the consumer that the product advertised is a really good buy. Internal reference prices are those prices (or price ranges) retrieved by the consumer from memory. Internal reference points are thought to play a major role in consumers' evaluations and perceptions of value of an advertised (external) price deal, as well as in the believability of any advertised reference price. However, consumers' internal reference prices change. For example, as the prices

TABLE 7-1 Three pricing strategies focused on perceived value

PRICING STRATEGY	PROVIDES VALUE BY . . .	IMPLEMENTED AS . . .
Satisfaction-based pricing	Recognizing and reducing customers' perceptions of uncertainty, which the intangible nature of services magnifies.	Service guarantees. Benefit-driven pricing. Flat-rate pricing.
Relationship pricing	Encouraging long-term relationships with the company that customers view as beneficial.	Long-term contracts. Price bundling.
Efficiency pricing	Sharing with customers the cost savings that the company has achieved by understanding, managing, and reducing the costs of providing the service.	Cost-leader pricing.

Source: Adapted from Leonard L. Berry and Yadav S. Manjit, 'Capture and Communicate Value in the Pricing of Services', *MIT Sloan Management Review*, Summer 1996, 41–51. © 1996 from MIT Sloan Management Review/Massachusetts Institute of Technology. All rights reserved. Distributed by Tribune Media Services.

of flat-screen televisions declined sharply due to competition and manufacturers' abilities to produce them more cheaply, consumers' reference prices for this product have declined as well, and many no longer perceive flat-screen televisions as a luxury product that only few can afford. One study showed that consumers' price reference points include past prices, competitors' prices and the cost of goods sold. The study also showed that these reference points do not adequately reflect the effects of inflation on costs, and that customers attribute price differentials to profit and fail to consider vendor costs.[20]

Some researchers proposed that two types of utility are associated with consumer purchases. **Acquisition utility** represents the consumer's perceived economic gain or loss associated with a purchase and is a function of product utility and purchase price. **Transaction utility** concerns the perceived pleasure or displeasure associated with the financial aspect of the purchase and is determined by the difference between the internal reference price and the purchase price.[21] For example, if a consumer wants to purchase a television set for which her internal reference price is approximately €500, and she buys a set that is priced at €500 in a sale, she receives no transaction utility. However, if either her internal reference price is increased or the sales price of the set is decreased, she will receive positive transaction utility, which increases the total utility she experiences with the purchase. Consumers' perceptions of the credibility and fairness of stated prices are an important factor in overall satisfaction. Although many marketers assume that the traditional phrases 'usual price' versus 'sale price' have the same meaning for all consumers, this is unlikely given the evidence that perceptions of marketing stimuli vary widely among consumers.[22]

Several studies showed that consumers believe that the selling prices of a product or service are considerably higher than their perceived fair prices.[23] Several studies have investigated the effects on consumer price perceptions of three types of advertised reference prices: plausible low, plausible high and implausible high. Plausible low prices are well within the range of acceptable market prices; plausible high are near the outer limits of the range but not beyond the realm of believability; and implausible high are well above the consumer's perceived range of acceptable market prices. As long as an advertised reference price is within a given consumer's acceptable price range, it is considered plausible and is assimilated. If the advertised reference point is outside the range of acceptable prices (i.e. implausible), it will be contrasted and thus will not be perceived as a valid reference point. This will adversely affect both consumer evaluations and the advertiser's image of credibility.[24] Another study showed that when consumers encounter prices that are significantly different from their expectations, they engage in dissonance reduction. That is, they seek

TABLE 7-2 Consumer encounters with unexpected prices

	Consumer Encounters with Unexpected Prices	
	↓	
	Consumers Reduce Dissonance using one of the following Modes	
↙	↓	↘
Seeking Consonant Information	**Changing Attitude**	**Trivializing**
↓	↓	↓
Evaluate alternative suppliers	Update Price Expectations	Reduce the importance of:
Evaluate substitute products	↓	(1) money
Plan to search for additional	Attribute higher prices to:	(2) shop around savings
information	(1) product quality	(3) saving money
↓	(2) updated product information	(4) a good deal
Seek consonant information from	(3) product attributes	(5) fair pricing
another retailer or a substitute	(4) general rising prices	(6) value
product (or) remain dissonant	↓	↓
↓	Dissonance is reduced	Dissonance is reduced
Change attitude, trivialize or remain		
dissonant		

Source: Adapted from Joan Lindsey-Mulliken, 'Beyond Reference Price: Understanding Consumers' Encounters with Unexpected Prices', *Journal of Product and Brand Management*, 12, 3, 2003, 141.

additional information to justify the high price or they trivialise their own expectations by, for example, saying that their expectations were unrealistic because it has been a while since they were last in the market to buy the product in question.[25] Table 7-2 depicts the possible changes in the perceptions of consumers who encounter unexpected prices. (The theory of cognitive dissonance is fully explored in Chapter 9.)

Perceived quality

Consumers often judge the quality of a product or service on the basis of a variety of informational cues that they associate with the product. Some of these **cues** are **intrinsic** to the product or service, whereas others are **extrinsic**. Either singly or in composite, such cues provide the basis for perceptions of product and service quality.

Perceived Quality of Products

Cues that are intrinsic concern physical characteristics of the product itself, such as size, colour, flavour or aroma. In some cases, consumers use physical characteristics (e.g. the flavour of ice cream or cake) to judge product quality. Consumers like to believe that they base their evaluations of product quality on intrinsic cues, because that enables them to justify their product decisions (either positive or negative) as being 'rational' or 'objective' product choices. More often than not, however, they use extrinsic characteristics to judge quality. For example, though many consumers claim they buy a brand because of its superior taste, they are often unable to identify that brand in blind taste tests. One study discovered that the colour of a powdered fruit drink product is a more important determinant than the label and the actual taste in determining the consumer's ability to identify the flavour correctly. The study's subjects perceived the purple or grape-coloured versions of the powdered product 'tart' in flavour and the orange-coloured version as 'flavorful, sweet, and refreshing'.[26] One study found that consumers often cannot differentiate among various cola drinks and that they base their preferences on such extrinsic

Non-personally-oriented perceptions			
Conspicuousness	Conspicuous	__:__:__:__:__:__	Noticeable
	Popular	__:__:__:__:__:__	Elitist*
	Affordable	__:__:__:__:__:__	Extremely expensive*
	For wealthy	__:__:__:__:__:__	For well-off
Uniqueness	Fairly exclusive	__:__:__:__:__:__	Very exclusive*
	Precious	__:__:__:__:__:__	Valuable
	Rare	__:__:__:__:__:__	Uncommon
	Unique	__:__:__:__:__:__	Unusual
Quality	Crafted	__:__:__:__:__:__	Manufactured
	Upmarket	__:__:__:__:__:__	Luxurious*
	Best quality	__:__:__:__:__:__	Good quality
	Sophisticated	__:__:__:__:__:__	Original
	Superior	__:__:__:__:__:__	Better
Personally-oriented perceptions			
Hedonism	Exquisite	__:__:__:__:__:__	Tasteful
	Attractive	__:__:__:__:__:__	Glamorous*
	Stunning	__:__:__:__:__:__	Memorable
Extended self	Leading	__:__:__:__:__:__	Influential
	Very powerful	__:__:__:__:__:__	Fairly powerful
	Rewarding	__:__:__:__:__:__	Pleasing
	Successful	__:__:__:__:__:__	Well regarded

* Indicates item is reverse-scored

FIGURE 7-9 Measuring perceptions of brand luxury

Source: Reprinted by permission from Macmillan Publishers Ltd. *Journal of Brand Management*, Franck Vigneron and Lester W. Johnson, 'Measuring Perceptions of Brand Luxury', London, 11, 6, July 2004, 484. Copyright 2004. Published by Palgrave Macmillan.

cues as packaging, pricing, advertising, and even peer pressure.[27] In the absence of actual experience with a product, consumers often evaluate quality on the basis of cues that are external to the product itself, such as price, brand image, manufacturer's image, retail store image, or even the country of origin.

Many consumers use country-of-origin stereotypes to evaluate products (e.g. 'German engineering is excellent' or 'Japanese cars are reliable'). Many consumers believe that a 'Made in . . .' label means a product is 'superior' or 'very good', or just the opposite; inferior or not very good. A recent study pointed out that consumers' perceptions of value, risk, trust, attitude towards the brand, satisfaction, familiarity, attachment and involvement moderate the impact of country-of-origin on perceived quality.[28] Several researchers developed a scale that measures perceptions of brand luxury – a construct that is often related to **perceived quality** (see Figure 7-9).

Perceived Quality of Services

It is more difficult for consumers to evaluate the quality of services than the quality of products. This is true because of certain distinctive characteristics of services: they are intangible, variable, perishable, and they are simultaneously produced and consumed. To overcome the fact that consumers are unable to compare competing services side by side as they do with competing products, consumers rely on surrogate cues (i.e. extrinsic cues) to evaluate service quality. In evaluating a doctor's services, for example, they note the quality of the office and examining room furnishings, the number (and source) of framed degrees on the wall, the pleasantness of the receptionist and the professionalism of the nurse; all contribute to the consumer's overall evaluation of the quality of a doctor's services.

Because the actual quality of services can vary from day to day, from service employee to service employee, and from customer to customer (e.g. in food, in service staff, in haircuts, even in classes taught by the same lecturer), marketers try to standardise their services in order to provide consistency of quality. The downside of service standardisation is the loss of customised services, which many consumers value.

Unlike products, which are first produced, then sold and then consumed, most services are first sold and then produced and consumed simultaneously. Whereas a defective product is likely to be detected by factory quality control inspectors before it ever reaches the consumer, an inferior service is consumed as it is being produced; thus, there is little opportunity to correct it. For example, a defective haircut is difficult to correct, just as the negative impression caused by an abrupt or careless waiter is difficult to correct.

During peak demand hours, the interactive quality of services often declines, because both the customer and the service provider are hurried and under stress. Without special effort by the service provider to ensure consistency of services during peak hours, service image is likely to decline. Some marketers try to change demand patterns in order to distribute the service more equally over time. Long-distance telephone services, for instance, have traditionally offered a discount on telephone calls placed during off-peak hours (e.g. after 6.00 p.m. or at weekends); some restaurants offer a significantly less expensive 'early bird' dinner for consumers who come in before 7.00 p.m. Research suggests that service providers can reduce the perceived waiting time and consequent negative service evaluation by filling the consumer's time. Diners may be invited to study the menu while waiting for a table; patients can view informative videos in the doctor's waiting room.[29]

The most widely accepted framework for researching service quality stems from the premise that a consumer's evaluation of service quality is a function of the magnitude and direction of the gap between the customer's expectations of service and the customer's assessment (perception) of the service actually delivered.[30] For example, a brand-new student enrolled in an introductory marketing course at a highly reputable university has certain expectations about the intellectual abilities of her classmates, the richness of classroom discussions and the lecturer's knowledge and communication skills. At the end of the term, her assessment of the course's quality is based on the differences between her expectations at the start of the term and her perceptions of the course at the end of it. If the course falls below her expectations, she will view it as poor quality. If her expectations are exceeded, she will view the course as a high-quality educational experience. Of course, the expectations of a given service vary widely among different consumers of the same service. These expectations stem from word-of-mouth the consumer has heard about the service, her past experience, the promises made about the service in its advertisements and by its salespeople, the purchase alternatives available and other situational factors.[31] Based on these factors, the sum total of a consumer's expectations of a service before receiving it is termed predicted service; services whose quality, as evaluated by the customer at the end of the service, significantly exceeds the predicted service are perceived as offerings of high quality and generate more customer satisfaction, increased probability of repeat purchase and favourable word-of-mouth.[32]

Perceptions of high service quality and high customer satisfaction lead to higher levels of purchase intentions and repeat buying. One model depicting this relationship states that service quality and consumer behavioural intentions are related, and that service quality is a determinant of whether the consumer ultimately remains with the company or defects to a competitor. When service quality evaluations are high, customers' behavioural intentions tend to be favourable to the company, and they are likely to remain customers. When service evaluations are low, customer relationships are more likely to weaken, resulting in defection to a competitor. Figure 7-10 portrays this model and depicts the behavioural service quality as it affects the retention or defection of customers and the financial consequences of such customer behaviours for the company.

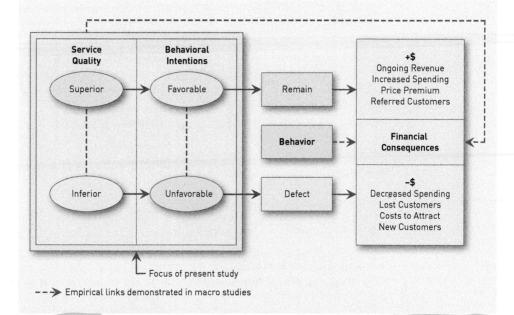

Focus of present study

- - - ▶ Empirical links demonstrated in macro studies

FIGURE 7-10 Conceptual model of behavioural and financial consequences of service quality

Source: Adapted from Valarie A. Zeithaml, Leonard L. Berry and A. Parasuraman, 'The Behavioural Consequences of Service Quality', *Journal of Marketing*, 60, April 1996, 33. Reprinted by permission of the American Marketing Association.

Price/quality relationship

Perceived product value has been described as a trade-off between the product's perceived benefits (or quality) and the perceived sacrifice – both monetary and non-monetary – necessary to acquire it. A number of research studies have found that consumers rely on price as an indicator of product quality, that consumers attribute different qualities to identical products that carry different price tags, and that such consumer characteristics as age and income affect the perception of value.[33] One study suggested that consumers using a **price/quality relationship** are actually relying on a well-known (and, hence, more expensive) brand name as an indicator of quality without actually relying directly on price per se.[34] A later study found out that consumers use price and brand to evaluate the prestige of the product but do not generally use these cues when they evaluate the product's performance.[35] Because price is so often considered an indicator of quality, some product advertisements deliberately emphasise a high price to underscore the marketers' claims of quality. Marketers understand that, at times, products with lower prices may be interpreted as of reduced quality. At the same time, when consumers evaluate more concrete attributes of a product, such as performance and durability, they rely less on the price and brand name as indicators of quality than when they evaluate the product's prestige and symbolic value.[36] For these reasons, marketers must understand all the attributes that customers use to evaluate a given product and include all applicable information in order to counter any perceptions of negative quality associated with a lower price.

In most consumption situations, in addition to price, consumers also use such cues as the brand and the shop in which the product is bought to evaluate its quality. Figure 7-11 presents a conceptual model of the effects of price, brand name and store name on perceived product quality. In summary, consumers use price as a surrogate indicator of quality if they have little information to go on, or if they have little confidence in their own ability to make the product

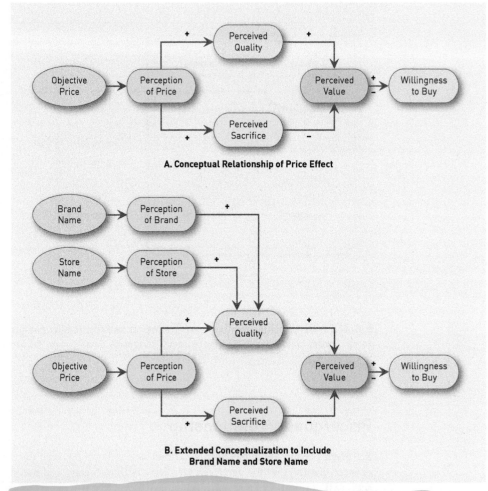

FIGURE 7-11 Conceptual model of the effects of price, brand name and store name on perceived value

Source: Reprinted by permission from Macmillan Publishers Ltd: *Journal of Brand Management*, 11, 6, July Measuring perceptions of brand luxury, p. 484 (Vigneron, F. and Johnson, L. W. 2004), copyright 2004 published by Palgrave Macmillan.

or service choice on other grounds. When the consumer is familiar with a brand name or has experience with a product (or service) or the shop where it is purchased, price declines as a determining factor in product evaluation and purchase.

Shop image

Shops have images of their own that serve to influence the perceived quality of products they carry and the decisions of consumers as to where to shop. These images stem from their design and physical environment, their pricing strategies and product assortments. A study that examined the effects of specific store environmental factors on quality inferences found that consumer perceptions were more heavily influenced by ambient factors (such as the number, type and behaviour of other customers within the shop and the sales personnel) than by store design features.[37]

A study of retail store image based on comparative pricing strategies found that consumers tend to perceive shops that offer a small discount on a large number of items (i.e. frequency of price advantage) as having lower prices overall than competing shops that offer larger discounts on a smaller number of products (i.e. magnitude of price advantage). Thus, frequent advertising that presents large numbers of price specials reinforces consumer beliefs about the competitiveness of a shop's prices.[38] This finding has important implications for retailers' positioning strategies. In times of heavy competition, when it is tempting to hold frequent, large sales, covering many items, such strategies may result in an unwanted change in store image. One study pointed out that some poorly chosen price promotions bring about discrepancies between the actual prices in the shop and consumers' perceptions of the retailer's overall store price image.[39]

The width of product assortment also affects retail store image. Grocery retailers, for example, are often reluctant to reduce the number of products they carry out of concern that perceptions of a smaller assortment will reduce the likelihood that consumers will shop there.[40] On the other hand, some small food markets have carved a profitable niche by carrying a much smaller but highly selective range of products in comparison to conventional supermarkets. Clearly, the unique benefit that a shop provides is more important than the number of items it carries in forming a favourable store image in consumers' minds.

The type of product the consumer wishes to buy influences his or her selection of a retail outlet; conversely, the consumer's evaluation of a product often is influenced by the knowledge of where it was bought. A consumer wishing to buy an elegant dress for a special occasion may go to a shop with an elegant, high-fashion image. Regardless of what she actually pays for the dress she selects (regular price or marked-down price), she will probably perceive its quality to be high. However, she may perceive the quality of the identical dress to be much lower if she buys it in a chain store with a low-price image. Most studies of the effects of extrinsic cues on perceived product quality have focused on just one variable – either price or store image. However, when a second extrinsic cue is available (such as price and store image), perceived quality is sometimes a function of the interaction of both cues on the consumer. For example, when brand and retailer images become associated, the less favourable image becomes enhanced at the expense of the more favourable image. Thus, when a low-priced shop carries a brand with a high-priced image, the image of the shop will improve, whereas the image of the brand will be adversely affected. For that reason, marketers of prestigious designer goods often attempt to control the outlets where these products are sold.

Manufacturers' image

Consumer imagery extends beyond **perceived price** and store image to the producers themselves. Manufacturers who enjoy a favourable image generally find that their new products are accepted more readily than those of manufacturers who have a less favourable or even a 'neutral' image. Researchers have found that consumers generally have favourable perceptions of pioneer brands (the first in a product category), even after follower brands become available. They also found a positive correlation between pioneer brand image and an individual's ideal self-image, which suggests that positive perceptions toward pioneer brands lead to positive purchase intentions.[41]

Some major marketers introduce new products under the guise of supposedly smaller, pioneering (and presumably more forward-thinking) companies. The goal of this so-called stealth (or faux) parentage is to persuade consumers that the new brands are produced by independent, nonconformist free spirits, rather than by giant corporate entities. Companies sometimes use stealth parentage when they enter a product category totally unrelated to the one with which their corporate name has become synonymous. For example, when Disney Studios – a company with a wholesome, family-focused image – produces films that include violence and sex, it does so under the name Touchstone Pictures.

Today companies are using advertising, exhibits and sponsorship of community events to enhance their images. Although some marketers argue that product and service advertising do more to boost the corporate image than institutional (image) advertising does, others see both types of advertising – product and institutional – as integral and complementary components of a total corporate communications programme.

PERCEIVED RISK

Consumers must constantly make decisions regarding what products or services to buy and where to buy them. Because the outcomes (or consequences) of such decisions are often uncertain, the consumer perceives some degree of 'risk' in making a purchase decision. **Perceived risk** is defined as the uncertainty that consumers face when they cannot foresee the consequences of their purchase decisions. This definition highlights two relevant dimensions of perceived risk: uncertainty and consequences. The degree of risk that consumers perceive and their own tolerance for risk-taking are factors that influence their purchase strategies. It should be stressed that consumers are influenced by risks that they perceive, whether or not such risks actually exist. Risk that is not perceived – no matter how real or how dangerous – will not influence consumer behaviour. The major types of risks that consumers perceive when making product decisions include functional, physical, financial, social, psychological and time risks (see Table 7-3).

Perception of risk varies

Consumer perception of risk varies, depending on the person, the product, the situation and the culture. The amount of risk perceived depends on the specific consumer. Some consumers tend to perceive high degrees of risk in various consumption situations; others tend to perceive little risk. For example, studies among adolescents have found that those who engage in high-risk consumption activities (such as smoking or drug use) have lower perceived risk than those who do not engage in high-risk activities.[42] High-risk perceivers are often described as **narrow categorisers** because they limit their choices (e.g. product choices) to a few safe alternatives. They would rather exclude some perfectly good alternatives than chance a poor selection. Low-risk perceivers have been described as **broad categorisers** because they tend to make their choices from a much wider range of alternatives. They would rather risk a poor selection than limit the number of alternatives from which they can choose.

An individual's perception of risk varies with product category. For example, consumers are likely to perceive a higher degree of risk (functional risk, financial risk, time risk) in the purchase of a plasma television set than in the purchase of a coffee-maker. In addition to product-category perceived risk, researchers have identified product-specific perceived risk.[43] One study found that consumers perceive service decisions to be riskier than product decisions, particularly in terms of social risk, physical risk and psychological risk.[44]

TABLE 7-3 Types of perceived risk

Functional risk is the risk that the product will not perform as expected. ('Can the new PDA operate a full week without needing to be recharged?')

Physical risk is the risk to self and others that the product may pose. ('Is a mobile phone really safe, or does it emit harmful radiation?')

Financial risk is the risk that the product will not be worth its cost. ('Will a new and cheaper model of a Plasma TV monitor become available six months from now?')

Social risk is the risk that a poor product choice may result in social embarrassment. ('Will my classmates laugh at my purple mohawk haircut?')

Psychological risk is the risk that a poor product choice will bruise the consumer's ego. ('Will I be embarrassed when I invite friends to listen to music on my five-year-old stereo?')

Time risk is the risk that the time spent in product search may be wasted if the product does not perform as expected. ('Will I have to go through the shopping effort all over again?')

The degree of risk perceived by a consumer is also affected by the shopping situation (e.g. a traditional shop, online, catalogue or direct-mail solicitations or door-to-door sales). High-risk perceivers are unlikely to purchase items online despite the expansion of online retailing, but as they gain experience online, it is believed that their levels of perceived risk regarding electronic buying will decline. However, the findings regarding the impact of perceived risk in shopping online are mixed. While some studies showed that the frequency of shopping online reduced consumers' perceived risk regarding such purchases, other studies showed no correlation between the two factors. Researchers also discovered that consumers' levels of involvement, brand familiarity and the perceived benefits of shopping online impacted the perceived risk of electronic buying.[45]

How consumers handle risk

Consumers characteristically develop their own strategies for reducing perceived risk. These risk-reduction strategies enable them to act with increased confidence when making product decisions, even though the consequences of such decisions remain somewhat uncertain. Some of the more common risk-reduction strategies are discussed in the following sections.

Consumers Seek Information

Consumers seek information about the product and product category through word-of-mouth communication (from friends and family and from other people whose opinions they value), from salespeople and from the general media. They spend more time thinking about their choice and search for more information about the product alternatives when they associate a high degree of risk with the purchase. This strategy is straightforward and logical because the more information the consumer has about the product and the product category, the more predictable the probable consequences and, thus, the lower the perceived risk.

Consumers Are Brand Loyal

Consumers avoid risk by remaining loyal to a brand with which they have been satisfied instead of purchasing new or untried brands. High-risk perceivers, for example, are more likely to be loyal to their old brands and less likely to purchase newly introduced products.

Consumers Select by Brand Image

When consumers have had no experience with a product, they tend to 'trust' a favoured or well-known brand name. Consumers often think well-known brands are better and are worth buying for the implied assurance of quality, dependability, performance and service. Marketers' promotional efforts supplement the perceived quality of their products by helping to build and sustain a favourable brand image.

Consumers Rely on Store Image

If consumers have no other information about a product, they often trust the judgement of the merchandise buyers of a reputable shop and depend on them to have made careful decisions in selecting products for resale. Store image also imparts the implication of product testing and the assurance of service, return privileges and adjustment in case of dissatisfaction.

Consumers Buy the Most Expensive Model

When in doubt, consumers often feel that the most expensive model is probably the best in terms of quality; that is, they equate price with quality. (The price/quality relationship was discussed earlier in this chapter.)

Consumers Seek Reassurance

Consumers who are uncertain about the wisdom of a product choice seek reassurance through money-back guarantees, government and private laboratory test results, warranties and pre-purchase trial. For example, it is unlikely that anyone would buy a new car without a test drive. Products that do not easily lend themselves to free or limited trial (such as a refrigerator) present a challenge to marketers.

The concept of perceived risk has major implications for the introduction of new products. Because high-risk perceivers are less likely to purchase new or innovative products than low-risk perceivers, it is important for marketers to provide such consumers with persuasive risk-reduction strategies, such as a well-known brand name (sometimes achieved through licensing), distribution through reputable retail outlets, informative advertising, publicity stories in the media, impartial test results, free samples and money-back guarantees. Also, most shops that carry a number of different brands and models of the same product, as well as manufacturers of such diverse model lines, now offer online consumers quick and easy ways to generate side-by-side comparisons with detailed charts of the features of all the available models.

ETHICS AND CONSUMER PERCEPTION

The ethical issues related to consumer perception focus on how marketers use the knowledge of perception to manipulate consumers. One technique marketers use is to blur the distinctions between figure and ground. For example, to combat fast-forwarding by consumers who wish to avoid television commercials, marketers are increasingly turning to product placements, where the line between television shows and advertisements is virtually non-existent. Predictions have indicated that marketers are likely to increase expenditures substantially on such branded entertainment. In addition, online editions of newspapers often embed advertisements within the content of news. Marketers also blend promotion and programme content by positioning a television commercial so close to the storyline of a programme that viewers are unaware they are watching an advertisement until they are well into it. In a growing number of countries, television stars or cartoon characters are now prohibited from promoting products during the children's shows in which they appear. Other potential misuses of figure-and-ground are print advertisements (called advertorials) that closely resemble editorial matter, making it increasingly difficult for readers to tell them apart. Thirty-minute commercials (called infomercials) appear to the average viewer as documentaries, and thus command more attentive viewing than obvious commercials would receive.

As discussed earlier, marketers use their knowledge of the just noticeable difference to ensure that reductions in product quantity or quality and increases in prices go unnoticed by consumers. Marketers can also increase the quantity of the product consumed by the way it is physically packaged or presented. For example, studies showed that:

1. both children and adults consume more juice when the product is presented in short, wide glasses than in tall slender glasses;
2. sweets placed in clear jars were eaten much more quickly than those presented in opaque jars;
3. sandwiches in transparent wrap generated more consumption than those in opaque wraps; and
4. the visibility and aroma of tempting foods generated greater consumption.[46]

Another study demonstrated that the organisation of the merchandise, the size of the package, the symmetry of the display and its perceived variety served to impact consumption quantities.[47]

Marketers can also manipulate consumers' perception and behaviour by using the physical setting where consumption occurs. It is widely known that supermarkets routinely move products around to encourage consumers to wander around the store, and keep the stores relatively cold because colder temperatures make people hungrier and so they increase their food purchases. (Some nutritionists advise consumers to go food shopping directly after a filling meal.) At theme parks, guests leaving rides, and presumably still under the spell of the thrill and enjoyment experienced, must exit through a corridor of shops featuring merchandise congruent with the themes of the rides. Marketers can also manipulate consumers' interpretations of marketing stimuli through the context in which they are featured. Inadvertently, marketers can also have an impact on the content of news to which consumers are exposed. For example, many marketers carefully screen the context in which their messages are shown, because they recognise that advertisements are perceived more positively when placed within more positive programmes. Thus, they may choose not to place advertisements in news broadcasts or programmes that cover serious issues, such as wars and world hunger, where some of the content is bound to be unpleasant.

Conveying socially undesirable stereotypes in products and advertisements is another ethical dilemma marketers may face. The makers of Barbie – a doll that has gradually become thinner and bustier – were accused of conveying an unrealistic body image to young girls.[48]

SUMMARY

Perception is the process by which individuals select, organise and interpret stimuli into a meaningful and coherent picture of the world. Perception has strategy implications for marketers because consumers make decisions based on what they perceive rather than on the basis of objective reality.

The lowest level at which an individual can perceive a specific stimulus is that person's absolute threshold. The minimal difference that can be perceived between two stimuli is called the differential threshold or just noticeable difference (JND). Most stimuli are perceived by consumers above the level of their conscious awareness; however, weak stimuli can be perceived below the level of conscious awareness (i.e. subliminally). Research refutes the notion that subliminal stimuli influence consumer buying decisions.

Consumers' selection of stimuli from the environment is based on the interaction of their expectations and motives with the stimulus itself. The principles of selective perception include the following concepts: selective exposure, selective attention, perceptual defence and perceptual blocking. People usually perceive things they need or want and block the perception of unnecessary, unfavourable or painful stimuli.

Consumers organise their perceptions into unified wholes according to the principles of Gestalt psychology: figure and ground, grouping and closure. The interpretation of stimuli is highly subjective and is based on what the consumer expects to see in the light of previous experience, on the number of plausible explanations he or she can envision, on motives and interests at the time of perception, and on the clarity of the stimulus itself. Influences that tend to distort objective interpretation include physical appearances, stereotypes, halo effects, irrelevant cues, first impressions and the tendency to jump to conclusions.

Just as individuals have perceived images of themselves, they also have perceived images of products and brands. The perceived image of a product or service (how it is positioned) is probably more important to its ultimate success than are its actual physical characteristics. Products and services that are perceived distinctly and favourably have a much better chance of being purchased than products or services with unclear or unfavourable images.

Compared with manufacturing firms, service marketers face several unique problems in positioning and promoting their offerings because services are intangible, inherently variable and perishable, and are simultaneously produced and consumed. Regardless of how well positioned a product or service appears to be, the marketer may be forced to reposition it in response to market events, such as new competitor strategies or changing consumer preferences.

Consumers often judge the quality of a product or service on the basis of a variety of informational cues; some are intrinsic to the product (such as colour, size, flavour and aroma), while others are extrinsic (e.g. price, store image, brand image and service environment). In the absence of direct experience or other information, consumers often rely on price as an indicator of quality. How a consumer perceives a price – as high, low or fair – has a strong influence on purchase intentions and satisfaction. Consumers rely on both internal and external reference prices when assessing the fairness of a price.

Consumer imagery also includes perceived images of shops that influence the perceived quality of products they carry, as well as decisions as to where to shop. Manufacturers who enjoy a favourable image generally find that their new products are accepted more readily than those of manufacturers with less favourable or even neutral images.

Consumers often perceive risk in making product selections because of uncertainty as to the consequences of their product decisions. The most frequent types of risk that consumers perceive are functional, physical, financial, social, psychological and time risks. Consumer strategies for reducing perceived risk include increased information search, brand loyalty, buying a well-known brand, buying from a reputable retailer, buying the most expensive brand and seeking reassurance in the form of money-back guarantees, warranties and pre-purchase trial. The concept of perceived risk has important implications for marketers, who can facilitate the acceptance of new products by incorporating risk-reduction strategies in their new-product promotional campaigns.

DISCUSSION QUESTIONS

1. How does sensory adaptation affect advertising effectiveness? How can marketers overcome sensory adaptation?

2. Discuss the differences between the absolute threshold and the differential threshold. Which one is more important to marketers? Explain your answer.

3. For each of these products – energy bars and expensive face moisturisers – describe how marketers can apply their knowledge of the differential threshold to packaging, pricing and promotional claims during periods of (a) rising ingredient and materials costs, and (b) increasing competition.

4. Does subliminal advertising work? Support your view.

5. How do advertisers use contrast to make sure that their advertisements are noticed? Would the lack of contrast between the advertisement and the medium in which it appears help or hinder the effectiveness of the advertisement? What are the ethical considerations in employing such strategies?

6. What are the implications of figure–ground relationships for print advertisements and for online advertisements? How can the figure–ground construct help or interfere with the communication of advertising messages?

7. Find two advertisements depicting two different types of perceptual distortion. Discuss your choices.

8. Why are marketers sometimes 'forced' to reposition their products or services? Illustrate your answers with examples.

9. a. Why is it more difficult for consumers to evaluate the quality of services than the quality of products?

   b. Apply two of the concepts used to explain consumers' evaluations of service quality to your evaluation of your course up to this point in the term.

10. Discuss the roles of extrinsic cues and intrinsic cues in the perceived quality of:
    a. wines
    b. restaurants
    c. digital cameras
    d. graduate education.

EXERCISES

1. Find three examples of print advertisements that use some of the stimulus factors discussed in this chapter to gain attention. For each example, evaluate the effectiveness of the stimulus factors used.
2. Define selective perception. Thinking back, relate one or two elements of this concept to your own attention patterns in viewing print advertisements and television commercials.
3. Find an advertisement or example in another form (e.g. an article) illustrating two of the positioning approaches discussed in this chapter. Evaluate the effectiveness of each advertisement or example selected.
4. Select a company that produces several versions of the same product under the same brand name (one that is not discussed in this chapter). Visit the firm's website and prepare a list of the product items and the positioning strategy for each of the products.
5. Construct a two-dimensional perceptual map of your university or business school using the two attributes that were most influential in your selection. Then mark the position of your business school on the diagram relative to that of another business school you considered. Discuss the implications of this perceptual map for the student recruitment function of the university that you did not choose.

NOTES

1. Martin Lindstrom, 'Smelling a Branding Opportunity', *Brandweek*, 14 March 2005, 26.
2. Philippa Ward, Barry J. Davies and Dion Kooijman, 'Ambient Smell and the Retail Environment: Retailing Olfaction Research to Consumer Behavior', *Journal of Business and Management*, Summer 2003, 289–303; Daniel Milotic, 'The Impact of Fragrance On Consumer Choice', *Journal of Consumer Behaviour*, December 2003, 179; Lawrence K. Altman, 'Unravelling Enigma of Smell Wins Nobel for 2 Americans', *New York Times*, 5 December 2004, A18.
3. Eric R. Spangenberg, Ayn E. Crowley and Pamela W. Henderson, 'Improving the Store Environment: Do Olfactory Cues Affect Evaluations and Behaviors?', *Journal of Marketing*, 60, April 1996, 67–80.
4. Stuart Elliott, 'Don't Call It a Store, Call It an Ad With Walls', *New York Times*, 7 December 2004, 6.
5. Jeffrey Kluger, 'Inside the Food Labs', *Time*, 6 October 2003, 56–60; Jon Gertner, 'Eat Chocolate, Live Longer?', www.nytimes.com, 10 October 2004.
6. Sharon E. Beatty and Del I. Hawkins, 'Subliminal Stimulation: Some New Data and Interpretation', *Journal of Advertising*, 18, 1989, 4–8.
7. Kathryn T. Theus, 'Subliminal Advertising and the Psychology of Processing Unconscious Stimuli: A Review of Research', *Psychology and Marketing*, 11, 3, May–June 1994, 271–90. See also Dennis L. Rosen and Surenra N. Singh, 'An Investigation of Subliminal Embed Effect on Multiple Measures of Advertising Effectiveness', *Psychology and Marketing*, 9, 2, March–April 1992, 157–73.

8. For example, Andrew B. Aylesworth, Ronald C. Goodstein and Ajay Kalra, 'Effects of Arche-typal Embeds of Feelings: An Indirect Route to Affecting Attitudes?', *Journal of Advertising*, Fall 1999, 73–81; Nicholas Epley, Kenneth Savitsky and Robert A. Kachelski, 'What Every Skeptic Should Know About Subliminal Persuasion', *Skeptical Inquirer*, September/October 1999, 4–58.

9. Carl L. Witte, Madhavan Parthasarathy and James W. Gentry, 'Subliminal Perception Versus Subliminal Persuasion: A Re-Examination of the Basic Issues', *American Marketing Associa-tion*, Summer 1995, 133–8. See also Jack Haberstroh, *Ice Cube Sex: The Truth about Subliminal Advertising* (Notre Dame, IN: Cross Cultural Publications, 1994).

10. Martha Rogers and Christine A. Seiler, 'The Answer Is No: A National Survey of Advertising Practitioners and Their Clients about Whether They Use Subliminal Advertising', *Journal of Advertising Research*, March–April 1994, 36–45; Martha Rogers and Kirk H. Smith, 'Pub-lic Perceptions of Subliminal Advertising: Why Practitioners Shouldn't Ignore This Issue', *Journal of Advertising Research*, March–April 1993, 10–18. See also Nicolas E. Synodinos, 'Subliminal Stimulation: What Does the Public Think about It?' in *Current Issues and Research in Advertising*, 11 (1 and 2), eds James H. Leigh and Claude R. Martin Jr., 1988, 157–87.

11. Keith Naughton, 'Gross Out, Smoke Out', *Newsweek*, 25 March 2002, 9.

12. Marsha L. Richins, 'Social Comparison and the Idealized Images of Advertising', *Journal of Consumer Research*, 18, June 1991, 71–83. See also Mary C. Martin and James W. Gentry, 'Stuck in the Model Trap: The Effects of Beautiful Models in Ads on Female Pre-Adolescents and Adolescents', *Journal of Advertising*, 26, 2, Summer 1997, 19–33.

13. Amanda B. Bower and Stacy Landreth, 'Is Beauty Best? Highly Versus Normally Attractive Models in Advertising', *Journal of Advertising*, 30, 1, Spring 2001, 1–12.

14. Kim Foltz, 'Campaign on Harmony Backfires on Benetton', *New York Times*, 20 November 1989, D8.

15. Brian Wansink, Koert van Ittersum and James E. Painter, 'How Descriptive Food Names Bias Sensory Perceptions in Restaurants', *Food Quality and Preference*, www.sciencedirect.com, June 2004.

16. Priya Raghubir and Aradhna Krishna, 'Vital Dimensions in Volume Perception: Can the Eye Fool the Stomach?', *Journal of Marketing Research*, August 1999, 313–26.

17. Steven S. Posavac, David M. Sanbonmatsu, Frank R. Kardes and Gavan J. Fitzsimons, 'The Brand Positivity Effect: When Evaluation Confers Preference', *Journal of Consumer Research*, December 2004, 643–52.

18. Ajay Kalra and Ronald C. Goodstein, 'The Impact of Advertising Positioning Strategies on Consumer Price Sensitivity', *Journal of Marketing Research*, 35, May 1998, 210–24.

19. Julie Baker, Leonard L. Berry and A. Parasuraman, 'The Marketing Impact of Branch Facility Design', *Journal of Retail Banking*, 10, 2, Summer 1988, 33–42.

20. Lisa E. Bolton, Luk Warlop and Joseph W. Alba, 'Consumer Perceptions of Price (Un)Fairness', *Journal of Consumer Research*, March 2003, 474–92.

21. Dhruv Grewal *et al.*, 'The Effects of Price Comparison Advertising on Buyers' Perceptions of Acquisition Value, Transaction Value, and Behavioral Intentions', *Journal of Marketing*, 62, April 1998, 46–59.

22. Larry D. Compeau, Joan Lindsey-Mullikin, Dhruv Grewal and Ross D. Petty, 'Consum-ers' Interpretations of the Semantic Phrases Found in Reference Price Advertisements', *The Journal of Consumer Affairs*, Summer 2004, 178–88.

23. Bolton *et al.*, 'Consumer Perceptions of Price (Un)Fairness'.

24. Katherine Fraccastoro, Scot Burton and Abhijit Biswas, 'Effective Use of Advertisements Pro-moting Sales Prices', *Journal of Consumer Marketing*, 1993, 61–79.

25. Joan Lindsey-Mulliken, 'Beyond Reference Price: Understanding Consumers' Encoun-ters with Unexpected Prices', *The Journal of Product and Brand Management*, 12, 2/3, 2003, 140–54.

26. Lawrence L. Garber Jr., Eva M. Hyatt and Richard G. Starr Jr., 'The Effects of Food Color on Perceived Flavor', *Journal of Marketing Theory and Practice*, Fall 2000, 59–72.

27. Michael J. McCarthy, 'Forget the Ads: Cola Is Cola, Magazine Finds', *Wall Street Journal*, 24 February 1991, B1.

28. Ting-Yu Chueh and Danny T. Kao, 'The Moderating Effects of Consumer Perception to the Impacts of Country-of-Design on Perceived Quality', *Journal of American Academy of Business*, March 2004, 70.

29. Shirley Taylor, 'Waiting for Service: The Relationship Between Delay and Evaluations of Service', *Journal of Marketing*, 58, April 1994, 56–69. See also Michael K. Hui and David K. Tse, 'What to Tell Consumers in Waits of Different Lengths: An Integrative Model of Service Evaluation', *Journal of Marketing*, 60, April 1996, 81–90.

30. Valarie A. Zeithaml, A. Parasuraman and Leonard L. Berry, *Delivering Quality Service: Balancing Customer Perceptions and Expectations* (New York: The Free Press, 1990).

31. Valarie A. Zeithaml, Leonard L. Berry and A. Parasuraman, 'The Nature and Determinants of Customer Expectation of Service', *Journal of the Academy of Marketing Science*, Winter 1993, 1–12.

32. Ibid.

33. For example, Kent Monroe, *Pricing: Making Profitable Decisions*, 2nd edn (New York: McGraw Hill, 1990); William Dodds, Kent Monroe and Dhruv Grewal, 'Effects of Price, Brand, and Store Information on Buyers' Product Evaluations', *Journal of Marketing Research*, 28, August 1991, 307–19; Tung Zong Chang and Albert R. Wildt, 'Price, Product Information, and Purchase Intention: An Empirical Study', *Journal of the Academy of Marketing Science*, 22, 1, 1994, 16–27; Indrajit Sinha and Wayne S. DeSarbo, 'An Integrated Approach toward the Spatial Model of Perceived Customer Value', *Journal of Marketing Research*, 35, May 1998, 236–49.

34. Donald R. Liechtenstein, Nancy M. Ridgway and Richard G. Nitemeyer, 'Price Perception and Consumer Shopping Behavior: A Field Study', *Journal of Marketing Research*, 30, May 1993, 242.

35. Merrie Brucks and Valarie A. Zeithaml, 'Price and Brand Name as Indicators of Quality Dimensions for Consumer Durables', *Journal of the Academy of Marketing Science*, Summer 2000, 359–74.

36. Ibid.

37. Julie Baker, Dhruv Grewal and A. Parasuraman, 'The Influence of Store Environment on Quality Inferences and Store Image', *Journal of the Academy of Marketing Science*, 22, 4, 1994, 328–39.

38. Joseph W. Alba, Susan M. Broniarczyk, Terence A. Shimp and Joel E. Urbany, 'The Influence of Prior Beliefs, Frequency Cues, and Magnitude Cues on Consumers' Perceptions of Comparative Price Data', *Journal of Consumer Research*, 21, September 1994, 219–35.

39. Kalpesh Kaushik Desai and Debabrata Talukdar, 'Relationship Between Product Groups' Price Perceptions, Shopper's Basket Size, and Grocery Store's Overall Store Price Image', *Psychology and Marketing*, 20, 10, 2003, 903.

40. Susan M. Broniarczyk *et al.*, 'Consumers' Perceptions of the Assortment Carried in a Grocery Category: The Impact of Item Reduction', *Journal of Marketing Research*, 35, May 1998, 166–76.

41. Frank H. Alpert and Michael A. Kamins, 'An Empirical Investigation of Consumer Memory, Attitude and Perceptions Toward Pioneer and Follower Brands', *Journal of Marketing*, 59, October 1995, 34–45.

42. Herbert H. Severson, Paul Slovic and Sarah Hampson, 'Adolescents' Perception of Risk: Understanding and Preventing High Risk Behavior', *Advances in Consumer Research*, 20, eds Leigh McAlister and Michael L. Rothschild (Provo, UT: Association for Consumer Research, 1993), 177–82.

43. Grahame R. Dowling and Richard Staelin, 'A Model of Perceived Risk and Intended Risk Handling Activity', *Journal of Consumer Research*, 21, June 1994, 119–34.

44. Keith B. Murray and John L. Schlacter, 'The Impact of Services versus Goods on Consumers' Assessment of Perceived Risk and Variability', *Journal of the Academy of Marketing Sciences*, 18, Winter 1990, 51–65.

45. For example, Wen-yeh Huang, Holly Schrank and Alan J. Dubinsky, 'Effect of Brand Name on Consumers' Risk Perceptions of Online Shopping', *Journal of Consumer Behaviour*, October 2004, 40–51; Guilherme Pires, John Stanton and Andrew Eckford, 'Influences on the Perceived Risk of Purchasing Online', *Journal of Consumer Behaviour*, December 2004, 118–32; Bill Doolin, Stuart Dillon, Fiona Thompson and James L. Corner, 'Perceived Risk, the Internet Shopping Experience and Online Purchasing Behavior: A New Zealand Perspective', *Journal of Global Information Management*, April–June 2005, 66–89.

46. Brian Wansink and Koert van Ittersum, 'Bottoms Up! The Influence of Elongation on Pouring and Consumption Value', *Journal of Consumer Research*, December 2003, 455–63; Brian Wansink, 'Environmental Factors That Increase the Food Intake and Consumption Volume of Unknowing Consumers', Annual Reviews, *Nutrition*, 2004, 24, 455–79.

47. Barbara E. Kahn and Brian Wansink, 'The Influence of Assortment Structure on Perceived Variety and Consumption Quantities', *Journal of Consumer Research*, March 2004, 519–34.

48. Natalie Angier, 'Drugs, Sports, Body Image and G.I. Joe', *New York Times*, 22 December 1998, F1.

CHAPTER 8
CONSUMER LEARNING

How individuals learn is a matter of great interest and importance to academics, psychologists, consumer researchers and to marketers. The reason that marketers are concerned with how individuals learn is that they are vitally interested in teaching them, in their roles as consumers, about products, product attributes and their potential benefits: where to buy them, how to use them, how to maintain them and even how to dispose of them. They are also vitally interested in how effectively they have taught consumers to prefer their brands and to differentiate their products from competitive offerings. Marketing strategies are based on communicating with the consumer – directly, through advertisements, and indirectly, through product appearance, packaging, price and distribution channels. Marketers want their communications to be noted, believed, remembered and recalled. For these reasons, they are interested in every aspect of the learning process.

However, despite the fact that learning is all-pervasive in our lives, there is no single, universal theory of how people learn. Instead, there are two major schools of thought concerning the learning process: one consists of behavioural theories, the other of cognitive theories. Cognitive theorists view learning as a function of purely mental processes, whereas behavioural theorists focus almost exclusively on observable behaviours (responses) that occur as the result of exposure to stimuli.

In this chapter, we examine the two general categories of learning theory: **behavioural learning theory** and **cognitive learning theory**. Although these theories differ markedly in a number of essentials, each theory offers insights to marketers on how to shape their messages to consumers to bring about desired purchase behaviour. We also discuss how consumers store, retain and retrieve information, and how learning is measured. The chapter concludes with a discussion of how marketers use learning theories in their marketing strategies.

THE ELEMENTS OF CONSUMER LEARNING

Because not all learning theorists agree on how learning takes place, it is difficult to come up with a generally accepted definition of learning. From a marketing perspective, however, consumer learning can be thought of as the process by which individuals acquire the purchase and consumption knowledge and experience that they can apply to future related behaviour. Several points in this definition are worth noting.

First, consumer learning is a process; that is, it continually evolves and changes as a result of newly acquired knowledge (which may be gained from reading, discussions, observation or thinking) or from actual experience. Both newly acquired knowledge and personal experience serve as feedback to the individual and provide the basis for future behaviour in similar situations.

The role of experience in learning does not mean that all learning is deliberately sought. Though much learning is intentional (i.e. it is acquired as the result of a careful search for information), a great deal of learning is also incidental, acquired by accident or without much effort. For example, some advertisements may induce learning (e.g. of brand names), even though the consumer's attention is elsewhere (on a magazine article rather than the advertisement on the facing page). Other advertisements are sought out and carefully read by consumers contemplating a major purchase decision.

The term **learning** encompasses the total range of learning, from simple, almost reflexive responses to the learning of abstract concepts and complex problem-solving. Most learning theorists recognise the existence of different types of learning and explain the differences through the use of distinctive models of learning.

Despite their different viewpoints, learning theorists in general agree that in order for learning to occur certain basic elements must be present. The elements included in most learning theories are motivation, cues, response and reinforcement. These concepts are discussed first because they tend to recur in the theories discussed later in this chapter.

Motivation

The concept of **motivation** is important to learning theory. Remember, motivation is based on needs and goals. Motivation acts as a spur to learning. For example, men and women who want to become good tennis players are motivated to learn all they can about tennis and to practise whenever they can. They may seek information concerning the prices, quality and characteristics of tennis racquets if they 'learn' that a good racquet is instrumental to playing a good game. Conversely, individuals who are not interested in tennis are likely to ignore all information related to the game. The goal object (proficiency in tennis) simply has no relevance for them. The degree of relevance, or involvement, determines the consumer's level of motivation to search for knowledge or information about a product or service. (*Involvement theory*, as it has come to be known, will be discussed later in the chapter.) Uncovering consumer motives is one of the prime tasks of marketers, who then try to teach motivated consumer segments why and how their products will fulfil the consumer's needs.

Cues

If motives serve to stimulate learning, **cues** are the stimuli that give direction to these motives. An advertisement for a tennis camp may serve as a cue for tennis buffs, who may suddenly 'recognise' that attending tennis camp is a concentrated way to improve their game while taking a holiday. The advertisement is the cue, or stimulus, that suggests a specific way to satisfy a salient motive. In the marketplace, price, styling, packaging, advertising and shop displays all serve as cues to help consumers fulfil their needs in product-specific ways.

Cues serve to direct consumer drives when they are consistent with consumer expectations. Marketers must be careful to provide cues that do not upset those expectations. For example, consumers expect designer clothes to be expensive and to be sold in upscale retail outlets. Thus, a high-fashion designer should sell his or her clothes only through exclusive shops and advertise only in upscale fashion magazines. Each aspect of the marketing mix must reinforce the others if cues are to serve as the stimuli that guide consumer actions in the direction desired by the marketer.

Response

How individuals react to a drive or cue – how they behave – constitutes their **response**. Learning can occur even when responses are not overt. The car manufacturer that provides consistent cues to a consumer may not always succeed in stimulating a purchase. However, if the manufacturer succeeds in forming a favourable image of a particular model in the consumer's mind, when the consumer is ready to buy, it is likely that he or she will consider that make or model.

A response is not tied to a need in a one-to-one fashion. Indeed, as was discussed in Chapter 5, a need or motive may evoke a whole variety of responses. For example, there are many ways to respond to the need for physical exercise besides playing tennis. Cues provide some direction, but there are many cues competing for the consumer's attention. Which response the consumer makes depends heavily on previous learning; that, in turn, depends on how related responses were reinforced previously.

Reinforcement

Reinforcement increases the likelihood that a specific response will occur in the future as the result of particular cues or stimuli. For example, the advertisement shown in Figure 8-1 has instructional text and is designed to generate consumer learning. It informs potential customers that the more you fly KLM the more bonus tickets you will receive. In other words, if you join the KLM Bluebiz loyalty programme you will get the same reinforcement whether your company is large or small. If John, a young businessman, joins the programme and finds the statements to be true, learning has taken place through positive reinforcement since the loyalty programme lived up to expectations. On the other hand, if the programme did not provide the benefits promised, John would have no reason to associate the loyalty programme with reinforcement in the future. Because of the absence of reinforcement, it is less likely that he would fly KLM again.

With these basic principles established, we can now discuss some well-known theories or models of how learning occurs.

BEHAVIOURAL LEARNING THEORIES

Behavioural learning theories are sometimes referred to as **stimulus-response theories** because they are based on the premise that observable responses to specific external stimuli signal that learning has taken place. When a person acts (responds) in a predictable way to a known stimulus, he or she is said to have 'learned'. Behavioural theories are concerned not so much with the process of learning as with the inputs and outcomes of learning; that is, in the stimuli that consumers select from the environment and the observable behaviours that result. Two behavioural theories with great relevance to marketing are classical conditioning and instrumental (or operant) conditioning.

Classical conditioning

Early **classical conditioning** theorists regarded all organisms (both animal and human) as relatively passive entities that could be taught certain behaviours through repetition (or 'conditioning'). In

FIGURE 8-1 Product usage leads to reinforcement
Source: © KLM Royal Dutch Airlines.

everyday speech, the word conditioning has come to mean a kind of 'knee-jerk' (or automatic) response to a situation built up through repeated exposure. If you get a headache every time you think of visiting your Aunt Molly, your reaction may be conditioned from years of boring visits.

Ivan Pavlov, a Russian physiologist, was the first to describe conditioning and to propose it as a general model of how learning occurs. According to Pavlovian theory, conditioned learning results when a stimulus that is paired with another stimulus that elicits a known response serves to produce the same response when used alone.

Pavlov demonstrated what he meant by **conditioned learning** in his studies with dogs. The dogs were hungry and highly motivated to eat. In his experiments, Pavlov sounded a bell and then immediately applied a meat paste to the dogs' tongues, which caused them to salivate. Learning (conditioning) occurred when, after a sufficient number of repetitions of the bell followed almost immediately by the food, the sound of the bell alone caused the dogs to salivate. The dogs associated the bell sound (the conditioned stimulus) with the meat paste (the unconditioned stimulus) and, after a number of pairings, gave the same unconditioned response (salivation) to the bell alone as they did to the meat paste. The unconditioned response to the meat paste became the conditioned response to the bell. Figure 8-2A models this relationship. An analogous situation would be one in which the smells of dinner cooking would cause your mouth to water. If you usually listen to the 6 o'clock news while waiting for dinner to be served, you would tend to associate the 6 o'clock news with dinner, so that eventually the sounds of the 6 o'clock news alone might cause your mouth to water, even if dinner was not being prepared and even if you were not hungry. Figure 8-2B shows this basic relationship.

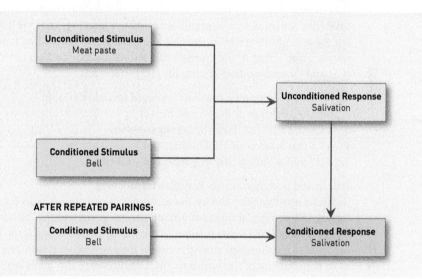

FIGURE 8-2A Pavlovian model of classical conditioning

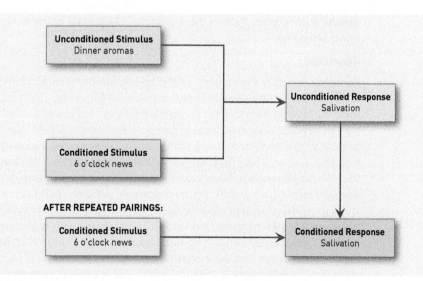

FIGURE 8-2B Analogous model of classical conditioning

In a consumer behaviour context, an unconditioned stimulus might consist of a well-known brand symbol (such as the BMW name) that implies technically superior and well-designed products. This previously acquired consumer perception of BMW is the unconditioned response. **Conditioned stimuli** might consist of new products bearing the well-known symbol (such as a new BMW motorcycle), and the conditioned response would be trying this product because of the belief that it embodies the same attributes with which the BMW name is associated.

Cognitive Associative Learning

Contemporary behavioural scientists view classical conditioning as the learning of associations among events that allows the organism to anticipate and 'represent' its environment. According to this view, the relationship (or contiguity) between the conditioned stimulus and the unconditioned stimulus (the bell and the meat paste) influenced the dogs' expectations, which in turn influenced their behaviour (salivation). Classical conditioning, then, rather than being a reflexive action, is seen as **cognitive associative learning** – not the acquisition of new reflexes, but the acquisition of new knowledge about the world.[1] According to some researchers, optimal conditioning – that is, the creation of a strong association between the conditioned stimulus (CS) and the unconditioned stimulus (US) – requires:

1. forward conditioning (i.e. the CS should precede the US);
2. repeated pairings of the CS and the US;
3. a CS and a US that logically belong together;
4. a CS that is novel and unfamiliar; and
5. a US that is biologically or symbolically salient.

This model is known as **neo-Pavlovian conditioning**.[2]

Under neo-Pavlovian theory, the consumer can be viewed as an information seeker who uses logical and perceptual relations among events, along with his or her own preconceptions, to form a sophisticated representation of the world. Conditioning is the learning that results from exposure to relationships among events in the environment; such exposure creates expectations as to the structure of the environment. Conditioning also generates more attention to subsequent advertisements and other promotions in the environment.[3]

Strategic Applications of Classical Conditioning

Three basic concepts derive from classical conditioning: *repetition, stimulus generalisation* and *stimulus discrimination*. Each of these concepts is important to the strategic applications of consumer behaviour.

Repetition

Repetition increases the strength of the association between a conditioned stimulus and an unconditioned stimulus and slows the process of forgetting. However, research suggests that there is a limit to the amount of repetition that will aid retention. Although some overlearning (i.e. repetition beyond what is necessary for learning) aids retention, at some point an individual can become satiated with numerous exposures, and both attention and retention will decline. This effect, known as **advertising wear-out**, can be moderated by varying the advertising message. Some marketers avoid wear-out by using *cosmetic variations* in their advertisements (using different backgrounds, different print types, different advertising spokespersons) while repeating the same advertising theme. For example, the classic, decades-old Absolut Vodka campaign has used the same theme with highly creative and varied backgrounds, relating the product to holidays, trends and cultural symbols across the world. Figure 8-3 portrays Absolut advertisements where the bottle is seen within the theme of cities, 8-3(A) in Brussels, 8-3(B) in Geneva. These two ads exemplify cosmetic variations of the same theme, as they have both placed the Absolut bottle in a context for which the city is famous (Manneken Pis in Brussels, and a Swiss watch in the Geneva ad).

(A)

FIGURE 8-3 Cosmetic variations of Absolut Vodka advertisments (*continues on next page*)
Source: © V&S Vin & Spirit AB. Used under permission from V&S Vin & Spirit AB.

One study showed that brand familiarity had an impact on the effectiveness of repeating advertisements. The effectiveness of repeats for an unfamiliar brand declined over time, but when the same advertising was used for a well-known and familiar brand, repetition wear-out was postponed.[4]

Substantive variations are changes in advertising content across different versions of an advertisement. For example, look at the advertisements in Figure 8-4. Figure 8-4(A) and 8-4(B) exemplify marketing of the Absolut product with a substantive variation when contrasted with the two advertisements in Figure 8-3. As mentioned, Figures 8-4(A) and 8-4(B) are both ads where the Absolut bottle is 'hidden' in a context for which the city is famous, and as such they might be viewed as cosmetic variations on the same underlying advertising theme. However, they might also be argued to be a substantive variation of the ads in Figure 8-3, since the concepts

(B)

FIGURE 8-3 Cosmetic variations of Absolut Vodka advertisments (*continued*)
Source: © V&S Vin & Spirit AB. Used under permission from V&S Vin & Spirit AB.

are different. For the ads in Figure 8.3 the common theme is cities, but there is no such common theme in Figure 8.4. Hence, there is a substantive variation both between the ads in Figures 8.3 and 8.4, but also to some degree between 8.4A and 8.4B. One study found that individuals exposed to substantively varied advertisements process more information about product attributes and have more positive thoughts about the product than those exposed to cosmetic variations. Attitudes formed as a result of exposure to substantively varied advertisements were also more resistant to change in the face of competitive attack.[5]

Although the principle of repetition is well established among advertisers, not everyone agrees on how much repetition is enough. Some marketing scholars believe that just three exposures to an advertisement are needed: one to make consumers aware of the product, a second

(A)

FIGURE 8-4 Substantive variations for the same product, when compared to the advertisements in Figure 8-3 (*continues on next page*)
Source: © V&S Vin & Spirit AB. Used under permission from V&S Vin & Spirit AB.

to show consumers its relevance and a third to remind them of its benefits. Others think it may take 11 to 12 repetitions to increase the likelihood that consumers will actually receive the three exposures basic to the so-called three-hit theory.

The effectiveness of repetition is somewhat dependent upon the amount of competitive advertising to which the consumer is exposed. The higher the level of competitive advertisements, the greater the likelihood that *interference* will occur, causing consumers to forget previous learning that resulted from repetition.

(B)

FIGURE 8-4 Substantive variations for the same product, when compared to the advertisements in Figure 8-3 (*continued*)
Source: © V&S Vin & Spirit AB. Used under permission from V&S Vin & Spirit AB.

Stimulus Generalisation

According to classical conditioning theorists, learning depends not only on repetition but also on the ability of individuals to generalise. Pavlov found, for example, that a dog could learn to salivate not only to the sound of a bell but also to the somewhat similar sound of jangling keys. If we were not capable of **stimulus generalisation** – that is, of making the same response to slightly different stimuli – not much learning would take place.

Stimulus generalisation explains why some imitative 'me-too' products succeed in the market-place: consumers confuse them with the original product they have seen advertised. It also explains why manufacturers of private-label brands try to make their packaging closely resemble the national brand leaders. They are hoping that consumers will confuse their packages with the leading brand and buy their product rather than the leading brand. Similarly packaged competitive products result in millions of lost sales for well-positioned and extensively advertised brands.

Product Line, Form and Category Extensions

The principle of stimulus generalisation is applied by marketers to product line, form and category extensions. In **product line extensions**, the marketer adds related products to an already established brand, knowing that the new product is more likely to be adopted when it is associated with a known and trusted brand name.

Marketers also offer product form extensions, such as Gillette Shaving Foam to Gillette Deodorant, or Honda motorcycles to Honda cars to Honda boat engines. Marketers also offer product category extensions that generally target new market segments, as Gillette did when they introduced a shaving product especially targeted at women.

The success of product extensions depends on a number of factors. If the image of the parent brand is one of quality and the new item is logically linked to the brand, consumers are more likely to bring positive associations to the new offerings introduced as product line, form or category extensions. The number of different products affiliated with a brand strengthens the brand name, as long as the company maintains a quality image across all brand extensions. Failure to do so, in the long run, is likely negatively to affect consumer confidence and evaluations of all the brand's offerings.

Family Branding

Family branding – the practice of marketing a whole line of company products under the same brand name – is another strategy that capitalises on the consumer's ability to generalise favourable brand associations from one product to others. BMW, for example, continues to add new car and motorcycle products under the BMW brand name, achieving ready acceptance for the new products from satisfied consumers of other BMW cars. Clearly, managing a family brand is more complex than managing a brand that includes only closely related items. It was demonstrated in a study that consumers are likely to expect variability in the performances of the products under the family brand if the company does not address this issue in the information provided with new products introduced; the study singles out the importance of consistent positioning even as the number of offerings under a given name increases.[6]

On the other hand, Volkswagen builds its strength on the many individual brands in the same product category. For example, the company offers car brands like Audi, Seat, Skoda and Volkswagen, with a variety of products offered under each specific brand (e.g. Audi A3, Audi A4 and Audi A6).

Licensing

Licensing – allowing a well-known brand name to be affixed to products of another manufacturer – is a marketing strategy that operates on the principle of stimulus generalisation. The names of designers, manufacturers, celebrities, corporations and even cartoon characters are attached for a fee (i.e. 'rented') to a variety of products, enabling the licensees to achieve instant recognition and implied quality for the licensed products. Some successful licensors include Tommy Hilfiger, Calvin Klein and Christian Dior, whose names appear on an exceptionally wide variety of products, from sheets to shoes and luggage to perfume.

Corporations also license their names and trademarks, usually for some form of brand extension, where the name of the corporation is licensed to the maker of a related product and thereby enters a new product category. Corporations also license their names for purely promotional licensing, in which popular company logos (such as 'Always Coca-Cola') are stamped on clothing, toys, coffee mugs and the like. Some magazines have also licensed their names to manufacturers of products similar to the magazines' own publishing focus. Municipal and state governments have begun licensing their names to achieve new sources of revenue. The Vatican Library licenses its name for a variety of products from luggage to bed linens, the Mormon Church has expanded its licensing activities to apparel and home decorating items.

The increase in licensing has made *counterfeiting* a booming business, as counterfeiters add well-known licensor names to a variety of products without benefit of contract or quality control. Apart from the loss of sales revenue because of counterfeiting, the authentic brands also suffer the consequences associated with zero quality control over counterfeit products that bear their names. It is also increasingly difficult to identify fakes of such expensive and upscale goods as Christian Dior bags, Gucci shoes and Chanel No. 5 perfume. Many firms are now legally pursuing retailers that sell counterfeit branded goods; many also are employing specialised technology to make their products more counterfeit-proof.[7]

Stimulus Discrimination

Stimulus discrimination is the opposite of stimulus generalisation and results in the selection of a specific stimulus from among similar stimuli. The consumer's ability to discriminate among similar stimuli is the basis of positioning strategy (discussed in Chapter 7), which seeks to establish a unique image for a brand in the consumer's mind.

Positioning

In our overcommunicated society, the key to stimulus discrimination is effective **positioning**, a major competitive advantage. The image – or position – that a product or service holds in the mind of the consumer is critical to its success. When a marketer targets consumers with a strong communications programme that stresses the unique ways in which its product will satisfy the consumer's needs, it wants the consumer to differentiate its product from among competitive products on the shelf. Unlike the imitator who hopes consumers will generalise their perceptions and attribute special characteristics of the market leader's products to its own products, market leaders want the consumer to discriminate among similar stimuli. Major marketers are constantly vigilant concerning store brand look-alikes, and they quickly take legal action against retailers that they believe are cannibalising their sales. They want their products to be recognised as uniquely fulfilling consumers' needs. Studies have shown that the favourable attitudes resulting from effective positioning and stimulus discrimination are usually retained long enough to influence future purchase behaviour.[8]

Product Differentiation

Most product differentiation strategies are designed to distinguish a product or brand from that of competitors on the basis of an attribute that is relevant, meaningful and valuable to consumers. However, many marketers also successfully differentiate their brands on an attribute that may actually be irrelevant to creating the implied benefit, such as a non-contributing ingredient or a colour.[9]

It often is quite difficult to unseat a brand leader once stimulus discrimination has occurred. One explanation is that the leader is usually first in the market and has had a longer period to 'teach' consumers (through advertising and selling) to associate the brand name with the product. In general, the longer the period of learning – of associating a brand name with a specific product – the more likely the consumer is to discriminate and the less likely to generalise the stimulus.

Classical Conditioning and Consumer Behaviour

The principles of classical conditioning provide the theoretical underpinnings for many marketing applications. Repetition, stimulus generalisation and stimulus discrimination are all major applied concepts that help to explain consumer behaviour in the marketplace. However, they do not explain all consumer behavioural learning. Although a great deal of consumer behaviour (e.g. the purchase of branded convenience goods) is shaped to some extent by repeated advertising messages stressing a unique competitive advantage, a significant amount of purchase behaviour results from careful evaluation of product alternatives. Our assessments of products are often based on the degree of satisfaction – the rewards – we experience as a result of making specific purchases; in other words, from instrumental conditioning.

Instrumental conditioning

Like classical conditioning, **instrumental conditioning** requires a link between a stimulus and a response. However, in instrumental conditioning, the stimulus that results in the most satisfactory response is the one that is learned.

Instrumental learning theorists believe that learning occurs through a trial-and-error process, with habits formed as a result of rewards received for certain responses or behaviours. This model of learning applies to many situations in which consumers learn about products, services and retail stores. For example, consumers learn which shops carry the type of clothing they prefer at prices they can afford to pay by shopping in a number of stores. Once they find a shop that carries clothing that meets their needs, they are likely to patronise that one to the exclusion of others. Every time they purchase a shirt or a sweater there that they really like, their store loyalty is rewarded (reinforced), and their patronage of that shop is more likely to be repeated. Whereas classical conditioning is useful in explaining how consumers learn very simple kinds of behaviours, instrumental conditioning is more helpful in explaining complex, goal-directed activities.

The name most closely associated with instrumental (operant) conditioning is that of the American psychologist B. F. Skinner. According to Skinner, most individual learning occurs in a controlled environment in which individuals are 'rewarded' for choosing an appropriate behaviour. In consumer behaviour terms, instrumental conditioning suggests that consumers learn by means of a trial-and-error process in which some purchase behaviours result in more favourable outcomes (i.e. rewards) than others. A favourable experience is 'instrumental' in teaching the individual to repeat a specific behaviour.

Like Pavlov, Skinner developed his model of learning by working with animals. Small animals, such as rats and pigeons, were placed in his 'Skinner box'; if they made appropriate movements (e.g. if they depressed levers or pecked keys), they received food (a positive reinforcement). Skinner and his many adherents have done amazing things with this simple learning model, including teaching pigeons to play ping-pong and even to dance. In a marketing context, the consumer who tries several brands and styles of jeans before finding a style that fits her figure (positive reinforcement) has engaged in instrumental learning. Presumably, the brand that fits best is the one she will continue to buy. This model of instrumental conditioning is presented in Figure 8-5.

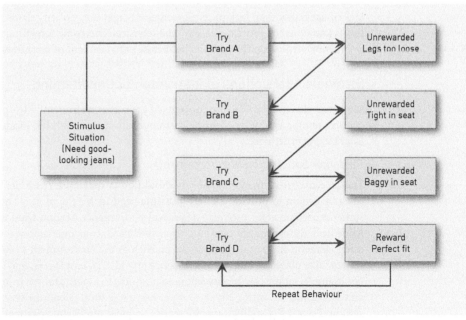

FIGURE 8-5 A model of instrumental conditioning

Reinforcement of Behaviour

Skinner distinguished two types of reinforcement (or reward) that influence the likelihood that a response will be repeated. The first type, **positive reinforcement**, consists of events that strengthen the likelihood of a specific response by adding something to the situation. Using a shampoo that leaves your hair feeling silky and clean is likely to result in a repeat purchase of the shampoo (the shampoo adds the feeling of your hair being silky and clean). In contrast, **negative reinforcement** removes something from the situation, which also serves to encourage a specific behaviour. For example, sunglasses stop the bright sunlight from bothering you, and thereby encourage the use of such glasses. An advertisement that shows a model with wrinkled skin is designed to encourage consumers to buy and use the advertised skin cream.

Fear appeals in advertising messages are examples of negative reinforcement. Many life insurance commercials rely on negative reinforcement to encourage the purchase of life insurance. The advertisements warn husbands of the dire consequences to their wives and children in the event of their sudden death. Marketers of headache remedies use negative reinforcement when they illustrate the unpleasant symptoms of an unrelieved headache, as do marketers of mouthwash when they show the loneliness suffered by someone with bad breath. In each of these cases, the consumer is encouraged to avoid the negative consequences by buying the advertised product.

Either positive or negative reinforcement can be used to elicit a desired response. However, negative reinforcement should not be confused with punishment, which is designed to discourage behaviour. For example, parking tickets are not negative reinforcement; they are a form of 'punishment' designed to discourage drivers from parking illegally.

Extinction and Forgetting

When a learned response is no longer reinforced, it diminishes to the point of extinction, that is, to the point at which the link between the stimulus and the expected reward is eliminated. If a consumer is no longer satisfied with the service a shop provides, the link between the stimulus (the shop) and the response (expected satisfaction) is no longer reinforced, and there is little likelihood that the consumer will return. When behaviour is no longer reinforced, it is 'unlearned'. There is a difference, however, between extinction and forgetting. A person who has not visited a once favourite restaurant for a very long time may simply forget how much he used to enjoy eating there and not think to return. Thus, his behaviour is unlearned because of lack of use rather than lack of reinforcement. Forgetting is often related to the passage of time; this is known as the process of decay. Marketers can overcome forgetting through repetition and can combat extinction through the deliberate enhancement of consumer satisfaction.

Strategic Applications of Instrumental Conditioning

Marketers effectively utilise the concepts of consumer instrumental learning when they provide positive reinforcement by ensuring customer satisfaction with the product, the service and the total buying experience.

Customer Satisfaction (Reinforcement)

The objective of all marketing efforts should be to maximise customer satisfaction. Marketers must be certain to provide the best possible product for the money and to avoid raising consumer expectations for product (or service) performance beyond what the product can deliver. Aside from the experience of using the product itself, consumers can receive reinforcement from other elements in the purchase situation, such as the environment in which the transaction or service takes place, the attention and service provided by employees, and the amenities provided. For example, an upscale beauty salon, in addition to a beautiful environment, may offer coffee and soft drinks to waiting clients and provide a free local telephone service at each hairdressing station. Even if the styling outcome is not so great, the client may feel so pampered with the atmosphere and service that she looks forward to her next visit. On the other hand, even with the other positive reinforcements in place, if the salon's employees are so busy talking to each other while the service is being rendered that the client feels ignored, she is not likely to return.

Research findings illustrate that many companies wrongly assume that lower prices and more diverse product lines make customers more satisfied. Instead, it appears that companies that create personal connections with customers, and also offer diverse product lines and competitive prices, are the ones providing the best reinforcement, resulting in satisfaction and repeat patronage.[10] Some hotels provide reinforcement in the form of small amenities, such as chocolates on the pillow or bottled water on the dressing table; others send bowls of fruit or even bottles of wine to returning guests to show their appreciation for continued patronage. Most frequent shopper programmes are based on enhancing positive reinforcement and encouraging continued patronage. The more a consumer uses the service, the greater the rewards (see Figure 8-1).

Relationship marketing – developing a close personalised relationship with customers – is another form of non-product reinforcement. Knowing that she will be advised of a forthcoming sale or that selected merchandise will be set aside for her next visit cements the loyalty that a consumer may have for a shop. The ability to telephone his 'personal' banker to transfer funds between accounts or to make other banking transactions without visiting the bank's office reinforces the satisfaction a consumer may have with his bank. Service companies are particularly vulnerable to interruptions in customer reinforcement because of service failures that cannot be controlled in advance. As a result, astute service providers have implemented service recovery measures that provide extra rewards to customers who have experienced service failures. Studies indicate that customers who bonded emotionally with the service provider were less forgiving than other customers because they felt truly 'betrayed', and that the effectiveness of service recovery measures had the strongest impact on loyal customers.[11]

Reinforcement Schedules

Marketers have found that product quality must be consistently high and provide customer satisfaction with each use for desired consumer behaviour to continue. However, they have also discovered that some non-product rewards do not have to be offered each time the transaction takes place; even an occasional reward provides reinforcement and encourages consumer patronage. For example, airlines may occasionally upgrade a passenger at the gate, or a clothing discounter may from time to time announce a one-hour sale over the store sound system. The promise of possibly receiving a reward provides positive reinforcement and encourages consumer patronage.

Marketers have identified three types of reinforcement schedules: total (or continuous) reinforcement, systematic (fixed ratio) reinforcement and random (variable ratio) reinforcement. An example of a total (or continuous) reinforcement schedule is the free after-dinner drink or fruit plate always served to patrons at certain restaurants. Needless to say, the basic product or service rendered is expected to provide total satisfaction (reinforcement) each time it is used.

A fixed ratio reinforcement schedule provides reinforcement every 'nth' time the product or service is purchased (say, every third time). For example, a local petrol station might give its customers a free car wash for every tenth car wash they purchase. A variable ratio reinforcement schedule rewards consumers on a random basis or on an average frequency basis. Gambling casinos operate on the basis of variable ratios. People pour money into slot machines (which are programmed to pay off on a variable ratio), hoping for the big win. Variable ratios tend to engender high rates of desired behaviour and are somewhat resistant to extinction – perhaps because, for many consumers, hope springs eternal. Other examples of variable ratio reinforcement are lotteries and competitions where the necessary input is unknown (e.g. an airline having a campaign where the customer who earns most frequent flyer miles between London and Paris in March will win an additional 500 miles).

Shaping

Reinforcement performed before the desired consumer behaviour actually takes place is called **shaping**. Shaping increases the probabilities that certain desired consumer behaviour will occur. For example, retailers recognise that they must first attract customers to their shops before they can expect them to do the bulk of their shopping there. Many retailers provide some form of preliminary reinforcement (shaping) to encourage consumers to visit only their store. For example, some retailers offer loss leaders – popular products at severely discounted prices – to the first hundred or so customers to arrive, since those customers are likely to stay to do much of their shopping. By reinforcing the behaviour that is needed to enable the targeted consumer behaviour to take place, marketers increase the probability that the desired behaviour will occur. Car dealers recognise that in order to sell new cars, they must first encourage people to visit their showrooms and to test-drive their cars. It is hoped that the test drive will result in a sale.

Massed Versus Distributed Learning

As illustrated previously, timing has an important influence on consumer learning. Should a learning schedule be spread out over a period of time (**distributed learning**), or should it be 'bunched up' all at once (**massed learning**)? The question is an important one for advertisers planning a media schedule, because massed advertising produces more initial learning, whereas a distributed schedule usually results in learning that persists longer. When advertisers want an immediate impact (e.g. to introduce a new product or to counter a competitor's blitz campaign), they generally use a massed schedule to hasten consumer learning. However, when the goal is long-term repeat buying on a regular basis, a distributed schedule is preferable. A distributed schedule, with advertisements repeated on a regular basis, usually results in more long-term learning and is relatively immune to extinction.

Modelling or observational learning

Learning theorists have noted that a considerable amount of learning takes place in the absence of direct reinforcement, either positive or negative, through a process psychologists call **modelling** or **observational learning** (also called vicarious learning). Consumers often observe how others behave in response to certain situations (stimuli) and the ensuing results (reinforcement) that occur, and they imitate (model) the positively reinforced behaviour when faced with similar situations. Modelling is the process through which individuals learn behaviour by observing the behaviour of others and the consequences of such behaviour. Their role models are usually people they admire because of such traits as appearance, accomplishment, skill and even social class.

Advertisers recognise the importance of observational learning in their selection of models – whether celebrities or unknowns. If a teenager sees an advertisement that depicts social success as the outcome of using a certain brand of shampoo, she will want to buy it. If her brother sees a commercial that shows a muscular young athlete drinking bottled water instead of Coca-Cola, he will want some water, too. Indeed, vicarious (or observational) learning is the basis of much of today's advertising. Consumer models with whom the target audience can identify are shown achieving positive outcomes to common problem situations through the use of the advertised product. Children learn much of their social behaviour and consumer behaviour by observing their older siblings or their parents. They imitate the behaviour of those they see rewarded, expecting to be rewarded similarly if they adopt the same behaviour. Figure 8-6 depicts an advertisement portraying modelling to advertise an upscale product.

Sometimes advertisements depict negative consequences for certain types of behaviour. This is particularly true of public policy advertisements, which may show the negative consequences of smoking, of driving too fast or of taking drugs. By observing the actions of others and the resulting consequences, consumers learn vicariously to recognise appropriate and inappropriate behaviour.

FIGURE 8-6 Consumers learn by modelling
Source: Patek Philippe.

COGNITIVE LEARNING THEORY

Not all learning takes place as the result of repeated trials. A considerable amount of learning takes place as the result of consumer thinking and problem-solving. Sudden learning is also a reality. When confronted with a problem, we sometimes see the solution instantly. More often, however, we are likely to search for information on which to base a decision, and we carefully evaluate what we learn in order to make the best decision possible for our purposes. This process was described in Chapter 4.

Learning based on mental activity is called *cognitive learning*. Cognitive learning theory holds that the kind of learning most characteristic of human beings is problem-solving, which enables individuals to gain some control over their environment. Unlike behavioural learning theory, cognitive theory holds that learning involves complex mental processing of information. Instead of stressing the importance of repetition or the association of a reward with a specific response, cognitive theorists emphasise the role of motivation and mental processes in producing a desired response.

Information processing

Just as a computer processes information received as input, so too does the human mind process the information it receives as input. **Information processing** is related to both the consumer's cognitive ability and the complexity of the information to be processed. Consumers process product information by attributes, brands, comparisons between brands or a combination of these factors. Although the attributes included in the brand's message and the number of available alternatives influence the intensity or degree of information processing, consumers with higher cognitive ability apparently acquire more product information and are more capable of integrating information on several product attributes than consumers with lesser ability.

Individuals also differ in terms of **imagery** – that is, in their ability to form mental images – and these differences influence their ability to recall information. Individual differences in imagery processing can be measured with tests of imagery vividness (the ability to evoke clear images), processing style (preference for and frequency of visual versus verbal processing) and daydream (fantasy) content and frequency.[12]

The more experience a consumer has with a product category, the greater his or her ability to make use of product information. Greater familiarity with the product category also increases cognitive ability and learning during a new purchase decision, particularly with regard to technical information. Some consumers learn by analogy; that is, they transfer knowledge about products they are familiar with to new or unfamiliar products in order to enhance their understanding.[13] One study found that when people exerted more cognitive effort in processing information about an alternative, they experienced a process-induced negative effect toward that alternative and were more likely to choose a product that required less effort to evaluate. However, the negative effect did not influence product choice for a clearly superior product.[14]

How Consumers Store, Retain and Retrieve Information

Of central importance to the processing of information is the human memory. A basic research concern of most cognitive scientists is discovering how information gets stored in memory, how it is retained and how it is retrieved.

Because information processing occurs in stages, it is generally believed that there are separate and sequential 'storehouses' in memory where information is kept temporarily before further processing: a sensory store, a short-term store and a long-term store.

Sensory Store

All data come to us through our senses; however, the senses do not transmit whole images as a camera does. Instead, each sense receives a fragmented piece of information (such as the smell, colour, shape and feel of a flower) and transmits it to the brain in parallel, where the perceptions of a single instant are synchronised and perceived as a single image, in a single moment of time. The image of a sensory input lasts for just a second or two in the mind's **sensory store**. If it is not processed, it is lost immediately. As noted in Chapter 7, we are constantly bombarded with stimuli from the environment and subconsciously block out a great deal of information that we do not 'need' or cannot use. For marketers, this means that although it is relatively easy to get information into the consumer's sensory store, it is difficult to make a lasting impression. Furthermore, studies suggest that the brain automatically and subconsciously 'tags' all perceptions with a value, either positive or negative; this evaluation, added to the initial perception in the first micro-second of cognition, tends to remain unless further information is processed.[15] This would explain why first impressions tend to last and why it is hazardous for a marketer to introduce a product prematurely into the marketplace.

Short-Term Store

The **short-term store** (known as 'working memory') is the stage of real memory in which information is processed and held for just a brief period. Anyone who has ever looked up a number in a telephone directory, only to forget it just before dialling, knows how briefly information lasts in short-term storage. If information in the short-term store undergoes the process known as rehearsal (i.e. the silent, mental repetition of information), it is then transferred to the long-term store. The transfer process takes from 2 to 10 seconds. If information is not rehearsed and transferred, it is lost in about 30 seconds or less. The amount of information that can be held in short-term storage is limited to about four or five items.

Long-Term Store

In contrast to the short-term store, where information lasts only a few seconds, the **long-term store** retains information for relatively extended periods of time. Although it is possible to forget something within a few minutes of the information reaching long-term storage, it is more common for data in long-term storage to last for days, weeks or even years. Almost all of us, for example, can remember the name of our first teacher. Figure 8-7 depicts the transfer of information received by the sensory store, through the short-term store, to long-term storage.

Rehearsal and Encoding

The amount of information available for delivery from short-term storage to long-term storage depends on the amount of **rehearsal** it is given. Failure to rehearse an input, either by repeating it or by relating it to other data, can result in fading and eventual loss of the information. Information can also be lost because of competition for attention. For example, if the short-term store receives a great number of inputs simultaneously from the sensory store, its capacity may be reduced to only two or three pieces of information.

The purpose of rehearsal is to hold information in short-term storage long enough for encoding to take place. **Encoding** is the process by which we select a word or visual image to represent a perceived object. Marketers, for example, help consumers encode brands by using brand symbols. Nike uses the 'swoosh' on its products; Audi cars have four circles in the front while Mercedes have a star. Dell Computer turns the e in its logo on its side for quick name recognition, while Microsoft uses a stylised window, presumably on the world.

'Learning' a picture takes less time than learning verbal information, but both types of information are important in forming an overall mental image. A print advertisement with both an illustration and body copy is more likely to be encoded and stored than an illustration without verbal information. A study that compared the effects of visual and verbal advertising found

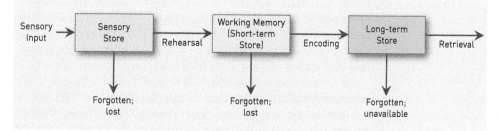

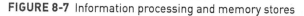

FIGURE 8-7 Information processing and memory stores

that, when advertising copy and illustrations focus on different product attributes, the illustrations disproportionately influence consumer inferences.[16]

Researchers have found that the encoding of a commercial is related to the context of the television programme during (or adjacent to) which it is shown. Some parts of a programme may require viewers to commit a larger portion of their cognitive resources to processing (e.g. when a dramatic event takes place rather than when there is a casual conversation). When viewers commit more cognitive resources to the programme itself, they encode and store less of the information conveyed by a commercial. This suggests that commercials requiring relatively little cognitive processing may be more effective within or adjacent to a dramatic programme setting than commercials requiring more elaborate processing.[17] Other research indicates that viewers who are very involved with a television show respond more positively to commercials adjacent to that show and have more positive purchase intentions.[18]

When consumers are presented with too much information (called **information overload**), they may encounter difficulty in encoding and storing it all. Findings suggest that it is difficult for consumers to remember product information from advertisements for new brands in heavily advertised categories.[19] Consumers can become cognitively overloaded when they are given a lot of information in a limited time. The result of this overload is confusion, resulting in poor purchase decisions.

Retention

Information does not just sit in long-term storage waiting to be retrieved. Instead, information is constantly organised and reorganised as new links between chunks of information are forged. In fact, many information-processing theorists view the long-term store as a network consisting of nodes (i.e. concepts), with links between and among them. As individuals gain more knowledge about a subject, they expand their network of relationships and sometimes their search for additional information. This process is known as activation, which involves relating new data to old to make the material more meaningful. Consumer memory for the name of a product may also be activated by relating it to the spokesperson used in its advertising. For many people, Cristiano Ronaldo means Nike football boots. The total package of associations brought to mind when a cue is activated is called a *schema*.

Product information stored in memory tends to be brand based, and consumers interpret new information in a manner consistent with the way in which it is already organised. Consumers are confronted with thousands of new products each year, and their information search is often dependent upon how similar or dissimilar (discrepant) these products are to product categories already stored in memory. Therefore, consumers are more likely to recall the information they receive on new products bearing a familiar brand name, and their memory is less affected by exposure to competitive advertisements.

Consumers recode what they have already encoded to include larger amounts of information (chunking). For example, those individuals new to a chessboard must carefully contemplate their every move, whereas experienced chess players can readily anticipate their opponents' moves and make their own moves accordingly. Marketers should research the kinds and numbers of groupings (chunks) of information that consumers can handle. When the chunks offered in an advertisement do not match those in the consumer's frame of reference, information recall may be hampered. The degree of prior knowledge is also an important consideration. Knowledgeable consumers can take in more complex chunks of information than those who are less knowledgeable in the product category. Thus, the amount and type of technological information contained in an advertisement for a yacht can be much more detailed in a specialised magazine such as *Yachting World* than in a general-interest magazine such as *Time*.

Information is stored in long-term memory in two ways: *episodically* (by the order in which it is acquired) and *semantically* (according to significant concepts). We may remember having gone to a film last Saturday because of our ability to store data episodically, and we may remember the plot, the stars and the director because of our ability to store data semantically. Learning theorists believe that memories stored semantically are organised into frameworks by which we integrate new data with previous experience. For information about a new brand or model of printer to enter our memory, for example, we would have to relate it to our previous experience with printers in terms of such attributes as speed, print quality, resolution and memory.

Retrieval

Retrieval is the process by which we recover information from long-term storage. For example, when we are unable to remember something with which we are very familiar, we are experiencing a failure of the retrieval system. Marketers maintain that consumers tend to remember the product's benefits rather than its attributes, suggesting that advertising messages are most effective when they link the product's attributes with the benefits that consumers seek from the product; this view is consistent with the previous discussion of product positioning strategies (Chapter 7). Consumers are likely to spend time interpreting and elaborating on information they find relevant to their needs and to activate such relevant knowledge from long-term memory.[20]

Studies indicate that incongruent (or unexpected) message elements pierce consumers' perceptual screens and improve the memorability of an advertisement when these elements are relevant to the advertising message.[21] For example, an advertisement for a brand of stain-resistant, easy-to-clean carpet shows an elegantly dressed couple in a beautiful dining room setting where the man inadvertently knocks the food, the flowers and the china crashing to the floor. The elegance of the actors and the sophisticated setting make the accident totally incongruous and unexpected, whereas the message remains highly relevant: the mess can be cleaned up easily without leaving a stain on the carpet.

Incongruent elements that are not relevant to an advertisement also pierce the consumer's perceptual screen but provide no memorability for the product. An advertisement showing a nude woman sitting on a piece of office furniture would very likely attract readers' attention, but would provide no memorability for the product or the advertiser because of the irrelevance of the nudity to the advertising message. One study discovered that false cues in post-experience advertising influence recollection. Also, when the false verbal cues and picture appeared together they were more likely to be integrated into memory than false verbal cues without pictures.[22]

Interference

The greater the number of competitive advertisements in a product category, the lower the recall of brand claims in a specific advertisement. These **interference effects** are caused by confusion with competing advertisements and make information retrieval difficult. Advertisements can also act as retrieval cues for a competitive brand. An example of such consumer confusion occurred when consumers attributed the long-running and attention-getting television campaign featuring the Eveready Energizer Bunny to the leader in the field, Duracell. This, however, might not be all that strange, as the Duracell Bunny is probably just as famous in some parts of the world as the Energizer Bunny is in others (see Figure 8-8).

(A)

(B)

FIGURE 8-8 The Energizer bunny (*left*) and the Duracell bunny (*right*)
Source: Courtesy of The Advertising Archives.

Advertisements for competing brands or for other products made by the same manufacturer can lower the consumer's ability to remember advertised brand information. Such effects occur in response to even a small amount of advertising for similar products. The level of interference experienced can depend on the consumer's previous experiences, prior knowledge of brand attribute information and the amount of brand information available at the time of choice. There are actually two kinds of interference. New learning can interfere with the retrieval of previously stored material, and old learning can interfere with the recall of recently learned material. With both kinds of interference, the problem is the similarity of old and new information. Advertising that creates a distinctive brand image can assist in the retention and retrieval of message contents.

Limited and Extensive Information Processing

For a long time, consumer researchers believed that all consumers passed through a complex series of mental and behavioural stages in arriving at a purchase decision. These stages ranged from awareness (exposure to information), to evaluation (preference, attitude formation), to behaviour (purchase), to final evaluation (adoption or rejection). This same series of stages is often presented as the consumer adoption process (discussed in Chapter 15).

A number of models have been developed over the years to express the same notion of sequential processing of information by consumers (see Table 8-1). Initially, marketing scholars believed that extensive and complex processing of information by consumers was applicable to all purchase decisions. However, as we recall from Chapter 4, some theorists argued that there were some purchase situations that simply did not call for extensive information processing and evaluation; that sometimes consumers simply went from awareness of a need to a routine purchase, without a great deal of information search and mental evaluation. Such purchases were considered of minimal personal relevance, as opposed to highly relevant, search-oriented purchases. Purchases of minimal personal importance were called low-involvement purchases, and complex, search-oriented purchases were considered high-involvement purchases. The following section describes the development of involvement theory and discusses its applications to marketing strategy.

Involvement theory

Involvement theory developed from a stream of research called **hemispheral lateralisation**, or split-brain theory. The basic premise of split-brain theory is that the right and left hemispheres of the brain 'specialise' in the kinds of information they process. The left hemisphere is primarily responsible for cognitive activities such as reading, speaking and attributional information processing. Individuals who are exposed to verbal information cognitively analyse the information through left-brain processing and form mental images. Unlike the left hemisphere, the right

TABLE 8-1 Models of cognitive learning

	PROMOTIONAL MODEL	TRICOMPONENT MODEL	DECISION MAKING MODEL	INNOVATION ADOPTION MODEL	INNOVATION DECISION PROCESS
Sequential Stages of Processing	Attention	Cognitive	Awareness Knowledge	Awareness	Knowledge
	Interest Desire	Affective	Evaluation	Interest Evaluation	Persuasion
	Action	Conative	Purchase Postpurchase Evaluation	Trial Adoption	Decision Confirmation

hemisphere of the brain is concerned with non-verbal, timeless, pictorial and holistic information. Put another way, the left side of the brain is rational, active and realistic; the right side is emotional, metaphoric, impulsive and intuitive.[23]

Involvement Theory and Media Strategy

Building on the notion of hemispheral lateralisation, a pioneer consumer researcher theorised that individuals passively process and store right-brain (non-verbal, pictorial) information – that is, without active involvement.[24] Because television is primarily a pictorial medium, television viewing was considered a right-brain activity (passive and holistic processing of images viewed on the screen), and television itself was therefore considered a low-involvement medium. This research concluded that **passive learning** occurs through repeated exposures to a television commercial (i.e. low-involvement information processing) and produces changes in consumer behaviour (e.g. product purchases) prior to changes in the consumer's attitude toward the product. This view contradicts the models presented in Table 8-1, all of which maintain that cognitive evaluation and favourable attitude towards a product take place before the actual purchase behaviour.

To extend this line of reasoning, cognitive (verbal) information is processed by the left side of the brain; thus, print media (e.g. newspapers and magazines) and interactive media (the Internet) are considered high-involvement media. According to this theory, print advertising is processed in the complex sequence of cognitive stages depicted in classic models of information processing (i.e. high-involvement information processing).

The right-brain theory of passive processing of information is consistent with classical conditioning. Through repetition, the product is paired with a visual image (e.g. a distinctive package) to produce the desired response: purchase of the advertised brand. According to this theory, in situations of passive learning (generated by low-involvement media), repetition is the key factor in producing purchase behaviour. In marketing terms, the theory suggests that television commercials are most effective when they are of short duration and repeated frequently, thus ensuring brand familiarity without provoking detailed evaluation of the message content.

The right-brain processing theory stresses the importance of the visual component of advertising, including the creative use of symbols. Under this theory, highly visual television commercials, packaging and in-store displays generate familiarity with the brand and induce purchase behaviour. Pictorial cues are more effective at generating recall and familiarity with the product, whereas verbal cues (which trigger left-brain processing) generate cognitive activity that encourages consumers to evaluate the advantages and disadvantages of the product.

There are limitations to the application of split-brain theory to media strategy. Although the right and left hemispheres of the brain process different types of cues, they do not operate independently of each other but work together to process information. Some individuals are integrated processors (they readily engage both hemispheres during information processing). Integrated processors show greater overall recall of both the verbal and the visual portions of print advertisements than individuals who exhibit more 'specialised' processing (i.e. right or left hemispheral processing).[25] If you look at Figure 8-9, the advertisement portrayed here builds on the notion of integrated processing as it shows an attention-getting illustration but also includes a description explaining why Bayer invests in medical science, and that their mission is to provide hope.

Involvement Theory and Consumer Relevance

From the conceptualisation of high- and low-involvement media, involvement theory next focused on the consumer's involvement with products and purchases. It was briefly hypothesised that there are high- and low-involvement consumers; then, that there are high- and low-involvement purchases. These two approaches led to the notion that a consumer's level of involvement depends on the degree of personal relevance that the product holds for that consumer. Under this definition, high-involvement purchases are those that are very important to the consumer (e.g. in terms of perceived risk) and thus provoke extensive problem-solving (information processing). A car and a dandruff shampoo may each represent high-involvement purchases under this scenario – the car because of high perceived financial risk, the shampoo because of high perceived social risk. Low-involvement purchases are purchases that are not very important to the consumer, hold little relevance and have little perceived risk, and thus provoke very limited information processing. Highly involved consumers find fewer brands acceptable (they are called **narrow categorisers**); uninvolved consumers are likely to be receptive to a greater number of advertising messages regarding the purchase and will consider more brands (they are **broad categorisers**).

Central and Peripheral Routes to Persuasion

The theory of **central and peripheral routes to persuasion** illustrates the concepts of extensive and limited problem-solving for high- and low-involvement purchase situations. The major premise of this theory is that consumers are more likely to evaluate carefully the merits and weaknesses of a product when the purchase is of high relevance to them. Conversely, the likelihood is great that consumers will engage in very limited information search and evaluation when the purchase holds little relevance or importance for them.[26] Thus, for high-involvement purchases, the central route to persuasion, which requires considered thought and cognitive processing, is likely to be the most effective marketing strategy. For low-involvement purchases, the peripheral route to persuasion is likely to be more effective. In this instance, because the consumer is less motivated to exert cognitive effort, learning is more likely to occur through repetition, the passive processing of visual cues and holistic perception.

Various researchers have addressed the relationship between the theory of central and peripheral routes to persuasion and consumer information processing. A number of studies have found that high involvement with a product produces more extensive processing of information, including extensive information search on the Internet.[27] It is apparent that highly involved consumers use more attributes to evaluate brands, whereas less involved consumers apply very simple decision rules. In marketing to highly involved consumers, the quality of the argument presented in the persuasive message, rather than merely the imagery of the promotional message, has the greater impact on the consumption decision.

Many studies investigated the relationship between the level of information processing and the product and promotional elements of the marketing mix. For example, one study found that comparative advertisements (see Chapter 10) are more likely to be processed centrally (purposeful processing of message arguments), whereas non-comparative advertisements are commonly processed peripherally (with little message elaboration and a response derived from other executional elements in the advertisement).[28] Another study found that the use of metaphors and figures of speech that deviate from the expected in print advertisements places added processing demands on the readers and increases an advertisement's persuasiveness and memorability. The metaphors examined in this study were such slogans as 'In the Caribbean, there's no such thing as a party of one' (Malibu Caribbean Rum).[29] Another study demonstrated that the correlation between a consumer's product involvement and objective product knowledge is higher for utilitarian products than in products designed to bring about pleasure (termed hedonic products); in the case of hedonic products, the correlation between subjective knowledge and product involvement is higher than for utilitarian products.[30] Assuming that subjective knowledge is the result of interpreting the imagery presented in the advertisement, while objective knowledge is the outcome of the factual information that the advertisement provides, marketers should consider the degree of the product's utilitarianism in selecting either the central or the peripheral route in promoting that product.

The Elaboration Likelihood Model

The **elaboration likelihood model (ELM)** suggests that a person's level of involvement during message processing is a critical factor in determining which route to persuasion is likely to be effective. For example, as the message becomes more personally relevant (i.e. as involvement increases), people are more willing to expend the cognitive effort required to process the message arguments. Thus, when involvement is high, consumers follow the central route and base their attitudes or choices on the message arguments. When involvement is low, they follow the peripheral route and rely more heavily on other message elements (such as the spokesperson or background music) to form attitudes or make product choices. The advertisement shown in Figure 8-9 illustrates using the central route to persuasion; Figure 8-10 shows an advertisement that takes the peripheral route.

FIGURE 8-9 Central route to persuasion
Source: Courtesy of The Advertising Archives.

FIGURE 8-10 Peripheral route to persuasion
Source: BBC World News/James Day.

Measures of Involvement

Given that involvement theory evolved from the notion of high- and low-involvement media, to high- and low-involvement consumers, to high- and low-involvement products and purchases, to appropriate methods of persuasion in situations of high and low product relevance, it is not surprising to find there is great variation in the conceptualisation and measurement of involvement itself. Researchers have defined and conceptualised involvement in a variety of ways, including ego involvement, commitment, communication involvement, purchase importance, extent of information search, persons, products, situations and purchase decisions.[31] Some studies have tried to differentiate between brand involvement and product involvement.[32] Others differentiate between situational, enduring and response involvement.[33]

The lack of a clear definition about the essential components of involvement poses some measurement problems. Researchers who regard involvement as a cognitive state are concerned with the measurement of ego involvement, risk perception and purchase importance. Researchers who focus on the behavioural aspects of involvement measure such factors as the search for and evaluation of product information. Others argue that involvement should be measured by the degree of importance the product has to the buyer.

Because of the many different dimensions and conceptualisations of involvement, many researchers agree that it makes more sense to develop an involvement profile rather than to measure a single involvement level. The suggested profile would include interest in the product category, the rewarding nature (perceived pleasure) of the product, its perceived ability to reflect the purchaser's personality and the perceived risk associated with the purchase.[34] This view is consistent with the notion that involvement should be measured on a continuum rather than as a dichotomy consisting of two mutually exclusive categories of 'high' and 'low' involvement.[35] Table 8-2 presents a semantic differential scale designed to measure involvement. Table 8-3

TABLE 8-2 Measuring involvement on a semantic differential scale

TO ME, [INSERT PRODUCT OR PRODUCT CATEGORY] IS:

	1	2	3	4	5	6	7	
1. Important	—	—	—	—	—	—	—	Unimportant
2. Interesting	—	—	—	—	—	—	—	Boring
3. Relevant	—	—	—	—	—	—	—	Irrelevant
4. Exciting	—	—	—	—	—	—	—	Unexciting
5. Meaningful	—	—	—	—	—	—	—	Meaningless
6. Appealing	—	—	—	—	—	—	—	Unappealing
7. Fascinating	—	—	—	—	—	—	—	Ordinary
8. Priceless	—	—	—	—	—	—	—	Worthless
9. Involving	—	—	—	—	—	—	—	Uninvolving
10. Necessary	—	—	—	—	—	—	—	Unnecessary

Source: Adapted from Judith Lynne Zaichowsky, 'The Personal Involvement Inventory: Reduction, Revision, and Application to Advertising', *Journal of Advertising*, 23, 4, December 1994, 59–70. Used by permission of M. E. Sharpe, Inc.

TABLE 8-3 Personal involvement inventory measuring a consumer's enduring involvement with a product

1. I would be interested in reading about this product.
2. I would read a *Consumer Reports* article about this product.
3. I have compared product characteristics among brands.
4. I usually pay attention to advertisements for this product.
5. I usually talk about this product with other people.
6. I usually seek advice from other people prior to purchasing this product.
7. I usually take many factors into account before purchasing this product.
8. I usually spend a lot of time choosing what kind to buy.

Source: Adapted from Edward F. McQuarrie and J. Michael Munson, 'A Revised Product Involvement Inventory: Improved Usability and Validity', *Diversity in Consumer Behavior: Advances in Consumer Research*, vol. 19 (Provo, UT: Association for Consumer Research, 1992), pp. 108–15. Reprinted by permission.

shows a personal involvement inventory developed to measure a consumer's 'enduring involvement' with a product.

Marketing Applications of Involvement

Involvement theory has a number of strategic applications for the marketer. For example, the left-brain (cognitive processing)/right-brain (passive processing) paradigm seems to have strong implications for the content, length and presentation of both print and television advertisements. There is evidence that people process information extensively when the purchase is of high personal relevance and engage in limited information processing when the purchase is of low personal relevance. Uninvolved consumers appear to be more susceptible to different kinds of persuasion than highly involved consumers. Therefore, for high-involvement purchases, marketers should use arguments stressing the strong, solid, high-quality attributes of their products, thus using the central (or highly cognitive) route. For low-involvement purchases, marketers should use the peripheral route to persuasion, focusing on the method of presentation rather than on the content of the message (e.g. through the use of a celebrity spokesperson or highly visual and symbolic advertisements).

Marketers can take steps to increase customer involvement with their advertisements. For example, advertisers can use sensory appeals, unusual stimuli and celebrity endorsers to generate more attention for their messages. Marketers should also focus on increasing customer involvement levels by creating bonds with their customers.[36] Of course, the best strategy for increasing the personal relevance of products to consumers is the same as the core of modern marketing itself: provide benefits that are important and relevant to customers, improve the product and add benefits as competition intensifies, and focus on forging bonds and relationships with customers rather than just engaging in transactions.

MEASURES OF CONSUMER LEARNING

For many marketers, the dual goals of consumer learning are increased market share and brand-loyal consumers. These goals are interdependent: brand-loyal customers provide the basis for a stable and growing market share, and brands with larger market shares have proportionately larger groups of loyal buyers.[37] Marketers focus their promotional budgets on trying to teach consumers that their brands are best and that their products will best solve the consumers' problems and satisfy their needs. Thus, it is important for the marketer to measure how effectively consumers have 'learned' its message. The following sections will examine various measures of consumer learning: recognition and recall measures, cognitive measures and the attitudinal and behavioural measures of brand loyalty.

Recognition and recall measures

Recognition and recall tests are conducted to determine whether consumers remember seeing an advertisement, the extent to which they have read it or seen it and can recall its content, their resulting attitudes towards the product and the brand, and their purchase intentions. Recognition tests are based on aided recall, whereas recall tests use unaided recall. In recognition tests, the consumer is shown an advertisement and asked whether he or she remembers seeing it and can remember any of its salient points. In recall tests, the consumer is asked whether he or she has read a specific magazine or watched a specific television show, and if so, can recall any advertisements or commercials seen, the product advertised, the brand and any salient points about the product. Generally, brand names that convey specific and relevant advantages are more easily recognisable. For example, one study found that a brand name explicitly conveying a product benefit leads to higher recall of an advertised benefit claim than a non-suggestive brand name.[38]

Cognitive Responses to Advertising

Another measure of consumer learning is the degree to which consumers accurately comprehend the intended advertising message. **Comprehension** is a function of the message characteristics, the consumer's opportunity and ability to process the information, and the consumer's motivation (or level of involvement).[39] To ensure a high level of comprehension, many marketers conduct copy testing either before the advertising is actually run in media (called **copy pre-testing**) or after it appears (**copy post-testing**). Pre-tests are used to determine which, if any, elements of an advertising message should be revised before major media expenses are incurred. Post-tests are used to evaluate the effectiveness of an advertisement that has already run and to identify which elements, if any, should be changed to improve the impact and memorability of future advertisements.

Attitudinal and Behavioural Measures of Brand Loyalty

Brand loyalty is the ultimate desired outcome of consumer learning. However, there is no single definition of this concept. The varied definitions of brand loyalty reflect the models presented earlier in Table 8-1. They are summarised in Table 8-4, together with their shortcomings and weaknesses in the context of potential competitive responses.

Marketers agree that brand loyalty consists of both attitudes and actual behaviours towards a brand and that both must be measured. **Attitudinal measures** are concerned with consumers' overall feelings (i.e. evaluation) about the product and the brand and their purchase intentions. **Behavioural measures** are based on observable responses to promotional stimuli – repeat purchase behaviour rather than attitude toward the product or brand. One study pointed out that marketers must distinguish between two attitudinal measures of brand loyalty (see Table 8-5); the study demonstrated that the degree of commitment towards buying the brand and the propensity to be brand loyal are two separate dimensions but did not conclusively determine which construct is more useful for explaining buying behaviour.[40]

TABLE 8-4 Definitions of brand loyalty and their shortcomings

STAGE	IDENTIFYING MARKER	VULNERABILITIES
Cognitive	Loyalty to information such as price, features and so forth.	Actual or imagined better competitive features or price through communication (e.g. advertising) and vicarious or personal experience. Deterioration in brand features or price. Variety seeking and voluntary trial.
Affective	Loyalty to a liking: 'I buy it because I like it.'	Cognitively induced dissatisfaction. Enhanced liking for competitive brands, perhaps conveyed through imagery and association. Variety seeking and voluntary trial. Deteriorating performance.
Conative	Loyalty to an intention: 'I'm committed to buying it.'	Persuasive counterargumentative competitive messages. Induced trial (e.g. coupons, sampling, point-of-purchase promotions). Deteriorating performance.
Action	Loyalty to action, coupled with the overcoming of obstacles.	Induced unavailability (e.g. stocklifts – purchasing the entire inventory of a competitor's product from a merchant). Increased obstacles generally. Deteriorating performance.

Source: Adapted from Richard L. Oliver, 'Whence Brand Loyalty?', *Journal of Marketing*, 63, 1999, 33–44.

TABLE 8-5 Two distinct attitudinal measures of brand loyalty

MEASURE DESCRIPTION						
Attitude toward the act of purchasing the brand						
Using a scale from 1 to 5, please tell me how committed you are to purchasing your preferred brand of directory advertising:						
x_1 Uncommitted	1	2	3	4	5	Committed
Purchasing advertising with my preferred brand of directory in the next issue would be:						
x_2 Bad	1	2	3	4	5	Good
x_3 Unpleasant	1	2	3	4	5	Pleasant
x_4 Unfavorable	1	2	3	4	5	Favorable
x_5 Negative	1	2	3	4	5	Positive
x_6 Undesirable	1	2	3	4	5	Desirable
x_7 Unwise	1	2	3	4	5	Wise
x_8 Unlikely	1	2	3	4	5	Likely
x_9 I would recommend my main brand to other people:						
Unlikely	1	2	3	4	5	Likely

Propensity to be loyal

x_1 I would rather stick with a brand I usually buy than try something I am not very sure of.

x_2 If I like a brand, I rarely switch from it just to try something different.

x_3 I rarely introduce new brands and products to my colleagues.

x_4 I rarely take chances by buying unfamiliar brands even if it means sacrificing variety.

x_5 I buy the same brands even if they are only average.

x_6 I would rather wait for others to try a new brand than try it myself.

x_7 I would rather stick to well-known brands when purchasing directory advertising.

Behavioral loyalty includes the dimensions of preference and allegiance. It was operationalized as the amount of money spent on the preferred brand (preference) over time (allegiance).

Source: Reprinted by permission from Macmillan Publishers Ltd: *Journal of Brand Management*, January, A comparison of attitudinal loyalty measurement approaches, pp. 193–209 (Bennett, R. and Rundle-Thiele, S. 2002), copyright 2002, published by Palgrave Macmillan.

Behavioural scientists who favour the theory of instrumental conditioning believe that brand loyalty results from an initial product trial that is reinforced through satisfaction, leading to repeat purchase. Cognitive researchers, on the other hand, emphasise the role of mental processes in building brand loyalty. They believe that consumers engage in extensive problem-solving behaviour involving brand and attribute comparisons, leading to a strong brand preference and repeat purchase behaviour. Therefore, brand loyalty is the synergy among such attitudinal components as perceived product superiority, customer satisfaction and the purchase behaviour itself.

Recently, brain imaging technologies, commonly used in medicine, were used to study brand loyalty and yielded some fascinating results. Brain scans of some Japanese women taken while they were answering questions about everyday events showed similar patterns, but these patterns became distinctive when women who were brand loyal to a given store responded to the statement 'this is the perfect store for me'. The brain scans of consumers who were split as to whether they preferred Coke or Pepsi and were given blind taste tests indicated that two different brain regions were at play. When the subjects tasted either of the soft drinks, their brain's reward system was activated. But when these persons were told which brand they were drinking, their brain's memory region (where information regarding brand loyalty is stored) was activated and overrode the preferences the participants indicated after tasting the soft drink, but before knowing which brand they had tasted.[41]

Behavioural definitions (such as frequency of purchase or proportion of total purchases) lack precision, because they do not distinguish between the 'real' brand-loyal buyer who is intentionally faithful and the spurious brand-loyal buyer who repeats a brand purchase because it is the only one available in the shop. Often consumers buy from a mix of brands within their acceptable range (i.e. their **evoked set**, see Chapter 4). The greater the number of acceptable brands in a specific product category, the less likely the consumer is to be brand loyal to one specific brand. Conversely, products having few competitors, as well as those purchased with great frequency, are likely to have greater brand loyalty. Thus, a more favourable attitude towards a brand, service or shop, compared to potential alternatives, together with repeat patronage, are seen as the requisite components of customer loyalty. One study related the attitudinal and purchase aspects of brand loyalty to market share and the relative prices of brands. The study showed that brand trust and brand affect, combined, determine purchase loyalty and attitudinal loyalty. Purchase loyalty leads to a higher market share and attitudinal loyalty often enables the marketer to charge a higher price for the brand relative to competition.[42]

An integrated conceptual framework views consumer loyalty as the relationship between an individual's relative attitude towards an entity (brand, service, store or vendor) and patronage behaviour.[43] The consumer's relative attitude consists of two dimensions: the strength of the attitude and the degree of attitudinal differentiation among competing brands. As Figure 8-11 indicates, a consumer with a high relative attitude and high degree of repeat purchase behaviour would be defined as brand loyal; a consumer with a low relative attitude and high repeat patronage would be considered spuriously loyal. This framework also reflects a correlation between brand loyalty and consumer involvement. High involvement leads to extensive information search and, ultimately, to brand loyalty, whereas low involvement leads to exposure and brand awareness and then possibly to brand habit (or spurious loyalty). Spuriously loyal consumers perceive little differentiation among brands and buy the brand repeatedly due to situational cues, such as package familiarity, shelf positioning, or special prices. On the other hand, truly brand-loyal consumers have a strong commitment to the brand and are less likely to switch to other brands in spite of the persuasive, promotional efforts of competitors.

Unlike tangible products where switching to another brand is relatively easy, it is often difficult to switch to another 'brand' of service. For example, it is costly and time-consuming to transfer one's business to a new accountant or even to get used to a new hairstylist. One study showed that the reasons that cause customers to switch service providers play a role in their loyalty behaviours towards subsequent providers. Thus, service marketers should research past customer behaviour and use these data to increase the loyalty of new customers.[44]

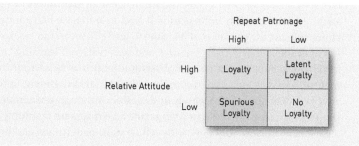

FIGURE 8-11 Brand loyalty as a function of relative attitude and patronage behaviour

Source: Adapted from Alan S. Dick and Kunai Basu, 'Customer Loyalty: Toward an Integrated Conceptual Framework', *Journal of the Academy of Marketing Science*, 22, 2, 1994, 101. Copyright © 1994 by *Journal of the Academy of Marketing Science*. With kind permission of Springer Science and Business Media.

Brand Equity

The term **brand equity** refers to the value inherent in a well-known brand name. This value stems from the consumer's perception of the brand's superiority and the social esteem that using it provides and the customer's trust and identification with the brand. For many companies, their most valuable assets are their brand names. Well-known brand names are referred to as **megabrands**. A selection of famous and internationally well-known brands could include American brands like Coca-Cola, Apple, Nike, Harley-Davidson or McDonald's. Or it could include European brands like Mercedes Benz, Carlsberg, Bang & Olufsen, Absolut or Guinness. Their names have become 'cultural icons' and enjoy powerful advantages over the competition.

Because of the escalation of new-product costs and the high rate of new-product failures, many companies prefer to leverage their brand equity through brand extensions rather than risk launching a new brand. Brand equity facilitates the acceptance of new products and the allocation of preferred shelf space, and enhances perceived value, perceived quality and premium pricing options. Brand equity is most important for low-involvement purchases, such as inexpensive consumer goods that are bought routinely and with little processing of cognitive information. A study found that very strong brand cues, such as the ones conveyed by brands with high equity, may actually 'block' the learning of quality-related cues for specific product attributes.[45] Thus, competitors of a strong brand will find it difficult to 'teach' brand-loyal customers about the benefits of their brands.

Because a brand that has been promoted heavily in the past retains a cumulative level of name recognition, companies buy, sell and rent (i.e. license) their brand names, knowing that it is easier for a new company to buy, rather than to create, a brand name that has enduring strength. Brand equity enables companies to charge a price premium – an additional amount over and above the price of an identical store brand. A relatively new strategy among some marketers is **co-branding** (also called double branding). The basis of co-branding, in which two brand names are featured on a single product, is to use another product's brand equity to enhance the primary brand's equity. Some experts believe that using a second brand's equity may imply that the host brand can no longer stand on its own. Others question whether a co-branded product causes consumer confusion as to who actually makes the product, and whether the host brand can survive if the second brand endorsement is taken away.

Brand equity reflects brand loyalty, which, as presented here, is a learned construct and one of the most important applications of learning theory to consumption behaviour. Brand loyalty and brand equity lead to increased market share and greater profits. To marketers, the major function of learning theory is to teach consumers that their product is best, to encourage repeat purchase, and, ultimately, to develop loyalty to the brand name and brand equity for the company.

ETHICS AND CONSUMER LEARNING

Previously, we discussed the ethics involved in using such factors as motivation and perception to arouse consumer needs and influence their cognitions of marketing offerings, with the assumptions that such influences will lead to purchase behaviour. This section discusses the ethics of using the elements of learning to lead consumers to engage in undesirable behaviours. For example, behavioural, cognitive and observational learning can sometimes lead to undesirable behaviour after a person observes a particular behaviour in an advertisement or commercial, and develops a cognition based on the advertisement. In trying to illustrate that some advertisements may bring about undesirable, although unintended, behaviour, a New Jersey professor showed his students a magazine advertisement featuring a fit, smiling young man on a pavement in New York City with yellow cabs, pedestrians and buildings in the background. The bright red headline read 'Just once a day!' All other copy elements were concealed in order to disguise the actual product advertised. When the professor asked his students to guess what kind of product was being promoted, the consensus of the guesses was that the advertisement was for some kind of a pill, probably a vitamin. In fact, it was for a medication that is used as part of HIV therapy by persons who are HIV positive. Since visual images are very persuasive, is it possible that the fit young man and the bright red caption 'Just once a day!' convey to young adults that being HIV positive is an easily 'manageable' condition, and that one can engage in unsafe sex? And, if a study indicates that such a perception is indeed created by the advertisement, what should the marketer do? Clearly, featuring an individual who looks unhealthy in an advertisement for a pharmaceutical product designed to control a serious medical condition will not be effective. The caption is an accurate representation of how often this drug should be taken (in combination, of course, with other drugs). This example demonstrates how difficult it is to develop advertisements that are free of any cues that may unintentionally cause some people to draw the wrong conclusions and engage in undesirable behaviour.

Since children are more likely than adults to imitate behaviour (observational learning) they see on television with little or no evaluative judgement, there are many ethical concerns regarding advertising to children. More and more countries have introduced or are thinking of introducing regulations relating to this issue. Such regulations will probably come in the form of statements saying that claims must not mislead children about a product's performance or benefits, exploit the child's imagination or create unrealistic expectations, that products be shown in safe situations and that advertisements must refrain from encouraging behaviour that is inappropriate for children. Following the direction of stimulus–response theory that children may easily form associations between stimuli and outcomes, we are likely to see directions for avoiding advertisements that (1) encourage children to pressure their parents to buy the products advertised, and (2) compel children to feel that ownership of a given product will make them more accepted by peers. Loyalty-building measures such as children's clubs, premiums and sweepstakes are other areas where the guidelines should recognise that children may not always understand the true purpose of such measures.[46]

Currently, a major concern regarding the impact of marketing on children's behaviour is whether food marketers 'teach' children to eat more than they should and thus cause the surging obesity and health problems among young consumers. Clearly, there are merits to the argument that ultimately any consumption behaviour, including excessive eating, is the responsibility of adult individuals and not the marketer who produced the food. However, it must always be remembered that children are a vulnerable population.

The principle of stimulus generalisation can also be used to confuse consumers and alter intended consumption behaviour. In some shops, less expensive brands of personal care products such as shampoo, dental floss, skin care lotions and soap come in packages that are extremely similar to instantly recognised and more expensive premium brands of these products, and are deliberately placed next to them on the shelves. Consumers can easily be confused by such displays and also by brand names or logos similar to those of premium offerings. Therefore, the marketers of premium brands often secure legal protection (in the form of patents or trademarks) for their brand names, packages and visual identities.

SUMMARY

Consumer learning is the process by which individuals acquire the purchase and consumption knowledge and experience they apply to future related behaviour. Although some learning is intentional, much learning is incidental. Basic elements that contribute to an understanding of learning are motivation, cues, response and reinforcement.

There are two schools of thought as to how individuals learn – behavioural theories and cognitive theories. Both contribute to an understanding of consumer behaviour. Behavioural theorists view learning as observable responses to stimuli, whereas cognitive theorists believe that learning is a function of mental processing.

Three major behavioural learning theories are classical conditioning, instrumental conditioning and observational (vicarious) learning. The principles of classical conditioning that provide theoretical underpinnings for many marketing applications include repetition, stimulus generalisation and stimulus discrimination. Neo-Pavlovian theories view traditional classical conditioning as cognitive associative learning rather than as reflexive action.

Instrumental learning theorists believe that learning occurs through a trial-and-error process in which positive outcomes (rewards) result in repeat behaviour. Both positive and negative reinforcement can be used to encourage the desired behaviour. Reinforcement schedules can be total (consistent) or partial (fixed ratio or random). The timing of repetitions influences how long the learned material is retained. Massed repetitions produce more initial learning than distributed repetitions; however, learning usually persists longer with distributed (i.e. spread-out) reinforcement schedules.

Cognitive learning theory holds that the kind of learning most characteristic of humans is problem-solving. Cognitive theorists are concerned with how information is processed by the human mind: how it is stored, retained and retrieved. A simple model of the structure and operation of memory suggests the existence of three separate storage units: the sensory store, short-term store (or working memory) and long-term store. The processes of memory include rehearsal, encoding, storage and retrieval.

Involvement theory proposes that people engage in limited information processing in situations of low importance or relevance to them and in extensive information processing in situations of high relevance. Hemispheral lateralisation theory gave rise to the theory that television is a low-involvement medium that results in passive learning and that print and interactive media encourage more cognitive information processing.

Measures of consumer learning include recall and recognition tests, cognitive responses to advertising, and attitudinal and behavioural measures of brand loyalty. A basic issue among researchers is whether to define brand loyalty in terms of the consumer's behaviour or the consumer's attitude towards the brand. Brand equity refers to the inherent value a brand name has in the marketplace.

For marketers, the major reasons for understanding how consumers learn are to teach them that their brand is best and to develop brand loyalty.

The ethical issues regarding consumer learning are centred on potential misuses of behavioural, cognitive and observational learning. Most importantly, these issues involve targeting children and young adults and, albeit unintentionally, 'teaching' them to engage in socially undesirable behaviours.

DISCUSSION QUESTIONS

1. How can the principles of (a) classical conditioning theory and (b) instrumental conditioning theory be applied to the development of marketing strategies?
2. Describe in learning terms the conditions under which family branding is a good policy and those under which it is not.
3. Assume that Gillette has introduced a new line of shaving products for men. How can the company use stimulus generalisation to market these products? Is instrumental conditioning applicable to this marketing situation? If so, how?
4. Which theory of learning (classical conditioning, instrumental conditioning, observational learning or cognitive learning) best explains the following consumption behaviours: (a) buying a Carlsberg beer six-pack, (b) preferring to purchase second-hand clothes, (c) buying a digital camera for the first time, (d) buying a new car, and (e) switching from one mobile phone service to another? Explain your choices.
5. a. Define the following memory structures: sensory store, short-term store (working memory) and long-term store. Discuss how each of these concepts can be used in the development of an advertising strategy.
   b. How does information overload affect the consumer's ability to comprehend an advertisement and store it in his or her memory?

6. Discuss the differences between low- and high-involvement media. How would you apply the knowledge of hemispheral lateralisation to the design of television commercials and print advertisements?
7. Why are both attitudinal and behavioural measures important in measuring brand loyalty?
8. What is the relationship between brand loyalty and brand equity? What role do both concepts play in the development of marketing strategies?
9. How can marketers use measures of recognition and recall to study the extent of consumer learning?

EXERCISES

1. Imagine you are the lecturer on this course and that you are trying to increase student participation in class discussions. How would you use reinforcement to achieve your objective?
2. Visit a supermarket. Can you identify any packages where you think the marketer's knowledge of stimulus generalisation or stimulus discrimination was incorporated into the package design? Note these examples and present them in class.

NOTES

1. N. J. Mackintosh, *Conditioning and Associative Learning* (New York: Oxford University Press, 1983), 10.
2. Terence A. Shimp, 'Neo-Pavlovian Conditioning and Its Implications for Consumer Theory and Research', in *Handbook of Consumer Behavior*, eds Thomas S. Robertson and Harold H. Kassarjian (Upper Saddle River, NJ: Prentice Hall, 1991), 162–87.
3. Chris Janiszewski and Luk Warlop, 'The Influence of Classical Conditioning Procedures on Subsequent Attention to the Conditioned Brand', *Journal of Consumer Research*, 20, September 1993, 171–89.
4. Margaret C. Campbell and Kevin Lane Keller, 'Brand Familiarity and Advertising Repetition Effects', *Journal of Consumer Research*, September 2003, 292ff.
5. Curtis P. Haugtvedt, David W. Schumann, Wendy L. Schneier and Wendy L. Warren, 'Advertising Repetition and Variation Strategies. Implications for Understanding Attitude Strength', *Journal of Consumer Research*, 21, June 1994, 176–89.
6. Zeynep Gurhan-Canli, 'The Effect of Expected Variability of Product Quality and Attribute Uniqueness on Family Brand Evaluations', *Journal of Consumer Research*, June 2003, 105ff.
7. Ken Bensinger, 'Can You Spot the Fake?', *Wall Street Journal*, 16 February 2001, W1, W14.
8. For example, Randi Priluck Grossman and Brian D. Till, 'The Persistence of Classically Conditioned Brand Attitudes', *Journal of Advertising*, 27, 1, Spring 1998, 23–31.
9. Gregory S. Carpenter, Rashi Glazer and Kent Nakamoto, 'Meaningful Brands from Meaningless Differentiation: The Dependence on Irrelevant Attributes', *Journal of Marketing Research*, 31, August 1994, 339–50.
10. William Taylor, 'Companies Find They Cannot Buy Love with Bargains', *New York Times*, 4 August 2004, C5.
11. Anna A. Mattila, 'The Impact of Service Failures on Customer Loyalty: The Moderating Role of Effective Commitment', *International Journal of Service Industry Management*, 15, 2, 2004, 134ff; and Tina L. Robbins and Janis L. Miller, 'Considering Customer Loyalty in Developing Service Recovery Strategies', *Journal of Business Strategies*, Fall 2004, 95–110.
12. Michael D. Johnson and Claes Fornell, 'The Nature and Methodological Implications of the Cognitive Representation of Products', *Journal of Consumer Research*, 14, September 1987, 214–27.

13. Jennifer Gregan Paxton and Deborah Roedder John, 'Consumer Learning by Analogy: A Model of Internal Knowledge Transfer', *Journal of Consumer Research*, 24, December 1997, 266–84.

14. Ellen C. Garbarino and Julie A. Edell, 'Cognitive Effort, Affect, and Choice', *Journal of Consumer Research*, 24, September 1997, 147–58.

15. Daniel Goleman, 'Brain May Tag All Perceptions with a Value', *New York Times*, 8 August 1995, C1.

16. Ruth Ann Smith, 'The Effects of Visual and Verbal Advertising Information on Consumers' Inferences', *Journal of Advertising*, 20, 4, December 1991, 13–23.

17. Kenneth R. Lord and Robert E. Burnkrant, 'Television Program Elaboration Effects on Commercial Processing', in *Advances in Consumer Research*, 15, ed. Michael Houston (Provo, UT: Association for Consumer Research, 1988), 213–18.

18. Kevin J. Clancy, 'CPMs Must Bow to "Involvement" Measurement', *Advertising Age*, 20 January 1992, 26.

19. Robert J. Kent and Chris T. Allen, 'Competitive Interference Effects in Consumer Memory for Advertising: The Role of Brand Familiarity', *Journal of Marketing*, 58, July 1994, 97–105.

20. Kevin Lane Keller, 'Memory and Evaluation Effects in Competitive Advertising Environments', *Journal of Consumer Research*, 17, March 1991, 463–76.

21. For example, Susan E. Heckler and Terry L. Childers, 'The Role of Expectancy and Relevancy in Memory for Verbal and Visual Information: What Is Incongruency?', *Journal of Consumer Research*, 18, March 1992, 475–92.

22. Kathryn A. Braun-LaTour, Michael S. LaTour, Jacqueline E. Pickrell and Elizabeth F. Loftus, 'How and When Advertising Can Influence Memory for Consumer Experience', *Journal of Advertising*, Winter 2004, 7–26.

23. Flemming Hansen, 'Hemispheral Lateralization: Implications for Understanding Consumer Behavior', *Journal of Consumer Research*, 8, June 1981, 23–36; Peter H. Lindzay and Donald Norman, *Human Information Processing* (New York: Academic Press, 1977); and Merlin C. Wittrock, *The Human Brain* (Upper Saddle River, NJ: Prentice Hall, 1977).

24. Herbert E. Krugman, 'The Impact of Television Advertising: Learning Without Involvement', *Public Opinion Quarterly*, 29, Fall 1965, 349–56; 'Brain Wave Measures of Media Involvement', *Journal of Advertising Research*, 11, February 1971, 3–10; and 'Memory Without Recall, Exposure Without Perception', *Journal of Advertising Research*, Classics 1, September 1982, 80–85.

25. Susan E. Heckler and Terry L. Childers, 'Hemispheric Lateralization: The Relationship of Processing Orientation with Judgment and Recall Measures for Print Advertisements', in *Advances in Consumer Research*, 14, eds M. Wallendorf and P. F. Anderson (Provo, UT: Association for Consumer Research, 1987), 46–50.

26. John T. Cacioppo, Richard E. Petty, Chuan Feng Kao and Regina Rodriguez, 'Central and Peripheral Routes to Persuasion: An Individual Difference Perspective', *Journal of Personality and Social Psychology*, 51, 5, 1986, 1032–43.

27. See, for example, Richard E. Petty and John T. Cacioppo, 'Issues Involvement Can Increase or Decrease Persuasion by Enhancing Message-Relevant Cognitive Responses', *Journal of Personality and Social Psychology*, 37, 1979, 1915–26; Cacioppo and Petty, 'The Need for Cognition', *Journal of Personality and Social Psychology*, 42, 1982, 116–31; Cacioppo, Petty and Katherine J. Morris, 'Effects of Need for Cognition on Message Evaluation, Recall and Persuasion', *Journal of Personality and Social Psychology*, 45, 1983, 805–18; and Liping A. Cai, Ruomei Feng and Deborah Breiter, 'Tourist Purchase Decision Involvement and Information Preferences', *Journal of Vacation Marketing*, March 2004, 138–49.

28. Sanjay Putrevu and Kenneth R. Lord, 'Comparative and Noncomparative Advertising: Attitudinal Effects Under Cognitive and Affective Involvement Conditions', *Journal of Advertising*, 23, 2, June 1994, 77–91.

29. Mark Toncar and James Munch, 'Consumer Responses to Tropes in Print Advertising', *Journal of Advertising*, Spring 2001, 55–65.

30. Chan-Wook Park and Byeong-Joon Moon, 'The Relationship Between Product Involvement and Product Knowledge: Moderating Roles of Product Type and Product Knowledge Type', *Psychology and Marketing*, November 2003, 977ff.

31. Theo B. C. Poiesz and J. P. M. de Bont, 'Do We Need Involvement to Understand Consumer Behavior?', *Advances in Consumer Research*, 22, eds Frank R. Kardes and Mita Sujan (Provo, UT: Association for Consumer Research, 1995), 448–52. See also the following articles in *Advances in Consumer Research*, 11, ed. Thomas C. Kinnear (Provo, UT: Association for Consumer Research, 1984): James A. Muncy and Shelby D. Hunt, 'Consumer Involvement: Definitional Issues and Research Directions', 193–6, John H. Antil, 'Conceptualization and Operationalization of Involvement', 203–9 and Michael L. Rothschild, 'Perspectives on Involvement: Current Problems and Future Directions', 216–17; Judith L. Zaichkowsky, 'Conceptualizing Involvement', *Journal of Advertising*, 15, 2, 1986, 4–34.

32. Banwari Mittal and Myung Soo Lee, 'Separating Brand Choice Involvement from Product Involvement via Consumer Involvement Profiles', in *Advances in Consumer Research*, 15, ed. Houston (1988), 43–9.

33. See Marsha L. Richins, Peter H. Bloch and Edward F. McQuarrie, 'How Enduring and Situational Involvement Combine to Create Involvement Responses', *Journal of Consumer Psychology*, 1, 2, 1992, 143–53.

34. Gilles Laurent and Jean Noel Kapferer, 'Measuring Consumer Involvement Profiles', *Journal of Marketing Research*, 22, February 1985, 41–53; Jean Noel Kapferer and Gilles Laurent, 'Consumer Involvement Profiles: A New Practical Approach to Consumer Involvement', *Journal of Advertising Research*, 25, 6, December 1985–January 1986, 48–56.

35. Kenneth Schneider and William Rodgers, 'An "Importance" Subscale for the Consumer Involvement Profile', *Advances in Consumer Research*, 23, eds Kim Corfman and John Lynch (Provo, UT: Association for Consumer Research, 1996), 249–54.

36. Simon Walls and David W. Schumann, 'Measuring the Customer's Perception of the Bond Between the Customer and the Company', *American Marketing Association Educators' Conference Proceedings*, 12, 2001, 388–400.

37. For example, Alan Dick and Kunal Basu, 'Customer Loyalty: Toward an Integrated Conceptual Framework', *Journal of the Academy of Marketing Science*, 22, Spring 1994, 99–113; Grahame R. Dowling and Mark Uncles, 'Do Customer Loyalty Programs Really Work?', *Sloan Management Review*, Summer 1997, 71–82.

38. Kevin Lane Keller, Susan E. Heckler and Michael J. Houston, 'The Effects of Brand Name Suggestiveness on Advertising Recall', *Journal of Marketing*, 62, January 1998, 48–57.

39. David Glen Mick, 'Levels of Subjective Comprehension in Advertising Processing and Their Relations to Ad Perceptions, Attitudes, and Memory', *Journal of Consumer Research*, 18, March 1992, 411–24.

40. Rebekah Bennett and Sharyn Rundle-Thiele, 'A Comparison of Attitudinal Loyalty Measurement Approaches', *Journal of Brand Management*, January 2002, 193–209.

41. Sandra Blakeslee, 'If You Have a "Buy Button" in Your Brain, What Pushes It?', *New York Times*, 19 October 2004, F5.

42. Arjun Chaudhuri and Morris B. Holbrook, 'The Chain of Effects from Brand Trust and Brand Affect to Brand Performance: The Role of Brand Loyalty', *Journal of Marketing*, April 2001, 81–93.

43. Dick and Basu, 'Customer Loyalty', 99–113.

44. Jaishankar Ganesh, Mark J. Arnold and Kristy E. Reynolds, 'Understanding the Customer Base of Service Providers: An Examination of the Differences Between Switchers and Stayers', *Journal of Marketing*, July 2000, 65–87.

45. Stijn M. J. Van Osselaer and Joseph W. Alba, 'Consumer Learning and Brand Equity', *Journal of Consumer Research*, 27, June 2000, 1–16.

46. 'Self-Regulatory Guidelines for Children's Advertising', www.caru.org.

CHAPTER 9
CONSUMER ATTITUDE FORMATION AND CHANGE

As consumers, each of us has a vast number of attitudes toward products, services, advertisements, direct mail, the Internet and shops. Whenever we are asked whether we like or dislike a product, a service, a particular retailer, a specific direct marketer, or an advertising theme, we are being asked to express our attitudes.

Within the context of consumer behaviour, an appreciation of prevailing attitudes has considerable strategic merit. For instance, there has been very rapid growth in the sales of natural ingredient bath, body and cosmetic products throughout the world. This trend seems linked to the currently popular attitude that things 'natural' are good and things 'synthetic' are bad. Yet, in reality, the positive attitude favouring things natural is not based on any systematic evidence that natural cosmetic products are any safer or better for consumers.

To get at the heart of what is driving consumers' behaviour, attitude research has been used to study a wide range of strategic marketing questions. For example, attitude research is frequently undertaken to determine whether consumers will accept a proposed new product idea, to gauge why a firm's target audience has not reacted more favourably to its new promotional theme or to learn how target customers are likely to react to a proposed change in the firm's packaging design. To illustrate, major athletic shoe marketers such as Nike or Reebok frequently conduct research among target consumers of the different types of athletic footwear products that they market. They seek attitudes of target consumers with respect to size, fit, comfort and fashion elements of their footwear, as well as test reactions to potential new designs or functional features. They also regularly gauge reactions to their latest advertising and other marketing messages designed to form and change consumer attitudes. All these marketing activities are related to the important task of impacting consumers' attitudes.

In this chapter we will discuss the reasons why attitude research has had such a pervasive impact on consumer behaviour. We also will discuss the properties that have made attitudes so attractive to consumer researchers, as well as some of the common frustrations encountered in attitude research. Particular attention will be paid to the central topics of attitude formation, attitude change and related strategic marketing issues.

WHAT ARE ATTITUDES?

Consumer researchers assess **attitudes** by asking questions or making inferences from behaviour. For example, if a researcher determines from questioning a consumer that he consistently buys Gillette shaving gel, and even recommends this to his friends, the researcher is likely to infer that the consumer possesses a positive attitude towards this brand of shaving gel. This example illustrates that attitudes are not directly observable but must be inferred from what people say or what they do.

Moreover, the illustration suggests that a whole universe of consumer behaviours – consistency of purchases, recommendations to others, top rankings, beliefs, evaluations and intentions are related to attitudes. What, then, are attitudes? In a consumer behaviour context, *an attitude is a learned predisposition to behave in a consistently favourable or unfavourable way with respect to a given object.* Each part of this definition describes an important property of an attitude and is critical to understanding the role of attitudes in consumer behaviour.

The attitude 'object'

The word *object* in our consumer-oriented definition of attitude should be interpreted broadly to include specific consumption- or marketing-related concepts, such as product, product category, brand, service, possessions, product use, causes or issues, people, advertisement, Internet site, price, medium or retailer.

In conducting attitude research, we tend to be object specific. For example, if we were interested in learning consumers' attitudes towards three major brands of DVD players, our 'object' might include Sony, Toshiba and Panasonic; if we were examining consumer attitudes towards major brands of mobile phones, our 'object' might include Nokia, Sony Ericsson, Samsung and Motorola.

Attitudes are learned predispositions

There is general agreement that attitudes are learned. This means that attitudes relevant to purchase behaviour are formed as a result of direct experience with the product, word-of-mouth information acquired from others, or exposure to mass-media advertising, the Internet and various forms of direct marketing (e.g. a retailer's catalogue). It is important to remember that although attitudes may result from behaviour, they are not synonymous with behaviour. Instead, they reflect either a favourable or an unfavourable evaluation of the attitude object. As learned predispositions, attitudes have a motivational quality, that is, they might propel a consumer towards a particular behaviour or repel the consumer away from a particular behaviour.

Attitudes have consistency

Another characteristic of attitudes is that they are relatively consistent with the behaviour they reflect. However, despite their consistency, attitudes are not necessarily permanent; they do change. (Attitude change is explored later in this chapter.)

It is important to illustrate what we mean by consistency. Normally, we expect consumers' behaviour to correspond with their attitudes. For example, if a French consumer reported preferring German to Japanese cars, we would expect that the individual would be more likely to buy a German brand when his current vehicle needed to be replaced. In other words, when consumers are free to act as they wish, we anticipate that their actions will be consistent with their attitudes. However, circumstances often preclude consistency between attitudes and behaviour. For example, in the case of our French consumer, the matter of affordability may intervene, and the consumer may find a particular Japanese car to be a more cost-effective choice than a German car. Therefore, we must consider possible situational influences on consumer attitudes and behaviour.

Attitudes occur within a situation

It is not immediately evident from our definition that attitudes occur within and are affected by the situation. By situation, we mean events or circumstances that, at a particular time, influence the relationship between an attitude and a behaviour. A specific situation can cause consumers to behave in ways seemingly inconsistent with their attitudes. For instance, let us assume that a Danish consumer, Marcus, purchases a different brand of deodorant each time the brand he is using runs low. Although his brand-switching behaviour may seem to reflect a negative attitude or dissatisfaction with the brands he tries, it actually may be influenced by a specific situation, for example, his wish to economise. Thus, he will buy whatever is the least expensive brand, and it is not a matter of a negative attitude.[1]

The opposite can also be true. If Elisabeth flies Lufthansa each time she goes out of town on business, we may erroneously infer that she has a particularly favourable attitude toward Lufthansa. On the contrary, Elisabeth may find Lufthansa to be 'just okay'. However, because she owns her own business and travels at her own expense, she may feel that Lufthansa is 'good enough', given that she may be paying less than she would be paying if she flew with another airline.

Indeed, individuals can have a variety of attitudes towards a particular behaviour, each corresponding to a particular situation. Dana may feel it is all right to eat lunch at Burger King but does not consider it appropriate for dinner. In this case, Burger King has its 'time and place', which functions as a boundary delineating the situations when Dana considers Burger King acceptable. However, if Dana is coming home late from school one night, feels exhausted and hungry and spots a Burger King, she may just decide to have dinner there. Why? Because it is late, she is tired and hungry, and Burger King is convenient. Has she changed her attitude? Probably not.

It is important to understand how consumer attitudes vary from situation to situation. For instance, it is useful to know whether consumer preferences for different burger chains (e.g. Burger King or McDonald's) vary in terms of eating situations (lunch or snack, evening meal when rushed for time, or evening meal with family when not rushed for time). Consumer preferences for the various burger restaurants might depend on the anticipated eating situation. Burger King, for example, might be favoured by a segment of consumers as a good place to have dinner with their families. This suggests that its management might position Burger King's restaurants as a nice place to take the family for a leisurely (and inexpensive) dinner.

Clearly, when measuring attitudes, it is important to consider the situation in which the behaviour takes place, or we can misinterpret the relationship between attitudes and behaviour.

STRUCTURAL MODELS OF ATTITUDES

Motivated by a desire to understand the relationship between attitudes and behaviour, psychologists have sought to construct models that capture the underlying dimensions of an attitude.[2] To this end, the focus has been on specifying the composition of an attitude to better explain or predict behaviour. The following section examines several important attitude models: the tricomponent attitude model, the multi-attribute attitude models, the trying to consume model and the attitude towards the ad models. Each of these models provides a somewhat different perspective on the number of component parts of an attitude and how those parts are arranged or interrelated.

Tricomponent attitude model

According to the **tricomponent attitude model**, attitudes consist of three major components: a cognitive component, an affective component and a conative component (see Figure 9-1).

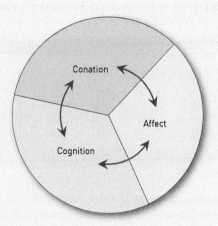

FIGURE 9-1 A simple representation of the tricomponent attitude model

The Cognitive Component

The first part of the tricomponent attitude model consists of a person's cognitions, that is, the knowledge and perceptions that are acquired by a combination of direct experience with the attitude object and related information from various sources. This knowledge and resulting perceptions commonly take the form of beliefs; that is, the consumer believes that the attitude object possesses various attributes and that specific behaviour will lead to specific outcomes.

Although it captures only a part of Ralph's belief system about two types of broadband Internet connections (e.g. cable and DSL), Figure 9-2 illustrates the composition of a consumer's belief system about these two alternatives. Ralph's belief system for both types of connections consists of the same basic four attributes: speed, availability, reliability and 'other' features. However, Ralph has somewhat different beliefs about the two broadband alternatives with respect to these attributes. For instance, he knows from friends that the local cable company's

Product	**BROADBAND INTERNET ACCESS**							
Brand	**Cable Internet Access**				**DSL Internet Access**			
Attributes	Speed	Availability	Reliability	Other Features	Speed	Availability	Reliability	Other Features
Beliefs	Faster than DSL	Offered now by my cable company	As reliable as my cable TV	No choice of provider and slows down when lots of subscribers are online	Slower than a cable modem but faster than dial-up service	Offered now by my local telephone company	Can be spotty	Bandwidth varies less than with a cable connection but can be more difficult to install and troubleshoot
Evaluations	[++++]	[+++]	[+++]	[–]	[++]	[+++]	[–]	[+]

FIGURE 9-2 A consumer's belief system for two methods of broadband Internet access
Source: Based on Todd Spangler, 'Crossing the Broadband Divide', *PC Magazine*, 12 February 2001, 92–103.

TABLE 9-1 Selected evaluative scale used to gauge consumers' attitudes towards Old Spice Aftershave

Compared to other aftershaves, Old Spice Aftershave is:							
Refreshing	[1]	[2]	[3]	[4]	[5]	[6]	[7]	Not refreshing
Positive	[1]	[2]	[3]	[4]	[5]	[6]	[7]	Negative
Pleasant	[1]	[2]	[3]	[4]	[5]	[6]	[7]	Unpleasant
Appealing to others	[1]	[2]	[3]	[4]	[5]	[6]	[7]	Unappealing to others

broadband connection is much faster than DSL, but he does not like the fact that he will also have to begin subscribing to cable television if he does not want to pay an extra €15 a month for the broadband Internet connection. Ralph is thinking of asking a few of his friends about the differences between cable and DSL broadband Internet services and will also go online to a number of websites that discuss this topic.

The Affective Component

A consumer's emotions or feelings about a particular product or brand constitute the affective component of an attitude. These emotions and feelings are frequently treated by consumer researchers as primarily evaluative in nature; that is, they capture an individual's direct or global assessment of the attitude object (the extent to which the individual rates the attitude object as 'favourable' or 'unfavourable', 'good' or 'bad'). To illustrate, Table 9-1 shows a series of evaluative (affective) scale items that might be used to assess consumers' attitudes towards Old Spice Aftershave.

Affect-laden experiences also manifest themselves as emotionally charged states (e.g. happiness, sadness, shame, disgust, anger, distress, guilt or surprise). Research indicates that such emotional states may enhance or amplify positive or negative experiences and that later recollections of such experiences may impact what comes to mind and how the individual acts.[3] For instance, a person visiting a shopping centre is likely to be influenced by his or her emotional state at the time. If the shopper is feeling particularly joyous at the moment, a positive response to the shopping centre may be amplified. The emotionally enhanced response to the shopping centre may lead the shopper to recall with great pleasure the time spent there. It also may influence the individual shopper to persuade friends and acquaintances to visit the same shopping centre and to make the personal decision to revisit the centre.

In addition to using direct or global evaluative measures of an attitude object, consumer researchers can also use a battery of affective response scales (e.g. that measure feelings and emotions) to construct a picture of consumers' overall feelings about a product, service or advertisement. Table 9-2 gives an example of a five-point scale that measures affective responses.

The Conative Component

Conation, the final component of the tricomponent attitude model, is concerned with the likelihood or tendency that an individual will undertake a specific action or behave in a particular way with regard to the attitude object. According to some interpretations, the conative component may include the actual behaviour itself.

In marketing and consumer research, the conative component is frequently treated as an expression of the consumer's intention to buy. Buyer intention scales are used to assess the likelihood of a consumer purchasing a product or behaving in a certain way. Table 9-3 provides two examples of common **intention-to-buy scales**. Interestingly, consumers who are asked to respond to an intention-to-buy question appear to be more likely actually to make a brand purchase for positively evaluated brands (e.g. 'I will buy it'), as contrasted to consumers who

TABLE 9-2 Measuring consumers' feelings and emotions with regard to using Old Spice
         Aftershave

For the past 30 days you have had a chance to try Old Spice Aftershave. We would appreciate it if
you would identify how your face felt after using the product during this 30-day trial period. For
each of the words below, we would appreciate it if you would mark an 'X' in the box corresponding
to how your face felt after using Old Spice Aftershave during the past 30 days.

	VERY				NOT AT ALL
Relaxed	[ ]	[ ]	[ ]	[ ]	[ ]
Attractive looking	[ ]	[ ]	[ ]	[ ]	[ ]
Tight	[ ]	[ ]	[ ]	[ ]	[ ]
Smooth	[ ]	[ ]	[ ]	[ ]	[ ]
Supple	[ ]	[ ]	[ ]	[ ]	[ ]
Clean	[ ]	[ ]	[ ]	[ ]	[ ]
Refreshed	[ ]	[ ]	[ ]	[ ]	[ ]
Younger	[ ]	[ ]	[ ]	[ ]	[ ]
Revived	[ ]	[ ]	[ ]	[ ]	[ ]
Renewed	[ ]	[ ]	[ ]	[ ]	[ ]

TABLE 9-3 Two examples of intention-to-buy scales

Which of the following statements best describes the chance that you will buy Old Spice
Aftershave the next time you purchase an aftershave product?

_____ I definitely will buy it.
_____ I probably will buy it.
_____ I am uncertain whether I will buy it.
_____ I probably will not buy it.
_____ I definitely will not buy it.

How likely are you to buy Old Spice Aftershave during the next three months?

_____ Very likely
_____ Likely
_____ Unlikely
_____ Very unlikely

are not asked to respond to an intention question.[4] This suggests that a positive brand commitment in the form of a positive answer to an attitude intention question impacts the actual brand
purchase in a positive way.

Multi-attribute attitude models

Multi-attribute attitude models portray consumers' attitudes with regard to an attitude object
(e.g. a product, a service, a direct-mail catalogue, a cause or an issue) as a function of consumers' perception and assessment of the key attributes or beliefs held with regard to the particular
attitude object. Although there are many variations of this type of attitude model, we have
selected the following four models to consider briefly here: the attitude towards object model,

the attitude towards behaviour model, the theory of reasoned action model and the theory of planned behaviour model.

The Attitude Towards Object Model

The **attitude towards object model** is especially suitable for measuring attitudes towards a product (or service) category or specific brands.[5] According to this model, the consumer's attitude towards a product or specific brands of a product is a function of the presence (or absence) and evaluation of certain product-specific beliefs and/or attributes. In other words, consumers generally have favourable attitudes towards those brands that they believe have an adequate level of attributes that they evaluate as positive, and they have unfavourable attitudes towards those brands they feel do not have an adequate level of desired attributes or have too many negative or undesired attributes. As an illustration, we return to the broadband Internet connection example (see Figure 9-2). Each alternative has a different 'mix' of features (a 'feature set'). The defining features might include speed, reliability, cost, availability of 24/7 technical assistance, maximum file size that can be emailed, and so on. For instance, one of the two types of connections might be found to excel on core features, whereas the other may be really good on a few of the core features but offer more additional features. It is also possible that neither the cable nor the DSL carriers may be more than 'second rate'. However, what consumers will purchase is likely to be a function of 'how much they know', 'what they feel are important features for them', and in the current example, their 'awareness as to which type of broadband service possesses (or lacks) the valued attributes'.

Conducting consumer attitude research with children, especially gauging their attitudes towards products and brands, is an ongoing challenge. What is needed are new and effective measurement approaches that allow children to express their attitudes towards brands. To this end, researchers have laboured to develop an especially simple and short attitude measurement instrument for questioning children between 8 and 12 years of age. In the case of the example presented in Table 9-4, the questionnaire is set up to assess children's attitudes towards the Kellogg's brand.[6]

The Attitude Towards Behaviour Model

The **attitude towards behaviour model** is the individual's attitude towards behaving or acting with respect to an object rather than the attitude towards the object itself.[7] The appeal of the attitude towards behaviour model is that it seems to correspond somewhat more closely to actual behaviour than does the attitude towards object model. For instance, knowing Sarah's attitude about the act of purchasing a top-range BMW (her attitude towards the behaviour) reveals more

TABLE 9-4 A scale used to measure attitude towards brands for 8- to 12-year-olds

	DEFINITELY DISAGREE	DISAGREE	AGREE	DEFINITELY AGREE
Kellogg's – I like it.	☐	☐	☐	☐
Kellogg's – It is fun.	☐	☐	☐	☐
Kellogg's – It is great.	☐	☐	☐	☐
Kellogg's – It is useful.	☐	☐	☐	☐
Kellogg's – I like it very much.	☐	☐	☐	☐
Kellogg's – It is practical/handy.	☐	☐	☐	☐
Kellogg's – It is useless.	☐	☐	☐	☐

Source: Adapted from Claude Pecheux and Christian Derbaix, 'Children and Attitude Toward the Brand. A New Measurement Scale', *Journal of Advertising Research*, July/August 1999, 19–27. Used by permission of M. E. Sharpe, Inc.

about the potential act of purchasing than does simply knowing her attitude towards expensive German cars or specifically BMWs (the attitude towards the object). This seems logical, for a consumer might have a positive attitude towards an expensive BMW but a negative attitude as to his or her prospects for purchasing such an expensive vehicle.

A study conducted in Taiwan examined the relationship between consumer characteristics and attitude towards the behaviour of online shopping. The researcher found that attitudes towards online shopping are significantly different based on various consumer behaviour factors. For example, the research identified the following nine benefits of online shopping:

1. effectiveness and modern,
2. purchase convenience,
3. information abundance,
4. multiform and safety,
5. service quality,
6. delivery speed,
7. homepage design,
8. selection freedom, and
9. company name familiarity.

These nine attributes were selected because they tend to reflect consumers' attitude towards online shopping.[8]

The researcher went on to explore a model (see Figure 9-3) that suggested that consumer characteristics (on the left side of the model) impact attitudes towards online shopping (in the middle of the model – the nine attitudinal attributes listed above) and the rating of the online shopping experience (on the right side of the model).

The Theory of Reasoned Action Model

The **theory of reasoned action (TRA)** represents a comprehensive integration of attitude components into a structure that is designed to lead to both better explanation and better

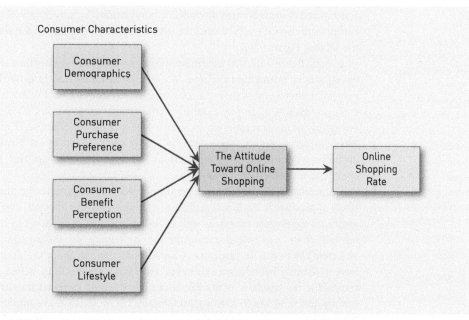

FIGURE 9-3 Consumer characteristics, attitude and online shopping

Source: Adapted from Shwu-Ing Wu, 'The Relationship Between Consumer Characteristics and Attitude Toward Online Shopping', *Marketing Intelligence and Planning*, 21, 2003, 40.

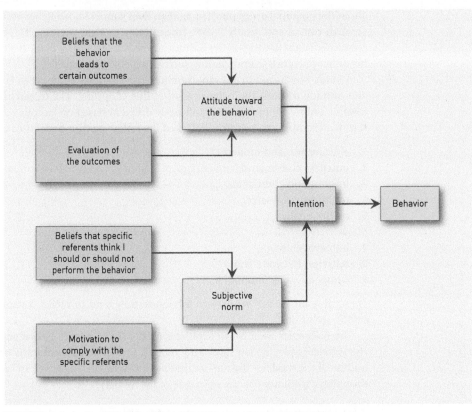

FIGURE 9-4 A simplified version of the theory of reasoned action
Source: Azjen, Iczek; Fishbein, Martin, *Understanding Attitudes and Predicting Social Behavior*, 1st edition, © 1980.
Printed and Electronically reproduced by permission of Pearson Education, Inc., Upper Saddle River, NJ.

predictions of behaviour. Like the basic tricomponent attitude model, the theory of reasoned action model incorporates a cognitive component, an affective component and a conative component; however, these are arranged in a pattern different from that of the tricomponent model (see Figure 9-4).

In accordance with this expanded model, to understand intention we also need to measure the subjective norms that influence an individual's intention to act. A subjective norm can be measured directly by assessing a consumer's feelings as to what relevant others (family, friends, room-mates, colleagues) would think of the action being contemplated; that is, would they look favourably or unfavourably on the anticipated action? For example, if an undergraduate student was considering purchasing a new VW Beetle and stopped to ask himself what his parents or girlfriend would think of such behaviour (i.e. approve or disapprove), such a reflection would constitute his subjective norm.

Consumer researchers can get behind the subjective norm to the underlying factors that are likely to produce it. They accomplish this by assessing the normative beliefs that the individual attributes to relevant others, as well as the individual's motivation to comply with each of the relevant others. For instance, consider the undergraduate student contemplating the purchase of a new VW Beetle. To understand his subjective norm about the desired purchase, we would have to identify his relevant others (parents and girlfriend); his beliefs about how each would respond to his purchase of the Beetle (e.g. 'Dad would consider the car an unnecessary luxury, but my girlfriend would love it'); and, finally, his motivation to comply with his parents and/or his girlfriend.[9] A recent study also indicates that incorporating the consumer's emotional experience into the multi-attribute model has the potential of enhancing the predictability of motives and preferences.[10]

The Theory of Planned Behaviour Model

An extension of the TRA model is the **theory of planned behavior (TPB)**, which included an additional factor leading to 'intention' – the construct of perceived behavioural control (PBC) – which is a consumer's perception of whether the behaviour is or is not within his or her control. For example, while brushing the teeth is clearly within an individual's control, weight loss may not be. It is believed that the addition of PBC permits better prediction of behaviours not completely under the individual's complete control.[11]

When applying the TPB model to the study of consumer behaviour, researchers typically treat behavioural intentions as determined by three variables. First are the attitude and the subjective norm from the TRA model. Remember that each of these is based on two elements, for example that the subjective norm consists of normative beliefs about relevant others, as well as the individual's motivation to comply with each of the relevant others. Perceived behavioural control also consists of two such inputs: the importance of a factor that will enable the individual to perform a certain behaviour, and the degree to which he or she has access to that factor. For example, in the toothbrush example mentioned in the last paragraph, the presence of a toothbrush and toothpaste is important for the ability to perform the behaviour, and if a consumer has access to these two factors, the PBC for brushing the teeth is more or less as high as it can get. However, if you are out camping in the mountains, and have left both these products at home, the behavioural control is likely to be perceived as very low. Hence, even though your attitude towards brushing the teeth and the subjective norm both result in a strong intention to brush the teeth, the fact that your behavioural control is low due to the absence of toothbrush and paste will probably end up with you curling up in your sleeping bag with teeth not brushed.

Theory of trying to consume model

There has been an effort under way to extend attitude models so that they might better accommodate consumers' goals as expressed by their 'trying' to consume.[12] The **theory of trying to consume** is designed to account for the many cases in which the action or outcome is not certain but instead reflects the consumer's attempts to consume (i.e. purchase). In trying to consume, there are often personal impediments (a consumer is trying to find just the right tie to go with a newly purchased suit for under €50 or is trying to lose weight but loves crisps) and/or environmental impediments (only the first 200 in the queue will be able to purchase this €300 DVD player for the special price of €179 available only on Saturday from 8.00 a.m. to 9.00 a.m.) that might prevent the desired action or outcome from occurring. Again, the key point is that in these cases of trying, the outcome (purchase, possession, use or action) is not and cannot be assumed to be certain. Table 9-5 lists a few examples of possible personal and environmental impediments that might negatively impact the outcome for a consumer trying to consume. Researchers have recently extended this inquiry by examining those situations in which consumers do not try to consume – that is, fail to try to consume. In this case, consumers appear to (1) fail to see or are ignorant of their options, and (2) make a conscious effort not to consume; that is, they might seek to self-sacrifice or defer gratification to some future time.[13]

Attitude towards the ad models

In an effort to understand the impact of advertising or some other promotional vehicle (e.g. a catalogue) on consumer attitudes towards particular products or brands, considerable attention has been paid to developing what has been referred to as **attitude towards the ad models**.

Figure 9-5 presents a diagram of some of the basic relationships described by an attitude towards the ad model. As the model depicts, the consumer forms various feelings (affects) and judgements (cognitions) as the result of exposure to an advertisement. These feelings and judgements in turn affect the consumer's attitude towards the advertisement and beliefs about the

TABLE 9-5 Selected examples of potential impediments that might impact trying

POTENTIAL PERSONAL IMPEDIMENTS

'I wonder whether my fingernails will be longer by the time of my wedding.'

'I want to try to lose 7 kilos by next summer.'

'I'm going to try to get tickets for a Robbie Williams concert for your birthday.'

'I'm going to attempt to give up smoking by my birthday.'

'I am going to increase how often I go to the gym from two to four times a week.'

'Tonight I'm not going to have dessert at the restaurant.'

POTENTIAL ENVIRONMENTAL IMPEDIMENTS

'The first 10 people to call in will receive a free T-shirt.'

'Sorry, the shoes didn't come in this shipment from Italy.'

'There are only three bottles of champagne in our stockroom. You'd better come in sometime later today.'

'I am sorry. We cannot serve you. We are closing the restaurant because of a problem with the oven.'

brand acquired from exposure to the advertisement. Finally, the consumer's attitude towards the advertisement and beliefs about the brand influence his or her attitude towards the brand.[14]

Researchers have explored attitudes towards 12 advertisements and purchase intention of six different products that the advertisements feature. The study found a positive relationship between attitude towards the advertisement and purchase intention for each of the advertised products; that is, if consumers 'like' the advertisement, they are more likely to purchase the product.[15]

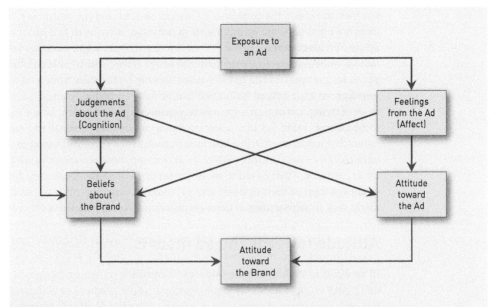

FIGURE 9-5 A conception of the relationship among elements in an attitude towards the ad model

Source: Inspired by and based on Julie A. Edell and Marian Chapman Burke, 'The Power of Feelings in Understanding Advertising Effects', *Journal of Consumer Research*, 14, December 1987, 431. Reprinted by permission of The University of Chicago Press as publisher. Copyright © 1987, JCR, Inc.

Additional research reveals that for a novel product (e.g. contact lenses for pets) consumers' attitude towards the advertisement has a stronger impact on brand attitude and purchase intention than for a familiar product (e.g. pet food).[16] This same research found that beliefs about a brand (brand cognition) that result from advertising exposure play a much stronger role in determining attitudes towards the brand for a familiar product. Thus, it is important to consider the nature of the attitude object in assessing the potential impact of advertising exposure.

Finally, consumer socialisation has also shown itself to be an important determinant of a consumer's attitudes towards advertising. One study, for example, found that parental communication, peer communication, social utility of advertising, amount of television watched, gender and race were all associated with attitude towards advertising.[17]

ATTITUDE FORMATION

How do people, especially young people, form their initial general attitudes towards 'things'? Consider their attitudes towards the clothing they wear: for example, underwear, casual wear and business attire. On a more specific level, how do they form attitudes towards Calvin Klein underwear, or Levi's casual wear or Armani business clothing? Also, what about attitudes towards the kind of shops in which they would buy their underwear, casual wear and business clothing? How do family members and friends, admired celebrities, mass-media advertisements, even cultural memberships, influence the formation of their attitudes concerning consuming or not consuming each of these types of clothing? Why do some attitudes seem to persist indefinitely while others change fairly often? The answers to such questions are of vital importance to marketers, for without knowing how attitudes are formed, they are unable to understand or to influence consumer attitudes or behaviour.

Our examination of attitude formation is divided into three areas: how attitudes are learned, the sources of influence on attitude formation and the impact of personality on attitude formation.

How attitudes are learned

When we speak of the formation of an attitude, we refer to the shift from having no attitude towards a given object (e.g. an MP3 player) to having some attitude towards it (e.g. having an MP3 player is great when you want to listen to music while on a treadmill at the gym). The shift from no attitude to an attitude (i.e. the attitude formation) is a result of learning (see Chapter 8 for detailed exploration of learning theories).

Consumers often purchase new products that are associated with a favourably viewed brand name. Their favourable attitude towards the brand name is frequently the result of repeated satisfaction with other products produced by the same company. In terms of classical conditioning, an established brand name is an unconditioned stimulus that through past positive reinforcement resulted in a favourable brand attitude. A new product, yet to be linked to the established brand, would be the conditioned stimulus. To illustrate, by giving a new game console the benefit of its well-known and respected family name, Microsoft counted on a transfer of the favourable attitude already associated with the brand name to the new product, Microsoft Xbox. The company counted on stimulus generalisation from the brand name to the new product. Research suggests that the 'fit' between a parent brand (e.g. Microsoft) and a brand extension (in this case Microsoft Xbox) is a function of two factors:

1. the similarity between the pre-existing product categories already associated with the parent brand (i.e. mostly products related to computer software) and the new extension, and
2. the fit or match between the images of the parent brand and the new extension.[18]

Sometimes attitudes follow the purchase and consumption of a product. For example, a consumer may purchase a brand name product without having a prior attitude towards it because it is the only product of its kind available (e.g. the last bottle of aspirin in a petrol station mini-mart). Consumers also make trial purchases of new brands from product categories in which they have little personal involvement (see Chapter 8). If they find the purchased brand to be satisfactory, then they are likely to develop a favourable attitude towards it.

In situations in which consumers seek to solve a problem or satisfy a need, they are likely to form attitudes (either positive or negative) about products on the basis of information exposure and their own cognition (knowledge and beliefs). In general, the more information consumers have about a product or service, the more likely they are to form attitudes about it, either positive or negative. However, regardless of available information, consumers are not always ready or willing to process product-related information. Furthermore, consumers often use only a limited amount of the information available to them. Research suggests that only two or three important beliefs about a product dominate in the formation of attitudes and that less important beliefs provide little additional input.[19] This important finding suggests that marketers should fight off the impulse to include all the features of their products and services in their advertisements; rather, they should focus on the few key points that are at the heart of what distinguishes their product from the competition.

Sources of influence on attitude formation

The formation of consumer attitudes is strongly influenced by personal experience, the influence of family and friends, direct marketing and mass media.

The primary means by which attitudes towards goods and services are formed is through the consumer's direct experience in trying and evaluating them.[20] Recognising the importance of direct experience, marketers frequently attempt to stimulate trial of new products by offering price cuts or even free samples. In such cases, the marketer's objective is to get consumers to try the product and then to evaluate it. If a product proves to be to their liking, then it is probable that consumers will form a positive attitude and be likely to repurchase the product.

As we come in contact with others, especially family, close friends and admired individuals (e.g. a respected teacher), we form attitudes that influence our lives.[21] The family is an extremely important source of influence on the formation of attitudes, for it is the family that provides us with many of our basic values and a wide range of less central beliefs. For instance, young children who are rewarded for good behaviour with sweets often retain a taste for (and positive attitude towards) sweets as adults.

Marketers are increasingly using highly focused direct-marketing programmes to target small consumer niches with products and services that fit their interests and lifestyles. (Niche marketing is sometimes called *micromarketing*.) Marketers very carefully target customers on the basis of their demographic, psychographic or geodemographic profiles with highly personalised product offerings (e.g. hunting rifles for left-handed people) and messages that show they understand their special needs and desires. Direct-marketing efforts have an excellent chance of favourably influencing target consumers' attitudes, because the products and services offered and the promotional messages conveyed are very carefully designed to address the individual segment's needs and concerns and, thus, are able to achieve a higher 'hit rate' than mass marketing.

In countries where people have easy access to newspapers and a variety of general and special-interest magazines and television channels, consumers are constantly exposed to new ideas, products, opinions and advertisements. These mass-media communications provide an important source of information that influences the formation of consumer attitudes. Other research indicates that for consumers who lack direct experience with a product, exposure to an emotionally appealing advertising message is more likely to create an attitude towards the product than for consumers who have earlier direct experience with the product category.[22] The net implications of these findings appear to be that emotional appeals are most effective with consumers who lack product experience.

Still another issue with regard to evaluating the impact of advertising messages on attitude formation is the level of realism that is provided. Research has shown that attitudes that develop through direct experience (e.g. product usage) tend to be more confidently held, more enduring and more resistant to attack than those developed via indirect experience (e.g. reading a print advertisement). And just as television provided the advertiser with more realism than is possible in a radio or print advertisement, the Internet has an even greater ability to provide *telepresence*, which is the simulated perception of direct experience. The World Wide Web also has the ability to provide the *flow experience*, which is a cognitive state occurring when the individual is so involved in an activity that nothing else matters. Research on telepresence suggests that 'perceptions of telepresence grew stronger as levels of interactivity and levels of vividness (i.e., the way an environment presents information to the senses) of web sites increased'.[23]

Personality factors

Personality also plays a critical role in attitude formation. For example, individuals with a high need for cognition (i.e. those who crave information and enjoy thinking) are likely to form positive attitudes in response to advertisements or direct mail that are rich in product-related information. On the other hand, consumers who are relatively low in need for cognition are more likely to form positive attitudes in response to advertisements that feature an attractive model or well-known celebrity. In a similar fashion, attitudes towards new products and new consumption situations are strongly influenced by specific personality characteristics of consumers.

STRATEGIES OF ATTITUDE CHANGE

It is important to recognise that much of what has been said about attitude formation is also basically true of attitude change. That is, attitude changes are learned; they are influenced by personal experience and other sources of information, and personality affects both the receptivity and the speed with which attitudes are likely to be altered.

Altering consumer attitudes is a key strategy consideration for most marketers. For marketers who are fortunate enough to be market leaders and to enjoy a significant amount of customer goodwill and loyalty, the overriding goal is to fortify the existing positive attitudes of customers so that they will not succumb to competitors' special offers and other inducements designed to win them over. For instance, in many product categories (e.g. wet shaving systems, in which Gillette has dominated), most competitors take aim at the market leaders when developing their marketing strategies. Their objective is to change the attitudes of the market leaders' customers and win them over. Among the attitude-change strategies that are available to them are:

1. changing the consumer's basic motivational function,
2. associating the product with a special group, event or cause,
3. resolving two conflicting attitudes,
4. altering components of the multi-attribute model, and
5. changing consumer beliefs about competitors' brands.

Changing the basic motivational function

An effective strategy for changing consumer attitudes towards a product or brand is to make particular needs prominent. One method for changing motivation is known as the **functional approach**.[24] According to this approach, attitudes can be classified in terms of four functions: the **utilitarian function**, the **ego-defensive function**, the **value-expressive function** and the **knowledge function**.

The Utilitarian Function

We hold certain brand attitudes partly because of a brand's utility. When a product has been useful or helped us in the past, our attitude towards it tends to be favourable. One way of changing attitudes in favour of a product is by showing people that it can serve a utilitarian purpose that they may not have considered. For example, the advertisement for Dell E6400 in Figure 9-6 points out that, with this computer you belong to the group of consumers with extraordinary demands.

FIGURE 9-6 Dell uses a utilitarian appeal

Source: Dell Corporation Ltd.

The Ego-Defensive Function

Most people want to protect their self-images from inner feelings of doubt – they want to replace their uncertainty with a sense of security and personal confidence.[25] Advertisements for cosmetics and personal care products, by acknowledging this need, increase both their relevance to the consumer and the likelihood of a favourable attitude change by offering reassurance to the consumer's self-concept. For example, in an advertising campaign for the Zippo lighter designed to counter the trend towards disposable lighters, the campaign used headlines such as 'True love is not disposable' (the advertisement showed a Zippo with an engraved love poem).[26] The campaign was an effort to equate the long-lasting relationship a consumer can have with his Zippo lighter with other things in life.

The Value-Expressive Function

Attitudes are an expression or reflection of the consumer's general values, lifestyle and outlook. If a consumer segment generally holds a positive attitude towards owning the latest designer jeans, then its members' attitudes towards new brands of designer jeans are likely to reflect that orientation. Similarly, if a segment of consumers has a positive attitude towards being 'high tech', then its members' attitudes towards thin wall-mountable high-definition television sets are likely to reflect this viewpoint. Thus, by knowing target consumers' attitudes, marketers can better anticipate their values, lifestyle or outlook and can reflect these characteristics in their advertising and direct-marketing efforts. The advertisement for Longines in Figure 9-7 addresses target consumers' attitudes.

The Knowledge Function

Individuals generally have a strong need to know and understand the people and things they encounter. The consumer's 'need to know', a cognitive need, is important to marketers concerned with product positioning. Indeed, many product and brand positionings are attempts to satisfy the need to know and to improve the consumer's attitudes towards the brand by emphasising its advantages over competitive brands. For instance, a message for an advanced-design toothbrush might point out how it is superior to other toothbrushes in controlling gum disease by removing more plaque and that this is important to overall good health. The message might even use a bar graph to contrast its plaque removal abilities with those of other leading toothbrushes. An important characteristic of such advertisements is the appeal and usefulness to consumers' need to know.

Combining Several Functions

Because different consumers may like or dislike the same product or service for different reasons, a functional framework for examining attitudes can be very useful. For instance, three consumers may all have positive attitudes towards one specific brand of haircare products. However, one may be responding solely to the fact that the products work well (the utilitarian function); the second may have the inner confidence to agree with the point 'When you know beautiful hair doesn't have to cost a fortune' (an ego-defensive function). The third consumer's favourable attitudes might reflect the realisation that the brand has for many years stressed value (equal or better products for less) – the knowledge function.

Associating the product with a special group, event or cause

Attitudes are related, at least in part, to certain groups, social events or causes. It is possible to alter attitudes towards products, services and brands by pointing out their relationships to particular social groups, events or causes. Companies regularly include mention in their advertising

FIGURE 9-7
Source: Courtesy of The Advertising Archives.

of the civic and public acts that they sponsor to let the public know about the good that they are trying to do.

Recent research into brand–cause alliances have investigated the relationship between the 'cause' and the 'sponsor'. For instance, one study found that while both the brand and the cause benefit from such alliances, a more unfamiliar cause benefited more from its association with

FIGURE 9-8 Cafedirect demonstrates its ongoing commitment to Fairtrade coffee
Source: Courtesy of The Advertising Archives.

a positive brand than did a highly familiar cause.[27] The results of another study further suggest that if corporate sponsors fail to indicate explicitly their motives for a company–cause or a product–cause association, it is likely that consumers will form their own motives for the association between the company, product or service and the cause.[28] This finding seems to indicate that it is likely to be a good idea for a sponsor to reveal to target consumers the reasoning behind its sponsorship, so that consumers know the sponsor's motives rather than form their own potentially inaccurate or negative motives.

Resolving two conflicting attitudes

Attitude-change strategies can sometimes resolve actual or potential conflict between two attitudes. Specifically, if consumers can be made to see that their negative attitude towards a product, a specific brand or its attributes is really not in conflict with another attitude, they may be induced to change their evaluation of the brand (i.e. moving from negative to positive).

For example, Stanley is a serious amateur photographer who has been thinking of moving from his point-and-shoot digital camera to a digital single reflex camera (DSLR) in order to take better pictures. However, with the recent improvements in point-and-shoot cameras, Stanley is unsure of whether his move to a DSLR will be worthwhile. Stanley loves the idea of having the ability to change lenses (attitude 1), but he may feel that purchasing a DSLR camera is an unwise investment because these cameras may be supplanted in the near future by newer types of cameras (attitude 2). However, if Stanley learns that Panasonic and Nikon are developing a 'micro four-thirds format' small point-and-shoot camera that will offer interchangeable lenses, he might change his mind and thereby resolve his conflicting attitudes.

Altering components of the multi-attribute model

Earlier in this chapter we discussed a number of multi-attribute attitude models. These models have implications for attitude-change strategies; specifically, they provide us with additional insights as to how to bring about attitude change:

1. changing the relative evaluation of attributes,
2. changing brand beliefs,
3. adding an attribute, and
4. changing the overall brand rating.

Changing the Relative Evaluation of Attributes

The overall market for many product categories is often set out so that different consumer segments are offered different brands with different features or benefits. For instance, within a product category such as cars, a brand such as Toyota is often associated with long-lasting quality, while the BMW brand is associated with driving comfort. These two brands of cars have historically appealed to different segments of the overall car market. Similarly, when it comes to cola, the market can be divided into regular colas and diet colas, or when it comes to teas, there is the division between regular teas and herbal teas.

In general, when a product category is naturally divided according to distinct product features or benefits that appeal to a particular segment of consumers, marketers usually have an opportunity to persuade consumers to 'cross over', that is, to persuade consumers who prefer one version of the product (e.g. a standard 'soft' contact lens) to shift their favourable attitudes towards another version of the product (e.g. a disposable contact lens).

Changing Brand Beliefs

A second cognitive-oriented strategy for changing attitudes concentrates on changing beliefs or perceptions about the brand itself. This is by far the most common form of advertising appeal.

FIGURE 9-9 Changing attitudes by altering beliefs about a brand
Source: Nikon. www.nikon-europe.com, Nikon BV.

Advertisers are constantly reminding us that their product has 'more' or is 'better' or 'best' in terms of some important product attribute. The Nikon advertisement in Figure 9-9 tells consumers that the Coolpix S600 camera is so fast that situations where the motive has changed during the time it takes from pressing the shutter button to the camera responds. Hence, Nikon states that with this camera 'You'll start loving fast things', implicitly teaching consumers that Nikon is the camera with speed. In a similar fashion, Pantene haircare products challenge the notion that you have to be stuck with 'flat hair'. Pantene suggests that when consumers use its volume care products, they can increase volume by as much as 80 per cent.

Within the context of brand beliefs, there are forces working to stop or slow down attitude change. For instance, consumers frequently resist evidence that challenges a strongly held attitude or belief and tend to interpret any ambiguous information in ways that reinforce their pre-existing attitudes.[29] Therefore, information suggesting a change in attitude needs to be compelling and repeated enough to overcome the natural resistance to letting go of established attitudes.

Adding an Attribute

Another cognitive strategy consists of adding an attribute. This can be accomplished by adding either an attribute that has previously been ignored or one that represents an improvement or technological innovation.

The first route, adding a previously ignored attribute, is illustrated by the point that yogurt has more potassium than a banana (a fruit associated with a high quantity of potassium). For consumers interested in increasing their intake of potassium, the comparison of yogurt and bananas has the power of enhancing their attitudes towards yogurt.

The second route of adding an attribute that reflects an actual product change or technological innovation is easier to accomplish than stressing a previously ignored attribute. An example is Dove Nutrium. Not only does it clean and moisturise like regular Dove, but it also replenishes the skin's nutrients because it contains vitamin E lotion (see Figure 9-10). Sometimes eliminating a characteristic or feature has the same enhancing outcome as adding a characteristic or attribute. For instance, a number of skin care or deodorant manufacturers offer versions of their products that are unscented (i.e. deleting an ingredient). Indeed, Dove also markets an unscented version of its original Dove product. When thinking of adding an attribute marketers should consider (1) whether the new attribute is of importance to consumers, and (2) whether the firm's product is perceived as superior on this attribute when compared to competitors. Adding a non-significant attribute on which competitors perform better is probably not a good strategy to get consumers to hold a more positive attitude towards a brand.

Changing the Overall Brand Rating

Still another cognitive-oriented strategy consists of attempting to alter consumers' overall assessment of the brand directly, without attempting to improve or change their evaluation of any single brand attribute. Such a strategy frequently relies on some form of global statement that 'this is the largest-selling brand' or 'the one all others try to imitate', or a similar claim that sets the brand apart from all its competitors. This strategy has regularly been part of Honda's advertising approach of affirming that its cars are used by other car manufacturers as the 'standard' to live up to.

Changing beliefs about competitors' brands

Another approach to attitude-change strategy involves changing consumer beliefs about the attributes of competitive brands or product categories. However, comparative advertising can boomerang by giving visibility to competing brands and claims. (Chapter 10 discusses comparative advertising in greater depth.)

The elaboration likelihood model (ELM)

Compared to the various specific strategies of attitude change that we have reviewed, the **elaboration likelihood model (ELM)** proposes the more global view that consumer attitudes are changed by two distinctly different 'routes to persuasion': a central route or a peripheral route (see also Chapter 8).[30] The central route is particularly relevant to attitude change when a consumer's motivation or ability to assess the attitude object is high; that is, attitude change occurs because the consumer actively seeks out information relevant to the attitude object itself. When consumers are willing to exert the effort to comprehend, learn or evaluate the available information about the attitude object, learning and attitude change occur via the central route.

FIGURE 9-10 Changing attitudes by adding an attribute
Source: Reproduced with kind permission of Unilever (from an original in Unilever Archives).

In contrast, when a consumer's motivation or assessment skills are low (e.g. low involve-ment), learning and attitude change tend to occur via the peripheral route without the consumer focusing on information relevant to the attitude object itself. In such cases, attitude change often is an outcome of secondary inducements (e.g. price promotions, free samples, beautiful back-ground scenery, great packaging or the encouragement of a celebrity endorsement). Research indicates that even in low-involvement conditions (such as exposure to most advertising), in which both central and secondary inducements are initially equal in their ability to evoke similar attitudes, it is the central inducement that has the greater 'staying power' – that is, over time it is more persistent.[31] Additionally, for subjects low in product knowledge, advertisements with terminology result in the consumer having a better attitude towards the brand and the advertisement.[32]

An offshoot of the elaboration likehood model is the dual mediation model (DMM). The DMM adds a link between attitude towards the advertisement and brand cognitions.[33] It acknowledges the possibility that the central route to persuasion could be influenced by a peripheral cue (i.e. attitude towards the advertisement). Thus, this model demonstrated the interrelationship between the central and peripheral processes.

BEHAVIOUR CAN PRECEDE OR FOLLOW ATTITUDE FORMATION

Our discussion of attitude formation and attitude change has stressed the traditional 'rational' view that consumers develop their attitudes before taking action (e.g. 'Know what you are doing before you do it'). There are alternatives to this 'attitude precedes behaviour' perspective, alternatives that, on careful analysis, are likely to be just as logical and rational. For example, cognitive dissonance theory and attribution theory each provide a different explanation as to why behaviour might precede attitude formation.

Cognitive dissonance theory

According to **cognitive dissonance theory**, discomfort or dissonance occurs when a consumer holds conflicting thoughts about a belief or an attitude object. For instance, when consumers have made a commitment – made a deposit or placed an order for a product, particularly an expensive one such as a car or a personal computer – they often begin to feel cognitive dissonance when they think of the unique, positive qualities of the brands not selected ('left behind'). When cognitive dissonance occurs after a purchase, it is called *post-purchase dissonance*. Because purchase decisions often require some amount of compromise, post-purchase dissonance is quite normal. Nevertheless, it is likely to leave consumers with an uneasy feeling about their prior beliefs or actions – a feeling that they would seek to resolve by changing their attitudes to conform with their behaviour.[34]

Thus, in the case of post-purchase dissonance, attitude change is frequently an outcome of an action or behaviour. The conflicting thoughts and dissonant information following a purchase are prime factors that induce consumers to change their attitudes so that they will be consonant with their actual purchase behaviour.

What makes post-purchase dissonance relevant to marketing strategists is the premise that dissonance propels consumers to reduce the unpleasant feelings created by the rival thoughts. A variety of tactics are open to consumers to reduce post-purchase dissonance. The consumer can rationalise the decision as being wise, seek out advertisements that support the choice (while avoiding dissonance-creating competitive advertisements), try to 'sell' friends on the positive features of the brand, or look to known satisfied owners for reassurance. For example, consider the response of a young man who just purchased an engagement ring for his girlfriend to the following headline: 'How can you make two months' salary last forever?' This thought is likely to catch his attention. It says to him that although an engagement ring costs a great deal of money, it lasts forever because the future bride will cherish it for the rest of her life. Such a message is bound to help him reduce any lingering dissonance that he might have about how much he has just spent on the ring.

While it has traditionally been thought that, with respect to a particular purchase, cognitive dissonance was something that a consumer either had or did not have, research has shown that there can exist different types and levels of dissonance. The research studied consumer durable purchases, and found three distinct segments of consumers: a high-dissonance segment, a low-dissonance segment, and a 'concerned about needing the purchase' segment.[35]

In addition to such consumer-initiated tactics to reduce post-purchase uncertainty, a marketer can relieve consumer dissonance by including messages in its advertising specifically aimed at reinforcing consumers' decisions by complimenting their wisdom, offering stronger guarantees or warranties, increasing the number and effectiveness of its services, or providing detailed brochures on how to use its products correctly.

Attribution theory

As a group of loosely interrelated social psychological principles, **attribution theory** attempts to explain how people assign causality (e.g. blame or credit) to events on the basis of either their own behaviour or the behaviour of others.[36] In other words, a person might say, 'I contributed to UNICEF because it really helps people in need', or 'She tried to persuade me to buy that unknown digital camera because she'd make a bigger commission'. In attribution theory, the underlying question is why: 'Why did I do this?', 'Why did she try to get me to switch brands?' This process of making inferences about one's own or another's behaviour is a major component of attitude formation and change.

Attribution theory is certainly part of our everyday life, as companies continue to have their names on football stadiums and sponsor all types of charitable events. Research results indicate that the better the 'match' between a sponsor and an event, the more positive the outcome is likely to be. Still further, there is evidence to suggest that consumers are willing to reward high-effort firms (i.e. they will pay more for a product and/or evaluate it more highly) if they feel that the company has made an extra effort to make a better product or provide better consumer services.[37]

Self-Perception Theory

Of the various perspectives on attribution theory that have been proposed, **self-perception theory** – individuals' inferences or judgements as to the causes of their own behaviour – is a good beginning point for a discussion of attribution.

In terms of consumer behaviour, self-perception theory suggests that attitudes develop as consumers look at and make judgements about their own behaviour. Simply stated, if a young Swedish doctor observes that she routinely purchases the newspaper *Expressen* on her way to the clinic, she is apt to conclude that she likes *Expressen* (i.e. she has a positive attitude towards this newspaper).[38] Drawing inferences from one's own behaviour is not always as simple or as clear-cut as the newspaper example might suggest. To appreciate the complexity of self-perception theory, it is useful to distinguish between **internal** and **external attributions**. Let us assume that Juan has just finished using a popular computer photo-editing program (e.g. Adobe's Photoshop) for the first time and that his digital photographs were well received when they were shown to the members of the photography club that he belongs to. If after receiving the compliments he says to himself, 'I'm really a natural at editing my digital photos', this statement would be an example of an internal attribution. It is an internal attribution because he is giving himself credit for the outcome (e.g. his ability, his skill or his effort). That is, he is saying, 'These photos are good because of me'. On the other hand, if Juan concluded that the successful digital photo-editing was due to factors beyond his control (e.g. a user-friendly program, the assistance of another club member or just 'luck'), this would be an example of an external attribution. In this case, he might be saying, 'My great photos are beginner's luck'.

This distinction between internal and external attributions can be of strategic marketing importance. For instance, it would generally be in the best interests of the firm that produces the photo-editing program if the users, especially inexperienced users, internalised their successful use of the software package. If they internalised such a positive experience, it is more likely that they will repeat the behaviour and become a satisfied regular user. Alternatively, however, if they were to externalise their success, it would be preferable that they attributed it to the particular program rather than to an incidental environmental factor such as 'beginner's luck' or another's 'foolproof' instructions. Additionally, recent studies suggest that when advertisers accurately target their message to consumers, with the proper cognitive generalisations about the self ('self-schema'), the consumer perceives the argument quality of the advertisement as being higher, and therefore has a more favourable attitude towards the message.[39]

According to the principle of **defensive attribution**, consumers are likely to accept credit personally for success (internal attribution) and to credit failure to others or to outside events (external attribution). For this reason, it is crucial that marketers offer uniformly high-quality products that allow consumers to perceive themselves as the reason for the success; that is, 'I'm competent.' Moreover, a company's advertising should serve to reassure consumers, particularly inexperienced ones, that its products will not let them down but will make them heroes instead.

Foot-in-the-Door Technique

Self-perception theorists have explored situations in which consumer compliance with a minor request affects subsequent compliance with a more substantial request. This strategy, which is commonly referred to as the **foot-in-the-door technique**, is based on the premise that individuals look at their prior behaviour (e.g. compliance with a minor request) and conclude that they are the kind of person who says 'yes' to such requests (i.e. an internal attribution). Such self-attribution serves to increase the likelihood that they will agree to a similar more substantial request. Someone who donates €10 to cancer research might be persuaded to donate a much larger amount when properly approached. The initial donation is, in effect, the foot in the door.

Research into the foot-in-the-door technique has concentrated on understanding how specific incentives (e.g. money-off coupons of varying amounts) ultimately influence consumer attitudes and subsequent purchase behaviour. It appears that different-sized incentives create different degrees of internal attribution which, in turn, lead to different amounts of attitude change. For instance, individuals who try a brand without any inducements or individuals who buy a brand repeatedly are more likely to infer increasingly positive attitudes towards the brand from their respective behaviours (e.g. 'I buy this brand because I like it'). In contrast, individuals who try a free sample are less committed to changing their attitudes towards the brand ('I tried this brand because it was free').

Thus, contrary to what might be expected, it is not the biggest incentive that is most likely to lead to positive attitude change. If an incentive is too big, marketers run the risk that consumers might externalise the cause of their behaviour to the incentive and be less likely to change their attitudes and less likely to make future purchases of the brand. Instead, what seems most effective is a moderate incentive, one that is just big enough to stimulate initial purchase of the brand but still small enough to encourage consumers to internalise their positive usage experience and allow a positive attitude change to occur.[40]

In contrast with the foot-in-the-door technique is the door-in-the-face technique, in which a large, costly first request that is probably refused is followed by a second, more realistic, less costly request. Under certain situations, this technique may prove more effective than the foot-in-the-door technique.[41]

Attributions Towards Others

In addition to understanding self-perception theory, it is important to understand **attributions towards others** because of the variety of potential applications to consumer behaviour and marketing. As already suggested, every time a person asks 'why?' about a statement or action of another or 'others' – a family member, a friend, a salesperson, a direct marketer, a shipping company – attribution theory is relevant. To illustrate, in evaluating the words or deeds of others (a salesperson, say), a consumer tries to determine if the salesperson's motives are in the consumer's best interests. If the salesperson's motives are viewed as favourable to the consumer, the consumer is likely to respond favourably. Otherwise, the consumer is likely to reject the salesperson's words and go elsewhere to make a purchase. In another case, a consumer orders a new digital camera from a major direct marketer. Because the consumer wants it immediately, she agrees to pay an extra €5 to €10 for next-day delivery by FedEx or TNT. If the next day the package with the digital camera fails to arrive as expected, the consumer has two possible 'others' to which she might attribute the failure – that is, the direct marketer (failing to get the product out on time) or the delivery service (failing to get the package to the consumer on time). In addition, she might blame them both (a dual failure); or if the weather was really bad, she might conclude that it was the bad weather (an attribution that neither of them was at fault).[42]

Attributions Towards Things

Consumer researchers also are interested in consumers' **attributions towards things** because products (or services) can readily be thought of as 'things'. It is in the area of judging product performance that consumers are most likely to form product attributions. Specifically, they want to find out why a product meets or does not meet their expectations. In this regard, they could attribute the product's successful performance (or failure) to the product itself, to themselves, to other people or situations, or to some combination of these factors.[43] To recap an earlier example, when Juan edited a set of challenging digital photos, he could attribute his success to the Photoshop software (product attribution), to his own skill (self- or internal attribution) or to a fellow photo club member who helped him (external attribution).

How We Test Our Attributions

After making initial attributions about a product's performance or a person's words or actions, we often attempt to determine whether the inference we made is correct. According to a leading attribution theorist, individuals acquire conviction about particular observations by acting like 'naive scientists', that is, by collecting additional information in an attempt to confirm (or disconfirm) prior inferences. In collecting such information, consumers often use the following criteria:[44]

1. *Distinctiveness* – The consumer attributes an action to a particular product (or person) if the action occurs when the product (or person) is present and does not occur in its absence.
2. *Consistency over time* – Whenever the person or product is present, the consumer's inference or reaction must be the same, or nearly so.
3. *Consistency over modality* – The inference or reaction must be the same, even when the situation in which it occurs varies.
4. *Consensus* – The action is perceived in the same way by other consumers.

To illustrate how the process of testing our attributions works, Table 9-6 provides three scenarios that depict (for three of the four 'attributions testing criteria') how people might use information to determine why a corporation has given a grant for an after-school programme to benefit schoolchildren, and whether the giving is either internally or externally driven or caused.

The following example illustrates how each of these criteria might be used to make inferences about product performance and people's actions.

If Nancy, a retired schoolteacher who loves to cook, observes that her apple pies seem to bake more evenly in her new gas range, she is likely to credit the new kitchen appliance with the improved appearance of her pies (i.e. distinctiveness). Furthermore, if Nancy finds that her new gas range produces the same high-quality results each time she uses it, she will tend to be more confident about her initial observation (i.e. the inference has consistency over time). Similarly, she will also be more confident if she finds that her satisfaction with the new kitchen appliance extends across a wide range of other related tasks, from cooking turkeys in the oven

TABLE 9-6 Testing attributions of a corporate grant to support an after-school programme

CONSENSUS	DISTINCTIVENESS	CONSISTENCY	RESULTING ATTRIBUTION
HIGH *Many groups support the after-school program*	**HIGH** *The corporation supports only the school*	**HIGH** *The corporation supports the school regularly*	➤ **EXTERNAL INFLUENCE** *Support of the school is related to the quality of the school*
LOW *Only the corporation supports the after-school program*	**LOW** *The corporation supports several schools and other programs*	**HIGH** *The corporation supports the school regularly*	➤ **INTERNAL DISPOSITION** *Support of the school is related to the benevolence of the corporation*
EITHER **High or Low**	**EITHER** **High or Low**	**LOW** *The corporation gave a grant to the school only once*	➤ **EXTERNAL INFLUENCE** *Support of the school is related to an undefined aspect of the particular situation that occurred at the time of the grant*

Source: Reprinted by permission from Macmillan Publishers Ltd. *Corporate Reputation Review*, 7, 1 October, From actions to impressions: Cognitive attribution theory and the formation of corporate reputation, p. 277, (Sjovall, A.M. and Talk, A.C. 2004). Copyright 2004, published by Palgrave Macmillan.

to cooking pasta on the gas range (i.e. consistency over modality). Finally, Nancy will have still more confidence in her inferences if her friends who own identical gas ranges also have similar experiences (i.e. consensus).

Much like Nancy, we go about gathering additional information from our experiences with people and things, and we use this information to test our initial inferences.

SUMMARY

An attitude is a learned predisposition to behave in a consistently favourable or unfavourable way with respect to a given object (e.g. a product category, a brand, a service, an advertisement, a website or a retail establishment). Each property of this definition is critical to understanding why and how attitudes are relevant in consumer behaviour and marketing.

Of considerable importance in understanding the role of attitudes in consumer behaviour is an appreciation of the structure and composition of an attitude. Four broad categories of attitude models have received attention: tricomponent attitude model, multi-attribute attitude models, trying to consume attitude model and attitude towards the ad models.

The tricomponent model of attitudes consists of three parts: a cognitive component, an affective component and a conative component. The cognitive component captures a consumer's knowledge and perceptions (i.e. beliefs) about products and services. The affective component focuses on a consumer's emotions or feelings with respect to a particular product or service. Evaluative in nature, the affective component determines an individual's overall assessment of the attitude object in terms of some kind of favourable rating. The conative component is concerned with the likelihood that a consumer will act in a specific fashion with respect to the attitude object. In marketing and consumer behaviour, the conative component is frequently treated as an expression of the consumer's intention to buy.

Multi-attribute attitude models (i.e. attitude towards object, attitude towards behaviour, the theory of reasoned action and theory of planned behaviour models) have received much attention from consumer researchers. As a group, these models examine consumer beliefs about specific product attributes (e.g. product or brand features or benefits). Recently, there has been an effort to better accommodate consumers' goals as expressed by their 'trying to consume' (i.e. a goal the consumer is trying or planning to accomplish). The theory of trying is designed to account for the many cases in which the action or outcome is not certain. The attitude towards the ad model examines the influence of advertisements on the consumer's attitudes towards the brand.

How consumer attitudes are formed and how they are changed are two closely related issues of considerable concern to marketing practitioners. When it comes to attitude formation, it is useful to remember that attitudes are learned and that different learning theories provide unique insights as to how attitudes initially may be formed. Attitude formation is facilitated by direct personal experience and influenced by the ideas and experiences of friends and family members and exposure to mass media. In addition, it is likely that an individual's personality plays a major role in attitude formation.

These same factors also have an impact on attitude change; that is, attitude changes are learned, and they are influenced by personal experiences and the information gained from various personal and impersonal sources. The consumer's own personality affects both the acceptance and the speed with which attitudes are likely to be altered.

Strategies of attitude change can be classified into six distinct categories:

1. changing the basic motivational function,
2. associating the attitude object with a special group, event or cause,
3. relating the attitude object to conflicting attitudes,
4. altering components of the multi-attribute model,
5. changing beliefs about competitors' brands, and
6. the elaboration likelihood model.

Each of these strategies provides the marketer with alternative ways of changing consumers' existing attitudes.

Most discussions of attitude formation and attitude change stress the traditional view that consumers develop attitudes before they act. However, this may not always, or even usually, be true. Both cognitive dissonance theory and attribution theory provide alternative explanations of attitude formation and change that suggest that behaviour might precede attitudes. Cognitive dissonance theory suggests that the conflicting thoughts, or dissonant information, following a purchase decision might propel consumers to change their attitudes to make them consonant with their actions. Attribution theory focuses on how people assign causality to events and how they form or alter attitudes as an outcome of assessing their own behaviour or the behaviour of other people or things.

DISCUSSION QUESTIONS

1. Explain how situational factors are likely to influence the degree of consistency between attitudes and behaviour.
2. Because attitudes are learned predispositions to respond, why don't marketers and consumer researchers just measure purchase behaviour and forget attitudes?
3. Explain a person's attitude towards visiting Legoland, Denmark, in terms of the tricomponent attitude model.
4. How can the marketer of a nicotine patch (a device that assists individuals to stop smoking) use the *theory of trying* to segment its market? Using this theory, identify two segments that the marketer should target and propose product positioning approaches to be directed at each of the two segments.
5. Explain how the product manager of a breakfast cereal might change consumer attitudes towards the company's brand by (a) changing beliefs about the brand, (b) changing beliefs about competing brands, (c) changing the relative evaluation of attributes and (d) adding an attribute.

6. Assume that Greenpeace is planning an advertising campaign that encourages people to switch from private cars to public transport. Give examples of how the organisation can use the following strategies to change commuters' attitudes: (a) changing the basic motivational function, (b) changing beliefs about public transport, (c) using self-perception theory and (d) using cognitive dissonance.

7. Assume that Toyota is faced with the problem that many European consumers perceive small and medium-sized Japanese cars to be of poorer quality than comparable German cars. Assuming that Toyota produces cars that are of a quality equal to or better than that of German cars, how can the company persuade consumers of this fact?

8. Should the marketer of a popular computer graphics program prefer consumers to make internal or external attributions? Explain your answer.

9. A university student has just purchased an iPad. What factors might cause the student to experience post-purchase dissonance? How might the student try to overcome it? How can the retailer who sold the computer help reduce the student's dissonance? How can the computer's manufacturer help?

EXERCISES

1. Find two print advertisements, one illustrating the use of the affective component and the other illustrating the cognitive component. Discuss each advertisement in the context of the tricomponent model. In your view, why has each marketer taken the approach it did in each of these advertisements?

2. What sources influenced your attitude about this course before classes started? Has your initial attitude changed since the course started? If so, how?

3. Describe a situation in which you acquired an attitude towards a new product through exposure to an advertisement for that product. Describe a situation in which you formed an attitude towards a product or brand on the basis of personal influence.

4. Find advertisements that illustrate each of the four motivational functions of attitudes. Distinguish between those that are designed to reinforce an existing attitude and those aimed at changing an attitude.

5. Think back to the time when you were selecting a university. Did you experience dissonance immediately after you made a decision? Why or why not? If you did experience dissonance, how did you resolve it?

NOTES

1. Jack Neff, 'Suave Strokes', *Advertising Age*, 20 August 2001, 12.

2. Richard J. Lutz, 'The Role of Attitude Theory in Marketing', in Harold H. Kassarjian and Thomas S. Robertson, eds, *Perspectives in Consumer Behavior*, 4th edn (Upper Saddle River, NJ: Prentice-Hall, 1991), 317–39.

3. Joel B. Cohen and Charles S. Areni, 'Affect and Consumer Behavior', in Kassarjian and Robertson, eds, *Perspectives in Consumer Behavior*, 188–240; and Madeline Johnson and George M. Zinkhan, 'Emotional Responses to a Professional Service Encounter', *Journal of Service Marketing*, 5, Spring 1991, 5–16. Also see John Kim, Jeen-Su Iim and Mukesh Bhargava, 'The Role of Affect in Attitude Formation: A Classical Condition Approach', *Journal of the Academy of Marketing Science*, 26, 1998, 143–52.

4. Jaideep Sengupta, 'Perspectives on Attitude Strength' (a special session summary), in *Advances in Consumer Research*, 25, eds Joseph W. Alba and J. Wesley Hutchinson (Provo, UT: Association for Consumer Research, 1998), 63–4.

5. Martin Fishbein, 'An Investigation of the Relationships Between Beliefs About an Object and the Attitude Toward the Object', *Human Relations*, 16, 1963, 233–40; and Martin Fishbein, 'A Behavioral Theory Approach to the Relations Between Beliefs About an Object and the Attitude Toward the Object', in Martin Fishbein, ed., *Readings in Attitude Theory and Measurement* (New York: Wiley, 1967), 389–400.

6. Claude Pecheux and Christian Derbaix, 'Children and Attitude Toward the Brand: A New Measurement Scale', *Journal of Advertising Research*, July/August 1999, 19–27.

7. Icek Ajzen and Martin Fishbein, *Understanding Attitudes and Predicting Social Behavior* (Upper Saddle River, NJ: Prentice-Hall, 1980); and Martin Fishbein and Icek Ajzen, *Belief, Attitude, Intentions, and Behavior* (Reading, MA: Addison-Wesley, 1975), 62–3. See also Robert E. Burnkrant, H. Rao Unnava and Thomas J. Page, Jr., 'Effects of Experience on Attitude Structure', in *Advances in Consumer Research*, 18, eds Rebecca H. Holman and Michael R. Solomon (Provo, UT: Association for Consumer Research, 1991), 28–9.

8. Shwu-Ing Wu, 'The Relationship between Consumer Characteristics and Attitude toward Online Shopping', *Marketing Intelligence and Planning*, 21, 2003, 37–44.

9. Terence A. Shimp and Alican Kavas, 'The Theory of Reasoned Action Applied to Coupon Usage', *Journal of Consumer Research*, 11, December 1984, 795–809; Blair H. Sheppard, Jon Hartwick and Paul R. Warshaw, 'The Theory of Reasoned Action: A Meta-Analysis of Past Research with Recommendations for Modifications and Future Research', *Journal of Consumer Research*, 15, September 1986, 325–43; Sharon E. Beatly and Lynn R. Kahle, 'Alternative Hierarchies of the Attitude-Behavior Relationship: The Impact of Brand Commitment and Habit', *Journal of the Academy of Marketing Science*, 16, Summer 1988, 1–10; Richard P. Bagozzi, Hans Baumgartner and Youjae Yi, 'Coupon Usage and the Theory of Reasoned Action', in *Advances in Consumer Research*, 18, eds Holman and Solomon, 24–7; and Hee Sun Park, 'Relationships Among Attitudes and Subjective Norms: Testing the Theory of Reasoned Action Across Cultures', *Communication Studies*, 51, 2, Summer 2000, 162–75.

10. Chris T. Allen, Karen A. Machleit, Susan Schultz Kleine and Arti Sahni Notani, 'A Place for Emotion in Attitude Models', *Journal of Business Research*, 58, April 2005, 494–9.

11. Rob van Zanten, 'Drink Choices: Factors Influencing the Intention to Drink Wine', *International Journal of Wine Marketing*, 17(2), 2005, 49–61.

12. Richard P. Bagozzi and Paul R. Warshaw, 'Trying to Consume', *Journal of Consumer Research*, 17, September 1990, 127–40; Richard P. Bagozzi, Fred D. Davis and Paul R. Warshaw, 'Development and Test of a Theory of Technological Learning and Usage', *Human Relations*, 45(7), July 1992, 659–86; and Anil Mathur, 'From Intentions to Behavior: The Role of Trying and Control', in Barbara B. Stern and George M. Zinkan, eds, *1995 AMA Educators' Conference Proceedings* (Chicago: American Marketing Association, 1995), 374–5.

13. Stephen J. Gould, Franklin S. Houston and Jonel Mundt, 'Failing to Try to Consume: A Reversal of the Usual Consumer Research Perspective', in *Advances in Consumer Research*, 24, eds Merrie Brucks and Deborah J. MacInnis (Provo, UT: Association for Consumer Research, 1997), 211–16.

14. Rajeev Batra and Michael L. Ray, 'Affective Responses Mediating Acceptance of Advertising', *Journal of Consumer Research*, 13, September 1986, 236–9; Julie A. Edell and Marian Chapman Burke, 'The Power of Feelings in Understanding Advertising Effects', *Journal of Consumer Research*, 14, December 1987, 421–33; and Marian Chapman Burke and Julie A. Edell, 'The Impact of Feelings on Ad-Based Affect and Cognition', *Journal of Marketing Research*, 26, February 1989, 69–83.

15. Durriya Z. Khairullah and Zahid Y. Khairullah, 'Relationships Between Acculturation, Attitude Toward the Advertisement, and Purchase Intention of Asian-Indian Immigrants', *International Journal of Commerce and Management*, 9, 3/4, 1999, 46–65.

16. Dena Saliagas Cox and William B. Locander, 'Product Novelty: Does It Moderate the Relationship Between Ad Attitudes and Brand Attitudes?', *Journal of Advertising*, 16, 1987, 39–44. See also Cynthia B. Hanson and Gabriel J. Biehal, 'Accessibility Effects on the Relationship Between

Attitude Toward the Ad and Brand Choice', in *Advances in Consumer Research*, 22, eds Frank R. Kardes and Mita Sujan (Provo, UT: Association for Consumer Research, 1995), 152–8.

17. Alan J. Bush, Rachel Smith and Craig Martin, 'The Influence of Consumer Socialization Variables on Attitude Toward Advertising: A Comparison of African-Americans and Caucasians', *Journal of Advertising*, 28, 3, Fall 1999, 13–24.

18. Subodh Bhat and Srinivas K. Reddy, 'Investigating the Dimensions of the Fit Between a Brand and Its Extensions', *1997 AMA Winter Educators' Conference Proceedings*, 8 (Chicago: American Marketing Association, 1997), 186–94.

19. Morris B. Holbrook, David A. Velez and Gerard J. Tabouret, 'Attitude Structure and Search: An Integrative Model of Importance-Directed Information Processing', in *Advances in Consumer Research*, 8, ed. Kent B. Monroe (Ann Arbor, MI: Association for Consumer Research, 1981), 35–41.

20. Richard P. Bagozzi, Hans Baumgartner and Youjae Yi, 'Coupon Usage and the Theory of Reasoned Action', in *Advances in Consumer Research*, 18, eds Holman and Solomon, 24–7.

21. For an interesting article on the impact of social interaction on attitude development, see Daniel J. Howard and Charles Gengler, 'Emotional Contagion Effects on Product Attitudes', *Journal of Consumer Research*, 28, September 2001, 189–201.

22. Haksik Lee, Gilbert D. Harrell and Cornelia L. Droge, 'Product Experiences and Hierarchy of Advertising Effects', in *2000 AMA Winter Educators' Conference*, 11, eds John P. Workman and William D. Perreault (Chicago: American Marketing Association, 2000), 41–2.

23. James R. Coyle and Esther Thorson, 'The Effects of Progressive Levels of Interactivity and Vividness in Web Marketing Sites', *Journal of Advertising*, 30, 3, Fall 2001, 65–77; and Lynn C. Dailey and C. Edward Heath, 'Creating the Flow Experience Online: The Role of Web Atmospherics', in *2000 AMA Winter Educators' Conference*, 11, eds Workman and Perreault, 58.

24. Daniel Katz, 'The Functional Approach to the Study of Attitudes', *Public Opinion Quarterly*, 24, Summer 1960, 163–91; Sharon Shavitt, 'Products, Personality and Situations in Attitude Functions: Implications for Consumer Behavior', in *Advances in Consumer Research*, 16, ed. Thomas K. Srull (Provo, UT: Association for Consumer Research, 1989), 300–5; and Richard Ennis and Mark P. Zanna, 'Attitudes, Advertising, and Automobiles: A Functional Approach', in *Advances in Consumer Research*, 20, eds Leigh McAlister and Michael L. Rothschild (Provo, UT: Association for Consumer Research, 1993), 662–6.

25. Maria Knight Lapinski and Franklin J. Boster, 'Modeling the Ego-Defensive Function of Attitudes', *Communication Monographs*, 68, 3, September 2001, 314–24.

26. Cara Beardi, 'Zippo's Eternal Flame', *Advertising Age*, 13 August 2001, 4.

27. Barbara A. Lafferty and Ronald E. Goldsmith, 'Cause-Brand Alliances: Does the Cause Help the Brand or Does the Brand Help the Cause?', *Journal of Business Research*, 58, April 2005, 423–9.

28. Nora J. Rifon, Sejung Marina Choi, Carrie S. Tripble and Hairong Li, 'Congruence Effects in Sponsorship', *Journal of Advertising*, 33, Spring 2004, 29–42.

29. Geoffrey L. Cohen, Joshua Aronson and Claude M. Steele, 'When Beliefs Yield to Evidence: Reducing Biased Evaluation by Affirming the Self', *Personality and Social Psychology Bulletin*, 26, 9, September 2000, 1151–64.

30. Richard E. Petty *et al.*, 'Theories of Attitude Change', in Harold Kassarjian and Thomas Robertson, eds, *Handbook of Consumer Theory and Research* (Upper Saddle River, NJ: Prentice Hall, 1991); and Richard E. Petty, John T. Cacioppo and David Schumann, 'Central and Peripheral Routes to Advertising Effectiveness: The Moderating Role of Involvement', *Journal of Consumer Research*, 10, September 1983, 135–46. Also see Curtis P. Haugtvedt and Alan J. Strathman, 'Situational Product Relevance and Attitude Persistence', in *Advances in Consumer Research*, 17, eds Marvin E. Goldberg, Gerald Gorn and Richard W. Pollay (Provo, UT: Association for Consumer Research, 1990), 766–9; and Scott B. Mackenzie and Richard A. Spreng, 'How Does Motivation Moderate the Impact of Central and Peripheral Processing on Brand Attitudes and Intentions?', *Journal of Consumer Research*, 18, March 1992, 519–29.

31. Jaideep Sgupta, Ronald C. Goldstein and David S. Boninger, 'All Cues Are Not Created Equal: Obtaining Attitude Persistence Under Low-Involvement Conditions', *Journal of Consumer Reserarch*, 23, March 1997, 351–61.

32. Shin-Chieh Chuang and Chia-Ching Tsai, 'The Impact of Consumer Product Knowledge on the Effect of Terminology in Advertising', *Journal of the American Academy of Business*, 6, March 2005, 154–8, and Sgupta, Goldstein and Boninger, 'All Cues Are Not Created Equal', 351–61.

33. Keith S. Coulter and Girish N. Punj, 'The Effects of Cognitive Resource Requirements, Availability, and Argument Quality on Brand Attitudes', *Journal of Advertising*, 33, Winter 2004, 53–64.

34. See, for example, David C. Matz and Wendy Wood, 'Cognitive Dissonance in Groups', *Journal of Personality and Social Psychology*, 88, January 2005, 22–37; Jillian C. Sweeney and Tanya Mukhopadhyay, 'Cognitive Dissonance After Purchase: A Comparison of Bricks and Mortar and Online Retail Purchase Situations', *American Marketing Association Conference Proceedings: 2004 AMA Winter Educators' Conference*, Chicago, 15, 190–91; Martin O'Neill and Adrian Palmer, 'Cognitive Dissonance and the Stability of Service Quality Perceptions', *Journal of Services Marketing*, 18, 6/7, 2004, 433–49; Robert A. Wicklund and Jack W. Brehm, 'Internalization of Multiple Perpectives or Dissonance Reduction?', *Theory and Psychology* (London), 14, June 2004, 355–71, and Alex R. Zablah, Danny N. Bellenger and Westley J. Johnson, 'Customer Relationship Management Implementation Gaps', *Journal of Personal Selling and Sales Management*, 24, Fall 2004, 279–95.

35. Geoffrey N. Soutar and Jillian C. Sweeney, 'Are There Cognitive Dissonance Segments?', *Australian Journal of Management*, 28, December 2003, 227–39.

36. Edward E. Jones *et al.*, *Attribution: Perceiving the Causes of Behavior* (Morristown, NJ: General Learning Press, 1972); and Bernard Weiner, 'Attributional Thoughts About Consumer Behavior', *Journal of Consumer Research*, 27, 3, December 2000, 382–7.

37. Rifon *et al.*, 'Congruence Effects in Sponsorship', 29; and Andrea C. Morales, 'Giving Firms an "E" for Effort: Consumer Responses to High-Effort Firms', *Journal of Consumer Research*, 3, March 2005, 806–12.

38. Chris T. Allen and William R. Dillon, 'Self-Perception Development and Consumer Choice Criteria: Is There a Linkage?', in *Advances in Consumer Research*, 10, eds Richard P. Bagozzi and Alice M. Tybout (Ann Arbor, MI: Association for Consumer Research, 1983), 45–50.

39. S. Christian Wheeler, Richard E. Petty and George Y. Bizer, 'Self-Schema Matching and Attitude Change: Situational and Dispositional Determinants of Message Elaboration', *Journal of Consumer Research*, 31, March 2005, 787–97.

40. See, for example, Leslie Lazar Kanuk, *Mail Questionnaire Response Behavior as a Function of Motivational Treatment* (New York: CUNY, 1974).

41. Angelos Rodafinos, Arso Vucevic and Georgios D. Sideridis, 'The Effectiveness of Compliance Techniques: Foot in the Door Versus Door in the Face', *Journal of Social Psychology*, 145, April 2005, 237–9.

42. John R. O'Malley, Jr., 'Consumer Attributions of Product Failures to Channel Members', in *Advances in Consumer Research*, 23, eds Kim P. Corfman and John F. Lynch, Jr. (Provo, UT: Association for Consumer Research, 1996), 342–5. Also see Charmine Hartel, Janet R. McColl Kennedy and Lyn McDonald, 'Incorporating Attributional Theory and the Theory of Reasoned Action Within an Affective Events Theory Framework to Produce a Contingency Predictive Model of Consumer Reactions to Organizational Mishaps', in *Advances in Consumer Research*, 25, eds Alba and Hutchinson, 428–32.

43. Valerie S. Folkes, 'Consumer Reactions to Product Failure: Attributional Approach', *Journal of Consumer Research*, 10, March 1984, 398–409; and 'Recent Attribution Research in Consumer Behavior: A Review and New Dimensions', *Journal of Consumer Research*, 14, March 1988, 548–65.

44. Harold H. Kelley, 'Attribution Theory in Social Psychology', in David Levine, ed., *Nebraska Symposium on Motivation*, 15 (Lincoln: University of Nebraska Press, 1967), 197.

The medium

The medium, or communications channel, can be **impersonal** (e.g. a mass medium) or **interpersonal** (a formal conversation between a salesperson and a customer or an informal conversation between two or more people that takes place face to face, by telephone, by post or online).

Mass media are generally classified as print (newspapers, magazines, hoardings), broadcast (radio, television), or electronic (primarily the Internet). New modes of interactive communication that permit the audiences of communication messages to provide direct feedback are beginning to blur the distinction between interpersonal and impersonal communications. For example, most companies encourage consumers to visit their websites to find out more about the product or service being advertised or to order online, but not all visitors receive the same message. The information visitors see or the ordering links they are routed to depend on their selections, in the form of clicking patterns, during that visit or even past visits to the site. **Direct marketing** – often called database marketing – also seeks individual responses from advertisements placed in all the mass media: broadcast, print and online, as well as from **direct mail**. Home shopping networks are expanding dramatically as consumers demonstrate their enthusiasm for television shopping. Direct marketers use data regarding recent buying behaviour of some consumers to generate purchases from subsequent consumers.

The message

The message can be verbal (spoken or written), non-verbal (a photograph, an illustration or a symbol), or a combination of the two. A verbal message, whether it is spoken or written, can usually contain more specific product (or service) information than a non-verbal message. However, a verbal message combined with a non-verbal message often provides more information to the receiver than either would alone.

Non-verbal information takes place in both interpersonal and impersonal channels and often takes the form of symbolic communication. Marketers often try to develop logos or symbols that are associated exclusively with their products and that achieve high recognition. The Coca-Cola Company, for example, has trademarked both the word Coke in a specific typographic style and the shape of the traditional Coke bottle, and both are instantly recognisable to consumers as symbols of the company's best-selling soft drink.[1] Figure 10-2 depicts an advertisement portraying non-verbal, symbolic communications (in the form of hand gestures) in three different cultures.

Feedback

Feedback is an essential component of both interpersonal and impersonal communications. Prompt feedback permits the sender to reinforce, to change or to modify the message to ensure that it is understood in the intended way. Generally, it is easier to obtain feedback (both verbal and non-verbal) from interpersonal rather than impersonal communications. For example, a good salesperson is usually alert to non-verbal feedback provided by consumer prospects. Such feedback may take the form of facial expressions (a smile, a frown, a look of total boredom, an expression of disbelief) or body movements (finger tapping, head nodding, head shaking or clenched hands). Because of the high cost of space and time in impersonal media, it is very important for sponsors of impersonal communications to devise methods to obtain feedback as promptly as possible, so that they may revise a message if its meaning is not being received as intended.

An excellent example of marketing based on shoppers' feedback, in the form of 'body language', is the selling method employed at the rapidly growing Diesel jeans stores. Unlike other clothing shops, Diesel stores are not user-friendly because the company believes that a disoriented customer is the best prospect. Diesel stores feature loud techno music and large television screens playing videos unrelated to the merchandise sold. There are no signs directing customers

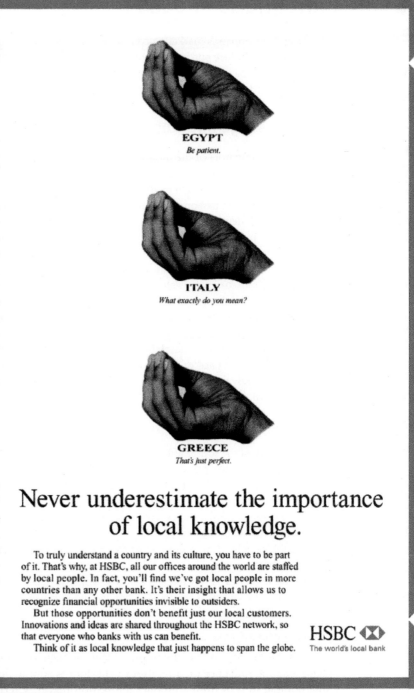

FIGURE 10-2 Advertisement depicting non-verbal communication
Source: Courtesy of HSBC Bank.

to different departments, no obvious salespeople, and jeans items have strange names accompanied by confusing charts intended to explain the clothing options. In the midst of this chaos, young and cool salespeople who are trained to spot 'wayward-looking', overwhelmed and confused shoppers 'rescue' them by becoming their 'shopping friends' and, of course, sell them as many pairs of jeans as possible.[2]

THE COMMUNICATIONS PROCESS

In general, a company's marketing communications are designed to make the consumer aware of the product, induce purchase or commitment, create a positive attitude towards the product, give the product a symbolic meaning or show how it can solve the consumer's problem better than a competitive product (or service).

The message initiator (source)

The sponsor (initiator) of the message must first decide to whom the message should be sent and what meaning it should convey. Then the sponsor must encode the message in such a way that its meaning is interpreted by the targeted audience in precisely the intended way.

The sources of impersonal communications usually are organisations (either business or charitable) that develop and transmit appropriate messages through special departments (e.g. marketing or public relations) or spokespeople. The targets, or receivers, of such messages are usually a specific audience or several audiences that the organisation is trying to inform, influence or persuade. For example, an Internet chat service wants to attract both online users and advertisers; a museum may wish to target both donors and visitors; and a mail-order company may want to persuade consumers to call a toll-free number for a copy of its catalogue.

Marketers have a large arsenal from which to draw in encoding their messages: they can use words, pictures, symbols, spokespeople and special channels. They can buy space or time in carefully selected media to advertise or broadcast their message, or they can try to have their message appear in space or time usually reserved for editorial messages. (The latter, called **publicity**, is usually the result of public relations efforts and tends to be more believable because its commercial origins and intent are not readily apparent.)

Credibility

The credibility of the source affects the decoding of the message. The sponsor of the communication – and his or her perceived honesty and objectivity – has an enormous influence on how the communication is accepted by the receiver(s). When the source is well respected and highly thought of by the intended audience, the message is much more likely to be believed. Conversely, a message from a source considered unreliable or untrustworthy is likely to be received with scepticism and may be rejected.

Credibility is built on a number of factors, of which the most important is the perceived intention of the source. Receivers ask themselves, 'Just what does he (or she) stand to gain if I do what is suggested?' If the receiver perceives any type of personal gain for the message sponsor as a result of the proposed action or advice, the message itself becomes suspect: 'He wants me to buy that product just to earn a commission.'

Credibility of Informal Sources

One of the major reasons why informal sources such as friends, neighbours and relatives have a strong influence on a receiver's behaviour is simply that they are perceived as having nothing to gain from a product transaction that they recommend. That is why word-of-mouth communication is so effective. Interestingly enough, informal communications sources, called **opinion leaders**, often do profit psychologically, if not tangibly, by providing product information to others. A person may obtain a great deal of ego satisfaction by providing solicited as well as unsolicited information and advice to friends. This ego gratification may actually improve the quality of the information provided, because the opinion leader often deliberately seeks out the latest detailed information in order to enhance his or her position as 'expert' in a particular product category. The fact that the opinion leader does not receive material gain from the recommended action increases the likelihood that the advice will be seriously considered.

Clever marketers initiate word-of-mouth (WOM) campaigns. Many firms enlist typical consumers to serve as their 'buzz agents', who agree to bring products they are promoting to gatherings of family and friends, read books they are promoting on public transport with the title clearly visible, suggest to shop owners who do not carry a given product that they should do so and talk other consumers into trying certain products during shopping trips. Generally, these 'agents' do not receive direct payment from the companies they represent, although they often receive free samples. They are motivated by having been identified by the marketers as opinion leaders, and they get an ego boost by appearing so knowledgeable to their peers and having access to new products before others do.[3]

Although marketers had long ago recognised the perils of negative word-of-mouth that can result in unfounded rumours about products (see Chapter 15), they are more acutely concerned about this issue than ever before. Digital technologies now enable disgruntled consumers to reach millions of people easily through chat rooms and their own websites to describe their often-exaggerated negative experiences with products and services. Persistent critics of marketers who initiate bad publicity online are called *determined detractors*. Many companies have been subject to such online attacks; perhaps the best-known example is the individual who ate nothing but McDonald's food for 30 days and produced an extremely critical documentary about this company entitled *Super Size Me*.[4]

Some of the factors that motivate consumers to engage in word-of-mouth are: consumer involvement with the product or message, self-involvement, alleviating post-purchase uncertainty and dissonance (by convincing others to make a similar purchase), seeking information and concern for others. One study identified the following factors as the primary motives behind WOM: venting negative feelings, concern for others, extraversion and positive self-enhancement, social benefits, economic incentives, helping the company and advice seeking.[5]

Credibility of Formal Sources

Not-for-profit sources generally have more credibility than commercial sources. Formal sources that are perceived to be 'neutral' have greater credibility than commercial sources because of the perception that they are more objective in their product assessments. That is why publicity is so valuable to a manufacturer: citations of a product in an editorial context, rather than in a paid advertisement, give the reader much more confidence in the message. One study discovered that the perceived trustworthiness of publicity was higher when the message involved stressed the company's altruistic motives (e.g. launching a recycling programme because of 'good corporate citizenship') than when the message stressed a commercial motive (e.g. launching a recycling venture in the form of a subsidiary).[6]

Because consumers recognise that the intentions of commercial sources (e.g. manufacturers, service companies, financial institutions, retailers) are clearly profit-oriented, they judge commercial **source credibility** on such factors as past performance, reputation, the kind and quality of service they are known to render, the quality and image of other products they manufacture, the image and attractiveness of the spokesperson used, the type of retail outlets through which they sell and their position in the community (e.g. evidence of their commitment to such issues as social responsibility or equal employment).

Firms with well-established reputations generally have an easier time selling their products than do firms with lesser reputations. The ability of a quality image to invoke credibility is one of the reasons for the growth of family brands. Manufacturers with favourable brand images prefer to give their new products the existing brand name in order to obtain ready acceptance from consumers. Furthermore, a quality image permits a company to experiment more freely in many more areas of marketing than would otherwise be considered prudent, such as independent retailers, new price levels and innovative promotional techniques. Recognising that a manufacturer with a good reputation generally has high credibility among consumers, many companies spend a sizeable part of their advertising budget on **institutional advertising**, which is designed to promote a favourable company image rather than to promote specific products. The advertisement depicted in Figure 10-3 exemplifies this strategy.

FIGURE 10-3 Institutional advertising
Source: Courtesy of The Advertising Archives.

In a crowded marketplace, many companies try to distinguish themselves and increase their credibility by being 'good corporate citizens'. These firms often engage in cause-related marketing, where they contribute a portion of the revenues they receive from selling certain products to such causes as helping people inflicted with incurable diseases or hurt by inclement weather. For example, fashion designers such as Armani and Ralph Lauren have donated selected portions of their sales to AIDS research and other charities (see also Figure 10-3).

Credibility of Spokespeople and Endorsers

Consumers sometimes regard the spokesperson who gives the product message as the source (or initiator) of the message. Thus, the 'pitchman' (whether male or female) who appears in person or in a commercial or advertisement has a major influence on message credibility. This accounts for the increasing use of celebrities to promote products. Many studies have investigated the relationship between the effectiveness of the message and the spokesperson or endorser employed. Here are some of the key findings of this body of research:

- The effectiveness of the spokesperson is related to the message itself. For example, when message comprehension is low, receivers rely on the spokesperson's credibility in forming attitudes towards the product, but when comprehension (and, thus, systematic information processing) is high, the expertise of the spokesperson has far less impact on a receiver's attitudes.[7]

- The synergy between the endorser and the type of product or service advertised is an important factor. One study found that, for attractiveness-related products (such as cosmetics), a physically attractive celebrity spokesperson significantly enhanced message credibility and attitude towards the advertisement; for products unrelated to attractiveness (e.g. a camera) an attractive endorser had little or no effect. This suggests a 'match-up' hypothesis for celebrity advertising.[8] Another study found that a celebrity endorser was more effective in terms of source credibility and consumer attitudes towards the advertisement for a hedonistic and 'experiential' service (e.g. a restaurant) than for a utilitarian service (e.g. a bank).[9] When a celebrity endorser has damaged his or her credentials through engaging in scandalous behaviour, the marketer immediately dissociates itself from the endorser in question.

- Endorsers who have demographic characteristics (e.g. age, social class and ethnicity) that are similar to those of the target audience are viewed as more credible and persuasive than those who do not. Also, consumers with strong ethnic identification are more likely to be persuaded by endorsers with similar ethnicity than individuals with weaker ethnic identification.[10]

- The endorser's credibility is not a substitute for corporate credibility. One study discovered that although the endorser's credibility strongly impacted the audience's attitudes towards the advertisement, the perceived corporate credibility had a strong impact on attitudes towards the advertised brand.[11] This study supports the development of multiple measures to evaluate the credibility and persuasiveness of advertising messages, such as attitudes towards the advertisement and towards the brand, and consumer purchase intentions.

- Marketers who use celebrities to give testimonials or endorse products must be sure that the specific wording of the endorsement lies within the recognised competence of the spokesperson. A tennis star can believably endorse a brand of analgesic with comments about how it relieves sore muscle pain; however, a recitation of medical evidence supporting the brand's superiority over other brands is beyond his expected knowledge and expertise and thus may reduce (rather than enhance) message credibility. Somewhat surprisingly, one study of advertising agencies found that none of the agencies surveyed had a written strategy regarding the selection of celebrity endorsers. The study's authors recommended a long list of factors to be considered in selecting celebrity endorsers, such as a careful match with the target audience, product and brand, the celebrity's overall image, prior endorsements, trustworthiness, familiarity, expertise, profession, physical attractiveness, and whether the celebrity is a brand user.[12]

In interpersonal communications, consumers are more likely to be persuaded by salespeople who engender confidence and who give the impression of honesty and integrity. Consumer confidence in a salesperson is created in diverse ways, whether warranted or not. A salesperson who 'looks you in the eye' is often perceived as more honest than one who evades direct eye contact. For many products, a sales representative who dresses well and drives an expensive, new car may have more credibility than one without such outward signs of success (and inferred representation of a best-selling product). For some products, however, a salesperson may achieve more credibility by dressing in the role of an expert. For example, a man selling home improvements may achieve more credibility by looking like someone who has just climbed off a roof or out of a basement than by looking like a banker.

Message Credibility

The reputation of the retailer who sells the product has a major influence on message credibility. Products sold by well-known quality shops seem to carry the added endorsement (and implicit guarantee) of the shop itself. The aura of credibility generated by reputable retail advertising reinforces the manufacturer's message.

The reputation of the medium that carries the advertisement also enhances the credibility of the advertiser. For example, the image of a prestige magazine like *Fortune* confers added status on the products advertised within. The reputation of the medium for honesty and objectivity also affects the believability of the advertising. Consumers often think that a medium they respect would not accept advertising for products it did not 'know' were good. Because specialisation in an area implies knowledge and expertise, consumers tend to regard advertising they see in special-interest magazines with more credibility than those they note in general-interest magazines.

Consumers today have more media options than ever before in new forms of media (such as the Web) and traditional media in new forms (such as online editions of well-established newspapers), but there is no single answer as to which medium has the most credibility, especially at a time when new forms are emerging and evolving. One study discovered that individuals interested in politics are shifting from television to the Web for political information.[13] Another study reported that the public generally considers opinion polls reported in traditional news media as more credible than online polls;[14] still another study reported that cable television newscasts are viewed as the most credible and that differences in the perceived credibility of various media were related to age.[15] As the number and types of media continue to evolve and grow, print, broadcast and digital media executives should survey their audiences periodically on such factors as perceived fairness, balance and accuracy in order to maximise their credibility with audiences and their attractiveness to advertisers.

The consumer's previous experience with the product or the retailer has a major impact on the credibility of the message. Fulfilled product expectations tend to increase the credibility accorded future messages by the same advertiser; unfulfilled product claims or disappointing product experiences tend to reduce the credibility of future messages. Thus, the key basis for message credibility is the ability of the product, service or brand to deliver consistent quality, value and satisfaction to consumers.

Effects of Time on Source Credibility: The Sleeper Effect

The persuasive effects of high-credibility sources do not endure over time. Although a high-credibility source is initially more influential than a low-credibility source, research suggests that both positive and negative credibility effects tend to disappear after six weeks or so. This phenomenon has been termed the **sleeper effect**.[16] Consumers simply forget the source of the message faster than they forget the message itself. Studies attribute the sleeper effect to dissociation (i.e. the consumer dissociates the message from its source) over time, leaving just the message content. The theory of differential decay suggests that the memory of a negative cue (e.g. a low-credibility source) simply decays faster than the message itself, leaving behind the primary message content.[17] However, reintroduction of the same or a similar message by the source serves to jog the audience's memory, and the original effect manifests itself again; that is, the high-credibility source remains more persuasive than the low-credibility source.[18] The implication for marketers who use high-credibility spokespeople is that they must repeat the same series of advertisements or commercials regularly in order to maintain a high level of persuasiveness. Somewhat surprisingly, the sleeper effect supports the use of negative attack advertising in political campaigns. The results of a study applying the sleeper effect to political advertising showed that the effectiveness of the attack advertisement increases considerably over a period of weeks, while the audience's initial negative perception of the political assailant as having low credibility fades and has only a temporary negative impact on the advertisement.[19] However, this logic must not be extended to advertising and marketers must not assume that consumers who become aware of a brand through a loud and intrusive advertising campaign will continue to remember the brand favourably and forget the negative experience of watching the advertisements that made them aware of the brand.[20]

The target audience (receivers)

Receivers decode the messages they receive on the basis of their personal experiences and personal characteristics. If Mrs Hawkins receives shoddy merchandise from an online retailer, she may be reluctant to buy online again. At the same time, her neighbour, Mrs Jones, may be so pleased with the merchandise she receives from a reliable online retailer in terms of quality, service and fit that she vows to do even more of her shopping online in the future. The level of trust each neighbour displays towards online communications is based on her own prior experience.

A number of factors affect the decoding and comprehension of persuasive messages, including the receiver's personal characteristics, involvement with the product or product category, the congruency of the message with the medium and the receiver's mood.

Personal Characteristics and Comprehension

The amount of meaning accurately derived from the message is a function of the message characteristics, the receiver's opportunity and ability to process the message and the receiver's motivation. In fact, all of an individual's personal characteristics (described in earlier chapters) influence the accuracy with which the individual decodes a message. A person's demographics (such as age, gender, marital status), sociocultural memberships (social class, race, religion) and lifestyle are key determinants in how a message is interpreted. A bachelor may interpret a friendly comment from his unmarried neighbour as a 'come-on'; a student may interpret a lecturer's comments as an indication of grading rigour. Personality, attitudes and prior learning all affect how a message is decoded. Perception, based as it is on expectations, motivation and past experience, certainly influences message interpretation. Not everyone reads and understands the marketing communications they receive in the same way that the sender intended.

For example, one study, focused on gender-based differences in responding to charity advertisements, reported that women found altruistic appeals that stressed helping others more persuasive, whereas men tended to choose self-oriented themes that stressed helping oneself.[21] Another study discovered that people who view themselves as more individualistic and unique and who tend to enjoy effortful thinking (i.e. they are high in the personality trait termed *need for cognition*) were more likely to be persuaded by comparative advertising than people who possess lower levels of these personality traits.[22] Other researchers discovered that people with a high need for cognition are more persuaded by messages that consist of high-quality arguments followed by implicit, rather than explicit, conclusions.[23] Another study found that the level of confidence that people have in their evaluations of an advertisement influence the type they preferred; people who were highly confident in their judgements were more persuaded by strong advertisements, rather than comparable weak advertisements, for a given product.[24]

Involvement and Congruency

A person's level of involvement (see Chapter 8) plays a key role in how much attention is paid to the message and how carefully it is decoded. People who have little interest (i.e. a low level of involvement) in golf, for example, may not pay much attention to an advertisement for a specially designed putter; people who are very interested (highly involved) in golf may read every word of a highly technical advertisement describing the new golf club. Thus, a target audience's level of involvement is an important consideration in the design and content of persuasive communications. One study discovered a relationship between level of involvement and the style and context of an advertisement. Subjects with low involvement with the product preferred messages placed within a congruent context (e.g. a humorous advertisement within a humorous television series) while people highly involved with the product preferred messages that contrasted the style of advertisement and the context within which it was placed (e.g. a humorous advertisement within a rational context such as a television documentary).[25] Another study showed that the congruency between the nature of the television programme and the advertisement affected the level of viewer recall. Cognitively involving commercials shown in a cognitively involving programme context had higher recall than low-involvement commercials placed within an affective programme context.[26]

Mood

Mood, or affect, plays a significant role in how a message is decoded. A consumer's mood (e.g. cheerfulness or unhappiness) affects the way in which an advertisement is perceived, recalled and acted upon. Marketers of many image-centred products such as perfume, fashion and alcohol have found that appeals focused on emotions and feelings associated with these products are more effective than rational appeals depicting the product's benefits. Advertisers have found that emotional appeals work well even for technologically complex products. For example, Apple Computer encourages consumers to 'Think Different',[27] Tag Heuer asks the question, 'What are you made of?'

Many studies have investigated the impact of mood on message comprehension and effectiveness. In one study, the subjects' moods were manipulated by showing humorous advertisements (generating a positive mood) to some subjects and informational advertisements (generating a neutral mood) to other subjects. The study found that a positive mood enhanced the learning of brand names and the product categories to which they belonged.[28] Also, research indicates that the consumer's mood is often influenced by the content of the advertisement and by the context in which the advertising message appears (such as the accompanying television programme or adjacent newspaper story); these in turn affect the consumer's evaluation and recall of the message.[29] One study showed that consumers with low familiarity with a service category prefer advertisements based on story appeals rather than lists of attributes and that such appeals work better when the receivers are in a happy mood while decoding the message.[30]

Barriers to Communication

Various 'barriers' to communication may affect the accuracy with which consumers interpret messages. These include selective perception and psychological noise.

Selective Exposure to Messages

Consumers selectively perceive advertising messages and tend to ignore advertisements that have no special interest or relevance to them. Furthermore, technology provides consumers with increasingly sophisticated means to control their exposure to media. Television remote controls offer viewers the ability to 'wander' among programme offerings with ease (often referred to as grazing), to skip commercials by muting the audio, and to channel surf – switch channels to check out other programme offerings during commercial breaks. Some marketers try to overcome channel surfing during commercials by 'roadblocking' (i.e. playing the same commercial simultaneously on competing channels).

Digital recorders enable viewers to fast-forward (zip) through commercials of prerecorded programmes. The majority of consumers zip indiscriminately through videotapes and DVDs to avoid all commercials, without first evaluating the commercials they skip. DVD recorders and digital services allow consumers not only to watch programmes whenever they want, but also to skip commercials more easily then ever before. In response, worried broadcasters have increased their product placements and expenditures on branded entertainment and have sought other means to make it more difficult for consumers to avoid exposure to television commercials. The growth of satellite radio allows consumers to avoid hearing radio advertisements. Caller ID, telephone answering machines, a government's 'do not call' list, and other devices allow consumers to screen out telemarketing and other unsolicited contacts from marketers.

Psychological Noise

Just as telephone static can impair reception of a message, so too can **psychological noise** (e.g. competing advertising messages or distracting thoughts). A viewer faced with the clutter of nine successive commercial messages during a programme break may actually receive and retain almost nothing of what he has seen. Similarly, an executive planning a departmental meeting while driving to work may be too engrossed in her thoughts to 'hear' a radio commercial. On a more familiar level, a student daydreaming about a Saturday night date may simply not 'hear' a direct question by the lecturer. The student is just as much a victim of noise – albeit psychological noise – as another student who literally cannot hear a question because of construction noise from the building next door. There are various strategies that marketers use to overcome psychological noise:

- Repeated exposure to an advertising message (through *repetition* or *redundancy* of the advertising appeal) helps surmount psychological noise and facilitates message reception. Thus, repeating an advertisement several times is a must. (The effects of repetition on learning were discussed in Chapter 8.) The principle of redundancy also is seen in advertisements that use both illustrations and copy to emphasise the same points. To achieve more advertising redundancy, many marketers now place their messages in such places as video games, cinemas, lifts, floors in supermarkets, and even public toilets.
- Copywriters often use *contrast* to break through the psychological noise and advertising clutter. Contrast (discussed in Chapter 7) entails using features within the message itself to attract additional attention. Such strategies include featuring an unexpected outcome, increasing the amount of sensory input (such as colour, scent or sound), and using tested message appeals that tend to attract more attention.
- Broadcasters and marketers also use *teasers* to overcome noise. For example, trivia quizzes shown at the beginning of a commercial break are designed to engage viewers in staying with the channel in order to find out at the end of the break whether their own answers were right.
- Thanks to new technologies, marketers can now place *customised* advertisements on such devices as mobile phones and television boxes with a unique user address; they can get consumers to register for promotional messages and giveaways more easily, and engage consumers with the product before the sales pitch.[31]
- The Web provides marketers with more options, and many advertisers have shifted considerable sums from television to Internet advertising. Online, marketers can place advertisements that consumers' PCs will automatically retrieve from the Internet, in such formats as *floater ads* that sometimes replace the more commonly used pop-ups, and on websites that use programming from television.[32] In fact, some large marketers like Pepsi and Unilever have implemented campaigns that run only online and that generally are more innovative and significantly cheaper than television advertisements.[33]

Of course, the most effective way to ensure that a promotional message stands out and is received and decoded appropriately by the target audience is through effective positioning and a unique selling proposition. Advertisements for products that are perceived to provide better value than competitive products are more likely to be received in their intended ways than other promotional messages within the advertising clutter.

Feedback – the receiver's response

Since marketing communications are usually designed to persuade a target audience to act in a desired way (e.g. to purchase a specific brand or product, to vote for a political candidate, to pay income taxes early), the ultimate test of marketing communications is the receiver's response. For this reason, it is essential for the sender to obtain feedback as promptly and as accurately as possible. Only through **feedback** can the sender determine whether and how well the message has been received.

As noted earlier, an important advantage of interpersonal communications is the ability to obtain immediate feedback through verbal as well as non-verbal cues. Experienced speakers are very attentive to feedback and constantly modify their messages based on what they see and hear from the audience. Immediate feedback is the factor that makes personal selling so effective. It enables the salesperson to tailor the sales pitch to the expressed needs and observed reactions of each prospect. Similarly, it enables a political candidate to stress specific aspects of his or her platform selectively in response to questions posed by prospective voters in face-to-face meetings. Immediate feedback in the form of inattention serves to alert the college lecturer to jolt a dozing class awake; thus, the lecturer may make a deliberately provocative statement such as: 'This material will probably appear on your final exam.'

Obtaining feedback is as important in impersonal (mass) communications as it is in interpersonal communications. Indeed, because of the high costs of advertising space and time in mass media, many marketers consider impersonal communications feedback to be even more essential. The organisation that initiates the message must develop some method for determining a priori whether its mass communications are received by the intended audience, understood in the intended way and effective in achieving the intended objectives.

Unlike interpersonal communications feedback, mass communications feedback is rarely direct; instead, it is usually inferred. Senders infer how persuasive their messages are from the resulting action (or inaction) of the targeted audience. Receivers buy (or do not buy) the advertised product; they renew (or do not renew) their magazine subscriptions; they vote (or do not vote) for the political candidate. Another type of feedback that companies seek from mass audiences is the degree of customer satisfaction (or dissatisfaction) with a product purchase. They try to discover and correct as swiftly as possible any problems with the product in order to retain their brand's image of reliability. Many companies have established 24-hour helplines to encourage comments and questions from their consumers and also solicit consumer feedback through online contact. Figure 10-4 shows a comprehensive model of the options and relationships among the basic communications elements discussed above.

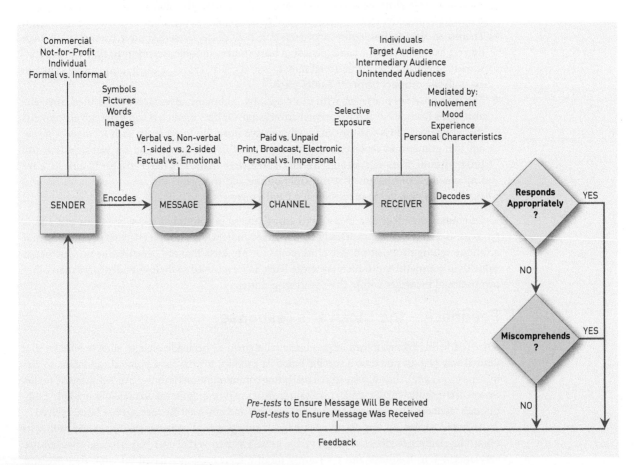

FIGURE 10-4 Comprehensive communication model

DESIGNING PERSUASIVE COMMUNICATIONS

In order to create persuasive communications, the sponsor (who may be an individual, a commercial company or a charitable organisation) must first establish the objectives of the communication, then select the appropriate audiences for the message and the appropriate media through which to reach them, and then design (encode) the message in a manner that is appropriate to each medium and to each audience. As noted earlier, the communications strategy should also include an a priori feedback mechanism that alerts the sponsor to any need for modifications or adjustments to the media or the message.

Communications strategy

In developing its communications strategy, the sponsor must establish the primary communications objectives. These might consist of creating awareness of a service, promoting sales of a product, encouraging (or discouraging) certain practices, attracting retail patronage, reducing post-purchase dissonance, creating goodwill or a favourable image, or any combination of these and other communications objectives.

There are numerous models claiming to depict how persuasive communications work. The cognitive models depict a process in which exposure to a message leads to interest and desire for the product and, ultimately, to buying behaviour. For many decades, this general model had been widely adopted by advertisers. A more recent and sophisticated model of advertising is shown in Figure 10-5. The authors of this paradigm maintain that it reflects the interrelationship among the key factors of persuasion – perception, experience and memory – in a manner more consistent with how the human mind really works than the older cognitive models, and that advertising messages based on this model are more likely to generate consumption behaviour.[34] The existence of these and many other models that claim to explain how persuasion works reflects the complexity of human information processing and the resulting challenges faced by advertisers trying to influence consumption behaviour.

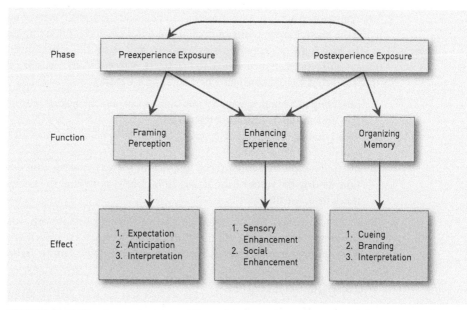

FIGURE 10-5 The three phases and flow of the perception/experience/memory model of advertising

Source: Adapted from Bruce F. Hall, 'A New Model for Measuring Advertising Effectiveness', *Journal of Advertising Research*, March/April 2002, 23–31, with permission from Warc.

Target audience

An essential component of a communications strategy is selecting the appropriate audience. It is important to remember that an audience is made up of individuals – in many cases, great numbers of individuals. Because each individual has his or her own traits, characteristics, interests, needs, experience and knowledge, it is essential for the sender to segment the audience into groups that are homogeneous in terms of some relevant characteristic. Segmentation enables the sender to create specific messages for each target group and to run them in specific media that are seen, heard or read by the target group. It is unlikely that a marketer could develop a single message that would appeal simultaneously to its total audience. Efforts to use 'universal' appeals phrased in simple language that everyone can understand invariably result in unsuccessful advertisements to which few people relate.

Companies that have many diverse audiences sometimes find it useful to develop a communications strategy that consists of an overall (or umbrella) communications message to all their audiences, from which they spin off a series of related messages targeted directly to the specific interests of individual segments. In addition, to maintain positive communications with all of their audiences, most large organisations have public relations departments or employ public relations consultants to provide favourable information about the company and to suppress unfavourable information.

Media strategy

Media strategy is an essential component of a communications plan. It calls for the placement of advertisements in the specific media read, viewed or heard by each targeted audience. To accomplish this, advertisers develop, through research, a **consumer profile** of their target customers that includes the specific media they read or watch. Media organisations regularly research their own audiences in order to develop descriptive **audience profiles**. A cost-effective media choice is one that closely matches the advertiser's consumer profile to a medium's audience profile.

Before selecting specific media vehicles, advertisers must select general media categories that will enhance the message they want to convey. Which media categories the marketer selects depends on the product or service to be advertised, the market segments to be reached and the marketer's advertising objectives. Rather than select one media category to the exclusion of others, many advertisers use a multimedia campaign strategy, with one primary media category carrying the major burden of the campaign and other categories providing supplementary support.

The Web is the newest advertising medium, and using it to communicate effectively with customers still represents a challenge to marketers. A recent study identified three groups of factors that marketers should consider when building a website:

1. providing information search tools such as easy site navigation, complete product information and ability to customise the content;
2. incorporating designs that enhance the enjoyment of the site's users (such as attractive visuals and colours); and
3. providing tools that support the transaction such as security, ease of entering the information, stating the rules of the transaction clearly, providing the company information and quick response time.[35]

Table 10-1 compares the potential persuasive impact of major advertising media along the dimensions of targeting precision (i.e. the ability to reach exclusively the intended audience), message development and execution, degree of psychological noise, feedback and relative cost.

Message strategies

The message is the thought, idea, attitude, image or other information that the sender wishes to convey to the intended audience. In trying to encode the message in a form that will enable the audience to understand its precise meaning, the sender must know exactly what he or she is

TABLE 10-1 Persuasive capabilities and limitations of major advertising media

	TARGETING PRECISION	MESSAGE DEVELOPMENT AND EXECUTION	DEGREE OF PSYCHOLOGICAL NOISE	OBTAINING FEEDBACK	RELATIVE COST
Newspapers	Access to large audiences. Not very selective in reaching consumers with specific demographics. Effective for reaching local consumers.	Flexible. Messages can be designed and published quickly. Limited production quality and short message life.	High clutter. Many messages competing for attention.	Sales volume. Redemptions of special promotions and level of store traffic provide immediate feedback.	Determined by size of ad and the medium's circulation. Affordable for local businesses. Permits joint (cooperative) advertising by national manufacturers and local sellers.
Magazines	High geographic and demographic selectivity. *Selective binding*[a] allows more precise targeting of subscribers with the desired demographics.	High quality of production. High credibility of ads in special-interest magazines. Long message life and pass-along readership. Long lead time required.	High clutter. Some magazines may not guarantee ad placement in a particular position within the magazine.	Delayed and indirect feedback, such as scores that measure recall and attention.	Determined by cost of page and circulation. Top magazines charge very high rates.
Television	Reaches very large audiences. Many programmes lack audience selectivity.	Appeals to several senses. Enables messages that draw attention and generate emotion. Short-duration messages must be repeated. Long lead time.	High clutter. Viewers can avoid message exposures by channel surfing or using advanced technologies.	Day-after recall tests measure how many consumers were exposed to the message and, to a lesser degree, their characteristics.	Very high costs based on how many consumers watch a given programme.
Radio	High geographic and demographic audience selectivity.	Audio messages only. Short exposure. Relatively short lead time.	High clutter. Listeners can easily switch among stations during commercials.	Delayed feedback, such as day-after recall tests.	Based on size of the audience reached. Local radio may be relatively inexpensive.
Internet	Potential for great audience selectivity. Audience may be demographically skewed. Enables tracking customers and building databases. Privacy issues make targeting more difficult.	Increasingly more advanced messages can be designed and shown relatively quickly. Marketers recognise that their home pages are advertisements and must be designed as persuasive tools.	Very high degree of clutter. Visitors can easily escape promotional messages. Banner ads and home pages can reinforce and expand promotional messages featured in other media.	Interactive medium with potential for gathering immediate feedback. Click rates on ads do not measure their impact accurately (since exposure to the brands featured occurs even without a click).	Great variation in establishing advertising rates since there is no standard measure of the impact of online advertising.

(Continued)

TABLE 10-1 (*Continued*)

	TARGETING PRECISION	MESSAGE DEVELOPMENT AND EXECUTION	DEGREE OF PSYCHOLOGICAL NOISE	OBTAINING FEEDBACK	RELATIVE COST
Direct Mail[b]	High audience selectivity. Enables personalisation. Perceived by many as 'junk mail' and discarded.	Enables novel, visually appealing, and dramatic messages (including the addition of sensory inputs).	No competing messages within the mailing.	Easy to measure feedback through limited pre-tests and cost-per-enquiry and cost-per-order. Delayed feedback.	Relatively high cost per person per mailing due to 'junk mail' image.
Direct Marketing[c]	Marketers can build and constantly refine an electronic database of qualified buyers based on enquiries and direct orders. Permits the development of highly selective customer segments. Privacy concerns makes this practice difficult.	A function of the medium used to solicit the direct response from the customer.	Can be relatively free of clutter, even in media where there is generally a lot of noise. For example, infomercials provide advertisers with a 'clutter-free' environment.	Generates measurable responses and enables marketers to measure the profitability of their efforts directly.	Determined through such variables as cost-per-enquiry, cost-per-sale, and revenue-per-advertisement.

Notes: [a]Selective binding is a technique that enables publishers to segment their subscription bases narrowly. When readers subscribe, they are asked to provide demographic information, which the publisher enters into a database. Through a sophisticated computerised system, the publisher is able to select specific subscribers, based on reader demographic profiles, to receive special sections that are bound into a limited number of magazines.
[b]Direct mail includes catalogues, letters, brochures, promotional offers and any materials mailed directly to customers at their homes or offices.
[c]Direct marketing is not a medium but an interactive marketing technique that uses various media (such as mail, print, broadcast, telephone and cyberspace) for the purpose of soliciting a direct response from a consumer. Electronic shopping (through home-shopping television channels or interactive cable) is also considered direct marketing.

trying to say and why (what the objectives are and what the message is intended to accomplish). The sender must also know the target audience's personal characteristics in terms of education, interests, needs and experience. The sender must then design a message strategy through words and/or pictures that will be perceived and accurately interpreted (decoded) by the targeted audience. One study developed a list of message elements designed to appeal to three personality types defined as the righteous buyer (who looks to recommendations from independent sources), the social buyer (who relies on the recommendations of friends, on celebrity endorsements and testimonials) and the pragmatic buyer (who looks for the best value for money, though not necessarily the least expensive).[36]

Involvement Theory

Involvement theory (see Chapter 8) suggests that individuals are more likely to devote active cognitive effort to evaluating the pros and cons of a product in a high-involvement purchase situation and more likely to focus on peripheral message cues in low-involvement situations. The elaboration likelihood model (ELM) proposes that, for high-involvement products, marketers should follow the **central route to persuasion**; that is, they should present advertisements with strong, well-documented, issue-relevant arguments that encourage cognitive processing. When involvement is low, marketers should follow the **peripheral route to persuasion** by emphasising non-content visual or symbolic material (e.g. background scenery, music or celebrity spokespeople) that provide the consumer with pleasant, indirect associations with the product and provoke favourable inferences about its merits. A recent study discovered that the level of involvement and the focus of the advertisement determined its persuasive effectiveness. Highly involved consumers were more influenced by advertisements stressing the outcome of using the product and less involved consumers were more influenced by those portraying the process of using it.[37]

Message structure and presentation

Some of the decisions that marketers must make in designing the message include the use of resonance, positive or negative message framing, one-sided or two-sided messages, comparative advertising and the order of presentation.

Resonance

Advertising resonance is defined as wordplay, often used to create a double meaning, used in combination with a relevant picture. Examples of advertising resonance are the phrase 'absolut masterpiece' appearing next to a bottle of Absolut Vodka, and Pepsi's slogan 'hit the beach topless' next to a Pepsi bottle cap lying in the sand. By using resonance marketers can improve the chances that their advertisements will be noticed by consumers and create favourable and lasting impressions. One study tested the effectiveness of metaphors and puns, such as a car seat with a package of motion sickness remedy serving as the seatbelt's buckle. The study concluded that using rhetorical figures and symbols in advertisements increased the recall and memory of these messages.[38]

Message Framing

Should a marketer stress the benefits to be gained by using a specific product (positive **message framing**) or the benefits to be lost by not using the product (negative **message framing**)? Research suggests that the appropriate message-framing decision depends on the consumer's attitudes and characteristics as well as the product itself. For example, one study found that people with a low need for cognition were more likely to be persuaded by negatively framed messages.[39] Another study found that an individual's self-image impacts the type of framing that he or she finds more persuasive. Individuals with an independent self-image (i.e. who view themselves as defined by unique characteristics) were more persuaded by messages stressing an approach goal (positive framing), and those with an interdependent self-view (i.e. who view themselves as defined by others) found messages that stress avoidance goals more convincing (negative framing).[40]

A study of a credit card company's customers who had not used their cards in the preceding three months found that negative message framing (i.e. what the consumer might lose by not using the credit card) had a much stronger effect on subsequent usage behaviour than positive message framing.[41] A study of advertised products that enabled the early detection of disease indicated that positively framed anecdotal messages were less persuasive than negatively framed anecdotal messages.[42] A recent study discovered that negative message framing was more effective than positive framing when respondents had less opportunity to process the information in the advertisement, but less effective when respondents had more opportunity to process its content.[43]

One-Sided Versus Two-Sided Messages

Should marketers tell their audiences only the good points about their products, or should they also tell them the bad (or the commonplace)? Should they pretend that their products are the only ones of their kind, or should they acknowledge competing products? These are very real strategy questions that marketers face every day, and the answers depend on the nature of the audience and the nature of the competition.

If the audience is friendly (e.g. if it uses the advertiser's products), if it initially favours the communicator's position or if it is not likely to hear an opposing argument, then a **one-sided message** (supportive message) that stresses only favourable information is most effective. However, if the audience is critical or unfriendly (e.g. if it uses competitive products), if it is well educated or if it is likely to hear opposing claims, then a **two-sided message** (refutational message) is likely to be more effective. Two-sided advertising messages tend to be more credible than one-sided advertising messages because they acknowledge that the advertised brand has shortcomings. Two-sided messages can also be very effective when consumers are likely to see competitors' negative counterclaims or when consumer attitudes towards the brand are already negative.[44]

Some marketers stress only positive factors about their products and pretend that competition does not exist. However, when competition does exist and when it is likely to be vocal, such advertisers tend to lose credibility with the consumer. The credibility of an advertised claim can often be enhanced by actually disclaiming superiority of some product features in relation to a competing brand or by not claiming that the product is a universal cure. In political marketing, a candidate will sometimes argue in generalities that a particular course of action is the correct one but give no details with which the audience can analyse, discuss or rebut the argument (a one-sided argument). Using a two-sided argument, the candidate may say something favourable about the reasonableness of an opponent's position before attacking it, thus gaining credibility by appearing objective, open-minded and fair in examining the issues.

Comparative Advertising

Comparative advertising is a widely used marketing strategy in which a marketer claims product superiority for its brand over one or more explicitly named or implicitly identified competitors, either on an overall basis or on selected product attributes. Comparative advertising is useful for product positioning, for target market selection, and for brand positioning strategies. Figure 10-6 presents an advertisement in which Saab Automobile compares its car to the Saab military aircraft AB Gripen, thus positioning the car as the motorway equivalent of Saab AB's precision manufactured military aircraft.

Some critics of the technique maintain that comparative advertisements often assist recall of the competitor's brand at the expense of the advertised brand. However, the wide use of comparative advertising and the research into its strategic effects do not support this view. Studies have found that comparative advertisements are capable of exerting more positive effects on brand attitudes, purchase intentions and purchase than non-comparative advertisements.[45] Studies of comparative advertising using an information-processing perspective found that comparative advertisements elicited higher levels of cognitive processing, had better recall and were perceived as more relevant than non-comparative advertisements.[46] A study that tested the degree of negativity in comparative messages (by using positive, negative and mildly negative comparative messages) for several products reported that negative elements in an advertisement contributed to its effectiveness as long as they were believable or were offset by some elements that made it appear neutral.[47]

There has been considerable concern expressed regarding the ability of comparative advertising to mislead consumers. A recent study advocates the development of concrete measures designed to gauge a comparative advertisement's ability to mislead consumers.[48]

Order Effects

Is it best to present your commercial first or last? Should you give the bad news first or last? Communications researchers have found that the order in which a message is presented affects audience receptivity. For this reason, politicians and other professional communicators often jockey for position when they address an audience sequentially; they are aware that the first and last speeches are more likely to be retained in the audience's memory than those in between. On television, the position of a commercial in a commercial pod can be critical. The commercials shown first are recalled the best, whereas those in the middle are recalled the least.

When just two competing messages are presented, one after the other, the evidence as to which position is more effective is somewhat conflicting. Some researchers have found that the material presented first produces a greater effect (primacy effect), whereas others have found that the material presented last is more effective (recency effect). One study found that in situations

FIGURE 10-6 Comparative advertising
Source: © Saab Cars USA Inc.

that foster high levels of cognitive processing, the initial message tends to be more influential, whereas in situations of low message elaboration, the second message had a greater impact.[49] Magazine publishers recognise the impact of order effects by charging more for advertisements on the front, back and inside covers of magazines than for the inside magazine pages because of their greater visibility and recall.

Order is also important in listing product benefits within an advertisement. If audience interest is low, the most important point should be made first to attract attention. However, if interest is high, it is not necessary to pique curiosity, so product benefits can be arranged in ascending order, with the most important point mentioned last. When both favourable information and unfavourable information are to be presented (as in an annual shareholders' report), placing the favourable material first often produces greater tolerance for the unfavourable news. It also produces greater acceptance and better understanding of the total message. A recent study found that revealing the brand name at the onset of a message enhances brand recall and message persuasiveness.[50]

Repetition

Repetition is an important factor in learning. Thus, it is not surprising that repetition, or frequency of the advertisement, affects persuasion, advertisement recall, brand-name recall and brand preferences. Multiple message exposures give consumers more opportunity to internalise product attributes to develop more or stronger cue associations, to develop more positive attitudes and an increased willingness to resist competitive counterpersuasion efforts. In low-involvement situations, individuals are more likely to regard message claims that are repeated frequently as more truthful than those repeated with less frequency. Different advertisements depicting different applications of the same promotional theme enhance the memorability of the brand advertised.

Advertising Appeals

Sometimes objective, factual appeals are more effective in persuading a target audience; at other times emotional appeals are more effective. It depends on the kind of audience to be reached and their degree of involvement in the product category. In general, however, logical, reason-why appeals are more effective in persuading educated audiences, and emotional appeals are more effective in persuading less-educated consumers. The following sections examine the effectiveness of several frequently used emotional appeals.

Fear

Fear is an effective appeal often used in marketing communications. Some researchers have found a negative relationship between the intensity of fear appeals and their ability to persuade, so that strong fear appeals tend to be less effective than mild fear appeals. A number of explanations have been offered for this phenomenon. Strong fear appeals concerning a highly relevant topic (such as cigarette smoking) cause the individual to experience cognitive dissonance, which is resolved either by rejecting the practice or by rejecting the unwelcome information. Because giving up a comfortable habit is difficult, consumers more readily reject the threat. This they do by a variety of techniques, including denial of its validity ('There still is no real proof that smoking causes cancer'), the belief that they are immune to personal disaster ('It can't happen to me'), and a diffusing process that robs the claim of its true significance ('I play it safe by smoking only filter cigarettes'). Therefore, marketers should use reasonable but not extreme fear appeals and also recognise that fear appeals are not always appropriate. For example, a study of warning information labels affixed to full-fat, reduced-fat and fat-free products concluded that, for products with credible and familiar risks, information labels were more effective than warning labels because they do not arouse psychological reactance.[51] Another study of adolescent responses to fear communications found that adolescents are more persuaded to avoid drug use by messages that depict negative social consequences of drug use rather than physical threats to their bodies.[52] A five-month study of students discovered that short-term cosmetic fear appeals (such as yellow teeth or bad breath) used in advertisements to stop or reduce smoking were more persuasive for males, while long-term health fear appeals (such as getting cancer later in life) were more persuasive for females.[53]

There is no single explanation of the relationship between fear appeals and persuasiveness. One theory proposes that individuals cognitively appraise the available information regarding the severity of the threat, then they appraise the likelihood that the threat will occur; they evaluate whether coping behaviour can eliminate the threat's danger, and if so, whether they have the ability to perform the coping behaviour. This theory is called the *ordered protection motivation* (OPM) model. The study also found that the personality variable 'sensation seeking' affected the processing of fear appeals. A high sensation seeker is more likely to use drugs and also to react negatively to fear-focused anti-drug messages, feeling that he or she is immortal.[54]

Marketers must also consider that the mention of possible detrimental effects of using a product while proclaiming its benefits may result in negative attitudes toward the product itself. For example, if a luxury car company features a new 24-hour emergency helpline in a series of advertisements (as an 'added value' product feature), some consumers may be 'turned off' by even the suggestion that a brand-new, expensive car would experience roadside mechanical problems – particularly late at night on a dark and lonely road.

Humour

Many marketers use humorous appeals in the belief that humour will increase the acceptance and persuasiveness of their advertising communications. Although the use of humour in advertising is significant, there are some risks associated with using this appeal.[55] For example, the effects of humorous advertisements vary by the audience's demographics, level of involvement (humour is more effective for promoting low-involvement products), and attitudes (humour is more effective when the audience already has positive attitudes towards the brand).[56] Table 10-2 summarises some research findings on the impact of humour on advertising.

Marketers believe that younger, better-educated, sophisticated and professional people tend to be receptive audiences for humorous messages. A study of how humour actually works within advertisements discovered that surprise is almost always needed to generate humour and that the effectiveness of humorous advertisements is also influenced by such message elements as warmth and playfulness.[57] One study developed a measure of a personality trait named *need for humour* (NFH) that is focused on a person's tendency to enjoy, engage in or seek out amusement and suggested that these cognitive factors can better explain how consumers respond to humorous advertisements.[58]

Abrasive Advertising

How effective can unpleasant or annoying advertisements be? Studies of the sleeper effect, discussed earlier, suggest that the memory of an unpleasant commercial that antagonises listeners or viewers may dissipate over time, leaving only the brand name in the minds of consumers.

All of us have at one time or another been repelled by so-called agony commercials, which depict in diagrammatic detail the internal and intestinal effects of heartburn, indigestion, clogged sinus cavities, hammer-induced headaches and the like. Nevertheless, pharmaceutical companies often run such commercials with great success because they appeal to a certain segment of the population that suffers from ailments that are not visible and thus elicit little sympathy from family and friends. Their complaints are legitimised by commercials with which they immediately identify. With the sponsor's credibility established ('They really understand the misery I'm going through'), the message itself tends to be highly persuasive in getting consumers to buy the advertised product.

TABLE 10-2 Impact of humour on advertising

- Humor attracts attention.
- Humor does not harm comprehension. (In some cases it may even aid comprehension.)
- Humor is not more effective at increasing persuasion.
- Humor does not enhance source credibility.
- Humor enhances liking.
- Humor that is relevant to the product is superior to humor that is unrelated to the product.
- Audience demographic factors (e.g., gender, ethnicity, age) affect the response to humorous advertising appeals.
- The nature of the product affects the appropriateness of a humorous treatment.
- Humor is more effective with existing products than with new products.
- Humor is more appropriate for low-involvement products and feeling-oriented products than for high-involvement products.

Source: Adapted from Marc G. Weinberger and Charles S. Gulas, 'The Impact of Humor in Advertising: A Review', *Journal of Advertising*, 21, 4, December 1992, 35–59. Reprinted by permission.

Sex in Advertising

In our highly permissive society, sensual advertising seems to permeate the print media and the airwaves. Advertisers are increasingly trying to provoke attention with suggestive illustrations, crude language and nudity in their efforts to appear cool and contemporary. In today's advertising, there is a lot of explicit and daring sexual imagery, extending far beyond the traditional product categories of fashion and fragrance into such categories as shampoo, beer, cars and home construction.

There is little doubt that sexual themes have attention-getting value, but studies show that they rarely encourage actual consumption behaviour. A widely quoted study that examined the effects of sexual advertising appeals on cognitive processing and communications effectiveness found that sexual appeals interfere with message comprehension, particularly when there is substantial information to be processed. It also found that more product-related thinking occurs in response to non-sexual appeals and that visual sexual elements in an advertisement are more likely to be processed than its verbal content, drawing cognitive processing away from product or message evaluation.[59] Some researchers have concluded that nudity may negatively impact the product message.[60] These and other findings support the theory that sexual advertising appeals often detract from the processing of message content.

The type of interest that sexually oriented advertising evokes often stops exactly where it starts – with sex. If a sexually suggestive or explicit illustration is not relevant to the product advertised, it has little effect on consumers' buying intentions. This highlights the potential risk of sexually oriented advertising: the advertiser may be giving up persuasiveness to achieve 'stopping power'. When using sex to promote a product, the advertiser must be sure that the product, the advertisement, the target audience and the use of sexual themes and elements all work together. When sex is relevant to the product, it can be an extremely potent copy theme.

Audience Participation

Earlier we spoke about the importance of feedback in the communications process. The provision of feedback changes the communications process from one-way to two-way communication. This is important to senders because it enables them to determine whether and how well communication has taken place. But feedback is also important to receivers because it enables them to participate, to be involved, to experience in some way the message itself. Participation by the receiver reinforces the message. An experienced communicator asks questions and opinions of an audience to draw them into the discussion. Many lecturers use the participative approach in classrooms rather than the more sterile lecture format because they recognise that student participation tends to facilitate internalisation of the information covered.

Although participation is easily accomplished in interpersonal and online communications, it takes a great deal of ingenuity to achieve in impersonal communications. Thus, it is a challenge for imaginative marketers to get consumers actively engaged in their advertising as soon as they see it.

MARKETING COMMUNICATION AND ETHICS

The keys to effective marketing communications are developing the right persuasive message and delivering it to the right audience. The corresponding ethical issues focus on: (1) identifying and locating specific audiences, and (2) the contents of the promotional messages they are sent.

Precision targeting

The consumer's loss of privacy is an increasingly problematic ethical issue as marketers manage to identify and reach out to increasingly smaller audiences through innovative media. As evident from discussions throughout this chapter, it is apparent that the old *broadcasting* model – where large audiences are reached with the same electronic or print messages – is rapidly becoming obsolete. Advertisers are increasingly adopting *narrowcasting* – a technique that allows them to send very directed messages to very small audiences on an ongoing basis. Narrowcasting is made possible through the efforts of sophisticated data providers who compile individual profiles from a variety of sources. Sophisticated analysis of such data enables the compilation of extremely specialised lists of consumers. Narrowcasting is also made possible because people have inadvertently yielded their privacy rights regarding their demographics and consumption habits.

Another ethical issue of targeted communications is reaching and possibly manipulating consumers who are, according to some, less capable of making sound consumption decisions. Public complaints have been made regarding the targeting of advertisements to pupils in classrooms and through the provision of materials and programmes that marketers provide to students as 'educational' tools when, in fact, they include a lot of persuasive advertising.

The contents of promotional messages

The ethical issues related to the content of marketing communications include the accuracy of the information provided, the impact of values portrayed in advertisements, and the potential misuse of the persuasive abilities of promotional messages. Regarding accuracy, a toothpaste advertisement stating that 'brand A is the best' is considered an acceptable form of advertising 'puffery' because consumers generally understand that there is no credible way to determine what 'best' means. A toothpaste advertisement stating that the brand was 'endorsed by the Dental Association' is an objective statement because it includes information that is easy to verify. However, is an advertisement stating that the brand 'provides more cavity protection than any other toothpaste' permissible advertising puffery, or is it false or misleading? The answer depends on how most reasonable consumers are likely to interpret it. Do they believe that there is a scientific way to measure the degree of cavity protection, that the maker of the brand has conducted a scientific study of all brands of toothpaste on the market and the study has proved the advertisement's claim? It is clear that determining how most reasonable consumers are likely to interpret the advertisement is a complex undertaking, and therefore there is no definitive answer to the question, 'At what point does puffery become deceptive?'

The potential manipulative impact of promotional messages on children was explored earlier (see Chapter 8). There is a consensus that even if children understand the purpose of promotional messages, marketers must take special care in advertising to children because of the amount of time children spend viewing television and online. Studies also show that parents significantly influence children's understanding and processing of advertisements.[61] Generally, advertising to children is more regulated in European countries than, for example, in the USA.

Since advertising is part of European culture, the cumulative persuasive impact of promotional messages on societal values must be considered. By itself, one tasteless advertisement has little impact on our values. However, cumulatively, such advertisements may persuade consumers to act unwisely or develop undesirable attitudes. For example, repeated exposure to advertisements depicting perfectly tanned people is likely to result in excessive sunbathing or tanning via ultraviolet light, despite the fact that it has been documented that such practices significantly increase the chances of developing cancer. Interestingly, not all advertisements that promote a practice that may negatively impact one's health are treated in the same way. For example, although it is known that tanning causes cancer, we have accepted advertisements portraying perfectly tanned models without criticism.

Following considerable research, it is now generally accepted that repeated exposure to very thin 'ideal' figures in promotional messages leads to negative self-perceptions (particularly in women) and is partially responsible for the increase in eating-related disorders. Marketers now recognise that advertisements focused on beauty and attractiveness, especially if they stress the importance of these attributes over other personal characteristics, are likely to be scrutinised by the media, consumers, campaign groups and religious organisations. Consequently, numerous advertisements now portray more realistic-looking models and some for beauty products integrate the notion that although the 'outside' is important, the person's self-worth or 'true beauty' comes from 'within'.

SUMMARY

This chapter has described how the consumer receives and is influenced by marketing communications. There are five basic components of communication: the sender, the receiver, the medium, the message and feedback (the receiver's response). In the communications process, the sender encodes the message using words, pictures, symbols or spokespeople and sends it through a selected channel (or medium). The receiver decodes (interprets) the message based on his or her personal characteristics and experience, and responds (or does not respond) based on such factors as selective exposure, selective perception, comprehension and psychological noise.

There are two types of communications: interpersonal and impersonal (or mass) communications. Interpersonal communications occur on a personal level between two or more people and may be verbal or non-verbal, formal or informal. In mass communications, there is no direct contact between source and receiver. Interpersonal communications take place in person, by telephone, by post or by email; mass communications occur through such impersonal media as television, radio, newspapers and magazines. Feedback is an essential component of all types of communications because it provides the sender with some notion as to whether and how well the message has been received.

The credibility of the source, a vital element in message persuasiveness, is often based on the source's perceived intentions. Informal sources and neutral or editorial sources are considered to be highly objective and, thus, highly credible. The credibility of a commercial source is more problematic and is usually based on a composite evaluation of its reputation, expertise and knowledge, and that of the medium, the retail channel and company spokespeople.

Media selection depends on the product, the audience and the advertising objectives of the campaign. Each medium has advantages and shortcomings that must be weighed in the selection of media for an advertising campaign. Following the emergence of new technologies, many advertisers are now developing more customised communications that can reach consumers via media with narrowcasting, rather than broadcasting, capabilities.

The manner in which a message is presented influences its impact. For example, one-sided messages are more effective in some situations and with some audiences; two-sided messages are more effective with others. High-involvement products (those with great relevance to a consumer segment) are best advertised through the central route to persuasion, which encourages active cognitive effort. Low-involvement products are best promoted through peripheral cues, such as background scenery, music or celebrity spokespeople.

The ethical issues related to marketing communications include invasion of consumer privacy, the potential manipulation of consumers who are less capable of making wise decisions due to age or other demographic factors, the distinction between advertising puffery and deception, misleading advertising, and the cumulative persuasive impact of messages that portray socially undesirable behaviour or values.

DISCUSSION QUESTIONS

1. Explain the differences between feedback from interpersonal communications and feedback from impersonal communications. How can the marketer obtain and use each kind of feedback?
2. List and discuss the effects of psychological noise on the communications process. What strategies can a marketer use to overcome psychological noise?
3. List and discuss factors that affect the credibility of formal communications sources of product information. What factors influence the perceived credibility of an informal communications source?

4. What are the implications of the sleeper effect for the selection of spokespeople and the scheduling of advertising messages?
5. Should marketers use more body copy than artwork in print advertisements? Explain your answer.
6. For what kinds of audiences would you consider using comparative advertising? Why?

EXERCISES

1. Bring two print advertisements to class: one illustrating a one-sided message and the other a two-sided message. Which of the measures discussed in the chapter would you use to evaluate the effectiveness of each advertisement? Explain your answers.
2. Find one example of each of the following two advertising appeals: fear and sex. One example must be a print advertisement and the other a television commercial. Analyse the placement of each advertisement in the medium where it appeared according to the media selection criteria presented in Table 10-1.
3. Watch one hour of television on a single commercial channel during prime time and also tape the broadcast. Immediately after watching the broadcast, list all the commercials you can recall seeing. For each commercial, identify: (a) the message-framing approach used, and (b) whether the message was one-sided or two-sided. Compare your list with the actual taped broadcast. Explain any discrepancies between your recollections and the actual broadcast on the basis of concepts discussed in this chapter.
4. For three of the commercials you watched in the preceding exercise, identify whether the marketer used the central or peripheral route to persuasion. Explain your answer and speculate on why each marketer chose the approach it used to advertise the product or service.
5. Find an example of a promotional message delivered by narrowcasting and discuss it in the light of the ethical issues discussed in this chapter.
6. Find an example of an advertisement that, in your view, depicts a socially undesirable practice and explain why.

NOTES

1. For an empirical analysis of some 200 logos designed to achieve corporate image and communication goals, see Pamela W. Henderson and Joseph A. Cote, 'Guidelines for Selecting or Modifying Logos', *Journal of Marketing*, April 1998, 14–30.
2. Warren St. John, 'A Store Lures Guys Who Are Graduating from Chinos', *New York Times on the Web*, 14 July 2002.
3. Rob Walker, 'The Hidden (in Plain Sight) Persuaders', 5 December 2004, www.nytimes.com.
4. Nat Ives, 'Marketing's Flip Side: The "Determined Detractor"', *New York Times*, 27 December 2004, C1.
5. Thorsten Hennig-Thurau, Kevin P. Gwinner, Gianfranco Walsh and Dwayne D. Gremler, 'Electronic Word-of-Mouth Via Consumer-Opinion Platforms: What Motivates Consumers to Articulate Themselves on the Internet?', *Journal of Interactive Marketing*, Winter 2004, 38–52.
6. Lynne M. Sallot, 'What the Public Thinks About Public Relations: An Impression Management Experiment', *Journalism and Mass Communication Quarterly*, Spring 2002, 150–71.
7. S. Ratneshwar and Shelly Chaiken, 'Comprehension's Role in Persuasion: The Case of Its Moderating Effect on the Persuasive Impact of Source Cues', *Journal of Consumer Research*, 18, June 1991, 52–62.
8. Michael A. Kamins, 'An Investigation into the "Match Up" Hypothesis in Celebrity Advertising: When Beauty May Be Only Skin Deep', *Journal of Advertising*, 19, 1, 1990, 4–13. See also

Marsha L. Richins, 'Social Comparison and the Idealized Images of Advertising', *Journal of Consumer Research*, 18, June 1991, 71–83.

9. Marla Royne Stafford, Thomas F. Stafford and Ellen Day, 'A Contingency Approach: The Effects of Spokesperson Type and Service Type on Service Advertising', *Journal of Advertising*, Summer 2000, 17–32.

10. Laura M. Arpan, 'When in Rome? The Effects of Spokesperson Ethnicity on Audience Evaluation of Crisis', *Journal of Business Communication*, July 2002, 314–39; Osei Appiah, 'Ethnic Identification and Adolescents' Evaluations of Advertisements', *Journal of Advertising Research*, September/October 2001, 7–22; Oscar W. DeShields Jr. and Ali Kara, 'The Persuasive Effect of Spokesperson Similarity Moderated by Source Credibility', *2000 American Marketing Association Education Proceedings*, 11, 132–43.

11. Ronald E. Goldsmith, Barbara A. Lafferty and Stephen J. Newell, 'The Impact of Corporate Credibility and Celebrity Credibility on Consumer Reaction to Advertisements and Brands', *Journal of Advertising*, Fall 2000, 43–54.

12. B. Zafer Erdogan, Michael J. Baker and Stephen Tagg, 'Selecting Celebrity Endorsers: The Practitioner's Perspective', *Journal of Advertising Research*, May/June 2001, 39–48.

13. Thomas J. Robinson and Barbara K. Kaye, 'Using Is Believing: The Influence of Reliance on the Credibility of Online Political Information Among Politically Interested Internet Users', *Journalism and Mass Communication Quarterly*, Winter 2000, 865–79.

14. Sung Tae Kim, David Weaver and Lars Willnat, 'Media Reporting and Perceived Credibility of Online Polls', *Journalism and Mass Communication Quarterly*, Winter 2000, 846–64.

15. Mineabere Ibelema and Lary Powell, 'Cable Television News Viewed as Most Credible', *Newspaper Research Journal*, Winter 2001, 41–51.

16. Carl I. Hovland, Arthur A. Lumsdaine and Fred D. Sheffield, *Experiments on Mass Communication* (New York: Wiley, 1949), 182–200.

17. See Joseph W. Alba, Howard Marmorstein and Amitava Chattopadhyay, 'Transitions in Preference over Time: The Effects of Memory on Message Persuasiveness', *Journal of Marketing Research*, 29, November 1992, 414.

18. Darlene B. Hannah and Brian Sternthal, 'Detecting and Explaining the Sleeper Effect', *Journal of Consumer Research*, 11, September 1984, 632–42.

19. Ruth Ann Weaver Lariscy and Spencer F. Tinkham, 'The Sleeper Effect and Negative Political Advertising', *Journal of Advertising*, Winter 1999, 13–30.

20. Kartik Pashupati, '"I Know This Brand, But Did I Like the Ad?" An Investigation of the Familiarity-Based Sleeper Effect', *Psychology and Marketing*, November 2003, 1017–28.

21. Frédéric F. Brunel and Michelle R. Nelson, 'Explaining Gender Responses to "Help-Self" and "Help-Others" Charity Ads Appeals: The Mediating Role of World-Views', *Journal of Advertising*, Fall 2000, 15–27.

22. Kawpong Polyorat and Dana L. Alden, 'Self-Construal and Need-for-Cognition Effects on Brand Attitudes and Purchase Intentions in Response to Comparative Advertising in Thailand and the United States', *Journal of Advertising*, Spring 2005, 37–49.

23. Bred A. S. Martin, Bodo Lang and Stephanie Wong, 'Conclusion Explicitness in Advertising: The Moderating Role of Need for Cognition (NFC) and Argument Quality (AQ) on Persuasion', *Journal of Advertising*, Winter 2003/2004, 57–66.

24. Pablo Brioni, Richard E. Petty and Zakary L. Tormala, 'Self-Validation of Cognitive Responses to Advertisements', *Journal of Consumer Research*, March 2004, 559–74.

25. Patrick De Pelsmacker, Maggie Geuens and Pascal Anckaert, 'Media Context and Advertising Effectiveness: The Role of Context Appreciation and Context/Ad Similarity', *Journal of Advertising*, Summer 2002, 49–61.

26. Andrew Sharma, 'Recall of Television Commercials as a Function of Viewing Context: The Impact of Program-Commercial Congruity on Commercial Messages', *Journal of General Psychology*, October 2000, 383–96.

27. Vijay Mahajan and Yoram Wind, 'Got Emotional Product Positioning?', *Marketing Management*, May/June 2002, 36–41.

28. Angela Y. Lee and Brian Sternthal, 'The Effects of Positive Mood on Memory', *Journal of Consumer Research*, September 1999, 115–29.

29. See Mahima Mathur and Amitava Chattopadhyay, 'The Impact of Moods Generated by Television Programs on Responses to Advertising', *Psychology and Marketing*, 8, 1, Spring 1991, 59–77.

30. Anna S. Mattila, 'The Role of Narratives in the Advertising of Experiential Services', *Journal of Service Research*, August 2000, 35–45.

31. Brian Steinberg and Suzanne Vranica, 'The Ad World's Message for 2005: Stealth', *Wall Street Journal*, 30 December 2004, B1.

32. Jonathan Miller, 'Floater Ads, the Cousins to Pop-Ups, Evade the Blockers', 24 February 2005, www.nytimes.com; Nat Ives, 'As TV Moves to the Web, Marketers Follow', 27 May 2005, www.nytimes.com; Louise Story, 'Marketers See Opportunity as a Web Tool Gains Users', 5 July 2005, www.nytimes.com.

33. Stuart Elliott, 'Pepsi One Goes on a Television-Free, Celebrity-Free Commercial Diet', 16 March 2005, www.nytimes.com; Stuart Elliott, 'Advertisers Want Something Different', 23 May 2005, www.nytimes.com; Stuart Elliott, 'I Can't Believe It's Not a TV Ad!', 26 July 2005, www.nytimes.com.

34. Bruce F. Hall, 'A New Model for Measuring Advertising Effectiveness', *Journal of Advertising Research*, March/April 2002, 23–31.

35. Sang M. Lee, Pairin Katerattanakul and Soongoo Hong, 'Framework for User Perception of Effective E-Tail Web Sites', *Journal of Electronic Commerce*, January–March 2005, 13–35.

36. Gary Hennerberg, 'The Righteous, Social, and Pragmatic Buyer', *Direct Marketing*, May 1993, 31–4.

37. Jennifer Edson Escalas and Mary Frances Luce, 'Understanding the Effects of Process-Focused versus Outcome-Focused Thought in Response to Advertising', *Journal of Consumer Research*, September 2004, 274–86.

38. Edward F. McQuarrie and David Glen Mick, 'Visual and Verbal Rhetorical Figures under Directed Processing versus Incidental Exposure to Advertising', *Journal of Consumer Research*, March 2003, 579–88.

39. Richard Buda and Bruce H. Charnov, 'Message Processing in Realistic Recruitment Practices', *Journal of Managerial Issues*, Fall 2003, 302ff.

40. Jennifer L. Aaker and Angela Y. Lee, '"I" Seek Pleasure and "We" Avoid Pains: The Role of Self-Regulatory Goals in Information Processing and Persuasion', *Journal of Consumer Research*, June 2001, 33–49.

41. Yoav Ganzach and Nili Karsahi, 'Message Framing and Buying Behavior: A Field Experiment', *Journal of Business Research*, 32, 1995, 11–17.

42. Dena Cox and Anthony D. Cox, 'Communicating the Consequences of Early Detection: The Role of Evidence and Framing', *Journal of Marketing*, July 2001, 91–103.

43. Baba Shiv, Julie A. Edell Britton and John W. Payne, 'Does Elaboration Increase or Decrease the Effectiveness of Negatively versus Positively Framed Messages?', *Journal of Consumer Research*, June 2004, 199–209.

44. Ayn E. Crowley and Wayne D. Hoyer, 'An Integrative Framework for Understanding Two-Sided Persuasion', *Journal of Consumer Research*, 20, March 1994, 561–74.

45. Randall L. Rose, Paul W. Miniard, Michael J. Barone, Kenneth C. Manning and Brian D. Till, 'When Persuasion Goes Undetected: The Case of Comparative Advertising', *Journal of Marketing Research*, 30, August 1993, 315–30; see also Cornelia Pechmann and S. Ratneshwar, 'The Use of Comparative Advertising for Brand Positioning: Association versus Differentiation', *Journal of Consumer Research*, 18, September 1991, 145–60, and Cornelia Pechmann and David W. Stewart, 'The Effects of Comparative Advertising on Attention, Memory, and Purchase Intentions', *Journal of Consumer Research*, 17, September 1990, 180–91.

46. Darrel D. Muehling, Jeffrey J. Stoltman and Sanford Grossbart, 'The Impact of Comparative Advertising on Levels of Message Involvement', *Journal of Advertising*, 19, 4, 1990, 41–50; see also Jerry B. Gotlieb and Dan Sarel, 'Comparative Advertising Effectiveness: The Role of Involvement and Source Credibility', *Journal of Advertising*, 20, 1, 1991, 38–45.

47. Alina B. Sorescu and Betsy D. Gelb, 'Negative Comparative Advertising: Evidence Favoring Fine-Tuning', *Journal of Advertising*, Winter 2000, 25–40.

48. Michael J. Barone, Randall L. Rose, Paul W. Miniard and Kenneth C. Manning, 'Enhancing the Detection of Misleading Comparative Advertising', *Journal of Advertising Research*, September/October 1999, 43–50.

49. Curtis P. Haugtvedt and Duane T. Wegener, 'Message Order Effect in Persuasion: An Attitude Strength Perspective', *Journal of Consumer Research*, 21, June 1994, 205–18.

50. William E. Baker, Heather Honea and Cristel Antonia Russell, 'Do Not Wait to Reveal the Brand Name: The Effect of Brand-Name Placement on Television Advertising Effectiveness', *Journal of Advertising*, Fall 2004, 77–86.

51. Brad J. Bushman, 'Effects of Warning and Information Labels on Consumption of Full Fat, Reduced Fat, and No Fat Products', *Journal of Applied Psychology*, 83, 1, 1998, 97–101.

52. Denise D. Schoenbachler and Tommy E. Whittler, 'Adolescent Processing of Social and Physical Threat Communications', *Journal of Advertising*, 35, 4, Winter 1996, 37–54.

53. Karen H. Smith and Mary Ann Stutts, 'Effects of Short-Term Cosmetic Versus Long-Term Health Fear Appeals in Anti-Smoking Advertisements on the Smoking Behaviour of Adolescents', *Journal of Consumer Behaviour*, December 2003, 157ff.

54. James B. Hunt, John F. Tanner Jr. and David R. Eppright, 'Forty Years of Fear Appeal Research: Support for the Ordered Protection Motivation Model', *American Marketing Association*, 6, Winter 1995, 147–53.

55. Dana L. Alden, Ashesh Mukherjee and Wayne D. Hoyer, 'The Effects of Incongruity, Surprise and Positive Moderators on Perceived Humor in Advertising', *Journal of Advertising*, Summer 2000, 1–15.

56. Ibid.

57. Ibid.

58. Thomas W. Cline, Moses B. Altsech, and James J. Kellaris, 'When Does Humor Enhance or Inhibit Ad Responses?: The Moderating Role of the Need for Humor', *Journal of Advertising*, Fall 2003, 31–46.

59. Jessica Severn, George E. Belch and Michael A. Belch, 'The Effects of Sexual and Non-Sexual Advertising Appeals and Information Level on Cognitive Processing and Communication Effectiveness', *Journal of Advertising*, 19, 1, 1990, 14–22.

60. Michael S. LaTour, Robert E. Pitts and David C. Snook Luther, 'Female Nudity, Arousal, and Ad Response: An Experimental Investigation', *Journal of Advertising*, 19, 4, 1990, 51–62.

61. For example, Albert Carvana and Rosella Vassallo, 'Children's Perception of Their Influence Over Purchases: The Role of Parental Communication Patterns', *Journal of Consumer Marketing*, 20, 1, 2003, 55–67.

PART 3

CONSUMERS IN THEIR SOCIAL AND CULTURAL SETTINGS

PART 3 DISCUSSES CONSUMERS IN THEIR SETTINGS

The four chapters in Part 3 are designed to provide the reader with a detailed picture of the social and cultural dimensions of consumer behaviour. Chapters 11 to 14 explain how social and cultural concepts affect the attitudes and behaviour of individuals, and show how these concepts are employed by marketing practitioners to achieve their marketing objectives.

CHAPTER 11
REFERENCE GROUPS AND FAMILY INFLUENCES

With the exception of those very few people who are classified as hermits, most individuals interact with other people on a daily basis, especially with members of their own families.

In the first part of this chapter, we will consider how group involvements and memberships influence our actions as consumers – that is, impact consumers' decision-making, shopping activities and actual consumption. The second part of this chapter deals with how the family influences its members' consumer behaviour. For instance, a child learning the use and value of money is often a 'family matter'; so are decisions about a new car, a holiday trip or where to go to university. The family commonly provides the opportunity for product exposure and trial and imparts consumption values to its members. As a major consumption group, the family is also a prime target for many products and services.

This chapter begins with a discussion of the basic concepts of group dynamics and how reference groups both directly and indirectly influence consumer behaviour. We then examine some basic family concepts. Next we discuss family consumer decision-making and consumption behaviour; last we explore the marketing implications of the family life cycle. (The three chapters that follow discuss other social and societal groupings that influence consumer buying processes: social class, culture and subculture, and cross-cultural exposure.)

WHAT IS A GROUP?

A **group** may be defined as two or more people who interact to accomplish either individual or mutual goals. The broad scope of this definition includes an intimate group of two neighbours who each summer Saturday drive to the local golf course to play a round of golf, and a larger, more formal group, such as a local diving club, whose members are mutually interested in equipment, training and diving trips and holidays. Included in this definition, too, is a kind of 'one-sided grouping' in which an individual consumer observes the appearance or actions of others, who unknowingly serve as consumption-related role models.

Sometimes groups are classified by membership status. A group to which a person either belongs or for membership of which he/she would qualify is called a **membership group**. For example, the group of women with whom a young executive plays tennis weekly would be considered, for her, a membership group. There are also groups in which an individual is not likely to receive membership, despite acting like a member by adopting the group's values, attitudes and behaviour. This is considered a **symbolic group**. For instance, professional golfers may constitute a symbolic group for an amateur golfer who identifies with certain players by imitating their behaviour whenever possible (e.g. by purchasing a specific brand of golf balls or golf clubs). However, the amateur golfer does not (and probably never will) qualify for membership as a professional golfer because he has neither the skills nor the opportunity to compete professionally.

UNDERSTANDING THE POWER OF REFERENCE GROUPS

Within the context of consumer behaviour, the concept of reference groups is an extremely important and powerful idea. A **reference group** is any person or group that serves as a point of comparison (or reference) for an individual in forming either general or specific values and attitudes, or a specific guide for behaviour. This basic concept provides a valuable perspective for understanding the impact of other people on an individual's consumption beliefs, attitudes and behaviour. It also provides insight into the methods marketers sometimes use to effect desired changes in consumer behaviour.

From a marketing perspective, reference groups are groups that serve as frames of reference for individuals in their purchase or consumption decisions. The usefulness of this concept is enhanced by the fact that it places no restrictions on group size or membership, nor does it require that consumers identify with a tangible group (i.e. the group can be symbolic such as owners of successful small businesses, leading corporate chief executive officers, rock stars or golf celebrities).

Reference groups that influence general or broadly defined values or behaviour are called **normative reference groups**. An example of a child's normative reference group is the immediate family, which is likely to play an important role in moulding the child's general consumer values and behaviour (such as which foods to select for good nutrition, appropriate ways to dress for specific occasions, how and where to shop or what constitutes 'good' value).

Reference groups that serve as benchmarks for specific or narrowly defined attitudes or behaviour are called **comparative reference groups**. A comparative reference group might be a neighbouring family whose lifestyle appears to be admirable and worthy of imitation (in terms of the way they maintain their home, their choice of home furnishings and cars, their taste in clothing or the number and types of holidays they take).

Both normative and comparative reference groups are important. Normative reference groups influence the development of a basic code of behaviour; comparative reference groups influence the expression of specific consumer attitudes and behaviour. It is likely that the specific influences of comparative reference groups to some measure depend on the basic values and behaviour patterns established early in a person's development by normative reference groups.

A broadened perspective on reference groups

The meaning of 'reference group' has changed over the years. As originally used, reference groups were narrowly defined to include only those groups with which a person interacted on a direct basis (such as family and close friends). However, the concept has gradually broadened to include both direct and indirect individual or group influences. **Indirect reference groups** consist of those individuals or groups with whom a person does not have direct face-to-face contact, such as film stars, sports heroes, political leaders, television personalities, or even well-dressed and interesting-looking people in the street. It is the power of the indirect reference group that helps sell the Nike clothing, football shoes and equipment used by Cristiano Ronaldo or Wayne Rooney.

Referents a person might use in evaluating his or her own general or specific attitudes or behaviour vary from one individual to several family members, to a broader kinship group or from a voluntary association to a social class, a profession, an ethnic group, a community, an age category or even a nation or culture. As Figure 11-1 indicates, the major societal groupings that influence an individual's consumer behaviour are family, friends, social class, selected subcultures, one's own culture and even other cultures. For instance, within the scope of selected subcultures, we would include various age categories (older consumers or young adults) that might serve as a reference group for their own or others' behaviour.

Factors that affect reference group influence

The degree of influence that a reference group exerts on an individual's behaviour usually depends on the nature of the individual and the product and on specific social factors. This section discusses how and why some of these factors influence consumer behaviour. Table 11-1 presents a broad view of the factors that influence conformity.

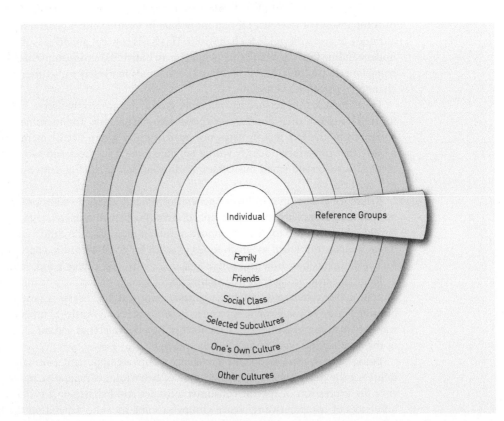

FIGURE 11-1 Major consumer reference groups

TABLE 11-1 Selective factors that positively influence conformity

CHARACTERISTICS	POSITIVE (+) EFFECT
Task/situational characteristics	Difficulty/complexity Ambiguity/subjectivity
Brand characteristics	No information Limited choice Prior conformity Crisis/emergency
Group characteristics	Attractiveness Expertise Credibility Clarity of group goals Likely future interaction with group Past success
Personal characteristics	Tendency to conform Need for affiliation Need to be liked Desire for control Fear of negative evaluation

Source: Adapted from Dana-Nicoleta Lascu and George Zinkhan, 'Consumer Conformity: Review and Applications for Marketing Theory and Practice', *Journal of Marketing Theory and Practice*, Summer 1999, 1–12. Used by permission of M. E. Sharpe, Inc.

Information and Experience

An individual who has first-hand experience with a product or service, or can easily obtain full information about it, is less likely to be influenced by the advice or example of others. On the other hand, a person who has little or no experience with a product or service and does not expect to have access to objective information about it (e.g. a person who believes that advertising may be misleading or deceptive) is more likely to seek out the advice or example of others. For instance, when a young corporate sales representative wants to impress his client, he may take him to a restaurant that he knows from experience to be good or to one that has been highly recommended by the local newspaper. If he has neither personal experience nor information he regards as valid, he may seek the advice of a friend or a parent or imitate the behaviour of others by taking him to a restaurant he knows is frequented by young business executives whom he admires.

Credibility, Attractiveness and Power of the Reference Group

A reference group that is perceived as credible, attractive or powerful can induce consumer attitude and behaviour change. For example, when consumers are concerned with obtaining accurate information about the performance or quality of a product or service, they are likely to be persuaded by those whom they consider trustworthy and knowledgeable. That is, they are more likely to be persuaded by sources with high credibility.

When consumers are primarily concerned with the acceptance or approval of others they like, with whom they identify, or who offer them status or other benefits, they are likely to adopt their product, brand or other behavioural characteristics. When consumers are primarily concerned with the power that a person or group can exert over them, they might choose products or services that conform to the norms of that person or group in order to avoid ridicule or punishment. However, unlike other reference groups that consumers follow because they are credible or because they are attractive, power groups are not as likely to cause attitude change. Individuals may conform to the behaviour of a powerful person or group but are not as likely to experience a change in their own attitudes.

Different reference groups may influence the beliefs, attitudes and behaviour of an individual at different points in time or under different circumstances. For example, the dress habits of a young staff member working for a conservative law practice may vary, depending on her place and role. She may conform to the dress code of her office by wearing by day conservative clothing and skirts or dresses that do not end above the knee and drastically alter her mode of dress after work by wearing more trendy, flamboyant, revealing styles.

Conspicuousness of the Product

The potential influence of a reference group on a purchase decision varies according to how visually or verbally conspicuous the product is to others. A visually conspicuous product is one that will stand out and be noticed (such as a luxury item or novelty product); a verbally conspicuous product may be highly interesting, or it may be easily described to others. Products that are especially conspicuous and status revealing (a new car, fashion clothing, sleek laptop computer or home furniture) are most likely to be purchased with an eye to the reactions of relevant others. Privately consumed products that are less conspicuous (fruit yogurt or laundry soaps) are less likely to be purchased with a reference group in mind.

Reference Groups and Consumer Conformity

Marketers may have divergent goals with regard to **consumer conformity**. Some marketers, especially market leaders, are interested in the ability of reference groups to change consumer attitudes and behaviour by encouraging conformity. To be capable of such influence, a reference group must accomplish the following:

1. inform or make the individual aware of a specific product or brand;
2. provide the individual with the opportunity to compare his or her own thinking with the attitudes and behaviour of the group;
3. influence the individual to adopt attitudes and behaviour that are consistent with the norms of the group;
4. legitimise the decision to use the same products as the group.

In contrast, marketers, especially those responsible for a new brand or a brand that is not the market leader, may wish to elect a strategy that asks consumers to strike out and be different and not just follow the crowd when making a purchase decision.

In reality the nonconformity appeal can be thought of as a request to shift one's reference (attitudes or behaviour) from one grouping (brand A users) to another reference (non-brand A users or brand B users).

SELECTED CONSUMER-RELATED REFERENCE GROUPS

As already mentioned, consumers are potentially influenced by a diverse range of people with whom they come in contact or observe. We will consider the following five specific reference groups because they give us a kind of cross-section of the types of groups that influence consumers' attitudes and behaviour:

1. friendship groups,
2. shopping groups,
3. work groups,
4. virtual groups or communities, and
5. consumer-action groups.

The family, possibly the most compelling reference group for consumer behaviour, will be fully covered in the second part of this chapter.

Friendship groups

Friendship groups are typically classified as **informal groups** because they are usually unstructured and lack specific authority levels. In terms of relative influence, after an individual's family, his or her friends are most likely to influence the individual's purchase decisions.

Seeking and maintaining friendships is a basic drive of most people. Friends fulfil a wide range of needs: they provide companionship, security and opportunities to discuss problems that an individual may be reluctant to discuss with family members. Friendships are also a sign of maturity and independence, for they represent a breaking away from the family and the forming of social ties with the outside world.

The opinions and preferences of friends are an important influence in determining the products or brands a consumer ultimately selects. Marketers of products such as brand-name clothing, fine jewellery, snack foods and alcoholic drinks recognise the power of peer group influence and frequently depict friendship situations in their advertisements.

Shopping groups

Two or more people who shop together, whether for food, for clothing, or simply to pass the time, can be called a **shopping group**. Such groups are often offshoots of family or friendship groups and, therefore, they function as what has been referred to as 'purchase pals'.[1] The motivations for shopping with a purchase pal range from a primarily social motive (to share time together and enjoy lunch after shopping) to helping reduce the risk when making an important decision (having someone along whose expertise will reduce the chance of making an incorrect purchase). In instances where none of the members of the shopping group knows much about the product under consideration (such as an expensive home entertainment centre), a shopping group may form for defensive reasons; members may feel more confident with a collective decision.

A special type of shopping group is the in-home shopping party, which typically consists of a group that gathers together in the home of a friend to attend a 'party' devoted to demonstrating and evaluating a specific line of products. The in-home party approach provides marketers with an opportunity to demonstrate the features of their products simultaneously to a group of potential customers. Early purchasers tend to create a bandwagon effect: undecided guests often overcome a reluctance to buy when they see their friends make positive purchase decisions. Furthermore, some of the guests may feel obliged to buy because they are in the home of the sponsoring host or hostess. Given the spirit and excitement of 'consumer gatherings' or 'parties', Tupperware, for example, generates 90 per cent of its annual sales from such consumer parties.[2]

Work groups

The sheer amount of time that people spend at their jobs, frequently more than 35 hours per week, provides ample opportunity for work groups to serve as a major influence on the consumption behaviour of members.

Both the formal work group and the informal friendship–work group can influence consumer behaviour. The formal work group consists of individuals who work together as part of a team and, thus, have a sustained opportunity to influence each other's consumption-related attitudes and actions. Informal friendship–work groups consist of people who have become friends as a result of working for the same firm, whether or not they work together as a team. Members of informal work groups may influence the consumption behaviour of other members during coffee or lunch breaks or at after-work meetings.

Recognising that work groups influence consumers' brand choices and that many women now go out to work, firms that in the past sold their products exclusively through direct calls on women in their homes are now redirecting their sales efforts to offices and plants during lunch-hour visits. For instance, Tupperware encourage their sales representatives to reach working women at their places of employment.

Virtual groups or communities

Thanks to computers and the Internet, we are witnessing the emergence of a new type of group – virtual groups or communities. Both adults and children are turning on their computers or cellphones, logging on to the Web and visiting special-interest websites, often with chat rooms. If you're a skier, you can chat online with other skiers; if you're an amateur photographer, you can chat online with others who share your interest. Local newspapers everywhere run stories from time to time about singles who met online, typically accompanied by a picture of their wedding. Some Internet providers, of which Facebook is the most famous, let their members create personal lists of their friends so that when they log on to the website they immediately know which of their friends are currently online and can send and receive instant messages. An elderly person in Hamburg or Dublin, for example, might not make it to the local senior citizen centre when it's freezing and snowing outside, but he or she can always log on.[3]

Whereas fifty years ago the definition of a community stressed the notion of geographic proximity and face-to-face relationships, today's communities are much more broadly defined as 'sets of social relations among people'.[4] In this spirit, there is also today wide-scale access to what is known as 'Internet communities' or 'virtual communities'. These terms refer to Web-based consumer groups. These communities provide their members with access to extensive amounts of information, fellowship and social interaction covering an extremely wide range of topics and issues (e.g. vegetarianism, cooking, collecting, trading, finance, film-making, romance, politics, technology, art, hobbies, spiritualism, age grouping, online game playing, voice-video chats, free email, tech assistance, travel and holidays, educational opportunities, living with illnesses and a host of lifestyle options). Virtual communities provide an opportunity for a marketer to address consumers with a particular common interest, which can be one of the primary pleasures a consumer has online, and also have the ability to enhance the consumption experience (via discussion with others).[5]

The exchange of knowledge that can take place within a virtual community can help a good product sell faster and a poor product fail faster. Indeed, there are a number of 'knowledge exchanges' that permit registered members and others to ask questions of experts on subjects germane to that exchange. And some virtual communities, hosted by a commercial source, are aimed at particular ethnic groups and contain online content targeted to a distinct ethnic community.

When visiting such communities, it does not matter if you are tall or short, thin or fat, handsome or plain-looking. On the Internet, people are free to express their thoughts, to be emotional and intimate with those they do not know and have never met, and even to escape from those they normally interact with by spending time on the Internet. The anonymity of the Web gives its users the freedom to express whatever views they wish and also to benefit from savouring the views of others. Because of this anonymity, Internet users can say things to others that they would not say in face-to-face interactions.[6] Communicating over the Internet permits people to explore the boundaries of their personalities (see the related discussion in Chapter 6) and to shift from one persona to another. For example, investigators have found that there are a surprisingly large number of men who adopt female personae online ('gender swapping').[7] Some community websites have attempted to control the limits of what is deemed appropriate and inappropriate by instituting codes of behaviour.

Brand Communities

Although relationship marketing has been discussed earlier in the text (see Chapter 8), the next step in its evolution is the establishment of brand communities. As one recent newspaper article noted, 'There is a definite feeling among marketers that if you want to build up loyalty to your brand, your product has to have an active social life'.[8] An example of such brand communities are the Harley-Davidson owner groups (abbreviated HOGs). A brand community has been defined as 'a specialized, non-geographically bound community, based on a structured set of social relationships among admirers of a brand . . . it is marked by a shared consciousness, rituals and traditions, and a sense of moral responsibility'.[9] It is this sense of community, for example, that causes Saab owners in some countries to beep or flash their lights at another Saab on the road (i.e. a greeting ritual).

Consumer-action groups

A particular kind of consumer group – a **consumer-action group** – has emerged in response to the consumerist movement. Today there are a very large number of such groups that are dedicated to providing consumers with assistance in their effort to make the right purchase decisions, consume products and services in a healthy and responsible manner, and generally to add to the overall quality of their lives. The following are just a few examples of the diverse range of consumer concerns being addressed by private and public consumer-action groups: neighbourhood crime watch, youth development, forests and wildlife concerns, children and advertising, race and ethnicity, community volunteerism, legal assistance, public health, disaster relief, energy conservation, education, smoking, the environment, access to telecommunications, science in the public interest, credit counselling, privacy issues and children and the Internet.

Consumer-action groups can be divided into two broad categories:

1. those that organise to correct a specific consumer abuse and then disband, and
2. those that organise to address broader, more pervasive problem areas and operate over an extended or indefinite period of time.

A group of irate parents who band together to protest at the opening of a cinema dedicated to showing X-rated films in their neighbourhood, or a group of neighbours who attend a meeting of the local highway department to protest at how poorly the streets in their area have been cleared of snow are examples of temporary, cause-specific consumer-action groups. The overriding objective of many consumer-action groups is to bring sufficient pressure to bear on selected members of the business community to make them correct perceived consumer abuses. Examples might include an attempt to ban gas-guzzling SUVs and/or genetically altered foods.[10]

CELEBRITY AND OTHER REFERENCE GROUP APPEALS

Appeals by celebrities and other similar reference groups are used very effectively by advertisers to communicate with their markets. Celebrities can be a powerful force in creating interest or actions with regard to purchasing or using selected goods and services. This identification may be based on admiration (of an athlete), aspiration (of a celebrity or a way of life), empathy (with a person or a situation), or on recognition (of a person – real or stereotypical – or of a situation). In some cases, the prospective consumer may think, 'If she uses it, it must be good. If I use it, I'll be like her.' In other cases, the prospective consumer says to himself, 'He has the same problems that I have. What worked for him will work for me.'

Five major types of reference group appeals in common marketing usage are celebrity, expert, common man, executive and employee, and trade or 'spokes-character'. These appeals, as well as others less frequently employed, are often operationalised in the form of testimonials or endorsements. In the case of the common man, they may be presented as slice-of-life commercials.

Celebrities

Celebrities, particularly film stars, television personalities, popular entertainers and sports icons, provide a very common type of reference group appeal. Indeed, a significant number of commercials

FIGURE 11-2 A consumer-action group appealing for involvement
Source: Friends of Animals (www.friendsofanimals.org).

TABLE 11-2 Types of celebrity appeals

TYPES	DEFINITION
Testimonial	Based on personal usage, a celebrity attests to the quality of the product or service.
Endorsement	Celebrity lends his or her name and appears on behalf of a product or service on which he or she may or may not be an expert.
Actor	Celebrity presents a product or service as part of character endorsement.
Spokesperson	Celebrity represents the brand or company over an extended period of time.

today include celebrity endorsers.[11] To their loyal followers and to much of the general public, celebrities represent an idealisation of life that most people imagine they would love to live. Advertisers spend enormous sums of money to have celebrities promote their products, with the expectation that the reading or viewing audience will react positively to the celebrity's association with them. Michael Jordan has been a particularly powerful product endorser. He has assisted many firms, whose products he promotes, to increase their stock market value substantially. Indeed, as an indication of his celebrity power, he is under contract to Nike until the year 2023.[12]

A firm that decides to employ a celebrity to promote its product or service has the choice of using the celebrity to give a **testimonial** or an **endorsement** as an actor in a commercial or as a company **spokesperson**. Table 11-2 distinguishes among these different types of celebrity appeals. Figure 11-3 presents the findings of a study that explored what marketing practitioners in the United Kingdom look for in selecting a celebrity endorser. What is apparent is that the importance of certain celebrity characteristics varies depending on whether the product being promoted is technical (e.g. PCs) or non-technical (e.g. jeans) in nature. Specifically, for a product like a PC the 'trustworthiness' of a celebrity is considered to be most important, whereas for a clothing item like jeans the 'physical attractiveness' of the celebrity is viewed as most important.

Of all the benefits that a celebrity might contribute to a firm's advertising programme – fame, talent, credibility or charisma – celebrity credibility with the consumer audience is the most important. By **celebrity credibility** we mean the audience's perception of both the celebrity's expertise (how much the celebrity knows about the product area) and trustworthiness (how honest the celebrity is about what he or she says about the product).[13] To illustrate, when a celebrity endorses only one product, consumers are likely to perceive the product in a highly favourable light and indicate a greater intention to purchase it. In contrast, when a celebrity endorses a variety of products, his or her perceived credibility is reduced because of the apparent economic motivation underlying the celebrity's efforts.[14] Figure 11-4 presents footballer Steven Gerrard as an endorser for Lucozade.

A recent study examining the impact of celebrity athlete endorsers on teens found that such endorsers had a positive influence on favourable word-of-mouth (WOM) and increased brand loyalty. Moreover, the research found that female teens tended to spread more favourable WOM about a product or brand endorsed by their favourite celebrity athlete than did male teens. The females were also more likely to agree that males who had athlete role models had influenced them to purchase certain brands.[15]

The expert

A second type of reference group appeal used by marketers is the expert, a person who, because of his or her occupation, special training or experience, is in a unique position to help the prospective consumer evaluate the product or service that the advertisement promotes. For example, an advertisement for a quality frying pan may feature the endorsement of a chef, one for fishing tackle may contain the endorsement of a professional fishing guide, or an advertisement for an allergy medication may contain the endorsement of a professional golfer.

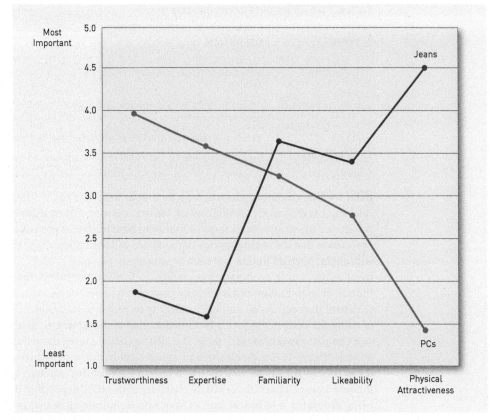

FIGURE 11-3 Importance of celebrity characteristics according to product types

Source: Adapted from B. Zafer Erdogan, Michael J. Baker and Stephen Tagg, 'Selecting Celebrity Endorsers: The Practitioner's Perspective', *Journal of Advertising Research*, May/June 2001, 46, with permission from Warc.

The 'common man'

A reference group appeal that uses the testimonials of satisfied customers is known as the common-man approach. The advantage of the common-man appeal is that it demonstrates to prospective customers that someone just like them uses and is satisfied with the product or service being advertised. The common-man appeal is especially effective in public health announcements (such as anti-smoking or high blood pressure messages), for most people seem to identify with people like themselves when it comes to such messages.[16]

Many television commercials show a typical person or family solving a problem by using the advertised product or service. These commercials are known as slice-of-life commercials because they focus on real-life situations with which the viewer can identify. For example, one commercial focuses on how a laundry detergent can deodorise clothes; another talks about how a certain breakfast cereal provides enough energy to get an individual through a hectic morning. When viewers identify with the situation, they are likely to adopt the solution that worked in the television commercial.

The executive and employee spokesperson

During the past two decades, an increasing number of firms have used their top executives as spokespeople in consumer advertisements. The popularity of this type of advertising is probably due to

FIGURE 11-4 Celebrity endorsement
Source: Courtesy of The Advertising Archives.

the success and publicity received by a number of executives. Like celebrity spokespeople, executive spokespeople seem to be admired by the general population because of their achievements and the status implicitly conferred on business leaders. The appearance of a company's chief executive in its advertising seems to imply that someone at the top is watching over the consumers' best interests, and it encourages consumers to have more confidence in the firm's products or services.

To apply a more grass-roots approach to such promotional programmes, some companies feature employees rather than top executives in selected advertising campaigns.

Trade or 'spokes-characters'

Trade or spokes-characters as well as familiar cartoon characters (e.g. Ninja Turtles, Bart Simpson) serve as quasi-celebrity endorsers. These trade spokes-characters present an idealised image and dispense information that can be very important for the product or service that they 'work for'.[17] With few exceptions, trade characters serve as exclusive spokespeople for a particular product or service. They sometimes provide a kind of personality for the product or service and make the product appear friendlier (e.g. Ronald McDonald).

Other reference group appeals

A variety of other promotional strategies can function creatively as frames of reference for consumers. Respected retailers and the editorial content of selected special-interest magazines can also function as frames of reference that influence consumer attitudes and behaviour. Also, seals of approval and even objective product ratings can serve as positive endorsements that encourage consumers to act favourably towards certain products. A high rating by an objective rating magazine can also serve as an endorsement for a brand.

The remainder of this chapter concentrates on the family – arguably the most important group influencing human behaviour in general and consumer behaviour in particular.

THE FAMILY IS A CONCEPT IN FLUX

Although the term **family** is a basic concept, it is not easy to define because family composition and structure, as well as the roles played by family members, are almost always in transition. Traditionally, however, family is defined as two or more persons related by blood, marriage or adoption who reside together. In a more dynamic sense, the individuals who constitute a family might be described as members of the most basic social group who live together and interact to satisfy their personal and mutual needs. According to many sources, the family remains the central or dominant institution in providing for the welfare of its members.

Although families are sometimes referred to as households, not all households are families. For example, a household might include individuals who are not related by blood, marriage or adoption, such as unmarried couples, family friends and room-mates. However, within the context of consumer behaviour, households and families are usually treated as synonymous, and we will continue this convention.

In most Western societies, three types of families dominate: the married couple, the nuclear family and the extended family. The simplest type of family, in number of members, is the married couple – a husband and a wife. As a household unit, the married couple is generally representative of either the newly married who have not yet started a family or older couples who have already raised their children.

A husband and wife and one or more children constitute a **nuclear family**. This type of family is still commonplace but has been on the decline. The nuclear family, together with at least one grandparent living within the household, is called an **extended family**. Within the past thirty years the incidence of the extended family has declined in a number of countries because of the geographic mobility that splits up families. Moreover, because of divorce, separation, and births outside marriage, there has been a rapid increase in the number of **single-parent family** households consisting of one parent and at least one child.

Not surprisingly, the type of family which is most typical can vary considerably from culture to culture. For instance, in an individualistic society such as that in Canada, the nuclear family is most common. In a kinship culture (with extended families) such as that in Thailand, a family would commonly include a head of household, married adult children and grandchildren.[18]

SOCIALISATION OF FAMILY MEMBERS

The **socialisation of family members**, ranging from young children to adults, is a central family function. In the case of young children, this process includes imparting to children the basic values and modes of behaviour consistent with the culture. These generally include moral and religious principles, interpersonal skills, dress and grooming standards, appropriate manners and speech and the selection of suitable educational and occupational or career goals.

A Dutch study found that younger juveniles spend most of their leisure time with their family, whereas older juveniles spend most of theirs with peers.[19] The transition period between these two age groups was 13, with 13-year-olds dividing their leisure time between parents, peers and being alone. The results further indicate that 14- and 15-year-old boys, especially from the higher social classes, were strongly focused on peer groups, whereas girls of the same age preferred dyadic friendships.

Parental socialisation responsibility seems to be constantly expanding. For instance, parents are often anxious to see their young children possess adequate computer skills, almost before they are able to talk or walk – as early as 12 months after their birth. Because of parents' intensive interest in their young children learning about using a computer, hardware and software developers are regularly developing products targeted at parents seeking to buy such items for their children.

Another sign of parents' constant pressure to help their young children secure an 'advantage' or 'keep ahead' are the demanding daily schedules that rule the lives of many children (e.g. daily pre-school classes, after-school classes, weekend enrichment and/or sports programmes). Such hectic schedules foster a concentration on competition and results and not on having fun or on being creative. In contrast, as children themselves present-day parents might have built forts out of blankets or pillows. However, with the structured activities of today and with the child constantly surrounded by media, there is less opportunity for the child to explore his or her world in such an imaginative fashion.[20]

Marketers frequently target parents looking for assistance in the task of socialising their children. To this end, marketers are sensitive to the fact that the socialisation of young children provides an opportunity to establish a foundation on which later experiences continue to build throughout life. These experiences are reinforced and modified as the child grows into adolescence, the teenage years and eventually into adulthood.

Consumer socialisation of children

The aspect of childhood socialisation that is particularly relevant to the study of consumer behaviour is **consumer socialisation**, which is defined as the process by which children acquire the skills, knowledge, attitudes and experiences necessary to function as consumers. A variety of studies have focused on how children develop consumption skills. Many pre-adolescent children acquire their consumer behaviour norms through observation of their parents and older siblings, who function as role models and sources of cues for basic consumption learning. In contrast, adolescents and teenagers are likely to look to their friends for models of acceptable consumption behaviour.[21] Other research has shown that younger children generally also react positively to advertisements employing a spokesperson who seems to fulfil a parental role, whereas teens often like products for the simple reason that their parents disapprove of them.[22]

Shared shopping experiences (i.e. co-shopping, when mother and child shop together) also give children the opportunity to acquire in-store shopping skills. Possibly because of their more harried lifestyles, working mothers are more likely to undertake co-shopping with their children than are non-working mothers. Co-shopping is a way of spending time with one's children while at the same time accomplishing a necessary task.

Consumer socialisation also serves as a tool by which parents influence other aspects of the socialisation process. For instance, parents frequently use the promise or reward of material goods as a device to modify or control a child's behaviour. A mother may reward her child with a gift when the child does something to please her, or she may withhold or remove it when the child disobeys. Research conducted by one of the authors supports this behaviour-controlling function. Specifically, adolescents reported that their parents frequently used the promise of chocolate sweets as a means of controlling their behaviour (such as getting them to complete homework or to clean their rooms).

There is research evidence to suggest that a child's age and sex, family size, social class and race are important factors in the consumer socialisation process. For example, parents have been found to be more active in the consumer socialisation of their daughters than their sons (e.g. parents co-shop more often with their daughters). Still further, wealthier parents appear to engage in more deliberate consumer training than those in lower socio-economic groups (e.g. co-shopping, talking about how buying decisions are made).[23]

Adult consumer socialisation

The socialisation process is not confined to childhood; rather, it is an ongoing process. It is now accepted that socialisation begins in early childhood and extends throughout a person's entire life. For example, when a newly married couple establishes their own household, their adjustment to living and consuming together is part of this continuing process. Similarly, the adjustment of a retired German couple who decide to move to Spain or Portugal is also part of the ongoing socialisation process. Even a family that is welcoming a pet into their home as a new family member must face the challenge of socialising the pet so that it fits into the family environment. Recent survey research reveals that pet owners commonly treat their pets as fully fledged family members. For instance, 58 per cent of those surveyed indicated that they have sent or received a holiday postcard from their dog or cat; and 78 per cent regularly talk in a different voice to their pets.[24]

Intergenerational socialisation

It appears that it is quite common for certain product loyalties or brand preferences to be transferred from one generation to another – intergenerational brand transfer – for perhaps even three or four generations within the same family. For instance, specific brand preferences for products such as peanut butter, mayonnaise, ketchup, coffee and canned soup are all product categories that are frequently passed on from one generation to another.

Figure 11-5 presents a simple model of the socialisation process that focuses on the socialisation of young children but that can be extended to family members of all ages. Note that the arrows run both ways between the young person and other family members and between the young person and his or her friends. This two-directional arrow signifies that socialisation is really a two-way street, in which the young person both is socialised and influences those who are doing the socialising. Supporting this view is the reality that children of all ages often influence the opinions and behaviour of their parents. As an example, recent research with school-aged children has found that parental warmth relates positively to:

1. the extent to which a child's interest in the Internet serves as a catalyst for increased parental Internet interest,
2. how much the child teaches a parent about the Internet, and
3. whether the child acts as the parent's Internet broker (e.g. the child shops for the parent on the Internet).[25]

Because children are often more comfortable than their parents with digital and electronic media, they are often the ones in the family who do the teaching. Another research study examined the influence of family on consumer innovativeness, and found that the perceptions of adult children regarding their parent's innovativeness influences their own innovativeness.[26]

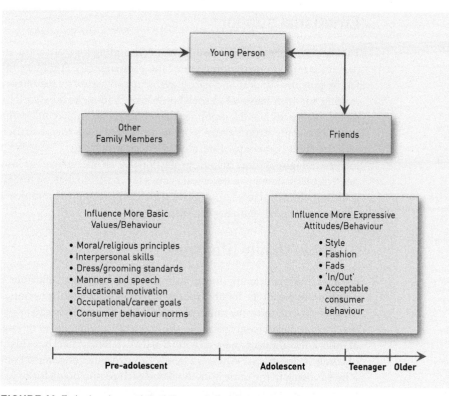

FIGURE 11-5 A simple model of the socialisation approach

OTHER FUNCTIONS OF THE FAMILY

Three other basic functions provided by the family are particularly relevant to a discussion of consumer behaviour. These include economic well-being, emotional support and suitable family lifestyles.

Economic well-being

Although families in affluent nations are no longer formed primarily for economic security, providing financial means to its dependants is unquestionably a basic family function. How the family divides its responsibilities for providing economic well-being has changed considerably during the past thirty years. No longer are the traditional roles of husband as economic provider and wife as homemaker and child bearer valid. Instead, in industrial countries married women with children are to an ever increasing extent employed outside the home, and they and their husbands share household responsibilities.

The last two decades have witnessed a growth in women's contributions to family income, as more and more women, now university educated, have careers rather than just jobs. According to some sociologists, the net effects of this income growth were largely positive on family outcomes and did not result in a decrease in the importance of men's earnings. The positive effects included greater marital stability and greater marital equality.[27]

The economic role of children has also changed. Today, despite the fact that many teenage children work, they rarely assist the family financially. Instead, many teenagers are expected to pay for their own amusements; others contribute to the costs of their formal education and prepare themselves to be financially independent. It is of interest to note that a recent study found that when parents are involved in a student's acquisition of a credit card, credit card balances tend to be lower.[28]

Emotional support

The provision of emotional nourishment (including love, affection and intimacy) to its members is an important core function of the contemporary family. In fulfilling this function, the family provides support and encouragement and assists its members in coping with decision-making and with personal or social problems.[29] To make it easier for working parents to show their love, affection and support to their children, greetings card companies have been increasingly using computer programs to create cards for parents to give to their children (or vice versa).

If the family cannot provide adequate assistance when it is needed, it may turn to a counsellor, psychologist or other helping professional as an alternative. For instance, in some communities, educational and psychological centres are available that are designed to assist parents who want to help their children improve their learning and communication skills or generally to adjust to their environments in a better way.

Suitable family lifestyles

Another important family function in terms of consumer behaviour is the establishment of a suitable lifestyle for the family. Upbringing, experience and the personal and jointly held goals of the spouses determine the importance placed on education or career, on reading, television viewing, the learning of computer skills, the frequency and quality of dining out and on the selection of other entertainment and recreational activities. Researchers have identified a shift in the nature of family 'togetherness'. Whereas a family being together once meant doing things together, today it means being in the same household and each person doing his or her own thing.[30]

Family lifestyle commitments, including the allocation of time, are greatly influencing consumption patterns. For example, a series of diverse pressures on mothers has reduced the time that they have available for household chores and has created a market for convenience products and fast-food restaurants. Also, with both parents working, an increased emphasis is being placed on the notion of 'quality time' rather than on the 'quantity of time' spent with children and other family members.

FAMILY DECISION-MAKING AND CONSUMPTION-RELATED ROLES

Although many marketers recognise the family as the basic consumer decision-making unit, they most frequently examine the attitudes and behaviour of the one family member whom they believe to be the major decision maker. In some cases, they also examine the attitudes and behaviour of the person most likely to be the primary user of the product or service. For instance, in the case of men's underwear, which is frequently purchased by women for their husbands and unmarried sons, it is commonplace to seek the views of both the men who wear the underwear and the women who buy it. By considering both the likely user and the likely purchaser, the marketer obtains a richer picture of the consumption process.

Key family consumption roles

For a family to function as a cohesive unit, tasks such as doing the washing, preparing meals, setting the dinner table, taking out the rubbish and walking the dog must be carried out by one or more family members. In a dynamic society, family-related duties are constantly changing (such as the greater performance of household tasks by men). However, we can identify eight distinct roles in the family decision-making process, as presented in Table 11-3. A look at these roles provides further insight into how family members interact in their various consumption-related roles.

TABLE 11-3 The eight roles in the family decision-making process

ROLE	DESCRIPTION
Influencers	Family member(s) who provide information to other members about a product or service
Gatekeepers	Family member(s) who control the flow of information about a product or service into the family
Deciders	Family member(s) with the power to determine unilaterally or jointly whether to shop for, purchase, use, consume, or dispose of a specific product or service
Buyers	Family member(s) who make the actual purchase of a particular product or service
Preparers	Family member(s) who transform the product into a form suitable for consumption by other family members
Users	Family member(s) who use or consume a particular product or service
Maintainers	Family member(s) who service or repair the product so that it will provide continued satisfaction
Disposers	Family member(s) who initiate or carry out the disposal or discontinuation of a particular product or service

The number and identity of the family members who fill these roles vary from family to family and from product to product. In some cases, a single family member will independently assume a number of roles; in other cases, a single role will be performed jointly by two or more family members. In still other cases, one or more of these basic roles may not be required. For example, a family member may be walking down the snack food aisle at a local supermarket when he picks out an interesting new chocolate bar. His selection does not directly involve the influence of other family members. He is the *decider*, the *buyer* and, in a sense, the *gatekeeper*; however, he may or may not be the sole consumer (or user). Products may be consumed by a single family member (deodorant, razor), consumed or used directly by two or more family members (orange juice, shampoo), or consumed indirectly by the entire family (central air conditioning, high-definition television set or art glass collection).

Dynamics of husband–wife decision-making

Marketers are interested in the relative amount of influence that a husband and a wife have when it comes to family consumption choices. Most husband–wife influence studies classify family consumption **decisions** as husband dominated, wife dominated, **joint** (either equal or syncratic) and **autonomic** (either solitary or unilateral).[31]

The relative influence of a husband and wife on a particular consumer decision depends in part on the product and service category. For instance, during the 1950s, the purchase of a new car was strongly husband dominated, whereas food and financial banking decisions more often were wife dominated. Forty years later, the purchase of the family's principal car is still often husband dominated in many households. However, in other contexts or situations (such as a second car or a car for a single or working woman), female car buyers are a rapidly expanding segment of the car market, a segment to which many car manufacturers are currently paying separate marketing attention. Also, in the case of financial decision-making, there has been a general trend over the past decade to have the female head of household make financial decisions.[32]

The expanding role of children in family decision-making

Over the past several decades, there has been a trend towards children playing a more active role in what the family buys, as well as in the family decision-making process. This shift in influence has occurred as a result of families having fewer children (which increases the influence of each child), more dual-income couples who can afford to permit their children to make a greater number of the choices and the encouragement by the media to allow children to 'express

TABLE 11-4 Tactics used by children to influence their parents

Pressure tactics	The child makes demands, uses threats, or intimidation to persuade you to comply with his/her request
Upward appeal	The child seeks to persuade you, saying that the request was approved or supported by an older member of the family, a teacher, or even a family friend
Exchange tactics	The child makes an explicit or implicit promise to give you some sort of service such as washing the car, cleaning the house, or taking care of the baby, in return for a favor
Coalition tactics	The child seeks the aid of others to persuade you to comply with his/her request or uses the support of others as an argument for you to agree with him/her
Ingratiating tactics	The child seeks to get you in a good mood or think favorably of him or her before asking you to comply with a request
Rational persuasion	The child uses logical arguments and factual evidence to persuade you to agree with his/her request
Inspirational appeals	The child makes an emotional appeal or proposal that arouses enthusiasm by appealing to your values and ideals
Consultation tactics	The child seeks your involvement in making a decision

Source: Adapted from 'Tactics Used by Children to Influence Their Parents', Joyantha S. Wimalasir, *Journal of Consumer Marketing* (2004, Vol. 21, No. 4). © MCB UP Limited. http://www.emeraldinsight.com/msq.htm.

themselves'. Still further, single-parent households often push their children towards household participation and self-reliance. As one example of children's influence, children accompanying a parent to a supermarket make an average of 15 requests, of which about half are typically granted.[33] Table 11-4 enumerates some of the tactics employed by children to influence their parents, and Table 11-5 presents the amount of influence children perceive they have with respect to their family's purchasing of a variety of items. As Table 11-5 indicates, children's influence was claimed to be higher when the purchase was for themselves, although many claimed to be influential in the purchase of 'family products', such as meals, holidays and cars.

Still other research reveals that children have considerable influence on family decision-making with respect to eating. The research found that about 17 per cent of the 9- to 12-year-old children studied considered themselves to be the main decision maker with respect to the

TABLE 11-5 Items the purchase of which children perceive themselves to have influenced

	%
Casual clothes for me	91
Trainers for me	88
CDs for me	84
Sweets for me	83
Computers for me	83
Soft drinks for me	80
School shoes for me	80
A family trip to the cinema	73
Food for me for lunch at the weekend	73
A holiday I would go on with the family	63
Going out for a family meal	52
A family car	37

Source: Adapted from Julie Tinson and Clive Nancarrow, *International Journal of Market Research*, 47, 1, 2005, 22.

TABLE 11-6 Who makes the decision to go to a restaurant? Children's perceptions by family type

	CHILD	FATHER	MOTHER	TOTAL
Traditional	12.0	52.0	36.0	100% 75.8
Nontraditional	25.0	12.5	62.5	100% 24.2
Total	15.2	42.4	42.4	100% 100%

Source: Reprinted from the *Journal of Business Research*, 54, JoAnne Labrecque and Line Ricard, 'Children's Influence on Family Decision Making: A Restaurant Study', p. 175, © November 2001, with permission from Elsevier.

decision to go to a restaurant, whereas 40 per cent thought of themselves as the main decision maker with respect to the choice of restaurants.[34] Interestingly, some 30 per cent of the parents of these children felt that their offspring were the main decision makers in deciding to eat out, and almost an equal number, 29 per cent, felt that the child (or children) was also the main decision maker with regard to which restaurant was patronised. Additionally, in traditional families, children most often felt that it was the father who made the decision to go to a restaurant, whereas in nontraditional families it was most often the mother (see Table 11-6). The results also reveal that a child was twice as likely to make the decision to go to a restaurant in nontraditional households as in a traditional household.

There is also research evidence supporting the notion that the extent to which children influence a family's purchases is related to family communication patterns. As might be expected, children's influence has been found to be highest in families where the parents are pluralistic parents (i.e. parents who encourage children to speak up and express their individual preferences on purchases) and consensual parents (i.e. parents who encourage children to seek harmony, but are nevertheless open to the children's viewpoint on purchases), because such parents allow their children a significantly greater amount of influence than do protective parents (i.e. parents who believe that children should not stress their own preferences, but rather go along with the parents judgement on what is to be purchased).[35]

Still further, there is research that has explored the concept of the teen Internet maven – teenagers who spend considerable time on the Internet and know how to search for and find information, and respond to requests from others to provide information. It has been shown that teen Internet mavens contribute significantly to the family's decision-making.[36] Specifically, they perceive themselves to be more influential in researching and evaluating family purchases; indeed, their parents tend to concur that they are more influential with regard to family decision-making.

Finally, advertisers have long recognised the importance of children's 'pester power', and therefore encourage children to 'pester' their parents to purchase what they see in advertisements. A recent study of the strategies children use to influence their parents' food-purchasing decisions began with the proposed framework that there are four types of influence – individual differences, interpersonal influences, environmental influences and societal influences – that children employ to influence their parents so that food-purchase decisions reflect their choices or preferences. This framework is depicted in Figure 11-6. This research goes on to reveal that ten-year-old French Canadian children (living in Montreal) considered it important to eat foods similar to those eaten by others, to eat in front of the television, to suggest that the family eat foods advertised on television, and to develop strategies to influence parental food-purchasing decisions. Still further, it was more important for boys than for girls to select foods eaten by others, and boys were more likely to eat in front of the television and to eat in their bedrooms. The strategies used by children to influence their parents' food-purchasing decisions included such persuasive strategies as stating their preferences or begging; and emotional strategies, such as asking repetitively for a product

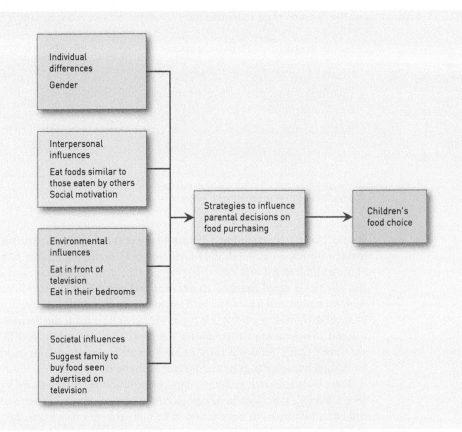

FIGURE 11-6 Conceptual framework related to factors explaining the development of strategies by ten-year-old children to influence parental decisions on food purchasing

Source: Adapted from M. Marie Marquis, 'Strategies for Influencing Parental Decisions on Food Purchasing', *Journal of Consumer Marketing*, 21, 2, 2004, 135.

(in a way that irritates the parents).[37] An additional point must be made about children and television viewing – networks today try to promote the branding process because it can change a child from a viewer into a consumer likely to purchase the advertised product.

THE FAMILY LIFE CYCLE

Sociologists and consumer researchers have long been attracted to the concept of the **family life cycle (FLC)** as a means of depicting what was once a rather steady and predictable series of stages through which most families progressed. However, with the advent of many diverse family and lifestyle arrangements, what was the rule has been on the decline. This decline in the percentage of families that progress through a traditional FLC (to be explored shortly) seems to be caused by a host of societal factors, including an increasing divorce rate, the explosive number of births outside marriage and the forty-year decline in the number of extended families that transpired as many young families moved to advance their job and career opportunities.

The notion of the FLC remains a useful marketing tool when one keeps in mind that there are family and lifestyle arrangements that are not fully accounted for by the traditional representation. FLC analysis enables marketers to segment families in terms of a series of stages spanning the life course of a family unit. The FLC is a composite variable created by systematically combining such commonly used demographic variables as marital status, size of family, age of family members (focusing on the age of the oldest or youngest child) and employment status of the head of household. The ages of the parents and the relative amount of disposable income are usually inferred from the stage in the family life cycle. To reflect the current realities of a wide range of family and lifestyle arrangements, our treatment of the FLC concept is divided into two sections. The first section considers the traditional FLC schema. This model is increasingly being challenged because it fails to account for various important family living arrangements. To rectify these limitations, the second section focuses on alternative FLC stages, including increasingly important nontraditional family structures.

Traditional family life cycle

The **traditional family life cycle** is a progression of stages through which many families pass, starting with bachelorhood, moving on to marriage (and the creation of the basic family unit), then to family growth (with the birth of children), to family contraction (as grown children leave the household) and ending with the dissolution of the basic unit (due to the death of one spouse). Although different researchers have expressed various preferences in terms of the number of FLC stages, the traditional FLC models proposed over the years can be synthesised into just five basic stages, as follows:

- Stage I: *Bachelorhood* – young single adult living apart from parents
- Stage II: *Honeymooners* – young married couple
- Stage III: *Parenthood* – married couple with at least one child living at home
- Stage IV: *Post-parenthood* – an older married couple with no children living at home
- Stage V: *Dissolution* – one surviving spouse

The following discussion examines the five stages in detail and shows how they lend themselves to market segmentation strategies.

Stage I: Bachelorhood

The first FLC stage consists of young single men and women who have established households apart from their parents. Although most members of this FLC stage are fully employed, many are university students who have left their parents' homes. Young single adults are apt to spend their incomes on rent, basic home furnishings, the purchase and maintenance of cars, travel and entertainment and clothing and accessories. Members of the bachelorhood stage frequently have sufficient disposable income to indulge themselves. Marketers target singles for a wide variety of products and services.

In most large cities, there are travel agents, housing developments, health clubs, sports clubs and other service and product marketers that find this FLC stage a lucrative target niche. Meeting, dating and mating are prominent concerns of many young adults who typically are beginning their working lives after recently completing university or some other form of career or job training. It is relatively easy to reach this segment because many special-interest publications target singles.

Stage II: Honeymooners

The honeymoon stage starts immediately after the marriage vows are taken and generally continues until the arrival of the couple's first child. This FLC stage serves as a period of adjustment to married life. Because many young husbands and wives both work, these couples have available a combined income that often permits a lifestyle that provides them with the opportunities of more indulgent purchasing of possessions or allows them to save or invest their extra income.

Honeymooners have considerable start-up expenses when establishing a new home (major and minor appliances, bedroom and living room furniture, carpeting, curtains, crockery, and a host of utensils and accessory items). During this stage, the advice and experience of other married couples is likely to be important to newly-weds. Also important as sources of new product information are the so-called shelter magazines (e.g. magazines that specialise in one specific topic of interest, like furnishing or gardening).

Stage III: Parenthood

When a couple has its first child, the honeymoon is considered over. The parenthood stage (sometimes called the full-nest stage) usually extends over more than twenty years. Because of its long duration, this stage can be divided into shorter phases, like the pre-school phase that occurs early at this stage and the university phase that occurs at the end of this FLC stage. Throughout several parenthood phases, the interrelationships of family members and the structure of the family gradually change. Furthermore, the financial resources of the family change significantly, as one (or both) parents progress in a career and as child-rearing and educational responsibilities gradually increase and finally decrease as children become self-supporting.

An increase in the number of births among baby boomers (born between 1946 and 1964) has resulted in a 'baby boomlet'. These parents are older, better educated, more affluent and more socially aware than previous generations. Many feel that they are better parents to their children than their parents were to them. Their children often become the focus of their lives, and they spend money accordingly. They also are an important market for many investment and insurance services.

Stage IV: Post-parenthood

Because parenthood extends over many years, it is only natural to find that post-parenthood, when all the children have left home, is traumatic for some parents and liberating for others. This so-called empty-nest stage signifies for many parents almost a 'rebirth', a time for doing all the things they could not do while the children were at home and they had to worry about soaring educational expenses. For the mother, it may be a time to further her education, to enter or re-enter the job market, or to seek new interests. For the father, it is a time to indulge in new hobbies. For both, it is the time to travel, to entertain, perhaps to refurnish their home or to sell it in favour of a new property.

It is during this stage that married couples tend to be most comfortable financially. Today's empty-nesters have more leisure time. They travel more frequently, take extended holidays and are likely to purchase a second home in a warmer climate. They have higher disposable incomes because of savings and investments and they have fewer expenses (no mortgage or college tuition bills). They look forward to being involved grandparents. For this reason, families in the post-parenthood stage are an important market for luxury goods, new cars, expensive furniture and holidays to faraway places.

Many empty-nesters retire while they are still in good health. Retirement provides the opportunity to pursue new interests, to travel and to fulfil unsatisfied needs. Hotels, airlines and car-hire companies have responded to this market with discounts to consumers over 60; some airlines have established special travel clubs with unlimited mileage for a flat fee. Of course, for older retired couples who do not have adequate savings or income, retirement is far different and very restrictive.

Older consumers tend to use television as an important source of information and entertainment. They favour programmes that provide the opportunity to 'keep up with what's happening', especially news and documentaries. In addition, a number of special-interest magazines cater exclusively to this market. (Chapter 13 contains a more detailed discussion of the older consumer as a subcultural market segment.)

Stage V: Dissolution

Dissolution of the basic family unit occurs with the death of one spouse. When the surviving spouse is in good health, is working or has adequate savings and has supportive family and friends, the adjustment is easier. The surviving spouse (usually, the wife) often tends to follow a more economical lifestyle. Many surviving spouses seek others out for companionship; others enter into second (or third and even fourth) marriages.

Marketing and the Traditional FLC

Whereas the foregoing discussion of the traditional family-life-cycle concept indicated the types of products and services that a household or family might be most interested in at each stage, it is also possible to trace how the FLC concept impacts a single product or service over time. One interesting study employed an eight-stage FLC scheme to investigate how consumers choose a bank.[38] As part of the research, the 3,100 respondents were asked to rate the relative importance of 18 product/service characteristics that might impact their choice of a bank. The research reveals that location is very important to all respondents (i.e. it was always ranked either first or second), but other bank attributes tended to be much more important to some FLC segments than to others. For instance, 'fast service' was ranked fifth by bachelor stage individuals and twelfth or thirteenth by full-nest II, empty-nest I, and empty-nest II respondents.

Modifications – the nontraditional FLC

As already noted, the traditional FLC model has lost its ability fully to represent the progression of stages through which current family and lifestyle arrangements move. To compensate for these limitations, consumer researchers have been attempting to search out expanded FLC models that better reflect diversity of family and lifestyle arrangements.[39] Figure 11-7 presents an FLC model that depicts along the main horizontal row the stages of the traditional FLC and above and below the main horizontal row are selected alternative FLC stages that account for some important nontraditional family households that marketers are increasingly targeting. The underlying sociodemographic forces that drive this expanded FLC model include divorce and later marriages, with and without the presence of children. Although somewhat greater reality is provided by this modified FLC model, it recognises only families that started in marriage, ignoring such single-parent households as unmarried mothers and families formed because a single person or single persons adopt a child.

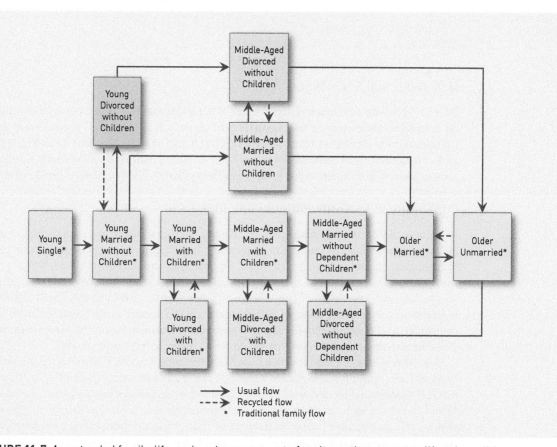

FIGURE 11-7 An extended family-life-cycle schema accounts for alternative consumer lifestyle realities

Source: Adapted from Patrick E. Murphy and William A. Staples, 'A Modern-Sized Family Life Cycle', *Journal of Consumer Research*, 6 June 1979, 17. Reprinted by permission of The University of Chicago Press as publisher. Copyright © 1979, JCR, Inc.

TABLE 11-7 Noteworthy nontraditional FLC stages

ALTERNATIVE FLC STAGES	DEFINITION/COMMENTARY
FAMILY HOUSEHOLDS	
Childless couples	It is increasingly acceptable for married couples to elect not to have children. Contributing forces are more career-oriented married women and delayed marriages.
Couples who marry later in life (in their late 30s or later)	More career-oriented men and women and greater occurrence of couples living together. Likely to have fewer or even no children.
Couples who have first child later in life (in their late 30s or later)	Likely to have fewer children. Stress quality lifestyle: 'Only the best is good enough.'
Single parents I	High divorce rates (about 50 per cent) contribute to a portion of single-parent households.
Single parents II	Young man or woman who has one or more children outside marriage.
Single parents III	A single person who adopts one or more children.
Extended family	Young single-adult children who return home to avoid the expenses of living alone while establishing their careers. Divorced daughter or son and grandchild(ren) return home to parents. Frail elderly parents who move in with children. Newly-weds living with in-laws.
NONFAMILY HOUSEHOLDS	
Unmarried couples	Increased acceptance of heterosexual and homosexual couples.
Divorced persons (no children)	High divorce rate contributes to dissolution of households before children are born.
Single persons (most are young)	Primarily a result of delaying first marriage; also, men and women who never marry.
Widowed persons (most are elderly)	Longer life expectancy, especially for women, means more over-75 single-person households.

Nontraditional FLC stages

Table 11-7 presents an extensive categorisation of nontraditional FLC stages that are derived from the dynamic sociodemographic forces operating during the past 25 years or so. These nontraditional stages include not only family households but also nonfamily households: those consisting of a single individual and those consisting of two or more unrelated individuals. At one time, nonfamily households were so uncommon that it was not really important whether they were considered or not.

Consumption in Nontraditional Families

When households undergo status changes (divorce, temporary retirement, a new person moving into the household or the death of a spouse), they often undergo spontaneous changes in consumption-related preferences and, thus, become attractive targets for many marketers. For example, divorce often requires that one (or both) former spouses find a new residence, get new telephones (with new telephone numbers), buy new furniture and perhaps find a job. These requirements mean that a divorced person might need to contact estate agents, call telephone companies, visit furniture shops and possibly contact a personnel agency or career consultant. There are also the special needs of the children who are experiencing the divorce.

In another sphere, the substantial increase in dual-income households (in which both the husband and wife work) has also tended to muddy the lifestyle assumptions implicit in the traditional FLC. Most dual-income families have children (the majority of those children are between 11 and 20 years of age). The most affluent dual-income segment is, not surprisingly, the 'crowded nesters'. This dual-income couple, with an adult child living at home, has the advantage of an additional potential source of income to contribute to the general well-being of the household.

The parallel existence of traditional and nontraditional FLC stages is another example of our recurring observation that the contemporary marketplace is complex in its diversity, and it is a challenge to segment and serve.

SUMMARY

Almost all individuals regularly interact with other people who directly or indirectly influence their purchase decisions. Thus, the study of groups and their impact on the individual is of great importance to marketers concerned with influencing consumer behaviour.

Consumer reference groups are groups that serve as frames of reference for individuals in their purchase decisions. Examples of reference groups include (1) friendship groups, (2) shopping groups, (3) work groups, (4) virtual groups or communities, and (5) consumer-action groups. Reference groups that influence general values or behaviour are called normative reference groups; those that influence specific attitudes are called comparative reference groups. The concept of consumer reference groups has been broadened to include groups with which consumers have no direct face-to-face contact, such as celebrities, political figures and social classes.

The credibility, attractiveness and power of the reference group affect the degree of influence it has. Reference group appeals are used very effectively by some advertisers in promoting their goods and services because they subtly induce the prospective consumer to identify with the pictured user of the product.

The five types of reference group appeals most commonly used in marketing are celebrities, experts, the common man, the executive and employee spokesperson and the trade 'spokescharacter'. Celebrities are used to give testimonials or endorsements as actors or as company spokespeople. Experts may be recognised experts in the product category or actors playing the part of experts (such as a car mechanic). The common-man approach is designed to show that individuals who are just like the prospect are satisfied with the advertised product. Increasingly, firms are using their top executives as spokespeople because their appearance in company advertisements seems to imply that someone at the top is watching over the consumer's interest.

For many consumers their family is their primary reference group for many attitudes and behaviours. The family is the prime target market for most products and product categories. As the most basic membership group, families are defined as two or more persons related by blood, marriage or adoption who reside together. There are three types of families: married couples, nuclear families and extended families. Socialisation is a core function of the family. Other functions of the family are the provision of economic and emotional support and the pursuit of a suitable lifestyle for its members.

The members of a family assume specific roles in their everyday functioning; such roles or tasks extend to the realm of consumer purchase decisions. Key consumer-related roles of family members include influencers, gatekeepers, deciders, buyers, preparers, users, maintainers and disposers (see Table 11-3). A family's decision-making style is often influenced by its lifestyle, roles and cultural factors.

The majority of consumer studies classify family consumption decisions as husband dominated, wife dominated, joint or autonomic decisions. The extent and nature of husband–wife influence in family decisions depends, in part, on the specific product or service and selected cultural influences.

Classification of families by stage in the family life cycle (FLC) provides valuable insights into family consumption-related behaviour. The traditional FLC begins with bachelorhood, moves on to marriage, then to an expanding family, to a contracting family and to an end with the death of a spouse. Dynamic sociodemographic changes in society have resulted in many nontraditional stages that a family or nonfamily household might pass through (such as childless couples, couples marrying later in life, single parents, unmarried couples or single-person households). These nontraditional stages are becoming increasingly important to marketers in terms of specific market niches.

DISCUSSION QUESTIONS

1. As a marketing consultant, you have been asked to evaluate a new promotional campaign for a large retail chain. The campaign strategy is aimed at increasing group shopping. What recommendations would you make?

2. Many celebrities who are considered to be persuasive role models often appear in television beer commercials. Does the use of such celebrities in beer advertising constitute an unethical marketing practice? Discuss.

3. You are the marketing vice president of a large soft-drink company. Your company's advertising agency is in the process of negotiating a contract to employ a superstar female singer to promote your product. Discuss the reference group factors that you would raise before the celebrity is hired.

4. How does the family influence the consumer socialisation of children? What role does television advertising play in consumer socialisation?

5. As a marketing consultant, you were retained by the Walt Disney Company to design a study investigating how families make holiday decisions. Who, within the family, would you interview? What kind of questions would you ask? How would you assess the relative power of each family member in making holiday-related decisions?

6. Which of the five stages of the traditional family life cycle constitute the most lucrative segment(s) for the following products and services: (a) newspaper subscription, (b) a cruise holiday, (c) takeaway pizza, (d) high-definition television, (e) unit trusts and (f) Harley-Davidson motor bikes? Explain your answers.

7. As the marketing manager of a high-quality, fairly expensive line of frozen dinners, how would you use the nonfamily household information listed in Table 11-7 to segment the market and position your product?

EXERCISES

1. Prepare a list of formal and informal groups to which you belong and give examples of purchases for which each served as a reference group. In which of the groups you listed is the pressure to conform the greatest? Why?

2. With a pen and paper, spend an hour watching a network television channel during prime time. Record the total number of commercials that were shown. For each commercial using a celebrity endorser, record the celebrity's name, the product or service advertised and whether the celebrity was used in a testimonial, as an endorser, as an actor or as a spokesperson.

3. Think of a recent major purchase your family has made. Analyse the roles performed by the various family members in terms of the following consumption roles: influencers, gatekeepers, deciders, buyers, preparers, users, maintainers and disposers (Table 11-3).

4. Select three product categories and compare the brands you prefer to those your parents prefer. To what extent are the preferences similar? Discuss the similarities in the context of consumer socialisation.

5. Identify one traditional family and one nontraditional family (or household) featured in a television sitcom or series. (The two families/households can be featured in the same or in different television shows.) Classify the traditional group into one stage of the traditional FLC. Classify the nontraditional group into one of the categories described in Table 11-7. Select two characters of the same gender and approximate age, one from each group, and compare their consumption behaviour (for items such as clothes and furniture, or stated or implied attitudes towards spending money).

NOTES

1. Pamela Kicker and Cathy L. Hartman, 'Purchase Pal Use: Why Buyers Choose to Shop with Others', in *1993 AMA Winter Educators' Proceedings*, 4, eds Rajan Varadarajan and Bernard Jaworski (Chicago: American Marketing Association, 1993), 378–84.

2. Eve M. Kahn and Julie Lasky, 'Out of the Pantry and Partying On', *New York Times*, 8 November 2001, F9.

3. Amitai Etzioni, 'E-Communities Build New Ties, But Ties That Bind', *New York Times*, 10 February 2000, G7.

4. Cara Okleshen and Sanford Grossbart, 'Usenet Groups, Virtual Community and Consumer Behavior', in *Advances in Consumer Research*, 25, eds Joseph W. Alba and J. Wesley Hutchinson (Provo, UT: Association for Consumer Research, 1998), 276–82.

5. Birud Sindhav, 'A Sociological Perspective on Web-Related Consumer Marketing', in *1999 AMA Educators' Proceedings*, 10, eds Stephen P. Brown and D. Sudharshan (Chicago: American Marketing Association, 1999), 226–7.

6. Eileen Fischer, Julia Bristor and Brenda Gainer, 'Creating or Escaping Community? An Exploratory Study of Internet Consumers' Behaviors', *Advances in Consumer Research*, 23, eds Kim P. Corfman and John F. Lynch, Jr. (Provo, UT: Association for Consumer Research, 1996), 178–82; Siok Kuan Tambyah, 'Life on the Net: The Reconstruction of Self and Community', *Advances in Consumer Research*, 23, eds Corfman and Lynch, 172–7.

7. Is the Net Redefining Our Identity?', *Business Week*, 12 May 1997, 100–101.

8. Kendra Nordin, *Christian Science Monitor*, 26 February 2001, 16.

9. Albert M. Muniz, Jr. and Thomas C. O'Guinn, 'Brand Community', *Journal of Consumer Research*, 27, March 2001, 412–32.

10. For example, see Robert V. Kozinets and Jay M. Handelman, 'Adversaries of Consumption: Consumer Movements, Activism, and Ideology', *Journal of Consumer Research*, 31, December 2004, 691–704; and Jill Gabrielle Klein, N. Craig Smith and Andrew John, 'Why We Boycott: Consumer Motivations for Boycott Participation', *Journal of Marketing*, 68, July 2004, 92–109.

11. B. Zafer Erdogan, Michael J. Baker and Stephen Tagg, 'Selecting Celebrity Endorsers: The Practitioner's Perspective', *Journal of Advertising Research*, May–June 2001, 39–48.

12. Lynette Knowles Mathur, Ike Mathur and Nanda Rangan, 'The Wealth Effects Associated with a Celebrity Endorser: The Michael Jordan Phenomenon', *Journal of Advertising Research*, 37, 3, May–June 1997, 25; and Jeff Manning, 'Jordan, Nike Linked Until 2023', *The Oregonian*, 14 January 1999, D1.

13. Roobina Ohanian, 'The Impact of Celebrity Spokespersons: Perceived Image on Consumers' Intention to Purchase', *Journal of Advertising Research*, February–March, 1991, 46–54.

14. Carolyn Tripp, Thomas D. Jensen and Les Carlson, 'The Effects of Multiple Product Endorsements by Celebrities on Consumers' Attitudes and Intentions', *Journal of Consumer Research*, 20, March 1994, 535–47; and David C. Bojanic, Patricia K. Voli and James B. Hunt, 'Can Consumers Match Celebrity Endorsers with Products?' in *Developments in Marketing Science*, ed. Robert L. King (Richmond, VA: Academy of Marketing Science, 1991), 303–7.

15. Alan J. Bush, Craig A. Martin and Victoria D. Bush, 'Sports Celebrity Influence on the Behavioral Intentions of Generation Y', *Journal of Advertising Research*, March 2004, 108–18.

16. 'Study Identifies Qualities of Effective Public Health Service Announcements', *Marketing News*, April 1981, 7.

17. Margaret F. Callcott and Wei-Na Lee, 'Establishing the Spokes-Character in Academic Inquiry: Historical Overview and Framework for Definition', in *Advances in Consumer Research*, 22, eds Frank R. Kardes and Mita Sujan (Provo, UT: Association for Consumer Research, 1995), 144–51.

18. Terry L. Childers and Akshay R. Rao, 'The Influence of Familial and Peer-Based Reference Groups on Consumer Decisions', *Journal of Consumer Research*, 19, September 1992, 198–211.

19. Elke Zeijl, Yolanda te Poel, Manuela du Bois-Reymond, Janita Ravesloot and Jacqueline J. Meulman, 'The Role of Parents and Peers in the Leisure Activities of Young Adolescents', *Journal of Leisure Research*, 32, 3, 2000, 281–302.

20. Pamela Kruger, 'Why Johnny Can't Play', *Fast Company*, August 2000, 271–2.
21. Deborah Roedder John, 'Consumer Socialization of Children: A Retrospective Look at Twenty-Five Years of Research', *Journal of Consumer Research*, 26, December 1999, 183–213.
22. Amy Rummel, John Howard, Jennifer M. Swinton and D. Bradley Seymour, 'You Can't Have That! A Study of Reactance Effects and Children's Consumer Behavior', *Journal of Marketing Theory and Practice*, Winter 2000, 38–45.
23. Sabrina Neeley, 'Influences on Consumer Socialization', *Young Consumers*, Quarter 1, 2005, 63–9.
24. John Fetto, '"Woof Woof" Means, "I Love You"', *American Demographics*, February 2002, 11.
25. Sanford Grossbart, Stephanie McConnell Hughes, Cara Okleshen, Stephanie Nelson, Les Carlson, Russell N. Laczniak and Darrel Muehling, 'Parents, Children, and the Internet: Socialization Perspectives', in *2001 AMA Winter Educators' Conference*, 12, eds Ram Krishnan and Madhu Viswanathan (Chicago: American Marketing Association, 2001), 379–85.
26. June Cotte and Stacy L. Wood, 'Families and Innovative Consumer Behavior: A Triadic Analysis of Sibling and Parental Influence', *Journal of Consumer Research*, 31, June 2004, 78–86.
27. Lynn White and Stacy J. Rogers, 'Economic Circumstances and Family Outcomes: A Review of the 1990s', *Journal of Marriage and the Family*, 62, November 2000, 1035–51.
28. Todd Starr Palmer, Mary Beth Pinto and Diane H. Parente, 'College Students' Credit Card Debt and the Role of Parental Involvement: Implications for Public Policy', *Journal of Public Policy and Marketing*, 20 (1), Spring 2001, 105–13.
29. Jonghee Park, Patriya Tanshuhaj, Eric R. Spangenberg and Jim McCullough, 'An Emotion-Based Perspective of Family Purchase Decisions', in *Advances in Consumer Research*, 22, eds Kardes and Sujan, 723–8.
30. Leah Haran, 'Families Together Differently Today', *Advertising Age*, 23 October 1995, 1, 12.
31. Kim P. Corfman, 'Perceptions of Relative Influence: Formation and Measurement', *Journal of Marketing Research*, 28, May 1991, 125–36. Also, for additional articles on family decision-making roles and structures, see Christina Kwai-Choi and Roger Marshall, 'Who Do We Ask and When: A Pilot Study About Research in Family Decision Making', in *Developments in Marketing Science*, 16, eds Michael Levy and Dhruv Grewal (Coral Gables, FL: Academy of Marketing Science, 1993), 30–35.
32. Joan Raymond, 'For Richer and for Poorer', *American Demographics*, July 2000, 58–64.
33. Joyantha S. Wimalasiri, 'A Cross-National Study on Children's Purchasing Behavior and Parental Response', *Journal of Consumer Marketing*, 21, 4, 2004, 274–84; Michael J. Dotson and Eva M. Hyatt, 'Major Influence Factors in Children's Consumer Socialization', *Journal of Consumer Marketing*, 22, 1, 2005, 35–42; Aviv Shoham, 'He Said, She Said . . . They Said: Parents' and Children's Assessment of Children's Influence on Family Consumption Decisions', *Journal of Consumer Marketing*, 22, 3, 2005, 152–60; and L. A. Flurry and Alvin C. Burns, 'Children's Influence in Purchase Decisions: A Social Power Theory Approach', *Journal of Business Research*, 58, May 2005, 593–601.
34. J. Labrecque and L. Ricard, 'Children's Influence on Family Decision-Making: A Restaurant Study', *Journal of Business Research*, 54, November 2001, 173–6.
35. Avis Shoham, Gregory M. Rose and Aysen Bakir, 'The Effect of Family Communication Patterns on Mothers' and Fathers' Perceived Influence in Family Decision Making', *Advances in Consumer Behavior*, 31, 2004, 692.
36. Michael A. Belch, Kathleen A. Krentler and Laura A. Willis-Flurry, 'Teen Internet Mavens: Influence in Family Decision Making', *Journal of Business Research*, 58, May 2005, 569–75.
37. N. Marie Marquis, 'Strategies for Influencing Parental Decisions on Food Purchasing', *Journal of Consumer Marketing*, 21, 2, 2004, 134–43.
38. Rajshekhar G. Javalgi and Paul Dion, 'A Life Cycle Segmentation Approach to Marketing Financial Products and Services', *Services Industries Journal*, 19, 3, July 1999, 74–96.
39. Charles M. Schaninger and William D. Danko, 'A Conceptual and Empirical Comparison of Alternative Household Life Cycle Models', *Journal of Consumer Research*, 19, March 1993, 580–94.

CHAPTER 12
SOCIAL CLASS AND CONSUMER BEHAVIOUR

Some form of class structure or social stratification has existed in all societies through-out the history of human existence. In contemporary societies, an indication that social classes exist is the common reality that people who are better educated or have more prestigious occupations such as doctors and lawyers often are more highly valued than those who are lorry drivers and farm labourers. This is so, even though all four occupations are necessary for a society's well-being. Moreover, as will be discussed later, a wide range of differences in values, attitudes and behaviour exists among members of different social classes.

The major topics that will be explored in this chapter are a definition of social class and how it is measured, lifestyle profiles of the social classes, social-class mobility, the affluent and non-affluent consumer, the arrival of the 'techno-class' and how attitudes and behaviour linked to social class influence consumer behaviour.

WHAT IS SOCIAL CLASS?

Although **social class** can be thought of as a continuum – a range of social positions on which each member of society can be placed – researchers have preferred to divide the continuum into a small number of specific social classes or strata. Within this framework, the concept of social class is used to assign individuals or families to a social-class category. Consistent with this practice, social class is defined as the division of members of a society into a hierarchy of distinct status classes, so that members of each class have relatively the same status and members of all other classes have either more or less status.

To appreciate more fully the complexity of social class, we will briefly consider several underlying concepts pertinent to this definition.

Social class and social status

Researchers often measure social class in terms of **social status**; that is, they define each social class by the amount of status the members of that class have in comparison with members of other social classes. In social-class research (sometimes called social stratification), status is frequently thought of as the relative rankings of members of each social class in terms of specific status factors. For example, relative wealth (amount of economic assets), power (the degree of personal choice or influence over others) and prestige (the degree of recognition received from others) are three status factors frequently used when estimating social class.

To secure an understanding of how status operates within the minds of consumers, researchers have explored the idea of social comparison theory. According to this social-psychological concept, individuals quite normally compare their own material possessions with those owned by others in order to determine their relative social standing. This is especially important in a marketing society where status is often associated with consumers' purchasing power (or how much can be purchased). Simply stated, individuals with more purchasing power or a greater ability to make purchases have more status. Those who have more restrictions on what they can or cannot buy have less status. Because visible or conspicuous possessions are easy to spot, they especially serve as markers or indicators of one's own status and the status of others. Not surprisingly, recent research confirmed that a key ingredient of status is a consumer's possessions compared with others' similar possessions (possibly one's home versus another person's home).[1] In making such a comparison, an individual consumer might decide to compare himself with someone who is worse off (i.e. a downward comparison) in order to bolster his self-esteem; or alternatively a consumer might elect to compare upwards with another consumer 'with more' or some idealised media image (e.g. a beautiful home in a magazine advertisement), which is likely to make the consumer feel somewhat inferior.

The dynamics of status consumption

A related concept is *status consumption* – the process by which consumers endeavour to increase their social standing through conspicuous consumption or possessions.[2] A number of research studies have validated the status consumption scale presented in Table 12-1. As the market for luxury or status products continues to grow, there is an even greater need for marketers to identify and understand which consumers especially seek out such status-enhancing possessions, as well as the relationship between status consumption and social class.[3]

It is important to mention that a recent study in Australia examined the two interrelated concepts of status consumption and conspicuous consumption with respect to fashion clothing and sunglasses (both products that are visible or conspicuous to others and capable of providing the possessor with 'status'). The research found that status consumption (i.e. the degree to which a consumer is likely to consume for status) and conspicuous consumption (i.e. the extent to which a consumer is to consume conspicuously) are different consumer measures, yet they

TABLE 12-1 A five-question status consumption scale[a]

1. I would buy a product just because it has status.
2. I am interested in new products with status.
3. I would pay more for a product if it had status.
4. The status of a product is irrelevant to me (negatively worded).
5. A product is more valuable to me if it has some snob appeal.

[a] Each of the five items is measured on a 7-point Likert (agree–disagree) scale.
Source: Adapted from Jacqueline K. Eastman, Ronald E. Goldsmith and Leisa Reinecke Flynn, 'Status Consumption in Consumer Behavior: Scale Development and Validation', *Journal of Marketing Theory and Practice*, Summer 1999, 44. Used by permission of M. E. Sharpe, Inc.

are related in that they are both affected by interpersonal or word-of-mouth communication. The research also revealed that females were more prone than males to consume conspicuously; whereas only status consumption was affected by self-monitoring (i.e. the tendency for consumers to use products as 'props').[4]

Although *social comparison theory* and its related activity of status consumption have the potential of being very enlightening about status and how it operates, consumer and marketing researchers most often approach the actual study of status in terms of one or more of the following convenient demographic (more precisely socio-economic) variables: family income, occupational status and educational attainment. These socio-economic variables, as expressions of status, are used by marketing practitioners on a daily basis to measure social class.

Social class is hierarchical and a natural form of segmentation

Social-class categories are usually ranked in a hierarchy, ranging from low to high status. Thus, members of a specific social class perceive members of other social classes as having either more or less status than they do. To many people, therefore, social-class categories suggest that others are either equal to them (about the same social class), superior to them (higher social class) or inferior to them (lower social class).

Within this context, social-class membership serves consumers as a frame of reference (or a reference group) for the development of their attitudes and behaviour. In the context of reference groups, members of a specific social class may be expected to turn most often to other members of the same class for cues (or clues) regarding appropriate behaviour. In other cases, members of a particular social class, for example the lower class, may aspire to advance their social-class standing by emulating the behaviour of members of the middle class. To accomplish this goal, they might read middle-class magazines, do 'middle-class things' (such as visit museums and advance their education), and patronise middle-class restaurants so that they can observe middle-class behaviour.[5]

The hierarchical aspect of social class is important to marketers. Consumers may purchase certain products because these products are favoured by members of either their own or a higher social class (e.g. a high-priced Swiss wristwatch), and consumers may avoid other products because they perceive the products to be 'lower-class' products (e.g. a 'no-name' brand of shoes). Thus, the various social-class strata provide a natural basis for market segmentation for many products and services. In many instances, consumer researchers have been able to relate aspects of product usage to social-class membership. For example, when it comes to the consumption of instant coffee throughout Europe, it appears that for German consumers instant coffee tends to be a particularly upmarket or upscale product; and in contrast, for French consumers instant coffee is a particularly downmarket or downscale product.[6]

The classification of society's members into a small number of social classes has also enabled researchers to note the existence of shared values, attitudes and behavioural patterns among members within each social class and differing values, attitudes and behaviour between social

TABLE 12-2 Variations in the number and types of social-class categories

TWO-CATEGORY SOCIAL-CLASS SCHEMA
- *Blue collar, white collar*
- *Lower, upper*
- *Lower, middle*

THREE-CATEGORY SOCIAL-CLASS SCHEMA
- *Blue collar, grey collar, white collar*
- *Lower, middle, upper*

FOUR-CATEGORY SOCIAL-CLASS SCHEMA
- *Lower, lower-middle, upper-middle, upper*

FIVE-CATEGORY SOCIAL-CLASS SCHEMA
- *Lower, working class, lower-middle, upper-middle, upper*
- *Lower, lower-middle, middle, upper-middle, upper*

SIX-CATEGORY SOCIAL-CLASS SCHEMA
- *Lower-lower, upper-lower, lower-middle, upper-middle, lower-upper, upper-upper*

SEVEN-CATEGORY SOCIAL-CLASS SCHEMA
- *Real lower-lower, a lower group of people but not the lowest, working class, middle class, upper-middle, lower-upper, upper-upper*

NINE-CATEGORY SOCIAL-CLASS SCHEMA
- *Lower-lower, middle-lower, upper-lower, lower-middle, middle-middle, upper-middle, lower-upper, middle-upper, upper-upper*

classes. Consumer researchers have been able to relate social-class standing to consumer attitudes concerning specific products and to examine social-class influences on the actual consumption of products.

Social-class categories

Little agreement exists among sociologists on how many distinct class divisions are necessary to describe adequately the class structures of different countries. Most early studies divided the members of specific communities into five or six social-class groups. However, other researchers have found nine-, four-, three-, and even two-class schemata suitable for their purposes. The choice of how many separate classes to use depends on the amount of detail that the researcher believes is necessary to explain adequately the attitudes or behaviour under study. Marketers are interested in the social-class structures of communities that are potential markets for their products and in the specific social-class level of their potential customers. Table 12-2 illustrates the number and diversity of social-class schemata.

THE MEASUREMENT OF SOCIAL CLASS

There is no general agreement on how to measure social class. To a great extent, researchers are uncertain about the underlying dimensions of social-class structure. To attempt to resolve this dilemma, researchers have used a wide range of measurement techniques that they believe give a fair approximation of social class.

Systematic approaches for measuring social class fall into the following broad categories: subjective measures, reputational measures and objective measures of social class.

Subjective measures

In the subjective approach to measuring social class, individuals are asked to estimate their own social-class positions. Typical of this approach is the following question:

Which one of the following four categories best describes your social class?

Lower class	[ ]
Lower-middle class	[ ]
Upper-middle class	[ ]
Upper class	[ ]
Do not know/refuse to answer	[ ]

The resulting classification of social-class membership is based on the participants' self-perceptions or self-images. Social class is treated as a personal phenomenon, one that reflects an individual's sense of belonging or identification with others. This feeling of social-group membership is often referred to as **class consciousness**.

Subjective measures of social-class membership tend to produce an over-abundance of people who classify themselves as middle class (thus understating the number of people – the 'fringe people' – who would, perhaps, be more correctly classified as either lower or upper class).[7] Moreover, it is likely that the subjective perception of one's social-class membership, as a reflection of one's self-image, is related to product usage and consumption preferences (see Chapter 6). For example, every year in Japan, a 'Life of the Nation' survey asks citizens to place themselves into one of five social-class categories: upper, upper-middle, middle-middle, lower-middle and lower class. Whereas in the late 1950s over 70 per cent of respondents placed themselves into one of the three middle-class categories, by the late 1960s, and continuing on to the present, close to 90 per cent categorise themselves as middle class.[8] Again, this demonstrates the tendency for consumers to report seeing themselves as middle class.

Reputational measures

The reputational approach for measuring social class requires selected community informants to make initial judgements concerning the social-class membership of others within the community. The final task of assigning community members to social-class positions, however, belongs to the trained researcher.

Sociologists have used the reputational approach to obtain a better understanding of the specific class structures of communities under study. Consumer researchers, however, are concerned with the measurement of social class to understand markets and consumption behaviour better, not social structure. In keeping with this more focused goal, the reputational approach has proved to be impractical.

Objective measures

In contrast to the subjective and reputational methods, which require people to envisage their own class standing or that of other community members, objective measures consist of selected demographic or socio-economic variables concerning the individual(s) under study. These variables are measured through questionnaires that ask respondents several factual questions about themselves, their families or where they live. When selecting objective measures of social class, most researchers favour one or more of the following variables: occupation, amount of income and education. To these socio-economic factors they sometimes add geodemographic clustering data in the form of postcode and residence-neighbourhood information. These socio-economic indicators are especially important as a means of locating concentrations of consumers with specific social-class membership.

Socio-economic measures of social class are of considerable value to marketers concerned with segmenting markets. Marketing managers who have developed socio-economic profiles of their target markets can locate these markets (i.e. identify and measure them) by studying socio-economic data periodically issued by national census bureaux and numerous commercial geodemographic data services. To reach a desired target market, marketers match the socio-economic profiles of their target audiences to the audience profiles of selected advertising media. Socio-economic audience profiles are regularly developed and routinely made available to potential advertisers by most of the mass media.

Objective measures of social class fall into two basic categories: **single-variable indexes** and **composite-variable indexes**.

Single-Variable Indexes

A single-variable index uses just one socio-economic variable to evaluate social-class membership. Some of the variables that are used for this purpose are discussed next.

Occupation

Occupation is a widely accepted and probably the best-documented measure of social class because it reflects occupational status.[9] The importance of occupation as a social-class indicator is dramatised by the frequency with which people ask others they meet for the first time, 'What do you do for a living?' The response to this question serves as a guide in sizing up (or evaluating and forming opinions of) others.

More important, marketers frequently think in terms of specific occupations when defining a target market for their products (such as 'Teachers are our best customers for summer cruises') or broader occupational categories ('We target our Caribbean cruises to executives and professionals'). Still further, the likelihood that particular occupations would be receptive to certain products or services often provides the basis for an occupational screener requirement for participation in focus groups or survey research and for marketers to select occupational databases to target with direct-marketing campaigns (e.g. a list of female lawyers practising in Vienna, Austria).

Within the domain of occupational status, there has been an increasing trend towards self-employment among business and professional people. Specifically, it appears that business executives and professionals who are self-employed or entrepreneurs are substantially more likely to be very wealthy than their counterparts who work for someone else.[10] This link between self-employment and higher incomes is consistent with the trend of increasing numbers of business school graduates seeking to work for themselves rather than going to work for a 'big business'.

Still further, it is also worth keeping in mind that although the status of a particular occupation may change significantly over time, evidence suggests that when it comes to the status of some 40 occupations (studied between 1976 and 2000) a high degree of status consistency was found.[11] Specifically, certain occupations (e.g. doctors) were consistently ranked high over the many years of the research, whereas other occupations (e.g. farm labourers and taxi drivers) were consistently ranked low during the same period of time.

Education

The level of a person's formal education is another commonly accepted approximation of social-class standing. Generally speaking, the more education a person has, the more likely it is that the person is well paid (or has a higher income) and has an admired or respected position (high occupational status).[12]

Income

Individual or family income is another socio-economic variable frequently used to approximate social-class standing. Researchers who favour income as a measure of social class use either

TABLE 12-3 Typical categories used for assessing amount or source of income

AMOUNT OF INCOME	SOURCE OF INCOME
Under €25,000 per year	Public welfare
€25,000 to €49,999	Private financial assistance
€50,000 to €74,999	Wages (hourly)
€75,000 to €99,999	Salary (yearly)
€100,000 to €124,999	Profits or fees
€125,000 to €149,999	Earned wealth
€150,000 to €174,999	Inherited wealth, interest, dividends, royalties
€175,000 to €199,999	
€200,000 and over	

amount or source of income. Table 12-3 illustrates the types of categories used for each of these income variables. Available research suggests that income works best in accounting for leisure consumption when measured in terms of ('engaging in' or 'doing or not doing') a particular leisure activity (such as skiing, bowling or playing golf).[13]

A recent effort to differentiate between 'income' and 'wealth' points out that:

1. wealth, not income, is the primary driver to financial freedom – wealth, not income, is a function of savings, so to achieve wealth you have to increase your net worth, and not just your income;
2. wealth and money are not the same – wealth deals with the creation of resources and money deals more with consumption;
3. for wealth you need to network and build personal alliances, because a great deal of the information needed to create wealth is passed along via such relationships; and
4. you need to find ways to minimise your taxes, because taxes reduce your ability to create wealth.[14]

Although income is a popular estimate of social-class standing, not all consumer researchers agree that it is an appropriate index of social class. Some argue that a blue-collar car mechanic and a white-collar assistant bank manager may have equal annual incomes, yet because of (or as a reflection of) social-class differences each will spend that income in a different way. How they decide to spend their incomes reflects different values. Within this context, it is the difference in values that is an important discriminant of social class between people, not the amount of income they earn.

Substantiating the importance of consumers' personal values, rather than amount of income, is the observation that affluence may be more a function of attitude or behaviour than of income level.[15] These 'adaptational affluent' consumers represent a broad segment who do not have the income needed to be considered affluent in today's society, yet they desire to have the best. They buy less but buy better quality, assigning priorities and gradually working their way towards having everything they want.

Other Variables

Quality of neighbourhood and monetary value of residence are rarely used as sole measures of social class. However, they are used informally to support or verify social-class membership assigned on the basis of occupational status or income.

Finally, possessions have been used by sociologists as an index of social class.[16] The best-known and most elaborate rating scheme for evaluating possessions is **Chapin's Social Status Scale**, which focuses on the presence of certain items of furniture and accessories in the living room (types of floor or floor covering, curtains, fireplace, library table, telephone or bookcases) and the condition of the room (cleanliness, organisation or general atmosphere).[17] Conclusions are drawn about a family's social class on the basis of such observations. To illustrate how home decorations reflect social-class standing, lower-class families are likely to place their television sets in the living room and bedrooms, whereas middle- and upper-class families usually place their television sets in one or more of the following rooms: bedrooms, family room or a media room (but not in the living room). The marketing implications of such insights suggest that advertisements for television sets targeted at lower-class consumers should show the set in a living room, whereas advertisements directed to middle- or upper-class consumers should show the set in a bedroom, a family room or a media room.

Composite-Variable Indexes

Composite indexes systematically combine a number of socio-economic factors to form one overall measure of social-class standing. Such indexes are of interest to consumer researchers because they may better reflect the complexity of social class than single-variable indexes. For instance, research exploring consumers' perceptions of mail order and telephone shopping reveals that the higher the socio-economic status (in terms of a composite of income, occupational status and education), the more positive are the consumers' ratings of mail order and telephone buying, relative to in-store shopping.[18] The same research also found that downscale consumers (a composite of lower scores on the three variables) were less positive towards magazine and catalogue shopping and more positive towards in-store shopping than more upscale socio-economic groupings. Armed with such information, retailers that especially target working-class consumers would have a real challenge using direct-marketing catalogues and telephone-selling approaches. In contrast, retailers concentrating on upscale consumers have been especially effective in developing catalogue programmes targeted to specific segments of affluent or upscale consumers.

LIFESTYLE PROFILES OF THE SOCIAL CLASSES

Consumer research has found evidence that within each of the social classes, there is a constellation of specific lifestyle factors (shared beliefs, attitudes, activities and behaviours) that tends to distinguish the members of each class from the members of all other social classes.

To capture the lifestyle composition of the various social-class groupings, Table 12-4 presents a consolidated portrait, pieced together from numerous sources, of the members of the following six social classes: upper-upper class, lower-upper class, upper-middle class, lower-middle class, upper-lower class and lower-lower class. Each of these profiles is only a generalised picture of the class. People in any class may possess values, attitudes and behavioural patterns that are a hybrid of two or more classes.

SOCIAL-CLASS MOBILITY

The extent to which social-class membership is hard and fixed varies between countries and cultures. Although individuals can move either up or down in social-class standing from the class position held by their parents, Europeans and citizens of the Western world have primarily thought in terms of **upward mobility** because of the availability of education and opportunities for self-development and self-advancement. Today many young men and women with ambition to get ahead dream of going to university and eventually starting their own successful businesses.

Where upward mobility has been attained, the higher social classes often become reference groups for ambitious men and women of lower social status. Familiar examples of upward mobility are the new management trainee who strives to dress like the boss; the middle manager who aspires to belong to the status golf club; or the blue-collar worker who wants to send his daughter to a prestigious university.

TABLE 12-4 Social-class profiles

THE UPPER-UPPER CLASS – COUNTRY CLUB ESTABLISHMENT

- *Small number of well-established families*
- *Serve as trustees for local schools and hospitals*
- *Prominent doctors and lawyers*
- *May be heads of major financial institutions, owners of major long-established firms*
- *Accustomed to wealth, so do not spend money conspicuously*

THE LOWER-UPPER CLASS – NEW WEALTH

- *Not quite accepted by the upper crust of society*
- *Represent 'new money'*
- *Successful business executives*
- *Conspicuous users of their new wealth*

THE UPPER-MIDDLE CLASS – ACHIEVING PROFESSIONALS

- *Have neither family status nor unusual wealth*
- *Career-oriented*
- *Young successful professionals, corporate managers and business owners*
- *Most are college graduates, many with advanced degrees*
- *Active in professional, community and social activities*
- *Have a keen interest in obtaining the 'better things in life'*
- *Their homes serve as symbols of their achievements*
- *Consumption is often conspicuous*
- *Very child-oriented*

THE LOWER-MIDDLE CLASS – FAITHFUL FOLLOWERS

- *Primarily non-managerial white-collar workers and highly paid blue-collar workers*
- *Want to achieve respectability and be accepted as good citizens*
- *Want their children to be well behaved*
- *Tend to be churchgoers and are often involved in church-sponsored activities*
- *Prefer a neat and clean appearance and tend to avoid faddish or highly styled clothing*
- *Constitute a major market for do-it-yourself products*

THE UPPER-LOWER CLASS – SECURITY-MINDED MAJORITY

- *The largest social-class segment*
- *Solidly blue collar*
- *Strive for security (sometimes gained from union membership)*
- *View work as a means to 'buy' enjoyment*
- *Want children to behave properly*
- *High wage earners in this group may spend impulsively*
- *Interested in items that enhance their leisure time (e.g. television sets, fishing equipment)*
- *Husbands typically have a strong 'macho' self-image*
- *Males are sports fans, heavy smokers, beer drinkers*

THE LOWER-LOWER CLASS – ROCK BOTTOM

- *Poorly educated, unskilled labourers*
- *Often out of work*
- *Children are often poorly treated*
- *Tend to live a day-to-day existence*

Recognising that individuals often aspire to the lifestyle and possessions enjoyed by members of a higher social class, marketers frequently incorporate the symbols of higher-class membership, both as products and props in advertisements targeted to lower social-class audiences. For example, advertisements often present or display marketers' products within an upper-class setting.

Sometimes a more direct appeal to consumers' sense of having products that are normally restricted to members of other social classes is an affective message. For instance, if a direct marketer of consumer electronics were to promote a top-of-the-range high-definition television set, usually purchased by wealthier homeowners, as 'now it's your turn to have what families living in the big houses have enjoyed' (it's been marked down to about 50 per cent of original price), this would be a marketing message that encourages household consumers to have a 'dream TV' in their homes.

Another characteristic of social-class mobility is that products and services traditionally within the realm of one social class may filter down to lower social classes. For instance, once only film stars and other wealthy consumers could afford plastic surgery. Today, however, consumers of all economic strata undergo cosmetic procedures.

Some signs of downward mobility

Although social class mobility is frequently associated with upward mobility, because it was more usual for each generation within a family to 'do better' than the last generation, there are also signs of some **downward mobility**. Social commentators have suggested that some young adults (such as members of the X-Generation described in Chapter 13) are not only likely to find it difficult to 'do better' than their successful parents (e.g. to get better jobs, own homes, have more disposable income and have more savings) but also may not even do as well as their parents.

There is some evidence of such a slide in social-class mobility. Specifically, researchers have found that the odds that young men's income will reach middle-class levels by the time they reach their thirtieth birthday have been slowly declining.[19] In some industrialised countries this regressive pattern holds true, regardless of race, parents' income and a young person's educational level.

THE AFFLUENT CONSUMER

Affluent households constitute an especially attractive target segment because members have incomes that provide them with a disproportionately larger share of all discretionary income – the 'extras' that allow the purchase of luxury cruises, sports cars, time-sharing ski-resort apartments, fine jewellery and ready access to home PCs, laptops and wireless surfing on the Internet. It has also been pointed out that there is a strong positive relationship between health and economic status – that is, 'the healthiest people are those who are economically advantaged' and 'poverty is bad for you'.[20] Indeed, more highly educated people with higher incomes are less likely to die of heart disease, strokes, diabetes and many types of cancer, and affluent consumers live longer and in better health than middle-class consumers, who live longer and in better health than individuals at the bottom of the social-class hierachy.[21] Conversely, evidence suggests that children of the affluent may have problems with substance abuse, anxiety and depression, which can be caused by excessive pressures to achieve and isolation from parents (both physically and emotionally).[22]

The **affluent market** is increasingly attracting marketers. Whirlpool Corporation, for example, a leading home appliance manufacturer, realises that as more and more consumers own household appliances, it can no longer rely on volume to increase profits. So the firm now focuses on upscale products that are so profitable they can sell fewer appliances and still make money.[23]

While the affluent market is most often defined by income or net worth, one research study explored whether such a definition was sufficient. The study proposed that an operational definition of 'affluent' should also include both lifestyle and psychographic factors because the heads of affluent households have a tendency to behave and think affluently. Using a richer mix of factors, researchers have been able to reclassify about one-third of the households, and to create a more useful definition for 'affluent consumers'.[24]

Figure 12-1 presents some further insights about affluent consumers in terms of a comparison of the sports participation of three segments of affluent consumers. The results reveal that

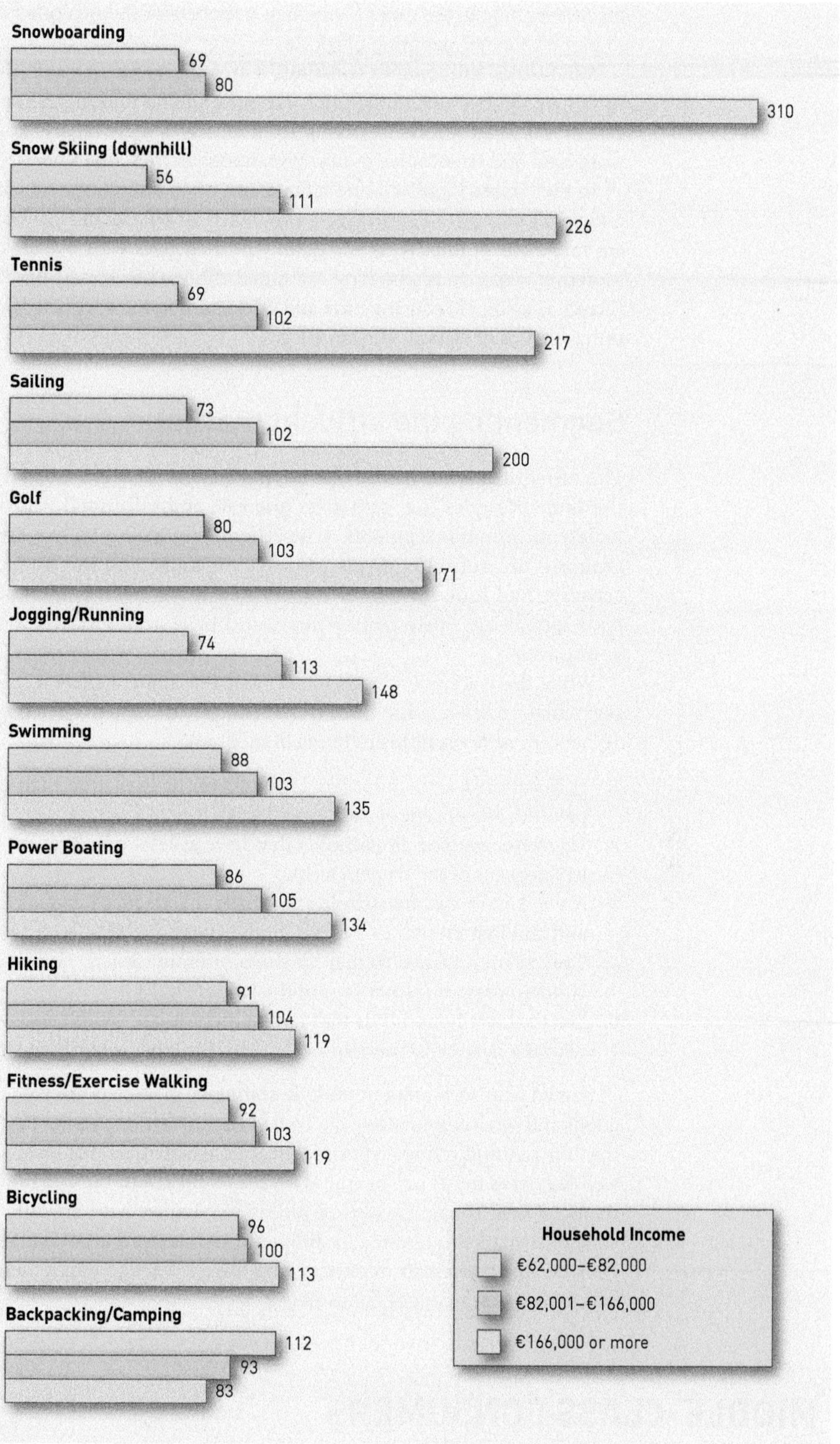

Snowboarding
69
80
310

Snow Skiing (downhill)
56
111
226

Tennis
69
102
217

Sailing
73
102
200

Golf
80
103
171

Jogging/Running
74
113
148

Swimming
88
103
135

Power Boating
86
105
134

Hiking
91
104
119

Fitness/Exercise Walking
92
103
119

Bicycling
96
100
113

Backpacking/Camping
112
93
83

Household Income
€62,000–€82,000
€82,001–€166,000
€166,000 or more

FIGURE 12-1 Affluent consumers' participation in selected sports (number of days in past year, indexed to each of the three income segments)
Source: Adapted from *The 2002 Mendelsohn Affluent Survey* (New York: Mendelsohn Media Research, Inc., 2002).

the 'most affluent' are more likely than members of the two other affluent consumer segments to participate in a sampling of sports.[25]

Still further, millionaires constitute a growing subcategory of the affluent. Contrary to common stereotypes, these millionaires are quite similar to non-millionaires. They are typically first generation wealthy, often working for themselves in 'ordinary' non-glamour businesses. They work hard and tend to live in non-pretentious homes, often next door to non-millionaires.

In the United Kingdom, the affluent are often empty-nesters with high disposable incomes and small or paid-off mortgages. They have an abundance of money, but are time-poor and are interested in improving the quality of their lives with overseas holidays and sports cars.[26] Moreover, researchers who have examined affluent consumers have found that they are likely to focus on saving or reducing time and effort and, not unsurprisingly, are willing to pay for many things that provide such convenience.[27]

Segmenting the affluent market

The affluent market is not one single market. Because not all affluent consumers share the same lifestyles (i.e. activities, interests and opinions), various marketers have tried to isolate meaningful segments. One scheme, for example, has divided the affluent into two groups – the upbeat enjoyers who live for today and the financial positives who are conservative and look for value. Still further, it has been commented that 'most people who have money are fairly conservative, and have accumulated wealth because they are very good savers'.[28]

While there are many ways to segment the affluent market, the following affluent market segmentation schema has been developed for the Upper Deck consumers (defined as the top 10 per cent of households in terms of income):[29]

1. *Well-feathered nests:* households that have at least one high-income earner and children present (38 per cent of the Upper Deck).
2. *No strings attached:* households that have at least one high-income earner and no children (35 per cent of the Upper Deck).
3. *Nanny's in charge:* households that have two or more earners, none earning high incomes, and children present (9 per cent of the Upper Deck).
4. *Two careers:* households that have two or more earners, none earning high incomes, and no children present (11 per cent of the Upper Deck).
5. *The good life:* households that have a high degree of affluence with no person employed or with the head of household not employed (7 per cent of the Upper Deck).

Armed with such affluent lifestyle segments, marketers are able to profile users of a variety of goods and services frequently targeted to the affluent consumer (e.g. travel services, leisure clothing, hire cars and various types of recreational activities). For instance, in terms of recreation, the well-feathered nester can be found on the tennis court, the good lifer may be playing golf, while the two-career couple may be off sailing.[30] What we have are different segments of the affluent consumer market interested in different products and activities. This type of information is of considerable interest to marketers who always want to target their marketing messages to the most suitable segment of consumers.

MIDDLE-CLASS CONSUMERS

Although it is not easy to define the boundaries of what is meant by 'middle class', there have nevertheless been many attempts to define it. For instance, 'middle market' has been defined as the 'middle' 50 per cent of household incomes.[31] Still another definition of 'middle class' envisages households composed of college-educated adults, who in some way use computers to make a living, are involved in their children's education, and are confident that they can maintain the quality of their family's life.[32]

For many marketers 'middle class' can be thought of as including households that range from lower-middle to middle-middle class in terms of some acceptable variable or combination of variables (e.g. income, education and/or occupation). This view of middle class does not include the upper-middle class, which over the years has increasingly been treated as a segment of affluent consumers.

A recent article differentiated between the children of middle-class parents and those from working-class and poor families. Working-class families often teach their children, at an early age, to do what they are told and to manage their own free time. In contrast, middle-class parents actively play a role in shaping their children's activities, want their children to get involved in extra-curricular activities that will add to their talents and encourage them to speak up and negotiate with figures of authority.[33]

Although the middle class has been shrinking in a variety of Western European countries, there has been a fairly rapid increase in the number of middle-class consumers in some Asian and Eastern European countries. For example, within the past few years Tropicana and other fruit juice companies have been successfully positioning their products to the expanding middle-class Indian consumers who are seeking more health-oriented products.[34] Similarly, both Japanese and Korean car manufacturers are now manufacturing vehicles and motorcyles in China, hoping that China's growing middle class will be attracted to purchasing them.

Moving up to more 'near' luxuries

Adding to the challenge of defining 'middle class' is the reality that luxury and technological products have been becoming more affordable for more consumers (often because of the introduction of near-luxury models by major luxury-brand firms and/or the downward price trend for many technology products) and, therefore, more middle-class consumers have access to products and brands that were once considered beyond their reach.[35]

Additionally, evidence suggests that some middle-class consumers are willing to pinch pennies on certain purchases in order to splash out on others. For example, a household might buy both groceries and clothes at low-priced retail chains in order to afford luxury or near-luxury goods that satisfy emotional needs, such as a luxury car. The luxury product purchased might even be premium food for their dog. One study found that people generally trade up in two to five categories, but at the same time they trade down in 20. For example, they might want the least expensive airfare they can get for a holiday trip to Fiji, but they want to stay at a luxury resort hotel when they get there.

Still further, while high-end retailers still consider their primary customer base to be the affluent, they are realising that middle-class customers have been purchasing more high-style items, often at not-so-high prices. Consequently, traditional marketers of luxury products have been expanding their offerings to more affordable merchandise. It is believed that a crucial factor in the growth of upscale retailers over the next few years will be how well they cater to middle-class buyers.[36]

However, companies offering 'luxury to the masses' must be careful how they position their products. Many loyal Jaguar owners, for example, 'went through the roof' when the company introduced the entry-level X-Type, and Jaguar's loyalty rate has dropped to 38 per cent from 85 per cent over the past few years. Trying to bring a luxury car to the masses appears to have been a flawed strategy for Jaguar.[37] Other companies, realising that they have made their offerings more accessible to the less than affluent marketplace, have been introducing high-priced collections in order to pull up their elite images.[38] These firms realise that if one of their products slips into the mass market, they will need a new product to take its place in the luxury market.

THE WORKING CLASS AND OTHER NON-AFFLUENT CONSUMERS

Although many advertisers would prefer to show their products as part of an affluent lifestyle, working-class or blue-collar people represent a vast group of consumers that marketers cannot ignore. Lower-income or lower-class consumers may actually be more brand loyal than wealthier consumers, because they cannot afford to make mistakes by switching to unfamiliar brands.

Understanding the importance of speaking to (not at) such consumers, companies such as MasterCard and McDonald's target 'average Joes' (and Janes) with advertisements reflecting the modest lifestyles of some of their customers.[39] For instance, marketers need to be sensitive to the reality that lower-class consumers often spend a higher percentage of their available income on food than do their middle-class counterparts. Moreover, food is a particularly important purchase area for low-income consumers because it represents an area of 'indulgence'. For this reason, they periodically trade-up the foods they purchase – especially favourite ethnic and natural foods – 'where taste and authenticity matter'.[40] A British writer, reflecting on a trend toward super-sized fast-food offerings in the United Kingdom, noted that 'It isn't the wealthy middle classes . . . that are generally obese – it's the under-class . . . with little budget, knowledge of diet . . . that is suffering'.[41]

RECOGNISING THE 'TECHNO-CLASS'

The degree of literacy, familiarity and competence with technology, especially computers and the Internet, appears to be a new basis for a kind of 'class standing', or status or prestige. Those who are unfamiliar with or lack computer skills are being referred to as 'technologically under-classed'.[42] Educators, business leaders and government officials have warned that the inability to use technology adequately is having a negative impact on the lifestyles and quality of life of those who are not computer-literate.

Not wanting to see their children left out of the 'sweep of computer technology', parents in all social-class groupings are seeking out early computer exposure for their children. Either based on their positive experiences using computers (or possibly on fears produced as a result of a lack of personal computer experience), parents sense that an understanding of computers is a necessary tool of competitive achievement and success. At the other end of the life and age spectrum, even 55-year-old professionals, who were initially reluctant to 'learn computers', are now seeking personal computer training – they no longer want to be left out, nor do they want to be further embarrassed by having to admit that they 'don't know computers'.

Consumers throughout the world have come to believe that it is critical to acquire a functional understanding of computers in order to ensure that they do not become obsolete or hinder themselves socially or professionally. In this sense, there is a technological class structure that centres around the amount of computer skills that one possesses. It appears that those without necessary computer skills will increasingly find themselves to be 'underclassed' and 'disadvantaged'.

The geek gets status

The importance of the computer and the prominent role it now plays in our lives has resulted in something of a reversal of fortune, in that the 'geek' is now often viewed by his or her peers as 'friendly and fun'. The increasingly positive image of geeks has made them and their lifestyles the target of marketers' messages designed to appeal to their great appetite for novel technological products.

Indeed, according to a British National Opinion Poll (NOP) of 7- to 16-year-olds, 'Computer geeks are now the coolest kids in class'.[43] The poll found that the archetypical geek is generally a

14- to 16-year-old boy who is the family computer expert, and he is willing to teach his parents, siblings and teachers about computers. Interestingly, in an environment where children naturally take to computers, it is often the parents who find themselves technologically disenfranchised. To remedy this situation, some schools are offering classes to bring parents up to speed in the use of computers.[44]

SUMMARY

Social stratification, the division of members of a society into a hierarchy of distinct social classes, exists in all societies and cultures. Social class is usually defined by the amount of status that members of a specific class possess in relation to members of other classes. Social-class membership often serves as a frame of reference (a reference group) for the development of consumer attitudes and behaviour.

The measurement of social class is concerned with classifying individuals into social-class groupings. These groupings are of particular value to marketers, who use social classification as an effective means of identifying and segmenting target markets. There are three basic methods for measuring social class: subjective measurement, reputational measurement and objective measurement. Subjective measures rely on an individual's self-perception; reputational measures rely on an individual's perceptions of others; and objective measures use specific socio-economic measures, either alone (as a single-variable index) or in combination with others (as a composite-variable index). Composite-variable indexes combine a number of socio-economic factors to form one overall measure of social-class standing.

Class structures range from two-class to nine-class systems. A frequently used classification system consists of six classes: upper-upper, lower-upper, upper-middle, lower-middle, upper-lower and lower-lower classes. Profiles of these classes indicate that the socio-economic differences among classes are reflected in differences in attitudes, in leisure activities and in consumption habits. This is why segmentation by social class is of special interest to marketers.

Particular attention is currently being directed to affluent consumers, who represent the fastest-growing segment in our population; however, some marketers are finding it extremely profitable to cater to the needs of non-affluent consumers.

Research has revealed social-class differences in clothing habits, home decoration and leisure activities, as well as saving, spending and credit habits. Thus, astute marketers tailor specific product and promotional strategies to each social-class target segment.

DISCUSSION QUESTIONS

1. Marketing researchers generally use the objective method to measure social class rather than the subjective or reputational methods. Why is the objective method preferred by researchers?
2. Under what circumstances would you expect income to be a better predictor of consumer behaviour than a composite measure of social class (e.g. based on income, education and occupation)? When would you expect the composite social-class measure to be superior?
3. Describe the correlation between social status (or prestige) and income. Which is a more useful segmentation variable? Discuss.
4. Which status-related variable – occupation, education or income – is the most appropriate segmentation base for: (a) expensive holidays, (b) opera subscriptions, (c) magazine subscriptions, (d) fat-free foods, (e) personal computers, (f) pocket-size mobile phones and (g) health clubs?
5. Consider the Rolex watch, which has a retail price range starting at about €2,000 for a stainless-steel model to thousands of euros for a solid gold model. How might the Rolex company use knowledge of lifestyle differences between social classes in its marketing efforts?

6. How would you use the descriptions of affluent households presented in this chapter to segment the market for (a) home exercise equipment, (b) holidays and (c) banking services?
7. How can a marketer use knowledge of consumer behaviour to develop financial services for affluent consumers? For lower-income consumers?
8. You are the owner of two furniture shops, one catering to upper-middle-class consumers and the other to lower-class consumers. How do social-class differences influence each shop's (a) product lines and styles, (b) advertising media selection, (c) communications style used in the advertisements and (d) payment policies?

EXERCISES

1. Make a list of 15 different occupations, and ask students studying in areas other than marketing (both business and non-business) to rank the relative prestige of these occupations. Are any differences in the rankings related to the students' own areas of study? Explain.
2. Find three print advertisements in a well-known publication. Using the social-class characteristics listed in Table 12-4, identify the social class targeted by each advertisement and evaluate the effectiveness of the advertising appeals used.
3. Select two households featured in two different television series or sitcoms. Classify each household into one of the social classes discussed in the text and analyse its lifestyle and consumption behaviour.

NOTES

1. Shaun Saunders, 'Fromm's Marketing Character and Rokeach Values', *Social Behavior and Personality*, 29(2), 2001, 191–6.
2. Jacqueline K. Eastman, Ronald E. Goldsmith, and Leisa Reinecke Flynn, 'Status Consumption in Consumer Behavior: Scale Development and Validation', *Journal of Marketing Theory and Practice*, Summer 1999, 41–52.
3. Ibid., 43.
4. Aron O'Cass and Emily McEwen, 'Exploring Consumer Status and Conspicuous Consumption', *Journal of Consumer Behaviour* (London), 4, October 2004, 25–39.
5. Douglas B. Holt, 'Does Cultural Capital Structure American Consumption?', *Journal of Consumer Research*, 25, June 1998, 19.
6. 'Brand Stats: Market Focus – Instant Coffee', *Brand Strategy* (London), 10 May 2005, 50.
7. Malcolm M. Knapp, 'Believing "Myth of the Middle Class" Can Be Costly Misreading of Consumer Spending', *Nation's Restaurant News*, 1 January 2001, 36.
8. Takashina Shuji, 'The New Inequality', *Japan Echo*, August 2000, 38–9.
9. Rebecca Piirto Heath, 'The New Working Class', *American Demographics*, January 1998, 52.
10. John P. Dickson and R. Bruce Lind, 'The Stability of Occupational Prestige as a Key Variable in Determining Social Class Structure: A Longitudinal Study 1976–2000', in *2001 AMA Winter Educators' Conference*, 12, eds Ram Krishnan and Madhu Viswanathan (Chicago: American Marketing Association, 2001), 38–44.
11. Rebecca Piirto Heath, 'Life on Easy Street', *American Demographics*, April 1997, 33–8.
12. Diane Crispell, 'The Real Middle Americans', *American Demographics*, October 1994, 28–35.
13. Eugene Sivadas, George Mathew and David J. Curry, 'A Preliminary Examination of the Continued Significance of Social Class to Marketing: A Geodemographic Replication', *Journal of Consumer Marketing*, 14, 6, 1997, 469.
14. David Hinson, 'Closing the Wealth Gap; How African-Americans Can Sustain a Middle-Class Lifestyle'. *Network Journal*, 11, 29 February 2004, 8.
15. Dennis Rodkin, 'Wealthy Attitude Wins over Healthy Wallet: Consumers Prove Affluence Is a State of Mind', *Advertising* Age, 9 July 1990, S4, S6.

16. Janeen Arnold Costa and Russell W. Belk, 'Nouveaux Riches as Quintessential Americans: Case Studies of Consumption in an Extended Family', *Advances in Nonprofit Marketing*, 3 (Greenwich, CT: JAI Press, 1990), 83–140.

17. F. Stuart Chapin, *Contemporary American Institutions* (New York: Harper, 1935), 373–97.

18. Robert B. Settle, Pamela L. Alreck and Denny E. McCorkle, 'Consumer Perceptions of Mail/Phone Order Shopping Media', *Journal of Direct Marketing*, 8, Summer 1994, 30–45.

19. Randy Kennedy, 'For Middle Class, New York Shrinks as Home Prices Soar', *New York Times*, 1 April 1998, A1, B6; 'Two Tier Marketing', *Business Week*, 17 March 1997, 82–90; and Keith Bradsher, 'America's Opportunity Gap', *New York Times*, 4 June 1995, 4.

20. Paul Bruder, 'Economic Health: The Key Ingredient in the Personal Health of Global Communities', *Hospital Topics*, 79, 1, Winter 2001, 32–5.

21. Janny Scott, 'In America, Living Better and Living Longer Is a Major Factor in Health Care and the Gaps Are Widening', *International Herald Tribune*, 17 May 2005, 2.

22. Suniya S. Luthar and Shawn J. Latendresse, 'Children of the Affluent; Challenges to Well-Being', *Current Directions in Psychological Science*, 14, February 2005, 49.

23. Lisa Singhania, 'Whirlpool Looks to Innovation to Boost Appliance Sales', *The Grand Rapids Press*, 6 February 2000, F1; and Gregory L. White and Shirley Leung, 'Stepping Up: Middle Market Shrinks as Americans Migrate Toward the High End – Shifting Consumer Values Create "Hourglass" Effect'; Quality Gets Easier to Sell – Six Air Bags, 22 Bath Towels', *Wall Street Journal*, 29 March 2002, A1.

24. Michael R. Hyman, Gopala Ganesh and Shaun McQuitty, 'Augmenting the Household Affluence Construct', *Journal of Marketing Theory and Practice*, 10, Summer 2002, 13–31.

25. *The 2002 Mendelsohn Affluent Survey* (New York: Mendelsohn Media Research Inc., 2002).

26. Geoffrey Holliman, 'Once a Teenager, Now Affluent and Best Not Ignored', *Marketing*, 2 December 1999, 22.

27. Martha R. McEnally and Charles Bodkin, 'A Comparison of Convenience Orientation Between U.S. and U.K. Households', in *2001 AMA Winter Educators' Conference*, 12, eds Ram Krishnan and Madhu Viswanathan (Chicago: American Marketing Association, 2001), 332–8.

28. Jeanie Casison, 'Wealthy and Wise', *Incentive*, January 1999, 78–81.

29. *The Upper Deck*, Mediamark Research, Inc., 2001.

30. For some further insights about the affluence of dual-income households, see Diane Crispell, 'The Very Rich Are Sort of Different', *American Demographics*, March 1994, 11–13.

31. Gayle Gerhardt and Pete Jacques, 'Is the Middle Market Still in the Middle?', *Life Insurance Marketing and Research Association's Market Facts Quarterly*, Fall 2001, 18–21.

32. Debra Goldman, 'Paradox of Pleasure', *American Demographics*, May 1999, 50–53.

33. Tamar Lewin, 'Up From the Holler: Living in Two Worlds, At Home in Neither; Class Matters', *New York Times*, 19 May 2005, A14.

34. Rasul Bailay, 'Juice Processors See Fruitful Future in India – Companies Hope to Lure Country's Middle Class – "The Taste of Good Health"', *Wall Street Journal*, 17 November 2000, 28; and Clay Chandler, 'GM to Make Small Cars in China; Buick Sail, Similar to Opel, Will Be Aimed at Middle Class', *Washington Post*, 24 October 2000, E1.

35. W. Michael Cox, 'The Low Cost of Living', *The Voluntaryist*, October 1999, 3.

36. Lorrie Grant, 'Scrimping to Splurge: Value-Conscious Middle-Class Buyers Pinch Pennies to Afford Luxuries', *USA Today*, 28 January, 2005, B1; Tiffany Meyers, 'Marketers Learn Luxury Isn't Simply for the Very Wealthy', *Advertising Age*, 13 September 2004, S2–S3; and 'America Loves to Trade Up', *Home Textiles Today*, 25, 26 January 2004, 4.

37. Jean Halliday and Lisa Sanders, 'Jaguar Hunts for Marketing Panacea', *Advertising Age*, 8 November 2004, 1, 64.

38. Stephanie Thompson, 'Marketers Hike Prices to Restake Luxury Claims', *Advertising Age*, 15 November 2004, 12.

39. Karen Benezra, 'Hardworking RC Cola', *Brandweek*, 25 May 1998, 18–19.

40. 'Small Budgets Yield Big Clout for Food Companies – 10.1 Million Low Income Consumers Can't (or Shouldn't) Be Ignored', *PR Newswire*, 22 August 2002, 1.

41. George Pitcher, 'Being Super-Sized Boils Down to Personal Choice', *Marketing Week* (London), 7 October 2004, 33.

42. Steve Rosenbush, 'Techno Leaders Warn of a "Great Divide"', *USA Today*, 17 June 1998, B1.

43. 'Computer Geeks Now the Cool Kids in Class', *The Press* (Christchurch, New Zealand), 20 July 2000, 31.

44. Sophia Lezin Jones, 'Parent Technology Nights: Classes to Help Boost Computer Savvy Riverside Elementary Moms, Dads Invited', *The Atlanta Journal – Constitution*, 19 October 1999, JJ1.

CHAPTER 13

THE INFLUENCE OF CULTURE AND SUBCULTURE ON CONSUMER BEHAVIOUR

The study of culture is a challenging undertaking because its primary focus is on the broadest component of social behaviour – an entire society. In contrast to the psychologist, who is principally concerned with the study of individual behaviour, or the sociologist, who is concerned with the study of groups, the anthropologist is primarily interested in identifying the very fabric of society itself.

This chapter explores the basic concepts of culture, with particular emphasis on the role that culture plays in influencing consumer behaviour. We will first consider the specific dimensions of culture that make it a powerful force in regulating human behaviour. After reviewing several measurement approaches that researchers use to understand the impact of culture on consumption behaviour, we will turn our attention to the notion of subculture.

In addition to segmenting in terms of cultural factors, marketers also segment overall societies into smaller sub-groups (subcultures) that consist of people who are similar in terms of their ethnic origin, their customs and the ways they behave. These subcultures provide important marketing opportunities for astute marketing strategists.

Our discussion of subcultures, therefore, has a narrower focus than the discussion of culture. Instead of examining the dominant beliefs, values and customs that exist within an entire society, this chapter explores the marketing opportunities created by the existence of certain beliefs, values and customs shared by members of specific subcultural groups within a society.

WHAT IS CULTURE?

Given the broad and pervasive nature of **culture**, its study generally requires a detailed examination of the character of the total society, including such factors as language, knowledge, laws, religions, food customs, music, art, technology, work patterns, products and other artefacts that give a society its distinctive flavour. In a sense, culture is a society's personality. For this reason, it is not easy to define its boundaries.

Because our objective is to understand the influence of culture on consumer behaviour, we define culture as *the sum total of learned beliefs, values and customs that serve to direct the consumer behaviour of members of a particular society.*

The *belief* and *value* components of our definition refer to the accumulated feelings and priorities that individuals have about 'things' and possessions. More precisely, beliefs consist of the very large number of mental or verbal statements (i.e. 'I believe . . .') that reflect a person's particular knowledge and assessment of something (another person, a shop, a product, a brand). Values also are beliefs. Values differ from other beliefs, however, because they meet the following criteria:

1. they are relatively few in number;
2. they serve as a guide for culturally appropriate behaviour;
3. they are enduring or difficult to change;
4. they are not tied to specific objects or situations; and
5. they are widely accepted by the members of a society.

Therefore, in a broad sense, both values and beliefs are mental images that affect a wide range of specific attitudes that, in turn, influence the way a person is likely to respond in a specific situation.[1] For example, the criteria a person uses to evaluate alternative brands in a product category (such as Volkswagen versus Peugeot cars), or his or her eventual preference for one of these brands over the other, are influenced by both a person's general values (perceptions as to what constitutes quality and the meaning of country of origin) and specific beliefs (particular perceptions about the quality of German-made versus French-made cars).

In contrast to beliefs and values, *customs* are overt modes of behaviour that constitute culturally approved or acceptable ways of behaving in specific situations. Customs consist of everyday or routine behaviour. For example, a consumer's routine behaviour, such as adding sugar and milk to coffee, putting ketchup on hamburgers, putting mustard on frankfurters and having a salad after rather than before the main course of a meal, are customs. Thus, whereas beliefs and values are guides for behaviour, customs are usual and acceptable ways of behaving.

By our definition, it is easy to see how an understanding of various cultures of a society helps marketers predict consumer acceptance of their products.

THE INVISIBLE HAND OF CULTURE

The impact of culture is so natural and automatic that its influence on behaviour is usually taken for granted. For instance, when consumer researchers ask people why they do certain things, they frequently answer, 'Because it's the right thing to do'. This seemingly superficial response partially reflects the ingrained influence of culture on our behaviour. Often it is only when we are exposed to people with different cultural values or customs (as when visiting a different country) that we become aware of how culture has moulded our own behaviour. Thus, a true appreciation of the influence that culture has on our daily life requires some knowledge of at least one other society with different cultural characteristics. For example, to understand that brushing our teeth twice a day with flavoured toothpaste is a cultural phenomenon requires some awareness that members of another society either do not brush their teeth at all or do so in a distinctly different manner from our own society.

Perhaps the following statement expresses it best:[2]

Consumers both view themselves in the context of their culture and react to their environment based upon the cultural framework that they bring to that experience. Each individual perceives the world through his own cultural lens.

CULTURE SATISFIES NEEDS

Culture exists to satisfy the needs of the people within a society. It offers order, direction and guidance in all phases of human problem-solving by providing 'tried-and-true' methods of satisfying physiological, personal and social needs. For example, culture provides standards and 'rules' about when to eat ('not between meals'), where to eat ('in a busy restaurant, because the food is likely to be good'), what is appropriate to eat for breakfast (juice and cereal), lunch (a sandwich), dinner ('something hot and good and healthy') and snacks ('something with quick energy'); and what to serve to guests at a dinner party ('a formal sit-down meal'), at a picnic (barbequed 'chicken and hamburgers'), or at a wedding (champagne). Culture is also associated with what a society's members consider to be a necessity and what they view as a luxury. For instance, when asked whether a cellphone or an iPod is a necessity or a luxury, the respondents' answers will vary between cultures.

Similarly, culture also provides insights as to suitable dress for specific occasions (such as what to wear around the house, what to wear to school, to work, to church, at a fast-food restaurant or to a cinema). Dress codes have shifted dramatically; people are dressing more casually most of the time. Today, fewer big-city restaurants and clubs have business dress requirements. With the relaxed dress code in the corporate work environment, fewer men are wearing formal shirts, ties and business suits, and fewer women are wearing dresses, suits and tights. In their place casual slacks, sports shirts and blouses, jeans and the emerging category of 'dress casual' have been increasing in sales.

Soft-drink companies would prefer that consumers received their morning 'jolt' of caffeine from one of their products rather than from coffee. Because so many people do not consider soda a suitable breakfast drink, the real challenge for soft-drink companies is to overcome culture, not competition. Indeed, coffee has been challenged on all fronts by juices, milk, teas (hot and iced), a host of different types of soft drinks and now even caffeinated waters. Not resting on their 'cultural advantage' as a breakfast drink and the namesake of the 'coffee break', coffee marketers have been fighting back by targeting gourmet and speciality coffees (e.g. espresso, cappuccino, and café mocha) to young adults (those 18–24 years of age). These efforts have been paying off as young adults (an important segment of the soft-drink market) have been responding positively to gourmet coffees.[3]

Cultural beliefs, values and customs continue to be followed as long as they yield satisfaction. When a specific standard no longer satisfies the members of a society, however, it is modified or replaced, so that the resulting standard is more in line with current needs and desires. For instance, it was once considered a sign of a fine hotel that it provided down or goose feather pillows in rooms. Today, with so many guests allergic to such materials, pillows with a polyester filling are becoming more the rule. Thus, culture gradually but continually evolves to meet the needs of society.

CULTURE IS LEARNED

Unlike innate biological characteristics (e.g. sex, skin or hair colour), culture is learned. At an early age, we begin to acquire from our social environment a set of beliefs, values and customs that make up our culture. For children, the learning of these acceptable cultural values and customs is reinforced by the process of playing with their toys. As children play, they act out and rehearse important cultural lessons and situations. This cultural learning prepares them for later real-life circumstances.

How culture is learned

Anthropologists have identified three distinct forms of cultural learning: formal learning, in which adults and older siblings teach a young family member 'how to behave'; informal learning, in which a child learns primarily by imitating the behaviour of selected others, such as family, friends or television heroes; and technical learning, in which teachers instruct the child in an educational environment about what should be done, how it should be done and why it should be done. Although a firm's advertising can influence all three types of cultural learning, it is likely that many product advertisements enhance informal cultural learning by providing the audience with a model of behaviour to imitate. This is especially true for visible or conspicuous products and products that are evaluated in public settings (such as designer clothing, mobile phones or status golf clubs), where peer influence is likely to play an important role.[4] Additionally, 'not only are cultural values cited in advertising copy, they also are often coded in the visual imagery, colours, movements, music, and other nonverbal elements of an advertisement'.[5]

The repetition of advertising messages creates and reinforces cultural beliefs and values. For example, many advertisers continually stress the same selected benefits of their products or services. Advertisements for wireless phone services often stress the clarity of their connection, or the coverage of their service, as well as the flexibility of their pricing plans. It is difficult to say whether wireless phone subscribers inherently desire these benefits from their wireless service providers or whether, after several years of cumulative exposure to advertising appeals stressing these benefits, they have been taught by marketers to desire them. In a sense, although specific product advertising may reinforce the benefits that consumers want from the product (as determined by consumer behaviour research), such advertising also 'teaches' future generations of consumers to expect the same benefits from the product category.

Figure 13-1 shows that cultural meaning moves from the culturally constituted world to consumer goods and from there to the individual consumer by means of various consumption-related

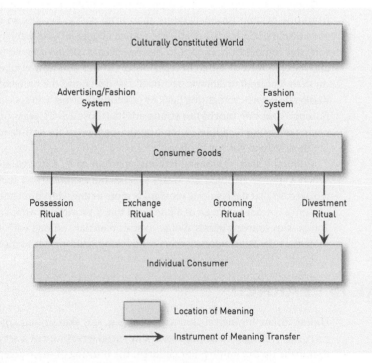

FIGURE 13-1 The movement of cultural meaning

Source: Adapted from Grant McCracken, 'Culture and Consumption: A Theoretical Account of the Structure and Movement of the Cultural Meaning of Consumer Goods', *Journal of Consumer Research*, 13, June 1986, 72. Reprinted by permission of The University of Chicago Press as publishers. Copyright © 1986, JCR, Inc.

vehicles (e.g. advertising or observing or imitating others' behaviour). Imagine the ever-popular T-shirt and how it can furnish cultural meaning and identity for wearers. T-shirts can function as trophies (as proof of participation in sports or travel) or as self-proclaimed labels of belonging to a cultural category. T-shirts can also be used as a means of self-expression, which may provide wearers with the additional benefit of serving as a topic initiating social dialogue with others. Still further, although we might expect that a Bucharest T-shirt would be worn by a person who has been to Bucharest in Romania (or has received it as a gift from someone else who has visited Bucharest), this is not necessarily so. In such a world of 'virtual identities', consumers can now just buy a Bucharest T-shirt at a local retailer and create the impression that they have been there.[6]

Enculturation and acculturation

When discussing the acquisition of culture, anthropologists often distinguish between the learning of one's own, or native, culture and the learning of some 'new' (other) culture. The learning of one's own culture is known as **enculturation**. The learning of a new or foreign culture is known as **acculturation**. In Chapter 14, we will see that acculturation is an important concept for marketers who plan to sell their products in foreign or multinational markets. In such cases, marketers must study the specific culture(s) of their potential target markets to determine whether their products will be acceptable to its members and, if so, how they can best communicate the characteristics of their products to persuade the target market to buy.

Language and symbols

To acquire a common culture, the members of a society must be able to communicate with each other through a common language. Without a common language, shared meaning could not exist, and true communication would not take place (see Chapter 10).

To communicate effectively with their audiences, marketers must use appropriate **symbols** to convey desired product images or characteristics. These symbols can be verbal or non-verbal. Verbal symbols may include a television announcement or an advertisement in a magazine. Non-verbal communication includes the use of such symbols as figures, colours, shapes and even textures to lend additional meaning to print or broadcast advertisements, to trademarks and to packaging or product designs (see Figure 13-2).

Basically, the symbolic nature of human language sets it apart from all other animal communication. A symbol is anything that stands for something else. Any word is a symbol. The word razor calls forth a specific image related to an individual's own knowledge and experience. The word tsunami calls forth the notion of waves and water and also has the power to stir us emotionally, arousing feelings of danger and the need for protection and safety. Similarly, the word jaguar has symbolic meaning: to some it suggests a fine luxury car, to others it implies wealth and status, to still others it suggests a sleek, wild animal to be seen in a zoo.

Because the human mind can process symbols, it is possible, for example, for a person to 'experience' cognitively a visualisation for a product, like an advertisement for skin moisturising gel, which contrasts two scenes – one of a parched desert without the gel and one of a rich green landscape with the gel. Such a comparison presents the idea that a skin-moisturising gel will transform a person's dry skin to a comfortable moist state. The capacity to learn symbolically is primarily a human phenomenon; animals learn by direct experience. Clearly, the ability of humans to understand symbolically how a product, service or idea can satisfy their needs makes it easier for marketers to sell the features and benefits of their offerings. Through a shared language and culture, individuals already know what the image means; thus, an association can be made without actively thinking about it.

A symbol may have several, even contradictory, meanings, so the advertiser must ascertain exactly what the symbol is communicating to its intended audience. For example, the

FIGURE 13-2 Advertisement using visual imagery as a symbol
Source: Courtesy of The Advertising Archives.

advertiser who uses a trademark depicting an old craftsman to symbolise careful workmanship may instead be communicating an image of outmoded methods and lack of style. The marketer who uses slang in an advertisement to attract a teenage audience must do so with great care; slang that is misused or outdated will symbolically date the marketer's firm and product.

Price and channels of distribution are also significant symbols of the marketer and the marketer's product. For example, price often implies quality to potential buyers. For certain products (such as clothing), the type of shop in which the product is sold is also an important symbol of quality. In fact, all the elements of the marketing mix – the product, its promotion, price and the shops at which it is available – are symbols that communicate ranges of quality to potential buyers.

Ritual

In addition to language and symbols, culture includes various ritualised experiences and behaviours that until recently have been neglected by consumer researchers. A **ritual** is a type of symbolic activity consisting of a series of steps (multiple behaviours) occurring in a fixed sequence and repeated over time.[7]

In practice, rituals extend over the human life cycle from birth to death, including a host of intermediate events (such as birthday celebrations, graduations and marriage). These rituals can be very public, elaborate, religious or civil ceremonies, or they can be as mundane as an individual's grooming behaviour or flossing.[8] Ritualised behaviour is typically rather formal and often is scripted behaviour (as a religious service requiring a prayer book or the code of proper conduct in a court of law). It is also likely to occur repeatedly over time (such as singing the national anthem before a rugby game).

Most important from the standpoint of marketers is the fact that rituals tend to be replete with ritual artefacts (products) that are associated with or somehow enhance the performance of the ritual. For instance, tree ornaments, stockings and various food items are linked to the ritual of Christmas celebrations; other rituals (such as a graduation, a wedding or wedding anniversary, a Wednesday night card game, or a Saturday afternoon visit to the hair salon) have their own specific artefacts associated with them. For special occasions, such as wedding anniversaries, some types of artefacts are perceived as more appropriate as gifts than others, for example, jewellery rather than everyday household items (see Table 13-1).

In addition to a ritual, which is the way that something is traditionally done, there is also ritualistic behaviour, which can be defined as any behaviour that is made into a ritual. For example, a tennis player may swing his racquet and kick the dirt before a serve to ensure a good swing.

TABLE 13-1 Selected rituals and associated artefacts

SELECTED RITUALS	TYPICAL ARTEFACTS
Wedding	White gown (something old, something new, something borrowed, something blue)
Birth of child	Silver baby spoon
Birthday	Card, present, cake with candles
50th wedding anniversary	Catered party, card and gift, display of photos of the couple's life together
Graduation	Pen, card, wristwatch
New Year's Eve	Champagne, party, fancy dress
Going to the gym	Towel, exercise clothes, water, portable tape player
Sunday football	Beer, crisps
Starting a new job	Get a haircut, buy some new clothing
Retirement	Company party, watch, plaque
Death	Send a card, give to charity in the name of the deceased

CULTURE IS SHARED

To be considered a cultural characteristic, a particular belief, value or practice must be shared by a significant portion of the society. Thus, culture is frequently viewed as group customs that link together the members of a society. Of course, common language is the critical cultural component that makes it possible for people to share values, experiences and customs.

Various social institutions within a society transmit the elements of culture and make the sharing of culture a reality. Chief among such institutions is the family, which serves as the primary agent for enculturation – the passing along of basic cultural beliefs, values and customs to society's newest members. A vital part of the enculturation role of the family is the consumer socialisation of the young. This includes teaching such basic consumer-related values and skills as the meaning of money; the relationship between price and quality; the establishment of product tastes, preferences and habits; and appropriate methods of response to various promotional messages.

In addition to the family, two other institutions traditionally share much of the responsibility for the transfer of selected aspects of culture: educational institutions and houses of worship. In some countries, educational institutions are specifically charged with imparting basic learning skills, history, patriotism, citizenship and the technical training needed to prepare people for significant roles within society. Religious institutions provide and perpetuate religious consciousness, spiritual guidance and moral training. Although the young receive much of their consumer training within the family setting, the educational and religious systems reinforce this training by teaching economic and ethical concepts.

A fourth, frequently overlooked, social institution that plays a major role in the transfer of culture throughout society is the mass media. Given the extensive exposure of European populations to both print and broadcast media, as well as the easily absorbed, entertaining format in which the contents of such media are usually presented, it is not surprising that the mass media are powerful vehicles for imparting a wide range of cultural values.

We are exposed daily to advertising, an important component of the media. Advertising not only underwrites, or makes economically feasible, the editorial or programming contents of the media, but it also transmits much about culture. Without advertising, it would be almost impossible to disseminate information about products, ideas and causes.

Consumers receive important cultural information from advertising. For example, it has been hypothesised that one of the roles of advertising in sophisticated magazines such as *Vanity Fair* and *Wine Spectator* is to instruct readers how to dress and what foods and wines to serve to guests, or in other words, what types of behaviour are most appropriate to their particular social class. Thus, although the scope of advertising is often considered to be limited to influencing the demand for specific products or services, in a cultural context advertising has the expanded mission of reinforcing established cultural values and aiding in the dissemination of new tastes, habits and customs. In planning their advertising, marketers should recognise that advertising is an important agent for social change in our society.

CULTURE IS DYNAMIC

To fulfil its need-gratifying role, culture must continually evolve if it is to function in the best interests of a society. For this reason, the marketer must carefully monitor the sociocultural environment in order to market an existing product more effectively or to develop promising new products.

This is not an easy task because many factors are likely to produce cultural changes within a given society (new technology, population shifts, resource shortages, wars, changing values and customs borrowed from other cultures). For example, major ongoing cultural changes in European societies reflect the expanded role options open to women. Today, more and more

TABLE 13-2 What is IN and what is OUT when visiting France

IN	OUT
Lesser-known cities	Paris
Languedoc	Provence
Recreational travel	Luxury travel
Small inns	Upscale hotels
Living in France	Visiting France
Driving	Riding the rails
Bringing your cell phone	Using a phone card
Packing light	Packing heavy

Source: Adapted from Kelby Carr, 'France Travel Trends – What's In & What's Out for 2005', accessed at http://gofrance.about.com/odissuesnewsshottopics/a/inandout.htm.

women work outside the home, frequently in careers that were once considered exclusively male-oriented. These career women are increasingly not waiting for marriage and a man to buy them luxury items – such as expensive wristwatches and diamond rings. More and more such women are saying, 'I earn a good living, why wait? I will buy it for myself.'[9]

The changing nature of culture means that marketers have consistently to reconsider why consumers are now doing what they do, who the purchasers and the users of their products are (males only, females only, or both), when they do their shopping, how and where they can be reached by the media, and what new product and service needs are emerging. Marketers who monitor cultural changes also often find new opportunities to increase corporate profitability. For example, marketers of such products and services as life insurance, financial and investment advice, casual clothing, toy electric trains and cigars are among those who have attempted to take advantage of shifts in what is feminine and how to communicate with female consumers.

Insights about cultural change are also secured from lists that trend observers create as to 'what's hot' and 'what's not'. Table 13-2 presents an example of such a comparison. Specifically, this one tells potential visitors to France that small, lesser-known cities are 'in', whereas Paris is 'out'; similarly, expensive or upmarket hotels are also 'out', while small inns are 'in'. Such lists often reflect the dynamic nature of a particular society or culture.

THE MEASUREMENT OF CULTURE

A wide range of measurement techniques is used in the study of culture. Some of these techniques were described in Chapter 2. For example, the projective tests used by psychologists to study motivation and personality and the attitude measurement techniques used by social psychologists and sociologists are relatively popular tools in the study of culture.

In addition, content analysis, consumer fieldwork and value measurement survey instruments are three research approaches that are frequently used to examine culture and to spot cultural trends. There are also several commercial services that track emerging values and social trends for businesses and government agencies.

Content analysis

Conclusions about a society, or specific aspects of a society, or a comparison of two or more societies can sometimes be drawn from examining the content of particular messages. **Content analysis**, as the name implies, focuses on the content of verbal, written and pictorial communications (such as the copy and art composition of an advertisement).

Content analysis can be used as a relatively objective means of determining what social and cultural changes have occurred in a specific society or as a way of contrasting aspects of two different societies. Content analysis is useful to both marketers and public policy makers interested in comparing the advertising claims of competitors within a specific industry, as well as for evaluating the nature of advertising claims targeted to specific audiences (e.g. women, the elderly or children).

Consumer fieldwork

When examining a specific society, anthropologists frequently immerse themselves in the environment under study through **consumer fieldwork**. As trained researchers, they are likely to select a small sample of people from a particular society and carefully observe their behaviour. Based on their observations, researchers draw conclusions about the values, beliefs and customs of the society under investigation. For example, if researchers were interested in how men selected ties, they might position trained observers in department and clothing stores and note how ties are selected (solid versus patterned, striped versus paisley and so on). The researchers may also be interested in the degree of search that accompanies the choice, that is, how often consumers tend to take a tie off the display, examine it, compare it to other ties on display and place it back again before selecting the tie that they finally purchase.

The distinct characteristics of **field observation** are that:

1. it takes place within a natural environment;
2. it is performed sometimes without the subject's awareness; and
3. it focuses on observation of behaviour.

Because the emphasis is on a natural environment and observable behaviour, field observation concerned with consumer behaviour often focuses on in-store shopping behaviour and, less frequently, on in-home preparation and consumption.

In some cases, instead of just observing behaviour, researchers become **participant-observers** (i.e. they become active members of the environment that they are studying). For example, if researchers were interested in examining how consumers selected computer software, they might take a sales position in a computer superstore to observe directly and even to interact with customers in the transaction process.

Both field observation and participant-observer research require highly skilled researchers who can separate their own emotions from what they actually observe in their professional roles. Both techniques provide valuable insight that might not easily be obtained through survey research that simply asks consumers questions about their behaviour.

In addition to fieldwork methods, depth interviews and focus-group sessions (see Chapter 2) are also often used by marketers to get a 'first look' at an emerging social or cultural change. In the relatively informal atmosphere of focus group discussions, consumers are apt to reveal attitudes or behaviour that may signal a shift in values that, in turn, may affect the long-term market acceptance of a product or service. For instance, focus group studies can be used to identify marketing programmes that reinforce established customer loyalty and goodwill (or relationship marketing). A common thread running throughout these studies showed that established customers, especially for services (such as investment and banking services), want to have their loyalty acknowledged in the form of personalised services. These observations have led various service and product companies to refine or establish loyalty programmes that are more personalised in the way that they treat their established customers (e.g. by recognising the individuality of such core customers). This is just one of numerous examples showing how focus groups and depth interviews are used to spot social trends.

Value measurement survey instruments

Anthropologists have traditionally observed the behaviour of members of a specific society and inferred from such behaviour the dominant or underlying values of the society. In recent years, however, there has been a gradual shift to measuring values directly by means of survey (questionnaire) research. Researchers use data collection instruments called value instruments to ask people how they feel about such basic personal and social concepts as freedom, comfort, national security and peace.

A variety of popular value instruments have been used in consumer behaviour studies, including the Rokeach Value Survey, the List of Values (LOV) and the Values and Lifestyles System – VALS (discussed in Chapter 3). The widely used **Rokeach Value Survey** is a self-administered value inventory that is divided into two parts, each part measuring different but complementary types of personal values (see Table 13-3). The first part consists of 18 terminal value items, which are designed to measure the relative importance of end states of existence (or personal goals). The second part consists of 18 instrumental value items, which measure basic approaches an individual might take to reach end-state values. Thus, the first half of the measurement instrument deals with ends and the second half considers means.

Using the Rokeach Value Survey, adult Brazilians were categorised into six distinctive value segments.[10] For example, Segment A (representing 13 per cent of the sample) was most concerned with 'world peace', followed by 'inner harmony' and 'true friendship'. Members of this segment were found to be especially involved in domestic-oriented activities (such as gardening, reading and going out with the family to visit relatives). Because of their less materialistic and non-hedonistic orientation, this segment also may be the least prone to experiment with new products. In contrast, Segment B (representing 9 per cent of the sample) was most concerned with self-centred values such as self-respect, a comfortable life, pleasure, an exciting life, a sense of accomplishment and social recognition. They were least concerned with values related to the family, such as friendship, love and equality. These self-centred, achievement-oriented pleasure seekers were expected to prefer provocative clothes in the latest fashion, to enjoy an active lifestyle and to be more likely to try new products.

The LOV is a related measurement instrument that is also designed to be used in surveying consumers' personal values. The LOV scale asks consumers to identify their two most important values from a nine-value list (such as 'warm relationships with others', 'a sense of belonging' or 'a sense of accomplishment') that is based on the terminal values of the Rokeach Value Survey.[11]

TABLE 13-3 The Rokeach Value Survey Instrument

TERMINAL VALUES	INSTRUMENTAL VALUES
A Comfortable Life (a prosperous life)	Ambitious (hardworking, aspiring)
An Exciting Life (a stimulating, active life)	Broad-Minded (open-minded)
A World at Peace (free of war and conflict)	Capable (competent, effective)
Equality (brotherhood, equal opportunity for all)	Cheerful (lighthearted, joyful)
Freedom (independence and free choice)	Clean (neat, tidy)
Happiness (contentedness)	Courageous (standing up for your beliefs)
National Security (protection from attack)	Forgiving (willing to pardon others)
Pleasure (an enjoyable life)	Helpful (working for the welfare of others)
Salvation (saved, eternal life)	Honest (sincere, truthful)
Social Recognition (respect and admiration)	Imaginative (daring, creative)
True Friendship (close companionship)	Independent (self-reliant, self-sufficient)
Wisdom (a mature understanding of life)	Intellectual (intelligent, reflective)

WHAT IS SUBCULTURE?

The members of a specific **subculture** possess beliefs, values and customs that set them apart from other members of the same society. In addition, they adhere to most of the dominant cultural beliefs, values and behavioural patterns of the larger society. We define subculture, then, as *a distinct cultural group that exists as an identifiable segment within a larger, more complex society.*

Thus, the cultural profile of a society or nation is a composite of two distinct elements:

1. the unique beliefs, values and customs subscribed to by members of specific subcultures; and
2. the central or core cultural themes that are shared by most of the population, regardless of specific subcultural memberships.

Figure 13-3 presents a simple model of the relationship between two subcultural groups (geographic or regional subcultures – i.e. citizens of Flemish north and Walloon south in Belgium) and the larger culture. As the figure depicts, each subculture has its own unique traits, yet both groups share some common traits of the Belgian culture.

Let us look at it in another way. Each German is, in large part, a product of the 'German way of life'. Each German, however, is at the same time a member of various subcultures. For example, an 11-year-old boy may simultaneously be a Catholic, a pre-teen and a classmate. We would expect that membership in each different subculture would provide its own set of specific beliefs, values, attitudes and customs. Table 13-4 lists typical subcultural categories and corresponding examples of specific subcultural groups. This list is by no means exhaustive: elementary school teachers, Girl Scouts and millionaires – in fact, any group that shares common beliefs and customs – may be classified as a subculture.

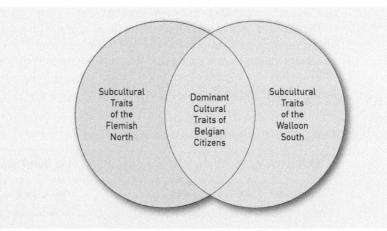

FIGURE 13-3 Relationship between culture and subculture

TABLE 13-4 Examples of major subcultural categories

CATEGORIES	EXAMPLES
Nationality	German, Polish, Lithuanian
Religion	Christian, Hindu, Muslim
Geographic region	Scandinavia, Walloon, Europe, Asia
Age	Senior citizen, teenager, Xers
Gender	Female, male
Occupation	Bus driver, mechanic, engineer
Social class	Lower, middle, upper

Subcultural analysis enables the marketing manager to focus on sizeable and natural market segments. When carrying out such analyses, the marketer must determine whether the beliefs, values and customs shared by members of a specific subgroup make them desirable candidates for special marketing attention. Subcultures, therefore, are relevant units of analysis for market research. And these subcultures are dynamic.

The following sections examine a number of important subcultural categories: nationality, religion, geographic location, age and sex. (Occupational and social-class subgroups were discussed in detail in Chapter 12.)

NATIONALITY SUBCULTURES

For many people, **nationality** is an important subcultural reference that guides what they value and what they buy. This is especially true for the populations of countries that have a history of attracting people from all over the globe. When it comes to consumer behaviour, this ancestral pride is manifested most strongly in the consumption of ethnic foods, in travel to the 'homeland' and in the purchase of numerous cultural artefacts (ethnic clothing, art, music, foreign-language newspapers). Interest in these goods and services has expanded rapidly as younger consumers attempt to understand better and associate more closely with their ethnic roots.

RELIGIOUS SUBCULTURES

In an area as geographically large and culturally varied as Europe, it is natural to find a substantial variety of **religious subcultures**. The members of all these religious groups at times are likely to make purchase decisions that are influenced by their religious identity. Commonly, consumer behaviour is directly affected by religion in terms of products that are symbolically and ritualistically associated with the celebration of various religious holidays. For example, for some religious subcultures, Christmas is indisputably the major gift-purchasing season of the year.

Religious requirements or practices sometimes take on an expanded meaning beyond their original purpose. For instance, dietary laws for an observant Jewish family represent an obligation, so there are toothpastes and artificial sweeteners that are kosher for Passover. In some countries, a 'U' and 'K' mark on food packaging are symbols that the food meets Jewish dietary laws. For non-observant Jews and an increasing number of non-Jews, however, these marks often signify that the food is pure and wholesome – a kind of 'Jewish *Good Housekeeping* Seal of Approval'. In response to the broader meaning given to kosher-certified products, a number of brands have secured kosher certification for their products. Indeed, most kosher food is consumed by non-Jews.[12] Figure 13-4 shows an advertisement for Hellmann's Real Mayonnaise. Note that the label displays a 'U' inside a circle and the word '*PARVE*'. This tells the shopper that the product is kosher and that it can be eaten with either meat or dairy products (but not both together). Targeting specific religious groups with specially designed marketing programmes can be really profitable.

GEOGRAPHIC AND REGIONAL SUBCULTURES

Europe is a large continent, one that enjoys a wide range of climatic and geographic conditions. Given the size and physical diversity, it is only natural that most Europeans have a sense of **regional** identification and use this identification as a way of describing others (such as 'he is a true Scandinavian'). These labels often assist us in developing a mental picture and supporting stereotype of the person in question.

FIGURE 13-4 Advertisement containing a 'U' seal indicating that the product is kosher
Source: Reproduced with kind permission of Unilever (from an original in Unilever Archives).

AGE SUBCULTURES

It is not difficult to understand why each major age sub-grouping of a population might be thought of as a separate subculture. After all, don't you listen to different music from your parents and grandparents, dress differently, read different magazines and enjoy different television shows? Clearly, important shifts occur in an individual's demand for specific types of products and services as he or she goes from being a dependent child to a retired senior citizen. In this chapter, we will limit our examination of **age subcultures** to four age groups, moving from youngest to oldest: Generation Y, Generation X, baby boomers and older consumers. These four age segments have been singled out because their distinctive lifestyles qualify them for consideration as subcultural groups.

The Generation Y market

This age cohort (a cohort is a group of individuals born over a relatively short and continuous period of time) includes the individuals born between the years 1977 and 1994 (i.e. the children of baby boomers). Although they are constantly getting older, members of **Generation Y** (also known as 'echo boomers' and the 'millennium generation') have usually been divided into three subsegments: Gen Y adults, Gen Y teens and Gen Y kids (or 'tweens').[13] Members of Generation Y are often described as pragmatic, clever, socially and environmentally aware and open to new experiences. Today, Generations Y'ers range in age from their mid-teens to their mid-thirties.

Appealing to Generation Y

The younger segment of Generation Y spends significant amounts of money annually and influences purchases by their parents of several times the amount they spend themselves. They have grown up in a media-saturated environment and tend to be aware of 'marketing hype'. For example, they would tend to understand immediately that when a shopping centre locates popular shops at opposite ends they are being encouraged 'to walk the mall'.[14]

This age cohort has shifted some of its television viewing time to the Internet and, when compared with their parents, they are less likely to read newspapers and often do not trust the shops that their parents use.[15] Astute retailers have found it profitable to develop websites specifically targeted to the interests of the Gen Y consumer.[16]

The Generation X market

This age grouping – often referred to as Xers, busters or slackers – consists of individuals born between about 1965 and 1979 (different experts quote different starting and ending years). As consumers, this segment does not like labels, is cynical and does not want to be singled out and marketed to. It matured during an era of soaring divorce rates and 'latchkey children'.[17]

Also, unlike their parents **Generation X** consumers have been in no rush to marry, start a family or work excessive hours to earn high salaries. For them, job satisfaction is typically more important than salary. It has been said, for example, that 'Baby Boomers live to work, Gen Xers work to live!' Xers reject the values of older colleagues who may neglect their families while striving to secure higher salaries and career advancement, and many have observed their parents getting laid off after many years of loyalty to an employer. They, therefore, are not particularly interested in long-term employment with a single company but instead prefer to work for a company that can offer some work–life flexibility and can bring some fun aspects into the environment. Gen Xers understand the necessity of money but do not view salary as a sufficient reason for staying with a company – the quality of the work itself and the relationships built on the job are much more important.[18] For Generation X, it is more important to enjoy life and to have a lifestyle that provides freedom and flexibility.

Appealing to Generation X

Members of Generation X often pride themselves on their sophistication. Although they are not necessarily materialistic, they do purchase good brand names (such as Sony) but not necessarily designer labels. They want to be recognised by marketers as a group in their own right and not as mini-baby boomers. Therefore, advertisements targeted to this audience must focus on their style in music, fashions and language. One key for marketers appears to be sincerity. Xers are not against advertising but only opposed to insincerity.

Baby boomer media do not work with Generation X members. For example, while between 55 and 65 per cent of 30- to 64-year-olds read a newspaper regularly, only 39 per cent of the youngest Xers regularly read a newspaper.[19] Xers are the MTV generation and they watch far more television shows and network channels than baby boomers do.

The baby boomer market

Marketers have found **baby boomers** a particularly desirable target audience because:

1. they are the single largest distinctive age category alive today;
2. they frequently make important consumer purchase decisions; and
3. they contain small subsegments of trendsetting consumers (sometimes known as yuppies, or young upwardly mobile professionals) who have influence on the consumer tastes of other age segments of society.[20]

Who Are the Baby Boomers?

The term *baby boomers* refers to the age segment of the population that was born between 1946 and 1964. Thus, baby boomers are in the broad age category that extends from about mid-40s to mid-60s. These baby boomers are usually found to represent more than 40 per cent of the adult population. The magnitude of this statistic alone would make them a much sought-after market segment. However, they are also valued because they often comprise about 50 per cent of all those in professional and managerial occupations and more than one-half of those with at least a college degree.

In addition, although each year more baby boomers turn 50 years of age, they do not necessarily like the idea. Increases in health club memberships and a boom in the sales of vitamin and health supplements are evidence that these consumers are trying hard to look and feel 'young' – they do not want to age gracefully but will fight and kick and pay whatever is necessary to look young. For example, in some countries 35- to 50-year-olds are the largest market for plastic surgery, and the majority of cosmetic dentistry patients are often 40 to 49 years of age.[21]

Consumer Characteristics of Baby Boomers

Baby boomers tend to be motivated consumers. They enjoy buying for themselves, for their homes or apartments and for others – they are consumption-oriented. As baby boomers age, the nature of the products and services they most need or desire changes. For example, because of the ageing of this market segment, sales of 'relaxed fit' jeans, and varifocal-lens glasses are up substantially, as is the sales of walking shoes. Men's and women's trousers with elasticated waistbands are also enjoying strong sales. Moreover, bank marketers and other financial institutions are beginning to pay more attention to boomers who are starting to think about retirement.

Yuppies are by far the most sought-after subgroup of baby boomers. Although they usually constitute only 5 per cent of a population, they are generally well off financially, well educated and in enviable professional or managerial careers. They are often associated with status brand names, such as BMW or Volvo cars, Rolex watches and cable television. Today, as many yuppies are maturing, they are shifting their attention away from expensive status-type possessions towards travel, physical fitness, planning for second careers or some other form of new direction for their lives.

Gen Yers, Gen Xers, and baby boomers differ in their purchasing behaviour, attitudes towards brands and behaviour towards advertisements. Table 13-5 captures some of the differences among these three age cohorts.

TABLE 13-5 Comparison of selected age cohorts across marketing-related issues

THEMES	GENERATION Y	GENERATION X	BOOMERS
Purchasing behaviour	Savvy, pragmatic	Materialistic	Narcissistic
Coming of age technology	Computer in every home	Microwave in every home	TV in every home
Price–quality attitude	Value oriented: weighing price–quality relationships	Price oriented: concerned about the cost of individual items	Conspicuous consumption: buying for indulgence
Attitude toward brands	Brand embracing	Against branding	Brand loyal
Behavior toward ads	Rebel against hype	Rebel against hype	Respond to image-building type

Source: Adapted from Stephanie M. Noble and Charles H. Noble, 'Getting to Know Y: The Consumption Behaviors of a New Cohort', in *2000 AMA Winter Educators' Conference*, 11 (Chicago: American Marketing Association, 2000), 294.

Older consumers

Europe is ageing. Increasing numbers of baby boomers are well into their fifties (or 'mature adults'), and there are plenty of 'pre-boomers' – those aged 60 to 67 years old.

It should be borne in mind that 'later adulthood' (i.e. those who are 50 years of age or older) is the longest adult life stage for most consumers (i.e. often 29 years or more in duration).[22] This is in contrast to 'early adulthood' (those who are 18 to 34 years of age), a stage lasting 16 years, and 'middle adulthood' (those who are 35 to 49 years of age), a stage lasting 14 years. Remember that people over the age of 50 comprise one-third or more of the adult market in most countries.

Although some people think of older consumers as consisting of people without substantial financial resources, generally in poor health and with plenty of free time on their hands, the fact is that a significant number of these consumers are employed. Additionally, millions of **seniors** are involved in the daily care of a grandchild, and many do voluntary work.[23] The annual discretionary income of this group amounts to 50 per cent of the discretionary income in some countries, and these older consumers are major purchasers of luxury products such as cars, alcohol, holidays and financial products.

Defining 'Older' in Older Consumer

Driving the growth of the elderly population as a proportion of the total population are three factors: the declining birth rate, the ageing of the huge baby boomer segment and improved medical diagnoses and treatment. Often, 'old age' is assumed to begin with a person's 65th birthday, or in some cultures at the age of 67 or perhaps 63. However, people over the age of 60 tend to view themselves as being 15 years younger than their chronological age. Research consistently suggests that people's perceptions of their ages are more important in determining behaviour than their chronological ages (or the number of years lived).[24] In fact, people may at the same time have a number of different perceived or **cognitive ages**. Specifically, elderly consumers perceive themselves to be younger than their chronological ages on four perceived age dimensions: *feel age* (how old they feel); *look age* (how old they look); *do age* (how involved they are in activities favoured by members of a specific age group); and *interest age* (how similar their interests are to those of members of a specific age group).[25] The results support other research that indicates that elderly consumers are more likely to consider themselves younger (to have a younger cognitive age) than their chronological age.

For marketers, these findings underscore the importance of looking beyond chronological age to perceived or cognitive age when appealing to mature consumers and to the possibility that cognitive age might be used to segment the mature market. The 'New-Age Elderly', when compared to the 'Traditional Elderly', are more adventurous, more likely to perceive themselves to be better off financially and more receptive to marketing information.[26]

Segmenting the Elderly Market

The elderly are by no means a homogeneous subcultural group. There are those who, as a matter of choice, do not have colour televisions or touch-tone telephone service, whereas others have the latest desktop computers and spend their time surfing the Internet.

One consumer gerontologist has suggested that the elderly are more diverse in interests, opinions and actions than other segments of the adult population.[27] Although this view runs counter to the popular myth that the elderly are uniform in terms of attitudes and life-styles, both gerontologists and market researchers have repeatedly demonstrated that age is not necessarily a major factor in determining how older consumers respond to marketing activities.

With an increased appreciation that the elderly constitute a diverse age segment, more atten-tion is now being given to identifying ways to segment the elderly into meaningful groupings.[28] One relatively simple segmentation scheme partitions the elderly into three chronological age categories: the young-old (65 to 74 years of age), the old (those 75 to 84); and the old-old (those 85 years of age and older). This market segmentation approach provides useful con-sumer-relevant insights.

The elderly can also be segmented in terms of motivations and quality-of-life orientation. Table 13-6 presents a parallel comparison of new-age elderly consumers and the more tradi-tional older consumers. The increased presence of the new-age elderly suggests that marketers need to respond to the value orientations of older consumers whose lifestyles remain rela-tively ageless. Clearly, the new-age elderly are individuals who feel, think and do according to

TABLE 13-6 Comparison of new-age and traditional elderly

NEW-AGE ELDERLY	TRADITIONAL/STEREOTYPICAL ELDERLY
• *Perceive themselves to be different in outlook from other people their age* • *Age is seen as a state of mind* • *See themselves as younger than their chronological age* • *Feel younger, think younger, and 'do' younger* • *Have a genuinely youthful outlook* • *Feel there is a considerable adventure to living* • *Feel more in control of their own lives* • *Have greater self-confidence when it comes to making consumer decisions* • *Less concerned that they will make a mistake when buying something* • *Especially knowledgeable and alert consumers* • *Selectively innovative* • *Seek new experiences and personal challenges* • *Less interested in accumulating possessions* • *Higher measured life satisfaction* • *Less likely to want to live their lives over differently* • *Perceive themselves to be healthier* • *Feel financially more secure*	• *Perceive all older people to be about the same in outlook* • *See age as more of a physical state* • *See themselves at or near their chronological age* • *Tend to feel, think, and do things that they feel match their chronological age* • *Feel that one should act one's age* • *Normal sense of being in control of their own lives* • *Normal range of self-confidence when it comes to making consumer decisions* • *Some concern that they will make a mistake when buying something* • *Low-to-average consumer capabilities* • *Not innovative* • *Seek stability and a secure routine* • *Normal range of interest in accumulating possessions* • *Lower measured life satisfaction* • *Have some regrets as to how they lived their lives* • *Perceive themselves to be of normal health for their age* • *Somewhat concerned about financial security*

Source: Adapted from 'The Value Orientation of New-Age Elderly: The Coming of an Ageless Market' by Leon G. Schiffman and Elaine Sherman in *Journal of Business Research* 22, March 1991, 187–94. Copyright © 1991 published by Elsevier Science Publishing Co., Inc. All rights reserved.

a cognitive age that is younger than their chronological age. An examination of several recent studies on ageing suggests an 'erosion of chronological age as a central indicator of the experience of aging'.

SEX AS A SUBCULTURE

Because sex roles have an important cultural component, it is quite fitting to examine **gender** as a subcultural category.

Sex roles and consumer behaviour

All societies tend to assign certain traits and roles to males and others to females. In American society, for instance, aggressiveness and competitiveness were often considered traditional masculine traits; neatness, tactfulness, gentleness and talkativeness were considered traditional feminine traits. In terms of role differences, women have historically been cast as homemakers with responsibility for childcare and men as the providers or breadwinners. Because such traits and roles are no longer relevant for many individuals, marketers are increasingly appealing to consumers' broader vision of gender-related role options. However, many studies are still suggesting that even with the large number of middle-class women in the workplace, men are not doing more in terms of housework (e.g. cleaning, cooking, laundry).[29] A recent study also found that men and women exhibit different reactions to identical print advertisements. Women show superior affect and purchase intention towards advertisements that are verbal, harmonious, complex and category-oriented. In contrast, men exhibit superior affect and purchase intention towards advertisements that are comparative, simple and attribute-oriented. Consequently, it may be best, where feasible, to advertise differently to men and women.[30]

Consumer products and sex roles

Within every society, it is quite common to find products that are either exclusively or strongly associated with the members of one sex. In Western Europe, for example, shaving equipment, cigars, trousers, ties and work clothing were historically male products; bracelets, hair spray, hair dryers and sweet-smelling perfumes were generally considered feminine products. For most of these products, the sex role link has either diminished or disappeared; for others, the prohibition still lingers. An interesting product category with regard to the blurring of a gender appeal is men's fragrances. Although men are increasingly wearing fragrances, it is estimated that 30 per cent of men's fragrances are worn by women.[31] Also, although women have historically been the major market for vitamins, men are increasingly being targeted for vitamins exclusively formulated for men.

In terms of its appeal, men and women seem to differ in their attraction to the Internet. For instance, women go online to seek out reference materials, online books, medical information, cooking ideas, government information and chatting. In contrast, men tend to focus on exploring, discovery, identifying free software and investments. This provides further support for the notion that men are 'hunters', whereas women are 'nurturers'.[32] Still further, although men and women are equally likely to browse commercial sites, women are less likely to purchase online (32 per cent for men versus 19 per cent for women). Evidence suggests that the lower incidence of women purchasing online is due to their heightened concerns with online security and privacy.[33] Table 13-7 presents a gender-oriented segmentation scheme that accounts for the type of online materials favoured by specific subsegments of males and females.

TABLE 13-7 Male and female Internet user segments

	KEY USAGE SITUATION	FAVORITE INTERNET MATERIALS
FEMALE SEGMENTS		
Social Sally	Making friends	Chat and personal Web page
New Age Crusader	Fight for causes	Books and government information
Cautious Mom	Nurture children	Cooking and medical facts
Playful Pretender	Role play	Chat and games
Master Producer	Job productivity	White Pages and government information
MALE SEGMENTS		
Bits and Bytes	Computers and hobbies	Investments, discovery, software
Practical Pete	Personal productivity	Investments, company listings
Viking Gamer	Competing and winning	Games, chat, software
Sensitive Sam	Help family and friends	Investments, government information
World Citizen	Connecting with world	Discovery, software, investments

Source: Adapted from Scott M. Smith and David B. Whitlark, 'Men and Women Online: What Makes Them Click?', *Marketing Research*, 13, 2, Summer 2001, 23.

The working woman

Marketers are keenly interested in the working woman, especially the married working woman. They recognise that married women who go out to work are a large and growing market segment, one whose needs differ from those of women who do not work outside the home (frequently self-labelled 'stay-at-home mums'). It is the size of the working woman market that makes it so attractive. For example, because approximately 40 per cent of all business travellers today are women, hotels have begun to realise that it pays to provide the services women want, such as healthy foods, gyms, spas and wellness centres. Female business travellers are also concerned about hotel security and frequently use room service because they do not want to go to the hotel bar or restaurant.

Segmenting the Working Woman Market

To provide a richer framework for segmentation, marketers have developed categories that differentiate the motivations of working and non-working women. For instance, a number of studies have divided the female population into four segments: stay-at-home housewives; plan-to-work housewives; just-a-job working women; and career-oriented working women.[34] The distinction between 'just-a-job' and 'career-oriented' working women is particularly meaningful. 'Just-a-job' working women seem to be motivated to work primarily by a sense that the family requires the additional income, whereas 'career-oriented' working women, who tend to be in a managerial or professional position, are driven more by a need to achieve and succeed in their chosen careers. Today, though, with increasing numbers of female university graduates in the workforce, the percentage of career-oriented working women is on the rise. Working women spend less time shopping than non-working women. They accomplish this 'time economy' by shopping less often and by being brand and store loyal. Not surprisingly, working women are also likely to shop during evening hours and at weekends, as well as to buy through direct-mail catalogues.

SUBCULTURAL INTERACTION

All consumers are simultaneously members of more than one subcultural segment (e.g. a consumer may be a young, Hungarian, Catholic student currently living in Barcelona). For this reason, marketers should strive to understand how multiple subcultural memberships interact to influence target consumers' relevant consumption behaviour. Promotional strategy should not be limited to targeting a single subcultural membership.

SUMMARY

The study of culture is the study of all aspects of a society. It is the language, knowledge, laws and customs that give that society its distinctive character and personality. In the context of consumer behaviour, culture is defined as the sum total of learned beliefs, values and customs that serve to regulate the consumer behaviour of members of a particular society. Beliefs and values are guides for consumer behaviour; customs are usual and accepted ways of behaving.

The impact of culture on society is so natural and so ingrained that its influence on behaviour is rarely noted. Yet culture offers order, direction and guidance to members of society in all phases of human problem-solving. Culture is dynamic and gradually and continually evolves to meet the needs of society.

Culture is learned as part of social experience. Children acquire from their environment a set of beliefs, values and customs that constitutes culture (i.e. they are encultured). These are acquired through formal learning, informal learning and technical learning. Advertising enhances formal learning by reinforcing desired modes of behaviour and expectations; it enhances informal learning by providing models for behaviour.

Culture is communicated to members of society through a common language and through commonly shared symbols. Because the human mind has the ability to absorb and to process symbolic communication, marketers can successfully promote both tangible and intangible products and product concepts to consumers through mass media.

All the elements in the marketing mix serve to communicate symbolically with the audience. Products project an image of their own; so does promotion. Price and retail outlets symbolically convey images concerning the quality of the product.

The elements of culture are transmitted by three pervasive social institutions: the family, religious institutions and the school. A fourth social institution that plays a major role in the transmission of culture is mass media, both through editorial content and through advertising.

A wide range of measurement techniques is used to study culture. The range includes projective techniques, attitude measurement methods, field observation, participant observation, content analysis and value measurement survey techniques.

Subcultural analysis enables marketers to segment their markets to meet the specific needs, motivations, perceptions and attitudes shared by members of a specific subcultural group. A subculture is a distinct cultural group that exists as an identifiable segment within a larger, more complex society. Its members possess beliefs, values and customs that set them apart from other members of the same society; at the same time, they hold to the dominant beliefs of the overall society. Major subcultural categories include nationality, religion, geographic location, age and sex. Each of these can be broken down into smaller segments that can be reached through special copy appeals and selective media choices. In some cases (such as the elderly consumer), product characteristics can be tailored to the specialised needs of the market segment. Because all consumers simultaneously are members of several subcultural groups, the marketer must determine for the product category how specific subcultural memberships interact to influence the consumer's purchase decisions.

DISCUSSION QUESTIONS

1. Distinguish between beliefs, values and customs. Illustrate how the clothing a person wears at different times or for different occasions is influenced by customs.
2. A manufacturer of low calorie crisps is considering targeting school-age children by positioning its product as a healthy, nutritious snack food. How can an understanding of the three forms of cultural learning be used in developing an effective strategy to target the intended market?
3. Sony is introducing a new 27-inch TV with a picture-in-picture feature. How should the company position and advertise the product to (a) Generation X consumers, and (b) affluent baby boomers?
4. For each of the following products and activities:
   a. Identify the core values most relevant to their purchase and use.
   b. Determine whether these values encourage or discourage use or ownership.
   c. Determine whether these core values are shifting and, if so, in what direction.

   The products and activities are:
   1. Donating money to charities
   2. Donating blood
   3. MP3 players
   4. Expensive wine
   5. Toothpaste
   6. Diet soft drinks
   7. Foreign travel
   8. Suntan lotion
   9. iPads
   10. Products in recyclable packaging.
5. Marketers realise that people of the same age often exhibit very different lifestyles. Using the evidence presented in this chapter, discuss how developers of retirement housing can use older consumers' lifestyles to segment their markets more effectively.

EXERCISES

1. Identify a singer or group whose music you like and discuss the symbolic function of the clothes that person (or group) wears.
2. Think of various routines in your everyday life (such as getting ready to go out or food preparation). Identify one ritual and describe it. In your view, is this ritual shared by others? If so, to what extent? What are the implications of your ritualistic behaviour to the marketer(s) of the product(s) you use during your routine?
3. Using one of the subculture categories listed in Table 13-4, identify a group that can be regarded as a subculture within your university or college.
   a. Describe the norms, values and behaviours of the subculture's members.
   b. Interview five members of that subculture regarding attitudes towards the use of credit cards.
   c. What are the implications of your findings for marketing credit cards to the group you selected?
4. Many of your perceptions regarding price versus value are likely to be different from those of your parents or grandparents. Researchers attribute such differences to cohort effects, which are based on the premise that consumption patterns are determined early in life. Therefore, individuals who experienced different economic, political and cultural environments during their youth are likely to be different types of consumers as adults. Describe instances in which your parents or grandparents disagreed with or criticised purchases you had made. Describe the cohort effects that explain each party's position during these disagreements.

NOTES

1. Thomas C. O'Guinn and L. J. Shrum, 'The Role of Television in the Construction of Consumer Reality', *Journal of Consumer Research*, 23, March 1997, 278–95.
2. Linda C. Ueltschy and Robert F. Krampf, 'Cultural Sensitivity to Satisfaction and Service Quality Measures', *Journal of Marketing Theory and Practice*, Summer 2001, 14–31.
3. 'U.S. Coffee Consumption Highest in Decade-Survey', Forbes.Com, 14 June 2002, at www.forbes.com/business/newswire/2002/06/14rtr632507.html.
4. Gwen Rae Bachmann, Deborah Roedder John and Akshay Rao, 'Children's Susceptibility to Peer Group Purchase Influence: An Exploratory Investigation', in *Advances in Consumer Research*, 20, eds Leigh McAlister and Michael L. Rothschild (Provo, UT: Association for Consumer Research 1993), 463–8.
5. Elizabeth C. Hirschman, 'Men, Dogs, Guns, and Cars: The Semiotics of Rugged Individualism', *Journal of Advertising*, 32, Spring 2003, 9–22.
6. Shaila K. Dewan, 'Can't Afford Hawaii? Get the Shirt', *New York Times*, 21 July 2001, B1, B6.
7. Dennis W. Rook, 'The Ritual Dimension of Consumer Behavior', *Journal of Consumer Research*, 12, December 1985, 251–64.
8. Dennis W. Rook, 'Ritual Behavior and Consumer Symbolism', in *Advances in Consumer Research*, 11, ed. Thomas C. Kinnear (Provo, UT: Association for Consumer Research, 1984), 279–84.
9. Tara Parker-Pope, 'All That Glitters Isn't Purchased by Men', *Wall Street Journal*, 7 January 1997, B1; and Dana Canedy, 'As the Purchasing Power of Women Rises, Marketers Start to Pay Attention to Them', *New York Times*, 2 July 1998, D6.
10. Wagner A. Kamakura and Jose Afonso Mazzon, 'Value Segmentation: A Model for the Measurement of Values and Value Systems', *Journal of Consumer Research*, 18, September 1991, 208–18.
11. Lynn R. Kahle, ed., *Social Values and Social Change: Adaption of Life in America* (New York: Praeger, 1983); Sharon E. Beatty *et al.*, 'Alternative Measurement Approaches to Consumer Values: The List of Values and the Rokeach Value Survey', *Psychology and Marketing*, 2, 1985, 181–200; and Lynn R. Kahle, Roger P. McIntyre, Reid P. Claxton and David B. Jones, 'Empirical Relationships Between Cognitive Style and LOV: Implications for Values and Value Systems', in *Advances in Consumer Research*, 22, eds Frank R. Kardes and Mita Sujan (Provo, UT: Association for Consumer Research 1995), 141–6.
12. Kevin Michael Grace, 'Is This Kosher', *Report Newsmagazine*, 27, 1, 8 May 2000, 37; Laura Bird, 'Major Brands Look for the Kosher Label', *Adweek's Marketing Week*, 1 April 1991, 18–19; and Judith Waldrop, 'Everything's Kosher', *American Demographics*, March 1991, 4.
13. Stephanie M. Noble and Charles H. Noble, 'Getting to Know Y: The Consumption Behaviors of a New Cohort', in *2000 AMA Winter Educators' Conference*, 11, eds John P. Workman and William D. Perreault (Chicago: American Marketing Association, 2000), 293–303; and Pamela Paul, 'Getting Inside Gen Y', *American Demographics*, 23, 9, September 2001, 42–9.
14. Lauren Keating, 'The In Crowds', *Shopping Center World*, 29, 5, May 2000, 160–65.
15. Joyce M. Wolburg and James Pokrywczynski, 'A Psychographic Analysis of Generation Y College Students', *Journal of Advertising Research*, 41, 5, September/October 2001, 33–52.
16. Chantal Todè, 'Evolution of Tweens' Tastes Keeps Retailers on Their Toes', *Advertising Age*, 12 February 2001, S6.
17. Keating, 'The In Crowds', 163.
18. Judi E. Loomis, 'Generation X', *Rough Notes*, 143, 9, September 2000, 52–4.
19. Paula M. Poindexter and Dominic L. Lasorsa, 'Generation X: Is Its Meaning Understood?' *Newspaper Research Journal*, 20, 4, Fall 1999, 28–36.
20. 'Boomer Facts', *American Demographics*, January 1996, 14. Also see Diane Crispell, 'U.S. Population Forecasts Decline for 2000, but Rise Slightly for 2050', *Wall Street Journal*, 25 March 1996, B3.

21. Cindy Hearn and Doug Hammond, 'Cosmetic Dentistry: The "Boom" Is upon Us!', *Dental Economics*, 91, 9, September 2001, 118–22.

22. John Nielson and Kathy Curry, 'Creative Strategies for Connecting with Mature Individuals', *Journal of Consumer Marketing*, 14, 4, 1997, 320.

23. Ibid., 3–40.

24. Kelly Tepper, 'The Role of Labeling Processes in Elderly Consumers' Responses to Age Segmentation Cues', *Journal of Consumer Research*, March 1994, 503–19; and Candace Corlett, 'Building a Successful 501 Marketing Program', *Marketing Review*, January 1996, 10–11, 19.

25. Benny Barak and Leon G. Schiffman, 'Cognitive Age: A Nonchronological Age Variable', in *Advances in Consumer Research*, 8, ed. Kent B. Monroe (Ann Arbor, MI: Association for Consumer Research, 1981), 602–6; Elaine Sherman, Leon G. Schiffman and William R. Dillon, 'Age/Gender Segments and Quality of Life Differences', in *1988 Winter Educators' Conference*, eds Stanley Shapiro and A. H. Walle (Chicago: American Marketing Association, 1988), 319–20; Stuart Van Auken and Thomas E. Barry, 'An Assessment of the Trait Validity of Cognitive Age', *Journal of Consumer Psychology*, 1995, 107–32; Robert E. Wilkes, 'A Structural Modeling Approach to the Measurement and Meaning of Cognitive Age', *Journal of Consumer Research*, September 1992, 292–301; and Chad Rubel, 'Mature Market Often Misunderstood', *Marketing News*, 28 August 1995, 28–9.

26. Elaine Sherman, Leon G. Schiffman and Anil Mathur, 'The Influence of Gender on the New-Age Elderly's Consumption Orientation', *Psychology and Marketing*, 18, 10, October 2001, 1073–89.

27. Elaine Sherman, quoted in David B. Wolfe, 'The Ageless Market', *American Demographics*, July 1987, 26–8, 55–6.

28. Carol M. Morgan and Doran J. Levy, 'Understanding Mature Consumers', *Marketing Review*, January 1996, 12–13, 25; and Elaine Sherman and Leon G. Schiffman, 'Quality-of-Life (QOL) Assessment of Older Consumers: A Retrospective Review', *Journal of Business and Psychology*, Fall 1991, 107–19.

29. James W. Gentry, Suraj Commuri and Sunkyu Jun, 'Review of Literature on Gender in the Family', *Academy of Marketing Science Review* (Vancouver), 2003, 1.

30. Sanjay Putrevu, 'Communicating with the Sexes', *Journal of Advertising*, 33, Fall 2004, 51–62.

31. Maxine Wilkie, 'Scent of a Market', *American Demographics*, August 1995, 40–49.

32. Scott M. Smith and David B. Whitlark, 'Men and Women Online: What Makes Them Click?', *Marketing Research*, 13, 2, Summer 2001, 20–25.

33. Kara A. Arnold and Lyle R. Wetsch, 'Sex differences and Information Processing; Implications for Marketing on the Internet', in *2001 AMA Winter Educators' Conference*, 12, eds Ram Krishnan and Madhu Viswanathan (Chicago: American Marketing Association 2001), 357–65.

34. Thomas Barry, Mary Gilly and Lindley Doran, 'Advertising to Women with Different Career Orientations', *Journal of Advertising Research*, 25, April–May 1985, 26–35.

CHAPTER 14
CROSS-CULTURAL CONSUMER BEHAVIOUR: AN INTERNATIONAL PERSPECTIVE

In our examination of psychological, social and cultural factors, we have consistently pointed out how various segments of the consuming public differ. If so much diversity exists among segments of a single society, then even more diversity is likely to exist among the members of two or more societies. To succeed, international marketers must understand the nature and extent of differences between the consumers of different societies – 'cross-cultural' differences – so that they can develop effective targeted marketing strategies to use in each foreign market of interest.

In this chapter, we broaden our scope of analysis and consider the marketing implications of cultural differences and similarities that exist between the people of two or more nations. We also compare the views that pit a global marketing perspective – one that stresses the similarities of consumers worldwide – against a localised marketing strategy that stresses the diversity of consumers in different nations and their specific cultural orientations. Our own view is that marketers must be aware of and sensitive to cross-cultural similarities and differences that can provide expanded sales and profit opportunities. Multinational marketers must be ready to tailor their marketing mixes to the specific customs of each nation that they want to target.

THE IMPERATIVE TO BE MULTINATIONAL

Today, almost all major corporations are actively marketing their products beyond their original national borders. In fact, the issue is generally not whether to market a brand in other countries but rather how to do it (as the same product with the same 'global' advertising campaign, or 'tailored' products and localised advertisements for each country). Because of this emphasis on operating multinationally, the vocabulary of marketing now includes terms such as *glocal*, which refers to companies that are both 'global' and 'local'; that is, they include in their marketing efforts a blend of standardised and local elements in order to secure the benefits of each strategy.[1]

This challenge has been given special meaning by the efforts of the European Union (EU) to form a single market. Although the movement of goods and services among community members has been eased, it is unclear whether this diverse market will really be transformed into a single market of approximately 500 million homogeneous 'Euroconsumers' with the same or very similar wants and needs. Many people hope that the introduction of the euro as a common EU currency will help shape Europe into a huge, powerful, unified market. Furthermore, the rapid acceptance of capitalism by many Eastern European countries also presents a major opportunity and challenge to marketers. Firms such as Coca-Cola and Gillette have been investing extensive sums on product development and marketing to satisfy the needs of Eastern European consumer markets.[2]

The North American Free Trade Agreement (NAFTA), which currently consists of the United States, Canada and Mexico, provides free-market access to more than 440 million consumers. The Association of South East Asian Nations (ASEAN), consisting of Indonesia, Singapore, Thailand, the Philippines, Malaysia and Brunei, is another important economic alliance that offers marketers new global markets. The members of this group have formed the ASEAN Free Trade Area (AFTA) to promote regional trade.

Many firms are developing strategies to take advantage of these and other emerging economic opportunities. A substantial number of firms are now jockeying for market share in foreign markets. Starbucks opened a store within the Forbidden City in Beijing, China, and MTV Networks has formed a partnership with @JapanMedia and is running a new 24-hour Japanese-language music television channel.[3]

With the build-up of 'multinational fever' and the general attractiveness of multinational markets, products or services originating in one country are increasingly being sought out by consumers in other parts of the world. For instance, a digital camera purchased by a tourist in France may contain a camera mechanism from a factory in China and LCD screen manufactured in the United States. While this particular camera was assembled and packaged in France, all the bits and pieces were produced by factories in Brazil, Mexico, Canada, India, China, Japan and Britain.

Firms are selling their products worldwide for a variety of reasons. First, many firms have learned that overseas markets represent the single most important opportunity for their future growth when their home markets reach maturity. This realisation is propelling them to expand their horizons and seek consumers scattered all over the world. Moreover, consumers all over the world are increasingly eager to try 'foreign' products that are popular in different and far-off places. Consider the following story:[4]

> There was this Englishman who worked in the London office of a multinational corporation based in the United States. He drove home one evening in his Japanese car. His wife, who worked in a firm which imported German kitchen equipment, was already home. Her small Italian car was often quicker through the traffic. After a meal which included New Zealand lamb, California carrots, Mexican honey, French cheese and Spanish wine, they settled down to watch a program on their television set, which was made in Finland. The program was a retrospective celebration of the war to recapture the Falkland Islands. As they watched it they felt warmly patriotic, and very proud to be British.

TABLE 14-1 The world's most valuable brands

RANK	BRAND	2011 BRAND VALUE ($ BILLIONS)
1	Apple	153.2
2	Google	111.4
3	IBM	100.8
4	McDonalds	81.0
5	Microsoft	78.2
6	Coca Cola	73.7
7	AT&T	69.9
8	Marlboro	67.5
9	China Mobile	57.3
10	GE	50.3

Source: BrandZ Top 100 Most Valuable Global Brands 2011, Milward Brown Optimor, WPP.

According to Milward Brown, Apple is the most valuable global brand in 2011, with a brand value of 153 billion dollars. Table 14-1 presents Milward Brown's BrandZ list of the world's ten most valuable brands.

Acquiring exposure to other cultures

As more and more consumers come in contact with the material goods and lifestyles of people living in other parts of the world, they have the opportunity to adopt these different products and practices. How consumers in one culture secure exposure to the goods of other people living in other cultures is an important part of consumer behaviour. It impacts the well-being of consumers worldwide and of marketers trying to gain acceptance for their products in countries that are often quite different from their home country.

Consider Mexico. While the Mexican culture shares many similarities with those of Central and South American nations, consumers in Mexico differ when it comes to attitude – they have an affinity for American values. Mexican consumers use brands to display status, making conspicuous consumption a part of life, even for the poor. For example, a working-class household might keep a large American refrigerator in the living room, instead of the kitchen, because it is viewed as a sign of financial success. Still further, the largest market for Martell cognac outside of France is Mexico, because the product allows the affluent to display their success and wealth.[5]

A portion of consumers' exposure to different cultures tends to come about through consumers' own initiatives – their travel, their living and working in foreign countries, or even their immigration to a different country. Additionally, consumers obtain a 'taste' of different cultures from contact with foreign films, theatre, art and artefacts and, most certainly, from exposure to unfamiliar and different products. This second major category of cultural exposure is often fostered by marketers seeking to expand their markets by bringing new products, services, practices, ideas and experiences to potential consumers residing in a different country and possessing a different cultural view. Within this context, international marketing provides a form of 'culture transfer'.

Country-of-origin effects

When consumers are making purchase decisions, they may take into consideration the countries of origin of their choices. Researchers have shown that consumers use their knowledge of where products are made in the evaluation of their purchase options.[6] Such a country-of-origin effect seems to come about because consumers are often aware that a particular firm or brand name is associated with a particular country. For example, as one article noted:[7]

> It's hard to think of BMW or Mercedes except in the context of their being German; a Rover or a Jaguar is linked with Britishness (despite the fact that both brands are now under overseas ownership); and Ferrari is a brand that is Italian before it's anything else at all . . . Brooklyn, Italy's leading brand of chewing gum, is manufactured near Milan by a company called Perfetti and, in its long history, has never been anywhere near the United States.

In general, many consumers associate France with wine, fashion clothing, and perfume and other beauty products; Italy with pasta, designer clothing, furniture, shoes and sports cars; Japan with cameras and consumer electronics; and Germany with cars, tools and machinery. Moreover, consumers tend to have an attitude or even a preference when it comes to a particular product being made in a particular country. This attitude might be positive, negative or neutral, depending on perceptions or experience. For instance, a consumer in one country might positively value a particular product made in another country (e.g. affluent Polish consumers may feel that an Italian Prada handbag or a Swiss Rolex watch are worthwhile investments). In contrast, another consumer might be negatively influenced when he learns that the personal digital assistant (PDA) he is considering buying is made in a country he does not associate with fine electronics, such as PDA Italy). Such country-of-origin effects influence how consumers rate quality and which brands they will ultimately select.[8] Research suggests, though, that when consumer motivation is high and when a specific model of a product is being evaluated (as opposed to a range of products manufactured in a particular country), then consumers are less likely to base judgements on country-of-origin information.[9] However, when consumers are less familiar with foreign products, country of origin becomes an important extrinsic cue.[10]

In addition to perceptions of a product's attributes based on its country of manufacture, research evidence exists that suggests that some consumers may refrain from purchasing products from particular countries due to animosity. A study of this issue found that high-animosity consumers in the People's Republic of China owned fewer Japanese products than low-animosity consumers (during the Second World War Japan occupied parts of China). Although some Chinese consumers might consider Sony to be a high-end, high-quality brand (or perceptions of the product itself might be very positive), they might nevertheless refuse to bring a product manufactured in Japan into the home. Similarly, some Jewish consumers might avoid purchasing German-made products due to the Holocaust, and some New Zealand and Australian consumers might boycott French products due to France's nuclear tests in the South Pacific.[11]

One way to explain why a consumer prefers buying products made in one country and does not wish to buy products made in another, or why consumers in different countries exhibit different behaviours, is the existence of a 'national identity'. As presented in Figure 14-1, national

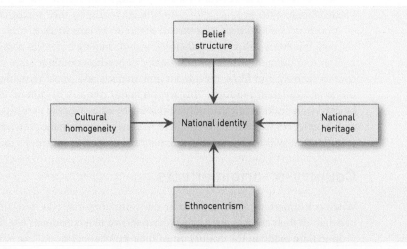

FIGURE 14-1 Dimensions of national identity

identity consists of four dimensions (for each dimension a sample item from a scale to measure it is included; the entire measure is composed of 17 items): belief structure (e.g. 'A true Italian would never reject their religious belief'), cultural homogeneity (e.g. 'People frequently engage in activities that identify them as Italian'), national heritage (e.g. 'Important people from the country's past are admired by people today'), and consumer ethnocentrism (e.g. 'Only those products that are unavailable in Italy should be imported'). Using the national identity scale, research has studied consumers in South Korea, Taiwan, Thailand and Singapore.[12] The research revealed that Thailand, for example, had the strongest national identity and Singapore the weakest. Generally, countries with a weak sense of national identity, coupled with low ethnocentric tendencies, are suitable for use as places to launch new products, because foreign firms are not viewed as threats.

CROSS-CULTURAL CONSUMER ANALYSIS

To determine whether and how to enter a foreign market, marketers need to conduct some form of cross-cultural consumer analysis. Within the scope of this discussion, **cross-cultural consumer analysis** is defined as the effort to determine to what extent the consumers of two or more nations are similar or different. Such analyses can provide marketers with an understanding of the psychological, social and cultural characteristics of the foreign consumers they wish to target, so that they can design effective marketing strategies for the specific national markets involved.

In a broader context, cross-cultural consumer analysis might also include a comparison of subcultural groups (see Chapter 13) within a single country (such as English and French Canadians, Flemish and Walloons in Belgium, or Protestants and Catholics in Northern Ireland). For our purposes, however, we will limit our discussion of cross-cultural consumer analysis to comparisons of consumers of different countries.

Similarities and differences among people

A major objective of cross-cultural consumer analysis is to determine how consumers in two or more societies are similar and how they are different. An understanding of the similarities and differences that exist between nations is critical to the multinational marketer who must devise appropriate strategies to reach consumers in specific foreign markets. The greater the similarity between nations, the more feasible it is to use relatively similar marketing strategies in each nation. On the other hand, if the cultural beliefs, values and customs of specific target countries are found to differ widely, then a highly individualised marketing strategy is indicated for each country. To illustrate, in addition to IKEA furniture company's generic global website that uses English, the firm also offers 14 localised websites and 30 mini-sites that only provide contact information. And whereas the IKEA Italian website shows a group of people frolicking on their IKEA furniture (nudity is acceptable and commonplace in Italian advertising), the Saudi Arabian website uses extremely conservative photographs.[13] As another example, while 88 per cent of adults in both France and Germany drink mineral water, French consumption is strongly associated with concern over the quality of tap water, while German consumption is closely linked to vegetarians.[14]

A firm's success in marketing a product or service in a number of foreign countries is likely to be influenced by how similar the beliefs, values and customs are that govern the use of the product in the various countries. For example, the worldwide television commercials of major international airlines (e.g. Lufthansa, KLM, Air France, American Airlines, Singapore Airlines, Qantas and British Airways) tend to depict the luxury and pampering offered their business-class and first-class international travellers. The reason for their general cross-cultural appeal is that these commercials speak to the same types of individuals worldwide – upscale international business travellers – who share much in common (Figure 14-2).

As another example of the importance of cultural differences or orientation, consider that South-east Asia is frequently the largest market for prestige and luxury brands from the West, and that luxury brand companies such as Louis Vuitton, Rolex, Gucci and Prada are looking to markets

(A)

FIGURE 14-2 The international business traveller seeks to be pampered with services (*continues on the next page*)
Source: © British Airways.

such as Hanoi and Guangzhou when they are thinking of expanding their market reach. Indeed, in fine-tuning their marketing, these luxury brand marketers need to be especially responsive to cultural differences that compel luxury purchases in the Asian and Western markets. Specifically, research suggests that whereas Western consumers tend to 'use' a prestige item to enhance their sense of individualism or serve as a source of personal pleasure, for South-east Asian consumers that same prestige item might serve to help the individual to bond with others and to provide visible evidence of the person's value to others.[15] Still further, within the scope of a visible luxury product, a woman in Hong Kong might carry a Fendi handbag (a visible and conspicuous item), but is not likely to be receptive to luxury lingerie because it is not an item that 'shows' in public.[16]

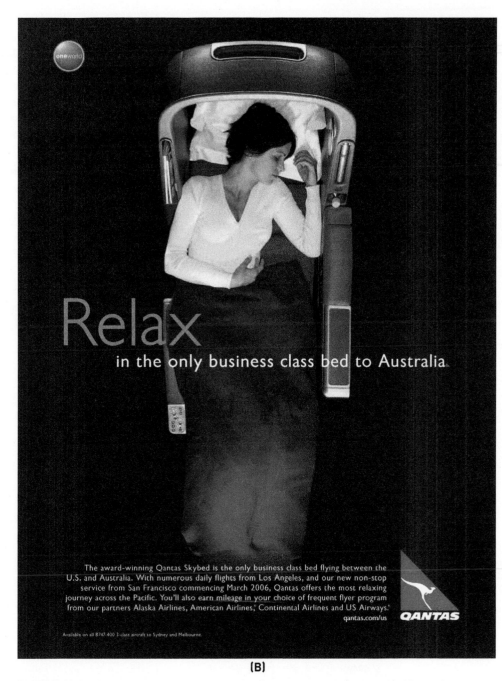

(B)

FIGURE 14-2 The international business traveller seeks to be pampered with services (*continued*)
Source: Qantas Airways.

Time Effects

When business people start dealing with their counterparts in other countries, one of the first things they must realise is that the pace of life differs from one nation to another. For example, whereas the average children's birthday party in Norway lasts approximately two or three hours, Brazilians are willing to wait a little more than two hours for a late arrival to turn up at a birthday party. Consequently, Brazilians are still waiting for guests to arrive as parents of Norwegian children are coming to take their children home. Interestingly, in contrast to Norway, fewer Brazilians wear watches.[17]

How time is spent on the job is also an issue that varies from country to country. In some Western countries, about 80 per cent of work time is spent on the task and perhaps 20 per cent is used for social activities. But in eastern countries such as India and Nepal, the balance is closer to 50 per cent on each; and in Japan, social time, such as having tea with peers in the middle of the day, is considered to be a part of work.[18] Research on the pace of life in 31 countries (basing overall pace on how long pedestrians take to walk 60 feet, the minutes it takes a postal clerk to complete a stamp-purchase transaction and the accuracy of public clocks) reveals substantial cross-cultural differences – whereas Switzerland had the fastest pace of life, Mexico had the slowest. Table 14-2 presents a summary of these findings.

TABLE 14-2 The pace of life in 31 countries

SPEED IS RELATIVE

(Rank of 31 countries for overall pace of life and for three measures: minutes downtown pedestrians take to walk 60 feet; minutes it takes a postal clerk to complete a stamp-purchase transaction; and accuracy in minutes of public clocks.)

	OVERALL PACE	WALKING 60 FEET	POSTAL SERVICE	PUBLIC CLOCK
Switzerland	1	3	2	1
Ireland	2	1	3	11
Germany	3	5	1	8
Japan	4	7	4	6
Italy	5	10	12	2
England	6	4	9	13
Sweden	7	13	5	7
Austria	8	23	8	3
Netherlands	9	2	14	25
Hong Kong	10	14	6	14
France	11	8	18	10
Poland	12	12	15	8
Costa Rica	13	16	10	15
Taiwan	14	18	7	21
Singapore	15	25	11	4
United States	16	6	23	20
Canada	17	11	21	22
South Korea	18	20	20	16
Hungary	19	19	19	18
Czech Republic	20	21	17	23
Greece	21	14	13	29
Kenya	22	9	30	24
China	23	24	25	12
Bulgaria	24	27	22	17
Romania	25	30	29	5
Jordan	26	28	27	19
Syria	27	29	28	27
El Salvador	28	22	16	31
Brazil	29	31	24	28
Indonesia	30	26	26	30
Mexico	31	17	31	26

Source: Adapted from Robert Levine, 'The Pace of Life in 31 Countries', *American Demographics*, November 1997, 20–29. Reprinted with permission. © Crain Communications, Inc. 2001.

The growing global middle class

Recent projections state that while the global population will grow by roughly 1 billion people over the next 10–12 years, the middle class will increase by 1.8 billion, of which 600 million will be Chinese. The growing middle class, particularly in developing countries, is a phenomenon that is very attractive to global marketers who are often eager to identify new customers for their products. The news media has given considerable coverage to the idea that the rapidly expanding middle class in countries of Asia, South America and Eastern Europe is based on the reality that, although per capita income may be low, there is nevertheless considerable buying power, for instance in a country such as China, where most income is largely discretionary income. In Beijing, top earners make about €9,000, while the middle class averages around €5,500. While this is not a particularly high income level compared to the standards of western Europe, it represents an impressive buying power in a low-cost market. In many parts of the world, an income equivalent to €3,600 is considered the point at which a person becomes 'middle class', and it has been estimated that more than 1 billion people in the world's developing countries meet this income standard.[19] This means that a Chinese family with an annual income of €3,600 is middle class and is a target customer for televisions, MP3 players and computers. Indeed, this same general pattern of the growing middle class has also been observed in many parts of South America, Asia and Eastern Europe.[20]

The rapid expansion of middle-class consumers over the past fifty years has attracted the attention of many well-established marketing powerhouses, who were already finding their home markets to be rather mature and reaching what was felt to be a saturation point in terms of sales opportunities. While in 1960 two-thirds of the world's middle class lived in industrialised nations, by the year 2000, some 83 per cent of middle-class citizens were living in developing countries. These changes strongly suggest that more people are now living longer, healthier and better lives – literacy rates in developing countries have risen dramatically in the past fifty years, and today two-thirds rather than only one-third of the people living in these nations are literate.[21] Table 14-3 captures the global progress over the past fifty years and projects it to the year 2050. Note how in 1950 the calorie intake in emerging markets was only 55 per cent of that in industrial countries, whereas today it is more than 80 per cent.

Although a growing middle class provides a market opportunity for products like Big Macs and fries, it should always be remembered that the same product may have different meanings in different countries. For example, whereas European consumers want their fast food to be fast, a Korean consumer is more likely to view a meal as a social or family-related experience. Consequently, convenient store hours may be valued more by a Korean consumer than shorter service time.[22] In China, despite a traditional emphasis on 'fresh' (just picked or killed) food, the emerging middle class, with rising incomes and rising demands on their time, are often willing to spend money to save time, in the form of alternatives to home-cooked meals.[23]

Many transnational corporations (a company that has direct foreign investments and owns or controls activities in more than one nation) think in terms of regions as markets, or even the entire world as their market. For example, Nestlé, a giant Swiss firm, generates only 2 per cent of its sales in Switzerland and bases only 4 per cent of its workers there. Whenever possible, transnational firms try to avoid having products identified with a particular country, rather they seek to make their product feel 'local and natural' to their target customers. Of course, there are exceptions to such strategy. In particular, we might speculate that people throughout the world might generally be expected to prefer a precision Swiss wristwatch to a wristwatch that is made in their own country. Also fashion clothing items, made in France or Italy, are likely to be perceived as more desirable than locally made clothing. The bottom line, though, is that more consumer goods are sold each year because of the growth of the world's middle-class population, and a marketer would do well to focus more on the emerging middle class in other nations than on people who cannot afford to buy its products in its home market. As a recent article concluded, 'Coke is the global soft drink, Macs the global fast-food, and CNN the global television. These are the commodities of a new global middle-class.'[24] We could probably add Facebook to the list, as the global Web page.

TABLE 14-3 Measured global progress 1950–2050

	1950	2000	2050
Global Output, Per Capita (€)	453.8	5,162.8	11,737.5
Global Financial Market			
Capitalization, Per Capita (€)	122.4	10,326.4	58,687.5
Percent of Global gdp			
Emerging Markets	5	50	55
Industrial Countries	95	75	45
Life Expectancy (years)			
Emerging Markets	41	64	76
Industrial Countries	65	77	82
Daily Calorie Intake			
Emerging Markets	1,200	2,600	3,000
Industrial Countries	2,200	3,100	3,200
Infant Mortality (per 1000)			
Emerging Markets	140	65	10
Industrial Countries	30	8	4
Literacy Rate (per 100)			
Emerging Markets	33	64	90
Industrial Countries	95	98	99

Note: The values were originally stated in US dollars, but have been recalculated to euros using an exchange rate of 0.7745.
Sources: Bloomberg, World Bank, United Nations, and author's estimates. Output and financial market capitalisation figures are inflation-adjusted. Peter Marber, 'Globalization and Its Contents', *World Policy Journal*, Winter 2004/05, 30.

Acculturation is a necessary marketing viewpoint

Too many marketers contemplating international expansion make the strategic error of believing that if its product is liked by local or domestic consumers, then everyone will like it. This biased viewpoint increases the likelihood of marketing failures abroad. It reflects a lack of appreciation of the unique psychological, social, cultural and environmental characteristics of distinctly different cultures. To overcome such a narrow and culturally myopic view, marketers must also go through an **acculturation** process. They must learn everything that is relevant about the usage or potential usage of their products and product categories in the foreign countries in which they plan to operate. Take the Chinese culture, for example. For Western marketers to succeed in China it is important for them to take into consideration *guo qing* (pronounced 'gwor ching'), which means 'to consider the special situation or character of China'.[25] An example of *guo qing* for Western marketers is the Chinese policy of limiting families to one child. An appreciation of this policy means that foreign businesses will understand that Chinese families are open to particularly high-quality baby products for their single child (or 'the little emperor').[26] One result of this one-child policy is that in the large cities in China, children are given more than €2.2 billion a year by their parents to spend as they wish, and they influence approximately 68 per cent of their parents' spending. These Chinese children are also less culture-bound than their parents and as a result are more open to Western ideas and products.[27]

In a sense, cross-cultural acculturation is a dual process for marketers. First, marketers must thoroughly orient themselves to the values, beliefs and customs of the new society so as to position and market their products appropriately (being sensitive to and consistent with traditional or prevailing attitudes and values). Secondly, to gain acceptance for a culturally new product in a foreign society, they must develop a strategy that encourages members of that society to modify or even break with their own traditions (to change their attitudes and possibly alter their behaviour). To illustrate the point, a social marketing effort designed to encourage consumers in developing nations to secure polio vaccinations for their children would require a two-step acculturation process. First, the marketer must obtain an in-depth picture of a society's present attitudes and customs with regard to preventive medicine and related concepts. Then the marketer must devise promotional strategies that will convince the members of a target market to have their children vaccinated, even if doing so requires a change in current attitudes.

Distinctive Characteristics of Cross-Cultural Analysis

It is often difficult for a company planning to do business in foreign countries to undertake **cross-cultural consumer research**. For instance, it is difficult in the Islamic countries of the Middle East to conduct Western-style market research: in Saudi Arabia it is illegal to stop people on the streets, and focus groups are impractical because most gatherings of four or more people (with the exception of family and religious gatherings) are outlawed.[28] Foreign firms desiring to do business in Russia have found information regarding consumer and market statistics somewhat limited. Similarly, marketing research information on China is generally inadequate, and surveys that ask personal questions arouse suspicion. So marketers have tried other ways to elicit the data they need. For example, one advertising agency has given cameras to Chinese children so that they can take pictures of what they like and do not like, rather than ask them to explain it to a stranger. Moreover, AC Nielsen conducts focus groups in pubs and children's playrooms rather than in conference rooms; and Leo Burnett has sent researchers to China simply to 'hang out' with consumers.[29]

Applying research techniques

Although the same basic research techniques used to study domestic consumers are useful in studying consumers in foreign lands (see Chapter 2), in cross-cultural analysis an additional burden exists because language and word usage often differ from nation to nation. Another issue in international marketing research concerns scales of measurement. Whereas a 5- or 7-point scale may be adequate in some countries, a 10- or even 20-point scale may be needed in other countries. Still further, research facilities, such as telephone interviewing services, may or may not be available in particular countries or areas of the world.

To avoid such research measurement problems, consumer researchers must familiarise themselves with the availability of research services in the countries they are evaluating as potential markets and must learn how to design marketing research studies that will yield useful data. Researchers must also keep in mind that cultural differences may make 'standard' research methodologies inappropriate. Table 14-4 identifies basic issues that multinational marketers must consider when planning cross-cultural consumer research.

TABLE 14-4 Basic research issues in cross-cultural analysis

FACTORS	EXAMPLES
Differences in language and meaning	Words or concepts (e.g. 'personal cheque account') may not mean the same in two different countries.
Differences in market segmentation opportunities	The income, social class, age and sex of target customers may differ dramatically between two different countries.
Differences in consumption patterns	Two countries may differ substantially in the level of consumption or use of products or services (e.g. mail catalogues).
Differences in the perceived benefits of products and services	Two nations may use or consume the same product (e.g. yogurt) in very different ways.
Differences in the criteria for evaluating products and services	The benefits sought from a service (e.g. bank cards) may differ from country to country.
Differences in economic and social conditions	The 'style' of family decision-making and family structure may vary significantly from country to country.
Differences in marketing research and conditions	The types and quality of retail outlets and direct-mail lists may vary greatly among countries.
Differences in marketing research possibilities	The availability of professional consumer researchers may vary considerably from country to country.

ALTERNATIVE MULTINATIONAL STRATEGIES: GLOBAL VERSUS LOCAL

Some marketers have argued that world markets are becoming increasingly similar and that standardised marketing strategies are, therefore, becoming more feasible. For example, Exxon Mobil sponsored a €125 million marketing campaign to promote its brands (Exxon, Esso, Mobil and General), and the firm wants all the advertisements to carry the same look and feel, regardless of in which of 100 countries in the world an advertisement will appear.[30] In contrast, other marketers feel that differences between consumers of various nations are far too great to permit a standardised marketing strategy. In a practical sense, a basic challenge for many executives contemplating multinational marketing is to decide whether to use shared needs and values as a segmentation strategy (i.e. to appeal to consumers in different countries in terms of their 'common' needs, values and goals) or to use national borders as a segmentation strategy (i.e. to use relatively different, 'local' or specific marketing strategies for members of distinctive cultures or countries).

Favouring a world brand

An increasing number of firms have created **world brand** products that are manufactured, packaged and positioned in exactly the same way regardless of the country in which they are sold. It is quite natural for a 'world class' upscale brand of wristwatches such as Patek Philippe to create a global or uniform advertising campaign to reach its sophisticated worldwide target market (see Figure 14-3). Although the advertising copy is in specific target languages, one might speculate that many of Patek Philippe's affluent target customers do read and write English. Nevertheless, to maximise their 'comfort zone', it is appropriate to speak to them in their native languages.

Marketers of products with a wide or almost mass-market appeal have also embraced a world branding strategy. Multinational companies, such as Gillette, Estée Lauder, Unilever and Fiat, also use global advertising for various products and services.

Still other marketers use a world branding strategy selectively. For example, you might think that Procter & Gamble (P&G), which markets more than 300 brands worldwide, is a company with an abundance of world brands. Recently, though, it was revealed that of its 16 largest brands, only three are truly global brands – Always/Whisper, Pringles and Pantene. Some of P&G's other brands, such as Pampers, Tide/Ariel, Safeguard and Oil of Olay, are just starting to establish common positioning in the world market.[31]

Are global brands different?

According to a 12-nation consumer research project, global brands are viewed differently compared with local brands, and consumers, worldwide, associate global brands with three characteristics: quality signal, global myth and social responsibility. First, consumers believe that the more people who purchase a brand, the higher the brand's *quality* (which often results in a global brand being able to command a premium price). Still further, consumers worldwide believe that global brands develop new products and breakthrough technologies at a faster pace than local brands. The second characteristic, *global myth*, refers to the fact that consumers view global brands as a kind of 'cultural ideal': their purchase and use makes the consumer feel like a citizen of the world, and gives them an identity, i.e. 'Local brands show what we are; global brands show what we want to be'. Finally, global companies are held to a higher level of corporate *social responsibility* than local brands, and are expected to respond to social problems associated with what they sell. For the 12 nations studied in this research, the importance of these three dimensions was consistent,

FIGURE 14-3 Leading wristwatch manufacturer using a global advertising strategy

Source: Patek Philippe Geneva.

and accounted for 64 per cent of the variation in the overall brand preferences (quality signal accounts for 44 per cent of the explanation, global myth for 12 per cent and social responsibility for 8 per cent).[32]

Additionally, while there was not much variation across the 12 nations studied, there were intracountry differences, which resulted in the conclusion that there were four major segments in each country with respect to how its citizens view global brands. *Global Citizens* (55 per cent of the total respondents) use a company's global success as an indication of product quality and innovativeness, and are also concerned that the firm acts in a socially responsible manner. *Global Dreamers* (23 per cent) view global brands as quality products, and are not particularly concerned about the social responsibility issue. *Anti-globals* (13 per cent) feel that global brands are higher quality than local brands, but they do not trust global companies to act responsibly. Generally, they try to avoid purchasing global brands. Lastly, *Global Agnostics* (8 per cent) evaluate global brands in the same way as they evaluate local brands.[33]

Adaptive global marketing

In contrast to the marketing communication strategy that stresses a common message, some firms embrace a strategy that adapts their advertising messages to the specific values of particular cultures. McDonald's is an example of a firm that tries to localise its advertising to consumers in each of the cross-cultural markets in which it operates, making it a 'glocal' company. For example, the Ronald McDonald that we all know has been renamed Donald McDonald in Japan, because the Japanese language does not contain the 'R' sound. Additionally, the McDonald's menu in Japan has been localised to include corn soup and green tea milkshakes.[34] And in Sweden McDonald's developed a new package using woodcut illustrations and a softer design to appeal to the interest that the consumers of that nation have in food value and the outdoors.[35]

Moreover, Coca-Cola is currently testing flavoured drinks containing vitamins and minerals that it hopes will find a large market among the 2 billion children of the world, primarily in underdeveloped nations, suffering from micronutrient deficiencies.[36] Responding to demanding market conditions, Coke's chairman-CEO has announced a new 'Think local – Act local' edict.[37] Other marketers, too, feel that the world brand concept may be going too far. Specifically, the computer game *Tomb Raider IV* had to be customised for different countries. Lara Croft, the heroine, was felt to be too tall and too British for the Japanese market, the Nazi icons had to be removed for the German market, and the naked priestess and zombies had to be clothed for the American market.[38]

Combining Global and Local Marketing Strategies

Some firms follow a mixed or combination strategy. For instance, Unilever and Black & Decker have augmented their global strategies with local executions. In taking such an adaptive approach, global advertisers with a knowledge of cross-cultural differences can tailor their supplemental messages more effectively to suit individual local markets. Because concepts and words often do not easily translate and many regions of the country have their own language, advertisements in China are likely to be more effective if they rely heavily on symbols rather than text.[39]

A study dealing with visual standardisation in print advertisements concluded that 'the standardized approach to global advertising may be able to convey a degree of uniformity in meaning when relying on visually explicit messages. . . . This suggests that there is an ability to create a general consensus of meaning across various cultures by using strong visual images whose fundamental message is highly apparent'.[40] It is also important to note that consumers in different countries of the world have vastly different amounts of exposure to advertisements. For instance, the daily amount of advertising aimed at Japanese consumers, around €5 a day, is 14 times the amount aimed at the average Laotian consumer in an entire year.[41]

A study of foreign advertisers in China found that 11 per cent employed a standardised (or global) strategy, 12 per cent used a localised strategy and the remaining 77 per cent favoured a combination strategy. Of the seven advertising components that were studied, localising language to blend with the local culture was considered to be the most important, followed by the need to localise product attributes, models, colours of advertisements, humour, scenic background and music.[42] Additionally, it has been reported that many of the Western companies that have not been successful in China have acted as if what had worked well in other parts of the world would also prove successful in China. This is too common a mistake.

Perhaps the latest creative hotbed for advertising is Thailand, a nation that generally requires a different advertising focus from most other countries. While over 90 per cent of the population is literate, Thais tend not to read as a leisure activity. Consequently, advertisements are designed visually to catch the attention of consumers, and are typically original, humorous and often slapstick. An example is an advertisement in which Coke is paired with kung fu, which is not how Coke would be advertised in other markets.[43]

Frameworks for assessing multinational strategies

Multinational marketers face the challenge of creating marketing and advertising programmes capable of communicating effectively with a diversity of target markets. To assist in this imposing task, various frameworks have been developed to determine the degree to which marketing and advertising efforts should be either globalised or localised.

To enable international marketers to assess the positions their products enjoy in specific foreign markets, Table 14-5 presents a five-stage continuum that ranges from mere awareness of a foreign brand in a local market area to complete global identification of the brand; that is, the brand is accepted 'as is' in almost every market, and consumers do not think about its country of origin.

Table 14-6 presents a framework that focuses on four marketing strategies available to a firm contemplating doing business on a global basis. A firm might decide either to standardise or localise its product and either standardise or localise its communications programme (thus forming a two-by-two matrix). The four possibilities that this decision framework considers range from a company incorporating a **global strategy** (or standardising both product and

TABLE 14-5 A product recognition continuum for multinational marketing

FACTORS	EXAMPLES
Stage One	Local consumers have heard or read of a brand marketed elsewhere but cannot get it at home; a brand is 'alien' and unavailable but may be desirable [e.g., Rover (English autos), Havana cigars (made in Cuba), or medicine not approved by the FDA but sold in Europe].
Stage Two	Local consumers view a brand made elsewhere as 'foreign', made in a particular country but locally available (e.g., Korean autos, French wine). The fact that the brand is foreign makes a difference in the consumer's mind, sometimes favorable, sometimes not.
Stage Three	Local consumers accord imported brand 'national status'; that is, its national origin is known but does not affect their choice (e.g., Molson beer in the United States, Ford autos in southern Europe).
Stage Four	Brand owned by a foreign company is made (wholly or partly) domestically and has come to be perceived by locals as a local brand; its foreign origins may be remembered but the brand has been 'adopted' ('naturalized'). Examples are Sony in the United States, Coca-Cola in Europe and Japan.
Stage Five	Brand has lost national identity and consumers everywhere see it as 'borderless' or global; not only can people not identify where it comes from but they never ask this question. Examples include the Associated Press and CNN news services, Nescafé, Bayer aspirin.

Source: Adapted from George V. Priovolos, 'How to Turn National European Brands into Pan-European Brands', Working paper, Hagan School of Business, Iona College, New Rochelle, NY.

TABLE 14-6 A framework for alternative global marketing strategies

PRODUCT STRATEGY	COMMUNICATION STRATEGY	
	Standardised Communications	Localised Communications
Standardised Product	**Global Strategy:** Uniform Product/ Uniform Message	**Mixed Strategy:** Uniform Product/ Customised Message
Localised Product	**Mixed Strategy:** Customised Product/Uniform Message	**Local Strategy:** Customised Product/ Customised Message

communications programme) to developing a completely **local strategy** (or customising both the product and communications programme) for each unique market. In the middle there are two mixed strategies. All four cells may represent growth opportunities for the firm. To determine which cell represents the firm's best strategy, the marketer must conduct cross-cultural consumer analysis to obtain consumer reactions to alternative product and promotional executions.

Another orientation for assessing whether to use a global versus local marketing strategy concentrates on a high-tech to high-touch continuum. **Product standardisation** appears to be most successful for high-involvement products that approach either end of the high-tech/high-touch continuum. In other words, products that are at either extreme are more suitable for positioning as global brands. In contrast, low-involvement products in the mid-range of the high-tech/high-touch continuum are more suitably marketed as local brands, using market-by-market executions.[44] To illustrate, on a worldwide basis, consumers interested in high-involvement, high-tech products share a common language (such as 'bytes' and 'microprocessors'), whereas advertisements for high-involvement, high-touch products tend to use more emotional appeals and to emphasise visual images. In either case, according to this perspective (high-involvement products that are either high-tech or high-touch), such products are candidates for global promotional communications.

Some researchers have written that globalisation (or standardisation) and localisation should be viewed as two ends of a continuum and that often the key to success is to 'be global but to act local'. It is also generally an error to assume that demographic segments in other nations would want to be or act like domestic consumers. When looking for success in a foreign market, it has been suggested, a company should remember the following three Ps – place, people and product. Table 14-7 presents the specific elements of these three Ps and cites the appropriate marketing strategy when using a standardisation approach and when using a localisation approach.[45]

TABLE 14-7 Degree of fit between marketing strategies and the 3 Ps

THE 3 Ps	SPECIFIC ELEMENTS	MARKETING STRATEGIES	
		STANDARDISATION	LOCALISATION
Place	Economy	Prosperous	Struggling
	Partners	Few	Plentiful
	Competition	Low	Intense
People	Tastes	Little preference	High preference
	Sophistication	High	Low
	Segments	Few	Many
	Classification	Industrial/consumer durables	Consumer nondurables
Products	Technology	High	Low
	Culture bound	Low	High
	Reputation	Sterling	Poor or unknown
	Product perception	High	Low

Source: Adapted from Sangeeta Ramarapu, John E. Timmerman and Narender Ramarapu, 'Choosing Between Globalization and Localization as a Strategic Thrust for Your International Marketing Effort', *Journal of Marketing Theory and Practice*, 7, 2, Spring 1999, 101. Used by permission of M. E. Sharpe, Inc.

CROSS-CULTURAL PSYCHOGRAPHIC SEGMENTATION

The paradox in cross-cultural consumer research is that although worldwide consumers may be similar in many ways (e.g. the increased number of women who go out to work), any differences in attitudes or behaviour can be crucial in determining satisfaction and may provide an opportunity for segmenting consumers in terms of cultural differences. One marketing authority aptly summed up the issues years ago by stating: 'The only ultimate truth possible is that humans are both deeply the same and obviously different …'.[46] This book endorses the same thesis. Earlier chapters have described the underlying similarities that exist between people and the external influences that serve to differentiate them into distinct market segments. If we believe in tailoring marketing strategies to specific domestic segments it follows then that we also believe in tailoring marketing strategies to the needs – psychological, social, cultural and functional – of specific foreign segments.

Global psychographic research often reveals cultural differences of great importance to marketers. For example, Roper Starch Worldwide, a major multinational marketing research company, interviewed 35,000 consumers in 35 countries in order to identify shared values, irrespective of national borders. The research sought to uncover the bedrock values in people's lives in order to understand the motivations that drive both attitudes and behaviour. After completing the interviews in North and South America, Asia and Europe, six global value groups were uncovered:[47]

Strivers (23%) values wealth, status, ambition, power, and consider material things extremely important. *Devouts* (22%) have more traditional values like faith, duty, obedience and respect for the elders. They are not especially involved with the media and similarly disinterested in western brands. This group is primarily concentrated to the Mideast, Africa and Asia. The *Altruists* (18%) are outer focused and interested in social issues and causes. They are generally well educated, older (median age 44), more female than the norm, and found in Russia and Latin America. The *Intimates* (15%) might be called 'people people,' and focus on relationships close to home, such as spouses, significant others, family, and friends. England, Hungary, the Netherlands, and the United States are where they are most typically found. Intimates are very heavy media users, as being updated gives them something to talk about to others. *Fun seekers* (12%) consist of the youngest consumer group. They value excitement, adventure, pleasure, and looking good, and leisure time is often spent at bars, clubs, and restaurants. This group loves electronic media and is more global in its lifestyle. The last group is the *Creatives* (10%), who are dedicated to technology, knowledge, and learning, and are the highest consumers of media. They especially like books, magazines, and newspapers. Creatives are also the group where you will find global trendsetters in owning and using PCs and in surfing the Web.

SUMMARY

With so much diversity to be found among the members of just one single nation, it is easy to appreciate that numerous larger differences may exist between citizens of different nations having different cultures, values, beliefs and languages. If international marketers are to satisfy effectively the needs of consumers in potentially very distinct markets, they must understand the relevant similarities and differences that exist between the peoples of the countries they decide to target.

When consumers make purchase decisions, they seem to take into consideration the countries of origin of the brands that they are assessing. Consumers frequently have specific attitudes or even preferences for products made in particular countries. These country-of-origin effects influence how consumers rate quality and, sometimes, which brands they will ultimately select.

As increasing numbers of consumers from all over the world come in contact with the material goods and lifestyle of people living in other countries and as the number of middle-class consumers grows in developing countries, marketers are eager to locate these new customers and to offer them their products. The rapidly expanding middle classes in the countries of Asia, South America and Eastern Europe possess relatively substantial buying power because their incomes are largely discretionary (for necessities like housing and medical care are often provided by the state at little or no cost).

For some international marketers, acculturation is a dual process. First, marketers must learn everything that is relevant to the product and product category in the society in which they plan to market, and then they must persuade the members of that society to break with their traditional ways of doing things to adopt the new product. The more similar a foreign target market is to a marketer's home market, the easier is the process of acculturation. Conversely, the more different a foreign target market, the more difficult the process of acculturation.

Some of the problems involved in cross-cultural analysis include differences in language, consumption patterns, needs, product usage, economic and social conditions, marketing conditions and market research opportunities. There is an urgent need for more systematic and conceptual cross-cultural analyses of the psychological, social and cultural characteristics concerning the consumption habits of foreign consumers. Such analyses would identify increased marketing opportunities that would benefit both international marketers and their targeted consumers.

DISCUSSION QUESTIONS

1. Will the elimination of trade barriers among the countries of the European Union change consumer behaviour in these countries? How can foreign companies take advantage of the economic opportunities emerging in Europe?
2. With all the problems facing companies that go global, why are so many companies choosing to expand internationally? What are the advantages of expanding beyond the domestic market?
3. Are the cultures of the world becoming more similar or more different? Discuss.
4. What is cross-cultural consumer analysis? How can a multinational company use cross-cultural research to design each factor in its marketing mix? Illustrate your answer with examples.
5. What are the advantages and disadvantages of global promotional strategies?
6. Consider a domestic brand of shampoo. Should this shampoo be sold worldwide with the same formulation? In the same package? With the same advertising theme? Explain your answers.
7. a. If you wanted to name a new product that would be acceptable to consumers throughout the world, what cultural factors would you consider?
   b. What factors might inhibit an attempt by Apple to position a new laptop computer as a world brand?
8. A Portuguese company is introducing a line of canned soups in Poland. (a) How should the company use cross-cultural research? (b) Should the company use the same marketing mix it uses in Portugal to target Polish consumers? (c) Which, if any, marketing mix components should be designed specifically for marketing canned soups in Poland? Explain your answers.
9. Mercedes-Benz, the German car manufacturer, is using cross-cultural psychographic segmentation to develop marketing campaigns for a new two-seater sports car directed at consumers in different countries. How should the company market the car in Turkey? How should it market the car in Japan?
10. What advice would you give to a Dutch retailer who wants to sell women's clothing in Japan?
11. Select two of the marketing mistakes discussed in the text. Discuss how these mistakes could have been avoided if the companies involved had adequately researched some of the issues listed in Table 14-4.

EXERCISES

1. Have you ever travelled outside Europe? If so, identify some of the differences in values, behaviour and consumption patterns you noted between people in a country you visited and the country which you are from.

2. Interview a student from another culture about his or her use of (a) credit cards, (b) fast-food restaurants, (c) shampoo and (d) trainers. Compare your consumption behaviour to that of the person you interviewed and discuss any similarities and differences you found.

3. Much has been written about the problems at Disneyland Resort, Paris, the Walt Disney Company's theme park and resort complex, which opened in France in April 1992. These difficulties were largely attributed to Disney's lack of understanding of European (particularly French) culture and the company's failure to modify its American theme-park concept to fit the preferences and customs of European visitors. Discuss how the Walt Disney Company could have used input from cross-cultural analysis in better designing and operating Disneyland Resort, Paris, using a computerised literature search about Disneyland Resort, Paris, from your business school's library.

4. Select one of the following countries: Switzerland, Brazil, Germany, Italy, Egypt, India, Japan or Australia. Assume that a significant number of people in the country you chose would like to visit the country in which you live, and that they have the financial means to do so. Now, imagine you are a consultant for your country's tourism agency and that you have been charged with developing a promotional strategy to attract tourists from the country you chose. Conduct a computerised literature search of the databases in your business school's library and select and read several articles about the lifestyles, customs and consumption behaviour of people in the country you chose. Prepare an analysis of the articles and, on the basis of what you read, develop a promotional strategy designed to persuade tourists from that country to visit your country.

NOTES

1. Thomas L. Friedman, 'Big Mac II', *New York Times*, 11 December 1996, A27.

2. Betsy McKay and Steven Gutterman, 'For Ads, Russian Revolution Lives', *Advertising Age*, 7 March 1994, 40.

3. Larry Roellig, 'Designing Global Brands: Critical Lessons', *Design Management Journal*, 12, 4, Fall 2001, 40–45; and 'MTV: Music Television and H&Q Asia Pacific's @JapanMedia Group to Launch New 24-Hour Channel in Japan', *PR Newswire*, 29 August 2000, 1.

4. Michael Silk and David L. Andrews, 'Beyond a Boundary? Sport, Transnational Advertising, and the Reimagining of National Culture', *Journal of Sport and Social Issues*, 25, 2, May 2001, 180–201.

5. 'Marketing to Mexican Consumers', *Brand Strategy* (London), 4 March 2005, 43.

6. Sharyne Merritt and Vernon Staubb, 'A Cross-Cultural Exploration of Country-of-Origin Preference', in *1995 AMA Winter Educators' Proceedings*, eds David W. Stewart and Naufel J. Vilcassim (Chicago: American Marketing Association, 1995), 380; Jill Gabrielle Klein, Richard Ettenson and Marlene D. Morris, 'The Animosity Model of Foreign Product Purchase: An Empirical Test in the People's Republic of China', *Journal of Marketing*, 62, January 1998, 89–100; and Gillian Sullivan Mort, Hume Winzar and C. Min Han, 'Country Image Effects in International Services: A Conceptual Model and Cross-National Empirical Test', in *2001 AMA Educators' Proceedings*, 12, eds Greg W. Marshall and Stephen J. Grove (Chicago: American Marketing Association, 2001), 43–4.

7. Simon Anholt, 'The Nation as Brand', *Across the Board*, 37, 10, December 2000, 22–7.

8. Israel D. Nebenzahl, Eugene D. Jaffe and Shlomo I. Lampert, 'Towards a Theory of Country Image Effect on Product Evaluation', *Management International Review*, 37, 1997, 27–49.

9. Zeynep Gurhan-Canli and Durairaj Maheswaran, 'Determinants of Country-of-Origin Evaluations', *Journal of Consumer Research*, 27, June 2000, 96–108.

10. Gary S. Insch and J. Brad McBride, 'The Impact of Country-of-Origin Cues on Consumer Perceptions of Product Quality: A Binational Test of the Decomposed Country-of-Origin Construct', *Journal of Business Research*, 57, 2004, 256–65.

11. Klein, Ettenson and Morris, 'The Animosity Model', 89–100.

12. Ian Phau and Kor-Weai Chan, 'Targeting East Asian Markets: A Comparative Study on National Identity', *Journal of Targeting, Measurement and Analysis for Marketing*, 12, December 2003, 157–72.

13. Olin Lagon, 'Culturally Correct Site Design', *Web Techniques*, 5, 9, September 2000, 49–51.

14. 'Market Focus: Bottled Mineral Water', *Brand Strategy* (London), 11 February 2004, 42.

15. Nancy Y. Wong and Aaron C. Ahuvia, 'Personal Taste and Family Face: Luxury Consumption in Confucian and Western Societies', *Psychology and Marketing*, 15, 5, August 1998, 423–41. See also Sarah Ellison, 'Sex-Themed Ads Often Don't Travel Well', *Wall Street Journal*, 31 March 2000, 87.

16. Kitty Go, 'Lessons in How to Love Lingerie: The Opening of Hong Kong's Largest Luxury Lingerie Store Heralds the Beginning of a Process to Educate Women on the Benefits of Wearing Their Wealth Close to the Skin', *Financial Times* (London), 28 May 2005, 9.

17. Robert Levine, 'The Pace of Life in 31 Countries', *American Demographics*, November 1997, 20–29.

18. Chip Walker, 'The Global Middle Class', *American Demographics*, September 1995, 40–46; Paula Kephart, 'How Big Is the Mexican Market?', *American Demographics*, October 1995, 17–18; and Rahul Jacob, 'The Big Rise', *Fortune*, 30 May 1994, 74–90.

19. Robert Levine, 'Re-Learning to Tell Time', *American Demographics*, January 1998, 20–25.

20. Rainer Hengst, 'Plotting Your Global Strategy', *Direct Marketing*, August 2000, 55.

21. Peter Marber, 'Globalization and its Contents', *World Policy Journal*, Winter 2004/05, 29–37.

22. Mookyu Lee and Francis M. Ulgado, 'Consumer Evaluations of Fast-Food Services: A Cross-National Comparison', *Journal of Services Marketing*, 11, 1, 1997, 39–52.

23. Ann Veeck and Alvin C. Burns, 'Changing Tastes: The Adoption of New Food Choices in Post-Reform China', *Journal of Business Research*, 58, 2005, 644–52.

24. Keith Suter, 'Transnational Corporations: Knitting the World Together', *Social Alternatives*, 23, 4, Fourth Quarter 2004, 42–5.

25. Rick Yan, 'To Reach China's Consumers, Adapt to Guo Qing', *Harvard Business Review*, September–October 1994, 66–7.

26. Kathy Chen, 'Chinese Babies Are Coveted Consumers', *Wall Street Journal*, 15 May 1998, B1; and Fara Warner, 'Western Markets Send Researchers to China to Plumb Consumers' Minds', *Wall Street Journal*, 28 March 1997, B5.

27. Mindy F. Ji and James U. McNeal, 'How Chinese Children's Commercials Differ from Those of the United States: A Content Analysis', *Journal of Advertising*, 30, 3, Fall 2001, 78–92.

28. Tara Parker-Pope, 'Nonalcoholic Beer Hits the Spot in Mideast', *Wall Street Journal*, 6 December 1995, B1.

29. Warner, 'Western Markets Send Researchers', B5.

30. Vanessa O'Connell, 'Exxon "Centralizes" New Global Campaign', *Wall Street Journal*, 11 July 2001, B6.

31. Robert L. Wehling, 'Even at P&G, Only 3 Brands Make Truly Global Grade So Far', *Advertising Age International*, January 1998, 8.

32. Douglas B. Holt, John A. Quelch and Earl L. Taylor, 'How Global Brands Compete', *Harvard Business Review*, September 2004, 68–75.

33. Ibid.

34. Friedman,'Big Mac II', A27; and Drew Martin and Paul Herbig, 'Marketing Implications of Japan's Social-Cultural Underpinnings', *Journal of Brand Management*, 9, 3, January 2002, 171–9.

35. Pamela Buxton, 'Helping Brands Take on the World', *Marketing* (London), 13 May 1999, 32.

36. Betsy McKay, 'Drinks for Developing Countries', *Wall Street Journal*, 27 November 2001, B1, B6.

37. Jack Neff, 'Rethinking Globalism', *Advertising Age*, 9 October 2000, 1, 100.

38. Silk and Andrews, 'Beyond a Boundary', 190.

39. Dean Foster, 'Playing with China Dollars', *Brandweek*, 10 November 1997, 20–23.

40. Michael Callow and Leon G. Schiffman, 'Sociocultural Meanings in Visually Standardised Print Ads', *European Journal of Marketing*, 38, 9/10, 2004, 1113–28.

41. Kip D. Cassino, 'A World of Advertising', *American Demographics*, November 1997, 60.

42. Jiafei Yin, 'International Advertising Strategies in China: A Worldwide Survey of Foreign Advertisers', *Journal of Advertising Research*, 39. 6, November/December 1999, 25–35.

43. Normandy Madden, 'Looking for the Next Brazil? Try Thailand', *Advertising Age*, 11 April 2005, 22.

44. Teresa Domzal and Lynette Unger, 'Emerging Positioning Strategies in Global Marketing', *Journal of Consumer Marketing*, 4, Fall 1987, 27–9.

45. Sangeeta Ramarapu, John E. Timmerman and Narender Ramarapu, 'Choosing Between Globalization and Localization as a Strategic Thrust for Your International Marketing Effort', *Journal of Marketing Theory and Practice*, 7, 2, 97–105.

46. Sidney J. Levy, 'Myth and Meaning in Marketing', in *1974 Combined Proceedings*, ed. Ronald C. Curhan (Chicago: American Marketing Association, 1975), 555–6.

47. Stuart Elliott, 'Research Finds Consumers Worldwide Belong to Six Basic Groups That Cross National Lines', *New York Times*, 25 June 1998, D8.

PART 4

MORE ON THE CONSUMER'S DECISION-MAKING PROCESS

PART 4 EXPLORES SOME FURTHER ASPECTS RELATED TO
CONSUMER DECISION-MAKING

Chapter 15 extends the previous discussion on the social influence on
consumer behaviour, and specifically presents the role of personal influence,
opinion leadership and the diffusion of innovations. The final chapter ties
together the psychological, social and cultural concepts examined throughout
the book and relates this to the decision-making process.

CHAPTER 15

CONSUMER INFLUENCE AND THE DIFFUSION OF INNOVATIONS

This chapter deals with two interrelated issues of considerable importance to consumers and marketers alike – the informal influence that others have on consumers' behaviour and the dynamic processes that impact consumers' acceptance of new products and services.

In the first part of this chapter we will examine the nature and dynamics of the influence that friends, neighbours and acquaintances have on our consumer-related decisions. This influence is often called word-of-mouth communications or the opinion leadership process (the two terms will be used interchangeably here). We will also consider the personality and motivations of those who influence (opinion leaders) and those who are influenced (opinion receivers). We will end the first part of this chapter with an exploration of how marketers are enhancing their consumer strategies by harnessing the power of natural word-of-mouth in the form of stimulated or market manipulated word-of-mouth. These contrived marketing efforts, unlike 'naturally occurring' word-of-mouth or opinion leadership, largely consist of either paid actors or largely unpaid volunteer agents who are engaged by marketers to create buzz and sales for new products that they often freely elect to talk up. In the second part of this chapter, we will explore factors that encourage and discourage acceptance (or rejection) of new products and services. For consumers, new products and services may represent increased opportunities to satisfy personal, social, and environmental needs and add to their quality of life. For the marketer, new products and services provide an important mechanism for keeping the firm competitive and profitable.

WHAT IS OPINION LEADERSHIP?

The power and importance of personal influence are captured in the following comment by an advertising agency executive: 'Perhaps the most important thing for marketers to understand about word-of-mouth is its huge potential economic impact.'[1]

Opinion leadership (or word-of-mouth communications) is the process by which one person (the opinion leader) informally influences the actions or attitudes of others, who may be opinion seekers or merely opinion recipients. The key characteristic of the influence is that it is interpersonal and informal and takes place between two or more people, none of whom represents a commercial selling source that would gain directly from the sale of something. Word-of-mouth implies personal, or face-to-face, communication, although it may also take place in a telephone conversation or within the context of email or a chat group on the Internet. This communication process is likely, at times, to be reinforced by non-verbal observations of the appearance and behaviour of others.

One of the parties in a word-of-mouth encounter usually offers advice or information about a product or service, such as which of several brands is best or how a particular product may be used. This person, the **opinion leader**, may become an **opinion receiver** when another product or service is brought up as part of the overall discussion.

Individuals who actively seek information and advice about products sometimes are called **opinion seekers**. For purposes of simplicity, the terms opinion receiver and opinion recipient will be used interchangeably in the following discussion to identify both those who actively seek product information from others and those who receive unsolicited information. Simple examples of opinion leadership at work include the following:

1. A family decides that they need a new gas barbecue for their back garden, and they ask a few of their neighbours which brand they should purchase.
2. During a coffee break, a colleague talks about the film he saw last night and recommends seeing it.
3. A person shows a friend photographs of his recent holiday on the Greek island of Corfu, and the friend suggests that learning to use the different manual settings instead of the auto function might produce better pictures in such a sunny place.

Most studies of opinion leadership are concerned with the measurement of the behavioural impact that opinion leaders have on the consumption habits of others. Available research, for example, suggests that 'influentials' or opinion leaders are almost four times more likely than others to be asked about political and government issues, as well as how to handle teens; three times more likely to be asked about computers or investments; and twice as likely to be asked about health issues and restaurants.[2] There is also research to suggest that when an information seeker feels that he or she knows little about a particular product or service, a 'strong-tie source' will be sought (such as a friend or family member), but when the consumer has some prior knowledge of the subject area, then a 'weak-tie source' is acceptable (acquaintances or strangers).[3]

Word-of-mouth in today's 'always in contact' world

Over the past decade, with the proliferation of mobile phone usage, wireless Internet access, Twitter and Facebook accounts, many people find themselves, by choice, 'always' available to friends, family and business associates. Along with the explosion of Web-capable mobile phones is the creation of the 'thumb generation', which is known in Japan as *oya yubi sedai*. Young people in Japan learn to send email messages from mobile phones by using their thumbs, and both Japanese television stations and other companies worldwide have held thumbing speed contests. This is just a natural extension of the thumb usage learned from using handheld computer games.[4]

Just How Important is Word-of-Mouth?

A study in the United Kingdom asked consumers which information sources would make them 'more comfortable' with a company. The answer at the top of the list was 'friend's recommendation' (the response of 71 per cent of respondents), whereas 'past experience' was the response of 63 per cent of respondents. Only 15 per cent of the consumers mentioned 'advertising'.[5] Additionally, some studies have reported that over 40 per cent of respondents will actively seek the advice of family and friends when in the market for a doctor, lawyer or car mechanic, and the importance of word-of-mouth is even greater with respect to the diffusion of new products.[6]

DYNAMICS OF THE OPINION LEADERSHIP PROCESS

The opinion leadership process is a very dynamic and powerful consumer force. As informal communication sources, opinion leaders are remarkably effective at influencing consumers in their product-related decisions. Some of the reasons for the effectiveness of opinion leaders are discussed next.

Credibility

Opinion leaders are highly credible sources of information because they are usually perceived as objective concerning the product or service information or advice they dispense. Their intentions are perceived as being in the best interests of the opinion recipients because they receive no compensation for the advice and apparently have no 'axe to grind'. Because opinion leaders often base their product comments on first-hand experience, their advice reduces for opinion receivers the perceived risk or anxiety inherent in buying new products. The average person is exposed to anywhere from 200 to 1,000 sales communications a day, but he or she is thousands of times more likely to act on the basis of a friend's or colleague's recommendation. Whereas the advertiser has a vested interest in the message being advertised, the opinion leader offers advice that does not have a commercial motive.[7]

Positive and negative product information

Information provided by marketers is invariably favourable to the product and/or brand. Thus, the very fact that opinion leaders provide both favourable and unfavourable information adds to their credibility. An example of an unfavourable or negative product comment is, 'The problem with those inexpensive digital cameras is that the images they produce are not nearly as sharp as those from a DSLR camera'. Compared with positive or even neutral comments, negative comments are relatively uncommon. For this reason, consumers are especially likely to note such information and to avoid products or brands that receive negative evaluations. Over the years, a number of films have failed due to negative 'buzz' about them, and one study found that negative word-of-mouth about a food product retarded sales more than twice as much as positive word-of-mouth promoted sales.[8] Consumers, it turns out, are generally three to ten times more likely to share a negative experience than a positive one.[9]

Information and advice

Opinion leaders are the source of both information and advice. They may simply talk about their experience with a product, relate what they know about a product or, more aggressively, advise others to buy or to avoid a specific product. The kinds of product or service information that opinion leaders are likely to transmit during a conversation include the following:

1. Which of several brands is best: 'In my opinion, when you consider picture quality versus cost, Sony offers the best value in small digital cameras'.

2. How best to use a specific product: 'I find that my walls look best when I paint with a roller rather than a pad.'
3. Where to shop: 'When Marks & Spencer has a sale, the values are remarkable.'
4. Who provides the best service: 'Over the last 10 years, I've flown Lufthansa several times a year, and I think its service can't be beaten.'

Opinion leadership is category specific

Opinion leadership tends to be category specific; that is, opinion leaders often 'specialise' in certain product categories about which they offer information and advice. When other product categories are discussed, however, they are just as likely to reverse their roles and become opinion receivers. A person who is considered particularly knowledgeable about boats may be an opinion leader in terms of this subject, yet when it comes to purchasing a new washing machine the same person may seek advice from someone else – perhaps even from someone who has sought his advice on boats.

Opinion leadership is a two-way street

As the preceding example suggests, consumers who are opinion leaders in one product-related situation may become opinion receivers in another situation, even for the same product. Consider the following example; Jeanette, a new mother contemplating the purchase of a baby car seat, may seek information and advice from other people to reduce her indecision about which brand to select. Once the car seat has been bought, however, she may experience post-purchase dissonance (see Chapter 9) and have a compelling need to talk favourably about the purchase to other people to confirm the correctness of her own choice. In the first instance, she is an opinion receiver (seeker); in the second, she assumes the role of opinion leader.

An opinion leader may also be influenced by an opinion receiver as the result of a product-related conversation. For example, a person may tell a friend about a favourite hotel in Glasgow, Scotland, and in response to comments from the opinion receiver, come to realise that the hotel is too small, too isolated and offers holidaymakers fewer amenities than other hotels.

THE MOTIVATION BEHIND OPINION LEADERSHIP

To understand the phenomenon of opinion leadership, it is useful to examine the motivation of those who provide and those who receive product-related information.

The needs of opinion leaders

What motivates a person to talk about a product or service? Motivation theory suggests that people may provide information or advice to others to satisfy some basic need of their own (see Chapter 5). However, opinion leaders may be unaware of their own underlying motives. As suggested earlier, opinion leaders may simply be trying to reduce their own post-purchase dissonance by confirming their own buying decisions. For instance, if Adam subscribes to a mobile phone service and then is uncertain that he made the right choice, he may try to reassure himself by 'talking up' the service's advantages to others. In this way, he relieves his own psychological discomfort. Furthermore, when he can influence a friend or neighbour also to subscribe to the service, he confirms his own good judgement in selecting the service first. Thus, the opinion leader's true motivation may really be self-confirmation or self-involvement. Furthermore, the information or advice that an opinion leader dispenses may provide all types of tangential personal benefits: it may confer attention, imply some type of status, grant superiority, demonstrate awareness and expertise and give the feeling of possessing inside information and the satisfaction of 'converting' less adventurous souls.

In addition to self-involvement, the opinion leader may also be motivated by product involvement, social involvement and message involvement. Opinion leaders who are motivated by product involvement may find themselves so pleased or so disappointed with a product that they simply must tell others about it. Those who are motivated by social involvement need to share product-related experiences. In this type of situation, opinion leaders use their product-related conversations as expressions of friendship, neighbourliness and love.

The needs of opinion receivers

Opinion receivers satisfy a variety of needs by engaging in product-related conversations. First, they obtain new-product or new-usage information. Secondly, they reduce their perceived risk by receiving first-hand knowledge from a user about a specific product or brand. Thirdly, they reduce the search time entailed in the identification of a needed product or service. Moreover, opinion receivers can be certain of receiving the approval of the opinion leader if they follow that person's product endorsement or advice and purchase the product. For all of these reasons, people often look to friends, neighbours and other acquaintances for product information. Indeed, research examining the importance of four specific information sources on a hypothetical purchase of consumer services revealed that advice from others was more important than the combined impact of sales representatives, advertising and promotion, and other sources.[10] Table 15-1 compares the motivations of opinion receivers with those of opinion leaders.

Purchase pals

Researchers have also examined the influence of 'purchase pals' as information sources who actually accompany consumers on shopping trips. Although purchase pals were used only 9 per cent of the time for grocery items, they were used 25 per cent of the time for purchases of

TABLE 15-1 A comparison of the motivations of opinion leaders and opinion receivers

OPINION LEADERS	OPINION RECEIVERS
SELF-IMPROVEMENT MOTIVATIONS	
• *Reduce post-purchase uncertainty or dissonance*	• *Reduce the risk of making a purchase commitment*
• *Gain attention or status*	• *Reduce search time (e.g. avoid the necessity of shopping around)*
• *Assert superiority and expertise*	
• *Feel like an adventurer*	
• *Experience the power of 'converting' others*	
PRODUCT-INVOLVEMENT MOTIVATIONS	
• *Express satisfaction or dissatisfaction with a product or service*	• *Learn how to use or consume a product*
	• *Learn what products are new in the marketplace*
SOCIAL-INVOLVEMENT MOTIVATIONS	
• *Express neighbourliness and friendship by discussing products or services that may be useful to others*	• *Buy products that have the approval of others, thereby ensuring acceptance*
MESSAGE-INVOLVEMENT MOTIVATIONS	
• *Express one's reaction to a stimulating advertisement by telling others about it*	

TABLE 15-2 Key differences between opinion leaders and surrogate buyers

OPINION LEADER	SURROGATE BUYER
1. Informal relationship with end users	1. Formal relationship; occupation-related status
2. Information exchange occurs in the context of a casual interaction	2. Information exchange in the form of formal instructions/advice
3. Homophilous (to a certain extent) to end users	3. Heterophilous to end users (that in fact is the source of power)
4. Does not get paid for advice	4. Usually hired, therefore gets paid
5. Usually socially more active than end users	5. Not necessarily socially more active than end users
6. Accountability limited regarding the outcome of advice	6. High level of accountability
7. As accountability limited, rigor in search and screening of alternatives low	7. Search and screening of alternatives more rigorous
8. Likely to have (although not always) used the product personally	8. May not have used the product for personal consumption
9. More than one can be consulted before making a final decision	9. Second opinion taken on rare occasions
10. Same person can be an opinion leader for a variety of related product categories	10. Usually specializes for a specific product/service category

Source: Adapted from Praveen Aggarwal and Taihoon Cha, 'Surrogate Buyers and the New Product Adoption Process: A Conceptualization and Managerial Framework', *Journal of Consumer Marketing*, 14, 5, 1997, 394.

electronic equipment (e.g. computers, television sets).[11] Interestingly, male purchase pals are more likely to be used as sources of product category expertise, product information and retail store and price information. Female purchase pals are more often used for moral support and to increase confidence in the buyer's decisions. Similarly, research evidence suggests that when a weak tie exists between the purchase pal and the shopper (e.g. neighbour, classmate or work colleague), the purchase pal's main contribution tends to be functional – the source's specific product experiences and general marketplace knowledge are being relied on. In contrast, when strong ties exist (such as mother, son, husband or wife), what is relied on is the purchase pal's familiarity with and understanding of the buyer's individual characteristics and needs (or tastes and preferences).[12]

Surrogate buyers versus opinion leaders

Although the traditional model of new product adoption shows opinion leaders influencing the purchase of many new products and services, there are instances in which surrogate buyers replace opinion leaders in this role. For example, working women are increasingly turning to wardrobe consultants for help in purchasing business attire, most new drugs start out requiring a doctor's prescription and many service providers make decisions for their clients (e.g. your service garage decides which brand of disc brake pads to install on your car). Consequently, in an increasing number of decision situations, it is a surrogate buyer who primarily influences the purchase.[13] Table 15-2 presents the key differences between opinion leaders and surrogate buyers.

MEASUREMENT OF OPINION LEADERSHIP

Consumer researchers are interested in identifying and measuring the impact of the opinion leadership process on consumption behaviour. In measuring opinion leadership, the researcher has a choice of four basic measurement techniques:

1. the self-designating method,
2. the sociometric method,

SINGLE-QUESTION APPROACH:
1.   In the last six months have you been asked your advice or opinion about *golf equipment*?*
     Yes _____ No _____

MULTIPLE-QUESTION APPROACH:
(Measured on a 5-point bipolar 'Agree/Disagree' scale)

1.   Friends and neighbours frequently ask my advice about *golf equipment*.
2.   I sometimes influence the types of *golf equipment* friends buy.
3.   My friends come to me more often than I go to them about *golf equipment*.
4.   I feel that I am generally regarded by my friends as a good source of advice about *golf equipment*.
5.   I can think of at least three people whom I have spoken to about *golf equipment* in the past six months.

*Researchers can insert their own relevant product/service or product/service category.

FIGURE 15-1 Self-designating questions for measuring opinion leadership

3. the key informant method, and
4. the objective method.

In the *self-designating method*, respondents are asked to evaluate the extent to which they have provided others with information about a product category or specific brand or have otherwise influenced the purchase decisions of others. Figure 15-1 shows two types of self-designating question formats that can be used to determine a consumer's opinion leadership activity. The first consists of a single question, whereas the second consists of a series of questions. The use of multiple questions enables the researcher to determine a respondent's opinion leadership more reliably because the statements are interrelated.[14] The self-designating technique is used more often than other methods for measuring opinion leadership because consumer researchers find it easy to include in market research questionnaires. Because this method relies on the respondent's self-evaluation, however, it may be open to bias should respondents perceive 'opinion leadership' (even though the term is not used) to be a desirable characteristic and, thus, overestimate their own roles as opinion leaders.

The *sociometric method* measures the person-to-person informal communication of consumers concerning products or product categories. In this method, respondents are asked to identify (a) the specific individuals (if any) to whom they provided advice or information about the product or brand under study, and (b) the specific individuals (if any) who provided them with advice or information about the product or brand under study. In the first instance, if respondents identify one or more individuals to whom they have provided some form of product information, they are tentatively classified as opinion leaders. In the second instance, respondents are asked to identify the individuals (if any) who provided them with information about a product under investigation. Individuals designated by the primary respondent are tentatively classified as opinion leaders. In both cases, the researcher attempts to validate the determination by asking the individuals named whether they did, in fact, either provide or receive the relevant product information.

Opinion leadership can also be measured through the use of a *key informant*, a person who is keenly aware of or knowledgeable about the nature of social communications among members of a specific group. The key informant is asked to identify those individuals in the group who are most likely to be opinion leaders. However, the key informant does not have to be a member of the group under study. For example, a professor may serve as the key informant for

TABLE 15-3 Scale items: Opinion leadership (Price)

STRONGLY DISAGREE	___:___:___:___:___:___:___ 1 2 3 4 5 6 7	STRONGLY AGREE

1. People ask me for information about prices for different types of products.
2. I'm considered somewhat of an expert when it comes to knowing the prices of products.
3. For many kinds of products, I would be better able than most people to tell someone where to shop to get the best buy.
4. I like helping people by providing them with price information about many kinds of products.
5. My friends think of me as a good source of price information.
6. I enjoy telling people how much they might expect to pay for different kinds of products.

Source: Donald R. Lichtenstein, Nancy M. Ridgeway and Richard G. Netemeyer (1993), Price perceptions and consumer shopping behavior: A field study, *Journal of Marketing Research*, 30 (May), 234–245.

a university class, identifying those students who are most likely to be opinion leaders with regard to a particular issue. This research method is relatively inexpensive because it requires that only one individual or at most several individuals be intensively interviewed, whereas the self-designating and sociometric methods require that a consumer sample or entire community be interviewed. However, the key informant method is not generally used by marketers because of the difficulties inherent in identifying an individual who can objectively identify opinion leaders in a relevant consumer group.

Finally, the *objective method* of determining opinion leadership is much like a controlled experiment – it involves placing new products or new-product information with selected individuals and then tracing the resulting web of interpersonal communication concerning the relevant product(s). In a practical sense, a new restaurant in a city's business district might apply this approach to speed up the creation of a core customer base by sending out invitations to young, influential business executives to dine with their friends at a reduced introductory price at any time during the first month of the restaurant's operations. If the restaurant's food and drink are judged to be superior, the restaurant is likely to enjoy the benefits of enhanced positive word-of-mouth generated by the systematic encouragement of the young clientele to try it out and who 'talk it up' to their friends after experiencing the new restaurant.

Table 15-3 presents a scale for measuring opinion leaderships related to price, or in other words – a self-reported tendency to be used by others as a good source of price information.

A PROFILE OF THE OPINION LEADER

Just who are opinion leaders? Can they be recognised by any distinctive characteristics? Can they be reached through specific media? Marketers have long sought answers to these questions, for if they are able to identify the relevant opinion leaders for their products, they can design marketing messages that encourage them to communicate with and influence the consumption behaviour of others. For this reason, consumer researchers have attempted to develop a realistic profile of the opinion leader. This has not been easy to do. As was pointed out earlier, opinion leadership tends to be category specific; that is, an individual who is an opinion leader in one product category may be an opinion receiver in another product category. Thus, the generalised profile of opinion leaders is likely to be influenced by the context of specific product categories.

TABLE 15-4 Profile of opinion leaders

GENERALISED ATTRIBUTES ACROSS PRODUCT CATEGORIES	CATEGORY-SPECIFIC ATTRIBUTES
Innovativeness	Interest
Willingness to talk	Knowledge
Self-confidence	Special-interest media exposure
Gregariousness	Same age
Cognitive differentiation	Same social status
	Social exposure outside group

Although it is difficult to construct a generalised profile of the opinion leader without considering a particular category of interest (or a specific product or service category), Table 15-4 does present a summary of the generalised characteristics that appear to hold true regardless of product category. The evidence indicates that opinion leaders across all product categories generally exhibit a variety of defining characteristics. First, they reveal a keen sense of knowledge and interest in the particular product or service area, and they are likely to be consumer innovators. They also demonstrate a greater willingness to talk about the product, service or topic; they are more self-confident; and they are more outgoing and gregarious ('more sociable'). Furthermore, within the context of a specific subject area, opinion leaders receive more information via non-personal sources and are considered by members of their groups to have expertise in their area of influence. Indeed, a recent study found expertise of the source (the opinion leader) to be strongly associated with likely influence on the information seeker's decision-making process.[15] They also usually belong to the same socio-economic and age groups as their opinion receivers.

When it comes to their mass-media exposure or habits, opinion leaders are likely to read special-interest publications devoted to the specific topic or product category in which they 'specialise'. For example, a sailing boat opinion leader might read publications such as *Yachting World*, *Sailing World*, *Cruising World* or *Sail*. These special-interest magazines not only serve to inform those who sail and those interested in sailing about new boats, equipment, harbours and routes over the seas of the world, but also provide readers with the specialised knowledge that enables them to make recommendations to friends and other sailors they meet both at home and while on their way. Thus, the opinion leader tends to have greater exposure to media specifically relevant to his or her area of interest than the non-leader. Summing it up for us, a recent study found that opinion leaders 'gain influence through their informational advantages relative to others in the same environment'.[16]

FREQUENCY AND OVERLAP OF OPINION LEADERSHIP

Opinion leadership is not a rare phenomenon. Often more than one-third of the people studied in a consumer research project are classified as opinion leaders with respect to some self-selected product category. The frequency of consumer opinion leadership suggests that people are sufficiently interested in at least one product or product category to talk about it and give advice concerning it to others.

This leads to the interesting question: do opinion leaders in one product category tend to be opinion leaders in other product categories? The answer to this question comes from an area of research aptly referred to as *opinion leadership overlap*. According to this, opinion leadership tends to overlap across certain combinations of interest areas. Overlap is likely to be highest among product categories that involve similar interests (such as high-definition television sets and Blu-ray players, high-fashion clothing and cosmetics, household cleaners and detergents, expensive wristwatches and writing instruments, hunting gear and fishing tackle). Thus, opinion leaders in one product area are often opinion leaders in related areas in which they are also interested.

Market mavens

Research does suggest the existence of a special category of opinion leader, the **market maven**.[17] These consumers possess a wide range of information about many different types of products, retail outlets and other dimensions of markets. They both initiate discussions with other consumers and respond to requests for market information. Market mavens like to shop, and they also like to share their shopping expertise with others. However, although they appear to fit the profile of opinion leaders in that they have high levels of brand awareness and tend to try more brands, unlike opinion leaders their influence extends beyond the realm of high-involvement products. For example, market mavens may help diffuse information on such low-involvement products as razor blades and laundry detergent.[18] Furthermore, market mavens appear to be motivated by a sense of obligation to share information, a desire to help others and the feeling of pleasure that comes with telling others about products.[19]

While both innovators and market mavens spend more time shopping than other consumers, innovators tend to be price insensitive. Market mavens are not primarily concerned with price, but are nevertheless more value conscious than other shoppers and are attentive to bargain prices.[20] Table 15-5 compares consumer innovators to market mavens, including breadth

TABLE 15-5 Consumer innovativeness and market mavenism compared

CONSTRUCT OF INTEREST	INNOVATIVENESS	MARKET MAVENISM
Information and Knowledge	Knowledgeable about specific product categories	Wide variety of market information; information seekers
Opinion Leadership	Act as opinion leaders for new products	Act as opinion leaders for many aspects of the marketplace
Search Behavior	Exposed to a variety of information sources	Exposed to a variety of information sources
Involvement	Involved in the marketplace; especially new products	Involved in many aspects of the marketplace
Promotion	Interested in information, heavy or centrally processed communications	Heavy users of coupons, shopping lists, grocery budgets, and ads
Brand Awareness	Aware of new brands in specific product fields	Aware of new brands in many fields
Assertiveness	No reason to expect an assertive style of shopping and buying	More assertive than other consumers
Value conscious	More interested in newness than price; not bargain conscious	More value conscious than other consumers; seek bargain prices
Fashion Consciousness	Fashion innovators are fashion conscious	Market Mavens are not fashion conscious

Source: Adapted from Ronald E. Goldsmith, Leisa R. Flynn and Elizabeth B. Goldsmith, 'Innovation Consumers and Market Mavens', *Journal of Marketing Theory and Practice*, 11, Fall 2003, 56. Used by permission of M. E. Sharpe, Inc.

TABLE 15-6 Market maven scale (six-point agree/disagree response format)

1. I like introducing new brands and products to my friends.
2. I like helping people by providing them with information about many kinds of products.
3. People ask me for information about products, places to shop, or sales.
4. If someone asked where to get the best buy on several products, I could tell him or her where to shop.
5. My friends think of me as a good source of information when it comes to new products or sales.
6. Think about a person who has information about a variety of products and likes to share this information with others. This person knows about new products, sales, stores, and so on, but does not necessarily feel he or she is an expert on one particular product. How well would you say that this description fits you?

Source: Adapted from Ronald E. Goldsmith, Leisa R. Flynn and Elizabeth B. Goldsmith, 'Innovation Consumers and Market Mavens', *Journal of Marketing Theory and Practice*, 11, Fall 2003, 58. Used by permission of M. E. Sharpe, Inc.

of knowledge and reaction to promotions. The table reveals, for example, that while the opinion leader's knowledge extends only to a specific product category, market mavens possess a wide range of market information. Table 15-6 presents a market maven scale that uses a six-point agree/disagree response format to identify market mavens.

It would be wrong to discuss market mavens without specifically citing the role played by teenagers. Seventy per cent of teens use the Internet regularly, and they know how to search for and find information both for themselves and in response to information requests from others. Research has found that in families where both parents and teenagers are heavy Internet users, both the teens and their parents recognise the teens' expertise and value their contribution to family decision-making.[21]

Just as the examination of the relationship between being an opinion leader and being an innovator led to the recognition of the existence of the market maven, research on the market maven has uncovered yet another category of consumers, the *social hub*. These are individuals who direct social traffic – they have relationships with many people, they frequently bring these people together, and they do so for personal pleasure (rather than for some tangible reward). It is possible that social hubs may prove to be an excellent way to predict the number of people that are told about a consumption experience.[22]

THE SITUATIONAL ENVIRONMENT OF OPINION LEADERSHIP

Product-related discussions between two people do not take place in a vacuum. Two people are not likely to meet and spontaneously break into a discussion in which product-related information is sought or offered. Rather, product discussions generally occur within relevant situational contexts, such as when a specific product or a similar product is used or served or as a result of a more general discussion that touches on the product category. For example, while drinking coffee, one person might tell the other person about a preferred brand of coffee.

Moreover, it is not surprising that opinion leaders and opinion receivers are often friends, neighbours or work associates, for existing friendships provide numerous opportunities for conversation concerning product-related topics. Close physical proximity is likely to increase the occurrences of product-related conversations. A local health club or community centre, for example, or even the local supermarket, provides opportunities for neighbours to meet and engage in informal communications about products or services. In a similar fashion, the rapid growth in the use of the Internet is also creating a type of close 'electronic proximity' or 'community' – one in which people of like minds, attitudes, concerns, backgrounds and experiences are coming together in 'chat sessions' to explore their common interests. Within this context, the Internet is proving to be a fertile environment for word-of-mouth communications of the kind that consumer marketers are interested in impacting.

THE INTERPERSONAL FLOW OF COMMUNICATION

A classic study of voting behaviour concluded that ideas often flow from radio and print media to opinion leaders and from them to the general public.[23] This so-called **two-step flow of communication theory** portrays opinion leaders as direct receivers of information from impersonal mass-media sources, who in turn transmit (and interpret) this information to the masses. This theory views the opinion leader as an intermediary between the impersonal mass media and the majority of society. Figure 15-2 presents a model of the two-step flow of communication theory. Information is depicted as flowing in a single direction (or one way) from the mass media to opinion leaders (Step 1) and then from the opinion leaders (who interpret, legitimise and transmit the information) to friends, neighbours and acquaintances, who constitute the 'masses' (Step 2).

Multi-step flow of communication theory

A more comprehensive model of the interpersonal flow of communication depicts the transmission of information from the media as a multi-step flow. The revised model takes into account the fact that information and influence are often two-way processes in which opinion leaders both influence and are influenced by opinion receivers. Figure 15-3 presents a model of the **multi-step flow of communication theory**. Steps 1a and 1b depict the flow of information from the mass media simultaneously to opinion leaders, opinion receivers/seekers, and information receivers (who neither influence nor are influenced by others). Step 2 shows the transmission of information and influence from opinion leaders to opinion receivers/seekers. Step 3 reflects the transfer of information and influence from opinion receivers to opinion leaders.

Advertising designed to stimulate/simulate word-of-mouth

In a world before the Internet, weblogs, and viral or buzz marketing, firms' advertising and promotional programmes largely relied on stimulating or persuading consumers to 'tell your friends how much you like our product'. This is one way in which marketers encourage

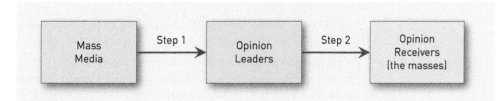

FIGURE 15-2 Two-step flow of communication model

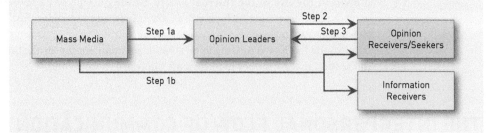

FIGURE 15-3 Multi-step flow of communication model

consumer discussions of their products or services. The objective of a promotional strategy of stimulation is to run advertisements or a direct-marketing programme sufficiently interesting and informative to provoke consumers into discussing the benefits of the product with others. In a classic study, a group of socially influential high school students (class presidents and sports captains) were asked to become members of a panel that would rate newly released musical recordings. As part of their responsibilities, panel participants were encouraged to discuss their record choices with friends. Preliminary examination suggested that these influential students would not qualify as opinion leaders for musical recordings because of their relatively meagre ownership of the product category.[24] However, some of the records the group evaluated made the Top 10 charts in the cities in which the members of the group lived; these same recordings did not make the Top 10 charts in any other city. This study suggests that product-specific opinion leaders can be created by taking socially involved or influential people and deliberately increasing their enthusiasm for a product category.

A more recent research effort explored the notion of increasing enthusiasm for a product category. Over a 12-week period, half the participants were assigned to look at corporate websites (i.e. marketer-generated information sources), and half were asked to look at online discussions (e.g. chat rooms, forums). Consumers who got their information from online discussions reported greater interest in the product category. It is felt that chat rooms and other forums provide consumers with personal experiences and may offer greater credibility, trustworthiness, relevance and empathy than marketer-generated Internet websites.[25] Another related form of advertising message (much less common than advertisements designed to *stimulate* word-of-mouth) is advertisements designed to *simulate* word-of-mouth and this was used occasionally by a small number of marketing firms to supplement their regular advertising image or brand advertising. Such advertisements designed to simulate word-of-mouth portrayed people in the act of informal communication.

Word-of-mouth may be uncontrollable

Although most marketing managers believe that word-of-mouth communication is extremely effective, one problem that they sometimes overlook is the fact that informal communication is difficult to control. Negative comments, frequently in the form of rumours that are untrue, can sweep through the marketplace to the detriment of a product.

Some common rumour themes that have plagued marketers in recent years and unfavourably influenced sales include the following:

1. the product was produced under unsanitary conditions,
2. the product contained an unwholesome or culturally unacceptable ingredient,
3. the product functioned as an undesirable depressant or stimulant,
4. the product included a cancer-causing element or agent, and
5. the firm was owned or influenced by an unfriendly or misguided foreign country, government agency or religious cult.

MARKETERS SEEK TO TAKE CONTROL OF THE OPINION LEADERSHIP PROCESS

Marketers have long been aware of the power that opinion leadership exerts on consumers' preferences and actual purchase behaviour. For this reason marketers are increasingly designing products with characteristics or design factors that make them easy to talk about and whip up interest about. They are also looking at ways to intervene more directly and take control of the word-of-mouth process. This effort to control the flow of word-of-mouth about a product is not new. However, what is new is the degree of interest and the available technologies that make it easier to accomplish (e.g. consumers' buddy lists).

Marketers are now moving beyond employing advertising primarily to stimulate or simulate word-of-mouth, to an environment where they are seeking to manage (i.e. to create and control) word-of-mouth. In this section we will consider marketers' efforts to create products with greater word-of-mouth potential, and to harness the power of word-of-mouth by either hiring paid actors to go out and create product buzz, or securing the involvement of largely unpaid consumer volunteers, who act as buzz agents to drum up awareness, interest and intention to purchase the clients' new products. As part of this discussion we will consider viral marketing and weblogs.

Creating products with built-in buzz potential

New-product designers take advantage of the effectiveness of word-of-mouth communication by deliberately designing products to have word-of-mouth potential. A new product should give customers something to talk about ('buzz potential'). Examples of products and services that have had such word-of-mouth appeal include iPods, mobile phones with digital cameras and a host of other sought-after technologies and luxury brands. Such high-demand products have attained market share advantages because consumers are willing to 'sell' them to each other by means of word-of-mouth. Films also appear to be one form of entertainment in which word-of-mouth operates with some degree of regularity and a large degree of impact. It is very common to be involved directly or to overhear people discussing which films they liked and which they advise others to miss. Proof of the power of word-of-mouth may be seen, for example, when critics hate a film but the viewing public like it and tell their friends.

Where informal word-of-mouth does not spontaneously emerge from the uniqueness of the product or its marketing strategy, some marketers have deliberately attempted to stimulate or to simulate opinion leadership.

Strategies designed to simulate buzz

The nature and scope of the Internet has inspired marketers to expand opportunities to take control of the process of word-of-mouth. For instance, they are increasingly hiring buzz marketing agencies that maintain large armies of largely volunteer consumer buzz agents who seem greatly to enjoy telling other consumers (often friends and family, and people on their buddy list) about a product that they have been exposed to and feel that they would like to talk about. Some marketers prefer to hire actors to go out and simulate buzz for a product. For instance, a campaign for Hennessy Cognac used paid actors to visit bars and nightclubs and order Cognac martinis made with Hennessy. Although they were instructed to act as if they were ordering a new fad drink, in reality they were attempting to create a new fad drink.[26] The objective of a promotional strategy of stimulation is to run advertisements or a direct-marketing programme that is sufficiently interesting and informative to provoke consumers into discussing the benefits of the product with others.

Viral Marketing

Also known as 'buzz marketing', 'wildfire marketing', 'avalanche marketing' or any one of a dozen other names, *viral marketing* 'describes any strategy that encourages individuals to pass on a marketing message to others, creating the potential for exponential growth in the message's exposure and influence'.[27] Viral marketing is the marriage of email and word-of-mouth. It is also named 'viral' because it allows a message to spread like a virus. Consider Hotmail, the first free Web email service. By giving away free email addresses and services, and by attaching a tag to the bottom of every message that reads 'Get your private, free email at http://www.hotmail. com', every time a Hotmail user sent an email, there was a good chance that the receiver of the email would consider signing up for a free Hotmail account. Vespa, the Italian motor scooter manufacturer, has its in-house agency hire models to hang out on scooters outside trendy nightclubs and cafés.[28]

There appear to be two principal types of 'buzz'. Uncodified buzz occurs when an innovator encounters a new product, film, etc., that he or she likes and passes on the information. While the level of trust and credibility that a consumer gives such communication, because it comes from a friend, is very high, this type of buzz is not something that is controllable by the firm, and could be either positive or negative. In contrast, codified buzz is something that is 'incubated, fostered, and underwritten by the firm', and may take the form of trial versions, testimonials, observable usage, endorsements, gift certificates, hosted chat rooms, and so on. The firm should understand that the observability and the trialability of the viral marketing programme for the new product (these two concepts will be fully discussed later in this chapter) are critical elements. For example, a money-back guarantee makes trialability a win-win undertaking for the consumers because it reduces the risk perceived with regard to making a purchase.[29]

One way in which the 'buzz' can spread quickly is through the forwarding of emails. It is estimated that 90 per cent of Internet users use email, and about 50 per cent of them use it daily. The term *Viral Maven* has been coined to refer to an individual who receives and sends pass-along emails frequently, as opposed to *Infrequent Senders*. One Viral Maven, for example, forwarded an email about the band Nsync to 500 of her friends because it contained video messages from band members that were not available anywhere else.[30] Recently, Nescafé Café con Leche (Nestlé Argentina) recruited 50 of the drink's target consumers who were 'big' email forwarders and asked them to forward a spot for the product to at least 15 people each. In the month after the product's introduction, the spot and link were forwarded 100,000 times, and 15 to 20 per cent of visitors to the site answered a four-question survey.[31]

Weblogs as Word-of-Mouth

One of the newest mediums for disseminating word-of-mouth is the blog (short for weblog), with millions of these Web journals appearing on the Internet over the past few years. *Fortune* magazine named the blog the number one tech trend, and estimated that over 23,000 new weblogs are created daily – by both consumers and companies. Consider the power and impact of blogs on a company's products. Specifically, when a person posted information on a group discussion site that U-shaped Kryptonite cycle locks could be picked with a Bic ballpoint pen, within a few days a number of blogs had videos demonstrating how this could be done. Four days after the original posting, Kryptonite issued a statement promising that their new line of cycle locks would be tougher. But bloggers kept up the pressure, and shortly afterwards newspapers started to publish articles about the problem. Over a ten-day period about 1.8 million people read postings about Kryptonite, and the company announced that it would offer free exchange for any affected lock.

Facebook and Twitter are also gaining ground as important arenas for word-of-mouth. With over 500 million users as of July 2010, a huge number of Facebook pages are designed to facilitate positive word-of-mouth (normally set up by a company), to spread negative word-of-mouth (usually designed by consumers) or to simply discuss and share consumption experiences. For example, by the end of October 2010, over 15.8 million consumers worldwide had signed up as 'friends' on the Coca Cola Facebook page. Similarly, more than 93,000 persons had signed up for the 'I hate Liverpool' page. The impact of these new channels of information distribution is enormous, as consumers can post their opinions and know for sure that they will pop up on the screens of all their Facebook friends, or on the screen of all the other consumers who are connected to a specific page.

DIFFUSION OF INNOVATIONS

The second part of this chapter examines a major issue in marketing and consumer behaviour – the acceptance of new products and services. The framework for exploring consumer acceptance of new products is drawn from the area of research known as the **diffusion of innovations**. Consumer researchers who specialise in the diffusion of innovations are primarily interested in understanding two closely related processes: the **diffusion process** and the **adoption process**. In the broadest sense, diffusion is a macro process concerned with the spread of a new product (an innovation) from its source to the consuming public. In contrast, adoption is a micro process that focuses on the stages through which an individual consumer passes when deciding to accept or reject a new product. In addition to an examination of these two interrelated processes, we present a profile of **consumer innovators**, those who are the first to purchase a new product. The ability of marketers to identify and reach this important group of consumers plays a major role in the success or failure of new-product introductions.

And why are new-product introductions so important? Well, the policy of Gillette is that 40 per cent of sales must come from products introduced within the past five years. Similarly, fully half of Hewlett-Packard's revenues are derived from products introduced to the market within the past 24 months.[32] It is also of interest to note that diffusion models for particular types of goods and services may change over time. For example, until the 1960s, it was assumed that new fashions diffused in a top-down or trickle-down manner – new styles are first adopted by the upper-class elites and gradually diffuse to the middle and lower classes. However, since the 1960s, the bottom-up model has served as the better explanation of fashion diffusion – new styles develop in lower-status groups and are later adopted by higher-status groups. These innovative fashions typically emanate from urban communities that also serve as seedbeds for other innovations, such as art and popular music.[33]

THE DIFFUSION PROCESS

The diffusion process is concerned with how innovations spread, that is, how they are assimilated within a market. More precisely, diffusion is the process by which the acceptance of an **innovation** (a new product, new service, new idea or new practice) is spread by communication (mass media, salespeople or informal conversations) to members of a social system (a target market) over a period of time. This definition includes the four basic elements of the diffusion process:

1. the innovation,
2. the channels of communication,
3. the social system, and
4. time.

The innovation

No universally accepted definitions of the terms *product innovation* or *new product* exist. Instead, various approaches have been taken to define a new product or a new service; these can be classified as firm-, product-, market- and consumer-oriented definitions of innovations.

Firm-Oriented Definitions

A *firm-oriented approach* treats the newness of a product from the perspective of the company producing or marketing it. When the product is 'new' to the company, it is considered new. This definition ignores whether or not the product is actually new to the marketplace (i.e. to competitors or consumers). Consistent with this view, copies or modifications of a competitor's product would qualify as new. Although this definition has considerable merit when the objective is to examine the impact that a 'new' product has on the firm, it is not very useful when the goal is to understand consumer acceptance of a new product.

Product-Oriented Definitions

In contrast to firm-oriented definitions, a *product-oriented approach* focuses on the features inherent in the product itself and on the effects these features are likely to have on consumers' established usage patterns. One product-oriented framework considers the extent to which a new product is likely to disrupt established behaviour patterns. It defines the following three types of product innovations:[34]

1. A **continuous innovation** has the least disruptive influence on established patterns. It involves the introduction of a modified product rather than a totally new product. Examples include the redesigned BMW 3-series, the latest version of Microsoft Windows or the BOSE Wave radio.
2. A **dynamically continuous innovation** is somewhat more disruptive than a continuous innovation but still does not alter established behaviour patterns. It may involve the creation of a new product or the modification of an existing product. Examples include digital cameras, digital video recorders, MP3 players and USB Flash drives.
3. A **discontinuous innovation** requires consumers to adopt new behaviour patterns. Examples include aircraft, radios, televisions, cars, PCs and videocassette recorders. Figure 15-4 shows how the telephone, a discontinuous innovation of major magnitude, has produced a variety of both dynamically continuous and continuous innovations and has even stimulated the development of other discontinuous innovations.

Market-Oriented Definitions

A *market-oriented approach* judges the newness of a product in terms of how much exposure consumers have to the new product. Two market-oriented definitions of product innovation have been used extensively in consumer studies:

1. A product is considered new if it has been purchased by a relatively small (fixed) percentage of the potential market.
2. A product is considered new if it has been on the market for a relatively short (specified) period of time.

Both of these market-oriented definitions are basically subjective because they leave the researcher with the task of establishing the degree of sales penetration within the market that qualifies the product as an 'innovation' (such as the first 5 per cent of the potential market to use the new product) or how long the product can be on the market and still be considered 'new' (i.e. the first three months that the product is available).

Consumer-Oriented Definitions

Although each of the three approaches described have been useful to consumer researchers in their study of the diffusion of innovations, some researchers have favoured a *consumer-oriented approach* in defining an innovation.[35] In this context, a 'new' product is any product that a potential consumer judges to be new. In other words, newness is based on the consumer's perception of the product rather than on physical features or market realities. Although the

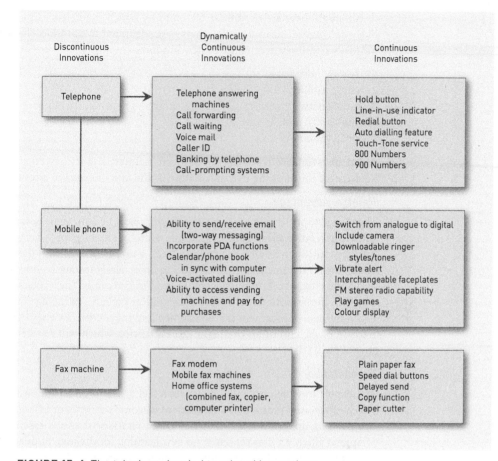

FIGURE 15-4 The telephone has led to related innovations

consumer-oriented approach has been endorsed by some advertising and marketing practitioners, it has received little systematic research attention.

Additionally, it should be pointed out that although this portion of the chapter deals primarily with what might be described as 'purchase' innovativeness (or time of adoption), a second type of innovativeness, 'use innovativeness', has been the subject of some thought and research. A consumer is being use innovative when he or she uses a previously adopted product in a novel or unusual way. In one study that dealt with the adoption of VCRs and PCs, early adopters showed significantly higher use innovativeness than those who adopted somewhat later along the cycle of acceptance of the innovation.[36]

Product Characteristics that Influence Diffusion

All products that are new do not have equal potential for consumer acceptance. Some products seem to catch on almost overnight (cordless telephones), whereas others take a very long time to gain acceptance or never seem to achieve widespread consumer acceptance (trash compactors).

The uncertainties of product marketing would be reduced if marketers could anticipate how consumers will react to their products. For example, if a marketer knew that a product contained inherent features that were likely to inhibit its acceptance, the marketer could develop a promotional strategy that would compensate for these features or decide not to market the product at all. Several car producers now design cars especially for the female driver, and manufacturers are careful to design door handles that do not break nails. Ford even offers adjustable accelerator and brake pedals.[37]

Although there are no precise formulas by which marketers can evaluate a new product's likely acceptance, diffusion researchers have identified five product characteristics that seem to influence consumer acceptance of new products:

1. relative advantage,
2. compatibility,
3. complexity,
4. trialability, and
5. observability.

Based on available research, it has been estimated that these five product characteristics account for much of the dynamic nature of the rate or speed of adoption.[38]

Relative Advantage

The degree to which potential customers perceive a new product as superior to existing substitutes is its relative advantage. For example, although many people carry cellphones so that their business offices or families can contact them, a mobile phone with the ability to read and send email, or surf the Internet, enables users to be in nearly instant communication with the world and allows users both to receive and to send information. The paper scanner is another example of an innovation that offers users a significant relative advantage in terms of their ability to communicate. A document can be scanned and transmitted by email in just a few seconds at a fraction of the cost of an overnight express service, which will not deliver the document until the following day.

Compatibility

The degree to which potential consumers feel a new product is consistent with their present needs, values and practices is a measure of its compatibility. For instance, an advantage of 3M's Scotch™ Pop-up Tape Strips is that they are easier to use than roll-tape for certain tasks (such as wrapping gifts), yet they represent no new learning for the user. Similarly, in the realm of shaving products, it is not too difficult to imagine that when Gillette introduced the MACH3 razor, some men made the transition from inexpensive disposable razors and other men shifted from competitive non-disposable razors (including Gillette's own Sensor razors). This new product is fully compatible with the established wet-shaving rituals of many men. However, it is difficult to imagine male shavers shifting to a new depilatory cream designed to remove facial hair. Although potentially simpler to use, a cream would be basically incompatible with most men's current values regarding daily shaving practices.

Complexity

Complexity, the degree to which a new product is difficult to understand or use, affects product acceptance. Clearly, the easier it is to understand and use a product, the more likely it is to be accepted. For example, the acceptance of such convenience foods as frozen chips, instant puddings and microwave dinners is generally due to their ease of preparation and use. Interestingly, although the digital television decoder is a well-known product to the majority of European consumers, millions of adults still need help from their children in programming the machine to record a particular television programme.

The issue of complexity is especially important when attempting to gain market acceptance for high-tech consumer products. Four predominant types of 'technological fear' act as barriers to new product acceptance: (1) fear of technical complexity, (2) fear of rapid obsolescence, (3) fear of social rejection and (4) fear of physical harm. Of the four, technological complexity was the most widespread concern of consumer innovators.[39]

Trialability

Trialability refers to the degree to which a new product is capable of being tried on a limited basis. The greater the opportunity to try a new product, the easier it is for consumers to evaluate it and ultimately adopt it. In general, frequently purchased household products tend to have qualities that make trial relatively easy, such as the ability to purchase a small or 'trial' size. Because a computer program cannot be packaged in a smaller size, many computer software companies offer free working models of their latest software to encourage computer users to try the program and subsequently buy it.

Aware of the importance of trial, marketers of new supermarket products commonly use substantial quantities of free samples to provide consumers with direct product experience. On the other hand, durable items, such as refrigerators or ovens, are difficult to try without making a major commitment. This may explain why consumer-oriented publications that include product tests are so widely consulted for their ratings of infrequently purchased durable goods.

Observability

Observability (or communicability) is the ease with which a product's benefits or attributes can be observed, imagined or described to potential consumers. Products that have a high degree of social visibility, such as fashion items, are more easily diffused than products that are used in private, such as a new type of deodorant. Similarly, a tangible product is promoted more easily than an intangible product (such as a service).

It is also important to recognise that a particular innovation may diffuse differently throughout different cultures. For example, although long-life milk (milk that does not require refrigeration) has been sold successfully for years in Europe, many consumers in other regions of the world have thus far resisted the aseptic milk package.[40]

Table 15-7 summarises the product characteristics that influence diffusion.

Resistance to Innovation

What makes some new products almost instant successes, while others must struggle to achieve consumer acceptance? To help answer such a question, marketers look at the product characteristics of an innovation. Such characteristics offer clues to help determine the extent of consumer resistance, which increases when perceived relative advantage, perceived compatibility, trialability and communicability are low, and perceived complexity is high. The term *innovation overload* is used to describe the situation in which the increase in information and options available to the consumer is so great that it seriously impairs decision-making. As a result, the consumer

TABLE 15-7 Product characteristics that influence diffusion

CHARACTERISTICS	DEFINITION	EXAMPLES
Relative Advantage	The degree to which potential customers perceive a new product as superior to existing substitutes	Air travel over train travel, cordless phones over corded telephones
Compatibility	The degree to which potential consumers feel a new product is consistent with their present needs, values, and practices	Gillette MACH3 over disposable razors, digital telephone answering machines over machines using tape to make recordings
Complexity	The degree to which a new product is difficult to understand or use	Products low in complexity include frozen TV dinners, electric shavers, instant puddings
Trialability	The degree to which a new product is capable of being tried on a limited basis	Trial size jars and bottles of new products, free trials of software, free samples
Observability	The degree to which a product's benefits or attributes can be observed, imagined, or described to potential customers	Clothing, such as a new Tommy Hilfiger jacket, a car, wristwatches, glasses

finds it difficult to make comparisons among the available choices. In a world in which consumers often find themselves with too little time and too much stress, increased complexity of products wastes time and may delay the acceptance of the product.[41]

The channels of communication

How quickly an innovation spreads through a market depends to a great extent on communication between the marketer and consumers, as well as communication among consumers (word-of-mouth communication). Of central concern is the uncovering of the relative influence of impersonal sources (advertising and editorial matter) and interpersonal sources (salespeople and informal opinion leaders). Over the past decade or so, we have also seen the rapid increase of the Internet as a major consumer-related source of information. The Internet is particularly interesting since it can on the one hand be seen as an interpersonal source of information (e.g. with Internet advertisements, e-commerce websites that function like a direct-mail category, and the introduction and growth of Webpods). On the other hand, the Internet can be seen at the same time as a highly personal and interpersonal source of information. In this second context, Internet consumers have an incredible number of company- and non- company-sponsored forums and discussion groups where they can chat with people who have expertise and experience that is vital to making an informed decision.

Still further, in recent years, a variety of new channels of communication have been developed to inform consumers of innovative products and services. Consider the growth of interactive marketing messages, in which the consumer becomes an important part of the communication rather than just a 'passive' message recipient. For example, for the past several years, an increasing number of companies, such as major car manufactures, have used CD-ROMs or USB-sticks to promote their products.

At the time of writing, one of the most rapidly growing media for word-of-mouth is the podcast, which a fast-growing number of consumers are seeking out as an alternative to television, radio and print. Thousands of podcasts are made available on the Internet every day, which the consumer can download as an audio file (e.g. to a computer or MP3 player). And maybe your university is among those that have already started to distribute lectures as podcasts?

The social system

The diffusion of a new product usually takes place in a social setting frequently referred to as a *social system*. In the context of consumer behaviour, the terms *market segment* and *target market* may be more relevant than the term social system used in diffusion research. A social system is a physical, social or cultural environment to which people belong and within which they function. For example, for a new hybrid seed corn, the social system might consist of all farmers in a number of local communities. For a new drug, the social system might consist of all doctors within a specific medical speciality (e.g. all neurologists). As these examples indicate, the social system serves as the boundary within which the diffusion of a new product is examined.

The orientation of a social system, with its own special values or norms, is likely to influence the acceptance or rejection of new products. When a social system is modern in orientation, the acceptance of innovations is likely to be high. In contrast, when a social system is traditional in orientation, innovations that are perceived as radical or as infringements on established customs are likely to be avoided. According to one authority, the following characteristics typify a modern social system:[42]

- a positive attitude towards change;
- an advanced technology and skilled labour force;
- a general respect for education and science;
- an emphasis on rational and ordered social relationships rather than on emotional ones;

- an outreach perspective, in which members of the system frequently interact with outsiders, thus facilitating the entrance of new ideas into the social system;
- a system in which members can readily see themselves in quite different roles.

The orientations of a social system (either modern or traditional) may be national in scope and may influence members of an entire society or may exist at the local level and influence only those who live in a specific community. The key point to remember is that a social system's orientation is the climate in which marketers must operate to gain acceptance for their new products.

Time

Time is the backbone of the diffusion process. It pervades the study of diffusion in three distinct but interrelated ways:

1. the amount of purchase time,
2. the identification of adopter categories, and
3. the rate of adoption.

Purchase Time

Purchase time refers to the amount of time that elapses between consumers' initial awareness of a new product or service and the point at which they purchase or reject it. Table 15-8 illustrates the scope of purchase time by tracking a hypothetical family's purchase of a new car.

Table 15-8 illustrates not only the length and complexity of consumer decision-making but also how different information sources become important at successive steps in the process. Purchase time is an important concept because the average time a consumer takes to adopt a new product is a predictor of the overall length of time it will take for the new product to achieve widespread adoption. For example, when the individual purchase time is short, a marketer can expect that the overall rate of diffusion will be faster than when the individual purchase time is long.

Adopter Categories

The concept of **adopter categories** involves a classification scheme that indicates where a consumer stands in relation to other consumers in terms of time (or when the consumer adopts a new product). Five adopter categories are frequently cited in the diffusion literature: innovators, early adopters, early majority, late majority and laggards. Diffusion is the sum of all individual adoption decisions, and Figure 15-5a portrays the cumulative diffusion curve with its expected S-shape. As can be seen, the steepest rate of diffusion is found when the larger part of the market is going through the adoption process. Also shown in Figure 15-5a is the different adopter categories, and an example of how adopters are distributed across these categories.[43]

As Figure 15-5b indicates, the adopter categories are generally depicted as taking on the characteristics of a normal distribution (a bell-shaped curve) that describes the total population that ultimately adopts a product. Some argue that the bell curve is an erroneous depiction because it may lead to the inaccurate conclusion that 100 per cent of the members of the social system under study (the target market) will eventually accept the product innovation. This assumption is not in keeping with marketers' experiences, because very few, if any, products fit the precise needs of all potential consumers. For example, all hirers/purchasers of films who have in the past rented DVDs could theoretically be expected to use (or try) Blu-rays. In fact, it is unrealistic for the film hire/sales industry to expect all hirers/purchasers of pre-recorded films to switch to Blu-ray. For this reason, it is appropriate to add an additional category, that of non-adopters. The non-adopter category matches marketplace reality – that not all potential consumers adopt a particular product or service innovation.

TABLE 15-8 Time line for selecting a new car

WEEK	
0	**PRECIPITATING SITUATIONS/FACTORS** The family (Mum and Dad are both schoolteachers and have two children in kindergarten) currently own one car, a mid-sized saloon, which is six years old and has done 140,000 kilometres. A month ago, the wife's parents, who retired recently, sold their home and moved to France. They hope that their daughter and family will visit them in Christmas week. But there is some concern that the family's current vehicle is too old to drive from Copenhagen to Marseilles.
1–4	**DECISION PROCESS BEGINS** For a few Saturday mornings, the family drive to a number of car dealerships to see, gather information about, test drive and price a number of mid-price, mid-sized family saloons.
5–9	The family's refrigerator breaks and has to be replaced. Because of the expense involved, the family put the notion of buying a new car on the back-burner for a while.
10	**INTEREST IS RETRIGGERED** As Christmas is now only two months away, the couple keep being prodded by the wife's parents about driving down and spending the Christmas holiday with them in Marseilles. So they decide to think once again about buying a new car in time for such a holiday trip. **CONSUMER ACQUIRES A MENTOR (OPINION LEADER)** The husband asks one of his colleagues, a fellow teacher who knows a great deal about cars, to serve as his mentor (opinion leader) with respect to cars, and he agrees.
11	**FEATURES AND BRAND OPTIONS ARE REVIEWED** With the advice of the mentor and bearing in mind their financial situation, the couple narrow down their search to vehicles that have four-cylinder engines, offer cruise control (for the long trip to Marseilles), and are equipped with airbags and antilock braking systems. Consequently, the choice has narrowed to the Toyota Avensis, Honda Accord and VW Passat.
12–13	The couple spend time on the Internet at both manufacturers' websites and the websites of independent auto services. They also return to their local Toyota, Honda and VW dealers to test drive these three vehicles again.
14–15	After spending evenings poring over brochures and information downloaded from the Internet, the couple decide that the VW Passat is the car they want to buy.
	ORDERING THE CAR The couple visit four VW dealers located in the Copenhagen area, and three of them have the desired car (colour, options, etc.) in stock. Volkswagen, through its dealers, is currently offering a low-interest, four-year financing plan, which the couple decide is the best way for them to pay for the car. After negotiating with the three dealerships that have the car they want, they decide to pay €300 more for the car (considering what the dealer wants for the new vehicle and what the dealer is willing to give them for their trade-in) than the lowest price they received, in order to purchase it from the dealership closest to their home. After signing the purchase agreement, the couple left the dealership singing 'France, here we come!'

Instead of the classic five-category adopter scheme, many consumer researchers have used other classification schemes, most of which consist of two or three categories that compare innovators or early triers with later triers or non-triers. As we will see, this focus on the innovator or early trier has produced several important generalisations that have practical significance for marketers planning the introduction of new products.

Rate of Adoption

The rate of adoption is concerned with how long it takes a new product or service to be adopted by members of a social system, that is, how quickly it takes a new product to be accepted by

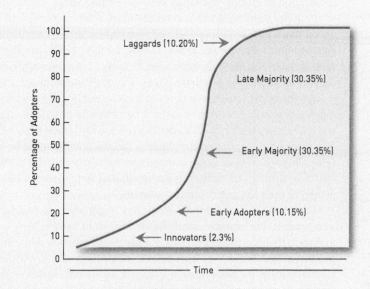

FIGURE 15-5a The S-shaped cumulative diffusion curve and adopter categories

Source: Elizabeth L. Jackson, Mohammed Quaddus, Nazrul Islam and John Stanton (2006) Hybrid vigour of behavioural theories in the agribusiness research domain. Is it possible? *Journal of International Farm Management*, Vol. 3, No. 3, July 2006.

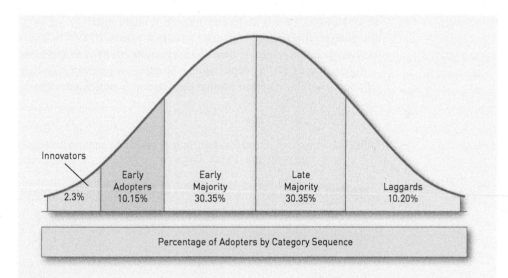

FIGURE 15-5b The sequence and proportion of adopter categories among the population that eventually adopts

Source: Elizabeth L. Jackson, Mohammed Quaddus, Nazrul Islam and John Stanton (2006) Hybrid vigour of behavioural theories in the agribusiness research domain. Is it possible? *Journal of International Farm Management*, Vol. 3, No. 3, July 2006.

those who will ultimately adopt it. The general view is that the rate of adoption for new products is getting faster or shorter. Fashion adoption is a form of diffusion, one in which the rate of adoption is important. Cyclical fashion trends or 'fads' are extremely 'fast', whereas 'fashion classics' may have extremely slow or 'long' cycles.

In general, the diffusion of products worldwide is becoming a more rapid phenomenon. For example, it took black-and-white television sets about 12 years longer to reach the same level of penetration in Europe and Japan as in the United States. For colour sets, the lag time dropped to about five years for Japan and several more years for Europe. In contrast, for VCRs there was only a three- or four-year spread, with the United States (with its emphasis on cable television) lagging behind Europe and Japan. Finally, for CD players, penetration levels in all three places were about even after only three years.[44] Table 15-9 presents the time required for a sample of electronic products to penetrate 10 per cent of the mass market in the United Kingdom.

The objective in marketing new products is usually to gain wide acceptance of the product as quickly as possible. Marketers desire a rapid rate of product adoption to penetrate the market and quickly establish market leadership (obtain the largest share of the market) before competition takes hold. A penetration policy is usually accompanied by a relatively low introductory price designed to discourage competition from entering the market. Rapid product adoption also demonstrates to marketing intermediaries (wholesalers and retailers) that the product is worthy of their full and continued support.

Under certain circumstances, marketers might prefer to avoid a rapid rate of adoption for a new product. For example, marketers who wish to use a pricing strategy that will enable them to recoup their development costs quickly might follow a skimming policy. They first make the product available at a very high price to consumers who are willing to pay top price and then gradually lower the price in steps to attract additional market segments at each price reduction plateau. As an example, new mobile phones are often priced high at the point of introduction, but after a relatively short period of time sell for as little as a tenth of the original price.

In addition to how long it takes from introduction to the point of adoption (or when the purchase actually occurs), it is useful to track the extent of adoption (the diffusion rate). For instance, a particular company might not upgrade its employees' computer systems to the Windows XP professional environment until after many other companies in the area have already begun to do so. However, once it decides to upgrade, it might install Windows XP professional software in a relatively short period of time on all of its employees' PCs. Thus, although the company was relatively late with respect to time of adoption, its extent of adoption was very high.

Although sales graphs depicting the adoption categories (again, see Figure 15-5) are typically thought of as having a normal distribution in which sales continue to increase prior to

TABLE 15-9 Time required for electronic products to penetrate 10 per cent of the mass market in the United Kingdom

PRODUCT	NUMBER OF YEARS
Pager	41
Telephone	38
Cable television	25
Fax machine	22
VCR	9
Cellular phone	9
Personal computer	7
CD-ROM*	6
Wireless data service*	6
Screen-phone*	6
Interactive television*	3

*Predicted.

Source: Adapted from Eric Chi-Chung Shiu and John A. Dawson, 'Cross-National Consumer Segmentation of Internet Shopping for Britain and Taiwan', *The Service Industries Journal* (London), 22, January 2002, 163. Reprinted by permission.

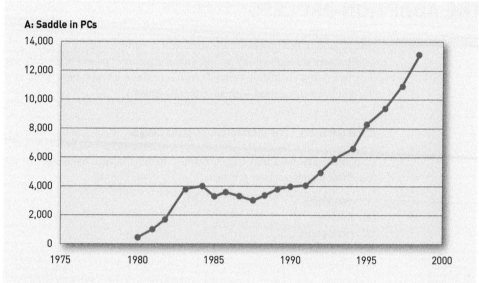

A: Saddle in PCs

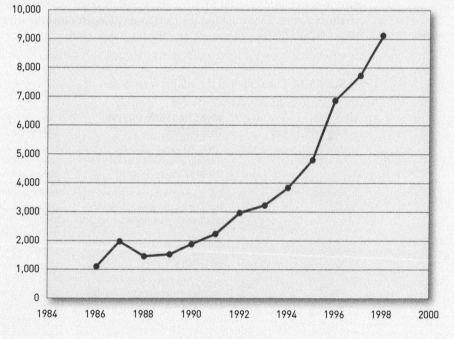

B: Saddle in VCR Decks with Stereo

FIGURE 15-6 'Sales saddle' differentiates early market adopters from the main market adopters

Source: Adapted from Jacob Goldenberg, Barak Libai and Eitan Muller, 'Riding the Saddle: How Cross-Market Communications Can Create a Major Slump in Sales', *Journal of Marketing*, 66, April 2000, 5.

reaching a peak (at the top of the curve), some research evidence indicates that a third to a half of such sales curves, at least in the consumer electronics industry, involve an initial peak, a trough and then another sales increase. Such a 'saddle' in the sales curve has been attributed to the early market adopters and the main market adopters being two separate markets.[45] Figure 15-6 presents two examples of sales curves with saddles – PCs and VCR decks with stereo.

THE ADOPTION PROCESS

The second major process in the diffusion of innovations is adoption. The focus of this process is the stages through which an individual consumer passes while arriving at a decision to try or not to try or to continue using or to discontinue using a new product. (The adoption process should not be confused with adopter categories.)

Stages in the adoption process

It is often assumed that the consumer moves through five stages in arriving at a decision to purchase or reject a new product:

1. awareness,
2. interest,
3. evaluation,
4. trial, and
5. adoption (or rejection).

The assumption underlying the adoption process is that consumers engage in extensive information search (see Chapter 8), whereas consumer involvement theory suggests that for some products a limited information search is more likely (for low-involvement products). The five **stages in the adoption process** are described in Table 15-10.

TABLE 15-10 The stages in the adoption process

NAME OF STAGE	WHAT HAPPENS DURING THIS STAGE	EXAMPLE
Awareness	Consumer is first exposed to the product innovation.	Janet sees an ad for a new MP3 player in a magazine she is reading.
Interest	Consumer is interested in the product and searches for additional information.	Janet reads about the MP3 player on the manufacturer's website and then goes to an electronics store near her apartment and has a salesperson show her the unit.
Evaluation	Consumer decides whether or not to believe that this product or service will satisfy the need – a kind of 'mental trial'.	After talking to a knowledgeable friend, Janet decides that this MP3 player will allow her to easily download the MP3 files that she has on her computer. She also feels that the unit's size is small enough to fit easily into her beltpack.
Trial	Consumer uses the product on a limited basis.	Since an MP3 player cannot be 'tried' like a small tube of toothpaste, Janet buys the MP3 player online from a local retailer, which offers a 30-day full refund policy.
Adoption (Rejection)	If trial is favourable, onsumer decides to use the product on a full rather than a limited basis – if unfavourable, the consumer decides to reject it.	Janet finds that the MP3 player is easy to use and that the sound quality is excellent. She keeps the MP3 player.

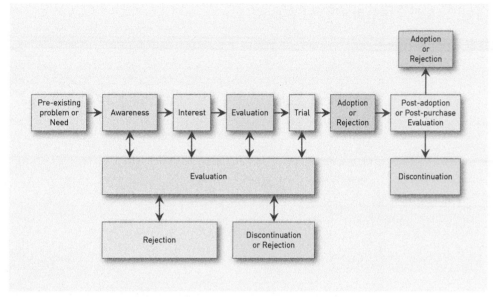

FIGURE 15-7 An enhanced adoption process model

Although the traditional adoption process model is insightful in its simplicity, it does not adequately reflect the full complexity of the consumer adoption process. For one, it does not adequately acknowledge that there is quite often a need- or problem-recognition stage that consumers face before acquiring an awareness of potential options or solutions (recognition of a need preceding the awareness stage). Moreover, the adoption process does not adequately provide for the possibility of evaluation and rejection of a new product or service after each stage, especially after trial (i.e. a consumer may reject the product after trial or never use the product on a continuous basis). Finally, it does not explicitly include post-adoption or post-purchase evaluation, which can lead to a strengthened commitment or to a decision to discontinue use. Figure 15-7 presents an enhanced representation of the adoption process model, one that includes the additional dimensions or actions described here.

The adoption of some products and services may have minimal consequences, whereas the adoption of other innovations may lead to major behavioural and lifestyle changes. Examples of innovations with such major impact on society include the car, the telephone, the electric refrigerator, the television, the aeroplane, the personal computer and the Internet.

The adoption process and information sources

The adoption process provides a framework for determining which types of information sources consumers find most important at specific decision stages. For example, early purchasers of USB storage devices or keys might first become aware of the service via mass-media sources. Then these early subscribers' final pre-trial information might be an outcome of informal discussions with personal sources. The key point is that impersonal mass-media sources tend to be most valuable for creating initial product awareness; as the purchase decision progresses, however, the relative importance of these sources declines while the relative importance of interpersonal sources (friends, salespeople and others) increases. Figure 15-8 depicts this relationship.

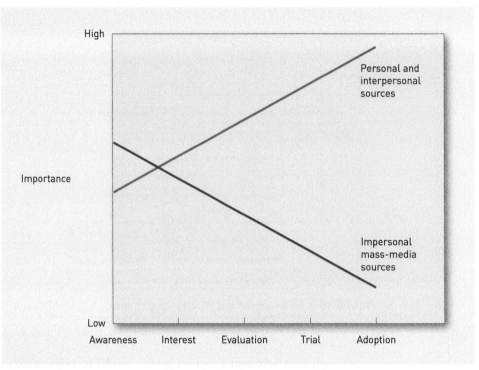

FIGURE 15-8 The relative importance of different types of information sources in the adoption process

A PROFILE OF THE CONSUMER INNOVATOR

Who is the consumer innovator? What characteristics set the innovator apart from later adopters and from those who never purchase? How can the marketer reach and influence the innovator? These are key questions for the marketing practitioner about to introduce a new product or service.

Defining the consumer innovator

Consumer innovators can be defined as the relatively small group of consumers who are the earliest purchasers of a new product. The problem with this definition, however, concerns the concept of earliest, which is, after all, a relative term. Sociologists have treated this issue by sometimes defining innovators as the first 2.5 per cent of the social system to adopt an innovation. In many marketing diffusion studies, however, the definition of the consumer innovator has been derived from the status of the new product under investigation. For example, if researchers define a new product as an innovation for the first three months of its availability, then they define the consumers who purchase it during this period as 'innovators'. Other researchers have defined innovators in terms of their innovativeness, that is, their purchase of some minimum number of new products from a selected group of new products. For instance, in the adoption of new fashion items, innovators can be defined as those consumers who purchase more than one fashion product from a group of 10 new fashion products. Non-innovators would be defined as those who purchase none or only one of the new fashion products. In other instances, researchers have defined innovators as those falling within an arbitrary proportion of the total market (e.g. the first 10 per cent of the population in a specified geographic area to buy the new product).

Interest in the product category

Not surprisingly, consumer innovators are much more interested than either later adopters or non-adopters in the product categories that they are among the first to purchase. If what is known from diffusion theory holds true in the future, the earliest purchasers of small electric cars are likely to have substantially greater interest in cars (they will enjoy looking at motoring magazines and will be interested in the performance and functioning of cars) than those who purchased conventional small cars during the same period or those who purchased small electric cars during a later period. Recent research examining early adopters of products containing a non-fat synthetic cooking oil were found to have a high interest in such a product because of health and diet concerns.[46] Consumer innovators are more likely than non-innovators to seek information concerning their specific interests from a variety of informal and mass-media sources. They are more likely to give greater deliberation to the purchase of new products or services in their areas of interest than non-innovators.

The innovator is an opinion leader

When discussing the characteristics of the opinion leader earlier in this chapter, we indicated a strong tendency for consumer opinion leaders to be innovators. In the present context, an impressive amount of research on the diffusion of innovations has found that consumer innovators provide other consumers with information and advice about new products and that those who receive such advice frequently follow it. Thus, in the role of opinion leader, the consumer innovator often influences the acceptance or rejection of new products.

When innovators are enthusiastic about a new product and encourage others to try it, the product is likely to receive broader and quicker acceptance. When consumer innovators are dissatisfied with a new product and discourage others from trying it, its acceptance will be severely limited and it may die a quick death. For products that do not generate much excitement (either positive or negative), consumer innovators may not be sufficiently motivated to provide advice. In such cases, the marketer must rely almost entirely on mass media and personal selling to influence future purchasers; the absence of informal influence is also likely to result in a somewhat slower rate of acceptance (or rejection) of the new product. Because motivated consumer innovators can influence the rate of acceptance or rejection of a new product, they influence its eventual success or failure.

Personality traits

In Chapter 6, we examined the personality traits that distinguish the consumer innovator from the non-innovator. In this section, we will briefly highlight what researchers have learned about the personality of the consumer innovator.

First, consumer innovators generally are less dogmatic than non-innovators. They tend to approach new or unfamiliar products with considerable openness and little anxiety. In contrast, non-innovators seem to find new products threatening to the point where they prefer to delay purchase until the product's success has been clearly established.

Consistent with their open-mindedness, it appears that innovative behaviour is an expression of an individual's need for uniqueness.[47] Those new products, both branded and unbranded, that represent a greater change in a person's consumption habits were viewed as superior when it came to satisfying the need for uniqueness. Therefore, to gain more rapid acceptance of a new product, marketers might consider appealing to a consumer's need for uniqueness.

Still further, consumer innovators also differ from non-innovators in terms of social character. Consumer innovators are inner-directed; that is, they rely on their own values or standards when making a decision about a new product. In contrast, non-innovators are other-directed, relying on others for guidance on how to respond to a new product rather than trusting their own personal values or standards. Thus, the initial purchasers of a new line of cars might be inner-directed, whereas the later purchasers of the same cars might be other-directed. This suggests that as acceptance of a product progresses from early to later adopters, a gradual shift occurs in the personality type of adopters from inner-directedness to other-directedness.

There also appears to be a link between optimum stimulation level and consumer innovativeness. Specifically, individuals who seek a lifestyle rich with novel, complex and unusual experiences (high optimum stimulation levels) are more willing to risk trying new products, to be innovative, to seek purchase-related information and to accept new retail facilities.

Researchers have isolated a link between variety seeking and purchase behaviour that provides insights into consumer innovators. Variety-seeking consumers tend to be brand switchers and purchasers of innovative products and services. They also possess the following innovator-related personality traits: they are open-minded (or low in dogmatism), extroverts, liberal, low in authoritarianism, able to deal with complex or ambiguous stimuli and creative.[48]

To sum up, consumer innovators seem to be more receptive to the unfamiliar and the unique; they are more willing to rely on their own values or standards than on the judgement of others. They also are willing to run the risk of a poor product choice to increase their exposure to new products that will be satisfying. For the marketer, the personality traits that distinguish innovators from non-innovators suggest the need for separate promotional campaigns for innovators and for later adopters.

Perceived Risk and Venturesomeness

Perceived risk, which is discussed in detail in Chapter 7, is another measure of a consumer's likelihood to try new brands or products. Perceived risk is the degree of uncertainty or fear about the consequences of a purchase that a consumer feels when considering the purchase of a new product. For example, consumers experience uncertainty when they are concerned that a new product will not work properly or as well as other alternatives. Research on perceived risk and the trial of new products overwhelmingly indicate that consumer innovators are low-risk perceivers; that is, they experience little fear of trying new products or services. Consumers who perceive little or no risk in the purchase of a new product are much more likely to make innovative purchases than consumers who perceive a great deal of risk. In other words, high-risk perception limits innovativeness.

Venturesomeness is a broad-based measure of a consumer's willingness to accept the risk of purchasing new products. Measures of venturesomeness have been used to evaluate a person's general values or attitudes toward trying new products. A typical measurement scale might include such items as:

1. I prefer to (try a shampoo when it first comes out), (wait and learn how good it is before trying it).
2. When I am shopping and see a brand of coffee I know about but have never used, I am (very anxious or willing to try it), (hesitant about trying it), (very unwilling to try it).
3. I like to be among the first people to buy and use new products that are on the market (measured on a five-point 'agreement' scale).

Research that has examined venturesomeness has generally found that consumers who indicate a willingness to try new products tend to be consumer innovators (as measured by their actual purchase of new products). On the other hand, consumers who express a reluctance to try new products are, in fact, less likely to purchase new products. Therefore, venturesomeness seems to be an effective barometer of actual innovative behaviour.

Purchase and Consumption Characteristics

Consumer innovators possess purchase and usage traits that set them apart from non-innovators. For example, consumer innovators are less brand loyal, that is, they are more apt to switch brands. This is not surprising, for brand loyalty would seriously impede a consumer's willingness to try new products.

Consumer innovators are more likely to be deal prone (to take advantage of special promotional offers such as free samples and money-off coupons). They are also likely to be heavy users of the product category in which they innovate. Specifically, they purchase larger quantities and consume more of the product than non-innovators. Finally, for products like DVDs, PCs, microwave ovens, digital cameras and food processors, usage variety is likely to be a relevant dimension of new-product diffusion. An understanding of how consumers might be 'usage innovators' – that is, finding or 'inventing' new uses for an innovation – might create entirely new market opportunities for marketers' products. Still further, a recent study of Indian consumers' attitudes towards the purchase of new food products found that 'intention to buy' was an accurate predictor of behaviour for highly innovative consumers, but failed to predict purchase behaviour for less innovative consumers.[49] This suggests that more innovative consumers are more likely to act on their reported intentions to purchase than less innovative consumers with the same intention of purchase.

To sum up, a positive relationship exists between innovative behaviour and heavy usage. Consumer innovators not only are an important market segment from the standpoint of being the first to use a new product, but also represent a substantial market in terms of product volume. However, their propensity to switch brands or to use products in different or unique ways and their positive response to promotional deals also suggest that innovators will continue to use a specific brand only as long as they do not perceive that a new and potentially better alternative is available.

Media Habits

Comparisons of the media habits of innovators and non-innovators across such widely diverse areas of consumption as fashion clothing and new motoring services suggest that innovators have somewhat greater total exposure to magazines than non-innovators, particularly to special-interest magazines devoted to the product category in which they innovate.

Consumer innovators are also less likely to watch television than non-innovators. This view is consistently supported by research that over the past decade or so has compared the magazine and television exposure levels of consumer innovators. The evidence indicates that consumer innovators have higher than average magazine exposure (see Figure 15-9) and lower than average television exposure. It will be interesting, though, to observe over the next few years what the impact of the convergence of computers and television will be. Studies concerning the relationship between innovative behaviour and exposure to other mass media, such as radio and newspapers, have been too few, and the results have been too varied to draw any useful conclusions.

Social characteristics

Consumer innovators are more socially accepted and socially involved than non-innovators. For example, innovators are more socially integrated into the community, better accepted by others and more socially involved, that is, they belong to more social groups and organisations than non-innovators. This greater social acceptance and involvement of consumer innovators may help explain why they function as effective opinion leaders.

Demographic characteristics

It is reasonable to assume that the age of the consumer innovator is related to the specific product category in which he or she innovates; however, research suggests that consumer innovators tend to be younger than either late adopters or non-innovators. This is no doubt because many of the products selected for research attention (such as fashion, convenience grocery products or new cars) are particularly attractive to younger consumers.

Consumer innovators have more formal education, have higher personal or family incomes, and are more likely to have higher occupational status (to be professionals or hold managerial

FIGURE 15-9 Where sport and style become one: adidas advertisement calls out to those who would be fashion innovators

Source: adidas, the adidas 3-bars logo and FOREVER SPORT are registered trademarks of the adidas group, used with permission.

positions) than late adopters or non-innovators. In other words, innovators tend to be more upscale than other consumer segments and can, therefore, better afford to make a mistake should the innovative new product or service being purchased prove to be unacceptable.

Table 15-12 summarises the major differences between consumer innovators and late adopters or non-innovators. The table includes the major distinctions examined in our current presentation of the consumer innovator profile.

TABLE 15-12 Comparative profiles of the consumer innovator and the non-innovator or late adopter

CHARACTERISTIC	INNOVATOR	NON-INNOVATOR (OR LATE ADOPTER)
Product Interest	More	Less
Opinion Leadership Personality	More	Less
Dogmatism	Open-minded	Closed-minded
Need for uniqueness	Higher	Lower
Social character	Inner-directed	Other-directed
Optimum stimulation level	Higher	Lower
Variety seeking	Higher	Lower
Perceived risk	Less	More
Venturesomeness	More	Less
PURCHASE AND CONSUMPTION TRAITS		
Brand loyalty	Less	More
Deal proneness	More	Less
Usage	More	Less
MEDIA HABITS		
Total magazine exposure	More	Less
Special-interest magazines	More	Less
Television	Less	More
SOCIAL CHARACTERISTICS		
Social integration	More	Less
Social striving (e.g. social, physical and occupational mobility)	More	Less
Group memberships	More	Less
DEMOGRAPHIC CHARACTERISTICS		
Age	Younger	Older
Income	Higher	Lower
Education	More	Less
Occupational status	Higher	Lower

Are there generalised consumer innovators?

Do consumer innovators in one product category tend to be consumer innovators in other product categories? The answer to this strategically important question is a guarded 'no'. The overlap of innovativeness across product categories, like opinion leadership, seems to be limited to product categories that are closely related to the same basic interest area. Consumers who are innovators of one new food product or one new appliance are more likely to be innovators of other new products in the same general product category. In other words, although no single or generalised consumer-innovativeness trait seems to operate across broadly different product categories, evidence suggests that consumers who innovate within a specific product category will innovate again within the same product category. For example, up to the point of 'innovator burn-out' (i.e. 'what I have is good enough'), a person who was an innovator in buying an early 2 megapixel digital camera in the 1990s was most likely again an innovator in buying a 3 megapixel camera, a 7 megapixel camera and a 12 megapixel camera, and is likely to be an innovator again when it comes to the next generation of digital cameras. For the marketer, such a pattern suggests that it is generally a good marketing strategy to target a new product to consumers who were the first to try other products in the same basic product category.

Technology and Innovators

In the realm of high-tech innovations, there is evidence suggesting that there is a generalised 'high-tech' innovator – known as a *'change leader'*.[50] Such individuals tend to embrace and popularise many of the innovations that are ultimately accepted by the mainstream population, such as computers, mobile phones and fax machines. They tend to have a wide range of personal and professional contacts representing different occupational and social groups; most often these contacts tend to be 'weak ties' or acquaintances. Change leaders also appear to fall into one of two distinct groups: a younger group that can be characterised as being stimulation seeking, sociable and having high levels of fashion awareness, and a middle-aged group that is highly self-confident and has very high information-seeking needs.

Similar to change leaders, *'technophiles'* are individuals who purchase technologically advanced products soon after their market debut. Such individuals tend to be technically curious people. Also, another group responding to technology are adults who are categorised as *'techthusiasts'* – people who are most likely to purchase or subscribe to emerging products and services that are technologically oriented. These consumers are typically younger, better educated and more affluent.[51]

The relationship between technology and consumer innovation has been explored within the context of the *technology acceptance model* (TAM). Within the domain of work, perceived usefulness or the utilitarian aspect of a technology has been revealed to be most important; however, within the context of consumers' responses to a new handheld Internet device, the most powerful determinant of attitudes towards usage was the 'fun' of using the device – a hedonic aspect. The implication for marketers is clear – a consumer may purchase a new bit of technology more for the fun they can have with the device than for the ability it gives them to accomplish particular functions.[52]

Research conducted with over 500 adult Internet users found that purchasing online was positively related to technology-related innovativeness. Moreover, the gathering of store or product information online was positively related to the number of years online and the weekly number of hours spent online.[53] Still further, when exploring the adoption of mobile gaming (games delivered via mobile phone), a market that passed €14.5 billion worldwide in 2006 (a growth from €785 million in 2001), researchers discovered important additions to the traditional list of product characteristics that influence the rate of adoption (e.g. relative advantage, complexity). What they perceived as risk were navigation (manoeuvring ergonomics associated with the mobile device), critical mass (the more people that have adopted the innovation, the more attractive it is to others), and payment options (because of the expense of the mobile device, trialability is not an option). Perceived risk was found to play the most important role in the adoption process, followed by complexity and compatibility.[54]

SUMMARY

Opinion leadership is the process by which one person (the opinion leader) informally influences the actions or attitudes of others, who may be opinion seekers or merely opinion recipients. Opinion receivers perceive the opinion leader as a highly credible, objective source of product information who can help reduce their search time and perceived risk. Opinion leaders, in turn, are motivated to give information or advice to others, in part because doing so enhances their own status and self-image and because such advice tends to reduce any post-purchase dissonance that they may have. Other motives include product involvement, 'other' involvement and message involvement.

Market researchers identify opinion leaders by such methods as self-designation, key informants, the sociometric method and the objective method. Studies of opinion leadership indicate that this phenomenon tends to be product specific, that is, individuals 'specialise' in a product or product category in which they are highly interested. An opinion leader for one product category may be an opinion receiver for another.

Generally, opinion leaders are gregarious, self-confident, innovative people who like to talk. Additionally, they may feel differentiated from others and choose to act differently (public individuation). They acquire information about their areas of interest through avid readership of special-interest magazines and by means of new-product trials. Their interests often overlap adjacent product areas; thus, their opinion leadership may extend into related areas. The market maven is an intense case of such a person. These consumers possess a wide range of information about many different types of products, retail outlets and other dimensions of markets. They both initiate discussions with other consumers and respond to requests for market information over a wide range of products and services. Market mavens are also distinguishable from other opinion leaders, because their influence stems not so much from product experience but from a more general knowledge or market expertise that leads them to an early awareness of a wide array of new products and services.

The opinion leadership process usually takes place among friends, neighbours and work associates who have frequent physical proximity and, thus, have ample opportunity to hold informal product-related conversations. These conversations usually occur naturally in the context of the product-category usage.

The two-step flow of communication theory highlights the role of interpersonal influence in the transmission of information from the mass media to the population at large. This theory provides the foundation for a revised multi-step flow of communication model, which takes into account the fact that information and influence are often two-way processes and that opinion leaders both influence and are influenced by opinion receivers.

Marketers recognise the strategic value of segmenting their audiences into opinion leaders and opinion receivers for their product categories. When marketers can direct their promotional efforts to the more influential segments of their markets, these individuals will transmit this information to those who seek product advice. Marketers try both to simulate and to stimulate opinion leadership. They have also found that they can create opinion leaders for their products by taking socially involved or influential people and deliberately increasing their enthusiasm for a product category.

The diffusion process and the adoption process are two closely related concepts concerned with the acceptance of new products by consumers. The diffusion process is a macro process that focuses on the spread of an innovation (a new product, service or idea) from its source to the consuming public. The adoption process is a micro process that examines the stages through which an individual consumer passes when making a decision to accept or reject a new product.

The definition of the term innovation can be firm-oriented (new to the firm), product-oriented (a continuous innovation, a dynamically continuous innovation or a discontinuous innovation), market-oriented (how long the product has been on the market or an arbitrary percentage of the potential target market that has purchased it), or consumer-oriented (new to the consumer). Market-oriented definitions of innovation are most useful to consumer researchers in the study of the diffusion and adoption of new products.

Five product characteristics influence the consumer's acceptance of a new product: relative advantage, compatibility, complexity, trialability and observability (or communicability).

Diffusion researchers are concerned with two aspects of communication – the channels through which word of a new product is spread to the consuming public and the types of messages that influence the adoption or rejection of new products. Diffusion is always examined in the context of a specific social system, such as a target market, a community, a region or even a nation.

Time is an integral consideration in the diffusion process. Researchers are concerned with the amount of purchase time required for an individual consumer to adopt or reject a new product, with the rate of adoption and with the identification of sequential adopters. The five adopter categories are innovators, early adopters, early majority, late majority and laggards.

Marketing strategists try to control the rate of adoption through their new-product pricing policies. Marketers who wish to penetrate the market to achieve market leadership try to acquire wide adoption as quickly as possible by using low prices. Those who wish to recoup their developmental costs quickly use a skimming pricing policy but lengthen the adoption process.

The traditional adoption process model describes five stages through which an individual consumer passes to arrive at the decision to adopt or reject a new product: awareness, interest, evaluation, trial and adoption. To make it more realistic, an enhanced model is suggested as one that considers the possibility of a pre-existing need or problem, the likelihood that some form of evaluation might occur through the entire process, and that even after adoption there will be post-adoption or post-purchase evaluation that might either strengthen the commitment or alternatively lead to discontinuation.

New-product marketers are vitally concerned with identifying the consumer innovator so that they may direct their promotional campaigns to the people who are most likely to try new products, adopt them and influence others. Consumer research has identified a number of consumer-related characteristics, including product interest, opinion leadership, personality factors, purchase and consumption traits, media habits, social characteristics and demographic variables that distinguish consumer innovators from later adopters. These serve as useful variables in the segmentation of markets for new-product introductions.

DISCUSSION QUESTIONS

1. **a.** Why is an opinion leader a more credible source of product information than an advertisement for the same product?
   b. Are there any circumstances in which information from advertisements is likely to be more influential than word-of-mouth?
2. Why would a consumer who has just purchased an expensive high-definition television set attempt to influence the purchase behaviour of others?
3. A company that owns and operates health clubs across your home country is opening a health club in your town. The company has retained you as its marketing research consultant and has asked you to identify opinion leaders for its service. Which of the following identification methods would you recommend: the self-designating method, the sociometric method, the key informant method or the objective method? Explain your selection. In your answer, be sure to discuss the advantages and disadvantages of the four techniques as they relate to the marketing situation just described.
4. Do you have any 'market mavens' among your friends? Describe their personality traits and behaviours. Describe a situation in which a market maven has given you advice regarding a product or service and discuss what you believe was his or her motivation for doing so.
5. Describe how a manufacturer might use knowledge of the following product characteristics to speed up the acceptance of the latest mobile phones:
   a. Relative advantage
   b. Compatibility
   c. Complexity
   d. Trialability
   e. Observability.
6. In 2010, Apple introduced its iPad, and competing firms are starting to launch their iPad equivalents. How can one of these companies use the diffusion-of-innovations framework to develop promotional, pricing and distribution strategies targeted to the following adopter categories?
   a. Innovators
   b. Early adopters
   c. Early majority
   d. Late majority
   e. Laggards.
7. Is the curve that describes the sequence and proportion of adopter categories among the population (Figure 15-5) similar in shape to the product life-cycle curve? Explain your answer. How would you use both curves to develop a marketing strategy?

8. Sony is introducing a 27-inch television set with a built-in Blu-ray player, a picture-in-picture feature, and a feature that allows the viewer simultaneously to view frozen frames of the last signals received from 12 channels.

   a. What recommendations would you make to Sony regarding the initial target market for the new TV model?

   b. How would you identify the innovators for this product?

   c. Select three characteristics of consumer innovators (as summarised in Table 15-12). Explain how Sony might use each of these characteristics to influence the adoption process and speed up the diffusion of the new product.

   d. Should Sony follow a penetration or a skimming policy in introducing the product? Why?

EXERCISES

1. Describe two situations in which you served as an opinion leader and two situations in which you sought consumption-related advice or information from an opinion leader. Indicate your relationship to the persons with whom you interacted. Are the circumstances during which you engaged in word-of-mouth communications consistent with those in the text's material? Explain.

2. a. Find advertisements that simulate and others that stimulate opinion leadership and present them in class.

   b. Can you think of negative rumours that you have heard recently about a company or a product? If so, present them in class.

3. Identify a product, service or style that was recently adopted by you or some of your friends. Identify what type of innovation it is and describe its diffusion process up until now. What are the characteristics of the people who adopted it first? What types of people did not adopt it? What features of the product, service or style are likely to determine its eventual success or failure?

4. With the advancement of digital technology, some companies plan to introduce interactive television systems that will allow viewers to select films from video libraries and view them on demand. Among people you know, identify two who are likely to be the innovators for such a new service and construct consumer profiles using the characteristics of consumer innovators discussed in the text.

NOTES

1. Chip Walker, 'Word of Mouth', *American Demographics*, July 1995, 40.

2. Ibid., 42.

3. Dale F. Duhan, Scott D. Johnson, James B. Wilcox and Gilbert D. Harrell, 'Influences on Consumer Use of Word-of-Mouth Recommendation Sources', *Journal of the Academy of Marketing Science*, 25, 4, 1997, 283–95.

4. James Brooke, 'Youth Let Their Thumbs Do the Talking in Japan', *New York Times*, 30 April 2002, A14.

5. David Fletcher, 'Advertising through Word-of-Mouth', *Brand Strategy* (London), June 2004, 38.

6. John E. Hogan, Katherine N. Lemon and Barak Libai, 'Quantifying the Ripple: Word-of-Mouth and Advertising Effectiveness', *Journal of Advertising Research*, September 2004, 271–80.

7. George Silverman, 'The Power of Word of Mouth', *Direct Marketing*, 64, 5, September 2001, 47–52.

8. S. Ramesh Kumar, 'The Might of the Word', *Businessline*, 2 September 1999, 1–2.

9. George Silverman, 'The Power of Word of Mouth'.

10. Pamala L. Alreck and Robert B. Settle, 'The Importance of Word-of-Mouth Communications to Service Buyers', in *1995 AMA Winter Educators' Proceedings*, eds David W. Stewart and Naufel J. Vilcassim (Chicago: American Marketing Association, 1995), 188–93.

11. Cathy L. Hartman and Pamela L. Kiecker, 'Marketplace Influencers at the Point of Purchase: The Role of Purchase Pals in Consumer Decision Making', in *1991 AMA Educators' Proceedings*, eds Mary C. Gilly and F. Robert Dwyer *et al.* (Chicago: American Marketing Association, 1991), 461–7.

12. Pamela Kiecker and Cathy L. Hartman, 'Predicting Buyers' Selection of Interpersonal Sources: The Role of Strong Ties and Weak Ties', in *Advances in Consumer Research*, 21, eds Chris T. Allen and Deborah Roedder John (Provo, UT: Association for Consumer Research, 1994), 464–9.

13. Praveen Aggarwal and Taihoon Cha, 'Surrogate Buyers and the New Product Adoption Process: A Conceptualization and Managerial Framework', *Journal of Consumer Marketing*, 14, 5, 1997, 391–400; and Stanley C. Hollander and Kathleen M. Rassuli, 'Shopping with Other People's Money: The Marketing Management Implications of Surrogate-Mediated Consumer Decision Making', *Journal of Marketing*, 63, 2, April 1999, 102–18.

14. Leisa Reinecke Flynn, Ronald E. Goldsmith and Jacqueline K. Eastman, 'The King and Summers Opinion Leadership Scale: Revision and Refinement', *Journal of Business Research*, 31, 1994, 55–64.

15. Mary C. Gilly, John L. Graham, Mary Finley Wolfinbarger and Laura J. Yale, 'A Dyadic Study of Interpersonal Information Search', *Journal of the Academy of Marketing Science*, 26, 2, 1998, 83–100.

16. Christine H. Roch, 'The Dual Roots of Opinion Leadership', *Journal of Politics*, 67, 1, February 2005, 110.

17. Lawrence F. Feick and Linda L. Price, 'The Market Maven: A Diffuser of Marketplace Information', *Journal of Marketing*, 51, January 1987, 85.

18. Michael T. Elliott and Anne E. Warfield, 'Do Market Mavens Categorize Brands Differently?', in *Advances in Consumer Research*, 20, eds Leigh McAlister and Michael L. Rothschild (Provo, UT: Association for Consumer Research 1993), 202–8; and Frank Alpert, 'Consumer Market Beliefs and Their Managerial Implications: An Empirical Examination', *Journal of Consumer Marketing*, 10, 2, 1993, 56–70.

19. Gianfranco Walse, Kevin P. Gwinner and Scott R. Swanson, 'What Makes Mavens Tick? Exploring the Motives of Market Mavens' Initiation of Information Diffusion', *Journal of Consumer Marketing*, 21, 2, 2004, 109–22.

20. Ronald E. Goldsmith, Leisa R. Flynn and Elizabeth B. Goldsmith, 'Innovation Consumers and Market Mavens', *Journal of Marketing Theory and Practice*, 11, Fall 2003, 54–65.

21. Michael A. Belch, Kathleen A. Krentler and Laura A. Willis-Flurry, 'Teen Internet Mavens: Influence in Family Decision Making', *Journal of Business Research*, 58, May 2005, 569–75.

22. Andrea C. Wojnicki, 'Social Hubs: A Valuable Segmentation Construct in the Word-of-Mouth Consumer Network', *Advances in Consumer Research*, 31, eds Barbara E. Kahn and Mary Frances Luce (Valdosta, GA: Association for Consumer Research, 2004), 521–2.

23. Paul F. Lazarsfeld, Bernard Berelson and Hazel Gaudet, *The People's Choice*, 2nd edn. (New York: Columbia University Press, 1948), 151.

24. Joseph R. Mancuso, 'Why Not Create Opinion Leaders for New Product Introduction?', *Journal of Marketing*, 33, July 1969, 20–25.

25. Barbara Bickart and Robert M. Schindler, 'Internet Forums as Influential Sources of Consumer Information', *Journal of Interactive Marketing*, 15, 3, Summer 2001, 31–9.

26. 'In the News: Ploys', *New York Times Magazine*, 13 February 1994, 19.

27. Ralph F. Wilson, 'The Six Simple Principles of Viral Marketing', *Web Marketing Today*, 70, 1 February 2000, accessed at www.wilsonweb.com/wmt5/viral-principles.htm; and search crm.techtarget.com/sDefinition/0,sid11_gci213514,00.html.

28. 'Virtual Viral Marketing Virus', *Wired*, November 2000, 116; Ren Dye, 'How to Create Explosive Self-Generating Demand', *Advertising Age*, 8 November 1999, S20; Thomas E. Weber, 'The Web's Newest Ploy May Not Make You a Very Popular Friend', *Wall Street Journal*, 13 September 1999, B1; Beth Snyder Bulik, 'Upping the Cool Quotient', *Business 2.0*, 22 August 2000, 94–6; and John Gaffney, 'The Cool Kids Are Doing It. Should You?', *Business 2.0*, November 2001, 140–41.

29. Greg Metz Thomas, Jr., 'Building the buzz in hive mind', *Journal of Consumer Behaviour*, 4, October 2004, 64–72.

30. Joseph E. Phelps, Regina Lewis, Lynne Mobilio, David Perry and Niranjan Raman, 'Viral Marketing or Electronic Word-of-Mouth Advertising: Examining Consumer Responses and Motivations to Pass Along Email', *Journal of Advertising Research*, December 2004, 333–48.

31. Charles Newbery, 'Nescafé Builds Buzz via Viral e-mail Effort', *Advertising Age*, 2 May 2005, 24.

32. Jan-Benedict E. M. Steenkamp, Frankel ter Hofstede and Michael Wedel, 'A Cross-National Investigation into the Individual and National Cultural Antecedents of Consumer Innovativeness', *Journal of Marketing*, 63, 2, April 1999, 55–69.

33. Diane Crane, 'Diffusion Models and Fashion: A Reassessment', *Annals of the American Academy of Political and Social Sciences*, 566, November 1999, 13–24.

34. Thomas S. Robertson, 'The Process of Innovation and the Diffusion of Innovation', *Journal of Marketing*, 31, January 1967, 14–19.

35. Everett M. Rogers, *Diffusion of Innovations*, 4th edn (New York: Free Press, 1995); and Hubert Gatignon and Thomas S. Robertson, 'Innovative Decision Processes', *in Handbook of Consumer Behavior*, eds Thomas S. Robertson and Harold H. Kassarjian (Upper Saddle River, NJ: Prentice Hall, 1991), 316–48.

36. S. Ram and Hyung-Shik Jung, 'Innovativeness in Product Usage: A Comparison of Early Adopters and Early Majority', *Psychology and Marketing*, 11, January–February 1994, 57–67; A. R. Petrosky, 'Gender and Use Innovation: An Inquiry into the Socialization of Innovative Behavior', in *1995 AMA Educators' Proceedings*, eds Barbara B. Stern and George M. Zinkan (Chicago: American Marketing Association, 1995), 299–307; Kyungae Park and Carl L. Dyer, 'Consumer Use Innovative Behavior: An Approach Toward Its Causes', in *Advances in Consumer Research*, 22, eds Frank R. Kardes and Mita Sujan (Provo, UT: Association for Consumer Research, 1995), 566–72.

37. Earle Eldridge, 'Pickups Get Women's Touch', *USA Today*, 13 June 2001, 1B, 2B.

38. Hsiang Chen and Kevin Crowston, 'Comparative Diffusion of the Telephone and the World Wide Web: An Analysis of Rates of Adoption', in Suave Lobodzinski and Ivan Tomek (eds), *Proceedings of WebNet '97 – World Conference of the WWW, Internet and Intranet, Toronto, Canada* (Charlottesville, VA: Association for the Advancement of Computing in Education, 1997), 110–15.

39. Susan H. Higgins and William L. Shanklin, 'Seeding Mass Market Acceptance for High Technology Consumer Products', *Journal of Consumer Marketing*, 9, Winter 1992, 5–14.

40. Richard Gibson, 'Shelf Stable Foods Seek to Freshen Sales', *Wall Street Journal*, 2 November 1990, B1.

41. Paul A. Herbig and Hugh Kramer, 'The Effect of Information Overload on the Innovation Choice Process', *Journal of Consumer Marketing*, 11, 2, 1994, 45–54.

42. Everett M. Rogers and F. Floyd Shoemaker, *Communication of Innovations*, 2nd edn (New York: Free Press, 1971), 32–3; see also Elizabeth C. Hirschman, 'Consumer Modernity, Cognitive Complexity, Creativity and Innovativeness', in *Marketing in the 80's: Changes and Challenges*, eds Richard P. Bagozzi *et al.* (Chicago: American Marketing Association, 1980), 135–9.

43. Elizabeth L. Jackson, Mohammed Quaddus, Nazrul Islam and John Stanton, 'Hybrid vigour of behavioural theories in the agribusiness research domain. Is it possible? *Journal of International Farm Management*, Vol. 3, No. 3, July 2006.

44. Kenichi Ohmae, 'Managing in a Borderless World', *Harvard Business Review*, May–June 1989, 152–61.

45. Jacob Goldenberg, Barak Libai and Eitan Muller, 'Riding the Saddle: How Cross-Market Communications Can Create a Major Slump in Sales', *Journal of Marketing*, 66, 2, April 2002, 1–16.

46. Dianne Neumark-Sztainer *et al.*, 'Early Adopters of Olestra-Containing Foods: Who Are They?', *Journal of the American Dietetic Association*, 100, 2, February 2000, 198–204.

47. David J. Burns and Robert F. Krampf, 'A Semiotic Perspective on Innovative Behavior', in *Developments in Marketing Science*, ed. Robert L. King (Richmond, VA: Academy of Marketing Science, 1991), 32–5.

48. Wayne D. Hoyer and Nancy M. Ridgway, 'Variety Seeking as an Explanation for Exploratory Purchase Behavior: A Theoretical Model', in *Advances in Consumer Research*, 11, ed. Thomas C. Kinnear (Provo, UT: Association for Consumer Research, 1984), 114–19.

49. HoJung Choo and Jae-Eun Chung, 'Antecedents to New Food Product Purchasing Behavior among Innovator Groups in India', *European Journal of Marketing*, 38, 5/6, 2004, 608–25.

50. Bruce MacEvoy, 'Change Leaders and the New Media', *American Demographics*, January 1994, 42–8.

51. Susan Mitchell, 'Technophiles and Technophobes', *American Demographics*, February 1994, 36–42.

52. Cordon C. Bruner II and Anand Kumar, 'Explaining Consumer Acceptance of Handheld Internet Devices', *Journal of Business Research*, 58, 2005, 553–8.

53. Mary Long, Leon Schiffman and Elaine Sherman, 'Exploring the Dynamics of Online Retail-Related Activities', in *Retailing 2003: Strategic Planning in Uncertain Times, Proceedings of the Seventh Triennial National Retailing Conference*, Academy of Marketing Sciences, Columbus, Ohio, November 2003.

54. Mirella Kleijnen, Ko de Ruyter and Martin Wetzels, 'Consumer Adoption of Wireless Services: Discovering the Rules While Playing the Game', *Journal of Interactive Marketing*, 18, Spring 2004, 51–61.

CHAPTER 16
CONSUMER DECISION-MAKING – AGAIN

The earlier chapters of this book have all focused on different aspects of consumer behaviour, and how consumer behaviour can be explained by a variety of insights from psychology, sociology, anthropology and economy (among others). While focusing on different issues, the chapters have in common that all the topics covered are in one way or another related to the behaviour consumers display in *searching for*, *purchasing*, *using*, *evaluating* and *disposing of products and services that they expect will satisfy their needs*. Consumer behaviour focuses on how individuals make decisions to spend their available resources (time, money, effort) on consumption-related items. That includes what they buy, why they buy it, when they buy it, where they buy it, how often they buy it, how often they use it, how they evaluate it after purchase, the impact of such evaluations on future purchases and how they dispose of it. And it is important to emphasise again that the focus must be on how consumers *make decisions*. To put it simply, a marketer's job is to make consumers in the target group choose its products instead of the ones offered by competitors. The focus of this book has been to portray how the outcomes of such choices are influenced by the characteristics of the decision-making individual and his or her social settings, while also offering insights on these topics. This final chapter links the content of the book back to the beginning: the simple model of consumer decision-making presented in Figure 1-1 (repeated here as Figure 16-1). Over the next few pages we offer some brief comments on how the contents of the previous chapters are linked to the different parts of the model.

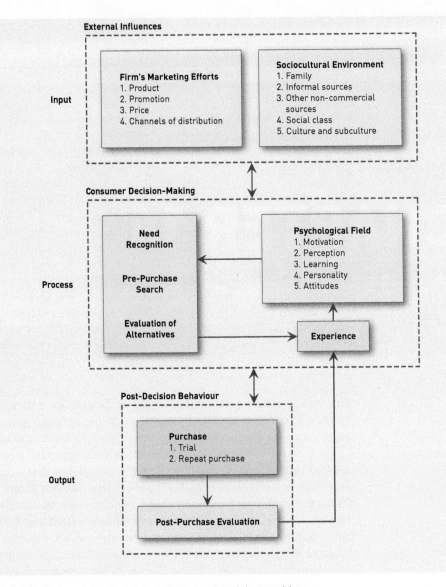

FIGURE 16-1 A simple model of consumer decision-making

When a consumer faces a need for a given product or service, this need is often triggered either by marketing efforts initiated by the firm offering the product, or by influences in the consumer's sociocultural environment. Part 3 of this book (Chapters 11–14) discusses some of the important aspects of the sociocultural environment, such as family, social class, culture and subculture. As can be seen from Figure 16-1, sociocultural issues not only act as input to the decision-making process, but also offer directions to the completion of the decision task. For example, if a specific need stems from the influence of a reference group, then the preferences of this group might be important when a consumer evaluates the alternative products that satisfy this need. In other words, sociocultural inputs will often be of importance during the decision-making process; a consumer using a weighted-score compensatory decision rule may in fact include the product's ability to satisfy reference group preferences as one attribute to consider, and this attribute may also be given higher weights than other product-related attributes. Thus, it is important to understand how the sociocultural environment not only gives rise to perceived needs, but also directly influences the outcome of a large variety of the purchase decisions consumers make.

The 'process' part of Figure 16-1 depicts the part of the model where decisions are actually made. How a consumer goes about searching for information and evaluating the information gathered on each alternative will depend on, and vary with, each individual's psychological characteristics. While each of the chapters in Part 2 (Chapters 4–10) gives a detailed overview of a specific theoretical topic, they are also crucial to the understanding of consumer decision-making. As can be seen from Figure 16-1, motivation, perception, learning, personality and attitudes are all distinct features influencing the decision process. Moreover, these are all subjective matters on which consumers differ. An important point to remember in this respect is that the explanatory mechanisms and models presented in Part 2 are somewhat generalised, implying that it is the input to the model that determines the output. The theory of reasoned action, for instance, may explain the purchase intentions of both a Swede and a Portuguese, but the difference between them stems from the input to the model and not the model itself. Due to cultural differences, the Portuguese may emphasise the reactions of significant others more than the Swede, thereby letting his behavioural intentions be more influenced by the subjective norm. On the other hand, the Swede may be other-directed and compliant, while the Portuguese is inner-directed and detached, implying that the Swede emphasises the reactions of significant others more than the Portuguese does. Accordingly, we must remember that consumers do not necessarily emphasise any given attribute to the same degree, and often such differences are due to a diversity of motivation, perception, learning, personality and attitudes. Furthermore, two consumers using a compensatory decision rule may evaluate the attributes of two competing products in a similar way, and still choose differently when they face a purchase situation. While our first consumer is highly involved and very familiar with the product category, the latter is a novice who cannot compete with the former in terms of product knowledge. Hence, their contrasting choices are not necessarily caused by differences in their evaluation of the attributes, but in their weighting of how important the product attributes are. This may result from differences in what quantity of cognitive resources they are willing to spend, or are able to spend, on learning the product category. Or other individual differences may be the cause.

How, then, can marketers cope with challenges like this? One answer, while not exhaustive, is that a thorough effort in identifying an accurate segment and reasonable target group will increase the probability of working towards a homogeneous group of consumers. In Part 1 (Chapters 2 and 3) research methods suitable to identify individual differences and the tools marketers can apply to identify a sensible segment are discussed. The goal for marketers is to define segments that will react equally to their attempts at persuasion and have similar needs, wants and characteristics. And again, as in Figure 16-1, important segmentation criteria include motivation, perception, learning, personality and attitudes.

The output phase of the model presented in Figure 16-1 consists of post-decision behaviour, which includes post-purchase evaluation. In several chapters throughout the book different aspects related to this phase are discussed. For example, the motivation process in Chapter 5 describes tension reduction as need fulfilment is achieved. Chapter 8 discusses customer satisfaction, and Chapter 9 describes cognitive dissonance (post-purchase dissonance). Related to this, Chapter 5 also presents defence mechanisms that may be activated should the consumer's need not be fulfilled or the goal reached. In addition, the experience consumers gain from purchases adds to their cognitive schemata, and purchases that satisfy their needs often lead to the purchased brand earning a place in the evoked set.

While the examples given in the previous paragraphs are only a selection, they still portray ways in which the knowledge we have on the topics covered in this book can be related to the decisions consumers make. For the marketer, the challenge is to develop such a fine-tuned conception of its target group that it is able to present its offer in a way that takes account of the psychological, sociological, anthropological and economic characteristics of the consumers in question. We hope that this book will be helpful in achieving this task.

GLOSSARY

Absolute Threshold. The lowest level at which an individual can experience a sensation.

Acculturation. The learning of a new or 'foreign' culture.

Acquired Needs. Needs that are learned in response to one's culture or environment (such as the need for esteem, prestige, affection, or power). Also known as *psychogenic* or *secondary needs*.

Acquisition–Transaction Utility. This theory suggests that there are two types of utilities that are associated with consumer purchases: acquisition utility, which represents the consumer's perceived economic gain or loss associated with a purchase, and transaction utility, which concerns the perceived pleasure or displeasure associated with the financial aspect of the purchase.

Activities, Interests and Opinions (AIOs). Psychographic variables that focus on activities, interests, and opinions. Also referred to as lifestyle.

Actual Self-Image. The image that an individual has of himself or herself as a certain kind of person, with certain characteristic traits, habits, possessions, relationships and behaviour.

Adopter Categories. A sequence of categories that describes how early (or late) a consumer adopts a new product in relation to other adopters. The five typical adopter categories are innovators, early adopters, early majority, late majority and laggards.

Adoption Process. The stages through which an individual consumer passes in arriving at a decision to try (or not to try), to continue using (or discontinue using) a new product. The five stages of the traditional adoption process are awareness, interest, evaluation, trial and adoption (rejection).

Advertising Resonance. Wordplay, often used to create a double meaning, used in combination with a relevant picture.

Advertising Wear-out. Overexposure to repetitive advertising that causes individuals to become satiated and their attention and retention to decline.

Affect Referral Decision Rule. A simplified decision rule by which consumers make a product choice on the basis of their previously established overall ratings of the brands considered, rather than on specific attributes.

Affluent Market. Upscale market segment that consists of households with incomes that are higher than average (e.g. income over €75,000).

Age Subcultures. Age sub-groupings of the population.

Approach Object. A positive goal towards which behaviour is directed.

Attitude. A learned predisposition to behave in a consistently favourable or unfavourable manner with respect to a given object.

Attitude Scales. Research measurement instrument used to capture evaluative data.

Attitude Towards Behaviour Model. A model that proposes that a consumer's attitude towards a specific behaviour is a function of how strongly he or she believes that the action will lead to a specific outcome (either favourable or unfavourable).

Attitude Towards Object Model. A model that proposes that a consumer's attitude towards a product or brand is a function of the presence of certain attributes and the consumer's evaluation of those attributes.

Attitude Towards the Ad Model. A model that proposes that a consumer forms various feelings (affects) and judgements (cognitions) as the result of exposure to an advertisement, which, in turn, affect the consumer's *attitude towards the advertisement* and *beliefs and attitudes towards the brand*.

Attitudinal Measures. Measures concerned with consumers' overall feelings (i.e. evaluation) about the product and the brand and their purchase intentions.

Attribution Theory. A theory concerned with how people assign causality to events, and form or alter their attitudes after assessing their own or other people's behaviour.

Attributions Towards Others. When consumers feel that another person is responsible for either positive or negative product performance.

Attributions Towards Things. Consumers judge a product's performance and attribute its success or failure to the product itself.

Audience Profile. Psychographic/demographic profile of the audience of a specific medium.

Autonomic (Unilateral) Decisions. Purchase decisions in which either the husband or the wife makes the final decision.

Avoidance Object. A negative goal from which behaviour is directed away.

Baby Boomers. Individuals born between 1946 and 1964 (approximately 40 per cent of the adult population).

Behavioural Learning Theory. Theory based on the premise that learning takes place as the result of observable responses to external stimuli. Also known as *stimulus response theory*.

Behavioural Measures. Measures based on observable responses to promotional stimuli.

Benefit Segmentation. Segmentation based on the kinds of benefits consumers seek in a product.

Brand Equity. The value inherent in a well-known brand name.

Brand Loyalty. Consumers' consistent preference and/ or purchase of the same brand in a specific product or service category.

Brand Personification. Specific 'personality-type' traits or characteristics ascribed by consumers to different brands.

Broad versus Narrow Categorisers. Broad categorisers are uninvolved consumers who are likely to be receptive to a greater number of advertising messages regarding a product category and will consider more brands. Narrow categorisers are highly involved consumers that find fewer brands acceptable.

Celebrity Credibility. The audience's perception of the endorser's expertise and trustworthiness.

Central and Peripheral Routes to Persuasion. A promotional theory that proposes that highly involved consumers are best reached through advertisements that focus on the specific attributes of the product (the central route) while uninvolved consumers can be attracted through peripheral advertising cues such as the model or the setting (the peripheral route).

Chapin's Social Status Scale. A social class rating scheme that focuses on the presence or absence of certain items of furniture and accessories in the home.

Class Consciousness. A feeling of social-group membership that reflects an individual's sense of belonging or identification with others.

Classical Conditioning. See **Conditioned Learning**.

Closure. A principle of gestalt psychology that stresses the individual's need for completion. This need is reflected in the individual's subconscious reorganisation and perception of incomplete stimuli as complete or whole pictures.

Co-branding. When two brand names are featured on a single product.

Cognitive Age. An individual's perceived age (usually 10 to 15 years younger than his or her chronological age).

Cognitive Associative Learning. The learning of associations among events through classical conditioning that allows the organism to anticipate and represent its environment.

Cognitive Dissonance Theory. The discomfort or dissonance that consumers experience as a result of conflicting information.

Cognitive Learning Theory. A theory of learning based on mental information processing, often in response to problem-solving.

Cognitive Personality. *Need for cognition* and *visualisers versus verbalisers* are two cognitive personality traits that influence consumer behaviour.

Communication. The transmission of a message from a sender to a receiver by means of a signal of some sort sent through a communications channel (e.g. medium) of some sort.

Comparative Advertising. Advertising that explicitly names or otherwise identifies one or more competitors of the advertised brand for the purpose of claiming superiority, either on an overall basis or on selected product attributes.

Comparative Reference Group. A group whose norms serve as a benchmark for highly specific or narrowly defined types of behaviour. (See also **Normative Reference Group**.)

Compensatory Decision Rule. A type of decision rule in which a consumer evaluates each brand in terms of each relevant attribute and then selects the brand with the highest weighted score.

Composite-Variable Index. An index that combines a number of socio-economic variables (such as education, income, occupation) to form one overall measure of social class standing. (See also **Single-Variable Index.**)

Comprehension. A function of the message characteristics, the consumer's opportunity and ability to process the information and the consumer's motivation to do so (e.g. level of involvement).

Compulsive Consumption. When buying becomes an addiction; consumers who are compulsive buyers are in some respects 'out of control', and their actions may have damaging consequences to them and to those around them.

Concentrated Marketing. Targeting a product or service to a single market segment with a unique marketing mix (price, product, promotion, method of distribution).

Conditioned Learning. According to Pavlovian theory, conditioned learning results when a stimulus paired with another stimulus that elicits a known response serves to produce the same response by itself.

Conditioned Stimuli. When consumers associate new products bearing a well-known symbol or brand name with the original product in the belief that it embodies the same attributes as the name it is associated with.

Conjunctive Decision Rule. A non-compensatory decision rule in which consumers establish a minimally acceptable cut-off point for each attribute evaluated. Brands that fall below the cut-off point on any one attribute are eliminated from further consideration.

Consumer–Action Group. Groups that are dedicated to providing consumers with assistance in making the 'right' purchase decisions and in avoiding 'poor' decisions; sometimes based on political activism such as avoiding products manufactured in sweatshops and other unhealthy worker environments. Also called consumer activists and consumer advocates.

Consumer Behaviour. The behaviour that consumers display in searching for, purchasing, using, evaluating and disposing of products, services and ideas.

Consumer Conformity. The willingness of consumers to adopt the norms, attitudes and behaviour of reference groups.

Consumer Decision-Making. The process of making purchase decisions based on cognitive and emotional influences such as impulse, family, friends, advertisers, role models, moods and situations that influence a purchase.

Consumer Decision Rules. Procedures adopted by consumers to reduce the complexity of making product and brand decisions.

Consumer Ethnocentrism. A consumer's predisposition to accept or reject foreign-made products.

Consumer Fieldwork. Observational research by anthropologists of the behaviours of a small sample of people from a particular society.

Consumer Imagery. Products and brands have symbolic value for individuals, who evaluate them on the basis of their consistency with their personal pictures of themselves.

Consumer Innovativeness. The degree to which consumers are receptive to new products, new services or new practices.

Consumer Innovators. Those who are among the first to purchase a new product.

Consumer Materialism. A personality-like trait of individuals who regard possessions as particularly essential to their identities and lives.

Consumer Profile. Psychographic/demographic profile of actual or proposed consumers for a specific product or service.

Consumer Research. Methodology used to study and interpret consumer behaviour.

Consumer Socialisation. The process, started in childhood, by which an individual learns the skills and attitudes relevant to consumer purchase behaviour.

Consumption Process. A process consisting of three stages: the *input stage* establishes the consumption set and consuming style; the *process* of consuming and possessing, which includes using, possessing, collecting and disposing of things; and the *output stage*, which includes changes in feelings, moods, attitudes and behaviour towards the product or service based on personal experience.

Content Analysis. A method for systematically analysing the content of verbal and/or pictorial communication. The method is frequently used to determine prevailing social values of a society in a particular era under study.

Continuous Innovation. A new product entry that is an improved or modified version of an existing product rather than a totally new product. A continuous innovation has the least disruptive influence on established consumption patterns.

Copy Post-testing. Testing an advertisement after it is run. A post-test is used to evaluate the effectiveness of an advertisement that has already appeared and to see which elements, if any, should be revised to improve the impact of future advertisements.

Copy Pre-testing. Testing an advertisement before it is run to determine which, if any, elements of the advertising message should be revised before major media expenses are incurred.

Counter-segmentation Strategy. A strategy in which a company combines two or more segments into a single segment to be targeted with an individually tailored product or promotion campaign.

Cross-Cultural Consumer Analysis. Research to determine the extent to which consumers of two or more nations are similar in relation to specific consumption behaviour.

Cross-Cultural Consumer Research. Research methods designed to find the similarities and differences among consumers in a marketer's domestic market and those it wants to target in a foreign country.

Cross-Cultural Psychographic Segmentation. Tailoring marketing strategies to the needs (psychological, social, cultural and functional) of specific foreign segments.

Cues. Stimuli that give direction to consumer motives (i.e. that suggest a specific way to satisfy a salient motive).

Culture. The sum total of learned beliefs, values and customs that serve to regulate the consumer behaviour of members of a particular society.

Customer Lifetime Value. Profiles based on the collection and analysis of internal secondary data.

Customer Retention. Providing value to customers continuously so that they will stay with the company rather than switch to a competitor.

Customer Satisfaction. An individual's perception of the performance of the product or service in relation to his or her expectations.

Customer Satisfaction Measurement. Quantitative and qualitative measures that gauge the level of customer satisfaction and its determinants.

Customer Value. The ratio between the customer's perceived benefits and the resources used to obtain those benefits.

Defence Mechanisms. Methods by which people mentally redefine frustrating situations to protect their self-images and their self-esteem.

Defensive Attribution. A theory that suggests consumers are likely to accept credit for successful outcomes (internal attribution) and to blame other persons or products for failure (external attribution).

Demographic Characteristics. Objective characteristics of a population (such as age, sex, marital status, income, occupation and education) which are often used as the basis for segmenting markets.

Demographic Segmentation. The division of a total market into smaller sub-groups on the basis of such objective characteristics as age, sex, marital status, income, occupation or education.

Depth Interview. A lengthy and relatively unstructured interview designed to uncover a consumer's underlying attitudes and/or motivations.

Differential Threshold. The minimal difference that can be detected between two stimuli. Also known as the *j.n.d.* *(just noticeable difference)*. (See also **Weber's Law**).

Differentiated Marketing. Targeting a product or service to two or more segments, using a specifically tailored product, promotional appeal, price and/or method of distribution for each.

Diffusion of Innovations. The framework for exploring the spread of consumer acceptance of new products throughout the social system.

Diffusion Process. The process by which the acceptance of an innovation is spread by communication to members of a social system over a period of time.

Direct Mail. Advertising that is sent directly to the mailing address of a targeted consumer.

Direct Marketing. A marketing technique that uses various media (e.g. mail, print, broadcast, Internet, telephone) to solicit a direct response from a consumer. Also known as database marketing.

Discontinuous Innovation. A dramatically new product entry that requires the establishment of new consumption practices.

Disjunctive Rule. A non-compensatory decision rule in which consumers establish a minimally acceptable cut-off point for each relevant product attribute; any brand meeting or surpassing the cut-off point for any one attribute is considered an acceptable choice.

Distributed Learning. Learning spaced over a period of time to increase consumer retention. (See also **Massed Learning.**)

Dogmatism. A personality trait that reflects the degree of rigidity a person displays towards the unfamiliar and towards information that is contrary to his or her own established beliefs.

Downward Mobility. Consumers who have a lower social class level than their parents in terms of the jobs they hold, their residences, level of disposable income and savings.

Dynamically Continuous Innovation. A new product entry that is sufficiently innovative to have some disruptive effects on established consumption practices.

Ego-Defensive Function. A component of the functional approach to attitude-change theory that suggests that consumers want to protect their self-concepts from inner feelings of doubt.

Elaboration Likelihood Model (ELM). A theory that suggests that a person's level of involvement during message processing is a critical factor in determining which route to persuasion is likely to be effective. (See also **Central and Peripheral Routes to Persuasion.**)

Emotional Motives. The selection of goals according to personal or subjective criteria (e.g. the desire for individuality, pride, fear, affection, status).

Encoding. The process by which individuals select and assign a word or visual image to represent a perceived object or idea.

Enculturation. The learning of the culture of one's own society.

Endorsements. When celebrities or the so-called man in the Street – who may or may not be users of a particular product or service – lend their names to advertisements for such products or services for a fee.

Evaluation of Alternatives. A stage in the consumer decision-making process in which the consumer appraises the benefits to be derived from each of the product alternatives being considered.

Evoked Set. The specific brands a consumer considers in making a purchase choice in a particular product category.

Expectations. What people expect to see based on familiarity or previous experience.

Expected Self. How individuals expect to see themselves at some specified future time.

Exploratory Study. A small-scale study that identifies critical issues to include in a large-scale research study.

Extended Family. A household consisting of a husband, wife, offspring and at least one other blood relative.

Extended Self. When a consumer uses self-altering products or services to conform to or take on the appearance of a particular type of person (e.g. a biker, a doctor, a lawyer, a university professor).

Extensive Problem-Solving. Decision-making efforts by consumers who have no established criteria for evaluating a product category or specific brands in that category, or have not narrowed the number of brands to a manageable subset.

External Attribution. A theory that suggests that consumers are likely to credit their successes to outside sources (e.g. their graduate degrees or other persons).

Extrinsic Cues. Cues external to the product (e.g. price, store image or brand image) that serve to influence the consumer's perception of a product's quality.

Family. Two or more persons related by blood, marriage or adoption who reside together.

Family Branding. The practice of marketing several company products under the same brand name.

Family Life Cycle. Classification of families into significant stages. The five traditional FLC stages are Bachelorhood, Honeymooners, Parenthood, Post-parenthood and Dissolution.

Feedback. Communication – either verbal or non-verbal (body language) – that is communicated back to the sender of a message by the receiver.

Field Observation. An anthropological measurement technique that focuses on observing behaviour within a natural environment (often without the subjects' awareness).

Figure and Ground. A gestalt principle of perceptual organisation that focuses on contrast. *Figure* is usually perceived clearly because (in contrast to (back) *ground*) it appears to be well defined, solid and in the forefront, while the *ground* is usually perceived as indefinite, hazy, and continuous. Music can be figure or (back) ground.

Focus Group. A qualitative research method in which about eight to ten people participate in an unstructured group interview focused on a product or service concept.

Foot-in-the-Door Technique. A theory of attitude change that suggests individuals form attitudes that are consistent with their own prior behaviour.

Formal Communications Source. A source that speaks on behalf of an organisation – either a commercial or a charitable organisation.

Freudian Theory. A theory of personality and motivation developed by the psychoanalyst Sigmund Freud. (See also **Psychoanalytic Theory.**)

Functional Approach. An attitude-change theory that classifies attitudes in terms of four functions: utilitarian, ego-defensive, value-expressive and knowledge functions.

Gender Subcultures. Sex roles are an important cultural component and require products that are either exclusively or strongly associated with the members of one sex.

Generation X. Born between 1965 and 1979, this is a post baby-boomer segment (also referred to as *Xers* or *busters*).

Generation Y. Consumers born between the years 1977 and 1994.

Generic Goals. The general classes or categories of goals that individuals select to fulfil their needs. (See also **Product-Specific Goals.**)

Geographic Segmentation. The division of a total potential market into smaller sub-groups on the basis of geographic variables (e.g. region, city or postcode).

Gestalt. A German term meaning 'pattern' or 'configuration' that has come to represent various principles of perceptual organisation.

Gifting Behaviour. The process of gift exchange that takes place between a giver and a recipient.

Global Strategy. Standardising both product and communications programmes when conducting business on a global basis.

Group. Two or more individuals who interact to accomplish either individual or mutual goals.

Grouping. A gestalt theory of perceptual organisation that proposes that individuals tend to group stimuli automatically so that they form a unified picture or impression. The perception of stimuli as groups or chunks of information, rather than as discrete bits of information, facilitates their memory and recall.

Hemispheral Lateralisation. Learning theory in which the basic premise is that the right and left hemispheres of the brain 'specialise' in the kinds of information that they process. Also called split brain theory.

Heuristics. See **Consumer Decision Rules**.

Hybrid Segmentation. The use of several segmentation variables to define more accurately or 'fine-tune' consumer segments.

Ideal Self-Image. How individuals would *like* to perceive themselves (as opposed to **Actual Self-Image** – the way they *do* perceive themselves).

Ideal Social Self-Image. How consumers would like others to see them.

Imagery. The ability to form mental images.

Impersonal Communication. Communication directed to a large and diffuse audience, with no direct communication between source and receiver. Also known as *mass communication*.

Indirect Reference Groups. Individuals or groups with whom a person identifies but does not have direct face-to-face contact, such as film stars, sports heroes, political leaders or television personalities.

Inept Set. Brands that a consumer excludes from purchase consideration.

Inert Set. Brands that a consumer is indifferent towards because they are perceived as having no particular advantage.

Informal Group. A group of people who see each other frequently on an informal basis, such as weekly poker players or social acquaintances.

Information Overload. A situation in which the consumer is presented with too much product- or brand-related information.

Information Processing. A cognitive theory of human learning patterned after computer information processing that focuses on how information is stored in human memory and how it is retrieved.

Innate Needs. Physiological needs for food, water, air, clothing, shelter and sex. Also known as *biogenic* or *primary needs*.

Inner-Directedness. Consumers who tend to rely on their own 'inner' values or standards when evaluating new products and who are likely to be consumer innovators.

Innovation. A totally new product, new service, new idea or new practice.

Institutional Advertising. Advertising designed to promote a favourable company image rather than specific products.

Instrumental Conditioning. A behavioural theory of learning based on a trial-and-error process, with habits formed as the result of positive experiences (reinforcement) resulting from specific behaviours. (See also **Conditioned Learning.**)

Intention-to-Buy Scales. A method of assessing the likelihood of a consumer purchasing a product or behaving in a certain way.

Interference Effects. The greater the number of competitive advertisements in a product category, the lower the recall of brand claims in a specific advertisement.

Internal Attributions. Consumers attribute their success in using a product or source to their own skill.

Interpersonal Communication. Communication that occurs directly between two or more people by post, telephone, email or in person.

Intrinsic Cues. Physical characteristics of the product (such as size, colour, flavour or aroma) that serve to influence the consumer's perceptions of product quality.

Involvement Theory. A theory of consumer learning postulating that consumers engage in a range of information processing activity, from extensive to limited problem-solving, depending on the relevance of the purchase.

Joint Decisions. Family purchase decisions in which the husband and wife are equally influential. Also known as *syncratic decisions*.

Just Noticeable Difference (j.n.d.). The minimal difference that can be detected between two stimuli. (See also **Differential Threshold** and **Weber's Law**.)

Knowledge Function. A component of the functional approach to attitude-change theory that suggests that consumers have a strong need to know and understand the people and products with which they come into contact.

Learning. The process by which individuals acquire the knowledge and experience they apply to future purchase and consumption behaviour.

Level of Aspiration. New and higher goals that individuals set for themselves.

Lexicographic Decision Rule. A non-compensatory decision rule in which consumers first rank product attributes in terms of their importance, then compare brands in terms of the attribute considered most important. If one brand scores higher than the other brands, it is selected; if not, the process is continued with the second ranked attribute, and so on.

Licensing. The use by manufacturers and retailers of well-known brands, celebrity or designer names (for a fee) to acquire instant recognition and status for their products.

Limited Problem-Solving. A limited search by a consumer for a product that will satisfy his or her basic criteria from among a selected group of brands.

Local Strategy. Customising both product and communications programmes by area or country when conducting business on a global basis.

Long-Term Store. In information-processing theory, the stage of real memory where information is organised, reorganised and retained for relatively extended periods of time.

Market Mavens. Individuals whose influence stems from a general knowledge and market expertise that lead to an early awareness of new products and services.

Market Segmentation. The process of dividing a potential market into distinct subsets of consumers and selecting one or more segments as a target market to be reached with a distinct marketing mix.

Marketing Concept. A consumer-oriented philosophy that suggests that satisfaction of consumer needs provides the focus for product development and marketing strategy to enable the firm to meet its own organisational goals.

Marketing Ethics. Designing, packaging, pricing, advertising and distributing products in such a way that negative consequences to consumers, employees and society in general are avoided.

Marketing Mix. The unique configuration of the four basic marketing variables (product, promotion, price and channels of distribution) that a marketing organisation controls.

Maslow's Hierarchy of Needs. A theory of motivation that postulates that individuals strive to satisfy their needs according to a basic hierarchical structure, starting with physiological needs, then moving to safety needs, social needs, egoistic needs and finally self-actualisation needs.

Mass Marketing. Offering the same product and marketing mix to all consumers.

Massed Learning. Compressing the learning schedule into a short time-span to accelerate consumer learning. (See also **Distributed Learning**.)

Megabrands. Well-known brand names.

Message Framing. Positively framed messages (those that specify benefits to be *gained* by using a product) are more persuasive than negatively framed messages (those that specify benefits *lost* by not using a product).

Modelling. See **Observational Learning**.

Mood. An individual's subjectively perceived 'feeling state'.

Motivation. The driving force within individuals that impels them to action.

Motivational Research. Qualitative research designed to uncover consumers' subconscious or hidden motivations. The basic premise of motivational research is that consumers are not always aware of, or may not wish to reveal, the basic reasons underlying their actions.

Multi-attribute Attitude Models. Attitude models that examine the composition of consumer attitudes in terms of selected product attributes or beliefs.

Multinational Strategies. Decisions that marketers make on how to reach all potential consumers of their products in countries throughout the world.

Multiple Self or Selves. Consumers have different images of themselves in response to different situations and are quite likely to act differently with different people and in different situations.

Multi-step Flow of Communication Theory. A revision of the traditional two-step theory that shows multiple communication flows: from the mass media simultaneously to opinion leaders, opinion receivers and information receivers (who neither influence nor are influenced by others); from opinion leaders to opinion receivers; and from opinion receivers to opinion leaders.

Nationality Subcultures. Subcultures in a larger society in which members often retain a sense of identification and pride in the language and customs of their ancestors.

Need for Cognition. The personality trait that measures a person's craving for or enjoyment of thinking.

Need Recognition. The realisation by the consumer that there is a difference between 'what is' and 'what should (or can) be'.

Negative Motivation. A driving force away from some object or condition.

Negative Reinforcement. An unpleasant or negative outcome that serves to encourage a specific behaviour. (Not to be confused with punishment, which discourages repetition of a specific behaviour.)

Neo-Freudian Theory. A school of psychology that stresses the fundamental role of social relationships in the formation and development of personality.

Neo-Pavlovian Conditioning. The creation of a strong association between the conditioned stimulus (CS) and the unconditioned stimulus (US) requiring (1) forward conditioning; (2) repeated pairings of the CS and the US; (3) a CS and US that logically belong together; (4) a CS that is novel and unfamiliar; and (5) a US that is biologically or symbolically salient.

Non-compensatory Decision Rule. A type of consumer decision rule by which positive evaluation of a brand attribute does not compensate for (i.e. is not balanced against) a negative evaluation of the same brand on some other attribute.

Non-probability Sample. Findings are representative of the population.

Normative Reference Group. A group that influences the general values or behaviour of an individual. (See also **Comparative Reference Group**.)

Nuclear Family. A household consisting of a husband and wife and at least one offspring.

Objectives. The goals for a research study that will help determine the type and level of information that is needed.

Observational Learning. A process by which individuals observe the behaviour of others, remember it and imitate it. Also known as *modelling*.

Observational Research. A form of consumer research that relies on observation of consumers in the process of buying and using products.

One-Sided Versus Two-Sided Messages. A one-sided message tells only the benefits of a product or service; a two-sided message also includes some negatives, thereby enhancing the credibility of the marketer.

Opinion Leader. A person who informally gives product information and advice to others.

Opinion Leadership. The process by which one person (the *opinion leader*) informally influences the consumption actions or attitudes of others, who may be *opinion seekers* or *opinion recipients*.

Opinion Receiver (Recipient). An individual who either actively seeks product information from others or receives unsolicited information.

Opinion Seekers. Individuals who actively seek information and advice about products from others.

Optimum Stimulation Level (OSL). A personality trait that measures the level or amount of novelty or complexity that individuals seek in their personal experiences. High OSL consumers tend to accept risky and novel products more readily than low OSL consumers.

Organisational Consumer. A business, government agency or other institution (commercial or charitable) that buys the goods, services and/or equipment necessary for the organisation to function.

Other-Directedness. Consumers who tend to look to others for direction and for approval.

'Ought-To' Self. Consists of traits or characteristics that an individual believes it is his or her duty or obligation to possess.

Participant-Observers. Researchers who participate in the environment that they are studying without notifying those who are being observed.

Passive Learning. Without active involvement, individuals process and store right-brain (non-verbal, pictorial) information.

Perceived Price. How a consumer perceives a price – as high, low or fair.

Perceived Quality. Consumers often judge the quality of a product or service on the basis of a variety of informational cues that they associate with the product; some of these cues are intrinsic to the product or service; others are extrinsic, such as price, store image, service environment, brand image and promotional messages.

Perceived Risk. The degree of uncertainty perceived by the consumer as to the consequences (outcome) of a specific purchase decision.

Perception. The process by which an individual selects, organises and interprets stimuli into a meaningful and coherent picture of the world.

Perceptual Blocking. The subconscious 'screening out' of stimuli that are threatening or inconsistent with one's needs, values, beliefs or attitudes.

Perceptual Distortion. The influences on an individual that separate that person's perception of a stimulus from reality.

Perceptual Mapping. A research technique that enables marketers to plot graphically consumers' perceptions concerning product attributes of specific brands.

Personal Consumer. The individual who buys goods and services for his or her own use, for household use, for the use of a family member or for a friend. (Also referred to as the *ultimate consumer* or *end-user*.)

Personality. The inner psychological characteristics that both determine and reflect how a person responds to his or her environment.

Positioning. Establishing a specific image for a brand in relation to competing brands. (See also **Product Positioning**.)

Positive Motivation. A driving force towards some object or condition.

Positive Reinforcement. A favourable outcome to a specific behaviour that strengthens the likelihood that the behaviour will be repeated.

Post-purchase Evaluation. An assessment of a product based on actual trial after purchase.

Prepotent Need. An overriding need, from among several needs, that serves to initiate goal-directed behaviour.

Pre-purchase Search. A stage in the consumer decision-making process in which the consumer perceives a need and actively seeks out information concerning products that will help satisfy that need.

Price/Quality Relationship. The perception of price as an indicator of product quality (e.g. the higher the price, the higher the perceived quality of the product).

Primary Needs. See **Innate Needs**.

Primary Research. Original research undertaken by individual researchers or organisations to meet specific objectives. Collected information is called *primary data*.

Probability Sample. Findings are projectable to the total population.

Product Line Extension. A marketing strategy of adding related products to an already established brand (based on the stimulus generalisation theory).

Product Positioning. A marketing strategy designed to project a specific image for a product.

Product-Specific Goals. The specifically branded or labelled products that consumers select to fulfil their needs. (See also **Generic Goals**.)

Product Standardisation. An orientation for assessing whether to use a global versus local marketing strategy concentrating on a high-tech to high-touch continuum.

Psychoanalytic Theory. A theory of motivation and personality that postulates that unconscious needs and drives, particularly sexual and other biological drives, are the basis of human motivation and personality.

Psychographic Inventory. A series of written statements designed to capture relevant aspects of a consumer's personality, buying motives, interests, attitudes, beliefs and values.

Psychographic Segmentation. Identifying segments of consumers based on their responses to statements about their activities, interests and opinions.

Psychological Noise. A barrier to message reception (i.e. competing advertising messages or distracting thoughts).

Psychological Reactance. When people become motivationally aroused by a threat to or elimination of a behavioural freedom.

Psychological Segmentation. The division of a total potential market into smaller sub-groups on the basis of intrinsic characteristics of the individual, such as personality, buying motives, lifestyle, attitudes or interests.

Publicity. When commercial or non-commercial messages appear in space or time that is not paid for and usually reserved for editorial messages.

Purchase Behaviour. Behaviour that involves two types of purchases: *trial purchases* (the exploratory phase in which consumers evaluate a product through direct use) and *repeat purchases*, which usually signify that the product meets with the consumer's approval and that the consumer is willing to use it again.

Qualitative Research. Research methods (e.g. interviews, focus groups, metaphor analysis, collage research, projective techniques) that are primarily used to obtain new ideas for promotional campaigns and products.

Quantitative Research. Research methods (e.g. experiments, survey techniques, observations) that enable researchers to understand the effects of various promotional inputs on the consumer, thus enabling marketers to predict consumer behaviour.

Rational Motives. Motives or goals based on economic or objective criteria, such as price, size, weight or miles per gallon.

Receivers. The recipients of a message.

Recognition and Recall Tests. Tests conducted to determine whether consumers remember seeing an advertisement, the extent to which they have read it or seen it and can recall its content, their resulting attitudes towards the product and the brand, and their purchase intentions.

Reference Group. A person or group that serves as a point of comparison (or reference) for an individual in the formation of either general or specific values, attitudes or behaviour.

Reference Prices. External or internal prices that a consumer uses as a basis for comparison in judging another price.

Regional Subcultures. Groups who identify with the regional or geographical areas in which they live.

Rehearsal. The silent, mental repetition of material.

Reinforcement. A positive or negative outcome that influences the likelihood that a specific behaviour will be repeated in the future in response to a particular cue or stimulus.

Relationship Marketing. Marketing aimed at creating strong, lasting relationships with a core group of customers by making them feel good about the company and by giving them some kind of personal connection to the business.

Reliability. The degree to which a measurement instrument is consistent in what it measures.

Religious Subcultures. Groups classified by religious affiliation that may be targeted by marketers because of purchase decisions that are influenced by their religious identity.

Repetition. A basic concept that increases the strength of the association between a conditioned stimulus and an unconditioned stimulus and slows the process of forgetting.

Repositioning. Changing the way a product is perceived by consumers in relation to other brands or product uses.

Response. How individuals react to a drive or cue.

Retention. The ability to retain information in the memory.

Retrieval. The stage of information processing in which individuals recover information from long-term storage.

Ritual. A type of symbolic activity consisting of a series of steps (multiple behaviours) occurring in a fixed sequence and repeated over time.

Rokeach Value Survey. A self-administered inventory consisting of 18 'terminal' values (i.e. personal goals) and 18 'instrumental' values (i.e. ways of reaching personal goals).

Role. A pattern of behaviour expected of an individual in a specific social position, such as mother, daughter, teacher, lawyer. One person may have a number of different roles, each of which is relevant in the context of specific social situations.

Routinised Response Behaviour. A habitual purchase response based on predetermined criteria.

Secondary Data. Data that has been collected for reasons other than the specific research project at hand.

Secondary Needs. See **Acquired Needs**.

Secondary Research. Research conducted for reasons other than the specific problem under study. Resulting data are called *secondary data*.

Self-Gifts. Gifts to one's self.

Self-Perception Theory. A theory that suggests that consumers develop attitudes by reflecting on their own behaviour.

Seniors. Individuals 65 years of age and older.

Sensation. The immediate and direct response of the sensory organs to simple stimuli (e.g. taste, colour, smell, brightness, loudness, feel).

Sensation Seeking. A trait characterised by the need for varied, novel and complex sensations and experience, and the willingness to take physical and social risks for the sake of such experience.

Sensory Adaptation. 'Getting used to' certain sensations; becoming accommodated to a certain level of stimulation.

Sensory Receptors. The human organs (eyes, ears, nose, mouth, skin) that receive sensory inputs.

Sensory Store. The place in which all sensory inputs are housed very briefly before passing into the short-term store.

Shaping. Reinforcement performed before the desired consumer behaviour actually takes place.

Shopping Group. Two or more people who shop together.

Short-Term Store. The stage of real memory in which information received from the sensory store for processing is retained briefly before passing into the long-term store or forgotten.

Single-Parent Family. Households consisting of only one parent and at least one child.

Single-Variable Index. The use of a single socio-economic variable (such as income) to estimate an individual's relative social class. (See also **Composite-Variable Index.**)

Sleeper Effect. The tendency for persuasive communications to lose the impact of source credibility over time (i.e. the influence of a message from a high-credibility source tends to *decrease* over time; the influence of a message from a low-credibility source tends to *increase* over time).

Social Class. The division of members of a society into a hierarchy of distinct status classes, so that members of each class have either higher or lower status than members of other classes.

Social Self-Image. How consumers feel others see them.

Social Status. The amount of status members of one social class have in comparison with members of other social classes.

Socialisation of Family Members. A process that includes imparting to children and other family members the basic values and modes of behaviour consistent with the culture.

Societal Marketing Concept. A revision of the traditional marketing concept that suggests that marketers adhere to principles of social responsibility in the marketing of their goods and services; that is, they must endeavour to satisfy the needs and wants of their target markets in ways that preserve and enhance the well-being of consumers and society as a whole.

Sociocultural Variables. Sociological and anthropological variables that provide further bases for market segmentation.

Source. The initiator of a message.

Source Credibility. The perceived honesty and objectivity of the source of the communication.

Spokesperson. A celebrity or company executive who represents a product, brand or company over an extended period of time, often in print, on television and in personal appearances.

Stages in the Adoption Process. See **Adoption Process.**

Stimulus Discrimination. The ability to select a specific stimulus from among similar stimuli because of perceived differences.

Stimulus Generalisation. The inability to perceive differences between slightly dissimilar stimuli.

Stimulus Response Theories. The premise that observable responses to specific external stimuli signal that learning has taken place.

Subcultural Interaction. Because consumers are simultaneously members of several subcultural groups, marketers must determine how consumer's specific subcultural memberships interact to influence the consumer's purchase decisions.

Subculture. A distinct cultural group that exists as an identifiable segment within a larger, more complex society.

Subliminal Perception. Perception of stimuli received *below* the level of conscious awareness.

Substitute Goal. A goal that replaces an individual's primary goal when that goal cannot be achieved.

Symbol. Anything that stands for something else.

Symbolic Group. A group with which an individual identifies by adopting its values, attitudes or behaviour despite the unlikelihood of future membership.

Targeting. The selection of a distinct market segment at which to direct a marketing strategy.

Testimonial. A promotional technique in which a celebrity that has used a product or service speaks highly of its benefits in order to influence consumers to buy.

Theory of Reasoned Action. A comprehensive theory of the interrelationship among attitudes, intentions and behaviour.

Theory of Trying to Consume. Recasts the theory of reasoned action model by replacing actual *behaviour* with *trying to behave* (i.e. consume) as the variable to be explained and/or predicted.

Traditional Family Life Cycle. A progression of stages through which many families pass.

Trait Theory. A theory of personality that focuses on the measurement of specific psychological characteristics.

Tricomponent Attitude Model. An attitude model consisting of three parts: a cognitive (knowledge) component, an affective (feeling) component and a conative (doing) component.

Two-Step Flow of Communication Theory. A communications model that portrays opinion leaders as direct receivers of information from mass-media sources who, in turn, interpret and transmit this information to the general public.

Upward Mobility. Movement upward in social-class standing from the social-class position into which the consumer was born.

Usage-Situation Segmentation. Segmentation that is based on the idea that the occasion or situation often determines what consumers will purchase or consume (i.e. certain products for certain situations, special usage occasions).

Use-Related Segmentation. Popular and effective form of segmentation that categorises consumers in terms of product, service or brand-usage characteristics, such as usage rate, awareness status and degree of brand loyalty.

Utilitarian Function. A component of the functional approach to attitude-change theory that suggests consumers hold certain attitudes partly because of the brand's utility.

Validity. The degree to which a measurement instrument accurately measures what it is designed to measure.

VALS. See **Values and Lifestyle System.**

Value-Expressive Function. A component of the functional approach to attitude-change theory that suggests that attitudes express consumers' general values, lifestyles and outlook.

Values and Lifestyle System. A research service that tracks marketing-relevant shifts in the beliefs, values and lifestyles of psychological segments of the population.

Variety or Novelty Seeking. A personality trait, similar to optimum stimulation level, which measures a consumer's degree of variety seeking.

Verbalisers. Consumers who prefer verbal or written information and products, such as membership in book clubs or audiotape clubs. (See also **Visualisers**.)

Virtual Personality or Virtual Self. A concept that provides an individual with the opportunity to 'try on' different personalities or different identities, such as creating a fictitious personality in an online chat room.

Visualisers. Consumers who prefer visual information and products that stress the visual, such as membership in a DVD club. (See also **Verbalisers**.)

Weber's Law. A theory concerning the perceived differentiation between similar stimuli of varying intensities; that is, the stronger the initial stimulus, the greater the additional intensity needed for the second stimulus to be perceived as different. (See also **Just Noticeable Difference**.)

Word-of-Mouth Communications. Informal conversations between friends concerning products or services.

World Brands. Products that are manufactured, packaged and positioned the same way regardless of the country in which they are sold.

INDEX